Productivity Growth, Inflation, and Ur.

This unique collection of seventeen pathbreaking essays treats the three
core topics of macroeconomics – economic growth, inflation, and unemployment. In all three topic areas, the essays have established the context
of macroeconomic discussions, including the author's early skepticism
that the New Economy and Internet warranted the hype and overblown
stock market valuations of the late 1990s, his reinterpretation of the roles
of capital accumulation and technological change in economic growth, his
reinvention of Keynesian macroeconomics as the interplay of shocks not
just to aggregate demand but also to aggregate supply, and his symmetric explanation of why inflation and unemployment were so high in the
1970s and so low in the late 1990s. This collection is unique not only in
the importance of its topics and conclusions, but in the novelty of its five
newly written introductions, one for the entire book and four new introductions to the separate parts of the book. Each introduction goes beyond
summarizing the contribution of the individual essays, setting them in the
context of past and current macroeconomic debates and tracing the origins of the ideas and their subsequent evolution. The collection contains
three previously unpublished essays on technology and productivity that
gain new relevance in today's economy. The foreword by Nobel Laureate
Robert M. Solow comments on the abiding importance of these essays for
the three core topics of macroeconomics.

Robert J. Gordon is Stanley G. Harris Professor in the Social Sciences
and Professor of Economics at Northwestern University. He is one of
the world's leading experts on the causes and consequences of inflation,
unemployment, and productivity growth, among other topics in macroeconomics. Professor Gordon is the author and editor of numerous books,
including the ninth edition of *Macroeconomics* (2003), *The Economics of
New Goods* (1997), *The Measurement of Durable Goods Prices* (1990),
and *The American Business Cycle* (1986). For more than twenty-five years,
Professor Gordon has been a research associate of the National Bureau
of Economic Research and a Fellow of the Centre for Economic Policy
Research in London. A Guggenheim Fellow, Fellow of the American
Academy of Arts and Sciences, Fellow and Treasurer of the Econometric
Society, and a senior adviser to the Brookings Panel of Econometric Ac-
tivity, Professor Gordon has also served as coeditor of the *Journal of
Political Economy* and as an elected member of the executive committee
of the American Economic Association.

Productivity Growth, Inflation, and Unemployment

The Collected Essays of Robert J. Gordon

ROBERT J. GORDON

Northwestern University

With a Foreword by ROBERT M. SOLOW

CAMBRIDGE
UNIVERSITY PRESS

CAMBRIDGE UNIVERSITY PRESS
Cambridge, New York, Melbourne, Madrid, Cape Town, Singapore,
São Paulo, Delhi, Dubai, Tokyo

Cambridge University Press
32 Avenue of the Americas, New York, NY 10013-2473, USA

www.cambridge.org
Information on this title: www.cambridge.org/9780521531429

First published 2004

A catalog record for this publication is available from the British Library

Library of Congress Cataloging in Publication data

Gordon, Robert J. (Robert James), 1940–
Productivity growth, inflation, and unemployment : the collected essays of Robert J. Gordon /
Robert J. Gordon.
   p. cm.
Includes bibliographical references and index.
ISBN 0-521-80008-0 – ISBN 0-521-53142-X (pb.)
1. Economics. 2. Macroeconomics. 3. Economic development. 4. Employment (Economic
theory) 5. Industrial productivity. 6. United States – Economic policy. I. Title.
HB119.G645 A25 2003
339–dc21   2002035080

ISBN 978-0-521-80008-2 Hardback
ISBN 978-0-521-53142-9 Paperback

Transferred to digital printing 2010

To the Memory of
Zvi Griliches,
1930-99

Contents

Foreword
Robert M. Solow

An Attentive and Thoughtful Reader (called ATR from now on) will learn an enormous amount from this book about the interactions among productivity, unemployment, and inflation in the contemporary American economy. There are no more important topics within economics and not many outside of economics either. These seventeen chapters do not contain sweet nothings.

On many of today's (and tomorrow's) headline issues, ATR will have been brought to the exploratory frontier of active research. By definition, nothing at the research frontier is settled. Every conclusion is debatable (and in macro-economics, where a lot is at stake, every conclusion is debated).

As early as Chapter One, for instance, ATR will learn many of the ins and outs involved in evaluating the belief that we now live in a "new economy," with a dramatically faster sustainable rate of increase of (total factor) productivity than before, mostly induced by the advent of the computer and information technology. Bob Gordon counts as a skeptic on the new economy. I do not mean a skeptic as compared with the hype that suffuses the trade press and the media. Any reasonable person would be a skeptic in that context. I mean that his estimate of the sustainable long-run growth rate of productivity, net of important cyclical and temporary factors, is near the low end among serious students of the theory and data of productivity growth. What I hope ATR will come to understand is that where one comes out on this issue depends not on native optimism or pessimism, but on such technical matters as the right way to allow for the fairly well understood fact that the pattern of year-to-year productivity growth is related to the stage of the business cycle. It is this kind of connection between technical analysis and the big picture that makes macroeconomics so fascinating; and Gordon is a master of just that conjunction, as ATR will discover.

To take a quite different example, the nature – even the existence – of a tradeoff between unemployment and inflation has been fought over by economists for almost fifty years, as if it were a disputed territory like Alsace–Lorraine, sometimes occupied by one side, sometimes by the other. Gordon has been actively engaged in that debate at least since the "stagflation" that followed the first OPEC (Organization of Petroleum Exporting Countries) oil shock of 1973–4. One of his distinctive contributions goes back to that episode.

The standard way to deal with the unemployment-inflation nexus had been to relate unemployment to wage inflation through a wage equation (or Phillips curve) and then to relate wage inflation to price inflation through a price equation, most often a mark-up on unit labor cost. After OPEC, there was serious need for a convenient way to allow for a variety of supply shocks. Gordon found it useful to collapse the wage and price equations into a single flexible reduced-form equation for price inflation, with niches for demand shocks, supply shocks, and the forces of inertia. In this context, the "Okun gap," the ratio of real GDP to potential GDP, replaced the unemployment rate as a comprehensive measure of demand pressure. All this is spelled out in Parts Three and Four, and in the introductory essays, along with much else.

In the course of attending and thinking, ATR will also pick up many clues about the right way to do macroeconomics. In Gordon's implicit view – or am I putting words in his mouth? – macroeconomics is a fundamentally pragmatic branch of economics, closely tied to everyday observation. Its relation to microeconomics is subtle, not simple. One would not want to rely on a relation between aggregates – even an apparently reliable one – that could not reasonably arise from interactions among individual agents. But price and quantity decisions are made by millions of producers, sellers, and buyers, all reacting as intelligently as they can to an environment that is not at all transparent. Gradual wage and price adjustment is a rational response in those circumstances, not some sort of abject foolishness.

So one would not wish to push the search for "microfoundations" of macroeconomics in the wrong direction. It would be too easy to fall into the trap of settling on inappropriate microeconomic assumptions for no better reason than that they are tidy and aggregate neatly. A consequence of a concern for microeconomic realism is that macroeconomics is not monolithic. Different models may be useful for different problems. There is, of course, an opposed view, possibly more popular among the elite, that there can be only one right model, and all of macroeconomics consists of minor variations on that theme. It appears from these essays that Gordon thinks that the monolithic view will not work, and I agree with him.

Bob Gordon was a graduate student at the Massachusetts Institute of Technology (MIT) in the mid-1960s. He was part of a magnificent cohort of supremely able and delightful students. I taught and advised many of them. To say that it was a privilege and a pleasure is like saying that the Mississippi is a river. One enterprising economics department tried (and failed) to hire six of them at job-market time. That would have been like having the first six picks in the National Basketball Association (NBA) draft. Those students, now grown up, are still my friends. To be able to introduce this book merely extends the pleasure of thirty-five years ago. ATR should only have such luck.

Preface

This book is the idea of Scott Parris, economics editor in the United States for Cambridge University Press. Scott was infinitely patient, waiting for several years before the appearance of a mere outline of chapters, and then two more years before the introductions were written and submitted. Throughout, I have valued his cautionary advice about keeping the book to modest size and about what kinds of articles to include and exclude.

My greatest debt is to the sponsor of this research over a period of more than 30 years dating back to 1971, the National Science Foundation. I am very grateful to the late James Blackman, director of the Economics Program at the NSF from 1967 to 1980, both for support of my research and for inviting me to participate in the peer-review process as a member of the NSF economics panel during the period 1973–76. Since 1980, the NSF economics program has been co-directed with a sure hand by Dan Newlon and, until recently, Lynn Pollnow. I am especially grateful to Dan for frequent consultation and advice on the direction and progress of my research. The successive NSF grants have made possible the support of several generations of graduate and undergraduate research assistants at Northwestern University, some of whom are acknowledged in the initial footnotes of the chapters in this book, and many more of whom worked on papers that could not be included within the space constraints of this book.

Throughout the three decades spanned by these papers, my primary intellectual inspiration has been Zvi Griliches, who was instrumental in hiring me for my first academic job at the University of Chicago and thereafter was my mentor and adviser, especially on the productivity research included here as Part One. The invention of e-mail converted our relationship into a personal friendship, and I was privileged in 1995–6 to serve as his colleague on the Boskin Commission that evaluated the Consumer Price Index (CPI). Zvi was a tough taskmaster and continually kept my eyes on the large issues and dissuaded me, with only partial success, from frittering my time away on minor and ephemeral projects.

While Zvi was my mentor on the papers about productivity contained in Part One of this book, the late Arthur Okun played an equally important role in setting the stage for the papers in Part Three. It was Okun's inspiration, in speeches and informal remarks during 1974, to develop the concept of "macroeconomic externalities" of supply shocks, and Chapter 10 of this volume was the first paper to formalize an idea that is properly attributed to Okun rather than to me. Throughout the period from 1970 to 1980, when he tragically died at a young age, Okun was the inventor of the Brookings Papers on Economic Activity (BPEA) and the inspiration of many ideas about macroeconomics. His colleague throughout that period in organizing BPEA, continuing until this day, has been George Perry, who has also provided many ideas related to Part Four of this book, and who, with Okun's successor William Brainard, has continued to provide me with frequent opportunities to publish papers on empirical macroeconomics.

Bob Solow was my hero as soon as I learned his name while at Oxford in 1962–4, when I was twenty-three and he was thirty-nine. I used to flip through the handwritten cards at the Oxford Bodleian library to gaze in wonderment at his incredible set of publications, seemingly a hit every six months and a home run every year or two. Luck allowed me to join the entering economics class at MIT in the fall of 1964 and take Bob Solow's famous course in growth theory. Then, more luck when he agreed to be my Ph.D. thesis supervisor despite the dry measurement issues tackled in my dissertation. Over the years, he has written trenchant comments and criticisms of several papers, as if I were still in the classroom, and I can only express my thanks that he was willing to provide the foreword to this volume.

On a separate and slightly irreverent note, Chapter One of this book reveals me to be a skeptic of the Internet as an invention, a mere pipsqueak in comparison with electricity and the internal combustion engine. There is a bit of personal hypocrisy in that role, since my professional and personal lives have been altered completely, in an unambiguously positive direction, by e-mail (just e-mail and its attachments, not the web itself). Bob Solow gives hope to the skeptic. He proudly announces to one and all that "I have neither sent nor received a single e-mail message." His chief technological advance over the past decade, as he reluctantly admits, is to move from writing on an old Olivetti typewriter to a personal computer using Wordperfect 5.1. (I tried to tell him, to no avail, that Wordperfect 6.0 for DOS, vintage 1992, was the ultimate development of word processing.)

Somewhat more advanced in the information revolution than Bob Solow is my wife Julie, who is swamped by personal and professional e-mail every day and uses modern Microsoft software in her role as Executive Director of the Econometric Society. My deepest thanks go to her for nagging me to move other projects aside to finish this book. I am grateful as well to her for understanding why, night after night, it was necessary for me to stay up late and write the long introductions that, I hope, will make this volume of more than usual interest.

Robert J. Gordon
Evanston, Illinois
September 2003

Introduction

Economic growth, inflation, and unemployment are the "big three" topics of macroeconomics. Explicitly embodied in legislation in the United States and other countries are the goals of achieving rapid economic growth, a low rate of inflation, and a low rate of unemployment. When I teach lecture classes on elementary or intermediate macroeconomics to large auditoriums full of fresh-faced undergraduates, the semester begins with simple examples to show how much better off they will be in thirty years with fast rather than slow economic growth, how rapid inflation could erode their savings and that of their parents, and how much easier it will be to find a job for the summer or after graduation if the nation's overall unemployment rate is low rather than high.

THE LAY OF THE LAND

This book, then, is about the big topics of macroeconomics. It is divided into four parts, of which the first is undeniably the most important. Why was American economic growth faster between 1913 and 1972 than before or after? What caused productivity growth to slow down after 1972 and accelerate after 1995? In my view the driving forces of twentieth-century growth were the "great inventions" of the late nineteenth century, especially electricity and the internal combustion engine. The central theme of Part One is the role of these inventions in creating faster growth early in the twentieth century and then, as their influence waned around 1970, slower economic growth. Along the way, Part One asks whether the new internet economy of the late 1990s measures up to the great inventions, how we disentangle the role of technical progress from raw data on output and inputs, and how America's famous job machine that created 23 million new jobs between 1992 and 2000 may also be, in a subtle way, a source of slow productivity growth.

Part Two asks why productivity growth fluctuates over shorter intervals of a decade or so. While this question may seem to be of less than cosmic importance, its interpretation turned out, somewhat surprisingly, to be the key issue on which debates about macroeconomic doctrine were centered in the past two decades. This question also must be addressed in trying to figure out how much of the post-1995 U.S. productivity growth revival was "structural" and how much was a temporary cyclical phenomenon caused by an unsustainable burst of output growth, especially in 1999–2000.

Then Part Three examines the theoretical relationship between output, inflation, and unemployment. Why cannot the central bank (Federal Reserve or "Fed") keep interest rates so low that the unemployment rate eventually declines to zero? The usual answer is that the Fed fears an acceleration of inflation if the unemployment rate is allowed to drop too low. But that answer presupposes that there is a negative "trade-off" between inflation and unemployment, a proposition that appeared to be effectively demolished in the late 1960s and early 1970s by two winners of the Nobel Prize in economics, Milton Friedman and independently by the equally perceptive Edmund S. Phelps.

The papers in Part Three constitute one of the most exciting developments in postwar macroeconomics, the introduction of a symmetric analysis of supply and demand shocks to replace the old-fashioned Keynesian analysis that was limited to the role of demand fluctuations. The traditional sources of demand shocks, investment cycles, wars, monetary policy, and fiscal policy boosted demand relative to supply and caused the same response that occurs in the elementary microanalysis of the supply and demand for corn or furniture – spurred by a positive demand shock, both aggregate output and the aggregate price level rise.

Starting in the mid-1970s, the analysis of business cycles was broadened to give an equal starring role to supply shocks, like the sharp increase in the price of farm products that occurred in 1972–3 or of oil in 1973–5. An adverse aggregate supply shock operates just like a crop failure in microeconomics – output declines but prices increase, moving in the opposite direction. The papers of Part Three show that when prices and wages in the economy outside of the "shocked" sector are slow to adjust (or "sticky"), the adverse supply shock creates a "macroeconomic externality." The total loss of output to the entire economy can be many times as large as the size of the crop shortfall or reduction in oil supplies that sets off the reaction. The teaching of macroeconomics today is much like it was in 1980. It was the five years between 1975 and 1980 that witnessed a revolutionary change in the development of the symmetric supply–demand analysis, as shown in Part Three, as well as its instantaneous introduction into undergraduate macro textbooks.

Then Part Four provides empirical evidence to support the theories of Part Three. Did those supply shocks actually cause the "twin peaks" of unemployment and inflation in the 1970s? Why was inflation so low in the late 1990s? Why was unemployment in the United States in the late 1980s and 1990s so much lower than in most of the large European countries? Was the American economic miracle of the late1990s due to good luck, the emergence of a new paradigm that loosened previous constraints, and can it continue?

There is no reason for anyone to be interested in a collection of papers. Many authors of collected essays choose the papers and publish them, without the connecting threads that show how they emerged, whether they are still interesting or valid, and why papers on the same topic written two decades apart reach the same or different conclusions. I take it as the job of the introductions in this book to make these papers interesting – to connect them to important themes and to each other and also to help the next generation of economists see where these ideas came from.

Each of the four parts of the book includes a substantive introduction to the main issues that, by and large, can be read independently of the papers themselves. The introduction to Part One is a new essay on twentieth-century growth that attempts to link together the themes of all six papers included there. The introductions to the other three parts are shorter and less ambitious but nevertheless provide a useful overview showing how the topic developed over the past twenty or thirty years.

HOW THE IDEAS AND PAPERS EMERGED

While the introductions are largely substantive, they do include a few remarks about the sources of ideas. Young economists may be interested in the circumstances that led to some of these papers. In many cases, an easy summary is that "events precede ideas." This is most obvious in the role of the inflation of the late 1960s and the inflationary recession of 1974–5 in revealing the inadequacy of then-current economic paradigms and pressing us to figure out what was wrong and how to fix it.

The initial catalyst for my interest in economic growth came during a two-year stay at Oxford, England, in 1962–4. There my previous interest in the microeconomic topic of industrial organization soon faded away. Britain in that era had finally recovered from the strains of postwar rationing and currency non-convertibility, but otherwise seemed to this outsider to be an economic basket case. The combative unions of "I'm All Right, Jack" held sway, the standard of living was far below that in the United States and had recently been overtaken by rapid recoveries in France and Germany, and history presented a dismal record in which the level of British productivity barely grew at all from 1895 to 1938. Clearly, the siren blared out that differences in the economic growth experience across nations and historical eras were the topic to study, and that is still true today. Perhaps the most important single piece of reading to which I was exposed at Oxford was Edward Denison's seminal 1962 study of the sources of growth (cited in Chapter Two), and especially his imaginative translation of dry data on educational attainment into implications for the sources of growth.

As described in the Introduction to Part One, much of my research on economic growth, and especially Chapter Two, can be traced to a summer job I had at MIT in 1965 as a new graduate student. Puzzles in then newly developed macro data on the history of U.S. economic growth led to my Ph.D. dissertation and to my interest in measurement errors of all types, but especially in important measurement problems that were big enough to skew the historical record over decades. From the beginning, my career developed along two parallel tracks. The first was to pursue these measurement puzzles and to make a serious investment in creating new data, particularly on the prices of investment goods, both structures and equipment. Much of this work could be likened to working as a medieval scribe in the library, converting data from the Sears catalogue, *Consumer Reports*, and other sources into alternative price indexes for investment goods. This work took almost twenty years before a book emerged (see the references to Chapter One). Yet along the way there were lots of ideas that involved substantive problems rather than measurement, and these were the sources for the six papers in Part One.

The second research track was motivated by the central debate in macroeconomics that was boiling as I moved in 1968 from a pleasant life as graduate student at MIT to the intellectual cauldron of the University of Chicago. Just as inflation was accelerating in the late 1960s, Chicago's most famous macroeconomist, Milton Friedman, had delivered his perfectly timed presidential address launching the natural rate hypothesis, contending that in the long run inflation is independent of the unemployment rate. As a new assistant professor, I had to plunge into the hot water and figure out how, if at all, to reconcile my Keynesian MIT training with Friedman's distinction between the negatively sloped short-run Phillips curve (based on expectational errors) and the vertical long-run Phillips curve. From then on, my major topic in time-series macroeconomics was the inflation–unemployment tradeoff, which created the papers in Parts Three and Four of this book.

My research on economic growth could have been carried out almost anywhere and did not require a particular university location. But the combination of graduate school at MIT and a first job at Chicago were crucial in making possible the research on the inflation–unemployment tradeoff. Being at Chicago with an MIT education was like watching two sticks rubbing together. The flame soon ignited, especially when I found that my students were teaching me more in my first Chicago graduate class than I was teaching them. But a second crucial piece of luck in timing and location came when Arthur M. Okun had the idea to start the Brookings Panel on Economic Activity as a triannual series of meetings, with the papers and discussions to be published almost immediately, within three months of the meeting rather than the two-year lag typical of conference volumes then and now.[1]

The original format of the Brookings panel (BPEA) was to have a core group of young macroeconomists who would become the resident expert on a particular topic, writing a major paper every year or two with "sector reports" in-between. While I was originally requested to cover consumption expenditures, I asked instead to handle the Phillips curve trade-off as my main topic. As a result, I wound up publishing no less than seven papers, most of them in print within four months after they were written, within the brief period 1970–3. Some

---

[1] The Brookings Panel held three meetings per year during 1970 to 1978 and two meetings per year since then, for a total of seventy-five meetings through the end of 2002. I have been to seventy-four of the seventy-five meetings, and coorganizer George Perry has been at every meeting.

of these papers had a lasting influence but none of them are included in this volume. Events, particularly the ongoing acceleration of inflation in 1969–70, the Nixon price controls, and the supply shocks of 1972–5, happened so fast that most of those papers were subject to rapid obsolescence. Nevertheless, the rapid publication schedule of BPEA gave me a rare and perhaps unfair advantage in always having the last word on the latest puzzle involving inflation. Another advantage conferred by BPEA also was of immeasurable value, the chance to interact with the top macroeconomists at the regular BPEA meetings, be exposed to the latest data that we could not explain, and start figuring out what to tackle next. In that sense, my two-track career was schizophrenic in nature, with the measurement research resembling a traditional cloistered ivory-tower experience, whereas the inflation research centered on the BPEA directed my communication and energy outside the confines of the local university campus.

Some acclaimed academics have succeeded by moving from topic to topic as the occasion emerged, often in collaboration with coauthors.[2] My professional hero, next to Bob Solow, was the late Zvi Griliches, whose prolific research career was exactly the opposite. Zvi "owned" the production function as a topic – when he moved to a new subtopic, whether hedonic price deflators, capital measurement, ability and human capital, patents, or research and development, it was part of a broad lifelong research plan to dig away at the outstanding puzzles related to the production process. My approach was similar but in a narrower area. I kept coming back to the same topics, whether price, output, and input measurement, cyclical productivity fluctuations, the Phillips curve, or aggregate supply shocks, both because macroeconomics is constantly creating new puzzles and new data, but also because I felt a responsibility to see whether my old theories and empirical results still worked. If they did not, I wanted to figure out why. There is no way to give advice to younger scholars on these different research strategies. To stick to the same topics over decades, those topics had better be important and longlasting in relevance. To move from topic to topic and have striking insights on a variety of unrelated topics, exactly the opposite of my own research approach, you had better be very smart.

CRITERIA FOR INCLUSION AND OMISSIONS

Selecting the seventeen papers for this volume was painful. The publisher set a page limit, which ruled out numerous long empirical time-series papers. Page limits also ruled out several long survey articles, including two from the *Journal of Economic Literature* on the sources of price and wage rigidities.

This volume includes papers that fit together tightly into the four themes, and three of the seventeen are papers have not been published before. Many of my other papers are ruled out on the basis of length or topics that do not fit within

---

[2] In Michael Szenberg's fascinating book *Passion and Craft: Economists at Work* (Michigan, 1998), I was struck at the ease with which such subjects as Greg Mankiw, Avinash Dixit, and others could move from topic to topic, reflecting their innate brilliance and analytical ability.

the framework of this volume, whether on corporate tax shifting, government investment during World War II, or remeasuring the volatility of U.S. GDP before 1929. Also, I have leaned toward including papers from lesser-known sources rather than my articles from well-known journals like the *American Economic Review* or the *Journal of Political Economy*.

The topics of the four parts of this book have the virtue that all are still relevant as the economy inches its way into the twenty-first century. We wonder when reading Part One whether productivity growth in the next decade will look more like the ebullient five years after 1995 or the dismal twenty-three years before 1995. Part Two makes us wait eagerly for the next quarterly productivity report, to see in retrospect how much of the post-1995 revival was cyclical rather than structural, and whether the 2001 recession and 2002–3 recovery adhered to old cyclical patterns or created a new one. Parts Three and Four help us to understand explicitly why inflation was so quiescent in the late 1990s and why, for the first time in decades, there was no sharp upward spike of interest rates as previously had been necessary to quell a significant acceleration of inflation. Since tight monetary policy did not cause the 2001 recession, its causes are to be found elsewhere, especially in the collapse of the New Economy investment boom.

A final word is needed on the ground rules for reproducing these papers. All of them have been newly typeset. Every paper is reproduced exactly in its original form, including any forecasts that were made long ago, no matter whether they turned out to be right or wrong (the introductions provide hindsight retrospective on several of these forecasts). No changes were made except to provide the final published reference for items of the reference lists that were originally "forthcoming," i.e., not yet published at the time the paper went to press, and also to clarify references to dates (e.g., "four years ago" in a 1982 paper is changed here to "in 1978").

PART ONE

THE HISTORY, THEORY, AND MEASUREMENT OF PRODUCTIVITY GROWTH

INTRODUCTION

STUDYING GROWTH AT THE FRONTIER

The gains to human welfare resulting from even minor increases in the rate of economic growth are enormous. In the oft-quoted words of Nobel Prize-winning University of Chicago economist Robert E. Lucas, Jr., "the consequences for human welfare are simply staggering. Once one starts thinking about them, it is hard to think of anything else" (Lucas, 1988, p. 5). Changes in the rate of economic growth in the history of the United States over long intervals have been sufficiently large to create the enormous differences that Lucas was thinking about. A slow growth rate of income per person, say 1 percent per year, causes the standard of living to double in seventy years, roughly every three generations. But a more rapid growth rate, say 3 percent per year, will cause the standard of living to double in a mere twenty-three years, making each generation twice as well off as that of its parents.

The consequences of differences in growth rates are most obvious in comparing rich and poor countries. In the past century, there has been little if any improvement in standards of living in some African countries and among rural populations in some Asian and Latin American nations. Yet the standard of living in the United States, at least as conventionally measured, has increased by a factor of about 8, and that of Japan by a factor of perhaps 25. While the average American is choosing among home entertainment systems and sport-utility vehicles, living in a suburb with clean water, reliable electricity, and constant propaganda to buy broadband cable access for the one or more family personal computers, life in the poorest countries involves a very different set of choices about obtaining sufficient food to survive and avoiding deadly diseases for which no medicines or cures are readily available.

My work on productivity and economic growth has focused mainly on the United States over the period since 1870, and particularly on the explanation of accelerations and decelerations in the rate of productivity growth. While a study of epochs in U.S. history may perhaps seem of less cosmic importance than asking why some nations are rich and some are poor, the U.S. experience has strong appeal as a research topic. First, starting sometime in the late nineteenth

7

century, when the per-capita income of the United States surpassed that of the United Kingdom, the level of productivity in the United States has defined the "frontier" of what is possible for the world's developed nations. Accelerations and decelerations in the growth rate at the frontier call out for explanations – are the sources of speed up and slow down unique to the United States, in which case Japan and the richer nations of Europe might overtake the U.S. frontier position, or are those sources of deceleration universal and without implication for the ranking of income per capita across nations?

Second, the focus on U.S. history helps to establish links between the pace of economic growth and the timing of the invention of new products and technologies.[1] More than in other countries, the development of the United States was spurred by economic opportunities based on a high ratio of land and natural resources to labor – these outsized potential returns not only rewarded investment in existing technologies, but they also fostered prolific inventions from McCormick's reaper to Edison's electric light and motor – and in turn the inventions created further opportunities for profitable investment. The "Great Inventions" emphasized in the first essay in this book were disproportionately American creations. The United States was directly involved in the invention of electricity through the work of Thomas A. Edison, as well as Alexander Graham Bell's telephone, George Eastman's roll film, and Lewis Waterman's fountain pen. The Germans Nikolaus Otto and Karl Benz played the major role in the development of the internal combustion engine and automobile. Nevertheless, America soon dominated the development and exploitation of motor transport, not to mention the Wright Brothers' first flight in 1903 that led two decades later to commercial air transport. So completely did the United States take over the development of the internal combustion engine that in 1929 the United States had 26 million registered automobiles and almost 5 million registered trucks, doubtless more than the rest of the world combined.[2]

Third, the lightbulb of guidance provided by economic data is not "turned off" by wartime destruction, as in Japan and most European countries. Students of U.S. economic growth do not have to be concerned with the destruction of substantial portions of the capital stock in World Wars I and II, and the loss of American lives and skills in both wars was sufficiently minor as to be safely ignored.[3] Nevertheless, as we shall see, the combined experiences of the Great

---

[1] My two favorite books on the interplay between inventions and economic growth, both written from a global rather than U.S. perspective, are Mokyr (1990) and Rosenberg-Birdzell (1986).

[2] Perhaps most important was that, judging from 1941 production figures, at the outbreak of World War II the U.S. had the capacity to manufacture 4 million automobiles and 1 million trucks, swamping the capacity of all other nations in the world combined. In one interpretation, World War II was a "war of engines" and, thanks to Lend-Lease, the Russian Army rode to victory in over 350,000 American trucks, which if delivered over the three years 1942–4 represented a mere 10 percent of American productive capacity to manufacture trucks (Overy, 1995, p. 214).

[3] U.S. military deaths in World War II were only 0.3 percent of the 1940 population of 131.7 million.

Depression and World War II create significant distortions in U.S. data that are important enough to alter the long-term growth record in a misleading way.

LABOR PRODUCTIVITY AND MULTIFACTOR PRODUCTIVITY

Whether talking about differences in economic growth across countries or across eras within one country, it matters whether one is talking about "average labor productivity" (ALP) or "multifactor productivity" (MFP). This distinction turns out to be central to an understanding of U.S. economic growth and of the role of technical change in creating that growth. ALP is output per labor hour, whereas MFP is output divided by a weighted average of labor input and capital input – the weights are usually the income shares of labor and capital, say 75 and 25 percent, respectively. The latter concept (MFP) almost always registers slower growth than the former (ALP) – the difference between them is the effect of "capital deepening," the boost to ALP that comes from the fact that capital input almost always grows faster than labor input.[4]

Another equivalent definition is that the growth rate of MFP is a weighted average of the growth in labor productivity or ALP (weighted by labor's share) and the growth rate of "capital productivity," that is, the growth rate of output minus the growth rate of capital input. This turns out to be crucial for understanding the "big wave" interpretation of U.S. economic growth in the twentieth century examined in Chapter Two. If labor productivity growth is steady but there is a big bulge in the growth of capital productivity, then MFP growth will soar relative to that of labor productivity. That is part of the story of the U.S. economy in the mid-twentieth century and, as we shall see below, much of the bulge in the growth of capital productivity reflects measurement errors rather than historical fact.[5] MFP is now often called "Solow's residual" as a tribute to Robert M. Solow's pathbreaking (1957) work that provided a

---

[4] An example clarifies these concepts. In the long run output growth and capital growth tend to be the same, say 4 percent per year. Growth in population or labor input is, say, 1 percent per year. Then ALP (average labor product) growth would be 4 minus 1, or 3 percent per year. If, as stated in the text, the weight on capital input is 25 percent, then input growth would be 1.75 percent (25 percent times capital growth of 4 percent plus 75 percent plus labor growth of 1 percent). MFP growth is 4 minus 1.75, or 2.25 percent per year. The "capital deepening" effect is the capital weight of 25 percent times the difference between capital and labor growth (4 – 1), or 0.75 percent. Thus MFP growth (2.25) equals ALP growth (3.0) minus the capital deepening effect (0.75).

[5] Continuing with the same example as in the previous footnote, MFP growth of 2.25 percent is a weighted average of ALP growth of 3 percent (4 minus 1) and capital productivity of zero percent (4 minus 4) with weights of 75 and 25 percent, respectively. Imagine that capital growth dropped from 4 to 0 while output growth remained at 4 and labor input growth remained at 1. MFP growth would accelerate from 2.25 to 3.25. MFP growth would exceed ALP growth, because the capital deepening effect is negative. To the extent that the decline in capital growth was a measurement error, so would be the acceleration of MFP growth in the opposite direction.

rigorous theoretical rationale for the near-universal practice since then of measuring the elasticity of output to changes of inputs by the income share of that
input.[6]

INTERPRETING THE ACCELERATIONS
AND SLOWDOWN

The recorded annals of U.S. productivity growth since the late nineteenth century have been marked by several notable turning points, which are examined
and interpreted in several of the papers in the first section of this book. When
did these turning points occur? The easiest way to remember the chronology
of productivity growth is "slow" 1870–1913, "fast" 1913–72, "slow" 1972–95,
and a recovery of debatable size and duration to somewhere between "fast"
and "slow" during 1995–2000. These long intervals are chosen to span several
business cycles and, in particular, to leap over the economic distortions of the
Great Depression and World War II by treating 1928–1950 as a single period
within the longer 1913–72 interval.

A marked acceleration distinguished the post-World War I half century from
the four decades prior to World War I and was one of the most important features of the historical record, noted by Solomon Fabricant in his introduction
to Kendrick's pathbreaking 1961 volume, that for the first time had set out the
historical record in annual data.[7] It took much less time for the post-1972 productivity growth slowdown to be recognized, and indeed it was analyzed by
William Nordhaus (1972) just as it was beginning by today's standard chronology.[8] The post-1995 productivity growth revival was preannounced by the
perceptive economics staff of *Business Week* just as it was commencing,[9] but
several years elapsed before it was recognized by academic economists.

The first two chapters of this book, Chapter One on the new economy and the
"great inventions," and Chapter Two on interpreting the "big wave" of U.S. economic growth, directly address the three turning points in U.S. growth history in
1913, 1972, and 1995. They share a common theme, that the "great inventions"
of the late nineteenth century (especially electricity and the internal combustion engine) were so powerful in their economic influence that they propelled a
fifty-year-long boom in productivity growth between 1913 and 1972, and that
the post-1972 slowdown could be interpreted as caused by diminishing returns,

---

[6] A short, revealing, and unique history of the "residual" is provided by Griliches (2000, Chapter
One).

[7] "The change in trend that came after World War I is one of the most interesting facts before us.
There is little question about it. . . . Some readers of the charts might prefer to see in them not a
sharp alteration of trend, but rather a gradual speeding up of the rate of growth over the period
as a whole. The latter reading is not entirely out of the question, but it seems to fit the facts less
well than the former" (Solomon Fabricant, p. xliii in the introduction to Kendrick, 1961).

[8] Nordhaus (1972) examined the slowdown that occurred in the late 1960s relative to the preceding
portion of the postwar era.

[9] See the cover banner in *Business Week*, October 9, 1995, "Productivity to the Rescue."

the gradual erosion of the payoff from the earlier inventions. Because Chapters One and Two are two of the most important and interesting papers included in this book, the following sections of this introduction devote disproportionate attention to their intellectual background and development.

THE "ONE BIG WAVE" AND THE "GREAT INVENTIONS"

While Fabricant's introduction to Kendrick's 1961 volume pointed to the post-1913 growth acceleration, this turning point did not attract much attention in the first decade following the 1961 publication of Kendrick's book. Indeed, the amount written about the post-1913 acceleration pales in contrast to the huge literature on the post-1972 productivity growth slowdown. Despite much effort by many talented economists, by the mid-1990s no consensus had emerged on the causes of the slowdown, and indeed numerous proposed causes, including energy prices, infrastructure, and mismeasurement, had been discarded as inconsistent with the facts. Equally puzzling was the apparent conflict between rapid growth of investment in computers and software and the failure to observe a payoff in faster productivity growth. Indeed growth in ALP was even slower during 1987–95 than in 1972–87, despite the invention of the personal computer and its adaptation in nearly every business.

As recently as 1998, economists were struggling to propose explanations of what had become known as the "Solow computer paradox," based on Robert Solow's (1987) inspired quip "You can see the computer age everywhere but in the productivity statistics." The prevailing reaction to Solow's paradox was "well, the computers are indeed everywhere, so there must be something wrong with the productivity statistics." A second possible solution was suggested by the important work of Stephen Oliner and Dan Sichel (Oliner and Sichel, 1994; Sichel, 1997), who criticized Solow's basic premise by arguing that "the computers are *not* everywhere," accounting for a mere 2 percent of the nation's capital stock.

Starting from this intellectual environment, we can trace the genesis of the main ideas in Chapters One and Two.

1. There was another logical exit out of Solow's paradox beyond the two listed above, namely, "perhaps there is something wrong with the computers."[10] Chapter One argues that the most unique attribute of the computer as an invention is its unprecedented rate of price decline, which inevitably implies an unprecedented onset of diminishing returns, so that the greatest contributions of computers to productivity lie in the past, not the future.[11] This skepticism is further extended in Chapter

---

[10] A masterful examination of every possible solution to Solow's paradox is Triplett (1999), where not just three but eight alternative solutions are proposed.

[11] Personal experience colors academic writing. I was an early convert to personal computers in 1983, relatively late to e-mail in 1993, and an adamant defender of DOS-based programs,

One to address the post-1995 development of the internet and web, and both are found lacking in contrast to the great inventions of the past.

2. The original source that created my fascination with the great old inventions was an unlikely paperback (Bettman, 1974) that I discovered long ago while staying at a quaint bed and breakfast in rural Michigan. The most entertaining part of Chapter One is the tale of the "bad old days" of the late nineteenth century, taken almost entirely from Bettman's book. What I added to Bettman's tale of widespread misery was the subsequent examination of how "we got from there to here," that is, how our standard of living made its transition from Bettman's bad old days to the new world of the 1950s. Much of the world established by the 1950s was made possible by the contribution of the great inventions and their spinoffs (i.e., consumer appliances and air conditioning as spinoffs of electricity, and supermarkets and superhighways as spinoffs of the internal combustion engine).

3. The idea of comparing the post-1995 "New Economy" to the great old inventions came as a reaction against the frenetic journalistic hype of 1998–9 that proclaimed the world to be in the midst of a true revolution: "The [computer] chip has transformed us at least as pervasively as the internal combustion engine or electric motor.[12] "When I thought about the transformation of Bettmann's dimly lit world of animal waste and rural isolation into the modern society of the 1950s and 1960s, I could not see how the internet and web could be placed in the same category in the pantheon of inventions. Instead, the web seemed more like a further step in the original 1844 invention of the telegraph and 1876 invention of the telephone.

4. The "big wave" examined in Chapter Two refers to the period of rapid growth in MFP between 1913 and 1972 at a rate much faster than before 1913 or after 1972. My interest in the chronology of long-term shifts in U.S. economic growth can be traced as far back as 1965, when I was working as a research assistant for Franklin Fisher and Edwin Kuh following my first year as a graduate student at MIT. Leaping out from the annals of U.S. economic growth in the newly published Kendrick data was a startling fact, namely a near-doubling in the average product of capital (the output-to-capital ratio) when the 1950s were compared with the 1920s and earlier decades. Why would something so basic as the productivity of capital take a one-time leap instead of changing slowly over time? As previewed above, a sharp

---

especially WordPerfect for DOS 6.0, against the onslaught of Windows/mouse-based programs. From 1984 on, I saw diminishing returns operating powerfully, and suffered when communicating with others in having to convert my documents from the elegant code-based interface of WordPerfect 6.0 to the unintelligible and uncontrollable Word 97 and its successors.

[12] *Fortune*, June 8, 1998, pp. 86–87.

jump in the productivity of capital translates into a sharp jump in MFP relative to ALP, and this is just what happened in the United States between 1928 and 1950. But I was suspicious of the validity of the data, which showed output surging ahead despite a complete cessation in the growth of the capital stock between the late 1920s and late 1940s. How did we produce so much in World War II with nothing more than the capital stock of 1929?

5. I discovered part of the answer in writing my 1967 Ph.D. dissertation, that the U.S. government had paid for a massive amount of plant and equipment investment during World War II, but this major increment to the capital stock had never been included in the capital input of the private sector. The rest of the explanation, however, waited until the early 1990s when the "big wave" essay, reproduced here as Chapter Two, began to emerge. In addition to the role of government-owned capital, Chapter Two shows that the growth of capital input in the 1928–50 period was radically understated by the universal practice of assuming that old capital is discarded on a fixed time schedule, regardless of whether new capital is built to replace it. Common sense suggests that old capital lives longer when economic conditions (the Great Depression and World War II) cause a near-cessation of new investment. When stirred together in Chapter Two with other factors, including government-financed highway investment and adjustments for advances in educational attainment in the early twentieth century, the 1965 puzzle of the leap in the output-capital ratio is completely resolved. In the new analysis the 1996 output-capital ratio is no higher than in 1870.

CONCEPTS OF INVESTMENT AND TECHNICAL CHANGE

Whereas Chapters One and Two are among my most recent papers, Chapter Three is among the earliest, written in 1968 and never published until now. Its main point is both fundamental and infrequently recognized. For decades economists have debated the relative importance of capital accumulation and technical change as sources of economic growth. But this is a false dichotomy if capital accumulation is not an independent source of growth but rather a by-product of technical change. Referring back to the previous discussion of MFP growth as being equal to ALP growth minus the contribution of capital deepening, Chapter Three argues that in the long run *all* capital deepening is caused by technical change rather than being an independent source of growth. With no technical change there will be no capital deepening. This accords with one's common sense that the long-run increase in a nation's standard of living is measured by income per capita, roughly equal to the growth in ALP (i.e., including the part of ALP growth caused by capital deepening that depends in turn on the rate of technical change), and not by the growth in MFP, which excludes the contribution of tech-driven capital deepening.

CAPITAL DEEPENING RESPONDS TO TECHNICAL CHANGE

The basic argument contained in Chapter Three was developed independently by Thomas K. Rymes (1971). A simple example demonstrates the deep truth that capital deepening – that is, the growth in the capital-labor ratio – must be directly attributable to technological change. If in the year 1770 all capital equipment consisted of vintage 1770 Watt-Bolton steam engines, and if technical change was all disembodied (that is, figuring out how to rearrange the Watt-Bolton steam engines to boost production) then capital accumulation would have ground to a halt within a few decades of 1770, exhausted by diminishing returns. The entire contribution of capital deepening to labor productivity growth since 1770 is attributable to trillions of dollars of investment in railroads, autos, trucks, airplanes, electrical machinery, computers, and much else, that was invented and further developed after 1770 and would not have occurred without those post-1770 inventions. Or, in the evocative words of Evsey Domar, one of my MIT professors quoted in Chapter Three, without technical change capital accumulation would just amount to "wooden ploughs piled up on top of existing wooden ploughs" (Domar, 1961, p. 712).

This point applies only to capital deepening, not to all capital accumulation. Technical change is not necessary for growth in the capital stock that keeps pace with growth in labor input, maintaining a fixed capital-labor ratio. Investment would then be entirely devoted to equipping the additional members of the population with additional machines of a given technology, whether wooden ploughs or personal computers. But because all capital deepening ultimately requires technical change, existing measures of MFP growth cannot be interpreted as measuring the pace of technical progress, since the capital-deepening effect (due also to technical change) is subtracted out in calculating MFP growth.

Chapter Three contains another important contribution. Its model of economic growth is a direct precursor of the "new growth theory" of the 1980s and 1990s associated with the names of Robert E. Lucas, Jr. (1988) and Paul Romer (1986, 1990). There is no "costless" or "disembodied" technical change. All technical improvements require the costly inputs of research workers, who are withdrawn from the pool of available production workers. The paper assumes a competitive market for capital and production workers but not necessarily for research workers, who may be "exploited" in the sense that they are unable to obtain as labor compensation the full marginal return of their research ideas. As a result, the contribution of technical change to economic growth is characterized by the excess of the social rate of return of research workers relative to production workers. This excess return both contributes directly to output growth and indirectly by causing the growth of capital input to be faster than without technical change. In short, capital deepening is fully endogenous and fully dependent on the flow of ideas from the research workers, not an independent source of growth.

The model of Chapter Three is set in a mid-1960s historical context as an evaluation of one of the great debates of that era, centered on the attack by Zvi Griliches and Dale Jorgenson (Griliches and Jorgenson, 1966; Jorgenson and Griliches, 1967) on the mainstream growth accounting framework originally created in the Nobel-recognized work of Robert M. Solow (1957), as well as by two pioneers of growth data and growth accounting, respectively, John W. Kendrick (1956) and Edward F. Denison (1962). Griliches and Jorgenson raised the rhetorical bar by claiming that Solow, Kendrick, and Denison were guilty of serious "errors of measurement" in their calculations of MFP.

The essence of the Griliches and Jorgenson attack was that previous authors had greatly overstated the share of economic growth attributable to technical change and understated that due to input growth, through an understatement of improvements in the growth of input quality. Yet the analysis of Chapter Three shows that most of the corrections to input growth made by Griliches and Jorgenson simply transferred the fruits of technical change into input growth, not just for capital input but also for labor input. The paper's treatment of education, showing that the returns to education are endogenous as well to the pace of technical change (in the sense that research workers would not be paid as much if they had no creative ideas), is still not widely recognized.[13]

Chapter Three shows that even those like Solow, Kendrick, and Denison, who had attributed a relatively large share of growth to technical change, had understated that share, and Griliches and Jorgenson (by transferring some of the achievements of technical change to input growth) had understated it even more.[14] The paper serves several purposes from this vantage point – its main point remains valid, that capital deepening is not an independent source of economic growth. It anticipates several themes of the new growth theory, including the endogeneity of investment in research and of the return to education. And at a more arcane level it provides useful insight into the mid-1960s debates on the sources of growth that help illuminate current discussions of the role

---

[13] This is part of a broader point in the study of cross-country differences in economic growth. Many of the so-called "causes" of economic growth, e.g., education, are themselves in large part the consequence of growth. Countries as they become richer can afford to spread the bounty to education, research subsidies, better infrastructure, and better justice systems that reduce crime and corruption.

[14] Griliches (2000, pp. 21–24) provides some "mea culpa" reflections on several directions in which the Griliches and Jorgenson critique was overstated, and on p. 89 refers both to my Chapter Three essay and to Rymes (1971) as legitimate arguments that the role of technical change is understated in conventional decompositions of economic growth. Unfortunately he dismisses the importance of our case and makes no mention of its relevance for the debate between Griliches and Jorgenson and Denison, Kendrick, and Solow, because we leave the underlying sources of technical change unexplained. Yes, but so does everyone else, at least at the empirical level of linking macro fluctuations in productivity growth to micro variations in patents, R&D spending, or specific inventions.

of computer investment in propelling the "new economy" boom of the late 1990s.[15]

The main point of Chapter Three can be applied to a further understanding of the productivity revival of the late 1990s in the United States. All calculations show that MFP growth revived, indicating an acceleration of technical change, but this understates the role of technical change, which together with an abundant supply of capital directly created the investment boom and hence the capital-deepening effect of the late 1990s. If the post-1995 acceleration in the rate of technical change were to disappear, this would erode the foundations of the investment boom, thus eliminating not just the revival of MFP growth but also the contribution of capital deepening.

HOW CAN WE MEASURE THE PREFERRED CONCEPT OF CAPITAL?

Much of my work related to economic growth has involved the measurement of capital goods prices, particularly in a detailed book-length project (Gordon, 1990). If over a long historical interval there has been a substantial upward bias in the price indexes of capital goods, by implication there has been a downward bias in the growth rate of capital input and an overstatement of the role of Solow's residual in economic growth. In one sense Chapter Three's argument reduces the importance of accurate measurement of investment goods prices, since it shows that measurement changes that increase the importance of capital deepening have no direct implications for the rate of technical change. However, from a broader perspective we need accurate measures of real investment and capital input, and my 1990 book attempted to explore the feasibility of more accurate price measurement across a wide array of capital goods.[16]

Throughout most of his life, Edward F. Denison represented one extreme in a spectrum of views on the measurement of capital goods prices. He had consistently opposed efforts to consider two machines as equal if they had the same performance attributes rather than the same cost of production. His earlier views would have considered two Dell computers priced at $1,000 to be equal amounts of investment and capital, even if the second had twice the computational capability of the first, as long as they cost the same to produce.

---

[15] In light of the retrospective importance of its ideas and its lack of recognition since 1968, I regret that the Chapter Three essay was not published. Indeed, I never submitted it for publication. At that age, I did not see clearly enough that much of the complexity could have been stripped away, and that the main points could have been made independently of the details of my critique of Griliches and Jorgenson. In that publication-driven stage of life prior to tenure, I felt that it was more important to work on "original" research rather than a critique of someone else's research, and yet in doing so I missed the chance to publish a shorter and "cleaner" version of Chapter Three that focussed on the main ideas, some of which seem quite original in retrospect.

[16] Ironically, in light of his role as a protagonist of Chapter Three, it was Dale Jorgenson (1966) who showed insightfully that measurement errors in capital goods price indexes have little impact on the accuracy of series on MFP, since a measured downward bias in capital input growth is largely or entirely offset by a measured downward bias in output growth, that is, output including investment.

Chapter Four provides a brief introduction to Denison's views, using the example of a computer "box" that in successive models produces ever greater quantities of computer "attributes," for example, speed, memory, hard drive capacity, speed of CD-ROM, etc. As explained in this short paper, the correct way to measure prices is to compare the "net revenue" (i.e., net of labor and fuel inputs) produced by a capital good. Thus an airplane represents more "real investment" if, for a constant purchase price, it provides more seats, uses fewer pilots, or uses less fuel under comparable operating conditions. This concept has the virtue that the notion of net revenue can be validated on the market for used assets. Thus, otherwise equivalent aircraft which have higher maintenance costs would have a lower ability to generate net revenue and hence be judged to represent less real capital input.

Denison was persuaded, in his last published essay (1993), that his previously endorsed method of equating costs of production was wrong, and that in principle I was right to implement my preferred method of considering two capital goods to be equal if they were equivalent in their ability to generate net revenue, for example, two aircraft or two computers. Chapter Four shows that our remaining disagreement reflected a different standard of consistency. Because he felt I had implemented my desirable criterion for only a few products, it should be rejected entirely since it was infeasible to implement it for every product. In my response in Chapter Four, I argued that "half a loaf is a waystation to three-quarters of a loaf, and half a loaf as a temporary solution is far better than a permanent solution of no loaf at all."

IS THERE A FEEDBACK FROM LABOR MARKETS TO PRODUCTIVITY GROWTH?

Once we have sorted out the role of technical change and input accumulation as sources of economic growth, what is left to explain differences over time and across countries? A hint appears at the end of Chapter Two, which shows that two major historical events contributed to the "big wave" of U.S. productivity growth in the middle of the twentieth century, namely restrictive immigration laws (and the world wars that inhibited immigration) that limited labor supply, and New Deal legislation that legitimized unions and allowed high school graduates to demand a rent for their labor services above their marginal product. Chapter Five broadens this theme by exploring those policy choices that can have outcomes that result in faster or slower productivity growth, not by stimulating faster or slower capital accumulation but by making labor more or less expensive to hire.

Are the apparently separate problems of high unemployment in Europe and slow productivity growth in America interrelated? A casual tourist's impression would suggest this possibility. The United States has millions of casual low-skilled service-sector jobs with few if any regulations on hiring, firing, qualifications, pensions, or medical care benefits. The U.S. jobs, which appear only rarely in Europe, include grocery baggers, bus boys, parking-lot attendants, and those ubiquitous valet-parking employees at urban restaurants. These jobs may reduce U.S. unemployment while also reducing productivity growth in the U.S. service sector.

Chapter Five shows how misleading is the facile contrast of Europe following a path of high productivity growth, high unemployment, and relatively greater income equality, in contrast to the opposite path being pursued by the United States. However plausible the notion that policy measures (like restrictive labor-market legislation) can create a positive correlation between unemployment and productivity growth (i.e., higher unemployment and faster productivity growth in Europe), that relation is likely soon to be eroded by changes in the rate of capital accumulation. The chapter finds that countries with the greatest increases in unemployment had the largest slowdowns in the growth rate of capital per potential labor hour. Europe entered the 1990s with much higher unemployment in the U.S., but with approximately the same rate of capacity utilization, indicating that there was no longer sufficient capital to equip all the employees who would be at work at the lower unemployment rates of the 1960s and 1970s.

The raw numbers show substantially more rapid growth in output per hour in the four large European countries than in the United States. Faster productivity growth in Europe mainly reflects the convergence effect, that is, that Europe started at a lower level of productivity and gradually converged toward the U.S. level, and the impact of more rapid capital accumulation. The fact that European productivity growth slowed down more than that in the U.S. after 1972 is attributed both to the gradual weakening of the convergence effect and also to the negative impact of wage-setting shocks that both increased the unemployment rate and reduced the growth rate of capital per potential labor hour.

CAN A SINGLE INDUSTRY BE TIED TO THE POST-1972 SLOWDOWN?

As suggested above, the post-1972 productivity growth slowdown can be linked in an informal sense to a "running out of ideas" hypothesis.[17] Two of those that I have studied closely, primarily in my durable goods prices book (Gordon, 1990), are electric utility generation and airlines. Once the airlines made the transition from propellers to jets in the period 1958–70, one could describe both industries with the same language. Starting in 1882 for the former (the date of Edison's first power station in New York) and starting in 1903 for the latter (the Wright brothers), both industries experienced quantum leaps in ratios of performance to price and performance to employment that suddenly ground to a halt in the late 1960s. As airline passengers, today we are still flying in 747's of roughly the same dimensions and speed as in 1969. Electric utility manufacturers faced a somewhat more complex technological environment, suddenly encountering a barrier (supercritical pressure, analogous to the sound barrier) and in addition facing a negative shock for productivity that the airlines did not have to face, namely antipollution regulations.

---

[17] This is closely related to Nordhaus's (1972) "depletion hypothesis."

Chapter Six looks closely at the electric utility generating industry, which is a prime culprit in the U.S. productivity growth slowdown after 1972. To examine labor productivity at the level of individual plants, Chapter Six develops econometric labor and fuel demand equations for a large panel data set covering almost all fossil-fueled electric generating capacity over the period 1948–87. Labor productivity and fuel efficiency both advanced rapidly until the late 1960s and then both reversed direction.

Chapter Six contains a unique methodological device in which I "interviewed the residuals" to find out why they were residuals in the econometric equations explaining labor productivity and fuel efficiency. The telephone interviews with individual plant managers support the view that after decades of increased scale, temperature, and pressure, a "technological frontier" was reached in which new large plants developed unanticipated maintenance problems requiring substantial additions of maintenance employees. Environmental regulations also contributed to the productivity reversal but were secondary in importance to the technological barriers. These reports both documented what one might expect but did not know (e.g., "we hired 25 percent more employees to do maintenance on our new air pollution equipment) or what we might not expect ("Oh, didn't you know, we run a hundred mile railroad to bring coal to our plant, and all of those railroad employees are included on our books.")

CONCLUSION ABOUT THEMES IN PART ONE

Without repeating the main themes in Part One, we can connect a few links among them. We start in Chapter One with the central role of the "great inventions" in creating the core of twentieth century economic growth in the "big wave" period between 1913 and 1972. The initial inventions generated spin-offs, including for electricity the major consumer appliances (radio, TV, washer, dryer, refrigerator, air conditioning) and for the internal combustion engine such follow-ons as the automobile, motor truck, propeller aircraft, superhighways, suburbs, and supermarkets. Yet each of these inventions could run out of steam, and this is the common theme in explaining the post-1972 slowdown. An obvious example is the interstate highway system, which "you could only build once."[18] Chapter Six points to a more precise example, electricity generation, one of the great inventions of the late nineteenth century, which ran into diminishing returns in the late 1960s.

The theoretical theme of these chapters is that the pace of technical change pervades all measures of factor inputs, not just the growth rate of capital but also the returns to education. Technical change and continuing opportunities to exploit the great inventions help to explain rapid productivity growth in the "Big

---

[18] Yes, the nooses of ring roads around suburbs are ever-expanding, but you could only build the basic system once. Look at any U.S. highway map and ask when an additional highway will be needed to supplement the existing four-lane interstate highway between, for example, Fargo, North Dakota, and Butte, Montana, on Interstate 94 (nearly 1,000 miles), or between Salt Lake City and Portland, Oregon, on I-84 (about 600 miles), or between El Paso, Texas, and Billings, Montana, on I-25 (more than 1,000 miles).

Wave" period between 1913 and 1972, while the extraneous factors of the Great Depression and World War II explain why these technological opportunities generated fast growth in capital input in the 1920s and 1945–70 but much slower growth in capital (even after correcting for measurement errors) during 1930–45. A period of slower technical change and fewer technological opportunities caused both capital deepening and MFP growth to decelerate after 1972. The jury is still out on the recent 1995–2000 productivity growth revival. The economy's growth and the U.S. stock market peaked in the first half of the year 2000. After that, profits, stock prices, and output growth tumbled, although productivity growth held up pretty well. Its deceleration confirmed my view that there had been a cyclical component in the 1998–2000 surge, but the growth rate was high enough to validate that something fundamental had changed after 1995.

Historical parallels are both compelling and inapplicable. The 1999–2000 NASDAQ bubble does resemble 1928–9, yet few critics expect the NASDAQ part of the U.S. economy to experience a Great Depression lasting a full decade, much less the entire economy. The 2001 recession was extremely shallow, suggesting one of the great contrasts with 1929–30, that is, the aggressive easing by the Fed in the recent episode compared with the much-analyzed bull-headedness of the Fed in the earlier episode.

The one chapter in Part One that stands out for special mention is Chapter Five, providing circumstantial evidence that countries having high unemployment also enjoy faster productivity growth. That chapter is motivated by the explosive growth of low-skilled jobs in the United States to a much greater extent than in many of the better off European countries. One can debate the virtues of the two systems, but Chapter Five argues that there is a choice to be made between tighter labor market regulations and faster productivity growth, as in the case of France, and looser labor market regulations, rapid growth of low skilled jobs, and slower productivity growth, as in the United States. The main theme of Chapter Five, that there are strong feedbacks from labor market conditions to productivity growth, is echoed at the end of Chapter Two, which argues that productivity growth in the United States was boosted in the period 1930–70 by two quite different types of restrictions on labor supply, the tight control of immigration initiated in the early 1920s, and the heyday of the labor union fostered by New Deal legislation in the 1930s.

References

Bettman, Otto. *The Good Old Days – They Were Terrible!* New York: Random House; 1974.

Denison, Edward F. *The Sources of Economic Growth in the United States and the Alternatives Before Us*. New York: Committee for Economic Development; 1962: Supplementary Paper no. 13.

"The Concept of Capital." *Review of Income and Wealth*. March, 1993; vol. 39, no. 1.

Domar, Evsey D. "On the Measurement of Technological Change." *Economic Journal*. December, 1961; vol. 71, no. 4, pp. 709–29.

Gordon, Robert J. *The Measurement of Durable Goods Prices*. Chicago: University of Chicago Press for NBER; 1990.

Griliches, Zvi. *R&D, Education, and Productivity: A Retrospective*. Cambridge MA: Harvard University Press; 2000.

and Jorgenson, Dale W. "Sources of Measured Productivity Change: Capital Input." *American Economic Review*. May, 1966; vol. 56, no. 2, pp. 50–61.

Jorgenson, Dale W. "The Embodiment Hypothesis." *Journal of Political Economy*. February, 1966; vol. 74, pp. 1–17.

and Griliches, Zvi. "The Explanation of Productivity Change." *The Review of Economic Studies*. July, 1967; vol. 34, no. 3, pp. 249–84.

Kendrick, John W. "Productivity Trends, Capital and Labor." *Review of Economics and Statistics*. August, 1956; vol. 38, no. 3.

Productivity Trends in the United States. Princeton: Princeton University Press for NBER; 1961.

Lucas, Robert E., Jr. "On the Mechanics of Economic Development." *Journal of Monetary Economics*. July, 1988; vol. 22, p. 5.

Mokyr, Joel. *The Lever of Riches: Technological Creativity and Economic Progress*. New York, Oxford: Oxford University Press; 1990.

Nordhaus, William D. "The Recent Productivity Slowdown," *Brookings Papers on Economic Activity*. 1972; vol. 3, no. 3, pp. 493–536.

Oliner, Stephen D. and Sichel, Daniel E. "Computers and Output Growth Revisited: How Big is the Puzzle?" *Brookings Papers on Economic Activity*. 1994; vol. 25, no. 2, pp. 273–317.

Overy, Richard. *Why the Allies Won*. New York: Norton; 1995.

Romer, Paul M. "Increasing Returns and Long-run Growth." *Journal of Political Economy*. 1986; vol. 94, pp. 1002–37.

"Endogenous Technical Change." *Journal of Political Economy*. 1990; vol. 98, pp. S71–103.

Rosenberg, Nathan, and Birdzell, L. E., Jr. *How the West Grew Rich: The Economic Transformation of the Industrial World*. New York: Basic Books; 1986.

Rymes, Thomas K. *On Concepts of Capital and Technical Change*. Cambridge, UK: Cambridge University Press; 1971.

Sichel, Daniel E. *The Computer Revolution: An Economic Perspective*. Washington: Brookings Institution Press; 1997.

Solow, Robert M. "Technical Change and the Aggregate Production Function." *Review of Economics and Statistics*. August, 1957; vol. 39, no. 3, pp. 312–20.

"We'd Better Watch Out." In the *New York Times Book Review*. July 12, 1987; p. 36.

Triplett, Jack E. "The Solow Productivity Paradox: What do Computers do to Productivity?" *Canadian Journal of Economics*. April, 1999; vol. 32, no. 2, pp. 309–34.

CHAPTER 1

Does the "New Economy" Measure Up to the Great Inventions of the Past?

A widespread belief seems to be emerging, at least in the popular press, that the U.S. economy is in the throes of a fundamental transformation, one which is wiping out the 1972–95 productivity slowdown, along with inflation, the budget deficit, and the business cycle. A typical recent comment, in a *Wall Street Journal* article, claimed that "when it comes to technology, even the most bearish analysts agree the microchip and Internet are changing almost everything in the economy" (Ip, 2000). Or as an article in *Fortune* (June 8, 1998, pp. 86–7) magazine put it, "The [computer] chip has transformed us at least as pervasively as the internal combustion engine or electric motor." Alan Greenspan (1999) appears to be among the technological enthusiasts. He recently stated: "A perceptible quickening in the pace at which technological innovations are applied argues for the hypothesis that the recent acceleration in labor productivity is not just a cyclical phenomenon or a statistical aberration, but reflects, at least in part, a more deep-seated, still developing, shift in our economic landscape." The true enthusiasts treat the New Economy as a fundamental industrial revolution as great or greater in importance than the concurrence of inventions, particularly electricity and the internal combustion engine, which transformed the world at the turn of the last century.

There is no dispute that the U.S. economy is awash in computer investment, that productivity has revived, and that the late 1990s were extremely good years for the U.S. economy. Indeed, Robert M. Solow has now declared obsolete his 1987 paradox that "we can see the computer age everywhere but in the productivity statistics" (Uchitelle, 2000). However, room remains for a degree of skepticism. Does the "New Economy" really merit treatment as a basic industrial revolution of a magnitude and importance equivalent to the great inventions of the late nineteenth and early twentieth century? These earlier changes, particularly electricity and the internal combustion engine, but also

Note. This research is supported by the National Science Foundation. I have benefitted from discussions on these topics with many people, especially Erik Brynjolfsson, Joel Mokyr, Jack Triplett, and the late Zvi Griliches. ("Does the New Economy Measure Up to the Great Inventions of the Past?" *Journal of Economic Perspectives.* Fall 2000; vol. 14, no. 4, pp. 49–74.)

including chemicals, movies, radio, and indoor plumbing, set off sixty years between roughly 1913 and 1972 during which multifactor productivity growth was more rapid than ever before or since, and during which everyday life was transformed.

The skeptic's case begins with a close examination of the recent productivity revival. While the aggregate numbers are impressive, the productivity revival appears to have occurred primarily within the production of computer hardware, peripherals, and telecommunications equipment, with substantial spillover to the 12 percent of the economy involved in manufacturing durable goods.[1] However, in the remaining 88 percent of the economy, the New Economy's effects on productivity growth are surprisingly absent, and capital deepening has been remarkably unproductive. Moreover, it is quite plausible that the greatest benefits of computers lie a decade or more in the past, not in the future. The essay then explores some of the intrinsic limitations of the computer in general and the Internet in particular for affecting productivity and the quality of life when evaluated in comparison with the great inventions of the past.

1.1 DISSECTING THE REVIVAL IN U.S. PRODUCTIVITY GROWTH

Since computer prices have been declining at rapid rates for the last fifty years, the phrase "New Economy" must mean that something more and different has happened in the last few years. Indeed, as shown in the top frame of Figure 1.1, at the end of 1995 there was an acceleration of the rate of price change in computer hardware (including peripherals) from an average rate of −14.7 percent during 1987–95 to an average rate of −31.2 percent during 1996–9. These growth rates do not mean that the prices of computers as listed on store shelves and websites literally fell by this amount. In the U.S. national accounts, computer prices since 1986 have been measured by the "hedonic" regression technique, in which the prices of a variety of models of computers are explained by the quantity of computer characteristics and by the passage of time. Thus, "decline in computer prices" actually means "a decline in the prices of computer attributes like a given level of speed, memory, disk drive access speed and capacity, presence and speed of a CD-ROM, and so on." Indeed, computers have seemed perhaps the ideal application for the hedonic regression technique since the work of Chow (1967).

One way to get a feel for the dramatic impact of this price decline is to consider the ratio of performance-to-price that is implicit in the BEA's calculations. From the fourth quarter of 1993 to the fourth quarter of 1999, the performance of a computer at a given price rose by a factor of 5.2. Improvements in performance-price ratios for individual computer components are substantially

---

[1] In 1996, current dollar value added in durable manufacturing was 11.6 percent of current dollar output in the nonfarm private business sector. See *Economic Report of the President* (February, 1999), Tables B-10 and B-12.

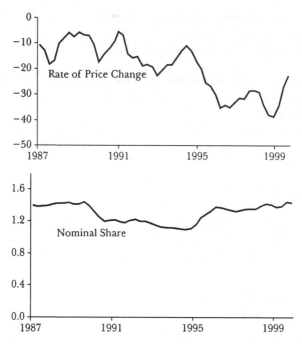

Figure 1.1. Final Sales of Computers and Peripherals, Four-Quarter Rate of Price Change and Nominal Share in Nonfarm Nonhousing Business GDP, 1987–99

larger, by a factor of 16.2 for computer processors, 75.5 for RAM, and 176.0 for hard disk capacity.[2] The driving force behind the greater rate of price decline was an acceleration in the rate of technological progress; apparently, the time cycle of Moore's Law, which has historically held that the price of computing power falls by half every 18 months, shortened from 18 months to about 12 months at this time.[3]

Most of the discussion in this paper will follow the lead of Figure 1.1 by focusing on computer hardware, rather than the universe of computer hardware, software, and telecommunications equipment, because the government deflators for software and telecommunications equipment exhibit implausibly low rates of price decline (Jorgenson and Stiroh, 2000). These adjustments for the "true" price of computer performance are essential, since over the period since 1987, spending on computers stagnated at around 1.3 percent of the nonfarm private business economy, as shown in the bottom frame of Figure 1.1. Within the computer industry, the productivity gains involve greater

---

[2] See "Computers, Then and Now," *Consumer Reports* (May 2000) p. 10, where the published reported comparisons in 1999 dollars have been converted to nominal dollars using the Consumer Price Index.

[3] This judgement is based on a conversation between Gordon Moore and Dale W. Jorgenson, related to the author by the latter.

Table 1.1. *Growth Rates of Output, Inputs, and Multifactor Productivity, Selected Intervals, 1870–1999*

	1870–1913	1913–1972	1972–1995	1995–1999
1. Output (y)	4.42	3.14	2.75	4.90
Without Composition Adjustment to Inputs				
2. Labor Hours (h)	3.24	1.28	1.71	2.25
3. Capital (k)	4.16	2.07	2.98	4.87
4. Capital per Hour (k-h)	0.92	0.79	1.27	2.62
5. Output per Hour (y-h)	1.18	1.86	1.04	2.65
6. Multifactor Productivity Growth (m)	0.77	1.60	0.62	1.79
With Composition Adjustment to Inputs				
7. Labor Hours (h)	3.73	1.72	2.09	2.71
8. Capital (k)	4.22	2.76	4.04	5.58
9. Capital per Hour (k-h)	0.49	1.04	1.95	2.87
10. Output per Hour (y-n)	0.69	1.42	0.66	2.19
11. Multifactor Productivity Growth (m)	0.47	1.08	0.02	1.25

Sources. 1870–1995. Lines 1–6 from Gordon (2000b), Table 1. Lines 7–11 from Gordon (2000b), Table 6. 1995–1999. All data are taken from Oliner and Sichel (2000) and are transformed as follows. Output (line 1): Table 1, line 1. Labor hours (line 2): Table 1, line 7, divided by 0.67, the implicit share of labor. Capital (line 3): Composition-adjusted capital (see below for source of line 7) minus 0.71, which is the difference between the growth of capital services and capital stock in Jorgenson and Stiroh (2000, Tables 1 and 2, column 1). MFP (line 6): Output growth minus input growth, using weights of 0.67 and 0.33 on labor and capital, respectively. Labor hours (line 7): Table 1, line 7 plus line 8, divided by 0.67, the implicit share of labor. Capital (line 8): Table 1, line 2 plus line 6, divided by 0.33, the implicit share of capital. MFP (line 11): Table 2, line 9.

amounts of computer speed and other capabilities from the same amount of total spending.

This acceleration in the price decline of computers since 1995 has been accompanied by a revival of productivity growth in the aggregate economy which is impressive in comparison with the American historical record dating back more than a century. Table 1.1 compares rates of output, input, and productivity growth achieved in the American economy during the four years 1995–9 as compared with three long earlier intervals: 1870–1913, 1913–1972, and 1972–1995.[4] The top line of the table shows the real growth rate of (nonfarm, nonhousing) output over these time periods.

Lines 2–6 show growth rates of inputs and productivity. Lines 2–3 show the growth rate of output for labor and capital, respectively. Line 4 is the growth

[4] The record compiled for 1870–1996 in Table 1.1 is based on Gordon (2000b), Chapter 2 in this volume, which merges data from Kendrick (1961) with BEA and BLS data for the postwar period and develops estimates for labor and capital composition to carry the postwar BLS composition adjustments back from 1948 to 1870.

rate of capital per hour worked. Line 5 shows the growth rate of output per hour or labor productivity, which can be calculated in the table by subtracting the growth rate of labor hours in line 2 from the growth rate of output in line 1. Line 6 is multifactor productivity growth, which is productivity growth based on a weighted average of several inputs, in this case labor and capital, with weights based on the share of each input in total income. The growth in output per hour (line 5) can be split up into multifactor productivity growth (line 6) and the contribution of capital deepening, which in turn is the growth in capital per hour (line 4) multiplied by capital's share of income, which is roughly one-third. Thus, the growth rate of output per hour minus one-third the growth rate of capital per hour equals multifactor productivity.[5]

Lines 6–9 repeat this exercise, but are based on alternative input concepts, which are adjusted for changes in composition of the inputs. For example, the growth in labor input is adjusted for changes in the dimensions of age, sex, and educational attainment. The shift in capital input is adjusted for the change in capital spending from structures to equipment, and from longer-lived equipment like railroad locomotives to shorter-lived equipment like computers.[6] These composition-adjusted estimates should be viewed as the preferred measures of the growth rates of labor and capital input. However, the estimates in lines 2–6 that exclude the composition adjustments are useful for comparability with other unadjusted quarterly data, some of which will be explored later in this paper.

In past writing, I have pointed to the historical patterns summarized through 1995 in the first three columns and have suggested that the basic question about historical productivity growth should not be "Why was growth so slow after 1972?" but rather "Why was growth so fast during the golden years 1913–72?" I have attributed the outstanding performance of the golden years to the role of the great inventions of the late nineteenth and early twentieth century mentioned in the introduction and discussed further below.

---

[5] The concepts can be related by considering a production function:

$$y = m + bh + (1 - b)k,$$

where y is the growth rate of output, m is the growth rate of multifactor productivity growth, b is the elasticity of output with respect to labor input, h is the growth rate of labor input. $1 - b$ is the elasticity of output with respect to capital input (implicity invoking constant returns to scale), and k is the growth rate of capital input. Thus, output growth is the sum of productivity growth and of the separate contributions of labor and capital input, weighted by the elasticity of output growth to each input. Now rewrite the equation as

$$y - h = m + (1 - b)(k - h).$$

Growth in output per hour $(y - h)$ is now equal to growth in multifactor productivity plus the contribution of "capital deepening," which is the elasticity of output with respect to capital $(1 - b)$ times the growth rate of the capital-labor ratio $(k - h)$.

[6] Likewise, housing is excluded to retain comparability with Table 1.2. Adjustments for labor composition were pioneered by Griliches (1960) and Denison (1962), and for capital composition by Jorgenson and Griliches (1967). Similar adjustments are incorporated in the official BLS series on multifactor productivity that currently covers 1948–97, and detailed annual data are available through 1998 in Jorgenson and Stiroh (2000).

Upon first examination, the data for 1995–9 are consistent with the beginning of a new golden age of productivity growth. Either with or without composition adjustments, multifactor productivity growth during 1995–9 exceeded that in the golden age from 1913–72. Capital deepening during 1995–9 proceeded at an extraordinary rate. The overall acceleration in output per hour, combining multifactor productivity growth and the impact of capital deepening, is more than a full percentage point per year when 1995–9 is compared to the 1972–95 slowdown period.

This performance is undeniably impressive. Yet there are two skeptical questions to be raised. First, when examined closely, it turns out that a major fraction of the revival in multifactor productivity growth has occurred within the part of the economy engaged in producing computers and peripherals, and within the rest of the durable manufacturing sector, which together comprise only about 12 percent of the private business economy. This raises the question of how far the New Economy actually reaches into the remaining 88 percent of economic activity. Second, the period from 1995 to 1999 is much shorter than the earlier three time periods and during at least part of that time, it seemed clear even to many of the New Economy optimists that output growth was running at a faster pace than the sustainable long-term growth trend. The idea that productivity varies procyclically dates back to Hultgren (1960) and "Okun's Law" (Okun, 1962) and was first interpreted by Oi (1962), who described labor as a "quasi-fixed factor" that adjusts only partially during cyclical swings of output. If output was growing faster than trend, then productivity was also growing faster than trend, and some part of the productivity revival recorded in Table 1.1 was transitory rather than permanent.

My recent research on the cyclical analysis of labor productivity in Gordon (2000c) updates the earlier results of Gordon (1993). In my econometric specification, the change in the growth of actual hours relative to the hours trend is explained by changes in its own lagged values and by changes in the growth of output relative to trend. Hours growth lags behind output growth and responds by roughly 0.75 of the output change; thus growth in output per hour exhibits a temporary acceleration when hours are lagging behind output changes, and in addition increases by roughly 0.25 of any excess in output growth relative to trend.[7]

Several decompositions between trend and cyclical productivity growth are displayed in Table 1.2. The first column refers to the aggregate economy, which in this case means the nonfarm private business sector including computers. Of

---

[7] I set the hours trend at a rate consistent with a nonaccelerating inflation rate of unemployment (NAIRU) in the fourth quarter of 1999 of 5.0 percent. Moreover, it is assumed that actual and trend output were equal in the later stages of upswings in 1954:Q1, 1963:Q3, 1972:Q2, 1978:Q2, 1987:Q3 and 1995:Q4. The task is to determine the optimal output trend after 1995:Q4. The decomposition of the recent productivity acceleration between cycle and trend is accomplished by specifying a value for the hours growth trend and then conducting a grid search to find the output growth trend that optimizes the fit of the equation. The regression equation is estimated for the period 1954:Q1–1999:Q4, and the growth in trend output is varied to minimize the root-mean-squared error over 1996:Q1–1999:Q4.

Table 1.2. *Decomposition of Growth in Output Per Hour, 1995:4–1999:4, into Contributions of Cyclical Effects and Structural Change in Trend Growth (Percentage Growth Rates at Annual Rate)*

	Nonfarm Private Business	NFPB Excluding Computer Hardware Manufacturing	NFPB Excluding Durable Manufacturing
1. Actual Growth	2.75	2.30	1.99
2. Contribution of Cyclical Effect	0.50	0.51	0.63
3. Growth in Trend (line 1–line 2)	2.25	1.79	1.36
4. Trend, 1972:2–1995:4	1.42	1.18	1.13
5. Acceleration of Trend (line 3–line 4)	0.83	0.61	0.23
6. Contribution of Price Measurement	0.14	0.14	0.14
7. Contribution of Labor Quality	0.05	0.05	0.05
8. Structural Acceleration in Labor Productivity (line 5–line 6)	0.64	0.42	0.04
9. Contribution of Capital Deepening	0.33	0.33	0.33
10. Contribution of MFP Growth in Computer and Computer-Related Semiconductor Manufacturing	0.29	0.19	–
11. Structural Acceleration in MFP (line 7–lines 8 through 10)	0.02	−0.10	−0.29

Sources and Notes. Actual and trend growth and contribution of price measurement (lines 1–6): Gordon (2000c), Tables 1.1 and 1.2. Lines 6, 9, and 10 are from Oliner and Sichel (2000), in each case comparing their growth rates for 1995–99 with a weighted average of 1973–90 and 1990–5. The table and line sources from Oliner and Sichel are as follows: Labor quality (line 7): Table 1.2, line 8. Capital deepening (line 9): Table 1.2, line 2. MFP growth in computers and computer-related semiconductors (line 10): Table 1.4, line 5. Comparing Table 1.4, lines 2 and 5, of the total effect of 0.29, 0.10 is due to computers (and hence is omitted from column 2 in our Table 1.2) and the remaining 0.19 is due to computer-related semiconductor manufacture.

the actual 2.75 percent annual growth of output per hour between 1995:Q4 and 1999:Q4, 0.50 percentage point are attributed to a cyclical effect and the remaining 2.25 points to trend growth. This is 0.83 points faster than the 1972–95 trend, as shown in lines 4 and 5. How can this acceleration be explained? A small part on lines 6 and 7 is attributed to changes in price measurement methods and to a slight acceleration in the growth of labor quality.[8] The remaining

[8] The price measurement effect consists of two components. While most changes in price measurement methods in the CPI have been backcast in the national accounts to 1978, one remaining

0.64 points can be directly attributed to computers. The capital-deepening effect of faster growth in capital relative to labor in the aggregate economy accounts for 0.33 percentage points of the acceleration (all due to computers), and an acceleration of multifactor productivity growth in computer and computer-related semiconductor manufacturing account for almost all of the rest.[9]

A different way of assessing the role of computers is displayed in the second column of Table 1.2. Here we carry out the same set of calculations, but in this case we subtract output and hours in computer hardware manufacturing (but not computer-related semiconductor manufacturing) from the nonfarm private business economy. In this calculation, the structural acceleration of labor productivity on line 8 is 0.42 percentage points, compared to 0.64 for the first column. Again, the impact of capital deepening has created a genuine revival in growth in output per hour in the noncomputer economy, and the contribution of the computer sector is reduced. But in either case, spillover effects on multifactor productivity in the noncomputer economy are absent (column 1) or slightly negative (column 2).

The third column of Table 1.2 carries out these calculations yet again, but this time excludes all durable goods manufacturing from hours worked and output. The starting growth rate in the first line is a much lower 1.99 percent. A slightly larger cyclical effect is subtracted, leaving an acceleration in trend on line 5 of only 0.23 percent. The cyclical effect is slightly larger here because between 1995 and 1999, there is no increase in the capacity utilization rate in manufacturing nor any acceleration in hours of growth in manufacturing. The cyclical effects in the economy over this time occur entirely outside of manufacturing, which accounts for the higher cyclical effect in this column. Almost all of the acceleration in productivity trend can be explained by price measurement and labor quality, leaving a structural acceleration in output per hour growth of only 0.04 percent. As a result, after taking capital deepening into account, line 11 shows a *substantial structural deceleration* in multifactor productivity growth in the economy outside of the durable goods manufacturing sector.

From the fourth quarter of 1995 to the fourth quarter of 1999, the annual growth of output per hour was 1.33 percentage points faster than from 1972:Q2

change – the 1993–4 shift in medical care deflation from the CPI to the slower-growing PPI – creates a measurement discontinuity of 0.09 percent. The fact that other measurement changes were carried back to 1978 rather than 1972 creates a further discontinuity of 0.05 when the full 1972–95 period is compared to 1995–9. The acceleration in labor quality growth is taken from Oliner and Sichel (2000, Table 2) and reflects the same compositional changes discussed in connection with Table 1.2; labor quality growth during 1972–95 was held down by a compositional shift toward female and teenage workers during the first half of that interval.

[9] In the Oliner-Sichel decomposition on which line 9 is based, computers account for all of the acceleration in the capital-deepening effect, and the additional acceleration attributable to semiconductors and telecommunications is exactly canceled out by a *deceleration* of capital deepening for all other types of equipment and structures (Oliner and Sichel, 2000, Table 2, lines 2 through 7).

to 1995:Q4 (as shown in Table 1.2, column 1, lines 1 and 4). The analysis here argues that 0.50 percentage points of that increase is a cyclical effect (column 1, line 2); 0.19 points of that increase results from changes in measurement of prices and labor quality; 0.33 points is the capital deepening from greater investment in computers; 0.29 points is the acceleration of multifactor productivity growth in manufacturing computers; 0.27 points is the acceleration in multifactor productivity growth in manufacturing other types of durable goods; and − 0.29 percent is a *deceleration* in trend productivity growth in the economy outside of durable goods manufacturing.

How credible is this decomposition? It depends on the accuracy of the cyclical adjustment. It would take a reduction in the cyclical effect in the right-hand column of Table 1.2 by .29 points (from 0.63 to 0.34) to eliminate the basic conclusion that trend productivity growth outside of durables has decelerated. Yet a cyclical effect of the magnitude estimated here is not unprecedented or unusual. Labor hiring always lags behind surges in output, and we would expect productivity to exhibit temporary growth in response to the astonishing 7.3 percent growth rate of nonfarm business output in the last half of 1999. At the end of 1999 the level of nonfarm business output per hour was 2.0 percent above trend, a smaller cyclical deviation than occurred in 1966, 1973, and 1992.[10]

These results imply that computer investment has had a near-zero rate of return outside of durable manufacturing. This is surprising, because 76.6 percent of all computers are used in the industries of wholesale and retail trade, finance, insurance, real estate, and other services, while just 11.9 percent of computers are used in five computer-intensive industries within manufacturing, and only 11.5 percent in the rest of the economy (McGuckin and Stiroh, 1998, Table 1, p. 42). Thus, three-quarters of all computer investment has been in industries with no perceptible trend increase in productivity. In this sense the Solow computer paradox survives intact for most of the economy, and the need to explain it motivates the rest of this paper.

1.2   HOW THE GREAT INVENTIONS HELPED US ESCAPE FROM THE BAD OLD DAYS

The First Industrial Revolution began largely in Britain and extended from about 1760 to 1830. But despite the list of innovations of this time period – the steam engine, the power loom, and so on – multifactor productivity grew at a snail's pace in the nineteenth century. As Brad De Long (2000) has observed: "Compared to the pace of economic growth in the 20th century, all other centuries – even the 19th . . . were standing still."[11] The Second Industrial Revolution took place simultaneously in Europe and the United States and can be dated roughly

---

[10] Compared to the 2 percent ratio in 1999:Q4, larger log ratios of actual to trend productivity in the nonfarm business sector occurred in 1966:Q1 (3 percent), 1973:Q1 (2.3 percent), and 1992:Q4 (2.2 percent).

[11] Quoted in "A Century of Progress," *Economist*, April 15, 2000, p. 86.

1860 to 1900. This is the revolution of electricity, the internal combustion engine, and so on, and it led to the golden age of productivity growth from 1913 to 1972.

The question at hand is whether the role of the computer and internet are likely to constitute a Third Industrial Revolution, with lasting productivity gains comparable to the second one. One might object that this comparison does not include the entirety of technological advance of the 1990s. For example, a broader perspective that included biology, pharmaceuticals, and medical technology might lead to a more sympathetic comparison of recent progress with the Second Industrial Revolution. But in common discourse, the New Economy is certainly more about computers than pharmaceuticals. Moreover, if one starts down the road of comparing changes in life expectancy, the yearly rate of increase in life expectancy at birth during 1900–50, resulting in substantial part from the inventions of the Second Industrial Revolution, was 0.72 percent per year, *triple* the 0.24 percent annual rate during 1950–95 (Nordhaus, 1999, Figure 3). Thus, it seems unlikely that taking gains in life expectancy into account will elevate the possible Third Industrial Revolution relative to the second one.

Life in the "Bad Old Days"

To understand the profound sense in which the great inventions of the Second Industrial Revolution altered the standard of living of the average American resident, we begin with a brief tour of some of the less desirable aspects of living in the late nineteenth century. An eye-opening introduction to the conditions of that era is provided in a little-known book by Otto Bettman (1974), the founder of the famed Bettman photographic archive, and I paraphrase and quote from that book in the next four paragraphs.

The urban streets of the 1870s and 1880s were full not just of horses but pigs, which were tolerated because they ate garbage. In Kansas City, the stench of patrolling hogs was so penetrating that Oscar Wilde observed, "They made granite eyes weep." The increasing production of animal waste caused pessimistic observers to fear that American cities would disappear like Pompeii – but not under ashes. Added to that was acrid industrial smog, sidewalks piled high with kitchen slops, coal dust, and dumped merchandise, which became a liquid slime after a rain. All of this was made worse in the summer, which was almost as unbearable outdoors as inside, especially with the heavy clothes of the day. Rudyard Kipling said of Chicago, "Having seen it, I desire urgently never to see it again. Its air is dirt." Added to putrid air was the danger of spoiled food – imagine meat and poultry hung unrefrigerated for days, spoiled fruit, bacteria-infected milk, and so on. Epidemics included yellow fever, scarlet fever, and smallpox. Many hospitals were deathtraps.

Before the invention of electricity, urban streets were a chaotic jungle of horse-drawn conveyances of all types, made even more congested in winter by horse-drawn snowplows that did little more than move the snow out of the way of the trolleys by dumping it on the sidewalks. Rural life was marked by isolation, loneliness, and the drudgery of fireplace cooking and laundry done by muscle power. Travel between cities on railroads was surprisingly dangerous; in 1890, railroad-connected accidents caused 10,000 deaths.

In 1882, only 2 percent of New York City's houses had water connections. Urban apartments were crowded, damp, airless, and often firetraps. Even middle-class apartment buildings were little more than glorified tenements. In the slums as many as eight persons shared a single small room.

Coal miners, steel workers, and many others worked sixty-hour weeks in dirty and dangerous conditions, exposed to suffocating gas and smoke. Danger was not confined to mines or mills; in 1890 one railroad employee was killed for every 300 employed. Sewing in a sweatshop might have been the most oppressive occupation for women, but was not as dangerous as soap-packing plants or the manual stripping of tobacco leaves.

The Great Inventions

Into this world of the late nineteenth and early twentieth century came a set of great inventions, which can be usefully grouped into five "clusters." Each of these clusters had a primary breakthrough invention that occurred during the period 1860–1900. For specific chronologies of these inventions as they developed, see Bunch and Hellemans (1993) or the website of the "Greatest Engineering Achievements of the 20th Century" recently released by the National Academic of Engineering at ⟨http://www.greatachievements.org⟩.

The first great invention in the "Group of Five" is electricity, including both electric light and electric motors. In the opening decades of the twentieth century, electric motors revolutionized manufacturing by decentralizing the source of power and making possible flexible and portable tools and machines. After a somewhat longer lag, electric motors embodied in consumer appliances eliminated the greatest source of drudgery of all, manual laundry; refrigeration virtually eliminated food spoilage; and air conditioning made summers enjoyable and opened the southern United States for modern economic development (David, 1990).[12]

Sharing the title with electricity for the most important invention that had its main diffusion in the twentieth century is the internal combustion engine, which made possible personal autos, motor transport, and air transport. Grouped in this category are such derivative inventions as the suburb, highway, and supermarket. Gradually eliminated or greatly reduced were many of the ills of the late nineteenth century, from manure to unplowed snow to rural isolation.

The third group of great inventions includes petroleum, natural gas, and various processes which "rearrange molecules," including chemicals, plastics, and pharmaceuticals. Some of these inventions were spontaneous and others were induced by the demands of motor and air transport. They helped to reduce air

---

[12] See Oi (1997) for an insightful analysis of the effect of air conditioning on productivity.

pollution created by industrial and heating uses of coal, and they made possible many new and improved materials and products. They aided in conquering illness and prolonging life.

The fourth cluster consists of the complex of entertainment, communication, and information innovations. This set of inventions that made the world smaller can be traced back to the telegraph (1844) and includes the telephone (1876), phonograph (1877), popular photography (1880s and 1890s), radio (1899), motion pictures (1881 to 1888), and television (1911). Television is the only one of these innovations that was diffused into the popular marketplace after World War II.

Perhaps the most tangible improvement in the everyday standard of living, besides electric light, came through the rapid spread after 1880 of running water, indoor plumbing, and urban sanitation infrastructure. Mokyr and Stein (1997, p. 146) credit Louis Pasteur's germ theory of disease for the great decline in mortality in the four decades prior to World War I, long before the invention of antibiotics, although in part the development of indoor plumbing was independent of the germ theory and dates to the invention of the indoor flush toilet.

These five clusters of inventions, in turn, created an increase in per capita income and wealth during the golden years of productivity growth from 1913–72 that allowed an improvement in living standards even in those aspects of consumption where inventions did not play a major role, particularly the ability of families to afford many more square feet of shelter (and in the suburbs more land surrounding that shelter) than in 1880.

Will the information revolution spawned by the computer create as great a change in living conditions as the major inventions of the late nineteenth and early twentieth century? At an intuitive level, it seems unlikely. For instance, we might gather together a group of Houston residents and ask: "If you could choose only one of the following two inventions, air conditioning or the internet, which would you choose?" Or we might ask a group of Minneapolis residents, "If you could choose only one of the following two inventions, indoor plumbing or the internet, which would you choose?" But there are deeper reasons, rooted in basic principles of economics like diminishing returns, as to why, half a century from now, it is unlikely that historians and economists will look back at the present surge in computer investment as the harbinger of a Third Industrial Revolution.

1.3 THE DECLINING COST OF COMPUTER POWER AND THE PERVASIVENESS OF DIMINISHING RETURNS

There are a number of differences between the computer and the great inventions of the Second Industrial Revolution, but perhaps the largest difference is the unprecedented rate of decline in the price of computing power. Although the price decline of computing power has accelerated from 1995–9 as opposed to the period from 1987–94, as shown earlier in Figure 1.1, over the last five decades these rapid rates of price decline are standard. The rate of price change has varied over time, but rapid price declines also occurred during the 1950–80 interval dominated by the mainframe computer and the 1980–95 interval dominated by the transition from mainframe to personal computer applications prior to the invention of the internet. Indeed, existing computer price deflators fail to take account of the radical decline in the price per calculation that occurred in the transition from mainframes to personal computers, which have been studied only separately, not together. Gordon (1990, p. 239) calculates that the annual rate of price decline between 1972 and 1987 would have been 35 percent per annum, rather than 20 percent per annum, if this transitional benefit had been taken into account. From this perspective, the technological advance created by the New Economy of the last five years may be less significant than it at first appears.

The top frame of Figure 1.2 shows the implicit price deflator for computers on the vertical axis, and real expenditures for computers and peripherals on the horizontal axis.[13] This set of points of price and quantity for given years has an intuitive supply and demand interpretation: there has been an outward shift of the supply curve for computers, driven by technological advance, happening at a rate much faster than the upward shift in the demand for computer services. In fact, the story is often told with a theoretical diagram like the bottom frame of Figure 1.2, in which the supply curve slides steadily downwards from S_1 to S_2 with no shift in the demand curve at all, as in Brynjolfsson (1996, p. 290), Gordon (1990, p. 46) and Sichel (1997, p. 17). The supply curves in this graph have been drawn as horizontal lines, both to simplify the subsequent discussion of consumer surplus and because there is no evidence of a rising marginal cost of producing additional computer speed, memory, and other characteristics at a given level of technology.

The shape of the graph offers evidence that the demand curve has not shifted much or at all. If there had been a discontinuous rightward shift in the demand curve for computer hardware, the slope of the price-quantity relationship in the top frame of Figure 1.2 should flatten noticeably, as the rate of increase of quantity accelerates relative to the rate of decline in price, but it does not. The rate of change of price and quantity both accelerate after 1995 (as indicated by the greater price declines and quantity increases between annual observations), but the slope becomes steeper rather than flatter. This pattern suggests that while the pace of technological change has speeded up in the last few years, the relationship between supply and demand is not qualitatively different than earlier advances in the computer industry.

---

[13] Domestic purchases in Figure 1.2 includes consumption, investment, and government expenditures on computers and peripherals. This differs from final sales of computers (the subject of Figure 1.1 and the middle column of Table 1.2) by excluding net exports (which are strongly negative). Final sales are relevant to issues involving domestic output and productivity in the computer sector, while domestic purchases are relevant for issues involving the domestic demand for computers.

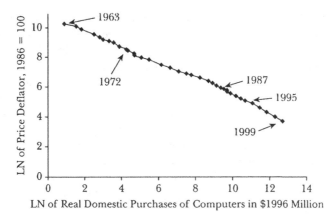

Figure 1.2. Real Gross Domestic Purchases of Computers and Peripherals and its Price Deflator, 1963–99

Source. Unpublished series provided by Christian Ehemann of the Bureau of Economic Analysis.

The data on the price and quantity of computer characteristics have previously been used to "map out" the demand curve (Brynjolfsson, 1996, p. 290). In fact, the slope of the price-quantity relationship was appreciably flatter during 1960–72 and 1972–87 than during 1987–95 or 1995–9. If the demand curve has not shifted, the inverse of these slopes is the price elasticity of demand, namely −2.03, −1.97, −1.64, and −1.36 in these four intervals, which can be compared with Brynjolfsson's (1996, p. 292) estimated price elasticity of −1.33 over the period 1970–89. The apparent decline in the price elasticity is the counterpart of the fact that the nominal share of computer hardware expenditures in the total economy (which implicitly holds income constant) rose rapidly before 1987 but barely increased at all after that year, and this shift in the price-quantity slope is consistent with the view that the most important uses of computers were developed more than a decade into the past, not currently.

A second distinguishing feature of the development of the computer industry, after the decline in price, is the unprecedented speed with which diminishing returns set in. While computer users steadily enjoy an increasing amount of consumer surplus as the price falls, the declining point of intersection of the supply curve with the fixed demand curve implies a rapid decline in the marginal utility or benefit of computer power. Since Gary Becker's (1965) seminal article on the economics of time, household production has been viewed as an activity that combines market goods and time. The fixed supply of time to any individual creates a fundamental limitation on the ability of exponential growth in computer speed and memory to create commensurate increases in output and productivity. As Zvi Griliches once said, "The cost of computing has dropped exponentially, but the cost of thinking is what it always was."[14]

In performing two of the activities that were revolutionized by the personal computer, namely word processing and spreadsheets, I cannot type or think any faster than I did with my first 1983 personal computer that contained 1/100th of the memory and operated at 1/60th of the speed of my present model. The capital stock with which I work has increased by a factor of almost 30, according to the hedonic price methodology, yet my productivity has hardly budged, occasionally benefitting for a few seconds when I can jump from the beginning to the end of a fifty-page paper much faster than in 1983. A price index that declines at 25 percent per year for seventeen years reaches a level of 1.4 in 2000 on a base of 1983 equals 100. This implies that my present $1,000 computer represents $70,100 in 1983 prices, or 28 times the $2,500 that I spent in 1983 on my first computer net of peripherals. As a result, there has been an exponential rate of decline in my output-to-capital ratio, and an equally sharp decline in the marginal productivity of computer capital.

The computer hardware and software industries are certainly not unique in running into some form of diminishing returns. Numerous industries have run into barriers to steady growth in productivity, most notably the airline industry when jet aircraft reached natural barriers of size and speed, and the electric utility industry when turbogenerator/boiler sets reached natural barriers of temperature and pressure. The apparent dearth of productivity growth in the construction and home maintenance industry reflects that electric portable power tools could only be invented once and have been subject to only marginal improvements in recent decades.

What makes diminishing returns particularly important in understanding the computer paradox is the sheer pace at which computer users are sliding down the computer demand curve to ever-lower marginal utility uses. Word processing offers an example of this point. The upper frame in Figure 1.3 conjectures a total utility curve for word processing, plotted against the speed of the computer measured in mHz. Plotted are successive improvements starting at point A with the memory typewriter, which eliminated much repetitive retyping. At point B

---

[14] The full remark continued, "That's why we see so many articles with so many regressions and so little thought." This comment was passed on to me by Jack Triplett.

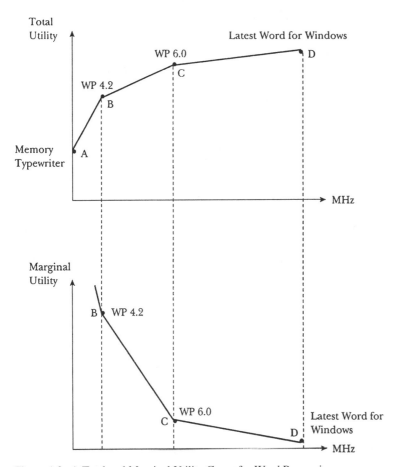

Figure 1.3. A Total and Marginal Utility Curve for Word Processing

comes the early slow DOS personal computer with WordPerfect 4.2. Much faster computer speeds allowed the development of WordPerfect 6.0 for DOS, with a fully graphical WYSIWYG interface, as at point C. Further order-of-magnitude increases in speed bring us today's state of the art at point D, Windows 98 with the latest version of Microsoft Word. Yet look at how the curve flattens out. The real revolution in word processing came at the beginning, by ending repetitive retyping and by allowing revisions to be inserted while the rest of the document would automatically reformat itself. The productivity enhancement of WYSIWYG was minor in comparison, and what was contributed by the final step to the latest version of Word for Windows, beyond some ease of training for novice users, escapes me. As the computer industry has developed, the steady decline in the prices of computer characteristics has fueled the development of increasingly complex software with high requirements for speed and memory required by graphical point-and-click interfaces that yield increasingly small increments of true functionality. The race between hardware capability and software requirements has been aptly summed up in the phrase, "What Intel giveth, Microsoft taketh away."

The bottom frame of Figure 1.3 replots the same relationship with marginal utility on the vertical axis. This is the demand curve for computers which is drawn on the simplified assumption that word processing is the only use of computers, but the point can be made in multiple dimensions. As the diagram is drawn, a large part of the consumer surplus occurred in going from A to B to C, and further gains are relatively small.[15]

When investment in computers was failing to provide much (or any) measurable increase in productivity from the 1970s up into the early 1990s, one response from economists was that the productivity gains would arrive eventually. Perhaps the most noteworthy formulation of this argument was by David (1990), who argued that it had taken electric light and electric motors some decades to diffuse after their invention in the 1870s, so that their productivity benefits did not arrive until the opening decades of the twenty-first century. Perhaps, David argued, the productivity gains from computers would follow a similar pattern.

But the fact of extreme diminishing returns in computers argues against the David (1990) delay hypothesis. The reason that electric light and electric motors took time to diffuse is that initially they were very expensive and did not work very well. But computers provided powerful benefits early on. Many of the industries that are the heaviest users of computer technology – like airlines, banks, and insurance companies – began in the 1960s and 1970s with mainframe technology and still perform the most computation-intensive activities on mainframes, often using personal computers as smart terminals to access the mainframe database. Personal computers are a secondary step in the evolution of computer technology, made practical by decreasing costs of computer power. The internet is yet another step in the evolution of computer technology, also made possible by decreasing costs of computer power. In this sense, computers have been around for almost fifty years. Instead of waiting for the productivity boost to arrive, it is more plausible that the main productivity gains of computers have already been achieved.

A final reason that computers run into diminishing returns is that there are real limitations to the replacement of human beings by computers. To be sure, some of the output of computers is, in principle, as productivity-enhancing as that of electric motors or motorized transport. Numerically controlled machine tools, robots, and other computer-driven machinery have some of the same potential for productivity improvement as the earlier great inventions and doubtless account for the robust rate of productivity growth apparent in much of the durable manufacturing sector. The use of ever-faster computers and peripherals to churn out securities transactions, bank statements, and insurance

---

[15] Even *Business Week*, normally enthusiastic about the benefits of the New Economy, admits that the latest increments in chip speed offer "a lot of speed you can't really use ... a speedier chip won't make you type faster or think faster." See Wildstrom (1999, p. 23).

policies has enhanced productivity growth in the finance/insurance sector. Just as the motor car enormously increased personal mobility and flexibility, so the computer has spawned inventions whose main output is convenience, perhaps most notably the automatic teller machine in the banking industry, but now also beginning to include various internet-based services.

However, computers are actually less pervasive in the economy than is generally thought, because some tasks are resistant to replacement of human beings by computers. Commercial aircraft will always need two human pilots, no matter how advanced the avionics in the cockpit. Trucks will always need at least one driver. In manufacturing, some critical functions have proven to be resistant to automation, such as the connecting of tubes and wires when an auto chassis is "married" to the body.[16] By their nature, many services involve in-person contact between clients and practitioners, whether doctors, nurses, dentists, lawyers, professors, investment bankers, management consultants, bartenders, wait staff, bus boys, flight attendants, barbers, or beauticians. Many other services require in-person contact between an object and the practitioner, such as grocery cashiers, grocery baggers, parking-lot attendants, valet parkers, auto repair, lawn maintenance, restaurant chefs, hotel housekeepers, and almost every type of maintenance of homes and machines. Computers are a relatively large share of capital in business, health, legal, and educational services, but in each of these the contribution of capital to productivity growth is relatively small. No matter how powerful the computer hardware and how user-friendly the software, most functions provided by personal computers, including word processing, spreadsheets, and database management, still require hands-on human contact to be productive, and that need for human contact creates diminishing returns for the productivity impact of the computer.

1.4 THE POSITIVE AND NEGATIVE SIDES OF THE INTERNET

The accelerated rate of price decline in computer attributes has been accompanied since 1995 by the invention of the internet, by which I really mean the widespread public use of the web using web browsers. In perhaps the most rapid diffusion of any invention since television in the late 1940s and early 1950s, by the end of the year 2000 the percentage of American households hooked up to the internet will have reached 50 percent.[17] Although the New Economy was

---

[16] Ford engineers explained to a group of National Bureau of Economic Research economists (including this author) touring a plant in Lakewood, Ohio, on November 1, 1996, that the "marriage" would be the last operation in automobile assembly to be fully automated. In another tour with some of the same economists at the Toyota plant in Georgetown, Kentucky, on April 3, 1998, officials explained their aversion to automation and replacing humans with robots: "Our philosophy is *kaizan* (continuous self-improvement), and machines cannot *kaizan*."

[17] This projection is made by Henry Harteveldt, Senior Analyst at Forrester Research, in communications with the author. The misleading data of Cox and Alm (1999, Figure 8.1, p. 162) suggests that it took more than twenty-five years for television to reach 50 percent household

defined at the beginning of this paper as the apparent acceleration around 1995 in the rate of technical progress in information technology broadly conceived, most of the optimistic interpretations of this development point to the internet, or more specifically the invention of web browsers, as the central development that warrants calling the present era a new Industrial Revolution. In terms of the supply and demand diagram in Figure 1.2, it might seem that the internet represents an expansion of possibilities that should shift the demand curve rightwards and raise consumer surplus substantially in exactly the same way that supermarkets and superhighways raised the consumer surplus associated with the invention of the automobile. But as noted earlier in the discussion of Figure 1.2, there is little evidence that the demand curve has shifted in this way. Why have the productivity effects of the internet been so moderate?

A useful starting point is the way in which Barua et al. (1999) divide the "internet economy" into four "layers:" (1) the internet infrastructure layer; (2) the internet applications layer; (3) the internet intermediary layer; and (4) the internet commerce layer. The first layer consists of hardware manufacturers, including IBM, Dell, HP, Cisco, Lucent, Sun, and many others, all included in either the computer hardware or telecommunications hardware industries. As we have seen in Table 1.2, this sector accounts for the largest single component of the post-1995 productivity growth acceleration, both the direct effect of faster multifactor growth in computer hardware (including computer-related semiconductors) and the indirect capital-deepening effect of the investment boom in information technology. There is little debate about the dynamism of this sector, but rather about the uses to which this exponentially exploding quantity of computer power is being put.

The second layer consists of software, consulting, and training, and includes such companies as Microsoft and its competitors. The impact of this sector is potentially substantial, since producers' durable equipment investment in software in 1999 was $143.3 billion, almost 50 percent larger than such investment in computer and peripheral hardware. The main debate concerning the productivity of this layer is whether the BEA software deflators decline too slowly to capture the increased capability of the software being produced as part of this massive investment effort. However, as shown by Jorgenson and Stiroh (2000), the outcome of the debate over the software deflators has almost no impact on the question of how this sector of the internet economy affects productivity in the rest of the economy. The reason is that using alternative software deflators with radically faster rates of price decline has two offsetting effects from the point of view of productivity calculations: capital inputs grow faster, but total output grows faster, too. Overall, there is more capital deepening and a higher share of the productivity acceleration accounted for by the software industry, but no change in any conclusions about spillovers from software to the rest of the economy.

penetration, but dating from the first commercial TV station in 1947 this penetration rate was reached in only seven years. See Kurian (1994, series R105 divided by A335).

The third and fourth layers of the internet economy consist of providers of intermediate goods and consumption goods. Many aggregators, portals, and content providers, like Yahoo and Travelocity, sell information and services both to business firms and to consumers. To the extent that e-commerce is provided by one business to another, it is an intermediate good and not directly relevant for computing the productivity of final output in the noncomputer economy. In this sense, we do not need to debate whether business-to-business e-commerce is a fruitful invention. If the development of more efficient links in the supply chain reduces costs and allows the elimination of people and paper in the chain of intermediate transactions, then we should see the payoff in faster productivity growth in the noncomputer economy. So far this payoff has appeared in other parts of durable manufacturing, but not in rest of the economy. Thus our primary remaining question concerns the benefits of the internet economy in the provision of final goods.

The consumer benefits of the internet are familiar. Perhaps the most important single consumer benefit at present, also now used universally within business firms, is e-mail. The use of the internet for e-mail long predated the invention of web browsers, and the hardware and software requirements for straight e-mail, as opposed to e-commerce, are very small. The benefits of e-commerce also include the provision of vast amounts of free information that was formerly expensive or inconvenient to obtain, including travel and sports schedules, hotel descriptions, maps, directions, news, security prices, and even entire encyclopedias. When items are purchased over the web rather than obtained for free, selection is often much better than at traditional bricks and mortar stores, and prices even net of shipping costs are often lower. Auctions on sites like e-Bay provide a new mechanism that allows the flea market to spread from local communities and neighborhoods to a worldwide community of potential buyers and sellers. According to Smith, Bailey and Brynjolfsson (1999), "[E]arly research suggests that electronic markets are more efficient than conventional markets with respect to price levels, menu costs, and price elasticity. . . . although several studies find significant price dispersion in internet markets."

If e-commerce contributes to holding down prices of goods traded in the noncomputer part of the economy, then this will provide an additional factor holding down inflation in addition to the direct impact of the falling prices of computer hardware discussed earlier. However, the low prices of many consumer web vendors have resulted in unsustainable financial losses financed temporarily – but surely not permanently! – by venture capitalists and stockholders. In 1999, it was common for well-known e-commerce companies to have losses that were 20 percent, 50 percent, or even more than 100 percent of sales revenues (Bulkeley and Carlton, 2000, p. A4). It remains to be seen how much the web reduces consumer prices once stockholders begin to require that e-commerce vendors actually earn profits (Byron, 2000).

The enormous variety of products and services available on the internet, both for free and for pay, might seem to be an invention worthy of comparison with the great inventions of the past. Yet the mere fact that new products and services are being developed is not sufficient for an Industrial Revolution, which requires that the extent of improvements must be greater than in the past. In Triplett's insightful critique (1999, pp. 326–7), the enthusiastic retelling of anecdotes about the New Economy ignores the distinction between arithmetic numbers and logarithmic growth rates. If an economy has ten products and invents a new one, the growth rate is 10 percent. If many years later the economy has one-hundred products, it must invent ten new ones to grow at the same rate and invent twelve or thirteen to register a significant increase in the growth rate. Today's U.S. real GDP is more than forty times greater than in 1880, but does anyone think that today we are inventing forty times as many important products as in the few decades that yielded the invention of electricity, the telephone, motion pictures, the phonograph, the indoor toilet, and the many others discussed above? No current development in communications has achieved a change in communication speed comparable to the telegraph, which between 1840 and 1850 reduced elapsed time per word transmitted by a factor of 3,000 (from ten days to five minutes for a one-page message between New York and Chicago), and the cost by a factor of 100 (Sichel, 1997, p. 127). The excitement of today's web access, taken in historical perspective, does not measure up to the first live electronic contact with the outside world achieved as radio spread in the early 1920s and television in the late 1940s.

The contribution of the internet to productivity is not the same as its contribution to consumer welfare. For consumers, the new combination of home personal computers and web access provides a valuable invention: Why else would internet access reach a 50 percent household penetration rate only six years after the invention of web browsers? But here again, as for computers in general, the vast variety of internet products collides with the fixed quantity of time available to each household member. Inevitably, much internet use represents a substitution from other forms of entertainment. Internet games replace hand-held games. Down-loaded internet music replaces purchased CDs. Internet pronography replaces purchased or rented adult videos. Other forms of internet entertainment and surfing for information replace hours previously spent watching television, reading books, or shopping. New evidence of diminishing returns is now emerging. Use of personal computers and of the internet is declining among newer purchasers who paid less for their machines and appear to value them less, and apparently only two-thirds of computer owners who subscribe to internet services actually use them (Clark, 1999). As Herbert Simon once said: "A wealth of information creates a poverty of attention."[18]

The essential question raised by the earlier productivity decomposition is to explain why the New Economy in general and the internet in particular have failed to boost multifactor productivity growth outside of the durable manufacturing sector. What explains the apparent contradiction between this unimpressive productivity performance and the eagerness with which millions of business firms and consumers have purchased business and home computers,

---

[18] This quotation was related to me by Hal Varian.

as well as internet infrastructure, spawning whole new industries and creating vast wealth? This conflict is highlighted by findings in microeconomic cross-section studies, discussed by Brynjolfsson and Hitt in this symposium, that the gross rate of return on investment in computers substantially exceeds investments in other areas.

At least four factors may play a role in resolving the conflict: market-share protection, recreation of old activities rather than creation of new activities, duplicative activity, and consumption on the job.

First, the need to protect market share against competitors explains much of the investment and maintenance expense of websites. Barnes and Noble and Borders would have been content to play a dominant role in the retailing of books, but were forced by competition from Amazon to become "clicks and mortar" organizations by developing their own websites that duplicated much of their previous retail activity and most of what Amazon had already pioneered. More generally, computers are used extensively to provide information aimed at taking customers, profits, or capital gains away from other companies. This is a zero-sum game involving redistribution of wealth rather than the increase of wealth, yet each individual firm has a strong incentive to make computer investments that, if they do not snatch wealth away from someone else, at least act as a defensive blockade against a hostile attack. This may be at the heart of the apparent contradiction between the Brynjolfsson-Hitt micro evidence on the high returns to computer investment and the failure of computers to spark a productivity growth revival outside of durable manufacturing; the high payoff to computers for individual firms may reflect redistributions to computer-using firms from firms that use computers less intensively. There is a "keeping up with the Joneses" aspect of hardware and software purchase motivated by competition, employee satisfaction, and employee recruitment.[19]

Second, much internet content is not truly new, but rather consists of preexisting forms of information now made available more cheaply and conveniently. Internet surfing of airline schedules provides a lower cost, although not necessarily faster, method of obtaining information already available in airline timetables, from the printed Official Airline Guide, and from travel agents. Obtaining stock quotes and performing trades on the web does not represent the invention of a new activity but rather a reduction in cost of performing an old activity. In contrast, the great inventions of the late nineteenth century created truly new products and activities.

A third factor subtracting from productivity is the duplicative aspect of the internet. Much e-commerce is an alternative to mail-order catalogue shopping (another invention of the 1870s, whose development is summarized in Gordon, 1990, pp. 419–23). Just as Wanamaker's and Macy's department stores began

---

[19] There seems to be a deeper contradiction between the macro and micro evidence that has not yet been resolved. For instance, in a study of multifactor productivity growth and computer capital across a number of industries, Stiroh (1998) finds: "For all computer-using sectors … the average growth rate of multifactor productivity fell while [computer] capital grew."

to issue catalogues to supplement their existing retail operations in the early 1870s, so currently Land's End, Spiegel's, and many other catalogue operators have supplemented their existing operations with websites in the late 1990s. Yet the catalogues have not disappeared. The full cost of printing and mailing the catalogues is still incurred, but on top of that must be expended many millions on developing and maintaining duplicative websites. While it is cheaper to take an order from a web customer than with a human worker answering a phone, much of the rest of the transaction involves the same physical input of labor in building and stocking warehouses, selecting items from warehouse shelves, packing them, and shipping them. The brown UPS trucks are thriving with e-commerce, but each truck still requires one driver. In fact, far from reducing or eliminating the use of paper, the electronic age seems to multiply paper. As the president of one dot com recently said: "For getting attention in a professional way, paper still matters. Nobody even asks anymore if paper is going away."[20]

An example closer to home for economists is the added cost to academic societies of developing websites to provide information already available in their printed journals. The Econometric Society now provides duplicate announcements of most of its activities through the back pages of its journal and through its website, and it like other societies is under increasing pressure to provide the contents of its journal and even papers given at its regional meetings to its members on the web without any additional fee. It costs money to develop and maintain these websites. Economists gain a consumer surplus in having more convenient access to research, but convenience for professors is not a final good. The final product, education and research, is affected little if at all by the ease of access of references.[21]

Finally, productivity on the job may be impaired by the growing use of business computers with continuous fast web access for consumption purposes. One research service found that people spend more than twice as much time online at the office as they do at home, and that web users at the office take advantage of high-speed connections to access entertainment sites more frequently at work than at home. In fact the most-visited site from the office is e-Bay, and three financial trading sites are not far behind (Farrell, 2000, p. A1). The media have gleefully reported that a large fraction of on-line equity trading is happening at the office, not at home (for instance, Bennett, 2000; "Workers Leaving Water Cooler for Internet," 1999). Employers are so disturbed by the continuing use of office computers for personal e-mail that the number of companies using "surveillance software" to monitor their employees' e-mail usage is "soaring" (Guernsey, 2000, p. C1).

---

[20] The speaker is the president of NowDocs.com, as quoted by Doan (2000, p. 140). On the growth in paper usage, see also "Bad News for Trees" (1998).

[21] In a related investigation of the payoff for academic research of information technology, Hamermesh and Oster (1987) find that articles with coauthors working at long distance from each other actually have fewer citations than other article; that is, "a greater case of overcoming distance does not enhance productivity" (p. 18). They interpret the rise in long-distance coauthorship as mainly a consumption good as academic friends find it easier to work together.

A final response from the New Economy optimists to the skeptics is that computers have added greatly to output, but that many of the benefits of computers have been mismeasured. While it is doubtless true that certain benefits of the current technology are not fully captured in national income accounts, a great many of the benefits should be captured. The heaviest uses of computers are in industries that provide mainly or entirely intermediate goods, especially wholesale trade, finance, many parts of the insurance industry, business services, and legal services. If computers truly raised the output of these intermediate industries in unmeasured ways, then the benefits should show up in the output of final goods industries that exhibit higher output in relation to their undermeasured inputs. Yet this spillover from intermediate to final goods industries is just what cannot be found in the official data on output and productivity growth, at least outside of the durable manufacturing sector.

Moreover, the presence of unmeasured outputs is certainly not new. Personal computers and the internet have doubtless created consumer surplus, but so did most of the great inventions of the past. Indeed, it is quite plausible that the additional consumer surplus from present technologies is less than the amount from diffusion of the great inventions during the golden age of productivity growth from about 1913 to 1972.

1.5 CONCLUSION

The New Economy, defined as the post-1995 acceleration in the rate of technical change in information technology together with the development of the internet, has been both a great success and a profound disappointment. The New Economy has created a dynamic explosion of productivity growth in the durable manufacturing sector, both in the manufacturing of computers and semiconductors and of other types of durables. This productivity explosion has boosted the economy's rate of productivity growth and created enormous wealth in the stock market. Also, by helping to hold down inflationary pressures in the last few years, the New Economy allowed the Federal Reserve to postpone the tightening of monetary policy for several years in the face of a steadily declining unemployment rate. However, the New Economy has meant little to the 88 percent of the economy outside of durable manufacturing. In that part of the economy, trend growth in multifactor productivity has actually *decelerated*, despite a massive investment boom in computers and related equipment.

The fundamental limitation on the contribution to productivity of computers in general and the internet in particular occurs because of the tension between rapid exponential growth in computer speed and memory on the one hand and the fixed endowment of human time. Most of the initial applications of mainframe and personal computers have encountered the rapid onset of diminishing returns. Much of the use of the internet represents a substitution from one type of entertainment or information-gathering for another.

In assessing the importance of the New Economy and the internet as an invention, we have applied a tough test. To measure up, the New Economy had to equal the great inventions that constitute what has been called the Second Industrial Revolution. Internet surfing may be fun and even informational, but it represents a far smaller increment in the standard of living than achieved by the extension of day into night achieved by electric light, the revolution in factory efficiency achieved by the electric motor, the flexibility and freedom achieved by the automobile, the saving of time and shrinking of the globe achieved by the airplane, the new materials achieved by the chemical industry, the first sense of live two-way communication achieved by the telephone, the arrival of live news and entertainment into the family parlor achieved by radio and then television, and the enormous improvements in life expectancy, health, and comfort achieved by urban sanitation and indoor plumbing.

References

"Bad News for Trees." 1998. *Economist*. December 19, pp. 123–26.

Barua, Anitesh; Pennell, Jon; Shutter, Jay, and Whinston, Andrew B. "Measuring the Internet Economy: An Exploratory Study." Working paper. June 10, 1999. Updated versions available at ⟨http://crec.bus.uteexas.edu⟩.

Basu, Susanto. "Procyclical Productivity: Increasing Returns of Cyclical Utilization?" *Quarterly Journal of Economics*. 1996; vol. 111, no. 4, pp. 719–51.

Becker, Gary S. "A Theory of the Allocation of Time." *Economic Journal*. 1965; vol. 75, no. 3, pp. 493–517.

Bennett, Johanna. "Placing Stock Trades While at the Office Adds a Little Risk." *Wall Street Journal*. March 15, 2000, p. B10D.

Bettmann, Otto L. *The Good Old Days – They Were Terrible!* New York: Random House; 1974.

Bresnahan, Timothy F. and Gordon, Robert J. eds. *The Economics of New Goods*. Chicago: University of Chicago Press for NBER; 1997.

Brynjolfsson, Erik. "The Contribution of Information Technology to Consumer Welfare." *Information Systems Research*. September, 1996; vol. 7, no. 3, pp. 281–300.

Brynjolfsson, Erik, and Hitt, Lorin M. "Paradox Lost? Firm-level Evidence on the Returns to Information Systems Spending." *Management Science*. 1996; vol. 42, no. 4, pp. 541–58.

Brynjolfsson, Erik, Hitt, Lorin M. and Yang Shinkyu. "Intangible Assets: How the Interaction of Computers and Organizational Structure Affects Stock Market Valuations." Presented at AEA meetings. Boston, MA: January, 2000.

Bulkeley, William M. and Carlton Jim. "E-Tail Gets Derailed, How Web Upstarts Misjudged the Game." *Wall Street Journal*. April 5, 2000, pp. A1, A4.

Bunch, Bryan, and Hellemans, Alexander. *The Timetables of Technology: A Chronology of the Most Important People and Events in the History of Technology*. New York: Touchstone; 1993.

Byron, Christopher. "Balance Due: In the Hunt for Elusive Profits, Consumer Web Sites will be the First Casualties." *Fortune*. February 21, 2000, pp. 104–8.

Checkland, S. G. "Industrial Revolution." In: *The New Palgrave: A Dictionary of Economics*. Eatwell, John; Milgate, Murray and Peter Newman, eds. London: Macmillan; 1987, pp. 811–15.

Chow, Gregory C. "Technological Change and the Demand for Computers." *American Economic Review*. December, 1967; vol. 57, pp. 1117–30.

Clark, Don. "Survey Finds PC Usage in Homes Has Dropped." *Wall Street Journal*. June, 1999, 21, p. B7.

Cortada, James W. *Before the Computer: IBM, NCR, Burroughs, and Remington Rand and the Industry They Created, 1865–1956*. Princeton: Princeton University Press; 1993.

Cox, W. Michael, and Alm, Richard. *Myths of Rich and Poor*. New York: Basic Books; 1999.

David, Paul A. "The Dynamo and the Computer: An Historical Perspective on the Modern Productivity Paradox." *American Economic Review*. Papers and Proceedings. 1990; vol. 80, no. 2, pp. 355–61.

Denison, Edward F. *The Sources of Economic Growth in the United States and the Alternatives Before Us*. New York: Committee for Economic Development. Supplementary Paper no. 13. 1962.

Doan, Amy. "Paper Boy." *Forbes*. February 21, 2000, p. 140.

Dudley, Leonard. "Communications and Economic Growth." *European Economic Review*. 1999; vol. 43, pp. 595–619.

Farrell, Greg. "Online Time Soars at Office; Not All Surfing Work-Related." *USA Today*. February 18, 2000, p. A1.

Flamm, Kenneth. *More for Less: The Economic Impact of Semiconductors*. Washington: Semiconductor Industry Association. December, 1997.

Gordon, Robert J. *The Measurement of Durable Goods Prices*. Chicago: University of Chicago Press for NBER; 1990.

"The Jobless Recovery: Does It Signal a New Era of Productivity-Led Growth?" *Brookings Papers on Economic Activity*. 1993; vol. 24, no. 1, pp. 271–316. **Chapter 9 in this book.**

"The Time-Varying NAIRU and its Implications for Economic Policy. *Journal of Economic Perspectives*. Winter, 1997, vol. 11, no. 1, pp. 11–32.

"Foundations of the Goldilocks Economy: Supply Shocks and the Time-Varying NAIRU." *Brookings Papers on Economic Activity*. 1998; vol. 29, no. 2, pp. 297–333. **Chapter 17 in this book.**

"U.S. Economic Growth Since 1870: One Big Wave?" *American Economic Review*. Papers and proceedings. 1999; vol. 89, no. 2, pp. 123–28.

Macroeconomics, eighth edition. Reading MA: Addison-Wesley; 2000a.

"Interpreting the 'One Big Wave' in U.S. Long-term Productivity Growth." In: Bart; van Ark, Kuipers, Simon, and Kuper, Gerard, eds. *Productivity, Technology, and Economic Growth*. Amsterdam: Kluwer Publishers; 2000b, pp. 19–65. **Chapter 2 in this book.**

"Has the New Economy Rendered the Productivity Slowdown Obsolete?" Unpublished working paper. Northwestern University; September, 2000c.

Greenspan, Alan. "The American Economy in a World Context." At the 35th Annual Conference on Bank Structure and Competition, Federal Reserve Bank of Chicago. May 6, 1999. At ⟨http://www.federalreserve.gov/board-docs/speeches/1999/19990506.htm⟩.

Griliches, Zvi. "Measuring Inputs in Agriculture: A Critical Survey." *Journal of Farm Economics*. 1960; vol. 42, no. 5, pp. 1411–33.

Guernsey, Lisa. "You've Got Inappropriate Mail: Monitoring of Office E-mail is Increasing." *New York Times*. April 5, 2000, pp. C1, C10.

Hamermesh, Daniel S., and Oster, Sharon M. "Tools or Toys? The Impact of High Technology on Scholarly Productivity." Manuscript. November, 1997.

Hultgren, Thor. "Changes in Labor Cost During Cycles in Production and Business." Occasional Paper 74. New York: National Bureau of Economic Research. 1960.

Ip, Greg. "Market on a High Wire." *Wall Street Journal.* January 18, 2000, p. Cl.

Jorgenson, Dale W., and Griliches, Zvi. "The Explanation of Productivity Change." *Review of Economic Studies.* 1967; vol. 34, no. 3, pp. 249–83.

Jorgenson, Dale W., and Stiroh, Kevin J. "Raising the Speed Limit: U.S. Economic Growth in the Information Age." *Brookings Papers on Economic Activity.* 2000; vol. 31, no. 1, pp. 125–211.

Katz, Lawrence F., and Krueger, Alan B. "The High-Pressure U.S. Labor Market of the 1990s." *Brookings Papers on Economic Activity.* 1999; vol. 30, no. 1, pp. 1–65.

Kendrick, John. "Productivity Trends in the United States." Princeton: Princeton University Press for the NBER; 1961.

Kurian, George Thomas. *Datapedia of the United States, 1790–2000.* Lanham, MD: Bernan Press; 1994.

McGuckin, Robert H., and Stiroh, Kevin J. "Computers Can Accelerate Productivity Growth." *Issues in Science and Technology.* Summer 1998; pp. 41–48.

Mokyr, Joel. "Are We Living in the Middle of an Industrial Revolution?" *Federal Reserve Bank of Kansas City Economic Review.* Second Quarter. 1997; pp. 31–43.

Mokyr, Joel, and Stein, Rebecca. "Science, Health, and Household Technology: The Effect of the Pasteur Revolution on Consumer Demand." In: Bresnahan, Timothy F., and Gordon, Robert J., eds. *The Economics of New Goods.* 1997; pp. 143–200.

Nordhaus, William D: "Do Real-Output and Real-Wage Measures Capture Reality? The History of Lighting Suggests Not." In: Bresnahan, Timothy J., and Gordon, Robert J., eds. *The Economics of New Goods.* 1997; pp. 29–66.

"The Health of Nations: The Contribution of Improved Health to Living Standards." In: Murphy, Kevin, and Topel, Robert Topel, eds. *The Economic Value of Medical Research.* Chicago: University of Chicago Press; 2000. Forthcoming.

Oi, Walter Y. "Labor as a Quasi-Fixed Factor." *Journal of Political Economy.* December, 1962; vol. 70, no. 4, pp. 538–55.

"The Welfare Implications of Invention." In: Bresnahan, Timothy J., and Gordon, Robert J., eds. *The Economics of New Goods.* 1997; pp. 109–41.

Okun, Arthur M. "The Gap between Actual and Potential Output." *Proceedings of the American Statistical Association.* 1962. Reprinted in *Problems of the Modern Economy.* Phelps, Edmund S. ed. New York: Norton; 1965.

Oliner, Stephen D., and Sichel, Daniel E. "The Resurgence of Growth in the Late 1990s: Is Information Technology the Story?" Working paper. Federal Reserve Board. February, 2000.

Schlesinger, Jacob M., and Dreazen, Yochi J. "Inflation Shows Signs of Stirring as Forces Restraining it Wane." *Wall Street Journal.* April 17, 2000, p. A1.

Sichel, Daniel E. *The Computer Revolution: An Economic Perspective.* Washington: Brookings; 1997.

Smith, Michael D.; Bailey, Joseph, and Brynjolfsson, Erik. "Understanding Digital Markets: Review and Assessment." In: Brynjolfsson, Erik, and Kahin, Brian, eds. *Understanding the Digital Economy.* Cambridge: MIT Press; 1999.

Staiger, Douglas; Stock, James H. and Watson, Mark W. "The NAIRU, Unemployment, and Monetary Policy." *Journal of Economic Perspectives.* Winter, 1997; vol. 11, pp. 33–49.

Stiroh, Kevin J. "Computers, Productivity and Input Substitution." *Economic Inquiry*. April, 1998; vol. 36, no. 2, pp. 175–91.

Triplett, Jack E. "The Solow Computer Paradox: What do Computers do to Productivity?" *Canadian Journal of Economics*. April, 1999; vol. 32, no. 2, pp. 309–34.

Uchitelle, Louis. "Economic View: Productivity Finally Shows the Impact of Computers." *New York Times*. March 12, 2000, Section 3, p. 4.

Wildstrom, Stephen H. "Pentium III: Enough Already?" *Business Week*. March 22, 1999, p. 23.

"Workers Leaving Water Cooler for Internet." *New York Times*. May 20, 1999, p. A1.

CHAPTER 2

Interpreting the "One Big Wave" in U.S. Long-term Productivity Growth

"The change in trend that came after World War I is one of the most interesting facts before us. There is little question about it. . . . the rate of growth in productivity witnessed by the present generation has been substantially higher than the rate experienced in the quarter-century before World War I."

Solomon Fabricant, introduction to Kendrick (1961, p. xliii)

It is now more than twenty-five years since the growth rate of labor productivity and of multifactor productivity (MFP) decelerated sharply both in the United States and in most other industrialized nations.[1] This slowdown in productivity growth, or "productivity slowdown" for short, has eluded many attempts to provide single-cause explanations, including fluctuations in energy prices, inadequate private investment, inadequate infrastructure investment, excessive government regulation, and declining educational test scores.[2] The wide

---

[1] The data in this paper end in 1996, because this was as far as the U.S. Bureau of Labor Statistics had extended its data on labor and capital composition, and multifactor productivity, at the time the conference draft of this paper was written. During the 1996–9 period the quarterly data on output per hour indicate a modest acceleration when growth over the recent 1995:Q4-1999: Q1 interval is compared with the slowdown interval 1972:Q2-1995:Q4. Gordon (1999b) argues that this acceleration can be entirely explained by (1) improved measurement of price deflators, (2) normal procyclical effects, and (3) the production of computer hardware, with nothing left over to indicate a structural revival in productivity growth in the 99 percent of the economy engaged in activities other than the manufacture of computers.

[2] Given that the productivity growth slowdown has continued over the period 1973–96, energy prices are ruled out as a cause, since by the early 1990s real energy prices had returned almost to their 1972 levels. Private investment is ruled out in that the productivity slowdown has occurred not just in output per hour but also in multifactor productivity, which takes into account the growth of capital input. If private investment in equipment has "super-normal" returns, as argued by De Long-Summers (1991), then a recalculated MFP exhibits an even more severe slowdown than in the official data. The infrastructure hypothesis proposed by Aschauer (1989) in research

"Interpreting the 'One Big Wave' in U.S. Long-term Productivity Growth." In van: Ark, Bart; Kuipers Simon, and Kuper Gerard, eds. *Productivity, Technology, and Economic Growth*. Boston: Kluwer Publishers; 2000, pp. 19–65.

variation in productivity slowdowns and accelerations across individual industries also argues against a single-cause explanation.[3] The slowdown has also been immune to multifaceted explanations, including those of the late Edward F. Denison (1962, 1979, 1985) to quantify the role of a slowdown in the growth of inputs and specific qualitative factors such as the movement out of agriculture and the spread of crime.

2.1 EXPLAINING THE "BIG WAVE"

When an important problem so completely eludes explanation, other possibilities are suggested. Perhaps we have been asking the wrong question. A basic theme of this paper is that slow productivity growth in the past 25 years echoes slow productivity growth in the late nineteenth century. Perhaps both were normal, and what needs to be explained is not the post-1972 slowdown but rather the post-1913 "speedup" that ushered in the glorious half century between World War I and the early 1970s during which U.S. productivity growth was much faster than before or after.

The timing of the productivity "golden age" is different in the U.S. from that in Europe and Japan, where there is no novelty in suggesting that the 1948–73 "golden age" may have been unsustainable, particularly insofar as it contained an element of catching up from lost opportunities during the previous dismal decades of the two world wars and the Great Depression.[4] However, the United States is another story. The low level of productivity and per-capita income in Europe relative to the U.S. in an early post-war year like 1950 reflects not only Europe's poor performance but also the rapid advance of the U.S. prior to that point.[5] Although most casual observers assume that 1948–73 was the "golden age" of U.S. productivity growth as it was in Europe and Japan, the data compiled in this paper suggest that the American golden age began much earlier, around the time of World War I, and that a substantial part of the great leap in the level of multifactor productivity had already occurred by the end of World War II.

on the aggregate economy has been criticised on the grounds of reverse causation and for failing to explain cross-country productivity differences (Ford-Poret, 1991). Environmental regulation provides only a partial explanation of the productivity slowdown, and only for a few specific industries, *e.g.*, electric utilities. Baily-Gordon (1988) use Bishops' earlier work to argue that declining test scores can explain at best 0.2–0.3 percentage points of the overall productivity growth slowdown.

[3] See Gordon (1998), Tables 3 and 4.

[4] Nordhaus (1982) christened his pessimistic interpretation the "depletion hypothesis," that we were running out of resources and ideas. Abramovitz (1986, 1991) regards the first twenty-five years after the war as a unique period when simultaneously the production possibility frontier expanded rapidly and as well the possibility of "realization" of this potential was unusually favorable.

[5] Abramovitz (1991, Table 2, col. 1) shows that mean productivity in Maddison's sample of fifteen countries (Europe and Japan) fell from 77 percent of the U.S. level in 1870, to 61 percent in 1913, to 46 percent in 1950, and then recovered to 69 percent by 1973 and 76 percent by 1986.

Unlike the common image of a step function, with steady MFP growth through 1973 and a post-1973 step down to a lower level, this paper shows that another image is more appropriate, that of "one big wave." Starting the record at 1870, MFP growth was slow until 1890, then accelerated and reached a crescendo in the five or six decades starting around World War I (1913–72), and then decelerated until in 1972–96 it reached a rate similar to that in 1870–1913.

The big wave image raises at least two big questions, (1) "Is it real?" and (2) "What caused it?" Was there indeed a "golden age" of economic growth that spanned the half century between 1913 and 1972, in contrast to a more normal situation of slow growth before and after?[6] If so, why did the big wave occur? Was there a happy coincidence of particular innovations that created unusually rapid MFP growth during this period? If so, are we forced to conclude pessimistically that slow growth since 1972 has been normal and that we may never return to the earlier years of glory?

This paper is about both questions, "Is it real?" and "What caused it?" We establish the existence of the big wave in the official U.S. data and then examine numerous measurement issues, which could either cut down the peak of the wave or boost its post-1972 wake. We construct and extend previous estimates of changes in the *composition* of labor and capital inputs, which depending on semantics could be considered as errors in the measurement of inputs or explanations of the growth rate in MFP, and in addition make corrections to the quantity of capital input. In explaining the big wave, we give primary attention to the many great inventions of the late nineteenth and early twentieth centuries. Compared with these, the information technology (IT) "revolution," which dates back to the first commercial mainframe computer in 1954, is smaller scale and less important than the real revolution caused by the earlier cluster of "great inventions." Other hypotheses are also examined, including the idea that immigration and flexible markets made labor cheap both before World War I and in the past two decades, thus driving down real wages and labor's marginal product, whereas during the "Big Wave" period controls on immigration and the growing influence of labor unions worked in the opposite direction.

Plan of the Chapter

The essay begins in Section 2.2 by examining data since 1870 on the growth rates of output, labor input, and two types of capital input, namely structures and equipment. We examine some critical relationships that have not received much attention, including the relationship between the big wave in MFP growth and the jump between the 1920s and 1950s in the output/structures ratio. Section 2.3 turns to existing postwar data on secular changes in the quality of labor and capital and then attempts to extend backward before World War II estimates

---

[6] Abramovitz (1991, Table 1) cites his own earlier research as indicating that MFP growth was only 0.45 percent per year over the entire nineteenth century, 1800–1905.

of changes in labor quality using a consistent methodology. Section 2.4 examines several issues in measuring the quantity and composition of capital that relate equally to the interwar and postwar period, and Section 2.5 provides new quantitative estimates of the secular growth in labor and capital input and in MFP itself. Section 2.6 provides an overview of several hypotheses that together are promising in providing an explanation of the big wave. The most important of these is the concurrence of five great clusters of inventions in the late nineteenth and early twentieth century. Complementary explanations involve the closing off of the U.S. economy to immigrant workers and to imported goods between the 1920s and 1960s. Section 2.7 concludes.

2.2   BASIC DATA ON OUTPUT AND INPUTS

Data Sources and their Main Features

While there are many sources of data on output and input growth in the U.S. economy over the last 125 years, three basic sources remain paramount. The U.S. National Income and Product Accounts (NIPA) provide a consistent set of accounts on the income and product side since 1929. For gross product originating (or value added) by industry the accounts are more difficult to use, since the current methodology has been extended back only to 1977, and previous estimates back to 1948 are based on a methodology that differs in many major and minor aspects. The NIPA also include data on employment and hours of labor input on a consistent basis, and the agency that produces the NIPA (Bureau of Economic Analysis, or BEA) also maintains data on capital stocks by industry since 1925.

Another complementary data set on aggregate output and input, available annually for 1948–96, is maintained by the Bureau of Labor Statistics (BLS).[7] While the BEA is the basic source for the output and capital input data used by the BLS, and the BLS is the basic source for the labor input data used by the BEA, there are two important differences. First, the BLS data are available only for three sectors – private business, private nonfarm business, and manufacturing. In contrast, the BEA data set is available for roughly 60 two-digit industries.[8] Second, the BLS data incorporate for the period since 1948 the results of extensive research on the composition of labor and capital, inspired in large part by the work of Denison on labor input and of Dale W. Jorgenson and Zvi Griliches (1967) on both labor and capital input, whereas the BEA data contain no information at all on the composition of labor or capital input.

The third data set is the classic work by John Kendrick (1961) which provides time series on output, labor input, and capital input for major (one-digit) industry

---

[7] Since the conference version of this paper was written, the data set described here has been extended to 1996 and will soon be extended to 1998.

[8] BEA data on hours of labor input are only available at the one-digit industry level while output, employment, and capital stock data are available at the two-digit level.

divisions over the long period between 1870 and 1953. The best match to extend the Kendrick data to the present on a consistent basis is the BEA data set, because it has much more disaggregated detail than the BLS data. Like the Kendrick data, the BEA data contain no compositional adjustments. We will turn in the next section to the BLS composition adjustments and how much they explain of the growth in the Kendrick/BEA MFP series. Subsequently we will explore the possibility of extending back before 1948 similar composition adjustments for labor and capital input.

MFP Growth and the Output–Capital Ratio Puzzle

This essay ignores inputs of energy and imported materials and considers only inputs of labor and capital. In this context it is obvious that the growth rate of MFP (m) is a weighted average of the growth of average labor productivity $(y\text{-}n)$ and of the average product of capital $(y\text{-}k)$:

$$m = y - \alpha n - (1 - \alpha)k = \alpha(y - n) + (1 - \alpha)(y - k) \tag{1}$$

Here α is the share of labor and reflects the standard joint assumptions of constant returns to scale and competitive factor pricing.

In the 1960s, largely as the result of data then newly published by Kendrick (1961) and Kuznets (1961), economists became aware of the puzzling behavior of the output–capital ratio. If one ignored the years within the 1929–48 interval in which economic relations were distorted by the Great Depression and World War II, it was clear that between the 1920s and 1950s there had been a sharp one-time leap in the output–capital ratio, $i.e.$, the average product of capital. In terms of equation (1), the growth rate $(y\text{-}k)$ was much faster during the decades of the 1930s and 1940s than in any other two-decade period in recorded U.S. history. Clearly, if the average product of labor grew steadily, then measured MFP growth (m) would be unusually high during the period of the spurt in $(y\text{-}k)$.[9]

Figure 2.1 begins our examination of the "standard" data on output and labor input based on splicing the Kendrick and BEA data sets at their intersection point of 1929. Details of data collection for the standard data are provided in the Data Appendix at the end of this chapter. Sectoral capital stock data come from Kendrick before 1925 and from the BEA capital stock study since 1925. As discussed below, there is a "rupture" in the BEA data source on capital, in that several data series previously compiled (e.g., capital retirements) have been discontinued, and this has required some improvisation to achieve a consistent historical record.

---

[9] The jump in the output-capital ratio intrigued me sufficiently to devote my Ph.D. dissertation (Gordon, 1967) to explaining it. This paper represents a return to several themes that remained unresolved at that time. My attention to the big wave was drawn by Duménil and Levy (1990), who call attention to this "rupture" in technical change without decomposing it by sector nor providing any link to the several aspects of capital input mismeasurement that in substantial part are responsible for it.

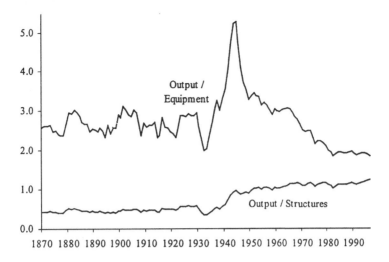

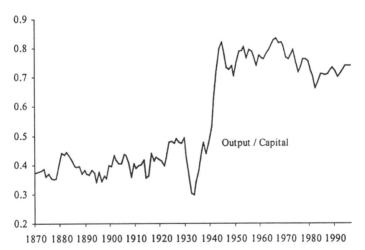

Figure 2.1. Alternative Ratios of Output to Capital, 1992 Prices, Nonfarm Nonhousing Private Economy, 1870–1996 (Sources: See data appendix).

Figure 2.1 displays the output–capital ratio separately for equipment and structures in the top frame and for the total capital stock, *i.e.*, equipment and structures together, in the bottom frame. The jump in the output–equipment ratio observed during 1936–44 was transitory. By 1966 the ratio had returned to its level of 1929, and the ratio declined steadily after 1966. But the jump for the output–structures ratio was huge and permanent. The average ratio for 1960–96 (1.13) was almost double the 1929 ratio of 0.59 and more than 2.5 times the average ratio for 1890–9 of 0.42. The ratio of output to total capital (equipment plus structures) in the bottom frame is dominated by structures (which were 5 times the constant-dollar value of equipment in 1929).

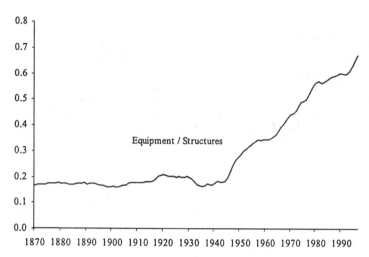

Figure 2.2. Ratio of Equipment to Structures, 1992 Prices, Nonfarm Non-housing Private Economy, 1870–1996 (Sources: See Data Appendix at the end of this chapter).

As shown in the top frame of Figure 2.1 the jump in the ratio for structures was permanent but that for equipment was temporary. A corollary is that the ratio of equipment to structures, as shown in Figure 2.2, exhibits a steady and relentless increase beginning in the mid-1930s from an average of about 0.18 for 1870–1913 to an average of 0.62 for 1990–6. This dramatic feature of the historical record has received surprisingly little attention. Clearly there has been a continuous bias toward space-saving innovation in the development of new equipment as compared to the equipment that was in place in the late 1920s.

Figure 2.3 compares average labor productivity (output per hour, or ALP) with MFP over the full period since 1870. While both ALP and MFP exhibit a high degree of cyclical volatility, the log-linear trends drawn through selected years reveal several features of long-run trends.[10] The first is that the "big wave" phenomenon is evident for both ALP and MFP, with faster growth during the middle period (1913–72) than in either the early or late periods. The second is

---

[10] The use of piecewise loglinear detrending implicitly involves the same method of separating trend and cycle as the more formal approach of Blanchard and Quah (1989), and this is to assume that the unemployment rate is stationary in the long run, that output is not, and that demand disturbances can be represented by shocks that occur in common to unemployment and to deviations of output from trend. The years used to identify trends are 1870, 1891, 1913, 1928, 1950, 1964, 1972, 1979, 1988, and 1996. These are "cyclically neutral" years chosen to smooth out the effects of recessions, depressions, and wartime booms. All the years chosen for the postwar have roughly the same unemployment rate, close to 5.5 percent. The long time span between 1928 and 1950 is intended to eliminate the impact of the Great Depression and World War II. While 1941 would be a possible interim year, distortions in output and labor markets (with rapid inflation, excess demand, and continuing residual unemployment) might create misleading results.

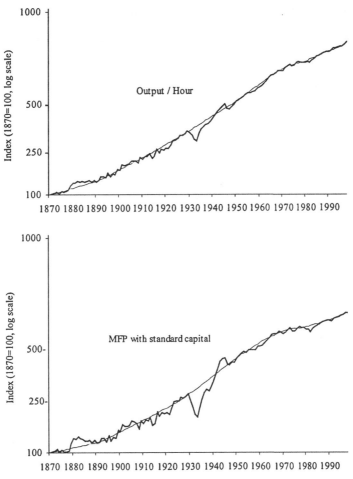

Figure 2.3. Output per Hour and Multifactor Productivity in the Nonfarm Nonhousing Private Economy, 1870–1996. (Sources: See Data Appendix at the end of this chapter).

that the big wave phenomenon is more pronounced for MFP than for ALP, and in the framework of equation (1) above this is the counterpart of the jump in the output-capital ratio in the middle period.

Several dimensions of the "big wave" phenomenon evident in Figure 2.3 are quantified more precisely in Table 2.1. Here are presented annual (logarithmic) percentage growth rates for output, inputs, and MFP in the nonfarm nonhousing private business sector. The top section of the table exhibits growth rates for nine medium-term intervals, the same as those used to draw the log-linear trends in Figure 2.3. The bottom section identifies long-term trends by dividing the full period into three intervals split at 1913 and 1972. The middle period has not only the fastest growth rate of MFP but also the slowest growth rates of

Table 2.1. *Outputs, Inputs, and MFP for Nonfarm Nonhousing Business GDP, Annual Growth Rates over Selected Intervals, 1870–1996*

Years	Output	Labor	Capital	MFP
1870–1891	4.41	3.56	4.48	0.39
1891–1913	4.43	2.92	3.85	1.14
1913–1928	3.11	1.42	2.21	1.42
1928–1950	2.75	0.91	0.74	1.90
1950–1964	3.50	1.41	2.89	1.47
1964–1972	3.63	1.82	4.08	0.89
1972–1979	2.99	2.38	3.46	0.16
1979–1988	2.55	1.09	3.35	0.59
1988–1996	2.74	1.74	2.26	0.79
Long-Term Trends				
Years	Output	Labor	Capital	MFP
1870–1913	4.42	3.24	4.16	0.77
1913–1972	3.14	1.28	2.07	1.60
1972–1996	2.75	1.71	2.98	0.62

Sources. See Data Appendix at the end of this chapter.

labor and capital.[11] We note that the "big wave" is roughly symmetric, in that the final 1972–96 period has about the same rate of MFP growth as the initial period 1870–1913.

2.3 COMPOSITION ADJUSTMENTS FOR LABOR AND CAPITAL

Dating from the pioneering work of Denison (1962) and Jorgenson-Griliches (1967), it has been conventional to explain part of the growth in MFP as the result of an improvement in the quality of labor. The BLS has adopted the framework of Jorgenson (1990) and publishes its indexes of labor and capital input, and of MFP, *after* correcting for changes in labor and capital composition.

In the rest of this paper, we shall use the word "composition" in preference to the somewhat misleading alternative label "quality" to describe the resulting adjustments to the growth of inputs. The increased growth in labor input that results from placing greater weight on more highly educated workers, in proportion to the incomes earned by those with higher educational attainments, clearly warrants labeling as an increase in labor quality. However, a decline in the growth rate of labor input, as in the 1970s, that results from rapid growth in the share of females in the labor force and the lower earnings weights attributable to females should not be called a "decline in quality" – this is not only inaccurate, but even offensive. Similarly, the adjustments to the growth

[11] The tendency for input growth and MFP growth to be negatively correlated over long time intervals was observed in Romer (1987).

in capital input reflect primarily the higher depreciation rate and hence rental price of equipment relative to structures, yielding a faster growth rate of capital input than in the dollar-weighted capital stock when the share of equipment is increasing relative to structures. Again, it is misleading to refer to this as an "increase in capital quality" instead of labeling it for what it is, a "shift to shorter-lived assets."

The Post-War Impact of Changing Input Composition

The labor composition adjustments are obtained by the BLS by developing Tornqvist-weighted aggregates of the hours worked by all persons, classified by education, work experience, and gender. Weights are shares of labor compensation in each group. Thus an increase in the share of higher-educated or more experienced employees will be interpreted as a positive change in labor composition, whereas an increase in the share of less-experienced teenagers would represent a negative change in labor composition.

The capital composition adjustments are obtained by weighting four types of capital (equipment, structures, inventories, and land) separately within each of fifty-three industries using estimated rental prices for each asset type. Since the rental price includes both the net return to capital and depreciation, any shift toward short-lived assets would be interpreted as an increase in the composition of capital. As we have seen in Figure 2.2, there has been a continuous shift from structures to equipment since the 1930s, and this emerges in the Jorgenson-BLS method as implying a continuous upward movement in the composition of capital.

The Kendrick and BEA data used to construct Table 2.1 do not contain any adjustments for labor or capital composition. Now we turn to Table 2.2 which indicates the magnitude of the composition adjustments. The top line of Table 2.2 displays growth rates of output, which in the BLS data are more rapid than the BEA data used in Table 2.1 for 1950–88 but slower for 1988–96.

The next section distinguishes the growth rates of composition-unadjusted hours of labor input (as used in Table 2.1) from the composition-adjusted growth rates that include the effects of changing composition across education, experience, and gender categories. During 1964–79 it appears that the benefits of increasing educational attainment were canceled out by a shift toward less experienced teenagers and the rapid inflow of females into the labor force. After 1979 the share of teenagers declined and the female labor force participation rate leveled off, allowing the positive impact of increasing educational attainment to be augmented by a slight increase in workforce experience.

The next section provides the composition adjustments for capital. Somewhat surprisingly, in view of the growing importance of short-lived computer capital, the compositional adjustment for capital grows more slowly in the most recent period (1988–96) than in any of the earlier periods. As a result of this phenomenon and of slower growth in the capital stock, the growth rate of composition-adjusted capital input falls by half when the most recent period is

Table 2.2. *Annual Percentage Growth Rates of Output, Inputs, and MFP, With and Without Composition Adjustments, for Nonfarm business GDP, 1950–1996*

	1950–64	1964–72	1972–79	1979–88	1988–96
Output (Y)	4.35	4.23	3.60	3.14	1.98
Labor					
Hours (H)	0.99	1.64	2.18	1.85	1.16
Composition	0.40	−0.03	0.00	0.54	0.52
Quality-Adjusted (L)	1.38	1.61	2.18	2.39	1.67
Capital					
Stock (K)	2.91	3.82	3.23	3.31	1.74
Composition	0.85	1.29	1.23	1.45	0.59
Quality-Adjusted (J)	3.76	5.11	4.46	4.76	2.33
MFP					
Based on H and K	2.69	1.83	1.08	0.84	0.70
Based on L and J	2.23	1.54	0.75	0.04	0.11
Effect of Quality Adj.	0.46	0.28	0.32	0.80	0.59
Addenda:					
Y/H	3.36	2.59	1.42	1.29	0.83
Y/L	2.97	2.61	1.42	0.75	0.31
Y/K	1.44	0.41	0.37	−0.17	0.25
Y/J	0.59	−0.88	−0.85	−1.63	−0.35

Sources. Y,L,J, Adjusted MFP from Multifactor Productivity Trends, 1995 and 1996, BLS, Release USDL 98–187, May 6, 1998.

H.K, and composition effects provided in unpublished e-mails from Michael Harper of the BLS. MFP based on *H* and *K* was calculated by aggregating *H* and *K* using the same implicit weights as are used by the BLS to aggregate *L* and *J*.

compared to the middle three periods. This helps to explain why composition-adjusted MFP growth ("based on *L* and *J*") in the next section of Table 2.2 is slightly faster in 1988–96 than in 1979–88, despite the fact that ALP growth measured by either *Y/H* or *Y/L* declines sharply in the final period.

Because the combined effect of the composition adjustments is greatest in the final two periods, the growth rate of MFP slows more sharply over the postwar period when the composition adjustments are included than when they are excluded, and indeed composition-adjusted MFP growth is barely positive over 1979–96. Similarly, the bottom section of Table 2.2 shows that ALP growth slows somewhat more from 1950–64 to 1988–96 when the effects of the labor composition adjustment are included. We also note in the bottom section of Table 2.2 that the output-capital ratio that takes account of capital composition change (*Y/J*) declines at about 1 percent per year after 1964. This decline in the average product of capital and the accompanying decline in capital's marginal product may raise a question as to the priority of increasing national saving and investment as a "cure" for the productivity slowdown.[12]

[12] The decline in the marginal product of capital was noted in this context by Baily and Schultze (1990).

Changes in Labor Composition, 1913–50

Further to understand the "big wave" phenomenon, we must develop measures of changes in labor composition for years prior to the postwar coverage of the BLS composition adjustments. Fortunately the elements of such adjustments back to 1909 have already been developed in Denison's seminal initial book (1962) on the sources of economic growth. However, Denison's techniques and assumptions are not consistent with the current BLS methodology, so in this section we lay out Denison's calculations and compute the changes needed to make them consistent with the BLS data discussed above for the postwar period.

Denison made two controversial assumptions in developing his labor composition adjustments. First, he did not use hours as his basic measure of labor input, but rather assumed that effort per hour increased as hours per week decreased from 52.0 in 1909 to 39.8 in 1957. Second, he adjusted downward by 40 percent the effect of increased educational attainment for the assumed contribution of ability to earnings differentials across educational categories. That is, if a college graduate earned 100 percent more than that of a high school graduate, Denison assumed that only 60 percent of this differential represented the contribution of higher education and the remaining 40 percent represented the contribution of the higher assumed innate ability of college graduates.[13]

Table 2.3 displays the ingredients in Denison's calculations and the changes needed to create a series that is consistent with BLS methodology. Since Denison's adjustments are presented as annual time series, we can calculate logarithmic percentage growth rates over the same intervals that are defined in Tables 2.1 and 2.2.[14] Line 1 lists the growth in total employment, while line 2 shows the negative rate of change of "potential" hours per employee (here "potential" is used in the sense of eliminating the effect of the business cycle). Growth in hours of labor input are then computed in line 3 as the sum of the first two lines and contrasted with Denison's computation of total labor input in line 4. The difference between line 4 and line 3, displayed separately in line 5, represents Denison's adjustment for the assumed effect of shorter hours per week on output per hour.

Denison made the assumption that at or above the hours per week prevailing in 1929 (48.6) a given percentage decrease in hours per week would increase productivity per hour by the same amount, for example, he assumed an elasticity of productivity to weekly hours of -1.0. At the lower level of weekly

---

[13] Partly stimulated by Denison's assumption, there was a vast outpouring of research on education and ability in the 1960s. As summarized by Griliches (2000), this research found no consistent or significant influence of ability on earnings differentials by educational category.

[14] Denison's 1962 book contained data through 1958 and projections through 1965 and later years. His 1985 book contained data for 1929 through 1982. As stated in the notes to Table 2.3, we use the 1962 data to cover our 1913–28 period and the 1985 book for 1928–79, backcasting the 1929 data in the 1985 book to 1928 using 1928–29 data as presented in the 1962 book.

Table 2.3. *Elements of Denison's Quality Corrections to Labor Input, Annual Percentage Growth Rates, Total Economy, 1913–79*

	1913–28	1928–50	1950–64	1964–72	1972–79
1. Employment	1.35	1.01	0.64	1.87	2.70
2. Potential hours per employee	−0.38	−0.75	−0.36	−0.63	−0.61
3. Hours of labor input (1 + 2)	0.97	0.36	0.28	1.24	2.10
4. Labor input (3 + 5)	1.36	0.78	0.46	1.43	2.23
5. Quality adjustment for hours (4 − 3)	0.39	0.42	0.18	0.19	0.14
6. Quality adjustment for education	0.57	0.62	0.60	0.67	0.75
7. Quality adjustment for age, gender	0.11	0.02	−0.06	−0.45	−0.47
8. Total quality adjustment (5 + 6 + 7)	1.07	1.06	0.72	0.40	0.42
9. Alternative education adjustment	0.49	0.48	0.54	0.71	0.84
10. Alt. total quality adjustment (7 + 9)	0.60	0.50	0.48	0.25	0.37

Elements of Education Adjustment	1910–30	1930–50	1950–64	1964–72	1972–76
11. Effect of increased years of education	0.30	0.38	0.43	0.56	0.67
12. Effect of increased days per year of education	0.27	0.23	0.17	0.11	0.08
13. Total education adjustment	0.57	0.62	0.60	0.67	0.75

Sources. For 1913–28 by line number. (1,2,4): Denison (1962), Table 5, p. 37.: (6,7): Denison (1962), Table 11, p. 85; (9): Line 11 divided by 0.6; (11,12): Denison (1962), Table 9, p. 72.

Sources. For 1928–79 by line number (note that 1929 data in sources below are extrapolated backward from 1929 to 1928 using sources for 1913–28 listed above): (1): Denison (1985), Table 3-1, p. 85, col. 1; (2) Denison (1985), Table 3-2, p. 86, col. 2; (5): Denison (1985), Table 3-1, p. 85, col. 9 divided by potential hours from the source of line 2; (9): Line 11 divided by 0.8; (11): Denison (1979), Table F-5, p. 169, col. 1; (13): Denison (1979), Table F-5, p. 169, col. 3.

hours (39.8) reached in 1957, he assumed an elasticity of −0.4, and he interpolated between the 1929 and 1957 values of weekly hours. Stated another way, Denison's approach assumes that a reduction from the 1929 level of weekly hours per employee has no impact on output per employee, while a 1 percent reduction from the 1957 level of weekly hours per employee reduces output per employee by 0.6 percent. The effect of Denison's approach can be seen in the shifting elasticity of productivity to reductions on hours per employee – the ratio of line 5 to line 2 – which amounts to –1.03 for 1913–28, –0.56 for 1928–50, –0.50 for 1950–64, –0.30 for 1964–72, and –0.23 for 1972–79.[15]

Denison's adjustment for education involves two changes from the standard Jorgenson/BLS technique of using observed wages by educational attainment category to attribute a productivity gain to increasing educational attainment over time. Denison multiplies the results of this compositional adjustment by 0.6, reflecting his assumption that differences in ability rather than educational attainment explains 40 percent of observed differences in earnings across educational attainment categories. Thus the estimated effect in the first column, line 11, of 0.30 percent per year represents the multiplication of the compositional adjustment of 0.5 by 0.6 to reflect the 40 percent deduction for the assumed ability contribution. Then on line 12 Denison boosts his estimate by assuming that any percentage increase in the number of school days per year has the same effect on productivity as a like percentage increase in the number of school years per person. The total education effect calculated by Denison for decadal intervals is listed on line 13 and translated into an annual series for individual years on line 6.[16]

Denison's final calculation is a compositional adjustment for age and sex, with an additional adjustment for the increased relative earnings of females. This age-sex adjustment as listed on line 7 makes only a small contribution to his final composition adjustment for labor input listed on line 8. Clearly, the Denison methodology leads to a very large labor composition effect, much larger than the BLS composition effect in Table 2.2 for the overlapping periods of 1950–79.

However, Denison's large adjustments do not correspond to the methodology currently used by the BLS, which does not make any adjustment for the effect of changing hours per week on productivity, any adjustment for changes in school days per school year, nor any adjustment for ability in calculating the impact of increasing educational attainment. To compute a new set of labor composition adjustments for 1913–79 using Denison's data, we eliminate the composition adjustment for changing hours per week. Then for the educational adjustment, we take only the impact of increasing school years per person (line 11) and ignore the impact of increasing school days per year (line 12), and subsequently divide the resulting composition adjustment by 0.6 for 1913–28 and 0.8 for 1928–79 to eliminate the assumed ability adjustment. The resulting "alternative" labor composition adjustment as displayed on line 10 is substantially smaller than the Denison concept on line 8, although the difference shinks through time. The alternative labor composition adjustment is

[15] The description here of Denison's procedure refers to his first (1962) book. His procedure in his 1985 book is more complex, treats different age-sex cohorts of part-time and full-time workers separately, and chooses somewhat lower elasticities than in the 1962 book.

[16] The 40 percent ability offset used in Denison's 1962 book was reduced to 20 percent in the 1985 book, and it is this later figure that is relevant in the columns of Table 2.3 covering the post-1928 period.

only slightly higher than the BLS adjustment for 1950–64 but much higher for 1964–79.

Claudia Goldin (1998, p. 346) provides some additional perspective on changes in education as an explanation of the "big wave": "Human capital accumulation and technological change were to the twentieth century what physical capital accumulation was to the nineteenth century – the engine of growth." She documents the revolution in secondary education attendance in the three decades after 1910, with enrollment rates rising from 18 to 73 percent between 1910 and 1940 and goes further in attributing to the secondary school revolution a substantial part of America's productivity advantage over European nations.[17] Goldin goes further by creating new estimates of graduation rates for 1910 that are substantially lower than implied by the 1940 census of population, implying a more rapid growth rate of educational attainment than in the official data. We do not pursue this bias further, because Denison was already aware of this bias and made an adjustment for it. Whether or not Denison's bias correction is consistent with Goldin's new results is a complex issue that lies beyond the scope of this paper.[18]

Changes in Labor Composition, 1870–1913

Denison's treatment of labor quality begins in 1909 but the current paper computes MFP starting in 1870. In this section we shall ignore changes in age-sex composition, which in Table 2.3 are negligible prior to 1964 and focus on changes in labor composition attributable to education. What information is available to compute a labor quality adjustment for the period 1870–1909? Goldin (1988, Figure 1, p. 348) shows that during the 1890–1910 interval the percentage of those aged 14–17 graduating from secondary school increased only from about 4 to 9 percent and thus had a much smaller effect on the quality of the labor force than the increase from 9 to 52 percent that occurred between 1910 and 1940. Was there an equivalent explosion in elementary school enrollment during 1870–1910 that would have implied an increase in educational attainment comparable to that after 1910?

Two measures of educational attainment prior to 1910 are displayed in Table 2.4. The first line displays enrollment in elementary schools (kindergarten plus grades 1–8), which can be compared with the population aged 5–14, as displayed on the second line. The percent of the population enrolled is displayed on the third line and displays remarkably little increase over the sixty years shown, only from 90 to 97 percent. Consistent with this evidence that elementary education was already standard by 1870 (at least for the white population) is the final line, which shows the illiteracy rate for the same years, implying

---

[17] "But the countries whose per capita incomes were closest to that of the United States in 1910 did not undergo an equivalent transformation at that time. Rather, their high school movements did not materialize for another thirty or more years. . . . Not only was the high school movement from 1910 to 1940 a uniquely American phenomenon, the secondary school as we know it today was a uniquely American invention" (Goldin, 1998, pp. 349–50).

[18] See Denison, 1962, pp. 70–71.

Table 2.4. *Elementary School Enrollment as a Share of Population Aged 5–14, and Illiterate Share of Total Population, Selected Years, 1870–1930*

	1870	1890	1910	1930
1. Enrollment in Kindergarten and Grades 1–8 (thousands)	7481	12520	16898	21278
2. Population aged 5–14 (thousands)	8287	12465	16393	21855
3. Percent of Population Enrolled	90.3	100.4	103.1	97.4
4. Illiterate as Percent of Population aged 10 and over	11.5	7.7	5.0	3.0

Source. Historical Statistics of the United States from Colonial Times to the Present, Bureau of the Census, 1960: (Line 1): series H226; (line 2): series A72 plus A73; (line 3) equals line 1 as a percent of line 2; (line 4): series H408.
Note: a. 1871 rather than 1870.

that literacy for whites was already 88.5 percent in 1870, reaching 97 percent in 1930.

It remains to translate this information into an estimate of the change in educational attainment. Goldin (1998, Table 1, p. 346) provides a distribution of educational attainment that distinguishes between the percentage distribution in each grade interval (8 or below, 9–11, 12, and over 12) and the mean years of attainment in each interval. This is presented for three cohorts, those born, respectively, in 1886–90, 1926–30, and 1946–50. To estimate years of educational attainment forty years earlier for the cohort born 1846–50, we take Goldin's attainments for the 1886–90 group, cut the percentage in each of the higher three intervals (9–11, 12, and over 12) in half, redistributing them to the 8 and below group, and then cut mean years for the elementary school group by half a year. This yields average attainment for our early cohort of 6.23 years, compared to Goldin's three cohorts of 7.58, 11.46, and 12.82, respectively.

The annual growth rate between our early cohort and Goldin's earliest is 0.49 percent per year, compared with annual growth between Goldin's three cohorts of 1.03 percent and 0.56, respectively. If we take a person aged forty-two to be in the midst of working life, then the implication is that the growth rate of educational attainment for adult workers was 0.49 percent per year between 1890 and 1930, 1.03 percent between 1930 and 1970, and 0.56 percent per year between 1970 and 1990.[19] There is a puzzling conflict between Denison's education adjustment (either line 9 or 11 of Table 2.3), which is most rapid in his final period of 1972–9, and Goldin's attainment series, which reaches its peak growth rate (when applied to the working-age adult population) around 1950 and then falls by half between 1950 and 1980.

[19] For instance, the first growth rate of 0.49 percent per year is between cohorts with a mean birth year of 1848 and 1888, who would be forty-two-year-old adult workers in 1890 and 1930, respectively. The final growth rate of 0.56 percent per year is between birth cohorts with a mean birth year of 1928 and 1948, who would be forty-two-year-old adult workers in 1970 and 1990, respectively.

The best we can do with our available information is to estimate that the growth of educational attainment in the late nineteenth century was about half that of the mid-twentieth century, which would reduce Denison's 0.54 percent for 1950–64 (Table 2.3, line 9) to 0.27 percent per annum. However, there is one additional step, which is to convert changes in educational attainment into changes in labor quality by applying earnings differentials across education-attainment groups. Translating changes in the growth rate of educational attainment directly into changes in labor quality would be valid only if the rate of return to increase in education had remained constant over time, which it clearly has not. In fact, Goldin and Katz (1999, Figure 2.4) estimate that the returns to high school education fell by half between 1914 and 1949, before recovering almost to their previous level. Since the rate of return on increases in high school enrollment were much higher around 1910 than in the middle of the century, this would appear roughly to cancel out the slower growth of educational attainment in the earlier period. As a result, we shall assume in the rest of this paper that labor quality increased during 1870–1913 at 0.5 percent per year, roughly the same as Denison's educational adjustment (Table 2.3, line 9) over the entire period 1913–64.

2.4 ISSUES IN THE MEASUREMENT OF CAPITAL

In addition to the questions raised in the previous section about techniques for computing labor composition adjustments, questions can be raised as well about output and capital input data in every interval. As we go back in time, price deflators on which output and capital input data are based become more problematical, as they rely on thinner and thinner samples of the final products actually sold at the time.

Here we concentrate on issues involving the growth of capital input. The close relationship of capital to the "one big wave" phenomenon is clear in comparing Figures 2.1 and 2.3 as discussed before, where the spike in the growth rate of MFP in the 1928–50 interval (the level of which is shown in the lower frame of Figure 2.3) corresponds to the period when the output–capital ratio (shown in the lower frame of Figure 2.1) made its one-time permanent jump. In addition to showing that the timing of the big wave and of the sharp jump in the output-capital ratio is identical, Figures 2.1 and 2.3 (and the Y/J ratio in Table 2.2) also show that the period of slow productivity growth since the mid-1960s has also been a period of a falling output-capital ratio. The latter phenomenon has been interpreted by Martin Baily and Charles Schultze (1990) as evidence of diminishing returns to capital, supporting the traditional Solow growth model against claims by Paul Romer (1990) and others that measured income shares understate the contribution of capital to output growth.

The purpose of this section is to consider several issues in the measurement of capital that, taken together, may help to explain the sharp jump in the output-capital ratio displayed in the bottom frame of Figure 2.1. These are the shifting composition of different types of capital, retirement patterns, and the role of government-owned capital in contributing to private production. The following sections introduce each issue and discuss the results of an attempt to provide a step-by-step remeasurement of capital input that deals with each issue in turn.

Adjustment for Changing Composition

Jorgenson and Griliches (1967) pioneered the use of service price weights for capital, based on the argument that the marginal product of each type of capital, for example, structures and equipment, is equal at the margin to its service price, and a more refined version of their approach has been adopted by the BLS in the capital composition adjustments displayed in Table 2.2 above. For instance, the service price of equipment is the relative price of equipment (p^E) times the sum of the real interest rate and depreciation rate ($r + \delta^E$), and similarly for structures. Since the depreciation rate for equipment is roughly four times that for structures, the use of service price weights substantially raises the share of equipment in capital input and diminishes the share of structures.

Since the big wave in MFP growth is related to the 1928–50 jump in the structures–output ratio (Figure 2.1), a reduction in the weight on structures indirectly dampens the big wave. Thus our task in this paper is to develop an adjustment for the shifting equipment-to-structures ratio (Figure 2.2) that applies to the period prior to the BLS postwar capital composition adjustments.

Already introduced in Table 2.2 and repeated in Table 2.5, column (2), are the capital composition adjustments provided by the BLS for the 1948–96 interval. These are obtained, as stated above, by weighting four types of capital (equipment, structures, inventories, and land) separately within each of fifty-three industries using estimated rental prices for each asset type. To extend these prior to 1948, our only information is on two types of capital, equipment and structures. Our approach is to create a crude composition index based only on reweighting equipment and structures for 1870–1996 and then compare it to the BLS capital composition index for the overlap period, 1948–96. Our crude index is the ratio of an index (1992 = 100) of the capital stock of equipment with a weight of three and structures with a weight of one (the "3:1 index") to a standard capital stock index which weights equipment and structures dollar-for-dollar (the "1:1 index"). The growth rate of this ratio is displayed in column (1) of Table 2.5.

Our capital composition index, that is, the ratio of the 3:1 to the 1:1 index displayed in column (1), grows steadily throughout the postwar period but more slowly than the BLS index shown in column (2) for the period after 1950, presumably because the BLS index contains additional reweighting within categories of equipment and across industries that has the effect of shortening the average lifetime of equipment and raising its service price. For the three intervals between 1950 and 1979, the growth rate of our crude composition index is slightly more or less than one-half the growth rate of the BLS capital composition index for various subperiods, averaging out to 0.56 for the full 1950–79

Table 2.5. *Adjustments to Capital Input, Annual Growth Rates over Selected Intervals, 1870–1996*

Years	Reweight Equipment 3:1 (1)	Back-Cast BLS Comp. Adjustment (2)	Effect of Variable Retirement			Add GOPO (6)	Add Highways (7)
			Equipment (3)	Structures (4)	Total (5)		
1870–1891	0.03	0.06	—	—	—	—	—
1891–1913	0.04	0.07	—	—	—	—	—
1913–1928	0.12	0.21	—	—	—	—	—
1928–1950	0.38	0.68	0.85	0.61	0.66	0.13	0.17
1950–1964	0.42	0.85	−1.11	−0.66	−0.76	−0.06	0.37
1964–1972	0.74	1.29	−0.69	−0.60	−0.64	−0.09	−0.01
1972–1979	0.77	1.23	−0.48	−0.49	−0.49	−0.03	−0.32
1979–1988	0.20	1.45	0.00	0.11	0.06	−0.02	−0.27
1988–1996	0.41	0.59	0.48	0.19	0.40	0.00	−0.13
Long-term Trends Years							
1870–1913	0.03	0.07	—	—	—	—	—
1913–1972	0.37	0.68	−0.05	−0.01	−0.03	0.02	0.20
1972–1996	0.43	1.10	−0.02	−0.10	−0.07	−0.02	−0.24

Sources by Column: (1): Equipment and structures data in 1992 dollars from same sources as Figures 2.1 and 2.2. Data shown in this column are the growth rate of the equipment and structures aggregate when each dollar of equipment capital is weighted 3 times one dollar of structures, minus the growth rate when equipment and structures are weighted dollar for dollar; (2): 1948–96, unpublished BLS series obtained from Michael Harper. 1870–1948, extrapolated backward by dividing the growth rate of column 1 by 0.56, which is the average ratio of column 1 to column 2 during 1950–79; (3)–(5):

Notes: Data listed for 1913–72 in columns (3)–(7) refer to 1925–72.

period.[20] Accordingly, we shall extrapolate the BLS composition index backward before 1948 by dividing the growth rate of our crude composition index in column (1) by 0.56. Moving backward, the BLS composition index in Table 2.2 grows by 1.29 percent per year in 1964–72 and 0.85 percent per year in 1950–64, and our extrapolated BLS index grows at 0.68 in 1928–50, 0.21 in 1913–28, mere 0.07 percent per year during 1870–1913. Thus the capital composition factor becomes important only after 1928, unlike changing labor composition which, at least along the educational dimension, is important throughout the 1870–1996 period. Subsequently we shall examine graphs which display the effects of the capital composition adjustment on the annual behavior of capital input and of MFP over the 1870–1996 period.

Variable Lifetimes

The single most important error in measuring capital input may be the inadequate allowance for quality change, the topic of my book on durable goods prices (1990). Unfortunately, a consistent set of new estimates of investment goods prices is available only for the period covered in that book, 1947–83, and only scattered evidence is available for earlier or later years. In particular, there is no readily available evidence that the bias in the growth rate of official price indexes for investment goods is higher or lower before or after the 1947–83 period than during that period. For the purposes of this paper, a continuous drift in measured price indexes relative to true prices does not have a major impact on the timing of MFP growth by decades. Even if the measurement error were different across decades, this would not skew our MFP calculations in a major way, simply because deflation errors affect both output and capital input growth in the same direction.[21]

Much more important in affecting the timing of capital input and MFP growth across decades is the universal assumption in standard capital data that service lifetimes and retirement patterns are constant. Yet Feldstein and Rothschild (1974) have argued that from a theoretical perspective a fixed retirement pattern is not optimal, and Feldstein and Foot (1971) showed on the basis of firm-level data that retirement patterns are variable and depend on firm cash flow and the state of the economy-wide business cycle. An "eyeball test" suggests that for both structures and equipment retirements occur when new investment occurs. Gross private investment was unusually low between 1930 and 1947 because of

---

[20] We omit the post-1979 period because it is most affected by the growing importance of computers, which play no role prior to 1948. It would make little difference to our results if we were to base the backcasting exercise only on the 1950–64 period; this would change our 0.56 backcasting factor to 0.49.

[21] For instance, I estimated for the 1947–83 period that the growth rate of capital input had been understated by 1.60 percent per year, but that this caused an overstatement of MFP growth by only 0.17 percent per year over the same 1947–83 period (Gordon, 1990, Table 12.14, column 5). Jorgenson (1966) showed theoretically that the impact of price measurement errors on MFP growth depends on the relative size of the share of investment in GDP and the share of capital in total income.

the Great Depression and World War II, and standard capital measures assume that buildings were being torn down on schedule during this period (leading to the implication that the annual growth rate of the capital stock dropped to nearly zero during 1928–50).[22] Yet Chicago's Loop and New York's Midtown were not littered with vacant lots during the 1930s and 1940s; the old buildings were still there.[23]

A simple way to allow for variable retirement patterns is to make the retirement rate depend on gross investment. This relationship can be derived from the empirical Equation estimated by Feldstein-Foot (1971):

$$\frac{R}{K} = \beta_0 + \beta_1 \left(\frac{F}{K} \right) + \beta_2 \left(\frac{N}{K} \right) + \beta_3 U \tag{2}$$

Here R/K is the ratio of retirements to the capital stock, *i.e.*, the retirement rate, F/K is the cash flow ratio, N/K is the net investment ratio, and U is the unemployment rate. To simplify this equation for use here, we assume that both the cash flow ratio and unemployment rate depend on the ratio of gross investment to capital:

$$\frac{F}{K} = \alpha_0 + \alpha_1 \left(\frac{G}{K} \right) ; U = \gamma_0 + \gamma_1 \left(\frac{G}{K} \right) \tag{3}$$

Using the identity that

$$\frac{N}{K} \equiv \frac{G}{K} - \frac{R}{K}, \tag{4}$$

we can combine (3) and (4) and write a relationship between the retirement rate and the gross investment ratio:

$$\frac{R}{K} = A_0 + A_1 \left(\frac{G}{K} \right). \tag{5}$$

To convert equation (5) into a specific adjustment in the capital stock series, we begin with BEA data on retirements and the ratio of gross investment to capital, available from 1925 to 1988.[24] No adjustment is performed before 1925, but this omission is not important since the motivation for the adjustment

---

[22] Our standard capital stock series summarized in Table 2.1 grows at only 0.04 percent per year between 1929 and 1945. All of its growth rate for 1928–50 shown in Table 2.1 occurs during 1928–9 and 1945–50.

[23] A vivid example of the cessation in office building construction in the 1930s and 1940s occurs in Chicago, where the tallest building from 1930 to 1957 was the Board of Trade, but after 1957 the title for tallest building changed every year or two until 1973. The story is similar in other cities.

[24] The basic computation was carried out on BEA gross investment and retirement data for the period 1925–88, as stated in the text. After these computations were carried out in 1992, the BEA changed the format of its historical capital stock data and no longer publishes gross investment or retirements. The current paper is based on the new BEA net investment data and bases its estimate of the effect of variable retirement on the previous results developed from the previous BEA gross investment and retirement data available for 1925–88.

is the delay in retirements in the 1930s and 1940s caused by unusually low gross investment during that period. The adjusted retirement rate $(R/K)^*$ is computed from the BEA data as follows:

$$\left(\frac{R}{K}\right)^*_t = \left(\frac{R}{K}\right)_t \frac{(G/K)_t}{\overline{(G/K)}} \tag{6}$$

Thus we simply multiply the BEA's retirement rate by the ratio of G/K in each year to its sample mean over 1925–1996. This procedure implies that retirements are reshuffled among the years between 1925 and 1996, but the average retirement rate over the entire period is maintained at the same level as in the BEA data.

The effect of the variable retirement adjustment is shown in Table 2.5 for equipment in column (3), for structures in column (4), and for the sum of equipment and structures in column (5). The effect is to make capital input grow faster over the 1928–50 period, as expected, and to grow slower during 1950–79. Over the entire 1925–96 period the effect of this adjustment is negligible, as is intended.

The adjustment is shown for the entire 1925–96 period in Figure 2.4, with the adjustment displayed for equipment in the top frame and for structures in the bottom frame. The shift to a variable retirement pattern substantially boosts the stock of both equipment and structures between 1929 and 1965 (for equipment) and 1970 (for structures). The ratio of the fixed-retirement capital stock for equipment reaches its low point relative to the variable retirement equipment stock in 1943–4 and for structures in 1945–50. As would be expected, the variable retirement pattern reduces the stock of both equipment and structures after 1975, since there was more capital existing in 1930–65 to be retired.

Omitted Capital

Part of the sharp rise in output during World War II was made possible by plants and equipment that were owned by the government but operated by private firms to produce goods and services. When the output–capital ratio puzzle was first discussed in the 1960s, the official statistics on capital input in the private sector did not keep track of this government-owned privately-operated (GOPO) capital, and thus the 1940–5 increase in the output–capital ratio (and hence in MFP) was exaggerated. After I studied this phenomenon and estimated its magnitude (1969), the BEA began to keep track of GOPO capital and includes it now as a separate category in its capital stock data bank. Thus we can show the impact of including GOPO capital, as in column (6) of Table 2.5, which is to boost the growth rate of capital input during 1928–50 (all of this occurs in 1940–5) and to reduce it after 1950.

A related issue is that a substantial part of government-owned infrastructure serves as an unmeasured input to production in the private sector. In particular, there has been a gradual shift over time in the transportation sector from privately-owned railroad capital to publicly-owned highways, airports, and

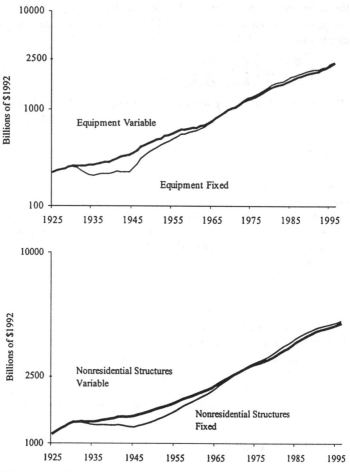

Figure 2.4. Effect of Variable Retirement Pattern, 1925–1996 (Sources: See data appendix).

air-traffic-control facilities. Sufficient data are available to allow us to add to private capital input two types of government capital, GOPO in column (6) and highway capital in column (7) of Table 2.5, relying on Fraumeni's (1999) recent estimates of the latter. The effect of adding highway capital is to boost the growth rate of capital input in both the 1928–50 and 1950–64 periods, but to reduce it thereafter, which has the effect of explaining a small part of the "big wave" of MFP growth during 1928–64 and a small part of the post-1972 MFP growth slowdown.[25]

---

[25] Highway capital data are included only beginning in 1925. To avoid an artificial jump in total capital between 1924–5, the total capital measure including highway capital is ratio-linked in 1925 to avoid having any impact on the growth rate of capital from 1924 (or any earlier year) to 1925.

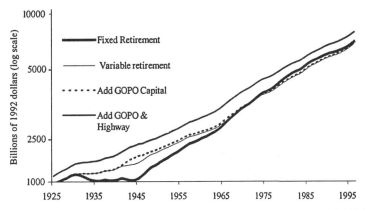

Figure 2.5. Alternative Nonresidential Fixed Capital Aggregates, 1925–1996 (Sources: See Data Appendix at the end of this Chapter).

The combined impact of changing from fixed to variable retirement, and of adding GOPO and highway capital, is illustrated for the 1925–96 period in Figure 2.5. Instead of declining by 7.4 percent between 1930 and 1944, total capital input actually increases by 28 percent (not counting the capital composition adjustment). This is clearly an important finding and highly relevant to the puzzle of how the United States succeeded in producing so much during World War II. Subsequently we will take a broader look at the revised input series over the entire 1870–1996 period.

2.5 SUMMARY OF INPUT DATA REVISIONS AND IMPLICATIONS FOR MFP

Corrections to Labor and Capital Input Data

We now take a tour of several graphs and tables that summarize the implications of our labor and capital composition adjustments, and of our capital quantity adjustments, for the full 1870–1996 period. The tables provide summary information on growth rates over the same intervals specified in Table 2.1, and the figures provide additional information by displaying all the years individually.

The effects of the labor composition adjustments on the level of labor input is shown in Figure 2.6 – the more rapid growth of composition-adjusted labor input combines the BLS composition series back to 1948, the Denison series adjusted to correspond with the BLS concept back from 1948 to 1913, and a guesstimate back to 1870 based on scattered evidence on enrollment rates, illiteracy, and the rate of return to high school education. The effects on growth rates over our standard intervals are shown in Table 2.6, where in column (3) the labor composition adjustment is shown to have about the same impact in raising labor input growth by about 0.5 percent per year in all periods except 1964–72 and 1972–9.

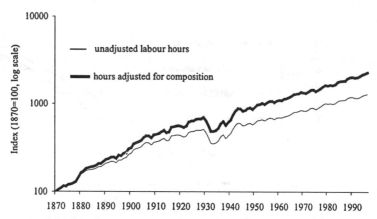

Figure 2.6. Labor Input with and without Composition Adjustment, Nonfarm Nonhousing Private Economy, 1870–1996 (Sources: See Data Appendix).

Columns (4) through (6) of Table 2.6 compare standard capital input with composition-adjusted capital input and with capital input adjusted both for composition and the three quantity adjustments quantified separately in Table 2.5 and Figure 2.5, namely the shift from fixed to variable retirement, the addition of GOPO capital, and the addition of highway capital. Unlike the labor composition adjustment, which has a similar effect in all intervals but 1964–79, the effect of the capital composition and quantity adjustments differ radically across intervals. By far the greatest impact is in 1928–50, the core period of the "big wave" in MFP growth, where there is a substantial impact of capital composition and where the other three adjustments (variable retirement, GOPO capital, and highway capital) all have sizeable effects. The combined capital adjustments also have substantial effects of close to 1 percentage point per year in three of the five postwar intervals, but virtually no impact prior to 1913. Thus the combined capital adjustments have the effect of reducing MFP growth after 1913 relative to pre-1913 MFP growth and reduce MFP most of all in 1928–50, 1964–72, and 1979–96. Figure 2.7 shows the same adjustments for each year back to 1870 and emphasizes that the quantity adjustments had their greatest proportional effect in the 1940s while the composition adjustment made the most difference between 1964 and 1988.

Implications for MFP Growth

We have now seen that the timing of our three types of input adjustments is quite different. The labor composition adjustment has a uniform effect in boosting labor input growth and reducing MFP growth across all periods except 1964–79. The capital composition adjustment is negligible before 1913 and has its largest effect in boosting capital input growth and reducing MFP growth during the postwar period, especially between 1964 and 1988. We have seen that several quantity adjustments made to the standard capital series have the effect

Table 2.6. *Summary of Input Adjustments, Selected Intervals, 1870–1996*

Years	Standard Labor Input (1)	Comp. Adjusted Labor Input (2)	Effect of Labor Adjustment (3)	Standard Capital Input (4)	Comp. Adjusted Capital Input (5)	Comp. & Quantity Adjusted Capital Input (6)	Effect of Capital Adjustment (7)
1870–1891	3.56	4.05	0.49	4.48	4.53	4.53	0.05
1891–1913	2.92	3.42	0.50	3.85	3.92	3.92	0.07
1913–1928	1.42	2.01	0.59	2.20	2.41	2.52	0.32
1928–1950	0.91	1.41	0.50	0.66	1.34	2.28	1.62
1950–1964	1.41	1.81	0.40	2.94	3.79	3.52	0.58
1964–1972	1.82	1.86	0.04	4.15	5.44	5.02	0.87
1972–1979	2.38	2.40	0.02	3.46	4.69	4.10	0.64
1979–1988	1.51	1.99	0.48	3.27	4.56	4.31	0.96
1988–1996	1.35	1.93	0.58	2.23	2.90	3.19	0.96

Long-term Trends
Years

1870–1913	3.24	3.73	0.49	4.16	4.22	4.22	0.06
1913–1972	1.28	1.72	0.44	2.06	2.75	3.01	0.95
1972–1996	1.71	2.09	0.38	2.98	4.04	3.87	0.99

Sources by Column. (1)–(2): Table 2 and Table 3, line 10, plus text discussion for 1870–1913; (3): column 2 minus column 1; (4): Same sources as Table 1; (5)–(6): Table 5; (7): column 6 minus column 4.

75

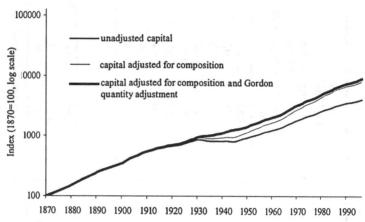

Figure 2.7. Alternative Measures of Capital Input, Nonfarm Nonhousing Private Economy, 1870–1996 (Sources: See Data Appendix).

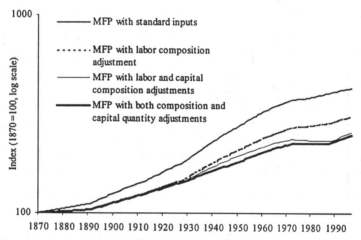

Figure 2.8. Alternative Measures of MFP, Nonfarm Nonhousing Private Economy, 1870–1996 (Sources: See Data Appendix).

of substantially raising the growth rate of capital input during the 1928–50 "big wave" interval relative to subsequent intervals, and indeed these adjustments reduce the growth rate of capital input in every interval but 1988–96, thus partly offsetting the positive impact on capital growth of the capital composition adjustment.[26]

The effects of these adjustments on MFP are displayed in Table 2.7 and Figure 2.8. Comparing the growth rates of MFP based on standard inputs in column (1) with the alternative growth rates of MFP based on fully adjusted

---

[26] Recall that the capital quantity adjustments do not extend before 1918 due to the absence of comparable data.

Table 2.7. *MFP for Nonfarm Nonhousing Business GDP, Annual Growth Rates for Selected Intervals, 1870–1996*

Years	Standard Inputs (1)	Standard Capital, Labor Composition Adjustment (2)	Labor and Capital Composition Adjustments (3)	L&K Composition Adjustment and Capital Quantity Adjustments (4)	Effect of all Adjustments (4)-(1)
1870–1891	0.54	0.22	0.20	0.20	−0.34
1891–1913	1.20	0.87	0.85	0.85	−0.35
1913–1928	1.43	1.03	0.96	0.93	−0.50
1928–1950	1.92	1.58	1.36	1.05	−0.87
1950–1964	1.59	1.32	1.04	1.13	−0.46
1964–1972	1.05	1.02	0.59	0.73	−0.32
1972–1979	0.25	0.24	−0.17	0.02	−0.23
1979–1988	0.73	0.41	−0.02	0.07	−0.66
1988–1996	0.82	0.43	0.21	0.12	−0.70
Long-Term Trends Years					
1870–1913	0.88	0.55	0.53	0.53	−0.35
1913–1972	1.60	1.30	1.08	0.99	−0.61
1972–1996	0.62	0.37	0.01	0.07	−0.55

Sources. MFP calculated from standard and adjusted input series as listed in Table 2.6.

inputs in column (4), we see that MFP growth is reduced in every period but by quite a different amount. The capital quantity adjustments have their biggest impact in 1928–50, the period in which MFP growth is reduced the most. The labor composition adjustments are close to zero in 1964–72 and 1972–9, the periods when MFP growth is reduced the least. And the capital composition and quantity adjustments are negligible prior to 1913, when the reduction in MFP is also relatively low. Overall, looking at the long-term trends in the bottom of Table 2.7, the middle period still has the most rapid MFP growth, although its margin of victory over 1870–1913 is substantially reduced. However the reduction in the growth rate of MFP after 1972 is almost as great as in 1913–72, and thus the contrast between the "big wave" period and the post-1972 "slowdown" period remains intact.

Figure 2.8 exhibits the same alternative MFP series for which the growth rates are displayed in Table 2.7. The input adjustments do create an important change in timing in contrast to MFP based on standard inputs. Instead of exhibiting a distinct acceleration in 1928–50 as compared to the periods immediately before or after, fully adjusted MFP growth appears as nearly a straight line all the way from 1891 to 1972, and indeed Table 2.7 shows that the growth rates over the five subperiods within 1891–1972 vary only between 0.77 and 1.17 percent, a

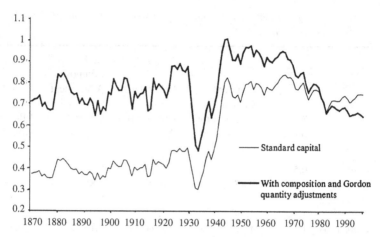

Figure 2.9. Alternative Ratios of Output to Capital, 1992 Prices, Nonfarm Nonhousing Private Economy 1870–1996 (Sources: See Data Appendix).

range of 0.40 percentage points compared to the range over the same subperiods of more than twice as much, 0.87 points, when MFP is based on standard inputs as in column (1) of Table 2.7.

Implications for the Output–Capital Ratio

This paper began by pointing to the permanent doubling in the output to capital ratio between the prewar and postwar eras, as depicted in Figure 2.1. Does this mysterious jump in the ratio survive the composition and quantity adjustments developed in this paper?

Figure 2.9 compares the output–capital ratio based on standard and adjusted capital input, while retaining the same measure of real output. It appears that the composition and quantity adjustments to capital input completely eliminate the permanency of this jump, a long-standing feature of the data that has previously resisted a coherent explanation.[27] Indeed, when both output and capital input are expressed in 1992 prices, the output–capital ratio is lower in 1996 (0.64) than in 1870 (0.71), in contrast to the doubling that occurs with the standard capital input date (0.37 to 0.74).

Two further differences stand out between the adjusted and standard data when shorter periods are examined. First, the increase between 1926 and 1953 in the output-capital ratio is substantially less with the adjusted than with the standard data, 9 percent (from 0.89 to 0.97) instead of by 65 percent (from 0.49 to 0.81). Second, there is a pronounced downdrift in the postwar period in the adjusted data, with the output-capital ratio declining from 0.97 in 1953 to

---

[27] The jump in the output-capital ratio depicted in Figures 2.1 and 2.9 using the standard capital series was the original motivation for my 1967 Ph.D. thesis on problems in measuring real investment.

0.64 in 1996 (a 34 percent decline) in contrast to a much milder decline from 0.81 in 1953 to 0.74 in 1996 (a 9 percent decline). The radical difference in the historical behavior of the output–capital ratio combines the influence of the steady increase in capital growth created by the composition effect after 1928 with the boost to capital growth in the 1928–50 interval created by the quantity adjustments.

2.6 SUBSTANTIVE HYPOTHESES

Now we turn to the task of explaining the "big wave" in U.S. growth in MFP, now expressed with the new data as the much faster growth between 1891 and 1972 than before or particularly after 1972. In discussing substantive explanations of the "big wave," we begin with the timing of the great inventions and then proceed to other complementary hypotheses.

The Great Inventions

In related research (Gordon, 1998) I have argued that the current information-technology revolution does not compare in its quantitative importance for MFP with the concurrence of many great inventions in the late nineteenth and early twentieth century that created the modern world as we know it. There are four major clusters of inventions to be compared with the computer, or chip-based IT broadly conceived. These are:

1. The first great invention in the "group of four" is electricity, including both electric light and electric motors. As shown by Nordhaus (1997), electricity drastically reduced the true price of light. Electric motors, after a developmental period of two or more decades emphasized by David (1990), revolutionized manufacturing by decentralizing the source of power and making possible flexible and portable tools and machines. After a somewhat longer lag, electric motors embodied in consumer appliances eliminated the greatest source of drudgery of all, manual laundry, and through refrigeration virtually eliminated food spoilage and through air conditioning made summers enjoyable and opened the southern United States for modern economic development.

2. Sharing the title with electricity for the most important invention that had its main diffusion in the twentieth century is the internal combustion engine, which made possible personal autos, motor transport, and air transport. Grouped in this category are such derivative inventions as the suburbs, interstate highways, and supermarkets.[28] Gradually eliminated or greatly reduced were many of the ills of the late nineteenth century, from manure to unplowed snow to putrid air to rural isolation.

---

[28] Bresnahan and Gordon (1997) in their introduction provide a formal analysis of how complementary inventions like supermarkets, suburbs, and highways increase the consumer surplus contributed by new inventions like the internal combustion engine and the motor car.

3. The third group of great inventions includes both petroleum and all the processes that "rearrange molecules," including petrochemicals, plastics, and pharmaceuticals. These are largely an independent invention, but some of the innovations were induced by the demands of motor and air transport. They helped to reduce air pollution created by industrial and heating uses of coal, and they made possible many new and improved products, as well as conquering illness and prolonging life.

4. The final member of the "group of four" is the complex of entertainment, communication, and information innovations that were developed before World War II. This set of inventions that made the world smaller can be traced back to the telegraph in 1844 and includes the telephone, radio, movies, television, recorded music, and mass-circulation newspapers and magazines. Television, which was invented in the 1920s and 1930s, is the only one of these innovations that was diffused after World War II. Otherwise, all the rest were well established before World War II and created a quantum leap in the standard of living when a year like, say, 1939 is compared with fifty years earlier.

The "group of four" inventions, in turn, created an increase in per capita income and wealth that allowed an improvement in living standards even in those aspects of consumption where inventions did not play a major role, particularly the ability of families to afford many more square feet of shelter (and in the suburbs more land surrounding that shelter) than at the turn of the century.

Has the information revolution spawned by the computer created as great a change in living conditions as any of the four major complexes of early twentieth-century inventions? While retrospective exercises are inevitably subjective, it is interesting to play an expanded version of what I like to call the "New Yorker game." A few years ago the New Yorker magazine commissioned a critic to sit in front of a television set for an entire week and record his impressions. He had many reactions, but the one most relevant for us is that he was surprised from the reruns of 1950 TV shows how similar were the living conditions of the 1950s Ozzie and Harriet families in comparison to those of today. Clearly living conditions were far better in the 1950s than in the 1890s, in large part because of the "group of four" inventions. We can surmise that a hypothetical critic revisiting the 1890s through a time machine would not have the same reaction as the New Yorker critic visiting the 1950s from the 1980s. For our purposes, it is a moot point whether life changed more between the 1890s and 1920s or between the 1920s and 1950s. What does seem sure is that society had cured most of the ills of late nineteenth century living conditions by the 1950s and 1960s without any help from computers.

To understand at a deeper level why the computer revolution does not measure up to the earlier great inventions, it is useful to consider some of the ways in which the great inventions created productivity growth. Electric light was a unique invention that extended the length of the day for reading, entertainment, and other pursuits. Both the electric motor and internal combustion engine created faster and more flexible movement, directly raising the productivity of factory workers, housewives, truck drivers, and airline pilots as the machines they powered could rotate ever faster. Petroleum refining, chemicals, plastics, and pharmaceuticals all involve the physical rearrangement of molecules in ways that change materials into more productive forms. The complex of electric and electronic entertainment and information industries arrived in a void in which nothing comparable existed and had, one may safely conjecture, a greater impact on everyday life of the average family than the second and third generation developments, for example, VCRs, CDs, the first generation of color TVs, and ever-larger TV screens, which provided merely better or more convenient ways of performing the same basic functions.

Some of the output of computers is, in principle, as productivity-enhancing as that of electric motors or motorized transport. From the earliest punch-card sorters, some applications of computer technology have involved movement and speed. Numerically-controlled machine tools, robots, and other computer-driven machinery has the same potential for productivity improvement as the earlier great inventions and doubtless accounts for the robust rate of productivity growth still apparent in some (but not all) manufacturing industries. The use of ever-faster computers and peripherals to churn out securities transactions, bank statements, and insurance policies should enhance productivity growth in the finance/insurance sector. And, just as the motor car enormously increased personal mobility and flexibility, so the computer has spawned inventions whose main output is convenience, most notably the ATM machine.

These productivity-enhancing aspects of computers suggest that MFP performance in the past two decades would have been even worse than the dismal record of Table 2.7 without the benefits of computers. Yet the benefits of computers have not been strong enough to bring us back to the rapid rates of MFP advance enjoyed before 1972. In my analysis (1998), the rapid price declines of computer power have resulting in diminishing returns to computers operating with unparalleled force. Just as the elementary textbook example explains diminishing returns as resulting from the application of additional units of labor to a fixed supply of land, so the computer revolution has resulted in the application of vastly multiplied units of computation power to a fixed supply of time and mental power for any given computer user. The computer revolution did not begin with the earliest PCs in the 1980s but with mainframes in the early 1950s. After more than four decades, the greatest benefits of computers have been achieved. The newest aspect of the computer revolution, the internet, can be viewed largely as a source of information and entertainment that substitutes for other forms of information and entertainment.

An intriguing connection of the time path of technical innovation with the "big wave" is Kleinknecht's (1987) count of "radically new products," which rises from six during 1850–1920 to 29 during 1920–1950 and then falls to five during 1950–70.[29] Kleinknecht's count is reproduced in Table 2.8.

---

[29] See Freeman (1986) for a collection of suggestive papers on long swings in design and innovation.

Table 2.8. *Types of Innovations in Ten-Year Periods*

	PI[1]	IP[2]	Scientific Instruments	Difficult Cases
1850–59	0	1	0	0
1860–69	1	2	0	1
1870–79	1	5	0	0
1880–89	3	4	0	0
1890–99	0	2	0	0
1900–09	1	5	0	1
1910–19	0	4	0	1
1920–29	6	2	0	0
1930–39	14	4	2	6
1940–49	9	5	4	1
1950–59	2	8	3	4
1960–69	3	4	9	2

Source. Kleinknecht (1987), p. 66

[1] PI = Product innovations (radically new products)

[2] IP = Improvement and process innovations

Other Substantive Hypotheses

Immigration and the Codependence of Productivity and Real Wages

Given the timing of the "big wave," it is striking that productivity growth was slow in the late nineteenth century when immigration was important, and then again in the 1970s and 1980s when the baby boom and renewed immigration created rapid labor-force growth. This observation is related to Romer's (1987, Figure 1) demonstration that productivity growth and labor-force growth in U.S. history is negatively correlated over twenty-year intervals since 1839. Thinking about immigration may be helpful in explaining why the U.S. MFP growth slowdown in the 1970–90 period has been concentrated in nonmanufacturing. My idea (further developed in Gordon, 1997 See Chapter 5) is that new entrants (teens and adult females in the 1970s and legal and illegal immigrants in the 1980s) have mainly gone into unskilled service jobs and have held down the real wage in services, in turn promoting the lavish use of unskilled labor in such occupations as grocery baggers, busboys, valet parkers, and parking lot attendants, jobs that barely exist in high-wage European economies. In contrast, immigrants in the 1890–1913 period were disproportionately employed in manufacturing, and their presence probably dampened real wage increases and delayed the introduction of labor-saving equipment.[30] The "big wave" period of rapid

[30] On the industrial and occupational composition of successive generations of immigrants, see Borjas (1994). On migration and economic development in an international context see Hatton-Williamson (1992) and Williamson (1992).

productivity growth coincides roughly with the shutting off of mass immigration in the 1920s and the slow labor-force growth of 1930–65.

Real Wage Convergence and Divergence

Goldin and Margo (1992) have recently studied the sharp convergence, that is, reduction in inequality, of real wages in the 1940s and subsequent divergence, and Goldin and Katz (1999) have shown the same type of V-shaped behavior for the rate of return to both high school and college education. If relative labor scarcity coincided with a technology that created a high demand for unskilled and semiskilled workers, then the relatively high wages for low-skill work in the 1940s may have in turn stimulated efficiency improvements that boosted productivity. Wages started diverging after 1950, with a sharp increase in inequality in the 1980s and 1990s that is reflected in a big jump in the rate of return to college education, mainly because the real wages of high school graduates fell. This process is the outcome of a complex process in which changing technology, an increased supply of cheap imported manufactured goods, and immigration interacted to erode the rents previously earned by union members with high school educational attainment. This, in turn, may have reversed the stimulus to higher efficiency that took place in the 1940s. The immigration and convergence stories are related, since Borjas (1992) shows that immigration in 1880–1913 introduced much of the inequality in skills and real wages that Goldin and Margo (1992) show was substantially eliminated in the 1940s.

Growing Openness to Trade

Trade theory teaches that trade in goods, not just labor mobility, can lead to convergence of incomes. This idea that trade simultaneously promotes convergence but also generates a slowdown of income growth in the leading country is closely related to several recent models, particularly that of Johnson and Stafford (1992). In this context a contribution to the "big wave" may have been a movement away from free trade in the Fordney-McCumber tariffs of 1922 and Smoot-Hawley Act of 1930. This movement away from trade may possibly help to explain some of the "big wave" and also the temporary cessation of convergence among nations in the 1913–1950 period previously noted by Abramovitz (1986, 1991) and many others.[31]

---

[31] The idea that protection can raise productivity is related to an idea that emerges from the McKinsey (1992) cross-country study, that West Germany boosts productivity in retailing by regulations that directly limit shop opening hours and indirectly stifle the development of shopping centers (thus creating crowded busy stores in contrast to the U.S. malls that are empty for many of their weekly opening hours).

*"Heavy" and "Light" Technology and the Upsurge in the
Equipment–Structures Ratio*

One of the most striking (and as yet little noticed) features of the historical record appears in the ratio of the capital stock of producers' equipment to that of nonresidential structures. This ratio (shown in Figure 2.2) remains constant between 1870 and 1945 and then rises rapidly and steadily by a factor of almost four through 1996.[32] I believe this phenomenon is related to Wright's (1990) emphasis on the raw-materials intensity of U.S. technology in the late nineteenth century, which favored "heavy" and space-intensive machinery (steel mills, railroad stock and track, *etc.*). Technological innovation beginning with the electric motor allowed a shift to lighter and less space-intensive equipment, so that more and more equipment could be stuffed into a given number of square feet of structures. Space-saving may have been an important part of the big wave, but this particular trend has continued throughout the period of slow MFP growth after 1972. Since computers have many of the same characteristics as electric motors (space-saving, energy-saving, materials-saving), a continuing puzzle is the failure of computers to boost productivity growth as electric motors apparently did.[33]

2.7 CONCLUSION

It is interesting that there is no mention of the big wave in recent commentaries on productivity by such prominent authors as Abramovitz (1986, 1991), Baumol-Blackman-Wolff (1989), Maddison (1982, 1987, 1989), and Nelson-Wright (1992). Most of the focus in the recent literature has been on the world-wide productivity slowdown, on convergence among leading industrial nations, and on catchup of these nations to the U.S. level of productivity. There has been remarkably little attention to the fact that in the century before 1973 U.S. productivity did not grow at a uniform rate, or at a peak rate during 1948–73, but rather displayed a sharp acceleration at some point after 1913. Yet this fact which makes up the early part of the big wave was evident as soon as Kendrick's (1961) results were computed, and Solomon Fabricant emphasizes it in his introduction to Kendrick's book (see the quote at the beginning of this chapter). This essay has shown that the standard data on output, labor input, and capital input imply "one big wave" in multifactor productivity (MFP) growth, with MFP growth exhibiting a symmetric wave that peaks in 1928–50 and slows

---

[32] Figure 2.2 is based on the "standard" capital series. With variable retirement the equipment/structures ratio rises slowly from 0.200 in 1929 to 0.248 in 1945, whereas with fixed retirement the ratio is 0.200 in 1929 and 0.199 in 1945.

[33] A development related to "heavy" materials and to the "big wave" is that the geographical concentration of U.S. manufacturing rose to a peak in 1940 and then fell (Kim, 1992). The economy may have received a one-time boost in MFP from the dispersion of manufacturing to more efficient locations in the 1940–70 period, made possible by "lighter" materials, motor transport, and the diffusion of air conditioning.

gradually moving backward to 1870–91 and forward to 1972–96. Much of this paper has discussed adjustments to MFP growth for changes in the composition of labor and capital input and adjustments to the quantity of capital input to take account of variable retirement, GOPO capital, and highway capital. These adjustments change the symmetry, flatten out the wave, and move it backward. MFP growth is very slow during 1870–91, relatively steady at roughly 1 percent per year from 1891 to 1972, and then almost completely disappears in 1972–96. The peak interval for MFP growth is now 1950–64 rather than 1928–50, although the margin is narrow and the 1928–50 period remains in second place despite the extensive data revisions that have the effect of boosting input growth and reducing MFP growth more in the 1928–50 interval than in any other period.

We have argued that previous attention to the post-1972 productivity slowdown is misguided. The question should be recast: Why was productivity growth so much faster between 1891 and 1972 than either before or after, and fastest of all between 1928 and 1964? Our preferred hypotheses combine several explanations, most notably the concurrence of a multitude of important inventions occurring simultaneously prior to and at the beginning of the rapid growth period. Two other leading explanations with the correct timing rely on a theoretical connection between open economies and slow growth in incomes, real wages, and productivity. The closing of American labor markets to immigration between the 1920s and 1960s, thus boosting wages and stimulating capital-labor substitution, contributed to the "big wave." So in like manner did the combination of high tariffs, depression, and war, in closing off American goods markets from the influence of imports, thus postponing the convergence of incomes with America's trading partners and temporarily boosting wage growth for American workers.

This chapter is undeniably pessimistic in its implications. If the "big wave" resulted from great inventions whose effects have now been fully diffused through the economy, together with a temporary shift toward closed labor and goods markets, the outlook for a revival of MFP growth is not promising. The optimists declare the arrival of a "new economy" in which the benefits of the hi-tech revolution and globalization will bring about a revival of rapid growth, but in my view the remorseless progression of diminishing returns has left the greatest benefits of the computer age in the past, not awaiting us in the future.

Data Appendix

This Appendix lists the sources of output and "standard" labor and capital input. The adjustments for changes in labor and capital composition and for variable retirement are described in the text and the notes to the tables. Sources of GOPO and highway capital are listed here.

BEA tables are cited by the number used in the *Survey of Current Business*, August 1998, and the most recent data are ratio-linked to earlier BEA sources for the same concept that sometimes use different table numbers.

Nonfarm Nonhousing Business Output

1870–1929: Kendrick (1961), Table A-III p. 298 (total output) less Table A-III
p. 298, (government) less Table A-III, P298 (farm) less Table A-XV p. 320
(housing).
    1929–96: BEA, Table 1.8.

Nonfarm Nonhousing Business Labor Hours

1870–1889: Kendrick (1961), Table A-XXII p. 332 (total hours) less Table A-X
p.312 (farm). Since the Kendrick data are based on decade averages, in order to
get cyclical variation, Kendrick's numbers are fitted by ordinary least squared
regression onto Balke-Gordon (1989) output.
    1889–1948: Kendrick (1961), Table A-XXIII p. 338
    1948–96: BEA, Table 6.9C for nonfarm private domestic hours minus hours
in real estate from Table 6.8C multiplied by hours per employee in the Finance,
insurance, and real estate sector obtained as the ratio of Table 6.9C to Table
6.8C.

Nonfarm Nonhousing Business Capital

1870–1929 Equipment: Kendrick (1961) Table A-XVI p. 323 (Equipment)
minus Table III, p. 367 (Farm Equipment).
    1929–1996 Equipment: BEA Fixed Reproducible Tangible Wealth CD-
ROM, Table Tw2a, nonresidential equipment minus farm equipment.
    1870–1929 Structures: Kendrick (1961) Table A-XVI p. 323 (Nonresidential
structures) minus Table III, p. 367 (farm structures). These are both interpolated
from decade averages. Because of the unusual behaviour of the Kendrick structures figures for 1890–1900, data from Raymond Goldsmith were substituted
instead.
    1929–1996 Structures: BEA Fixed Reproducible Tangible Wealth CD-ROM,
Table Tw2a, nonresidential structures minus farm structures.

GOPO (Government-Owned, Privately Operated) Capital

1870–1925: It was assumed that most government-owned, privately-operated
capital in the early 1920s is merchant vessels built by U.S. shipyards in World
War I, and so GOPO is set equal to zero prior to 1918.
    1925–1988: BEA wealth data tape.
    Highway Capital
    1925–1996: Fraumeni (1999).

References

Abramovitz, Moses. "Catching Up, Forging Ahead, and Falling Behind." *Journal of
    Economic History* 1986, vol. 46, pp. 385–406.
    "The Post-war Productivity Spurt and Slowdown: Factors of Potential and

Realisation." In: G. Bell (ed.), *Technology and Productivity: The Challenge for Economic Policy*. Paris: OECD; 1991; pp. 19–37.

Aschauer, David A. "Is Public Expenditure Productive?" *Journal of Monetary Economics* 1989; vol. 23, pp. 177–200.

Baily, Martin Neil, and Gordon, Robert J. "The Productivity Slowdown, Measurement Issues, and the Explosion of Computer Power." *Brookings Papers on Economic Activity*. 1988; vol. 19, pp. 347–420.

Baily, Martin Neil, and Schultze, Charles L. "The Productivity of Capital in a Period of Slower Growth." *Brookings Papers on Economic Activity: Microeconomics 1990*. 1990; vol. 21, pp. 369–420.

Balke, Nathan S., and Gordon, Robert J. "The Estimation of Pre-war GNP: Methodology and New Results." *Journal of Political Economy*. 1989; vol. 97, pp. 38–92.

Baumol, William J., Batey Blackman, Sue Anne, and Wolff, Edward N. *Productivity and American Leadership: the Long View*. Cambridge MA: MIT Press; 1989.

Berndt, Ernst R., and Triplett, Jack. *Fifty Years of Economic Measurement: the Jubilee of the Conference on Research in Income and Wealth*. Chicago: University of Chicago Press for NBER; 1990.

Blanchard, Olivier J., and Danny Quah, Danny. "The Dynamic Effects of Aggregate Demand and Supply Disturbances." *American Economic Review*. 1989; vol. 79, pp. 655–73.

Borjas, George J. "Long-run Convergence of Ethnic Skill Differentials: The Children and Grandchildren of the Great Migration." *Industrial Labor Relations Review*. 1994; vol. 7, pp. 553–73.

Bresnahan, Timothy F., and Gordon, Robert J., eds. *The Economics of New Goods*. Chicago: University of Chicago Press for NBER; 1997.

David, Paul A. "The Dynamo and the Computer: An Historical Perspective on the Modern Productivity Paradox." *American Economic Review Papers and Proceedings*. 1990; vol. 80, pp. 355–61.

De Long, J. Bradford, and Summers, Lawrence H. "Equipment Investment and Economic Growth." *Quarterly Journal of Economics*. 1991, vol. 106, pp. 445–502.

Denison, Edward F. *The Sources of Economic Growth in the United States and the Alternatives Before Us*. Supplementary Paper no. 13. New York: Committee for Economic Development; 1962.

Accounting for Slower Economic Growth: The United States in the 1970s. Washington: Brookings; 1979.

Trends in American Economic Growth, 1929–82. Washington: Brookings; 1985.

Duménil, Gérard, and Levy, Dominique. "Continuity and Ruptures in the Process of Technological Change." Working paper. CEPREMAP; August, 1990.

Feldstein, Martin S., and Foot, David K. "Towards an Economic Theory of Replacement Investment." *Econometrica*. 1974; vol. 42, pp. 393–423.

"The Other Half of Gross Investment: Replacement and Modernization Expenditures." *Review of Economics and Statistics*. 1971; vol. 53, pp. 49–58.

Ford, Robert, and Poret, Pierre. "Infrastructure and Private-Sector Productivity." *OECD Economic Studies*. 1991; vol. 7, pp. 63–89.

Fraumeni, Barbara M. "Productive Highway Capital Stock Measures." Paper written under subcontract to Battelle Memorial Institute, Federal Highway Administration, Department of Transportation; January, 1999.

Freeman, C. ed. *Design, Innovation and Long Cycles in Economic Development*. New York: St. Martin's Press; 1986.

Goldin, Claudia. "America's Graduation from High School: The Evolution and Spread of Secondary Schooling in the Twentieth Century." *Journal of Economic History.* 1998; vol. 58, pp. 345–74.

Goldin, Claudia, and Katz, Lawrence F. "The Returns to Skill in the United States across the Twentieth Century," NBER working paper 7126, May, 1999.

Goldin, Claudia, and Margo, Robert A. "The Great Compression: The Wage Structure in the United States at Mid-Century." *Quarterly Journal of Economics.* 1992; vol. 107, pp. 1–34.

Gordon, Robert J. "Problems in the Measurement of Real Investment in the U.S. Private Economy." Ph. D. Dissertation. MIT; 1967.

"$45 Billion of U.S. Private Investment Has Been Mislaid." *American Economic Review.* 1969; vol. 59, pp. 221–38.

The Measurement of Durable Goods Prices. Chicago: University of Chicago Press for NBER; 1990.

"Is There a Tradeoff between Unemployment and Productivity Growth?" In: D. Snower and G. de la Dehesa, eds., *Unemployment Policy: Government Options for the Labour Market.* Cambridge, UK: Cambridge University Press; 1997, pp. 433–63. **Chapter 5 in this book.**

"Monetary Policy in the Age of Information Technology: Computers and the Solow Paradox." Paper presented to Bank of Japan conference, Monetary Policy in a World of Knowledge-based Growth, Quality Change, and Uncertain Measurement; June 19, 1998.

"U.S. Economic Growth Since 1870: One Big Wave?" *American Economic Review Papers and Proceedings.* 1999a; vol. 89, pp. 123–8.

"Has the 'New Economy' Rendered the Productivity Slowdown Obsolete?" Unpublished working paper. Northwestern University. June, 1999b.

Griliches, Zvi. *Research and Development, Education, and Productivity: A Personal Retrospective.* Cambridge MA: Harvard University Press; 2000.

Hatton, Timothy J., and Williamson, Jeffrey G. "International Migration and World Development: A Historical Perspective." NBER Historical Paper no. 41. September, 1992.

Johnson, George, and Stafford, Frank. "Models of Real Wages and International Competition." Unnumbered University of Michigan working paper. July, 1992.

Jorgenson, Dale W. "The Embodiment Hypothesis." *Journal of Political Economy.* 1966; vol. 74, pp. 1–17.

Jorgenson, Dale W. "Productivity and Economic Growth." In: Berndt, Ernst, and Jack Triplett. *Fifty Years of Economic Measurement: the Jubilee of the Conference on Research in Income and Wealth.* Chicago: University of Chicago Press for NBER; 1990, pp. 19–118.

Jorgenson, Dale W., and Griliches, Zvi. "The Explanation of Productivity Change." *Review of Economic Studies.* 1967; vol. 34, pp. 249–83.

Kendrick, John W. *Productivity Trends in the United States.* Princeton: Princeton University Press for NBER; 1961.

Kim, Sukkoo. "Expansion of Markets and the Geographic Distribution of Economic Activities: The Trends in U.S. Regional Manufacturing Structure, 1860–1987." Unnumbered UCLA working paper. October 14, 1992.

Kleinkencht, Alfred. *Innovation Patterns in Crisis and Prosperity: Schumpeter's Long Cycle Reconsidered.* London: Macmillan; 1987.

Kuznets, Simon. *Capital in the American Economy: Its Formation and Financing.* Princeton: Princeton University Press for NBER; 1961.

Maddison, Angus. *Phases of Capitalist Development.* New York: Oxford University Press, 1982.

"Growth and Slowdown in Advanced Capitalist Economies: Techniques of Quantitative Assessment." *Journal of Economic Literature.* 1987; vol. 25, pp. 649–98.

The World Economy in the 20th Century. Paris: OECD; 1989.

McKinsey Global Institute. *Service Sector Productivity.* Washington: McKinsey & Company; 1992.

Nelson, Richard R., and Wright, Gavin. "The Rise and Fall of American Technological Leadership: The Post-war Era in Historical Perspective." *Journal of Economic Literature.* 1992; vol. 30, pp. 1931–64.

Nordhaus, William D. "Economic Policy in the Face of Declining Productivity Growth." *European Economic Review.* 1982; vol. 18, pp. 131–58.

Nordhaus, William D. "Do Real-Output and Real-Wage Measures Capture Reality? The History of Lighting Suggests Not." In: Bresnahan, Timothy F. and Gordon, Robert, J. eds. *The Economics of New Goods.* Chicago: University of Chicago Press for NBER. 1997; vol. 29, p. 66.

Romer, Paul M. "Crazy Explanations for the Productivity Slowdown," *NBER Macroeconomics Annual 1987.* 1987; pp. 163–201.

"Capital, Labour, and Productivity." *Brookings Papers on Economic Activity: Microeconomics 1990.* 1990; vol. 21, pp. 337–67.

Williamson, Jeffrey G. "The Evolution of Global Labour Markets in the First and Second World Since 1830: Background Evidence and Hypotheses." NBER Historical paper no. 36. February, 1992.

Wright, Gavin. "The Origins of American Industrial Success: 1879–1940," *American Economic Review.* 1990; vol. 80, pp. 651–68.

CHAPTER 3

The Disappearance of Productivity Change

Most empirical studies of economic growth attempt to determine the relative importance of increases in inputs and advances in technology in the achievement of growth in per-capita output. This approach is motivated by a desire to explain the sources of that output growth: How much less rapidly would the U.S. economy have expanded in the last fifty years if it had continued to operate with 1918 levels of technology or if technology had advanced but no net investment in tangible or human capital had occurred? Answers to these questions help us to maximize our future rate of growth by guiding policymakers to an optimal allocation of resources among investment in tangible capital, in education, and in technology-increasing activities, and they help in explaining the reasons for international differences in per-capita income.[1]

Since the mid-1950s a common technique for the separation of the respective contributions of input growth and advances in technology has been the calculation of indexes of total factor productivity. Pioneering studies by Solow (1957, pp. 312–20) (Abramovitz, pp. 5–23; Kendrick, 1956; Schmookler, 1952, pp. 214–231) and others have suggested capital played only a minor role in per-capita growth, and that most of the long-term increase in U.S. output per capita was due to an increase in the output obtainable per unit of appropriately weighted input. While it was recognized that some of this increase in total factor productivity or "the residual" might have been due to the spread of education, most of it was assumed to have represented technical change. A more refined study in 1962 by Denison (1962) reduced the size of the residual by making

---

[1] In this discussion we adopt Mansfield's definition of technical change as the advance of technology, which is "society's pool of knowledge regarding the industrial arts. It consists of knowledge used by industry regarding the principles of physical and social phenomena . . . knowledge regarding the application of these principles to production . . . and knowledge regarding the day-to-day operations of production" (Mansfield, 1968, p. 10).

Note. The author gratefully acknowledges research support from the Project for Quantitative Research in Economic Development at Harvard University, operating under grants from the Agency for International Development and the National Science Foundation. (*Source.* "The Disappearance of Productivity Change." Previously unpublished. Harvard Institute of Economic Research. Discussion Paper 44, September 1968).

adjustments for the impact of education on the quality of labor but continued to attribute most of the remaining residual to technological advance. In his later book (1967, p. 334) Denison confirmed the earlier studies of long-term U.S. growth by showing that only 28 percent of the 1960 difference in per-capital income levels between the U.S. and Northwest Europe can be explained by differences in capital and in the quality of labor, and that the remainder is primarily due to differences in the "state of knowledge."

But in a recent duet of papers (1966, pp. 50–61; 1967, pp. 249–84) Griliches and Jorgenson make the startling claim that all previous investigators have committed serious "errors of measurement," resulting in a sizable exaggeration of the size of the residual. When these errors are eliminated and "if real product and real factor input are accurately accounted for, the observed growth in total factor productivity is negligible" (Jorgenson and Griliches, 1967). The habits of a decade have led to the association of advances in total factor productivity with technical change, so that Griliches and Jorgenson appear to be concluding that technical change has been almost nonexistent as a source of U.S. growth. Bewildered businessmen and economists, who previously thought that they had been observing rapid advances in managerial techniques and production technology in the postwar United States, may now wonder whether their eyes have been deceiving them. How are they to interpret industry studies (for example, Hollander, 1965) which emphasize the importance of technological progress? If we accept Griliches and Jorgenson's results, are we then forced to conclude that industries enjoying technical change have been atypical and that their achievements have been counterbalanced by technical regress in unstudied industries?

But a closer evaluation, attempted in this paper, suggests that the Griliches and Jorgenson conclusion is misleading. Increases in total factor productivity appear to be negligible because Griliches and Jorgenson raise the rate of growth of inputs relative to output, but they ignore the important role of technological change in achieving this rapid growth of inputs. Thus the Griliches and Jorgenson paper forces us to break our ingrained mental habit of thinking of technological advances as a number equal to or smaller than the increase in total factor productivity or "residual," and instead, to realize that the contribution of technical change to economic growth may in fact be much larger than the "error-corrected" residual. Unfortunately, Griliches and Jorgenson repeatedly promote the illusion that their conclusion about total factor *productivity* change provides information on *technological* change, contrary to our analysis below. For instance, they argue that "our results suggest that the . . . advance of knowledge has been substantially overstated, even by Denison" (Griliches, May, 1966, p. 61) and that "Identification of measured growth in total factor productivity with embodied or disembodied technical change provides methods for measuring technical change" (Jorgenson and Griliches, 1967, p. 249). Again they imply that calculations of changes in total factor productivity yield information on technical change when they claim their results to "suggest that social rates of return to expenditures on research and development are comparable to rates of return on other types of investment" (Jorgenson and Griliches, 1967, p. 274). Most directly, they predict on the basis of their results that "perhaps the day is not far off when economists can remove the intellectual scaffolding of technical change altogether" (Griliches and Jorgenson, 1966, p. 61).[2]

This essay demonstrates that the measures of total factor productivity provided by Griliches and Jorgenson tell us nothing about the importance of advances in technology. In addition, traditional methods of productivity measurement used by Kendrick (1956), Solow (1957, pp. 312–20), and others provide no direct evidence on technical change, partly because they ignore cost-increasing advances in knowledge. The Kendrick-Solow methods, however, both algebraically and in computer simulations, appear to give more accurate evidence on the importance of technical change than the "error-free" Griliches and Jorgenson methods. Therefore the Griliches and Jorgenson paper is both misleading and irrelevant for the study of economic growth; misleading, since it appears to claim that advances in technology have been unimportant, and irrelevant, since it provides no new information to help us measure the relative contribution of technological advance and other sources of economic growth. In short, Griliches and Jorgenson have thrown the baby out with the error-ridden bathwater.

3.1   TOTAL FACTOR PRODUCTIVITY AND THE SOCIAL RETURN TO RESEARCH

Griliches and Jorgenson begin by identifying a change in total factor productivity with a shift in the production function, that is, a "costless" advance in knowledge. They conclude that the 1945–65 increase in total factor productivity has been substantially overstated. Their argument, however, focuses exclusive attention on "costless" advances in knowledge, which Nordhaus has called a "pleasant fiction" (1967, p. 3). Consider in contrast an economy in which knowledge has been advancing steadily, but only by means of "the employment of scarce resources with alternative uses" – for example, managers and research workers. If these workers discover new techniques which were previously unknown, a production function relating output to *production labor and capital alone* may be said to have shifted, even though the fruits of research work have not been "costless." Furthermore, if the research workers are able to appropriate the full social returns of their efforts and if the research portion of labor input is properly weighted to reflect these returns, there will be no apparent increase in indexes of total factor productivity.

---

[2] These statements are contradicted by the remark, "our conclusion is not that advances in knowledge are negligible" (Mansfield, 1968, p. 274), but are nowhere retracted or rescinded. In fact, the admission that no conclusion is reached regarding technological change is immediately followed by the statement on the comparability of social returns to research and other kinds of investment, which requires the identification of advances in knowledge (that is, the returns to research) with changes in total factor productivity.

Solow (1965, pp. 16–28) and Schultz (1967, pp. 293–7) have previously argued the advantages of thinking in terms of the rate of return of alternative forms of tangible and intangible capital. But the constancy of total factor productivity in the example of the previous paragraph tells us nothing about the social rate of return of research workers. If the net social rate of return of a research worker is positive, an economy can increase output by reallocating labor from the production to the research sector, even if no increase in total factor productivity occurs because research workers appropriate their full social returns.

Thus the Griliches and Jorgenson measures of total factor productivity are misleading, both regarding the contribution of technological change to economic growth, and in the implication that social rates of return to expenditures on research are comparable to rates of return on other types of investment. The rest of the section illustrates this point more precisely with a simple economic model incorporating a distinction between research and nonresearch workers. It is demonstrated that the approach not only of Griliches and Jorgenson but also of their predecessors inaccurately measures the true contribution of advances in knowledge to economic growth.

A.   The Model

In our simple economy there are no "costless" shifts in the production function, yet advances in knowledge play a crucial role in economic growth. All technological change is created by research workers, and the model incorporates both embodied and disembodied research using technical change. Our aim is to describe the contribution of advances of knowledge to output growth in the hypothetical economy, and then compute how accurately Griliches and Jorgenson and earlier investigators would measure this contribution. At this initial stage no separate attention is given to education, which will be discussed later in Section Three.

In the economy output $Y(t)$ is produced by effective production-worker man-hours $L(t)$, and effective machine-hours $J(t)$. In addition there is disembodied technical progress which raises output in response to increase in the accumulated stock of research knowledge $R(t)$:

$$Y(t) = F(L(t), J(t), R(t)) \tag{1}$$

where

$$R(t) = \int_0^t S(g)\, dg \tag{2}$$

and $S(g)$ is the number of workers engaged in knowledge-increasing activities (including not just conventionally measured research and development workers but anyone who thinks about or implements new techniques, including managers, foremen, summer interns, and even the share of production worker man hours spent contributing to suggestion boxes).

The effective machine-hours $J(t)$ available from a given stock of capital $K(t)$ may be increased by means of embodied technical progress, which also takes place through increases in the accumulated stock of research knowledge:

$$J(t) = G(K(t), R(t)) \tag{3}$$

where (3) is a shorthand representation of the following embodiment process:

$$J(t) = \int_0^t I(v)\,\Phi(R(v))\,dv \tag{3a}$$

and

$$K(t) = \int_0^t I(v)\,dv \tag{3b}$$

$I(v)$ is investment in period v, and to simplify matters, we assume no depreciation.[3]

The production process in our economy has constant returns to L, K, and R.[4] The sum of the elasticities of output with respect to the three inputs is unity:

$$E_{YL} + E_{YK} + E_{YR} = 1 \tag{4}$$

where

$$E_{YL} = \frac{F_L L}{Y} \tag{4a}$$

$$E_{YK} = \frac{F_J G_K K}{Y} \tag{4b}$$

$$E_{YR} = \frac{(F_R + F_J G_R)R}{Y} \tag{4c}$$

These elasticities, however, do not necessarily describe the distribution of income. In the model, as in most economies, research is not carried on in separate accounting units. Instead, there are only two such units – employees and firms. Firms obtain both production (L) and research man-hours (S) by offering a wage to workers. The market for production workers is perfectly competitive,

---

[3] Since all capital-embodied technical change is capital-augmenting, it is legitimate to write the capital aggregate $J(t)$. (See Fisher, 1965, pp. 263–88). For a more precise description of the production process in such an economy, see Solow (1965, p. 75).

[4] Possible justifications for this assumption, which implies diminishing returns to the "conventional" factors K and L alone, have been enumerated by Nordhaus (1967, pp. 172–4). There are no strong reasons to expect that this assumption is more realistic than the alternative of constant returns in L and K, but it simplifies the exposition. The computer simulations below include experiments assuming both diminishing and constant returns to L and K. One reason to expect at least slightly diminishing returns to L and K is that a doubling of L and K probably requires some improvements in managerial techniques and distribution and handling techniques, and if these technological improvements do not occur, Y may not be able to double in size.

and thus the observed value share of production workers in the national income V_L is equal to E_{YL}. But we make no such restrictive assumption about the market for research workers, and simply write their share as V_R, allowing their wage to be larger or smaller than their marginal product. The share of all workers ($M = L + S$) is then $V_M = V_L + V_R = E_{YL} + V_R$. The share of capital can then be derived from the constant returns assumption (4):

$$V_K = 1 - V_M = E_{YK} + E_{YR} - V_R. \tag{5}$$

If $E_{YR} > V_R$, firms are exploiting research workers and pushing the observed rate of return on capital above the marginal product of capital.

Our aim is to isolate in this model the contribution of advances of knowledge to economic growth. To do this, we can compare two economies A and B at time t, each with production and distribution arrangements described by (1)–(6). The only difference between the two economies is that suddenly at time t advances in knowledge cease in economy B. Thus, after time t:

$$ECONOMY \ A \qquad T_R > 0; \ G_R > 0$$
$$ECONOMY \ B \qquad T_R = G_R = 0$$

The next step is to separate observed changes in output in the two economies into portions attributable to changes in the three inputs L, K, and R. This can be accomplished by differentiating (1) totally with respect to time and converting to elasticities for the two economies. This is straightforward for economy A:

$$\frac{\dot{Y}_A}{Y_A} = E_{YL}\frac{\dot{L}}{L} + E_{YK}\frac{\dot{K}_A}{K_A} + E_{YR}\frac{\dot{R}}{R} \tag{6}$$

No subscript is attached to the symbols L or R, since population growth is assumed exogenous and therefore is the same in the two economies. In economy B, all research workers, barren of new ideas, return to production work, where they behave and are paid exactly like all other production workers:[5]

$$\frac{\dot{Y}_B}{Y_B} = E_{YL}\frac{\dot{M}}{M} + E_{YK}\frac{\dot{K}_B}{K_B} = E_{YL}\frac{\dot{L}}{L} + E_{YK}\frac{\dot{K}_B}{K_B} + V_R^*\frac{\dot{R}}{R} \tag{7}$$

where V_R^* is the share of research workers when they are paid the same wage as production workers.

---

[5] The expression for economy B is derived as follows. We differentiate (1) with respect to time on the condition that the marginal product of research workers is the same as that of production workers.

$$\dot{Y}_B = F_L\dot{L} + F_J G_K \dot{K}_B + F_L\dot{S} \tag{a}$$

Now we divide both sides by Y_B, multiply the three right-hand terms by $\frac{L}{L}, \frac{K}{K}, \frac{LS}{LS}$, respectively, and note that, on the assumption of steady-state exponential growth in S, $\frac{\dot{R}}{R} = \frac{\dot{S}}{S}$:

$$\frac{\dot{Y}_B}{Y_B} = \frac{F_L L}{Y_B}\frac{\dot{L}}{L} + \frac{F_J G_K K_B}{Y_B}\frac{\dot{K}_B}{K_B} + \frac{F_L S}{Y_B}\frac{\dot{R}}{R} \tag{b}$$

The contribution of advances of knowledge ($\dot{C}/C$) is simply the difference between the growth rates of the two economies:

$$\frac{\dot{C}}{C} = \frac{\dot{Y}_A}{Y_A} - \frac{\dot{Y}_B}{Y_B} = (E_{YR} - V_R^*)\frac{\dot{R}}{R} + E_{YK}\left(\frac{\dot{K}_A}{K_A} - \frac{\dot{K}_B}{K_B}\right)$$

This can be simplified is we assume steady-state growth with a proportional saving rate, so that $\frac{\dot{Y}_A}{Y_A} = \frac{\dot{K}_A}{K_A}$ and $\frac{\dot{Y}_B}{Y_B} = \frac{\dot{K}_B}{K_B}$. In that case:

$$\frac{\dot{C}}{C} = \frac{\dot{Y}_A}{Y_A} - \frac{\dot{Y}_B}{Y_B} = \left(\frac{E_{YR} - V_R^*}{1 - E_K}\right)\frac{\dot{R}}{R} \tag{8}$$

The factor inside the parentheses represents the social rate of return to research workers in economy A. When this factor is zero, the contribution of research workers in A just offsets their opportunity cost, the output which they could be producing as production workers. In this case, their research efforts make no extra contribution to economic growth.

B.   The Kendrick-Solow Method

Now let us expose economy A to two pairs of energetic economic detectives, who can observe only the rates of growth of inputs and outputs and factor shares, but not the underlying structure of production. The first pair to arrive on the scene are Kendrick and Solow (K-S), who propose to measure the contribution of knowledge or the "residual" by the following formula:

$$\frac{\dot{C}_{K\text{-}S}}{C_{K\text{-}S}} = \frac{\dot{Y}_A}{Y_A} - V_M\frac{\dot{M}}{M} - V_K\frac{\dot{K}_A}{K_A} \tag{9}$$

Since $V_M\frac{\dot{M}}{M} = V_L\frac{\dot{L}}{L} + V_R\frac{\dot{S}}{S}$, $E_{YL} = V_L$, $E_{YK} + E_{YR} = V_K + V_R$, and assuming $\frac{\dot{R}}{R} = \frac{\dot{S}}{S}$, the K-S residual equals:

$$\frac{\dot{C}_{K\text{-}S}}{C_{K\text{-}S}} = (E_{YR} - V_R)\left(\frac{\dot{R}}{R} - \frac{\dot{K}_A}{K_A}\right) \tag{10}$$

Does the K-S "residual" correctly identify the contribution of advances of knowledge to the growth of economy A? By subtracting (10) from (8), we can derive an expression for the K-S "error" in measuring the contribution of advances in knowledge:

$$\frac{\dot{C}}{C} - \frac{\dot{C}_{K\text{-}S}}{C_{K\text{-}S}} = \left(\frac{E_{YK}(E_{YR} - V_R) + V_R - V_R^*}{1 - E_{YK}}\right)\frac{\dot{R}}{R} + (E_{YR} - V_R)\frac{\dot{K}_A}{K_A} \tag{11}$$

There are several possible cases:

1. Research workers are not exploited, and their marginal product is larger than that of production workers, $E_{YR} = V_R > V_R^*$. In this case the K-S error becomes:

$$\frac{\dot{C}}{C} - \frac{\dot{C}_{K\text{-}S}}{C_{K\text{-}S}} = \left(\frac{E_{YR} - V_R^*}{1 - E_{YK}}\right)\frac{\dot{R}}{R} \tag{12}$$

By identifying the contribution of advances of knowledge with increases in total factor productivity, K-S erroneously conclude that there is no residual, even though the true contribution of knowledge from (8) is $(\frac{E_{YR}-V_R^*}{1-E_{YK}})\frac{\dot{R}}{R}$. The mistake stems from counting the salary advantage of research workers over production workers as part of the contribution of labor, rather than as a consequence of the advance of knowledge which causes the salary differentials.[6]

2. Firms exploit research workers by paying them the production worker wage, even though their marginal product exceeds the marginal product of production workers, $E_{YR} > V_R = V_R^*$. The K-S error is:

$$\frac{\dot{C}}{C} - \frac{\dot{C}_{K\text{-}S}}{C_{K\text{-}S}} = (E_{YR} - V_R)\left(\frac{E_{YK}}{1-E_{YK}}\frac{\dot{R}}{R} + \frac{\dot{K}_A}{K_A}\right) \tag{13}$$

If capital is not growing ($\dot{K}_A/K_A = 0$), K-S err again, although the mistake may not be too serious if E_{YK} is small.

3. If $\dot{K}_A/K_A > 0$, Kendrick-Solow underestimate the contribution of knowledge by erroneously using all of capital's share as a weight on the growth of capital, ignoring the fact that a portion of capital's share really represents the contribution of research. Thus a finding by Kendrick and Solow that their residual (10) is equal to zero should not be accepted as evidence that advances in knowledge have been unimportant or that the social rate of return to research is zero.

C.   The Griliches-Jorgenson Method

After the team of Kendrick and Solow has issued its report on economy A using formula (9), the team of Griliches and Jorgenson arrives on the scene and discovers "errors of measurement" in the work of Kendrick and Solow. The earlier investigators err in (9) by using the stock of capital K as a measure of capital input, and Griliches and Jorgenson recalculate their procedure "correctly," replacing K in (9) by effective capital J.[7] Thus the Griliches and Jorgenson measure of the contribution of advances of knowledge ($C_{G\text{-}J}$) is

---

[6] This point has been made before: "Surely it is a mistake to measure the contribution of technological change to economic growth after subtracting the higher incomes that R&D scientists and engineers receive" (Nelson, 1964, p. 591). One might add that this point is valid also for a large portion of managerial salaries, for fewer and less well-paid managers would be necessary if there were no technological change.

[7] At this point it is important to clarify a disagreement between Griliches-Jorgenson and Denison (Jorgenson and Griliches, 1967, p. 254, fn. 1). Denison claims:

Since advances in knowledge cannot increase national product without raising the marginal product of one or more factors of production, they, of course, disappear as a source of growth if an increase in a factor's marginal product resulting from the advance of knowledge is counted as an increase in the quantity of factor input.

Griliches and Jorgenson respond that Denison's interpretation implies the measurement of input growth as the sum of the growth of input prices and input quantities, whereas Griliches and

$$\frac{\dot{C}_{G\text{-}J}}{C_{G\text{-}J}} = \frac{\dot{Y}_A}{Y_A} - V_M \frac{\dot{M}}{M} - V_K \frac{\dot{J}_A}{J_A} \tag{14}$$

which can be solved like (9):[8]

$$\frac{\dot{C}_{G\text{-}J}}{C_{G\text{-}J}} = E_{YL}\frac{\dot{L}}{L} + E_{YR}\frac{\dot{R}}{R} + E_{YK}\frac{\dot{K}_A}{K_A} - V_L\frac{\dot{L}}{L} - V_R\frac{\dot{R}}{R}$$

$$- V_K\left(E_{JR}\frac{\dot{R}}{R} + E_{JK}\frac{\dot{K}_A}{K_A}\right)$$

$$= (E_{YR} - V_R - V_K E_{JR})\left(\frac{\dot{R}}{R} - \frac{\dot{K}_A}{K_A}\right) \tag{15}$$

Again we can compare the Griliches and Jorgenson estimate (14) with the actual contribution of knowledge to gauge the accuracy of their approach.

Jorgenson clearly state in their equation (4) that input growth only includes the growth of input quantities.

In fact, Denison is partly right. Consider the model in the text above. On the assumption that factor shares equal factor elasticities, Griliches and Jorgenson measure the growth of inputs as:

$$\frac{\dot{X}}{X} = E_{YL}\frac{\dot{L}}{L} + E_{YJ}\frac{\dot{J}}{J} \tag{a}$$

That is, they measure the sum of growth in input *quantities*. But what is $\dot{J}/J$? Substituting from (4) above:

$$\frac{\dot{X}}{X} = E_{YL}\frac{\dot{L}}{L} + E_{YJ}E_{JK}\frac{\dot{K}}{K} + E_{YJ}E_{JR}\frac{\dot{R}}{R} \tag{b}$$

This last term is what Denison means as "an increase in a factor's marginal product resulting from the advance of knowledge," and Griliches and Jorgenson indeed include it in their measurement of input, as long as the "factor" to which Denison refers is understood to be K, not J. However, Denison is not correct that advances in knowledge "disappear as a source of growth" through this procedure, as can be seen by subtracting the Griliches and Jorgenson expression for the growth of inputs (b) from (4) above:

$$\frac{\dot{P}}{P} = \frac{\dot{Y}}{Y} - \frac{\dot{X}}{X} = E_{YL}\frac{\dot{L}}{L} + E_{YK}\frac{\dot{K}}{K} + E_{YR}\frac{\dot{R}}{R}$$

$$- E_{YL}\frac{\dot{L}}{L} - E_{YJ}E_{JK}\frac{\dot{K}}{K} - E_{YJ}E_{JR}\frac{\dot{R}}{R} \tag{c}$$

$$= \frac{F_R R}{Y}\frac{\dot{R}}{R}$$

This last term is the contribution of research-using *disembodied* advances of knowledge to output growth, which the Griliches and Jorgenson procedure does allow them to identify. In short, Denison is right to the extent that advances in knowledge operate in the form of embodied technical change, but not to the extent that they are disembodied.

[8] This ignores the Griliches and Jorgenson recalculation of output as a weighted average of the output of consumers' goods and "effective" investment goods. As long as the share of capital exceeds the share of investment goods in output, as in the United States, our algebraic manipulations can safely ignore this adjustment to output. (See Jorgenson and Griliches, 1967, p. 259, fn. 1. Also, we ignore the Griliches and Jorgenson treatment of education, which is discussed later.

Subtracting (15) from (10), we can write the Griliches and Jorgenson error as:

$$\frac{\dot{C}}{C} - \frac{\dot{C}_{G\text{-}J}}{C_{G\text{-}J}} = \left(\frac{E_{YR} - V_R^*}{1 - E_{YK}}\right)\frac{\dot{R}}{R} - (E_{YR} - V_R - V_K E_{JR})\left(\frac{\dot{R}}{R} - \frac{\dot{K}_A}{K_A}\right)$$

(16)

Again, there are several possible cases:

1. Research workers are not exploited: $E_{YR} = V_R > V_R^*$. It appears from (15) that, if $\dot{R}/R > \dot{K}_A/K_A > 0$, Griliches and Jorgenson are further from the truth than Kendrick and Solow, since the former calculate a *negative* contribution of knowledge in the amount $-V_K E_{JR}(\dot{R}/R - \dot{K}_A/K_A)$. This occurs because they double-count the impact of research in making capital more "effective," i.e., in raising the ratio of J to K. In this no-exploitation case, the marginal product of research workers is already fully counted in the research share V_R, but Griliches and Jorgenson add to the growth of input an extra quantity reflecting the contribution of research workers in making capital more effective. This is in addition to the basic mistake which Griliches and Jorgenson make (in common with Kendrick and Solow) in counting the wage differential between research and production workers as part of the contribution of labor. In sum, the Griliches-Jorgenson error in this case is:

$$\frac{\dot{C}}{C} - \frac{\dot{C}_{G\text{-}J}}{C_{G\text{-}J}} = \left(\frac{E_{YR} - V_R^*}{1 - E_{YK}}\right)\frac{\dot{R}}{R} - E_{JR}V_K\left(\frac{\dot{R}}{R} - \frac{\dot{K}_A}{K_A}\right)$$

(17)

2. When research workers are exploited and paid a wage equal to the marginal product of production workers (so that $E_R > V_R = V_R^*$), Griliches and Jorgenson still underestimate the contribution of advances of knowledge, even when $\dot{K}_A/K_A = 0$. This again occurs because Griliches and Jorgenson count the contribution of research workers in making capital more effective as an increase in input rather than as a contribution of advances in knowledge. Their error in the $\dot{K}_A/K_A = 0$ case is:

$$\frac{\dot{C}}{C} - \frac{\dot{C}_{G\text{-}J}}{C_{G\text{-}J}} = \left(\frac{E_{YK}(E_{YR} - V_R) + (1 - E_{YK})E_{JR}V_K}{1 - E_{YK}}\right)\frac{\dot{R}}{R}$$

(18)

3. And, as was true with Kendrick and Solow, in the exploitation case where $\dot{R}/R > \dot{K}_A/K_A > 0$, Griliches and Jorgenson underestimate the contribution of knowledge by erroneously applying all of capital's share as a weight on the growth of capital, even though part of capital's share represents the contribution of research rather than capital. In this case their error can be written as equation (16) above.

In short, neither the Kendrick and Solow nor Griliches and Jorgenson calculations of changes in total factor productivity are reliable indicators of the contribution of advances in knowledge to economic growth. Nor can a finding of negligible growth in total factor productivity be accepted as evidence that the social returns to research activity are similar to returns for those in other kinds of employment. Both methods tend to underestimate the contribution of knowledge by including in the weights on input growth the portion of labor and capital compensation which really represents the return to research workers. In addition, the Griliches and Jorgenson insistence on measuring "effective capital" further understates the contribution of advances in knowledge by ignoring the role of research in raising capital's "effectiveness." (Note that in each of the three cases above, the Griliches-Jorgenson "error" is larger than that of Kendrick-Solow). It is easy to conceive of examples, using (14), in which the social return to research workers is strongly positive, yet at the same time Griliches and Jorgenson could be calculating virtually no growth in total factor productivity.

After a few brief remarks on the Griliches and Jorgenson treatment of education, we shall use computer simulations of a hypothetical economy to suggest orders of magnitude for the Kendrick and Solow and Griliches and Jorgenson errors.

3.2 THE TREATMENT OF EDUCATION

To simplify the discussion in the preceding section, the labor force was divided into two homogeneous groups, production and research workers, and no account was taken of possible differences in the quality of labor within these groups. Now, however, we should recognize the role of education in creating quality differences among workers and should consequently examine Griliches and Jorgenson's method of measuring the contribution of education to economic growth.

Just as embodied research can make some machines more productive than others, so can embodied education make some workers more productive than others. In addition, the efficiency of workers with given education endowments will vary with their "native ability" or intelligence, as well as with their environment, amount of encouragement from parents, and other factors. Thus the input of effective labor $L(t)$ into the production function (1) is itself a function of education, ability (where "ability" stands for influences on labor quality other than education), and man hours:

$$L(T) = \sum_i G(E_i) \sum_j H(A_j)B_{ij}(t) \tag{19}$$

Here total man-hours B are allocated into groups according to native ability A_j and educational attainment E_i. B_{ij} is the number of man hours in each education-ability group; $H(A_j)$ represents the contribution of ability to effective labor input, and $G(E_i)$ similarly stands for the impact of differing levels of educational attainment on effective labor input. The respective contributions of ability and education to economic growth can be separated as follows. First, we define b_{ij}, the proportion of man hours of a given ability group j in an education group i:

$$b_{ij} = B_{ij}/B_i \tag{20}$$

and e_i, the proportion of aggregate man hours in a group with educational attainment i:

$$e_i = B_i/B. \tag{21}$$

Substituting (20) and (21) into (19), differentiating with respect to time, and dividing by L, we obtain:

$$\frac{\dot{L}}{L} = \frac{B}{L} \sum_i G(E_i) \left(\dot{e}_i \sum_j H(A_j)b_{ij} + e_i \sum_j H(A_j)\dot{b}_{ij} \right) + \frac{\dot{B}}{B} \tag{22}$$

The average wage within an educational group can be written as follows (if workers are paid their marginal products):

$$w_i = \frac{\sum_j w_{ij} B_{ij}}{B_i} = \sum_j \frac{\partial L}{\partial B_{ij}} b_{ij} = G(E_i) \sum_j H(A_j)b_{ij} \tag{23}$$

Substituting (23) into (22), and noting that the average wage in the economy is $\overline{w} = L/B$, we can write:

$$\frac{\dot{L}}{L} = \sum_i \frac{w_i}{\overline{w}} \left[\dot{e}_i + \frac{\sum_j H(A_j)\dot{b}_{ij}}{\sum_j H(A_j)b_{ij}} \right] + \frac{\dot{B}}{B} \tag{24}$$

Here the relative wage $w_i/\overline{w}$ times the first term inside the brackets represents the contribution to economic growth of the changing educational distribution of the labor force. Even with a stationary population, effective labor input L will increase as a larger fraction of the labor force enters the educational groups with high relative wages $w_i/\overline{w}$. The second term is an adjustment for the changing average ability of each educational group. As a larger and larger fraction of the nation's population attains a twelfth-grade educational level, the average ability of the twelfth-grade group is likely to decline, so the net effect of the second term on economic growth is almost certainly negative.

Stated in another way, differences in the relative wages $w_i/\overline{w}$ used to weight the educational groups occur for reasons other than education. The relative earnings of college-educated workers are high not just because they went to college, but also because of the relatively high percentage of college graduates "who had obtained high marks in earlier schooling, who had scored well on standardized intelligence tests, who had attended the better schools at lower educational levels, and who also had parents who were themselves well educated and had substantial incomes" [Denison, 1966 p. 83].[9]

---

[9] Note that our discussion above ignores Denison's adjustment for the secular increase in the number of school days per school year, which is explained by him in detail in "Measuring the Contribution of Education (and the Residual) to Economic Growth (1965, p. 28) and which has the effect of doubling the contribution of education to growth. This adjustment has been questioned recently by Schwartzman (1968).

Equation (17) above can be compared with Griliches and Jorgenson's equation (12), which in our notation can be written:

$$\frac{\dot{L}}{L} = \sum \frac{w_i}{w}\dot{e}_i + \frac{\dot{B}}{B} \tag{25}$$

Griliches and Jorgenson, therefore, allow for the first term inside the brackets in (17), the positive contribution of education to economic growth, but they make no mention of the second term, the changing ability mix of each educational group. Thus Griliches and Jorgenson substantially exaggerate the rate of growth of labor input "with errors in the aggregation of labor services eliminated." The order of magnitude of this exaggeration can never be known exactly, although Denison has recently cited several pieces of evidence supporting his original estimate that education is responsible for 60 percent of observed wage differentials among educational groups, not the 100 percent assumed by Griliches and Jorgenson.[10]

3.3   ADVANCES IN KNOWLEDGE AND TOTAL FACTOR PRODUCTIVITY IN A HYPOTHETICAL ECONOMY

Sections 3.1 and 3.2 demonstrated that the measurement techniques of Griliches and Jorgenson tend to underestimate the contribution of advances in knowledge to economic growth. But, unfortunately, we can never obtain accurate estimates of the magnitude of their errors, since we can never know how rapidly the U.S. economy would have grown from 1945 to 1965 without any advances in knowledge. As a second-best alternative, it is possible to construct a numerical model of economic growth in a hypothetical economy to reveal the accuracy of the Griliches and Jorgenson measurement techniques, given the stated assumptions of the numerical model. The model has been designed for computer simulation to facilitate the inclusion of numerous "realistic" assumptions, and so several different experiments can be run to test the sensitivity of the conclusions to alternative parameter values.

A.   Outline of the Model

1.   The Effective Input of Labor

The model is completely production-oriented and has no demand mechanism. Full employment is maintained continuously, since investment is always set equal to saving. There are two production sectors, one producing consumption goods with effective production workers, effective capital, and part of the accumulated stock of knowledge. Effective capital is produced by effective production workers in the investment sector and the rest of the accumulated stock of knowledge. There is no capital input in the investment goods sector.

---

[10] See Denison, 1965; 1967, pp. 86–100, p. 84.

The allocation of the labor force between research workers and the two groups of production workers is arbitrary. An allocation obtained through the equalization of marginal returns is not desired, since one of the main purposes of the model is to exhibit the effects on growth and productivity measurement of large differences between the marginal returns to research and investment. So the allocation of production workers between the two sectors is governed by a fixed proportional savings rate, and the proportion of the total labor force engaged in research activity is completely exogenous.[11]

The first equation of the model describes the determination of the effective labor force M_t, given the exogenous supply of "brute force" or "raw" labor B_t, the proportion e_{it} of the labor force in each of n education-ability classes, and the multiplicative education (G_i) and ability (H_i) factors which convert the units of raw labor in each class into units of effective labor:

$$M_t = B_t \sum_{i=1}^{n} e_{it} G_i H_i \tag{26}$$

The multiplicative factors are based on U.S. data on the relative compensation of workers in different educational groups, using Denison's assumption that 60 percent of compensation differences are due to differences in education and the remainder to differences in ability.[12] The proportions in the different education-ability groups are based on Griliches and Jorgenson's figures on the education attainment of the U.S. labor force, and in addition on the assumption that all people moving from one educational level to a higher one have the native ability of an average member of the former class.[13]

---

[11] Thus the model differs considerably, both in form and in purpose, from the models of Phelps (1966, pp. 133–46), Uzawa (1965, pp. 18–31), and Nordhaus (1967), which are designed to calculate the *optimal* allocation of the labor force between research and nonresearch work. Here we want the allocation to be *nonoptimal*, as it may well be in the real world due to bottlenecks and long gestation periods in the supply of research workers.

[12] The figures on relative compensation were obtained from Denison (1967, p. 68).

[13] Resources to furnish education are not specified in the model, for they are assumed to be provided from outside the private sector. Specific assumptions on our seven education-ability classes are:

Class (i)	Educational Attainment (1)	Native Ability (2)	Education Coefficient G_i (3)	Ability Coefficient H_i (4)	Proportion in Class i at	
					$t = 1$ (5)	$t = 25$ (6)
1	0–4 grade	0–4 grade	.70	.71	.10	.04
2	5–11 grade	0–4 grade	1.00	.71	.00	.06
3	5–11 grade	5–11 grade	1.00	1.00	.63	.34
4	12–15 grade	5–11 grade	1.24	1.00	.00	.29
5	12–15 grade	12–15 grade	1.24	1.13	.22	.14
6	16+ grade	12–15 grade	1.81	1.13	.00	.08
7	16+ grade	16+ grade	1.81	1.30	.05	.05

Data for columns (5) and (6) from Jorgenson and Griliches (1967, p. 279, Table XI, columns 1 and 8).

As noted above in section 3, Griliches and Jorgenson do not allow for differences in native ability. Their procedure implies that the native ability of persons moving to a higher educational attainment is effortlessly converted to the average native ability of those in the higher educational category.[14] The application by Griliches and Jorgenson of ability coefficients $H_i^{G\text{-}J}$ which differ from the H_i values used in (26) requires us to calculate a separate series showing Griliches and Jorgenson's measure of the labor force:[15]

$$M_t^{G\text{-}J} = B_t \sum_{i=1}^{n} e_{it} G_i H_i^{G\text{-}J} \tag{27}$$

Research workers are assumed to constitute a given (and growing) fraction u_t of "raw" labor, but their share S_t/L_t of effective labor input is considerably greater than this, since they are assumed to be the most-educated members of the labor force.[16]

$$\frac{S_t}{M_t} = \sum_{i=0}^{n-1} x_{it} e_{n-i,t} G_{n-i} H_{n-i} \begin{cases} x_{it} = 1; \quad i = 1, \ldots, m-1 \\[2mm] x_{it} = \dfrac{e_{n-i,t} + u_t - \sum_{i=0}^{m} e_{n-i,t}}{e_{n-i,t}} \\[2mm] x_{it} = 0; \quad i = m+1, \ldots, n-1 \\[2mm] \text{where } m \text{ is the lowest number at which} \\[2mm] u_t < \sum_{i=0}^{m} e_{n-i,t} \end{cases} \tag{28}$$

The portion of effective labor input M_t which is not devoted to research work is available as production labor in the investment (L_t^{PI}) and consumption (L_t^{PC}) sectors:

$$L_t = L_t^{PI} + L_t^{PC} = M_t - S_t \tag{29}$$

The effective input of research workers (S_t) is apportioned arbitrarily to three different research laboratories. One group works on disembodied *process*

---

[14] Thus their ability coefficients $H_i^{G\text{-}J}$ for the seven groups would be, respectively, 0.71, 1.00, 1.00, 1.13, 1.13, 1.30, 1.30.

[15] Recently David Schwartzman (June 1968, pp. 508–13) has claimed that the earnings statistics used by Denison and Griliches-Jorgenson (and copied for use here) exaggerate the contribution of education, due to the inclusion of agricultural workers, the unemployed, and those not in the labor force. An offsetting bias may be the failure to allow for differences in experience. Since inexperienced young workers are on the average better educated than older, more experienced workers, the figures on relative compensation by educational attainment of all workers may understate the effect of education with experience held constant. For calculations of the contribution of experience, see Thurow, *The Economics of Poverty and Discremenation* (in press, Chapter 5).

[16] The annual rate of growth of u_t was determined by the increase in the proportion of professional, technical, and kindred workers (excluding teachers) plus managers, officials, and proprietors (excluding retail trade proprietors) in the U.S. labor force from 1900 to 1950 (U.S. Department of Commerce, 1965, p. 75). The 1900 proportion was 0.054 and had increased by 1950 to 0.121.

improvement in the machinery industry; a second is engaged in *product* improvement in the machinery industry (performing what we usually mean by "technical change embodied in capital"); and the third group works on disembodied process improvements in the production of consumer goods (improvements in management, organization, etc.). There is no product research in the consumption sector built into the model, reflecting the real-life failure of the national accounts properly to measure quality change in consumer goods.

In keeping with our deliberately arbitrary allocation of the labor force, we shall assume that the research labor force is evenly divided among the three research laboratories. Effective labor input in each laboratory (s_t) is:

$$s_t = S_t/3 \tag{30}$$

Technical progress takes place in the model in response to increases in the accumulated stock of the three different types of knowledge produced by the three groups of research workers. The accumulated stock of knowledge in each laboratory (R_t) is:

$$R_t = \sum_{g=0}^{t-1} s_g e^{-\lambda(t-g)} \tag{31}$$

where λ represents the obsolescence of ideas.[17] Old ideas lose their usefulness when replaced by newer versions, just as do old machines.

2.   *Technology in the Consumption Sector*

A simple Cobb-Douglas production function is assumed for the consumption goods industry:

$$Q_t = (R_t)^{\alpha_1} \left(L_t^{PC} \right)^{\alpha_2} J_t^{\alpha_3} \tag{32}$$

Output is a function of the accumulated stock of research knowledge on production processes in the consumption industry R_t, the effective input of production workers (L_t^{PC}), and the effective stock of capital (J_t), which is measured not in tons or dollars but in machine revolutions per unit of time. If there are constant returns to all factors, so that $\alpha_1 + \alpha_2 + \alpha_3 = 1$, and if $\alpha_1 > 0$, then there are diminishing returns to effective labor and capital alone. A possible rationalization for this assumption is that any economy which grows without process research in the consumption sector becomes disorganized and inefficient.[18] An alternative assumption is increasing returns to the three factors $(\alpha_1 + \alpha_2 + \alpha_3 > 1)$

[17] (31) is similar to Mansfield's expression for the stock of research (Mansfield, 1968, equation (1)). This expression has the undesirable property that obsolescence will continue even if new research ceases, which is unrealistic, since obsolescence is *caused* by the appearance of new ideas.

[18] (32) implies that with a constant population, a constant share of research workers in the labor force, and no obsolescence of ideas, the rate of increase of technology would approach zero because of decreasing returns $(\alpha_1 < 1)$.

and constant and returns to L^{PC} and J alone. If the stock of knowledge is growing exponentially, this assumption makes (32) into the traditional constant-returns Cobb-Douglas production function with neutral disembodied technical progress which has been used so often in studies of economic growth. We are not committed to any particular values of the factor elasticities, and below we shall present results for values of $\alpha_1 + \alpha_2 + \alpha_3$ both equal to and greater than one.

The wage rate for production workers in the consumption industry is competitively determined, for each unit of effective labor receives its marginal product. In the increasing returns case, the wage is assumed to be proportional to the marginal product:

$$w_t = \frac{\partial Q_t}{\partial L_t^{PC}} \left(\frac{1}{\alpha_1 + \alpha_2 + \alpha_3} \right) = \frac{\alpha_2 Q_t}{(\alpha_1 + \alpha_2 + \alpha_3)L_t^{PC}} \tag{33}$$

Research workers, however, are not paid their marginal product but are paid the same wage *per unit of effective input* as production workers. Since research workers are all the best-educated members of society, their annual earnings per man will be greater than those of the less-educated production workers. This payment system corresponds to the observable fact in the real world that salaries for research workers are similar to the earnings of employees with similar educational backgrounds.

The compensation of capital A_t^K is simply the residual product in the consumption sector after all workers have been paid:

$$A_t^K = Q_t - w_t \left(L_t^{PC} + s_t \right) \tag{34}$$

3.   Technology in the Investment Goods Sector

The conversion of labor into machine revolutions (J_t) takes place in two stages. First, production workers in the investment sector join with the accumulated stock of process knowledge to produce structures and equipment (I_t):

$$I_t = (R_t)^{\beta_1} \left(L_t^{PI} \right)^{\beta_2} \tag{35}$$

This production function, like (32), can exhibit either constant or increasing returns in R and L^{PI}. I_t is measured in units of effective labor input.[19]

Although only equipment is used in (32) to produce consumption goods, structures are necessary to house the equipment, in the ratio μ units of structures to every $1 - \mu$ units of equipment. Thus, if I_t^X is the portion of investment output available for expansion after replacement needs have been satisfied, K_t^S is the accumulated stock of structures, δ the depreciation rate of effective machine

---

[19] See Solow, 1963, pp. 623–46 for another model in which investment is measured in units of labor input.

revolutions, and η the depreciation rate for structures, we have:

$$I_t^X = I_t - \delta J_t - \eta K_t^S \tag{36}$$

$$I_t^E = (1 - \mu)I_t^X + \delta J_t \tag{37}$$

$$I_t^S = \mu I_t^X + \eta K_t^S [2pt] \tag{38}$$

with I_t^E and I_t^S as gross investment in equipment and structures, respectively. The machine revolutions Z_t obtainable from a unit of gross equipment investment I_t^E do not remain constant over time but are constantly increased through product research in the investment sector. The production function for *effective* equipment investment is similar to (35):

$$Z_t = (R_t)^{\gamma_1} \left(I_t^E\right)^{\gamma_2} \tag{39}$$

If the stock of research knowledge grows exponentially and $\gamma_2 = 1$, this equation represents exponential capital-augmenting, capital-embodied technical progress.[20] Only machines improve, however, and structures always remain the same.

Finally, we write two accounting equations which describe the accumulation of capital:

$$K_t^S = \sum_{g=0}^{t-1} I_t^S \, e^{-\delta(t-g)} \tag{40}$$

$$J_t = \sum_{g=0}^{t-1} Z_t \, e^{-\delta(t-g)} \tag{41}$$

Another set of equations is necessary to determine the allocation of the production labor force between the consumption and investment sectors. On the assumption of a constant propensity to save and invest (ω) out of current-dollar income (Y_t^*), current dollar investment ($p_t^I I_t$) can be written:

$$p_t^I I_t = \omega Y_t^* \tag{42}$$

But current-dollar income and product is:

$$Y_t^* = Q_t + p_t^I I_t \tag{43}$$

where the relative price of investment goods is just the wage bill in the investment sector W_t^I divided by real investment (in labor units) I_t:

$$p_t^I = \frac{W_t^I}{I_t} = \frac{w_t \left(2s_t + L_t^{PI}\right)}{I_t} \tag{44}$$

Note that production labor input in the investment sector is paid the same wage (w_t) as in the consumption sector, implying a competitive market for production workers. The three equations (42), (43) and (44) can be combined with (33)

---

[20] And we are allowed to write the capital aggregate J_t, since all capital-embodied technical change is capital-augmenting. See Fesher, 1965, pp. 263–88.

to yield an expression for the input of production labor in the consumption sector.

$$L_t^{PC} = \frac{\alpha_2(1 - \omega)}{\omega + \alpha_2(1 - \omega)}(M_t - s_t) \tag{45}$$

and then L_t^{PI} is a residual determined by (29).

A final unknown in the model is the rate of return on the book value of capital (r_t), which is:

$$r_t = \frac{A_t^K}{p_t^K K_t} \tag{46}$$

and

$$p_t^K K_t = \sum_{g=0}^{t-1} p_t^I \left(I_t^E e^{-\delta(t-g)} + I_t^S e^{-\eta(t-g)} \right) \tag{47}$$

B.   Total Factor Productivity and the Contribution of Advances in Knowledge

1.   Growth in Economies A and B

Following the scheme laid out in section II above, the contribution of advances in knowledge to economic growth $\dot{C}/C$ is the difference between the growth rates of two economies, A and B, which are the same in every detail except that research workers are productive in economy A and completely barren of ideas in economy B:

$$\frac{\dot{C}}{C} = \frac{\dot{Y}^A}{Y^A} - \frac{\dot{Y}^B}{Y^B} \tag{48}$$

where Y_t^A is constant-dollar output of consumption goods plus the real gross output of capital services in economy A,

$$Y_t^A = Q_t + Z_t + I_t^S \tag{49}$$

and Y_t^B is a similar expression for economy B. Economy B differs from the model outlined above in that $\alpha_1 = \beta_1 = \gamma_1 = 0$, and research workers abandon their desks and drawing boards to return to production work in the same sector (i.e., L_t^{PC} in economy B equals $L_t^{PC} + S_t$ from economy A above and $L_t^{PI} = L_t - L_t^{PC}$). In the cases where there are constant returns to both research and nonresearch factors, this implies, of course, that the elasticity of Q_t and I_t with respect to the remaining nonresearch inputs is less than one. Diminishing returns would not be implausible in an economy with no advances in technical or managerial knowledge, since capital accumulation would just amount, in Domar's phrase, to "wooden ploughs piled up on top of existing wooden ploughs" (Domar, 1961, p. 712). The alternative of increasing returns to all inputs with constant returns to nonresearch inputs will also be included in the experiments.

In practice, the above model can be written down as a computer program, and given arbitrary values of the parameters $(\lambda, \alpha_1, \alpha_2, \alpha_3, \beta_1, \beta_2, \gamma_1, \gamma_2, \delta, \eta, \omega, \mu)$ and initial period values of capital and research stocks, the time path of economies A and B can be traced and the contribution of advances in knowledge $\dot{C}/C$ can be calculated. The purpose of the exercise is to compare $\dot{C}/C$ with the measures of total factor productivity which would be calculated by the rival teams of Kendrick and Solow and Griliches and Jorgenson, if they had access to data on the dependent variables in economy A, but not the parameter values. It is important to evaluate the accuracy of their methods, of course, since we can never learn how a real-world economy B would have behaved without advances of knowledge. Hence we cannot calculate $\dot{C}/C$ for the United States and must rely on some indirect technique.[21]

2. The Measurement of Output

The first difference between Kendrick-Solow and Griliches-Jorgenson is in the measurement of real output. Griliches and Jorgenson measure real investment as the real gross output of capital services, so that their output measure $Y_t^{G\text{-}J}$ agrees with (49) above:

$$Y_t^{G\text{-}J} = Y_t^A = Q_t + Z_t + I_t^S \tag{50}$$

The Kendrick-Solow measure of output $Y_t^{K\text{-}S}$ differs in two ways, due both to a conceptual difference and to an error in measurement. First, Kendrick and Solow include in output not the gross output of equipment services, but the gross output of equipment in units of base-year cost I_t^E. And, second, Kendrick and Solow use erroneous structures deflators which are merely averages of input costs and ignore technological advance in the construction part of the investment sector. Since the only input in the sector is labor, the Kendrick-Solow price deflator is the wage w_t, and their measure of the real output of structures is $I_t^{SKS} = I_t^S(p_t^I/w_t)$. K-S therefore calculate output as:

$$Y_t^{K\text{-}S} = Q_t + I_t^E + I_t^S\left(p_t^I/w_t\right) \tag{51}$$

If β_1 and γ_1 are positive, the growth of Z_t will be faster than I_t^E, and w_t will grow more rapidly than P_t^I, so that $Y^{G\text{-}J}$ will grow at a faster rate than $Y^{K\text{-}S}$.

---

[21] As Nelson (1964, pp. 591–2) points out, the returns to education would be lower if there were no technological change, and thus the growth of effective labor input in economy A would probably be greater than in economy B. This point would cause our procedure to underestimate the contribution of technological advance to the growth of economy A.

3.   *The Measurement of Input*

Griliches and Jorgenson make an advance over Kendrick and Solow (as did Denison [1966, pp. 76–8] in 1962) by recognizing that labor is heterogeneous and should be weighted by educational attainment. But, as shown above in equation (27), Griliches and Jorgenson ignore differences in native ability, with the result that their measure of effective labor input $M_t^{G\text{-}J}$ grows more rapidly than the true measure M_t, and both grow more rapidly than the homogeneous Kendrick and Solow labor force B_t.

The differences between Griliches-Jorgenson and Kendrick-Solow in the measurement of capital parallel those in the measurement of investment. The Kendrick-Solow aggregate capital stock is:

$$K_t^{K\text{-}S} = \sum_{g=0}^{t} I_t^E e^{-\delta(t-g)} + \frac{P_t^I}{w_t} I_t^S e^{-\eta(t-g)} \tag{52}$$

Griliches-Jorgenson, on the other hand, weight together the effective capital input of structures and equipment into a Divisia index:

$$\frac{\dot{K}^{G\text{-}J}}{K^{G\text{-}J}} = v_t^J \frac{\dot{J}}{J} + v_t^S \frac{\dot{K}^S}{K^S} \tag{53}$$

where the definitions of J_t and K_t^S are given above in (40) and (41), and the respective weights are determined by the relative prices of capital services C_t^J and C_t^S.[22]

$$v_t^J = \frac{c_t^J J_t}{c_t^J J_t + c_t^S K_t^S} \tag{54}$$

$$v_t^S = 1 - v_t^J \tag{55}$$

$$c_t^J = P_t^I (r_t + \delta_t) \tag{56}$$

$$c_t^S = P_t^I (r_t + \eta_t) \tag{57}$$

Finally, both Kendrick-Solow and Griliches-Jorgenson calculate the rate of growth of total input and total factor productivity ($C^{K\text{-}J}$ and $C^{G\text{-}J}$) by weighting together capital and labor with weights based on share of total compensation:

$$\frac{\dot{C}^{K\text{-}S}}{C^{K\text{-}S}} = \frac{\dot{Y}^{K\text{-}S}}{Y^{K\text{-}S}} - v_t^M \frac{\dot{B}}{B} - v_t^K \frac{\dot{K}^{K\text{-}S}}{K^{K\text{-}S}} \tag{58}$$

$$\frac{\dot{C}^{G\text{-}J}}{C^{G\text{-}J}} = \frac{\dot{Y}^{G\text{-}J}}{Y^{G\text{-}J}} - v_t^M \frac{\dot{M}^{G\text{-}J}}{M^{G\text{-}J}} - v_t^K \frac{\dot{K}^{G\text{-}J}}{K^{G\text{-}J}} \tag{59}$$

where

$$v_t^M = \frac{w_t M_t}{Y_t^*} \tag{60}$$

---

[22] In practice, year-to-year growth rates are calculated from (53) and averaged over the period of the simulation.

and

$$v_t^K = \frac{A_t^K}{Y_t^*} = 1 - v_t^M \tag{61}$$

4.   *The Social Rate of Return to Research and Physical Capital*

Griliches and Jorgenson have claimed that their finding of negligible growth in total factor productivity implies that "social rates of return to this type of investment are comparable to rates of return on other types of investment" (Jorgenson and Griliches, 1967, p. 274). To evaluate this claim, we can calculate the social rates of return of investment to research and to physical capital in each of our simulations, and observe true differences in rates of return in cases where $\dot{C}^{G\text{-}J}/C^{G\text{-}J}$ is very small.

To calculate the one-period rate of return on investment in physical capital, we follow Solow and "sacrifice one unit of consumption at time t in favor of investment, and then ask what is the largest increment of consumption that can be enjoyed at time $t + 1$ without impairing consumption possibilities in any later period.... This last condition means that the effective stock of capital bequeathed to period $t + 2$ must be no smaller than would have been the case had the extra saving in period t and the extra consumption in period $t + 1$ not taken place" (Solow, 1965, p. 60). In practice we begin the calculation by switching one production worker from the consumption to the investment sector. Similarly, the one-period rate of return on investment in research involves the switch of one man from production work in the consumption sector to research work with one third of the man going to each of the three research laboratories for one time period. We calculate the maximum consumption increment at time period $t + 1$ compared to the original "control solution" on the condition that the effective stock of physical capital *and* accumulated research bequeathed to period $t + 2$ must not be altered by the experiment. In practice, we must extend our calculations over two time periods, since extra research performed at time t raises consumption at time $t + 1$ *directly* through disembodied change in the consumption sector, but also raises consumption *indirectly* at time $t + 2$ as a consequence of the increased research input in the investment sector at time $t + 1$ and higher resulting quantity of J_{t+2}. The experimental switch in the allocation of labor lasts only for the one period t, and in period $t + 1$ the allocation of labor is unchanged from the basic simulation. The labor allocation is affected at time $t + 2$, however. Since the J_{t+3} and R_{t+3} must return to the original values of the control solution and since J_{t+2} and R_{t+2} are higher than in the control solution, less investment and research work are necessary in time period $t + 2$ than in the control solution, leaving extra workers for the production labor force in the consumption sector and giving an additional boost to Q_{t+2}. To preserve symmetry, the rate of return on physical capital, like the rate of return on research, is calculated over two periods.

3.4 SIMULATION RESULTS

Initial experimentation revealed that variations in several structural parameters made little difference in the results, so that arbitrary values were assigned to the three depreciation parameters ($\lambda = 0.05, \delta = 0.10, \eta = 0.04$) and the structures requirements parameter ($\mu = 0.40$). In the first part of this section results will be reported for a saving rate (ω) of 0.20, but later the effect of alterations in ω will be examined. Growth rates were calculated over fifteen periods.

A.   Embodied and Disembodied Change

1.   Constant Returns

Information on the first simulation is presented in Table 3.1. Technical progress takes place in all three laboratories in economy A; there is disembodied progress in the consumption and investment sectors as well as embodied progress, which improves the quality of equipment. There are constant returns to scale in production labor, the stock of knowledge, and effective equipment services in the consumption sector, and to production labor and the stock of knowledge in the equipment sector. The effect of altering this assumption to increasing returns will be examined shortly.[23] The technological parameters are listed in line C of Table 3.1, and the results are summarized in line D. The rate of growth of output in economy A (Y_A) is 4.30 percent per year, but only 1.44 percent in economy B (Y_B). The difference between the two rates is the contribution of advances of technology (2.86 percent per year). In their pioneer calculations of the growth of total factor productivity ("the residual") in economy A, Kendrick and Solow arrive at the figure of 1.91 percent per year. And shortly thereafter Griliches-Jorgenson announce that the Kendrick and Solow study suffers from "errors in measurement" and that the corrected rate of growth of total factor productivity is really only 0.97 percent per year. The social rates of return to investment in research and tangible capital are 0.3645 and 0.0095, respectively, so that a considerable increase in the growth rate could be achieved by switching production workers into the research laboratories.[24]

Line E describes the components of the Griliches and Jorgenson corrections. First, the Kendrick and Solow index of output, aggregated by adding together quantities at constant prices, is replaced by a Divisia index of consumption and investment goods output. There are no corresponding errors of aggregation

---

[23] The constant returns assumption here, which refers to capital services (J), thus differs somewhat from the constant returns assumption in the theoretical model of Section II, which referred to the capital stock (K) *uncorrected* for improvements in equipment quality. The present/assumption is more convenient in the two-sector model of the simulations and does not differ for an instantaneous doubling of L, J, and R, since the increased stock of knowledge would have no time to affect the ratio of J to K.

[24] In the calculations of social rates of return the initial switch of a production worker from the consumption sector takes place in period 8.

Table 3.1.

A. Types of Technical Progress: Disembodied in Consumption Sector
Disembodied in Investment Sector
Embodied

B. Returns to scale in all factors: Constant

C. Parameter values of the technology:

$\alpha_1 = .20 \; \alpha_2 = .60 \; \alpha_3 = .20 \; \beta_1 = .20 \; \beta_2 = .80 \; \gamma_1 = .20 \; \gamma_2 = .80$

D. Summary of results (percentage growth rates):

$$\frac{\dot{Y}_A}{Y_A} = 4.30 \; \frac{\dot{Y}_B}{Y_B} = 1.44 \; \frac{\dot{C}}{C} = 2.86 \; \frac{\dot{C}_{K\text{-}S}}{C_{K\text{-}S}} = 1.91 \; \frac{\dot{C}_{G\text{-}J}}{C_{G\text{-}J}} = .97 \; \rho_8^R = .365 \; \rho_8^K = .010$$

E. Components of Griliches-Jorgenson (G-J) Correction of Kendrick-Solow (K-S):

	Output Aggregation	Price of Structures	Effective Equipment	Education
1. Percentage points subtracted from residual	−.17	.23	.26	.55
2. Percent of output growth explained by input growth after correction	52.4	58.4	64.8	77.5

F. Explanation of discrepancies between calculations of residual and true contribution of advances in knowledge:

(percentage points)	True	K-S	G-J
1. Calculated contribution	2.86	1.91	.97
2. Sources of Discrepancies:			
a. Growth capital input		.51	.68
b. Price of structures		−.16	
c. Capital share		.61	.84
d. Growth labor input		−.29	.18
e. Labor share		.11	.19
f. Growth of output		.17	
3. True contribution	$\overline{2.86}$	$\overline{2.86}$	$\overline{2.86}$

4. Addendum: Sources of true contribution of advances in knowledge
  a. Direct impact of research   2.61
  b. Indirect impact on capital   .74
  c. Indirect impact on prod'n labor   −.49

of labor and capital input, since in (58) and (59) above Kendrick-Solow and Griliches-Jorgenson both calculate Divisia indexes of total input. After the error in output aggregation is corrected, growth in total inputs explains 52.4 percent of the growth in total output. Next, the Kendrick-Solow input-cost price index for structures, which does not adjust for improvements in labor productivity in the construction industry, is replaced by a true price index. With this error corrected, input growth explains 58.4 percent of output growth. Next, the measurement of the stock of equipment in terms of base-year cost is replaced by a measure of effective equipment services (J). This is equivalent to Griliches and Jorgenson's replacement of the official producers' durable price index by the price index for consumers' durables, and their adjustment for the secular improvement in the utilization of equipment.[25] This third adjustment on line E also includes a switch to the use of service prices as weights for the aggregation of structures and equipment. After these corrections, input growth explains 64.8 percent of output growth in economy A. Finally, the Kendrick and Solow measure of man hour-labor input is replaced by Griliches and Jorgenson's estimate of effective labor input, in which different educational categories of labor are aggregated, using relative wages as weights. With this final correction completed, input growth explains 77.5 percent of output growth. Notice that the Griliches and Jorgenson corrections do not lead to a conclusion that the growth in total factor productivity has been zero. This occurs, as we shall see below, only if all advances in technology are embodied in new equipment.

Section F of Table 3.1 analyzes the sources of discrepancies between the Kendrick-Solow and Griliches-Jorgenson measures of growth in total factor productivity and the true contribution of advances in knowledge to the growth of economy A. First, the stock of capital (measured at base-year cost) in economy A grows much faster than in economy B, due to the faster rate of output growth in economy A and the proportional saving assumption (Line F.2.a of Table 3.1). Thus, even if there had been no embodied technical change, disembodied change would have indirectly caused an increase in the rate of growth of the capital stock, and both the Kendrick-Solow and Griliches-Jorgenson techniques would exaggerate the growth of capital, which would have occurred in the absence of any advances in technology (i.e., in economy B). For this reason alone, calculations of the growth in total factor productivity may be unreliable guides to the importance of advances in technology. The Griliches and Jorgenson discrepancy in line F.2.a is larger than that of Kendrick and Solow because the Griliches and Jorgenson effective capital series grows faster than the Kendrick and Solow capital stock series measured at base-year cost. In line F.2.b. the Kendrick and

---

[25] Griliches and Jorgenson attempt a parallel treatment of labor and capital utilization, implying that the secular improvement in equipment utilization has been caused, like any reduction in the unemployment rate, by an improvement in aggregate demand. But in fact, the main cause of the secular improvement in equipment utilization has probably been technical change, for example, improvements in machine quality which reduce downtime and allow the stretching of maintenance and overhaul intervals. Otherwise, why wouldn't manufacturing firms in the 1920s have chosen to invest less and utilize their existing capital more?

Solow discrepancy is reduced by the use of an erroneous input-cost price index for structures, which reduces the rate of growth of their capital measure.

Next, in line F.2.c., both Kendrick-Solow and Griliches-Jorgenson exaggerate the contribution of capital to economic growth through the use of an oversized weight on capital based on the share of capital compensation in current-dollar output. Since in this model research workers are exploited, part of the reward to capital represents the contribution of research to output growth. The Griliches and Jorgenson error is larger despite their use of the same capital share as Kendrick and Solow, because that capital share is applied to a more rapidly growing capital series. Line F.2.d. shows the effect of the failure of Kendrick and Solow to adjust for the contribution of education to economic growth, and the effect of the overcorrection by Griliches and Jorgenson. The Kendrick and Solow underestimate of the growth rate of labor input reduces the discrepancy between $\dot{C}/C$ and their calculation of the "residual," so that a correct measure of labor input by Kendrick and Solow would reduce their residual to only 1.57.[26]

As shown in line F.2.e., another discrepancy is due to the use by Griliches-Jorgenson and Kendrick-Solow of weights which exaggerate the contribution of production workers to output. As we shall see, this discrepancy is eliminated when we assume increasing returns to all factors and raise the elasticity of output with respect to production workers. A final source of discrepancy for Kendrick and Solow is the underestimation of the rate of growth of output, causing an underestimate of the residual relative to the contribution of advances in knowledge.

Line F.4 separates $\dot{C}/C$ into components showing the routes by which advances in technology affect the growth rate of economy A relative to that of economy B. The direct impact of disembodied technical change is an improvement in the growth rate of 2.61 percent, of which 1.77 occurs through the growth rate of consumption and 0.84 through the growth rate of effective investment.[27] The indirect impact of research through the rate of growth of capital is 0.74 percent, of which 0.28 percent represents the contribution of embodied technical change to the growth of consumption, and the remainder is due to the overall impact of faster output growth on capital growth through the proportional saving rate. In fact, the stock of capital measured in base-year cost (i.e., excluding embodiment effects) grows 40 percent faster in economy A than economy B. The influence of research on the supply of production workers serves to reduce the growth rate. Since the portion of the labor force engaged in research in economy A is steadily rising, the rate of growth of production workers in economy A is slower than in economy B, where all research workers do production work.

---

[26] This calculation assumes a value of 0.00 for line F.2.d. and 0.16 for line F.2.e.

[27] Although the share of effective investment in total real output is only about one fifth, the direct impact of research is relatively greater than this implies, since there are twice as many research workers in the investment sector as in the consumption sector.

In short, the simulation results confirm the analysis of Section 3.1 above. Both Kendrick-Solow and Griliches-Jorgenson underestimate the contribution of advances in knowledge to economic growth. The underestimate by Griliches and Jorgenson is larger, both because they count the effects of embodied technical change as part of the growth of input and because they exaggerate the contribution of education to growth. But even if these two "corrections" in the Griliches and Jorgenson procedure were to be omitted, the calculated increase in total factor productivity would still be only 1.32 percent, less than half of the true contribution of advances in knowledge. This, for instance, would be the Kendrick and Solow measure of the residual if Kendrick and Solow (as is likely) were to agree with Griliches and Jorgenson on the use of correct structures deflators, on Divisia indexes for output and input aggregation, and on a "correct" adjustment for education. We can call this 1.32 percent figure the "compromise residual," and it is striking that it explains so little of the true contribution of advances in knowledge.

Other interesting features of the first experiment are not shown in Table 3.1. Over the fifteen time periods of the simulation, the relative price of investment rises by 55 percent, due to the more rapid pace of productivity change in the consumption than in the investment sector, combined with the fact that wage rates in the two sectors are the same. The wage rate increases by 64 percent over this interval, and since the wage rate is used by Kendrick and Solow to measure the price of structures, they overestimate the growth of the latter by 9 percent. Due to the relatively greater burden of replacement investment in equipment and the rising importance of replacement, the ratio of gross investment in structures to equipment (I_t^S/I_t^E) declines over the simulation period from 64 to 53 percent. The ratio of gross investment in structures to the gross production of equipment *services* (I_t^S/Z_t) declines even more, from 54 percent to 35 percent.

Although the assumed saving rate in current prices is 20 percent, the actual share of gross constant-price investment in output (when investment is measured at base-year cost) is only 16 percent in the final period, because the rising relative price of investment goods cuts down on the investment goods that can be purchased with a given sacrifice of consumption goods. But the share of *effective* investment in output (defined to include consumption plus effective investment) is 23 percent, due to the contribution of technical change to increasing the equipment services obtainable from a given amount of base-year-cost investment.

2.   *Increasing Returns*

As shown in Table 3.2, the main points of the first simulation are confirmed if we introduce increasing returns in all factors, which can be accomplished if the technological elasticities of output with respect to production labor and effective capital are raised in proportion by enough to yield constant returns to production labor and effective capital alone. But the magnitudes of the discrepancies between $\dot{C}/C$ and the two measures of growth in total factor productivity are reduced considerably, enough so that the Kendrick and Solow residual is

Table 3.2.

A. Types of Technical Progress: Disembodied in Consumption Sector
                                    Disembodied in Investment Sector
                                    Embodied

B. Returns to scale in all factors: Increasing

C. Parameter values of the technology:

$\alpha_1 = 0.20\ \alpha_2 = 0.75\ \alpha_3 = 0.25\ \beta_1 = 0.20\ \beta_2 = 1.00\ \gamma_1 = 0.20\ \gamma_2 = 1.00$

D. Summary of results (percentage growth rates):

$$\frac{\dot{Y}_A}{Y_A} = 5.29\ \frac{\dot{Y}_B}{Y_B} = 2.31\ \frac{\dot{C}}{C} = 2.98\ \frac{\dot{C}_{K\text{-}S}}{C_{K\text{-}S}} = 3.01\ \frac{\dot{C}_{G\text{-}J}}{C_{G\text{-}J}} = 1.73\ \rho_8^R$$

$$= 0.351\ \rho_8^K = 0.147$$

E. Components of G-J Correction of K-S:

	Output Aggregation	Price of Structures	Effective Equipment	Education
1. Percentage points subtracted from residual	−0.02	0.20	0.55	0.55
2. Percent of output growth explained by input growth after correction	42.7	46.5	56.9	67.2

F. Explanation of discrepancies between calculations of residual and true contribution of advances in knowledge:

(percentage points)	True	K-S	G-J
1. Calculated contribution	2.98	3.01	1.73
2. Sources of Discrepancies:			
a. Growth capital input		0.31	0.78
b. Price of structures		−0.17	...
c. Capital share		0.22	0.33
d. Growth labor input		−0.37	0.22
e. Labor share		−0.04	−0.08
f. Growth of output		0.02	...
3. True contribution	2.98	2.98	2.98

4. Addendum: Sources of true contribution of advances in knowledge
  a. Direct impact of research   2.76
  b. Indirect impact on capital   0.90
  c. Indirect impact on prod'n labor   −0.68

---

actually slightly larger than the true contribution of advances in knowledge. The Griliches and Jorgenson residual is 58 percent of $\dot{C}/C$, as opposed to only 34 percent in the constant returns case.

The reasons for the main differences between Tables 3.1 and 3.2 may be briefly noted. The increase in the α_2, α_3, β_2, and γ_2 parameters raises the growth rate of output in economy A, but economy B, where the output growth rate had been held down by diminishing returns in labor and capital, benefits relatively more. Thus the contribution of advances in knowledge, the difference in the growth rates of the two economies, is only slightly larger here than in Table 3.1. Since the increased growth rate of economy A has been achieved with no increase in the growth rate of labor input and only a moderate increase in the growth rate of capital, both the Kendrick-Solow and Griliches-Jorgenson "residuals," i.e., output growth minus weighted input growth, are raised considerably. Another result in line D is the reduction in the social rate of return to research (since shifting a unit of labor out of production work now involves more of a sacrifice, given the unchanged elasticity of output with respect to research) and a substantial increase in the social rate of return to tangible capital (which again makes sense, since output is now more responsive to the efforts of production workers in the investment sector).

The difference between the Kendrick-Solow and Griliches-Jorgenson residuals is a bit larger than before – 1.28 percentage points in the increasing returns case as opposed to 0.94 with constant returns. The Griliches-Jorgenson correction, which converts capital K into effective capital J is more important here, since the increased r_2 coefficient raises the magnitude of the embodiment effect. Another reason for the increase in the difference between Kendrick-Solow and Griliches-Jorgenson is the slightly increased share of labor, which raises the importance of the Griliches and Jorgenson correction for education.

In Section F we notice first that the Kendrick and Solow overstatement of the contribution of capital input is less serious now, mainly because of the faster growth of capital in economy B. In line F.2.c. both overestimates of the capital share are less serious. This occurs because the higher elasticity with respect to labor raises the marginal product of production workers in the consumption sector, hence the wage of research workers relative to the marginal product of research, and thus reduces the degree of exploitation of research workers. The value shares understate the true share of labor, as shown in line F.2.e. An important change in the last section is in line F.4.c., where the negative impact of research on the contribution of production workers is larger, since a larger sacrifice is now involved in switching a worker from production to research employment.

Although the Kendrick and Solow residual overestimates the contribution of knowledge, this is not true after corrections are made for the erroneous price of structures, for the contribution of education, and for errors in output aggregation. This "compromise residual" is 2.48 percent, or 83 percent of the true contribution of advances in knowledge. This may be compared to a "compromise residual" in the initial constant-returns trial which is only 46 percent of the contribution of advances in knowledge. Thus the degree of returns to scale in the economy is very important in assessing the actual deviation of the "compromise residual" from the true contribution of technical change, but is not decisive in determining the *direction* of that deviation (unless there are significantly increasing returns in capital and production labor alone).

B.   Disembodied and Embodied Change Introduced Separately

Tables 3.3 and 3.4 present results for the case of technological advance which takes place only in the form of disembodied improvements in the consumption sector. This brings the Kendrick-Solow and Griliches-Solow residuals much closer together, with the only important differences being due to the Griliches and Jorgenson corrections for errors in output aggregation and education. Kendrick and Solow would probably agree with these corrections, at least after the educational correction has been adjusted for ability differences, and a "compromise residual" can be calculated. As in Tables 3.1 and 3.2, this only explains a fraction of the true contribution of advances in technology – 48 percent in Table 3.3 and 81 percent in Table 3.4. Incidentally, we are reminded in Tables 3.3 and 3.4 that there is nothing about the Griliches and Jorgenson measurement techniques that forces the contribution of advances in knowledge to be zero by definition, as Denison appears to have implied (see note 7).

Results in Tables 3.5 and 3.6 depict the case of embodied quality improvements in equipment, with no disembodied technical change in either the consumption or investment sectors. The results are qualitatively similar to the initial cases considered in Tables 3.1 and 3.2, but the growth rates of all the variables in line D are much smaller, since only one third as much research is being carried on and its effect is dampened by an elasticity of output with respect to effective capital of only 0.20. Taking aside the Griliches and Jorgenson exaggeration of the contribution of education, the Griliches and Jorgenson residual would be 0.19 percentage points in the constant returns case and 0.30 in the increasing returns case. The residual in this embodied-only example would be equal to zero but for a peculiarity of the simulation model – in the simulations it is only effective *equipment* that directly contributes to output, but the Griliches and Jorgenson measure of effective capital includes both equipment and slower-growing structures. If the model had been designed so that both structures and equipment contributed directly to output, Y_A would have grown more slowly and the small remaining Griliches and Jorgenson residual would have been wiped out.

If the Kendrick and Solow residual is corrected for the true contribution of education, the price of structures, and errors of output aggregation, we again have the "compromise residual," which is 0.45 percent per year in Table 3.5 and 0.63 in Table 3.6, and thus explains 88 and 112 percent of the true $\dot{C}/C$. The percentage of explanation is higher in the pure embodied case, since the compromise capital index for economy A does not grow markedly faster than

Table 3.3.

A. Types of Technical Progress: Disembodied in Consumption Sector Only

B. Returns to scale in all factors: Constant

C. Parameter values of the technology:

$\alpha_1 = 0.20$ $\alpha_2 = 0.60$ $\alpha_3 = 0.20$ $\beta_1 = 0.00$ $\beta_2 = 1.00$ $\gamma_1 = 0.00$ $\gamma_2 = 1.00$

D. Summary of results (percentage growth rates):

$$\frac{\dot{Y}_A}{Y_A} = 3.52 \quad \frac{\dot{Y}_B}{Y_B} = 1.76 \quad \frac{\dot{C}}{C} = 1.76 \quad \frac{\dot{C}_{K\text{-}S}}{C_{K\text{-}S}} = 1.00 \quad \frac{\dot{C}_{G\text{-}J}}{C_{G\text{-}J}} = 0.64 \, \rho_8^R$$

$$= 0.574 \, \rho_8^K = 0.040$$

E. Components of G-J Correction of K-S:

	Output Aggregation	Price of Structures	Effective Equipment	Education
1. Percentage points subtracted from residual	−0.13	. . .	0.05	0.54
2. Percent of output growth explained by input growth after correction	67.9	67.9	66.5	81.8

F. Explanation of discrepancies between calculations of residual and true contribution of advances in knowledge:

(percentage points)	True	K-S	G-J
1. Calculated contribution	1.76	1.00	0.64
2. Sources of Discrepancies:			
a. Growth capital input		0.17	0.15
b. Price of structures		. . .	. . .
c. Capital share		0.81	0.78
d. Growth labor input		−0.34	0.21
e. Labor share		−0.01	−0.02
f. Growth of output		0.13	. . .
3. True contribution	1.76	1.76	1.76

4. Addendum: Sources of true contribution of advances in knowledge
   a. Direct impact of research   1.72
   b. Indirect impact on capital   0.17
   c. Indirect impact on prod'n labor   −.13

Table 3.4.

A. Types of Technical Progress:　Disembodied in Consumption Sector

B. Returns to scale in all factors:　Increasing

C. Parameter values of the technology:

$\alpha_1 = 0.20\ \alpha_2 = 0.75\ \alpha_3 = 0.25\ \beta_1 = 0.00\ \beta_2 = 1.00\ \gamma_1 = 0.00\ \gamma_2 = 1.00$

D. Summary of results (percentage growth rates):

$$\frac{\dot{Y}_A}{Y_A} = 4.37 \quad \frac{\dot{Y}_B}{Y_B} = 2.31 \quad \frac{\dot{C}}{C} = 2.06 \quad \frac{\dot{C}_{K\text{-}S}}{C_{K\text{-}S}} = 2.02 \quad \frac{\dot{C}_{G\text{-}J}}{C_{G\text{-}J}} = 1.60\ \rho_8^R$$

$$= 0.505\ \rho_8^K = 0.080$$

E. Components of G-J Correction of K-S:

	Output Aggregation	Price of Structures	Effective Equipment	Education
1. Percentage points subtracted from residual	0.09	. . .	−0.04	0.55
2. Percent of output growth explained by input growth after correction	51.7	51.7	50.8	63.4

F. Explanation of discrepancies between calculations of residual and true contribution of advances in knowledge:

(percentage points)	True	K-S	G-J
1. Calculated contribution	2.06	2.02	1.60
2. Sources of Discrepancies:			
a. Growth capital input		0.12	0.09
b. Price of structures		. . .	. . .
c. Capital share		0.24	0.23
d. Growth labor input		−0.37	0.22
e. Labor share		−0.04	−0.08
f. Growth of output		0.09	. . .
3. True contribution	2.06	2.06	2.06

4. Addendum: Sources of true contribution of advances in knowledge
  a. Direct impact of research　　　　2.06
  b. Indirect impact on capital　　　　0.13
  c. Indirect impact on prod'n labor　−0.13

Table 3.5.

A. Types of Technical Progress: Embodied Only

B. Returns to scale in all factors: Constant

C. Parameter values of the technology:

$\alpha_1 = 0.00 \; \alpha_2 = 0.80 \; \alpha_3 = 0.20 \; \beta_1 = 0.00 \; \beta_2 = 1.00 \; \gamma_1 = 0.20 \; \gamma_2 = 0.80$

D. Summary of results (percentage growth rates):

$$\frac{\dot{Y}_A}{Y_A} = 2.46 \quad \frac{\dot{Y}_B}{Y_B} = 1.95 \quad \frac{\dot{C}}{C} = 0.51 \quad \frac{\dot{C}_{K\text{-}S}}{C_{K\text{-}S}} = 0.58 \quad \frac{\dot{C}_{G\text{-}J}}{C_{G\text{-}J}} = -0.03 \quad \rho_8^R$$

$$= 0.0995 \quad \rho_8^K = -0.0003$$

E. Components of G-J Correction of K-S:

	Output Aggregation	Price of Structures	Effective Equipment	Education
1. Percentage points subtracted from residual	0.20	−0.03	0.23	0.62
2. Percent of output growth explained by input growth after correction	72.4	72.0	76.2	1.013

F. Explanation of discrepancies between calculations of residual and true contribution of advances in knowledge:

(percentage points)	True	K-S	G-J
1. Calculated contribution	0.51	0.58	−0.03
2. Sources of Discrepancies:			
a. Growth capital input		0.05	0.26
b. Price of structures		0.03	. . .
c. Capital share		0.02	0.03
d. Growth labor input		−0.38	0.22
e. Labor share		0.02	0.03
f. Growth of output		0.20	. . .
3. True contribution	$\overline{0.51}$	$\overline{0.51}$	$\overline{0.51}$

4. Addendum: Sources of true contribution of advances in knowledge
  a. Direct impact of research   0.29
  b. Indirect impact on capital   0.39
  c. Indirect impact on production labor   −0.17

Table 3.6.

A. Types of Technical Progress: Embodied Only

B. Returns to scale in all factors: Increasing

C. Parameter values of the technology:

$\alpha_1 = 0.00 \; \alpha_2 = 0.80 \; \alpha_3 = 0.20 \; \beta_1 = 0.00 \; \beta_2 = 1.00 \; \gamma_1 = 0.20 \; \gamma_2 = 1.00$

D. Summary of results (percentage growth rates):

$$\frac{\dot{Y}_A}{Y_A} = 2.70 \; \frac{\dot{Y}_B}{Y_B} = 2.14 \; \frac{\dot{C}}{C} = 0.56 \; \frac{\dot{C}_{K\text{-}S}}{C_{K\text{-}S}} = 0.80 \; \frac{\dot{C}_{G\text{-}J}}{C_{G\text{-}J}} = 0.07 \; \rho_8^R$$

$$= 0.0852 \; \rho_8^K = 0.0536$$

E. Components of G-J Correction of K-S:

	Output Aggregation	Price of Structures	Effective Equipment	Education
1. Percentage points subtracted from residual	−0.05	0.00	0.16	0.62
2. Percent of output growth explained by input growth after correction	66.4	65.7	74.6	97.5

F. Explanation of discrepancies between calculations of residual and true contribution of advances in knowledge:

(percentage points)	True	K-S	G-J
1. Calculated contribution	0.56	0.80	0.07
2. Sources of Discrepancies:			
a. Growth capital input		−0.13	0.19
b. Price of structures		...	...
c. Capital share		0.05	0.07
d. Growth labor input		−0.38	0.23
e. Labor share		0.00	0.00
f. Growth of output		0.23	...
3. True contribution	$\overline{0.56}$	$\overline{0.56}$	$\overline{0.56}$

4. Addendum: Sources of true contribution of advances in knowledge
   a. Direct impact of research   0.44
   b. Indirect impact on capital   0.33
   c. Indirect impact on prod'n labor 0.21

the growth of capital in economy B, as occurs in the presence of disembodied technical change.

C.   Other Examples

Table 3.7 summarizes the results of the previous tables and several additional trials. Two lines of results are given for each trial, one for constant returns and a second for increasing returns (where in each case the Cobb and Douglas exponents on capital and production labor are raised in proportion by enough to yield constant returns in capital and production labor alone).

Trial 1 duplicates the experiment presented in Tables 3.1 and 3.2 Trial 2 is the same with higher research elasticities in the investment sector, which appears further to widen the gap between $\dot{C}/C$ and the "residuals." The "compromise residual" explains only 48 and 76 percent of $\dot{C}/C$ in the constant and increasing returns cases, respectively. In general, the higher the coefficients on disembodied change in either sector, the less accurate the "compromise residual." This is confirmed in Trial 3, in which the parameters on capital and disembodied research in the consumption sector are raised, resulting in a "compromise residual" which only explains 33 and 70 percent of $\dot{C}/C$. Trial 4 returns to the β_1 and γ_1 parameters of the initial trial but lowers the disembodied consumption research parameter (α_1) and raises the capital parameter (α_3). The result is a narrowing of the gap between $\dot{C}/C$ and all versions of the residual; the "compromise residual" explains 54 and 85 percent of $\dot{C}/C$. Trial 5 reverses the change in the α_1 and α_3 parameters, with a slight alteration of the explanation of $\dot{C}/C$ by the compromise residual to 48 and 86 percent. In general, the gap between the social rates of return to investment in research and tangible capital widens in favor of research when α_1 is increased and narrows when α_3 is increased. The increase in β_1 and γ_1 (Trial 2 compared to Trial 1) appears to raise the gap in the constant returns case and reduce it with increasing returns. Trial 6 corresponds to Tables 3.3 and 3.4. In Trial 7 there is disembodied technical change only in the investment sector, with results very similar to the embodied-only case in Trial 8, except that the "compromise residual" explains a considerably smaller fraction of $\dot{C}/C$. In Trial 9 γ_1 in the embodied-only case is raised over its value in Trial 8, with a "compromise" residual which continues to explain most or all of $\dot{C}/C$. depending on the degree of returns to scale. Finally, in Trial 10, there is another variant which differs from the first trial by omitting disembodied change in the consumption sector, but in which the explanation of $\dot{C}/C$ by the "compromise residual" is about the same – 58 and 86 percent.

An interesting feature of Table 3.7 is the existence of several Trials, 7, 8, and 10, in which the Griliches and Jorgenson version of the residual is virtually zero, but in which the social rate of return to research exceeds the social rate of return to investment in tangible capital (an exception is the increasing returns version of Trial 10). As pointed out above in Section II, this contradicts the Griliches and Jorgenson statement that a small value of their residual implies virtual equality of the two social rates of return.

Table 3.7. Summary Data for Experiments

Trial	DC	DI	E	α_1	α_3	β_1	γ_1	Inc.	Dec.	$\dot{Y}_A/Y_A$	$\dot{C}/C$	$\dot{C}_{K\text{-}S}/C_{K\text{-}S}$	$\dot{C}_{G\text{-}J}/C_{G\text{-}J}$	CR	ρ_8^R	ρ_8^K
1.	×	×	×	0.20	0.20	0.20	0.20		×	4.30	2.86	1.91	0.97	1.32	0.365	0.010
								×		5.29	2.98	3.01	1.73	2.48	0.351	0.147
2.	×	×	×	0.20	0.20	0.30	0.30		×	4.92	3.74	2.15	1.02	1.78	0.480	−0.044
								×		6.13	3.79	3.33	1.57	2.87	0.402	0.323
3.	×	×	×	0.30	0.30	0.30	0.30		×	6.52	5.45	2.38	0.94	1.80	0.921	0.065
								×		9.67	6.60	5.46	2.88	4.67	0.808	0.701
4.	×	×	×	0.10	0.30	0.20	0.20		×	4.11	2.36	1.64	0.66	1.28	0.267	0.085
								×		4.94	2.29	2.33	1.02	1.94	0.260	0.370
5.	×	×	×	0.30	0.10	0.20	0.20		×	4.48	3.42	2.00	1.03	1.65	0.464	−0.067
								×		5.46	3.52	3.45	2.18	3.02	0.360	0.127
6.	×	×	×	0.20	0.20	0.00	0.00		×	3.52	1.76	1.00	0.64	0.85	0.574	0.040
								×		4.37	2.06	2.02	1.60	1.43	0.505	0.080
7.	×	×		0.00	0.20	0.20	0.00		×	2.60	0.64	0.79	0.01	0.22	0.176	−0.033
								×		2.77	0.61	0.75	−0.03	0.18	0.146	0.027
8.			×	0.00	0.20	0.00	0.20		×	2.46	0.51	0.58	−0.03	0.45	0.100	0.000
								×		2.70	0.56	0.80	0.07	0.63	0.085	0.054
9.			×	0.00	0.20	0.00	0.30		×	2.78	1.01	0.78	0.15	0.75	0.200	−0.017
								×		3.21	1.05	1.08	0.34	1.16	0.156	0.068
10.		×	×	0.00	0.20	0.20	0.20		×	2.58	0.85	0.91	0.04	0.49	0.100	−0.015
								×		2.87	0.71	0.97	0.01	0.61	0.092	0.158

New Abbreviations:
CR: The "compromise residual."
DC: Disembodied technical change in consumption sector.
DI: Disembodied technical change in investment sector.
E: Embodied technical change.

Table 3.8. *Effect of Increase in Saving Rate from 20 to 25 Percent*

Case	Type of Technical Change DC	DI	E	α_1	α_3	β_1	γ_1	Returns to Scale Inc.	Dec.	Increase in $\dot{Y}_A/Y_A$ Points	%
1.	×	×	×	0.20	0.20	0.20	0.20		×	0.11	2.6
								×		0.22	4.2
2.	×			0.20	0.20	0.00	0.00		×	0.09	2.6
3.			×	0.00	0.20	0.00	0.20		×	0.10	4.1

D.   Effect of a Higher Saving Rate

Denison has argued on several occasions (1962, 1964, pp. 90–4) that a substantial boost in the proportion of fixed investment in national income would yield inconsequential increases in the growth rate of output. In his initial study of the United States, for instance, Denison calculated that "A change of 0.1 points in the growth rate over perhaps sixty years would be achieved by continuing additional net investment equal to ... 0.75 percent [of the national income] if none of the additional investment were devoted to nonfarm housing" (Denison, 1962, p. 277). The present simulations lead to smaller effect, as illustrated in Table 3.8. With the parameter values of the initial trial, as shown on line 1, a 5 percent increase in the ratio of gross investment to gross national product (both measured in current prices) yields an increase of only 0.11 points in the fifteen-period average annual growth rate in the constant returns case (from 4.30 to 4.41 percent), and only 0.22 with increasing returns. Thus a 25 percent boost in the saving rate produces only a 2.6 (or 4.2) percent increase in the growth rate.

Further, the results confirm Denison's argument that the yield of extra saving is little affected by the existence of embodied technical change. For instance, the assumed increase in the saving rate by one quarter yields a 2.6 percent (0.09 points) increase in the growth rate in the trial which assumes disembodied technical change in the consumption sector, and an increase of 4.1 percent (0.10 points) in the embodied-only trial. In fact, these calculations may overstate the effect of higher saving on the growth rate, since no allowance is made for Denison's point [1964, p. 92] that new capital goods are heterogeneous; some new pieces of equipment, which are vastly superior in quality to older vintages, will be installed even at low rates of saving and investment. Marginal increments in the saving rate, however, will be used to purchase lower-priority items which are less superior in quality to earlier vintages and which will thus yield smaller increments in the growth rate than suggested in Table 3.8.[28]

[28] Alterations in the saving rate do not yield important changes in our comparisons of $\dot{C}/C$ with the Griliches-Jorgenson, Kendrick-Solow, and "compromise" residuals. Experiments were run with saving rates of 0.15, 0.20, and 0.25. Smaller saving rates cannot in general be used, since

3.5 CONCLUSION: SUMMARY AND IMPLICATIONS

A.   Summary

This paper has demonstrated that total factor productivity or "residual" indexes, whether calculated with or without correction for the "errors" discovered by Griliches and Jorgenson, are not reliable estimates of the contribution of techno-logical change to economic growth. In a theoretical model and in computer sim-ulations the true contribution of advances in technology is, in most cases, greater than indexes of total factor productivity as calculated by Kendrick-Solow and Griliches-Jorgenson. In all cases the full list of corrections for "errors in mea-surement" proposed in the Griliches and Jorgenson papers makes the Griliches and Jorgenson "residual" smaller than that of Kendrick and Solow, and hence a more inaccurate estimate of the contribution of technological advance.

Of the numerous Griliches and Jorgenson corrections, Kendrick and Solow might agree on the use of accurate price indexes for structures, Divisia indexes for the growth of input and output, and some adjustment of labor input for education – although not as much of an adjustment as made by Griliches and Jorgenson. An index of total factor productivity adjusted for these corrections can be called a "compromise residual." But Kendrick and Solow would not go beyond this and approve the Griliches and Jorgenson substitution of mea-sures of effective capital (J) for the base-year-cost stock of capital (K), since this measure of effective input disguises the role of advances in technology in achieving the increase in J relative to K, that is, it rules out embodied technical change by definition. And, as we saw above in Tables 3.5 and 3.6, the Griliches and Jorgenson residual (after their erroneous educational adjustment is cor-rected) is zero in the case of embodied technical change. It is this feature which makes the Griliches and Jorgenson residual in all of the above simulations fur-ther from the true contribution of technological progress than the "compromise residual."

A more novel conclusion is that even the "compromise residual" almost always underestimates the contribution of advances of knowledge to economic growth. The magnitude of this discrepancy varies over a considerable range in the computer simulations, depending on assumptions made in the model regarding the underlying production coefficients and payment arrangements for research workers. The discrepancy depends mainly on:

1.   The Degree of Returns to Scale

Simulations with constant returns to scale in production labor, capital, and re-search, produced larger discrepancies than the assumption of increasing returns

simulations with β_1 and γ_1 positive required a saving rate of at least 0.15 to pay the salaries of the research workers in the two laboratories in the investment sector. And even then, with $\omega = 0.15$, there was little of the wage bill left over for production workers in the investment sector, resulting in some cases in negative net investment.

in these three factors and constant returns in production labor and capital alone. This is natural, since constant returns to labor and capital is an underlying assumption of the Kendrick-Solow and Griliches-Jorgenson techniques for calculating indexes of total factor input. If the true elasticity of output with respect to labor and capital is actually less than one, their weights on the growth of labor and capital (which add to one) are too high, their measures of total factor input grow too rapidly, and their residual is too small. Of course this source of the discrepancy between the "compromise residual" and the true contribution of advances in technology is eliminated or reversed if the true elasticity of output with respect to production labor and capital is sufficiently greater than one. But it seems unlikely that an economy with absolutely no advances in knowledge could avoid diminishing returns to production labor and capital. It could endlessly duplicate plants operating with 1918 or 1818 technology, but how could it overcome problems of transport, organization, and distribution when no one takes time out to think about them? In fact, this is the fate of economy B in Tables 3.1, 3.3, and 3.5, in which there is no research, significantly decreasing returns in labor and capital, and a large discrepancy between the "compromise residual" and the true contribution of advances in knowledge.

2.   The True Growth Rate of Capital Input

Whether returns to scale are constant or increasing in the three factors, disembodied technical change increases the rate of growth of economy A relative to economy B, and this, due to the proportional saving assumption, raises the growth rate of capital in economy A relative to B, even if there is no embodied technical change. Since the Kendrick-Solow and Griliches-Jorgenson indexes of total factor productivity are based on the observed growth of capital in economy A, they overstate the growth of capital that would have occurred without technical change and, consequently, understate the contribution of advances of technology to economic growth. There is no way this error can be avoided, so that even the "compromise residual" will not accurately identify the contribution of technical change unless in the real world there is no disembodied change at all.

3.   Research Compensation in the Capital and Labor Shares

In the computer simulations research workers are paid the same wage as production workers of the same educational attainment, so that they are exploited if the social rate of return to research is positive. For this reason the observed capital share in economy A overstates the elasticity of output with respect to capital, and the Kendrick-Solow and Griliches-Jorgenson measures of the contribution of the growth of capital to output growth are overstated due to the application of oversized capital shares. This source of error in the approximation of $\dot{C}/C$ by the Kendrick-Solow and Griliches-Jorgenson residuals would not be eliminated if capital were to be paid its marginal product. In this case it would be the oversized value share of *labor* that would disguise the contribution of research workers, and the contribution of the growth of labor would be overstated. Only with constant returns to scale in production labor and capital, and increasing returns to all factors, will there be no error when the extra research compensation is included in the shares of the conventional factors.[29]

B.   Implications

Griliches and Jorgenson claim that "the equality between private and social rates of return is a testable hypothesis within our framework," that is, that a finding by Griliches and Jorgenson of no change in total factor productivity would imply that the "contribution of investment to economic growth is.... compensated by the private returns to investment" (Jorgenson and Griliches, (1967, p. 274). Presumably a positive Griliches and Jorgenson residual would suggest that social returns exceed private returns. Yet in our simulations above there are numerous trials in which the Griliches and Jorgenson residual is positive, yet private returns exceed the contribution of investment to growth, due to the exploitation of research workers. Without exploitation the social and private returns are equal, but the Griliches and Jorgenson residuals would be raised due to a smaller weight on the growth of capital input. Thus there is no correspondence between the Griliches and Jorgenson residual and the difference between the social and private rates of return to investment, since research using disembodied technical change creates a positive Griliches and Jorgenson residual without causing the social rate of return to diverge from the private. This point reminds us that previous writers on total factor productivity, including Griliches and Jorgenson, have been led to misleading conclusions through excessive concentration on "costless" technical change and insufficient attention to cost-increasing advances in technology.

In the simulations above the Griliches and Jorgenson residual is much smaller in trials in which all technical change is embodied than those in which part or all of technological advance is disembodied. Does the small Griliches and Jorgenson residual in for U.S. growth from 1945 to 1965 therefore imply that in reality most U.S. technological advance has been of the embodied type? (Jorgenson and Griliches, July 1967, pp. 249–84). As yet we do not have sufficient information to answer this question, since the Griliches and Jorgenson corrections for "errors" in the price of equipment and utilization of capital are notoriously unreliable, as pointed out by Denison [1966, pp. 76–78]:

> Whether the [equipment] deflator on balance can be assumed to have an upward bias rather than random error depends on the criterion adopted for judging appropriate behavior. I think there is no such presumption if the criterion is the same as for other price indexes, including those for consumers' durables....

---

[29] More precisely, there will be no error when (a) there are constant returns to capital and labor, and (b) the excess of the contribution of research workers over the marginal product of production workers is distributed between capital and labor in proportion to the contribution of each to output growth.

Power-driven machinery in manufacturing, to which the [utilization] data refer, is so small a component of total capital input that an increase in the hours it is used would have only a minor effect on the growth rate ... [Griliches and Jorgenson] assume, with no attempt at justification, that the average hours worked by inventories, by structures, and by all producers' durables, including such components as office furniture and restaurant equipment, increased in all industries in proportion to the increase in hours worked by manufacturing machinery driven by electric motors.

There is a noticeable assymetry in the models outlined in Sections II and IV, since, following the U.S. national accounts, investment in tangible capital is considered a part of output and investment in research is excluded from output. If output were redefined to include investment in research and if "investment in scientific research and development could be. ... cumulated into stocks" (as Griliches and Jorgenson, 1967, suggest, p. 275) and included in total factor input, changes in total factor productivity would be eliminated in the above models, which do not allow for any shifts in the consumption or investment production functions. But this would be an unrewarding effort for students of economic growth, since such a redefinition would further disguise the true contribution of advances in knowledge to economic growth. No useful information about growth could be gained from such a "broader accounting framework." We could not discover, for instance, how much growth had been due to research, for we would have no way of estimating the contribution of research inputs to growth without *assuming in advance* that the private earnings of research workers are equal to their social marginal product. Yet the social returns to research are one of the elements that calculations of the "residual" are designed to reveal. This difficulty is in addition to the insuperable problem of measuring the proportion of the labor force which is really engaged in technology-advancing activities. We would include those formally designated as research and development employees, to be sure, but how many managers would we include, and what fraction of the time of foremen and innovative production workers?

A full evaluation of previous research in the light of our simulation studies is beyond the scope of this paper. But it is interesting to reflect that the work of Denison (1962; 1967), which basically follows the Kendrick and Solow techniques but corrects for the contribution of education to growth, is a close approximation of what we have called the "compromise residual." In most of our simulations the "compromise residual" substantially underestimates the contribution of advances in knowledge to economic growth, suggesting Denison's "state of knowledge" source of U.S. and European growth may be too low.[30]

For potential econometric production function studies, this paper introduces a new note of caution into a file drawer already overstuffed with warnings.

[30] In addition, Schwartzman (1968, pp. 508–13) presents evidence that Denison's educational adjustment is too high, further raising the probable contribution of advances in knowledge.

Investigators attempting to identify the relative importance of input growth and advances in technology as sources of economic growth should study the results of our simulations, which suggest that the growth in the base-year-cost capital stock that actually occurred in a technologically advancing economy is larger than that which would have occurred without technical change, so that statistically-estimated "residuals" are likely to underestimate the true contribution of technical change. Also, it is probable that the observed rate of growth of the labor force is greater than the rate of growth of workers actually engaged in production work. Further, as Nelson has pointed out (1964, p. 597), a cyclical correlation between investment in research and development and investment in tangible capital will produce estimated capital parameters that are biased upward in regressions which exclude a research variable. This in turn would foil any attempt to estimate the true degree of returns to scale, leading us to be skeptical of Griliches and Jorgenson's statement that "such production functions provide one means of testing the assumptions of constant returns to scale and equality between price ratios and marginal rates of transformation. . . ." (1967, p. 276).

Griliches and Jorgenson claim that their results "suggest a new point of departure for econometric studies of production functions at every level of aggregation" (1967, p. 276). Econometricians should view this advice with caution, for literal interpretation would require the replacement of capital stock data by "surrogate" or "effective" capital series. This would prevent econometric studies from identifying the portion of output growth which is explainable by technological advance, since part of the advance in technology would be disguised in the growth of effective capital. Griliches and Jorgenson might counter that econometric production function studies based on "error-corrected" data are at least a guide to *disembodied* change, but this is true only if we can trust the reliability of the Griliches and Jorgenson techniques for estimating the ratio of effective capital services to the capital stock – and Denison's remarks suggest that this is very doubtful. (Of course, econometricians should continue to heed Jorgenson's warning that embodied and disembodied technical change cannot in principle be distinguished with standard capital stock data).

Where does research go from here? Since studies of economic growth with existing macro data are suspect for so many reasons, increased resources should be devoted to micro studies of technological improvement at the plant and product level. Nothing in this paper criticizes the laudable earlier attempts of Griliches and others to compute quality-corrected price indexes for machinery and other durables. While we have warned against the use of input indexes computed from such quality-corrected data in studies that attempt to determine the importance of technological advance by residual-type methods, quality-corrected data are clearly desirable for measuring improvements in welfare and the true rate of inflation. And, in the field of human capital, the task of separating the relative contributions of education, ability, experience, and environmental differences to wage differentials has only begun.

References

Abramovitz, M. "Resource and Output Trends in the United States Since 1870." *American Economic Review*. May, 1956; vol. 46, no. 2, pp. 5–23.

Denison, E. F. *The Sources of Economic Growth in the United States and the Alternatives Before Us*. Supplementary Paper No. 13. New York: Committee for Economic Development; 1962.

"The Unimportance of the Embodied Question." *American Economic Review*. March, 1964; vol. 54, no. 1, pp. 90–4.

"Measuring the Contribution of Education (and the Residual) to Economic Growth." In "Organisation for Economic Co-operation and Development." *The Residual Factor and Economic Growth*. Paris; 1965, pp. 13–100.

"Discussion" (see 9 below). *American Economic Review*. May, 1966; vol. 56, no. 2, pp. 76–8.

Why Growth Rates Differ: Postwar Experience in Nine Western Countries. Washington: The Brookings Institution; 1967.

Domar, E. D. "On the Measurement of Technological Change." *Economic Journal*. December, 1961; vol. 71, no. 4, pp. 709–29.

Fisher, F. M. "Embodied Technical Change and the Existence of an Aggregate Capital Stock." *The Review of Economic Studies*. October, 1965; vol. 32, no. 4, pp. 263–88.

Griliches, Z., and Jorgenson, D. "Sources of Measured Productivity Change: Capital Input." *American Economic Review*. May, 1966; vol. 56, no. 2, pp. 50–61.

Hollander, S. *The Sources of Increased Efficiency*. Cambridge: The MIT Press; 1965.

Jorgenson, D., and Griliches, Z. "The Explanation of Productivity Change." *The Review of Economic Studies*. July, 1967; vol. 34, no. 3, pp. 249–84.

Kendrick, J. W. "Productivity Trends, Capital and Labor." *Review of Economics and Statistics*. August, 1956; vol. 38, no. 3.

Mansfield, E. "Rates of Return from Industrial Research and Development." *American Economic Review*. May, 1965; vol. 55, no. 2, pp. 310–22.

The Economics of Technological Change. New York: W. W. Norton; 1968.

Nelson, R. R. "Aggregate Production Functions and Medium-Range Growth Projections." *American Economic Review*. September, 1964; vol. 54, no. 5, pp. 575–606.

Nordhaus, W. D. "The Optimal Rate and Direction of Technical Change." In Shell, K., ed. *Essays on the Theory of Optimal Economic Growth*. Cambridge: MIT Press; 1967.

Invention, Growth, and Welfare: A Theoretical Treatment of Technological Change. Cambridge MIT Press; 1969.

Phelps, E. S. "Models of Technical Progress and the Golden Rule of Research." *The Review of Economic Studies*. April, 1966; vol. 33, no. 2, pp. 133–46.

Schmookler, J. "The Changing Efficiency of the American Economy, 1869–1938." *Review of Economics and Statistics*. August, 1952; vol. 34, no. 3, pp. 214–231.

Schultz, T. W. "The Rate of Return in Allocating Investment Resources to Education." *The Journal of Human Resources*. Summer 1967; vol. 2, no. 3, pp. 293–309.

Schwartzman, D. "Education and the Quality of Labor, 1929–63." *American Economic Review*. June, 1968; vol. 68, no. 3, pp. 508–13.

Solow, R. M. "Technical Change and the Aggregate Production Function." *Review of Economics and Statistics*. August, 1957; vol. 39, no. 3, pp. 312–20.

"Heterogeneous Capital and Smooth Production Functions." *Econometrica*. October, 1963; vol. 31, no. 4, pp. 623–46.

Capital Theory and the Rate of Return, Chicago, Rand-McNally, 1965.

Thurow, L. C. *The Economics of Poverty and Discrimination.* To be published by The Brookings Institution.

U. S. Department of Commerce, Bureau of the Census. *The Statistical History of the United States.* Stamford: Fairfield Publishers; 1965.

Uzawa, H. "Optimal Technical Change in an Aggregative Model of Economic Growth." *International Economic Review.* January, 1965; vol. 6, no. 1, pp. 18–31.

CHAPTER 4

The Concept of Capital

Edward F. Denison was a great economist. Following on Robert Solow's (1957) demonstration that one could proxy the elasticity of output to changes in an input by that input's income share (assuming competitive factor pricing and constant returns to scale), Denison went on to invent and develop the field of growth accounting. Many of the basic innovations in this field were his, especially the treatment of labor input as human capital, the use of incomes stratified by educational attainment to obtain a measure of labor quality, and the recognition that some of these income differences reflect innate ability rather than the contribution of education.[1]

Perhaps the most contentious issue in the field of growth accounting has been the concept of capital input, and especially the allocation of the fruits of technical advance between the contribution of capital and the residual factor that Denison variously called "advances in knowledge," "residual productivity," or "output per unit of input." Thus it is fitting that Denison's last published article is devoted to an insightful and probing analysis of the concept of capital, taking as his point of departure my recent book, *The Measurement of Durable Goods Prices*. I am honored that my book served as a catalyst for his final thoughts on capital measurement.

4.1 POINTS OF AGREEMENT AND DISAGREEMENT

My book was the first to advocate a criterion for comparing capital goods based on their ability to produce real net revenue, defined as gross output

[1] Most of his seminal innovations in growth accounting were introduced in his first (1962) book on the topic, which remains a landmark in the study of economic growth. I first read his book in an Oxford tutorial in 1962, an experience that played a major role in redirecting my main interest in economics from its previous focus on industrial organization to its subsequent focus on macroeconomics, economic growth, and the measurement of capital.

Note. This research has been supported by the National Science Foundation. This paper benefitted greatly from an exchange of correspondence with Edward Denison in late 1991. (*Source.* "The Concept of Capital." *Review of Income and Wealth.* March 1993; vol. 39, no. 1, pp. 103–110).

minus variable costs spent on labor, energy, and other intermediate inputs. One chapter was devoted to an analysis of this concept and its relation to other approaches, including Denison's earlier writing, and the rest of the book attempted to implement the theoretical approach by providing quantitative estimates of quality and price changes for a wide variety of durable goods. Data were available to implement the theory completely for just two products, commercial aircraft and electric generating equipment. Estimates were produced for a wide variety of other products, including computers, automobiles, and appliances, where data allowed only a partial implementation of the theoretical formulation.

When aggregated into a new price deflator for producers' durable equipment, the book concluded that the official deflator had overstated price changes at a rate of about 3 percent per annum over the interval 1947–83, and that the growth of real equipment investment had been understated at the same rate. I argued that, although this estimate of price index bias may have seemed large, it was doubtless an understatement, and I ended my introductory chapter by listing twenty-three separate examples of unmeasured quality change that had not been taken into account in the estimates of the book.

Despite the appearance of major disagreement, Denison's paper endorses the two most important contributions of the book, the theoretical approach that compares capital goods by the net revenue criterion, and the empirical result that my new price deflators rise much less rapidly than the official deflators and doubtless understate the extent of the bias. On theory, he views my study as the first to apply the criterion of comparing capital goods by the marginal products "defined correctly," that is, by deducting operating costs. He views my approach not as a minor extension of previous analyses but as differing in a "major and fundamental way."[2] On empirical implementation, he emphasizes that I fail to adjust completely for operating cost on products other than aircraft and electric generating equipment, and so my estimates for other products understate the importance of quality change. In short, Denison concludes more forcefully than I did that the estimates of price index bias are understated, probably by a large amount.

Where, then, do we disagree? Denison concludes that my empirical work goes only part of the way toward a complete implementation of the net revenue criterion that both he and I endorse, that is, I have baked only "half a loaf." He believes that half a loaf is worse than none, while I think that half a loaf is better than none and is a good start toward everyone's objective of a "full loaf." As this analogy suggests, our ultimate disagreement concerns research strategy and is largely subjective.

Denison's paper is complex and may be hard to follow for readers who are unfamiliar with his previous classifications of measures of capital by methods

---

[2] " . . . doing so is not *extending* the definition of marginal product but *implementing* it. Nor is the 'extension' slight; it is major and fundamental" Denison, 1993, p. 92.

"1," "2," and "3." Here I provide a bare-bones formalization of the central distinctions in order to clarify both his position and mine.[3]

The economy produces output (y) with the characteristics of capital goods (x), e.g., computer calculations (MIPS) or trucking ton-miles, as well as variable inputs (q) like computer operators, truck drivers, and fuel. Here it is important that the measure of capital which enters the production function is the attribute of capital that actually produces output, e.g., computer calculations, not the particular unit in which a piece of capital is packaged (the computer "box"):

$$y = y(x, q), \quad y_x > 0; \quad y_q > 0. \tag{1}$$

The real net revenue generated from production is output minus the real cost of variable inputs, which in turn is equal to the real price of these inputs (w) times their quantity:

$$n = y(x, q) - wq(x, \sigma), \tag{2}$$

where the demand for inputs depends on the quantity of capital used and a technological shift parameter that can alter the requirements for variable inputs, e.g., as the result of fuel-saving technological change.[4]

The cost (v) of producing a capital good at any given time depends on its physical attributes (z), which in turn depend on the net revenue it can generate, as well as on a shift parameter that can change net revenue relative to physical attributes:[5]

$$v = v[z(n), \lambda], \quad v_z > 0; \quad v_\lambda < 0; \quad z_n > 0. \tag{3}$$

This distinction between the physical attributes that determine cost (z) and net revenue (n) applies with most force in the computer industry. At any given moment of time computers generating more n (faster speed, greater memory) cost more to purchase in the marketplace, but a continuous increase in λ over time has allowed firms to increase n by many orders of magnitude without any appreciable increase in the price of a computer "box." The same goes for fuel economy; at any given moment of time more fuel-efficient models that generate higher n cost more to produce, but technological progress can improve the fuel economy of models of a given cost.

---

[3] What follows is a stripped-down version of the analysis on my book (1990, Chapter 2). The notation in the book has been retained where possible, although the emphasis here has been changed to focus on the concerns raised by Denison. The most important simplification is to eliminate a number of terms that allow the demand for characteristics of capital goods to respond to changes in the relative prices of output and inputs.

[4] Real net revenue in (2) is nominal net revenue divided by the price of output (P). Nominal net revenue is:

$$N = Py(x, q) - Wq(x, \sigma).$$

[5] In this analysis there is no distinction between the cost of a capital good and its market price; hence v represents both cost and price.

4.2 THE CORRECT MEASURE OF CAPITAL AND ITS VALIDATION BY USED ASSET PRICES

The debate over alternative methods of measuring capital involves the choice of alternative price deflators. We observe a given stream of investment on capital goods of various types measured in nominal dollars, and we need a deflator to convert this stream into constant dollars. The approach proposed in my book (1990) is to consider two goods as representing the same amount of capital if they yield the same net revenue at a given set of prices (w) of variable inputs. The implied deflator compares "model 1" with "model 0" at a given time, dividing their market price ratio by the ratio of the net revenue that they can generate:

$$P^3 = \frac{v_1/v_0}{n_1/n_0} = \frac{v[z(n_1), \lambda_1]/v[z(n_0), \lambda_0]}{[y(x_1, q_1) - w_0 q(x_1, \sigma_1)]/[y(x_0, q_0) - w_0 q(x_0, \sigma_0)]}. \tag{4}$$

This price deflator is labeled P^3 because it is what Denison calls a correct implemention of his "method 3" of measuring capital. Note that in comparing the two models, the price of output and the real price of variable inputs (w_0) is held constant.

Several examples can be provided to illustrate the versatility of this concept. If the market price of a new model is double that of an old model, yet they produce the same real net revenue, the price deflator doubles. If the market price doubles but net revenue rises by a factor of 2, the price deflator is unchanged. This would be a typical event when a larger model replaces a smaller model without any shift in the cost of production parameter (λ) or in the efficiency of use of variable inputs (σ). When the first generation of jet planes was introduced, market price doubled, while net revenue increased by a factor of 10 as a result of both faster speed and reduced fuel use, so that the price index declined from 1.0 to 0.2.

As shown by the theoretical analysis in my book, the market for used assets should establish used prices (a) of two models of a given age in proportion to their ability to generate net revenue:

$$\frac{a_1}{a_0} = \frac{n_1}{n_0}. \tag{5}$$

This relationship is important both theoretically and in empirical implementation. In theory it shows why net revenue rather than gross marginal product is the correct criterion for comparing capital goods. For instance, jet aircraft with similar speeds and seating capacities (e.g., the Boeing 757 and McDonnell-Douglas DC8-61) have very different prices on the used aircraft market (corrected for age) because the latter model uses more pilots and consumes much more fuel. In empirical implementation the availability of used asset prices provides data that can be used directly to compare models or to double-check computations of net revenue by model.

THE OTHER METHODS FOR MEASURING CAPITAL

Much of Denison's paper involves the contrast between "method 1," "modified method 1," and "method 3." Originally "method 1" considered two capital goods to be equivalent if they had the same production cost in a particular base year. Making the same comparison between "model 1" and "model 0," and treating year "0" as the base year, the original method 1 deflator would be:

$$P^1 = \frac{v_1/v_0}{c_1/c_0} = \frac{v[z(n_1), \lambda_1]/v[z(n_0), \lambda_0]}{v[z(n_1), \lambda_0]/v[z(n_0), \lambda_0]}. \tag{6}$$

Notice that here the numerator is the same as in (4), but the denominator is the ratio of the cost of the new and old model at the base-period level of production technology (λ_0), that is, ignoring any changes in λ that make it possible to boost the productive characteristics of a machine of given base-period cost or to reduce the cost of obtaining improved fuel efficiency.

An intermediate step between methods 1 and 3 (introduced in Triplett's 1983 paper) is a reformulation of method 1 to consider as equivalent two capital goods that have the same productive characteristics (x), while continuing to ignore any differences in operating efficiency.

$$P^{1*} = \frac{v_1/v_0}{m_1/m_0} = \frac{v[z(n_1), \lambda_1]/v[z(n_0), \lambda_0]}{y(x_1)/y(x_0)}. \tag{7}$$

Again, the numerator is the same as before, but now the denominator is the ratio of the gross output that can be produced with the new and old models, neglecting any role for variable inputs (hence the terms in q in the denominator of 4 are omitted in 7). In most of his description, Denison intends this formulation to apply to hedonic price indexes for computers, in which the ratio of output produced by two computer models is determined by the ratio of their prices at a given time, ignoring any other input that is used cooperatively with computers.

"Method 2" is to consider two capital goods as equivalent if they produce the same output. Denison rightly dismisses this as eliminating the distinction between output and capital. Note that method 1* would be equivalent to method 2 only if the elasticity of output with respect to an increase in characteristics is unity.[6] What Denison elsewhere calls "method 4" is to measure capital as consumption foregone, i.e., apply the price deflator for consumption goods rather than to attempt to compute a separate price deflator for investment goods. We return to this suggestion below.

---

[6] Denison is not entirely consistent in his terminology. In the first part of his paper he refers to the reformulation of method 1 by Triplett in characteristics space as "reformulated method 1." But then he refers to the use by the BEA of a hedonic price index for computers as "modified method 2."

4.3 PROBLEMS OF IMPLEMENTING THE CORRECT CAPITAL MEASURE

The preferred "method 3" is implemented in my book for commercial aircraft and electric generating plants. Both of these have the great advantage of separable technology, so that the output, net revenue, and market price of each unit of capital can be measured separately. In the case of aircraft, net revenue for pairs of models was calculated and then roughly confirmed by ratios on the used aircraft market. Price indexes based on the net revenue and used asset ratios behaved similarly and differed radically from conventional indexes based on a "method 1" approach.

The analysis of aircraft prices reveals that there are good reasons why asset prices can differ (other than age) that are hard to measure in comparisons of net revenue. If model "1" produces an output of higher quality than model "0" (e.g., less vibration for a jet plane than for a piston plane), but the market for this product (airline travel) is such that no price differential exists between the product of the old and new model (the benefit being passed on to the consumer), then the net revenue method will "miss" the improvement in this quality attribute. However, the used asset price will capture the improvement, since the bids by potential equipment purchasers will reflect their knowledge that consumers prefer the new model. Also, the used price method is superior, since used prices incorporate current expectations about useful lifetimes.

Once we go beyond the aircraft and electric utility chapters, the empirical implementation in the book does not make explicit calculations of net revenue for other products. For such products as appliances and TV sets, rough adjustments are made for the value of reduced energy use and repair frequency, and data on the prices of used automobiles and tractors are also employed. The bias to which Denison calls attention applies to any price comparison, especially by the hedonic method, which ignores operating costs.

Denison's criticism applies with particular force to computers, where I find that between 1951 and 1984 the computer price index fell by a factor of 1,337. Since the nominal price of computers changed little, the implied quality of computers measured by method 1^* increased by a factor of 1,337. Denison dramatizes his criticism by arguing that I implicitly assumed that a 1984 computer processor "required 1,337 times as much labor to operate it. Requirements for structures, inventories, land, and purchased materials and services are also assumed to be 1,337 times as great in 1984 as in 1951." In truth, 1984 computers doubtless required less of most types of variable inputs than 1951 computers, not more. Denison's criticism applies to all hedonic regression studies of high-tech products, not just those in my book.

The bias that Denison identifies goes unambiguously in the direction of causing my price indexes to understate quality improvements by a significant amount. Denison provides no guidance on the size of the bias, but it is easy to work out a formal assessment. We want a price index that divides the price ratio of a new and old model by their net revenue ratios, as in (4). Yet the hedonic regression methodology makes the mistake of comparing the gross marginal products, i.e., compares two models by $y(x_1)/y(x_0)$ instead of n_1/n_0. To simplify, let us assume that a new model of, say, a computer has more computation power (a higher x) but uses an unchanged quantity of labor, electricity, and other input characteristics. Then the net revenue ratio from (4) is:

$$\frac{n_1}{n_0} = \frac{y(x_1) - w_0 q_0}{y(x_0) - w_0 q_0}. \tag{8}$$

Dividing through by $y(x_1)$, defining the base-period share of variable cost as $\alpha = w_0 q_0 / y(x_0)$, and defining the ratio of marginal products as $R = [y(x_1)/y(x_0)]$, we can rewrite (8) as:

$$\frac{n_1}{n_0} = \frac{R - \alpha}{1 - \alpha}. \tag{9}$$

Now it is easy to compute the bias in hedonic price indexes that measure the quality superiority of the new model over the old model by the ratio R. Let us consider a value for R of 1.25, equivalent to the 25 percent annual rate of price decline that emerges from many studies of mainframe and personal computers. Then the proper comparison based on the net revenue ratio comes out at 1.25 only if the variable cost share (α) is zero. The net revenue ratio ranges from 1.28 at $\alpha = 0.1$ to 1.5 at $\alpha = 0.5$ to 3.5 at $\alpha = 0.9$. Thus if the true variable cost ratio is one-half, the hedonic method understates the increase in the quality of computers (and their rate of price decline) by half.

Clearly, Denison has identified an important problem that has been ignored previously. Yet it is not fatal. Rough order-of-magnitude calculations of the variable costs involved in operating a computer center would suffice to avoid most of the bias. And computers are special. There has not been any such radical change in labor used relative to the characteristics of most other types of capital goods. Trucks may be more fuel efficient but still require one driver, broadcast TV cameras still require one cameraman, electric drills and other power tools still require one operator, and so on.

4.4   THE CRITERION OF CONSUMPTION FOREGONE

Daunted by the difficulties of implementing the correct method 3 across the board, Denison rejects it as infeasible. His final section then ponders the relative advantages of the criterion of consumption foregone as compared with the alternative of using unmodified method 1 (which, as in equation 6 above, ignores cost-reducing shifts in production technology that allow an increase in the quantity of productive characteristics relative to base-period production cost). The consumption foregone method simply deflates the nominal value of investment goods by the consumption goods deflator, while method 1 corresponds roughly to the practices used in the official investment deflator for goods other than computers. Denison, who had previously (1989) endorsed the consumption foregone criterion, now criticizes it for failing to provide any detail on changes in the relative price of investment goods, and as a result he comes back to his original (1957) preference for method 1, since this allows the development of "different price indexes . . . to deflate different capital goods." We note that this distinction is of little practical importance. The 1929–91 annual growth rates of the official deflators were 3.45 percent for consumption, 3.64 percent for fixed nonresidential investment, and 3.29 percent for producers' durable equipment (PDE). These differences are trivial compared to the three percent annual difference between the official PDE deflator and that developed for my book for 1947–83, or the 20-to-25 percent annual rate of price decline for computers.

4.5 CONCLUSION: IS HALF A LOAF BETTER THAN NONE?

In correspondence and in the body of his paper (1993), Denison recognizes that my chapters on aircraft and electric generating plants represent a full-blown implementation of method 3. He also recognizes that some of my other empirical work represents a significant step toward method 3, including the adjustments for improved energy efficiency of automobiles and appliances, and the reduced repair frequency of TV sets. Nevertheless, he rejects method 3 because it is currently difficult to provide a *comprehensive* set of investment goods deflators based on method 3, even though it is clearly feasible for particular products with good data. Thus, while he recognizes that my PDE deflator is biased upward because of its incomplete implementation of method 3, he nevertheless recommends going back to method 1 that contains a much larger upward bias.

Through the centuries scientists have adopted new paradigms when the old ones have been rendered obsolete, even if instantaneously they could not provide precise measures of the new concepts. Only method 3 makes any sense as a theory that provides a unified approach to both economic growth and economic behavior at the individual and industry level. Only method 3 allows us to explain why for some products net revenue is not proportional to cost, or why used asset prices for assets of a given age are not proportional to cost. Only method 3 allows us to allocate properly the fruits of research and development, crediting the manufacturers who do the R&D with productivity gains rather than the users who (like airlines) do virtually no R&D. Only method 3 treats the first-generation DC-8 jet aircraft that generated ten times more net revenue than the old DC-7 as ten times the capital, not just as a larger version of the clunky fuel-guzzling piston DC-7 lumbering along at 350 miles per hour (as is implied by a method 1 treatment of aircraft).

In the end, Denison wants our measures of capital and output to ignore a "vastly greater" range of choice and quality available to today's consumer, including the ability to fly across the continent for roughly 10–15 times the average hourly wage, instead of 400 times the average wage as in the 1930s. I want to go as far as possible toward quantifying the increase in consumer welfare in a way that makes microeconomic sense. For me, the "half a loaf" that I have achieved is a way-station to "3/4 loaf" in the next generation and maybe a "full loaf" in the generation after that. Should we follow the other route and prefer no loaf at all?

References

Denison, Edward F. "The Sources of Economic Growth in the United States and the Alternatives Before Us." Supplementary Paper No. 13. New York: Committee for Economic Development; 1962.

   "The Concept of Capital." *Review of Income and Wealth*. March, 1993; series 39, no. 1, pp. 89–108.

Gordon, Robert J. *The Measurement of Durable Goods Prices*. Chicago: University of Chicago Press for NBER; 1990.

Solow, R. M. "Technical Change and the Aggregate Production Function." *Review of Economics and Statistics*. August, 1957; vol. 39, no. 3, pp. 312–20.

Triplett, Jack E. "Concepts of Quality in Input and Output Price Measures: A Resolution of the User-Value Resource-Cost Debate." In Foss, Murray F. (ed). *The U.S. National Income and Product Account: Selected Topics*. Studies in Income and Wealth. Chicago: University of Chicago Press; 1983; vol. 47, pp. 296–311.

CHAPTER 5

Is There a Tradeoff between Unemployment and Productivity Growth?

The Transatlantic Divide

Over the past decade there has been a steady divergence in the interests of European and American macro and labor economists. Persistently high unemployment in Europe has held center stage in the concerns of Europeans, and little consensus has emerged regarding the share of blame to be attributed to cyclical or structural factors, nor on the particular mix of structural factors to be held responsible. In the United States, by contrast, there is near total agreement that fluctuations in unemployment have been cyclical in nature, and that the underlying "Non-Accelerating Inflation Rate of Unemployment" (NAIRU) has changed little over the past two decades. Since there are few puzzles in the behavior of unemployment, American economists have increasingly shifted their emphasis toward the view that the central problems of the U.S. economy are (1) slow growth in productivity and in real wages, and (2) an increasing dispersion of the income distribution that has resulted in an absolute decline in real wages for workers below the twentieth or even the fiftieth percentile (depending on the exact measure used).

This chapter explores the hypothesis that the divergence of emphasis across the Atlantic is misplaced, and that the apparently separate problems of high unemployment in Europe and low productivity growth in America may be interrelated. Is there a trade-off between low unemployment and high productivity growth? If so, what factors have caused Europe and America to move to different positions on the unemployment–productivity trade-off (UPT) schedule? What events and policies can cause this schedule to shift in a favorable or

This research was supported by the National Science Foundation. David Rose and Gareth Siegel provided outstanding help with the data and tables. Bart van Ark, Eric J. Bartlesman, and Charles Bean provided essential data on hours per employee. Charles Bean and Dennis Snower provided important comments on an earlier draft. Because of the chapter's length, it is not possible to include here either appendix tables or the explanation of data sources. These are readily available from the author.
Source. "Is There a Tradeoff between Unemployment and Productivity Growth?" In Snower, D., and de la Dehesa, G., eds. *Unemployment Policy: Government Options for the Labour Market.* Cambridge, MA: Cambridge University Press; 1997, pp. 433–63.

unfavorable direction? Are there policies that Europe could adopt that would reduce structural unemployment without eroding its advantage over the United States of faster productivity growth? In parallel, could the United States adopt policies that would boost productivity growth without creating extra structural unemployment?

Not only is there a transatlantic divide in the interests of European and American economists, but there is also an asymmetry in the degree to which they look to the other side of the Atlantic for solutions. While American economists have devoted little attention to European practices and institutions as providing lessons for the United States, in contrast many Europeans have pointed to the "flexibility" of the U.S. labor market as a likely source of the lower unemployment rate in the United States than in Europe, and as providing a desirable model for European reforms. However, the fact that buoyant U.S. employment growth has been accompanied by growing income inequality has more recently caused European economists to draw back from unqualified admiration of U.S. labor market institutions.[1] In Europe at present there is an active search for policies that might reduce unemployment without having adverse side effects on productivity or the income distribution – these are policies that we shall describe as shifting the UPT schedule in a favorable direction.

Contribution of this Chapter

This chapter provides a new perspective on alternative policies designed to reduce European unemployment. It introduces the idea of the UPT schedule and distinguishes between policies that move a country along a given schedule and those that shift the schedule. The productivity impact of alternative anti-unemployment policies therefore becomes a criterion, little discussed previously, for choosing among these policies. However, the chapter shows how misleading is the facile contrast of Europe following a path of high productivity growth, high unemployment, and relatively greater income equality, in contrast to the opposite path being pursued by the United States. Many structural shocks that initially create a positive trade-off between productivity and unemployment set in motion a dynamic path of adjustment involving capital accumulation or decumulation that in principle can eliminate the trade-off.

5.1 BASIC ANALYTICS

Our theoretical discussion begins by setting out the UPT schedule. We then provide an interpretation of this schedule in terms of the standard labor market model so often used to analyze the persistence of European unemployment. That model then helps us to distinguish between factors that cause movements along the UPT schedule and those factors that cause the UPT schedule to shift its position.

---

[1] Saint-Paul (1994) is a particularly articulate and convincing example.

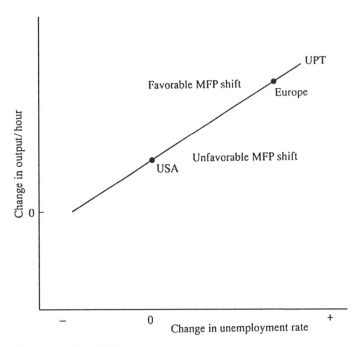

Figure 5.1. The UPT Schedule

The UPT Schedule

The UPT schedule can be drawn in terms of levels or changes. Figure 5.1 illustrates the version expressed in terms of changes, plotting the change in output per hour on the vertical axis against the change in the unemployment rate on the horizontal axis. The "change" version of the UPT schedule is intended to focus on developments over the length of one business cycle or longer, for example, causes of changes in the unemployment rate over the fifteen-year period between 1979 and 1994. The point labeled "U.S.A." is plotted at zero on the horizontal axis, reflecting the fact that the United States had no change in its unemployment rate between 1979 and 1994, while the point labeled "Europe" is plotted further to the right, reflecting the fact that the unemployment rate for the EC/EU more than doubled, from 5.7 percent in 1979 to 11.8 percent in 1994. In the vertical direction the change in productivity for Europe is greater than for the United States.

Why do we focus on the change version of the UPT schedule rather than the level? By most measures the *level* of labor productivity is still higher in the United States than in Europe, and so a plot of the level of productivity versus the level of unemployment for the United States and Europe would have a negative slope. The high level of productivity in the United States is assumed to reflect historical factors dating back before 1960, whereas we want to examine the consequences of more recent changes in structure and in policies on the evolution of productivity and the unemployment rate. The change version of the UPT schedule allows us to "factor out" contributions to the high level of U.S. productivity that predate the period of interest.

It is important to note that the vertical axis of the UPT diagram refers to the change in output per hour, not the change in multifactor productivity (hereafter MFP, that is output relative to both labor and capital inputs, not just labor input). We can establish some basic relationships starting with the definition that labor's income share (S) is equal to the real wage (W/P) divided by output per hour (Q/H). Using lower-case letters for logs, this definition implies that the growth rate of the real wage is equal to the growth rate of productivity plus the growth rate of labor's share:

$$(\Delta w - \Delta p) = (\Delta q - \Delta h) + \Delta s. \tag{1}$$

Using the same notation as in (1), and designating the change (or growth rate) of MFP as Δa, the growth rate of capital as Δk, and the elasticity of output to a change in capital as $(1 - \alpha)$, the change in output per hour is:

$$\Delta q - \Delta h = \Delta a + (1 - \alpha)(\Delta k - \Delta h). \tag{2}$$

Equation (2) neatly separates factors that account for the positive slope of the UPT schedule from those that account for shifts in that schedule. Any positive change in Δa shifts the schedule up and a negative change shifts the schedule down. In contrast, any event (labeled below as a "wage-setting shock") that causes an increase in $\Delta k - \Delta h$ by simultaneously raising unemployment while reducing employment (and hours), for a given growth rate of capital, causes the economy to move northeast along the UPT schedule from a point like that marked "USA" to a point like that marked "Europe." Finally, for any given change in unemployment and employment, a downward shift in the growth rate of capital shifts the UPT schedule downward, just as does a reduction in Δa.

The initial focus in our analysis is on factors that cause movements along the UPT schedule, while subsequently we examine factors that cause adverse or favorable shifts in the schedule. The ultimate goal is to distinguish unemployment-reducing policies for Europe that tend to have an adverse impact on productivity (moving Europe southwest from its position in Figure 5.1) from those that do not.

The Standard Labor Market Model

The relationship between unemployment and productivity is implicit in the standard labor market model so often used to discuss the persistence of European unemployment.[2] Figure 5.2 incorporates three relationships. First, the kinked line N^S is a labor-supply curve, relating the total labor force plotted horizontally to the levels of the real wage plotted vertically. At the level of unemployment

---

[2] This section provides a bare-bones graphical discussion of a model developed in more detail by Alogoskoufis and Manning (1988), Blanchard (1990), Bean (1994), and Layard *et al.* (1991).

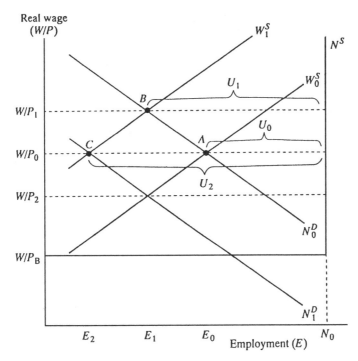

Figure 5.2. Unemployment and Productivity in the Standard Labor Market Model

benefits $(W/P)_B$ the schedule is horizontal while at higher levels of the real wage the schedule is vertical, following the weight of evidence suggesting that this relationship is highly inelastic.

Second, the downward-sloping N^D curves represent the negative relationship between the level of employment and the real wage. In elementary textbooks, this relationship is interpreted as reflecting the price-taking, profit-maximizing behavior of firms operating in competitive labor markets. For such firms, employment is determined by setting the real wage equal to the marginal product of labor, which is assumed to be subject to diminishing returns with increased employment. Thus, for this analysis to be consistent with a production function exhibiting constant returns to scale, the quantity of other factors of production (especially capital, energy, and materials) is held constant along any particular N^D curve. However, in much of the recent literature this graphical analysis has been shown to be consistent with imperfectly competitive product markets in which prices are set as a mark-up on marginal labor cost. In this case, any tendency for the mark-up to increase with the level of employment would increase the negative slope of the schedule. In the imperfectly competitive case these downward-sloping schedules reflect the joint outcome of pricing and employment decisions by firms and are sometimes called "price-setting" schedules.

In contrast to the traditional textbook diagram, in which the upward-sloping lines are called labor supply schedules, in the recent literature these are called wage-setting schedules (W^S). Higher employment is postulated to elicit higher real wages as the outcome of bargaining between unions and employer associations and is also consistent with the efficiency wage model. As employment increases, the bargaining power of workers is postulated to increase.

In Figure 5.2, the economy is initially in equilibrium at point A along curves N_0^D and W_0^S, equilibrium employment is represented by E_0 and equilibrium unemployment (U_0) by N_0-E_0. In the competitive interpretation of the labor demand curve, the marginal product of labor is $(W/P)_0$, and in the special Cobb–Douglas case, the average product of labor is $(W/P)_0/s$, where s is labor's income share.

Wage-Setting Shocks

Now, let us examine two types of shocks and inquire into the circumstances in which an increase in unemployment could coincide with an increase in the level of productivity (which in our discussion of the labor market diagram refers to output per employee, since hours per employee are assumed fixed, as is MFP). First, consider a wage-setting shock that shifts the W_0^S curve upward to the position W_1^S. Such a shock might be caused by an autonomous increase in the bargaining power of trade unions, or any event (like the French general strike of spring 1968) in which a given group of workers band together and autonomously raises the wages that it requires to supply a particular amount of employment. The result of such a wage-setting shock is to move the economy from point A to point B, where the original labor demand curve N_0^D intersects the new higher W_1^S curve.

Such a wage-setting shock establishes a trade-off between higher unemployment and higher output per employee. At point B unemployment has risen from U_0 to U_1, while the marginal product of labor has risen from $(W/P)_0$ to $(W/P)_1$. In the Cobb–Douglas case, the average product of labor increases in proportion to the marginal product.

The economy, however, is unlikely to settle at point B for long. Compared to point A, at point B output and employment are lower, and the marginal product of capital has fallen because the fixed stock of capital is being combined with less labor input. The demand for capital will fall, and a period of disinvestment will occur that shifts the labor demand curve down and to the left to a position like N_1^D. If the higher wage-setting schedule remains in effect, then on standard assumptions about the structure of the model, the labor demand curve must shift downward to the point at which the new wage-setting schedule intersects the original real wage $(W/P)_0$, as shown at point C in Figure 5.2.[3]

---

[3] Consider a Cobb–Douglas production function $Y = AH^\alpha K^{1-\alpha}$, the same as (2) in the text (where the latter is converted into logs). The marginal product of labor and the real wage are equal to $\alpha Y/H$ and the marginal product of capital is equal to $(1-\alpha)Y/K$. Designating

Once the process of adjustment in capital input is completed, unemployment has grown from the initial level U_0 to the intermediate level U_1 to the final level U_2. However, at point C we do not observe a trade-off between unemployment and output per hour, since the marginal and average products of labor have returned to their initial values (the same as point C as at point A), while unemployment has increased greatly. However, this model does help capture a key feature of the European unemployment puzzle of the 1980s and 1990s – at point C there has been a substantial increase in the unemployment rate without any decline in the rate of capacity utilization, which is assumed to be constant in the model. At point C Europe has "disinvested" and substantially reduced the ratio of capital to the labor force, without reducing at all the ratio of capital input to labor input. Unemployment has occurred in an environment of disinvestment in which there is now insufficient capital fully to employ the labor force (N_0).

Indeed, a notable feature of the permanent rise in European unemployment in the 1980s is that this rise was not accompanied by a permanent drop in capacity utilization. For instance, German unemployment was higher in 1990 than in 1979 but so was the rate of capacity utilization. As shown by Franz and Gordon (1993), the mean utilization unemployment rate ("MURU") for Germany has increased almost as much as the actual unemployment rate, implying that there no longer exists sufficient productive capacity to provide jobs for enough people to attain the unemployment rates of the 1970s, much less the 1960s. Bean (1994, p. 613) shows that the same phenomenon has occurred for the EC/EU as a whole.

Energy Price Shocks

Most European discussions of the productivity–unemployment connection have in mind not wage-setting shocks but rather the effects of the oil shocks, and these can be illustrated in Figure 5.3. An increase in the real price of oil shifts down the labor demand curve to schedule N_1^D, by reducing the quantity of energy and hence the marginal product of labor.[4] Starting from point A, the economy's equilibrium position shifts southwest to point D. As before, unemployment

the initial equilibrium situation at point A with asterisks, the wage-setting curve is $w = \alpha(1 + \lambda)(Y^*/H^*)(H/H^*)^\lambda$, where at point A the "wage push" parameter (λ) is initially set at zero. A hypothetical "wage push" of 3 percent ($\lambda = 0.03$) pushes the economy from point A to point B, and assuming $\alpha = 0.75$ and $\lambda = 0.5$, we can calculate that there will follow at point B an increase in the real wage of 1 percent and a decline in labor input of 3.9 percent. Once we allow subsequent disinvestment that decreases the capital stock, and if the capital stock continues to adjust until the marginal product of capital is equal to a fixed supply price of capital, then output, labor input, and capital input must all decline in proportion, so that the Y/H and Y/K ratios return to their original values. With the assumed parameters of the wage setting curve, this requires a decline in output and factor inputs of 5.8 percent at point C.

[4] If MFP is defined as output relative to the weighted inputs of not just labor and capital but also energy, then MFP remains constant and the entire cause of the downward shift of the schedule N_1^D is the reduced quantity of energy. However, if as in the empirical research in this chapter, MFP is calculated relative to the weighted inputs of just labor and capital input, then MFP is lower along schedule N_1^D than along schedule N_0^D.

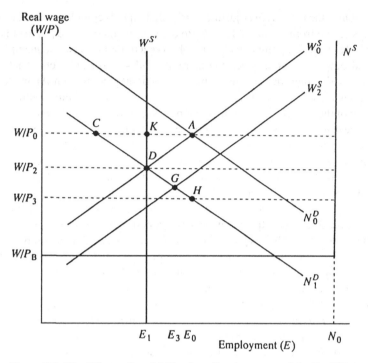

Figure 5.3. The Effects of an Oil Shock on Employment and the Real Wage

has increased and the marginal product of labor has fallen from $(W/P)_0$ to $(W/P)_2$ and (in the Cobb–Douglas case) the average product of labor falls in proportion.

Thus far we have learned that a shock that increases unemployment may either raise or lower productivity. An adverse productivity shock can create a negative correlation between the level of unemployment and the level of productivity, while a wage-setting shock can create a positive correlation between the level of unemployment and the level of productivity, at least over the period of time prior to the downward adjustment of the capital stock to the wage-setting shock.

How does the economy adjust to an energy price shock? Several possibilities are illustrated in Figure 5.3, where points A and C represent the same situation as in Figure 5.2. During the early 1980s the seminal work of Branson and Rotemberg (1980), Sachs (1979) and Bruno and Sachs (1985), emphasized the contrast between real wage rigidity in Europe and real wage flexibility in the United States. Taken literally, this dichotomy would imply that a given adverse energy price shock would shift Europe from point A to point C, as the result of a horizontal wage-setting curve. In contrast, the same shock would shift the U.S.A. from point A to point H, as the result of flexible wage-setting institutions that cause the wage-setting curve to shift down until it intersects the lower labor demand curve at the original level of employment.

Other possibilities are suggested by Elmeskov and MacFarlan (1993), who use the same diagram to interpret the concept of hysteresis. With full hysteresis, the equilibrium unemployment rate depends on the current unemployment rate. Following an energy price shock (or an adverse aggregate demand shock) that shifts the labor demand curve in Figure 5.3 from N_0^D to N_1^D the economy moves from A to D, as before. But under full hysteresis there is a vertical long-run wage-setting schedule $W^{S'}$ which moves to the current level of employment. Under partial hysteresis or "slow adjustment," the wage-setting schedule does not shift down all the way to point H but comes to rest at a schedule like W_2^S, and employment is prevented from rising above E_3. In short, points C, D, G and H (all of which lie along the lower labor demand curve N_1^D) represent alternative responses to an adverse productivity shock under the extremes of real wage rigidity and full flexibility, and the intermediate cases of full and partial hysteresis.

We note that, while the *event* of an adverse energy price shock can create a negative correlation between unemployment and productivity, any *adjustment following the shock* along the labor demand curve (e.g., between points C and H) can create a positive correlation. In this sense any slow or gradual adjustment of wage-setting following a shock creates the same positive correlation between unemployment and productivity as occurs in Figure 5.2 following a wage-setting shock.

Much of the literature in the early 1980s (e.g., Bruno and Sachs, 1985), emphasized that labor's share of national income had risen in Europe at the time of the first energy price shock, and took this as *prima facie* evidence that European unemployment was structural, caused by excessive real wage rigidity. As pointed out by Krugman (1987, pp. 60–5), Bean (1994, p. 577), and others, there is no such necessary link between real wage rigidity and labor's share. If the labor demand curve N_1^D is derived from a Cobb–Douglas production function, then labor's share cannot change at all under the assumptions of perfect competition and constant returns. Any observed increase in labor's share must be interpreted as the result of a temporary disequilibrium, i.e., that the economy is operating off of its labor demand curve at a point like K, so that the real wage has risen above labor's average product. A subsequent decline in labor's share, such as that which occurred in the EC in the 1980s, can then be interpreted as the result of lagged or partial adjustment that moves the economy from a point like K to a point like G.

5.2 AN EXAMPLE: THE MINIMUM WAGE

Data and Theory

The minimum wage provides the most straightforward example of a wage-setting shock that can simultaneously change the unemployment rate and the level of productivity. France and the United States differ along many dimensions, but three stand out from the perspective of this chapter. First, French

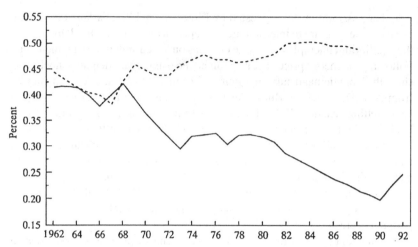

Figure 5.4. The Minimum Wage Relative to Average Hourly Compensation, 1962–92 (*Source.* France: Bazan and Martin (1991, chart 2, p. 204); U.S.A.: Statutory minimum wage divided by average hourly compensation)

unemployment, which was previously well below the U.S. rate, climbed to exceed the U.S. rate in every year after 1983 (and to exceed the EC/EU average in every year after 1988). The 1994 French unemployment rate of 12.6 percent exceeded by a wide margin the U.S. rate of 6.1 percent.[5] Second, French productivity growth exceeded that in the United States during the 1979–92 period, but by a much wider margin of 1.51 points per annum outside of manufacturing than the 0.25 margin of French superiority in manufacturing.[6] Third, the effective minimum wage (SMIC) continued its slow upward creep in France during the 1980s, as shown in Figure 5.4, while in the United States the effective minimum wage had fallen from roughly the French level in the late 1960s to well under half of the French level after 1982.[7] Figure 5.4 understates the importance of the SMIC, since the proportion of the French workforce covered by the SMIC is much higher than the equivalent proportion in the United States (Bazan and Martin, 1991, p. 214).

[5] These comparisons refer to the official U.S. 1994 unemployment rate and the projection of the French 1994 unemployment rate, *OECD Economic Outlook* (December 1994, annex table 5.4, p. A58).

[6] The French and U.S. output per hour growth rates for 1979–92 are, respectively, 2.14 and 0.63 percent per year in private nonfarm, nonmanufacturing, nonmining, and 2.85 and 2.50 percent per year in manufacturing.

[7] Note that the data in Figure 5.4 use the Bazan and Martin (1991) data for France but not for the USA. The denominator for the US minimum wage used by Bazan and Martin, that is, average hourly earnings for non-farm private production workers, is well known to be biased downward quite severely as a measure of the growth of nominal compensation (see Bosworth and Perry, 1994). In Figure 5.4 we use as a denominator average hourly compensation.

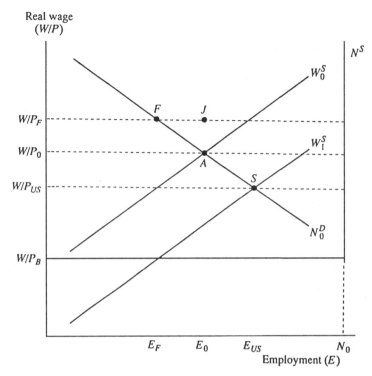

Figure 5.5. The Effect of an Increase in the Real Minimum Wage in France and a Decrease in the U.S.A.

The labor market diagram in Figure 5.5 provides an analysis of an increase in the French real minimum wage and a decrease in the U.S. real minimum wage. Note that, to use the same labor market analysis provided in Figures 5.2 and 5.3, we define the minimum wage in real terms, that is, divided by the product price deflator, in contrast to the data plotted in Figure 5.4, which define the effective minimum wage in terms of the ratio of the statutory minimum wage to nominal labor compensation. Since real labor compensation for low-paid workers grew in France much faster than in the United States during this period, Figure 5.4 understates the divergence between the two countries in the real minimum wage.

In the theoretical labor market diagram of Figure 5.5, both economies are assumed to share the same wage-setting and labor demand schedules, as well as the same total labor supply schedule. The economy is initially in equilibrium at point A, as in Figures 5.2 and 5.3. Now let us introduce an increase in the French real minimum wage that is sufficient to raise the overall French real wage from $(W/P)_0$ to $(W/P)_F$. The economy moves to point F, and employment falls from E_0 to E_F. Assuming competitive labor markets and instantaneous adjustment, the marginal product of labor rises in France in proportion to the increase in the real wage.

A different interpretation is required for the decline in the effective minimum wage in the United States. If the economy starts out in equilibrium at point A, then a decline in the minimum wage to the lower level $(W/P)_{US}$ will be ineffective, since the minimum wage will be below the market-clearing wage. In this case, we would still observe a contrast between France and the United States represented by the difference between points F and A; in France productivity would grow and employment would shrink relative to the United States.

Another possibility is that the steady erosion of the real minimum wage in the United States has contributed to a downward shift in the wage-setting curve to a position like W_1^S – this downward shift may have been partly due to other causes, such as the decline in U.S. union density. Such a downward shift in the wage-setting curve would reduce the U.S. real wage from $(W/P)_0$ to $(W/P)_{US}$, shift the economy to point S and boost employment from E_0 to E_{US}. In this analysis, the divergent behavior of the real minimum wage can help to explain the divergent behavior of both unemployment and productivity in France and the United States in the 1980s.

Beyond affecting the evolution of unemployment and productivity, what would be the other major effects of the divergence in effective minimum wages depicted in Figures 5.4 and 5.5? The real earnings of low-paid French workers would be boosted and those of low-paid American workers would be depressed, thus helping to explain the contrast between an income dispersion that widened in the United States in the 1980s while remaining roughly constant in France. If there were no unemployment compensation system, there would be an increased dispersion in incomes between the employed French, now making more, and the unemployed, now making zero. But in the extreme case of an unemployment compensation system with a 100 percent replacement ratio (ignoring taxes), an increase in the real minimum wage would raise the welfare not only of the employed but of the unemployed as well. The French government would be obliged to pay out extra unemployment compensation shown in Figure 5.5 by the rectangle FJE_0E_F. This amount takes the form of a transfer to the current unemployed from some combination of current workers and future generations of taxpayers.[8]

If the labor demand curve in Figure 5.5 had a unitary elasticity, then labor income (and labor's income share) would be the same at points A and F. With full-replacement unemployment compensation, the most obvious effect would be to create an increase in government transfer expenditures as a share of GDP, with possible side-effects in the form of higher taxes or a higher public debt–GDP ratio, which in the latter case might lead as well to higher real interest rates.

---

[8] Saint-Paul (1994, p. 3) argues that

> an increase in the minimum wage may well have adverse impacts on inequality. This is because while it redistributes income from the skilled to the unskilled workers, by creating unemployment it also redistributes income from the poorest to the lower-middle class.

This argument appears to neglect the unemployment compensation received by those who lose their jobs as a result of a higher minimum wage.

Another effect, often discussed in connection with the hysteresis hypothesis, would be an erosion of the skills of the newly unemployed (E_0-E_F). Ironically, measured national productivity could increase while the skills of the population deteriorate, because a decrease in the employment–population ratio would be accompanied by a decline in the skills of the unemployed.

Literature on the Effects of the Minimum Wage

There is a contradiction between the analysis of Figure 5.5 and the recent literature on the effects of the minimum wage. Studies like those of Bazan and Martin (1991) for France, Dickens *et al.* (1993) for the United Kingdom, and Card (1992), Card, Katz and Krueger (1993), Card and Krueger (1994), and Krueger (1994) for the United States, all seem to indicate that the minimum wage has small or negligible effects on employment. These results occur despite findings that minimum wages "spill over" to other wages, for instance the finding by Bazan and Martin (1991) that a one percentage point increase in the real value of the SMIC increases the real value of real youth earnings by 0.4 of a percentage point.

There are at least two interpretations of the small measured employment effects of changes in the minimum wage. An equilibrium interpretation is that the labor demand curve in Figure 5.5 is extremely steep, accounting for the absence of employment effects in the studies cited above. Under this interpretation an increase in the minimum wage is an excellent way to boost productivity with minimal employment effects. However, one doubts that the hypothesis of a near-vertical long-run labor demand curve can be supported, as this would conflict with a large production function literature supporting an elasticity of substitution in the range of 0.5 to 1.0 (Bean, 1994, p. 614), and with the long-run constancy of labor's share that is consistent with an elasticity of 1.0. Indeed, Bazan and Martin (1991, p. 215) "believe it to be the case" that an increase in real youth labor costs have reduced youth employment, despite their inability to establish this response "satisfactorily."

An alternative view is that the short-run response is small while the long-run response is large, that is, that the process of substitution caused by a significant increase in the minimum wage (or any other shock to the wage-setting curve) takes a significant time to occur. In this interpretation the labor demand curve gradually rotates through time, starting steep and becoming flatter, and this lagged adjustment process is inadequately captured in studies that focus on short-run responses.

The same problems may affect the studies of the U.S. minimum wage by Card and his coauthors. These studies found no adverse employment effects following increases in the minimum wage above the Federal level in particular states of the United States. But there is a different problem as well. It is very likely that by 1990 the U.S. minimum wage had dropped so low as to be ineffective, that is, to be below the market-clearing wage rate like point A in Figure 5.5. The U.S. studies cited here focused on increases in the minimum wage from a low level, and if at this level the minimum wage was ineffective, then it is no surprise that no employment effects could be found.

Finally, even when academic studies fail to provide convincing demonstrations of effects that seem theoretically plausible, anecdotal evidence seems compelling that the divergent evolution of the French and U.S. minimum wages plotted in Figure 5.4 has resulted in very different employment practices, particularly in the service sector. United States supermarkets (often in some places, always in others) employ two people at each check-out lane, one to ring up the purchases and the other to place the purchases in bags. French supermarkets expect customers to bag their own groceries and sometimes to provide their own bags. Similarly, American restaurants, from the high-priced gourmet level down to the midlevel, employ "busboys" to set and clear tables (these are often recent legal or illegal immigrants) while "waitpeople" take orders and serve food. In contrast, in much of Europe staffing levels in restaurants are noticeably lower, and waitpeople set and clear tables in addition to taking orders and serving food.

5.3 MECHANISMS

As we have seen, a positive correlation between unemployment and the level of productivity can be generated by any factor that shifts the wage-setting curve, and this correlation can persist for as long as it takes for the capital stock to adjust. In this section we distinguish those variables that shift the wage-setting schedule and cause movements *along* the UPT schedule of Figure 5.1 from those other factors that may cause changes in productivity or in unemployment without simultaneously changing both; these cause shifts in Figure 5.1's UPT schedule.

Shifts in the UPT Schedule

First we translate the preceding labor market analysis in terms of the UPT schedule, which reappears in Figure 5.6. Recall from our discussion of Figure 5.1 that movements in MFP and in capital relative to a fixed level of employment and unemployment cause shifts in the UPT schedule, while changes in employment and unemployment occurring with a fixed level of MFP and capital input cause movements along the UPT schedule.

The economy begins at point A in Figure 5.6, the same situation of initial equilibrium as at point A of Figure 5.2, where the initial unemployment rate is U_0. Next, an adverse wage-setting shock shifts the economy to point B, as in Figure 5.2, with a higher marginal and average product of labor and a higher unemployment rate U_1. The initial UPT_0 schedule drawn between points A and B in Figure 5.6 shows that over the period of time encompassed by situations A and B, the unemployment rate increases by the amount U_1-U_0, while growth in productivity (output per employee) is boosted above whatever rate prevailed at point A.

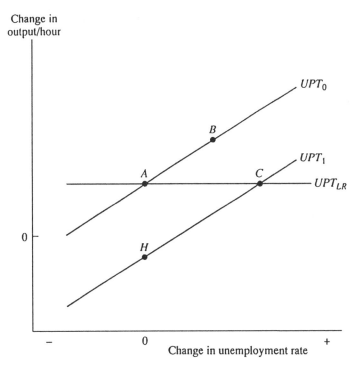

Figure 5.6. Movements Along and Shifts in the UPT Schedule

In the long run there will be a period of disinvestment that, as shown in Figure 5.2, reduces productivity and the real wage to the original level at point C while further boosting the unemployment rate from U_1 to U_2. The same situation is shown in Figure 5.6 by the downward shift in the UPT schedule to UPT_1. A point like C depicts the cumulative change from the initial equilibrium situation at point A. There is a cumulative change in unemployment (U_2-U_0), while productivity growth is unchanged from the initial situation at point A. Thus one conclusion from this analysis is that the process of capital accumulation implies that in the long run the UPT schedule becomes flat or even horizontal, as implied by the horizontal schedule UPT_{LR}.

The movements in Figure 5.6 from point A to B to C are caused by a wage-setting shock followed by capital decumulation. Other factors that might shift the UPT schedule in an unfavorable (downward) direction include an adverse oil price shock, while better education or an exogenous improvement in the rate of innovation would shift the UPT schedule in a favorable (upward direction). Figure 5.6 suggest that we might fruitfully distinguish those causes of higher European unemployment that can be interpreted as initially causing a northeast movement along the UPT schedule from those that can be interpreted as causing shifts in that schedule. Similarly, we might investigate the suggested causes of slow productivity growth and increased inequality in the United States by applying the same distinction involving movements along versus shifts in the UPT schedule.

Sources of Upward Shifts in the Wage-Setting Schedule

Bean (1994, pp. 579) interprets the wage-setting mechanism in terms of this equation:

$$w - p^e = -\gamma_1 U + (1 - \gamma_2)(w - p)_{-1} + Z_w \Gamma + \epsilon_w, \tag{3}$$

where lower-case letters are logs, w is the log wage, p is the log price, U is the unemployment rate, and Z_w is a vector of variables "that include the reservation wage and whatever factors are thought to influence the markup over the reservation wage." Thus any element in Z_w may in principle be a source of a shift in the wage-setting schedule and at the same time a source of a movement along a given UPT schedule.

The typical European list of elements that would shift Z_w upward (drawn from Bean, 1994, pp. 587–96) includes the following.

1. A *higher minimum wage*, as discussed previously.
2. An *increase in the level and/or coverage of unemployment benefits*, which raise the effective replacement ratio of the unemployment benefits system and hence the reservation wage.[9]
3. An *increase in the price wedge*. Since firms care about the product-price real wage and workers care about the consumption-price real wage, any increase in consumer prices relative to product prices would shift up the wage-setting schedule. An increase in this wedge occurred at the time of the first oil shock, which also marks the beginning of the productivity growth slowdown. An increase in the price wedge can also be caused by a decline in the terms of trade that raises import prices relative to the prices of domestic production.
4. An *increase in the tax wedge*. Since firms pay pre-tax wages but workers receive after-tax wages, any increase in payroll or income taxes can shift up the wage-setting schedule. Tax wedges in Europe range from 40 to 70 percent, in contrast to a range of 20–25 percent in the United States and Japan.[10]
5. An *increase in worker militancy*. An increase in union power would shift up the wage-setting schedule, raising both unemployment and productivity. Trade union membership as a share of the labor force is only 15 percent in the United States but is much higher in most

---

[9] See Lindbeck (1994b, p. 1)

It is a commonplace that very generous unemployment benefits with low or even unlimited duration and with lax work tests contribute to unemployment persistence.

[10] Lindbeck (1994b, p. 9).

European countries, in the 30–40 percent range in Germany, Italy, and Britain, and 80 percent in Sweden (France is an exception with a share below that of the United States). One problem with this explanation is that, while relatively high, the trade union membership share fell in most European countries in the 1980s (primarily as a result of the growing share of employment in the service sector).

Factors that May Shift the UPT Schedule

Numerous other factors have been cited as causes of high European unemployment, but these do not involve causation going initially from wage-setting behavior to subsequent response by productivity and the unemployment rate. Hence they are best interpreted as factors causing an adverse (downward) shift in the UPT schedule of Figure 5.6.

6. *Supply shock combined with real wage rigidity.* As in Figure 5.3, an adverse supply shock (e.g., a higher real price of oil) can simultaneously cause unemployment to rise and productivity to fall, thus shifting the UPT schedule downward. The dichotomy between real wage rigidity and real-wage flexibility determines where the economy winds up on the lower UPT schedule, so that the position of Europe might be interpreted as similar to point C on the lower UPT schedule of Figure 5.6, and that of the USA at a point like H.

7. *Mismatch.* A shift in technology may create unemployment if there are barriers to labor mobility across occupations, regions and industrial sectors. An increased pace of technological change or growing openness to foreign trade might increase structural unemployment without causing a change in productivity, either up or down. Thus mismatch can be interpreted as shifting the UPT schedule to the right, i.e., down.

8. *Labor market regulations.* Numerous forms of employment regulation lead to the general diagnosis that European labor markets are more "rigid" than in the United States. The exhaustive analysis of Grubb and Wells (1993) includes among these regulations restrictions on employers' freedom to dismiss workers; limits on the use or the legal validity of fixed-term contracts; limits on the use of temporary work; restrictions on weekly hours of regular or overtime work; and limits on use of part-time work. Also included in this category is mandated severance pay. Here the important point is that when aggregate demand is high, such regulations can stabilize employment and reduce the incidence of temporary layoffs in response to mild recessions. But when a major decline in demand occurs, perhaps amplified by an upward shift in the wage-setting schedule for the reasons outlined above, such regulations can stabilize *unemployment* by raising

the present discounted value of the cost to employers of hiring an extra worker in response to an upturn in demand.[11] Again, such regulations may increase unemployment without necessarily changing productivity and should be interpreted as causing a rightward shift in the UPT schedule.

9. *Product market regulations.* A particular form of regulation that potentially boosts both unemployment and productivity is the draconian type of shop-closing rules imposed in Germany and some other countries. A movement to Sunday and evening opening, underway currently in Britain, clearly creates jobs but reduces retailing productivity by spreading the same transactions over more labor hours. While such regulations push unemployment and productivity in the same direction as a wage-setting shock, there is no reason why the mix of unemployment and productivity responses should trace out a labor demand curve, and hence we treat such regulations as shifting the UPT schedule rather than causing a movement along it.

Sources of Slow Productivity Growth and Increasing Inequality in the United States

Bean (1994) effectively criticizes much of the research attributing the rise in European unemployment to particular items on the above list and concludes that there must be multiple causes, rather than a single cause. Can we identify some of the above items as promising explanations by comparing behavior in the United States and Europe? While the replacement ratio of unemployment benefits (item (1) on the above list) changed little in either the European Community or in the United States between the late 1960s and late 1980s, the fraction of U.S. employees eligible for benefits has fallen substantially. While the price wedge (3) behaved similarly in the European Community and the United States, the tax wedge (4) in the European Community is both higher and increased more between the late 1960s and late 1980s (Bean, 1994, p. 586). The rigid real wage hypothesis (6) seems consistent with the observed bulge in the European Community labor share between 1974 and 1982. While there is no reason for mismatch (7) to have difference between Europe and the United States, there is clearly a major difference between the United States and particular European countries in the extent of labor market and product market regulation (8) and (9).

Perhaps the leading candidate for causing divergent behavior across the Atlantic is the marked decline in U.S. union membership (5), from 26.2 percent in 1977 to 15.8 percent in 1993 (union members as a fraction of wage and salary workers). Together with the sharp reduction in the real minimum wage (1), this decline in union representation plausibly exerted downward pressure on the U.S. wage-setting schedule throughout the 1970s and 1980s.

---

[11] See Lindbeck (1994a, pp. 2–3).

The result was the well known dichotomy between rapid growth in U.S. employment relative to Europe, but a less widely recognized implication is that some part of the continuing productivity growth divergence must have occurred as well.

In addition to unions and the minimum wage, any U.S. list of factors causing depressed real wages and productivity must include immigration and imports. Annual *legal* immigration as a percent of the population has steadily increased in each decade of the postwar period (Simon, 1991), although this percentage is still far below the records set during 1890–1914 (also a period of slow productivity growth). In addition, a large and undetermined amount of illegal immigration has added substantially to the supply of unskilled labor and plausibly added to downward pressure on the wage-setting schedule. Finally, Johnson and Stafford (1993) have argued convincingly that an increased supply of medium-technology goods from newly industrializing countries can cause an absolute decline in the real wage of an advanced country (or group of countries) that previously had a monopoly on the manufacturing of those goods. To the extent that the United States was more open to Asian imports than some European countries that imposed quantitative trade restrictions (notably France and Italy), imports of goods can put the same kind of downward pressure on the wage-setting schedule as imports of people, that is, immigration.

5.4 PRODUCTIVITY GROWTH DIFFERENCES ACROSS COUNTRIES AND SECTORS

The growth rates of output per hour and of MFP for seven countries, nine sectors, and three alternative aggregates (private, private nonfarm, and private nonfarm, nonmanufacturing, nonmining – PNFNMNM) are provided in tables available from the author. Also available are tables showing *levels* of output per hour for each sector in 1992, converted into dollars at OECD 1992 exchange rates.

Means and Variances of Output per Hour Growth Rates

Some of the main features of the data are summarized in Table 5.1, which displays in the top frame unweighted means and variances across the nine sectors for each of the seven countries, and in the bottom frame unweighted means and variances across the seven countries for each of the nine sectors. The averages show the now familiar post-1973 slowdown and indicate that post-1973 productivity growth for all countries averaged together was about the same in 1973–9 as in 1973–92. This would appear to rule out the energy price shocks as a major causative factor.

Every country experienced a post-1973 slowdown, but some (United States, Canada, and Japan) did better during 1979–92 than 1973–9, while the four European countries all experienced slower productivity growth after 1979 than during 1973–9. The bottom section of Table 5.2 shows that every sector

Table 5.1. *Growth Rates of Output Per Hour, Mean and Variance by Country and Sector*

Country	1960–73	1973–9	1979–92
United States	2.15 (3.99)	−0.95 (13.83)	2.01 (3.93)
Canada	3.53 (3.14)	0.77 (10.14)	1.64 (1.17)
Japan	8.47 (5.68)	2.68 (6.14)	3.17 (0.91)
France	4.64 (4.13)	3.68 (2.08)	3.14 (2.86)
Germany	4.97 (2.01)	4.23 (3.18)	2.36 (2.05)
Italy	6.38 (2.05)	1.91 (3.09)	1.87 (3.38)
United Kingdom	4.02 (5.67)	3.32 (23.59)	2.91 (9.27)
Average	4.88 (3.81)	2.23 (9.57)	2.44 (3.37)

Sector	1960–73	1973–9	1979–92
Agriculture	6.59 (3.87)	2.59 (7.77)	4.49 (2.09)
Mining	5.67 (17.07)	1.83 (97.82)	3.55 (6.64)
Manufacturing	5.93 (5.57)	2.89 (5.48)	2.82 (0.98)
Utilities	6.08 (1.30)	3.25 (5.65)	2.45 (3.48)
Construction	3.49 (10.74)	0.74 (2.01)	1.67 (0.84)
Trade	4.35 (5.02)	1.92 (2.03)	2.09 (0.89)
Transport/communication	5.15 (1.18)	2.91 (3.61)	2.93 (3.21)
FIRE[a]	2.40 (5.94)	2.22 (1.60)	1.09 (0.94)
Services	3.52 (7.03)	1.42 (2.32)	0.62 (3.17)
Average	4.80 (6.30)	2.20 (14.25)	2.41 (2.37)
Av. excluding mining	4.69 (4.95)	2.24 (3.80)	2.27 (1.84)

Note. [a]Fire, insurance and real estate.

experienced a post-1973 slowdown. In agriculture, mining and construction, productivity growth was more rapid after 1979 than during 1973–9, while for manufacturing and trade there was no difference, and for transport/communication, FIRE, and services, there was a further slowdown after 1979.

Is productivity growth more variable across countries or across sectors? The variances across countries within given sectors are averaged with and without mining, because of the huge variance of mining (including oil production) productivity during the oil shock period, 1973–9. Comparing the first (1960–73) and last (1979–92) periods, the variance across sectors for given countries was smaller than the variance across countries for given sectors in the earlier period, whereas the reverse was true in the latter period. The relatively low cross-country within-sector variance during 1979–92 suggests that technological convergence may have played a role in causing rapid productivity growth outside the United States prior to 1973 or 1979, followed by more modest rates as individual sectors neared the frontier achieved by American technology.

Table 5.2. Growth Rates of Output Per Hour, the Contribution of Capital, and Multifactor Productivity, Nonfarm Private Business Sector, 1960–92

	Output per Hour			Contribution of Capital			Multifactor Productivity		
	1960–73	1973–9	1979–92	1960–73	1973–9	1979–92	1960–73	1973–9	1979–92
United States	1.92	0.46	1.20	0.57	0.60	0.82	1.35	−0.14	−0.38
Canada	3.02	1.27	1.41	0.72	0.91	1.45	2.30	0.36	−0.04
Japan	8.23	3.08	3.22	–	1.79	1.59	–	1.29	1.63
France	4.90	3.94	2.55	1.26	1.55	0.98	3.64	2.39	1.57
Germany	5.33	4.38	2.36	1.90	1.69	0.92	3.43	2.69	1.44
Italy	6.71	1.99	1.90	1.15	−0.64	0.19	5.56	2.63	1.71
United Kingdom	3.53	2.20	1.27	1.21	1.04	0.05	2.32	1.16	1.22

What Did Capital Contribute to the Productivity Slowdown?

Our theoretical analysis treats MFP growth as exogenous. The growth rate of output per hour relative to MFP growth can be affected by wage-setting shocks that boost real wages and productivity, or by subsequent disinvestment that reduces real wages and productivity.

The relation between growth in output per hour and in MFP is defined in (2) above, which is repeated here:

$$\Delta q - \Delta h = \Delta a + (1 - \alpha)(\Delta k - \Delta h). \tag{4}$$

Thus the growth rate of output per hour $(\Delta q - \Delta h)$ is simply the growth rate of MFP (Δa) plus the contribution of the growth in capital per hour $[(1 - \alpha)(\Delta k - \Delta h)]$.

Table 5.2 decomposes the observed growth rate of output per hour for the non-farm business sector in the G-7 countries between the separate contributions of capital and MFP. For most countries all three columns reveal a slowdown in growth rates between the first period (1960–73) and the final period (1979–92), but there are some anomalies. Between the first and last periods the capital contribution actually accelerates in both the United States and Canada, and consequently the slowdown in MFP growth is greater than in the growth rate of output per hour. Table 5.2 also reveals that for 1979–92 the excess of growth in output per hour for Europe versus the United States is more than explained by MFP growth. Because the 1979–92 contribution of capital in France and Germany is only slightly more than in the United States, capital contributes almost nothing to explaining the excess of growth in output per hour for these two countries over that in the United States. Because the 1979–92 contribution of capital in Italy and the United Kingdom is much less than in the United States, capital makes a *negative* contribution to the explanation for those two countries.

The contribution of capital growth to the slowdown in growth in output per hour is exhibited in Table 5.3 not just for nonfarm private business, but also for manufacturing and a large "residual" sector, private nonfarm, nonmanufacturing, nonmining (PNFNMNM). Here we note that the contribution of capital to the slowdown in all three sectors is negative for both the United States and Canada, while it is positive in the four European countries (except for manufacturing in Italy, where there is a negative contribution of capital to the slowdown in growth of output per hour, and for United Kingdom manufacturing, where there is no slowdown in the growth of output per hour, but rather an acceleration).

There is some support in Tables 5.2 and 5.3 for the relationships suggested in this chapter. For the aggregate economy (the nonfarm economy displayed in Table 5.2 and the first three columns of Table 5.3), there was a very substantial slowdown in the contribution of capital in Europe but not in the United States. This supports the emphasis placed above on the role of wage-setting shocks in setting into motion a process of capital decumulation, while also causing an increase in unemployment. A notable exception is provided by Canada, where

Table 5.3. *The Contribution of Capital and of MFP to Slowdown in Growth Rate of Output Per Hour, 1979–92 as Compared to 1960–73, by Major Sector*

	Private Nonfarm Business			Manufacturing			Private NFNMNM[a]		
	Slowdown	% Share Capital	% Share MFP	Slowdown	% Share Capital	% Share MFP	Slowdown	% Share Capital	% Share MFP
United States	−0.72	−35	135	−0.78	−40	140	−0.71	−24	124
Canada	−1.61	−45	145	−2.03	−49	149	−1.03	−61	161
France	−2.35	12	88	−4.05	4	96	−1.52	26	74
Germany	−2.97	33	67	−3.83	24	76	−2.32	54	46
Italy	−4.81	20	80	−3.02	−11	110	−5.49	27	73
United Kingdom	−2.26	51	49	0.66	88	12	−2.07	51	49

Note. [a] Nonfarm, nonmining, nonmanufacturing.

the contribution of capital accelerated rather than slowed down, while Canadian unemployment increased between 1960–73 and 1979–92 almost as much as in the four large European economies.

Productivity Growth Regressions

This chapter has examined the dynamic interaction of unemployment and productivity. It has shown that the correlation between unemployment and productivity can be positive, zero, or negative, and the same carries over to the correlation between the *change* in unemployment and the *growth rate* of productivity.

However, the above analysis makes a definite prediction about at least one correlation, that there should be a negative correlation between the change in unemployment and the change in capital per member of the labor force. To the extent that increased unemployment is initially caused by a positive wage-setting shock, we should observe a decline in capital relative to the labor force (or relative to the initial level of employment).

To examine these interrelations, we run a set of regression equations in which the dependent variables are alternatively growth in output per hour, growth in capital per member of the labor force, and growth in MFP. Each variable is measured as the growth rate for a particular country and sector over the three time intervals shown in Tables 5.2 and 5.3, that is, 1960–73, 1973–9, and 1979–92. The explanatory variables are a set of dummy variables for country effects, sector effects, time effects, as well as two economic variables. First, in common with numerous recent studies of the convergence process, we include the level of productivity in a given country sector relative to that for the United States in the same sector at the beginning of a particular interval. The coefficient on this relative level variable should be negative, indicating that country sectors with a low initial *level* of productivity grow relatively rapidly. Second, we include the change in a country's unemployment rate over each time interval, since our analysis above relates the level of the unemployment rate to the level of productivity, or the change in the unemployment rate to the growth rate of productivity.

Thus the regression equation is:

$$(\Delta q - \Delta h)_{ikt} = \alpha_0 + \alpha_1 \Delta U_{kt} + \alpha_2 \frac{(Q/H)_{ikt}}{(Q/H)_{itUS}} + \Sigma \beta_k DC_k$$
$$+ \Sigma \gamma_i DS_i + \Sigma_t \delta_t DT_t + \epsilon_{ikt}. \tag{5}$$

Here DC is a set of country dummies (with the United States taken as the base), DS is a set of sector dummies (with manufacturing taken as the base), and DT is a set of time interval dummies (with 1960–73 taken as the base).

The results are presented in Table 5.4. The equation explaining the growth rate of output per hour is presented three times in columns (1) to (3). The first two columns differ only in that (1) excludes the country sector level effect.

Table 5.4. *Regression Equations Explaining Growth Rates by Country and Sector, Three Intervals, 1960–92*

	Output per Hour			Capital per Potential Hour	Multifactor Productivity
	(1)	(2)	(3)	(4)	(5)
Constant	2.55**	4.77**	5.12**	4.93**	4.33**
Productivity level relative to United States	–	−2.45**	−2.48**	−2.63**	−2.36**
Change in unemployment	−0.46	−0.43	–	−0.56*	–
Canada	1.37*	0.35	−0.06	0.27	−0.48
France	3.81**	2.34**	1.35	2.45**	0.68
Germany	3.35**	2.34**	1.68**	2.29**	0.91
Italy	2.48**	2.79**	2.28**	1.97**	2.10**
United Kingdom	3.55**	2.36**	1.43*	1.78*	0.75
Agriculture	1.53*	0.87	0.86	0.96	−1.74**
Mining	−0.64	−0.68	−0.68	2.28**	−1.63**
Utilities	0.42	0.36	0.36	−0.93	−0.43
Construction	−1.87**	−2.13**	−2.13**	−0.38	−2.07**
Transport/ communication	0.11	0.17	0.16	−1.47	0.56
Trade	−0.11	−0.90	−0.89	−0.30	−1.02
FIRE	−1.99**	−2.13**	−2.14**	−2.77**	−2.16**
Services	−1.76**	−1.30	−1.29	−0.32	−1.67**
1973–9	−1.41**	−1.12*	−1.65**	0.10	−1.33**
1979–92	−0.74	−0.23	−1.28**	0.13	−0.82*
$\bar{R}^2$	0.34	0.39	0.39	0.43	0.37
SEE	2.30	2.20	2.21	2.19	1.90

Notes. *Indicates that coefficient is significant at 5 percent level;
** at 1 percent level.

Inclusion of this effect in (2) substantially reduces the size of the country dummies, indicating that part of the more rapid productivity growth in the European countries relative to the United States can be attributed to the convergence effect. Inclusion of this effect in (2) has no impact on the unemployment change coefficient, which is negative but insignificant in both columns (1) and (2). Exclusion of this variable in column (3) further reduces the size of the country effects, indicating that the high values of the country effects in columns (1) and (2) are in part offsetting the negative coefficient on the change in unemployment for the European countries. Several sector dummies are highly significant, indicating that across all countries productivity growth is significantly slower in construction and FIRE (Finance, Insurance, and Real Estate) than in manufacturing (the base sector). Interestingly, exclusion of the unemployment variable in column (3) yields a highly significant slowdown coefficient on the 1979–92 time effect. In columns (1) and (2) the productivity slowdown is spuriously explained by the increase in unemployment.

In column (4) the dependent variable is capital per potential hour, where "potential hours" is defined as the hours that would have been worked if a country had the unemployment rate at the beginning of the period rather than at the end of the period. Here the country-sector productivity level effect is again highly significant, and the change in the unemployment rate has the expected negative sign at a significance level of 5 percent.[12] Country-specific dummy variables for the four European countries are positive and significant, indicating that a substantial part of the productivity growth advantage of several European countries is explained by their more rapid rate of capital accumulation (holding constant the change in their unemployment rates). The pattern of sector-specific dummy coefficients is somewhat different, with mining experiencing unusually rapid capital accumulation and FIRE experiencing unusually slow capital accumulation. Somewhat unexpectedly, there are no time-specific slowdown effects, indicating that whatever slowdown in capital accumulation has occurred is entirely explained by the country sector productivity level variable and by the change in unemployment.

Finally, column (5) presents the same regression with the change in MFP as dependent variable. Here the country-specific effect is significant only for Italy. Thus it appears that most of the productivity advantage of France, Germany, and the United Kingdom over the United States, so evident in column (1), can be explained by convergence and capital accumulation. Significantly negative sector-specific effects are now present for MFP growth in agriculture, mining, construction, FIRE, and services (again, relative to manufacturing). The time-specific dummy coefficients indicate that between two-thirds and three-quarters of the productivity slowdown in column (3) can be attributed to a slowdown in MFP growth, and the rest can be attributed to a slowdown in capital accumulation associated with higher unemployment.

To summarize, we find that much of the productivity growth advantage of Europe countries over the United States is explained by convergence and more rapid capital accumulation. Only for Italy does more rapid growth in MFP explain a significant part of the productivity growth differential. The element of our theoretical analysis that is validated by the regression results concerns the growth of capital per potential hour, which seems to have decelerated more in countries with larger increases in unemployment. The theoretical analysis showed that productivity could be either positively or negatively correlated with unemployment in a world exposed to a mixture of wage-setting shocks and oil price shocks, and so it is not surprising that the regressions do not identify a significant correlation between productivity (output per hour or MFP) and unemployment.

---

[12] If the growth rate of capital per potential hour is replaced by the growth of capital per actual hour, the coefficient on the change in unemployment declines from -0.56 to -0.47, and the significance level changes from 5 percent to about 9 percent.

5.5 CONCLUSIONS

The point of departure for this chapter is the divergence between the concerns of European and American economists. The persistence of high unemployment dominates European policy discussions, whereas American economists are increasingly concerned with the slow growth rate of real wages and a large increase in the dispersion of incomes. This chapter argues that these phenomena may be more closely related than is commonly recognized. The many factors that are believed to have contributed to European unemployment by shifting upward the European wage-setting schedule may also have increased the growth rate of European productivity relative to that in the United States.

However plausible the notion that wage-setting shocks can create a positive correlation between unemployment and productivity, that relation is likely soon to be eroded by changes in the rate of capital accumulation. We find that countries with the greatest increases in unemployment had the largest slowdowns in the growth rate of capital per potential labor hour, a correlation that is consistent with the important role that capital accumulation plays in our analysis. Europe entered the 1990s with much higher unemployment in the United States but with approximately the same rate of capacity utilization, indicating that there was no longer sufficient capital to equip all the employees who would be at work at the unemployment rates of the late 1970s.

The raw numbers show substantially more rapid growth in output per hour in the four large European countries than in the United States. Our empirical analysis shows that none of this is related to the large increase in unemployment in Europe between the 1960s and the 1980s. Instead, faster productivity growth in Europe mainly reflects the convergence effect, i.e. that Europe started at a lower level of productivity and gradually converged toward the U.S. level, and the impact of more rapid capital accumulation. The fact that European productivity growth slowed down more than that in the United States is attributed both to the gradual weakening of the convergence effect and also to the negative impact of wage-setting shocks which both increased the unemployment rate and reduced the growth rate of capital per potential labor hour.

The policy implications of this analysis apply both to the European and U.S. settings. In Europe there is an increasing call for eliminating regulations and for more labor market flexibility. Yet there has thus far been little discussion of the fact that different types of reforms may help reduce structural unemployment but may have different effects on productivity. Proposed structural reforms to make European labor markets more "flexible" – such as reducing the real minimum wage, reducing unemployment compensation, reducing the price and tax wedges, and weakening the power of labor unions – can all be interpreted as attempts to shift down the wage-setting schedule. In the language of this chapter, they cause a country to move southwest along the UPT schedule, thus imposing a cost of reduced productivity that offsets some of the benefits of reduced unemployment. Some or all of this productivity cost may be offset in the medium run by more rapid capital accumulation, as the improved environment for profitability creates a stimulus for investment.

Rather than working indirectly through the wage-setting schedule, policy-makers would be better advised to adopt policies that reduce unemployment directly, especially policies to reduce mismatch and improve the efficiency of labor markets by better training or fewer employment regulations. Reform of product market regulations, such as a liberalization of German shop-closing hours, might reduce measured productivity while improving consumer welfare through extra convenience that is omitted from GDP.

Policy implications for the United States can be developed from the same analysis. Attention should be directed to policies that shift the UPT schedule upwards, for example by reducing mismatch and eliminating unnecessary regu-lations. Placing upward pressure on the U.S. wage-setting schedule by boosting the real minimum wage, and policies that attempt to reverse the decline in union penetration, would move the United States northeast along the UPT schedule. Some or all of the short-run productivity benefit might be offset in the medium run by slower capital accumulation, as the deteriorating environment for prof-itability squeezes investment. Policies that attempt to exploit the UPT trade-off seem likely to boost unemployment without creating any lasting benefit in the form of faster productivity growth.

References

Alogoskoufis, G.S., and Manning, A. "On the Persistence of Unemployment" *Economic Policy*. 1988; vol. 7, pp. 427–69.

Baily, M., and Gordon, R.J. "The Productivity Slowdown, Measurer Issues, and the Explosion of Computer Power." *Brookings Papers on Economic Activity*. 1988; vol. 9, pp. 348–420.

Baumol, W.J., Blackman, S.A.B., and Wolff, E.N. *Productivity and American Leadership: The Long View*. Cambridge, MA: MIT Press; 1989.

Bazan, B., and Martin, J.P. "The Impact of the Minimum Wage on Earnings and Employment in France," *OECD Economic Studies*. 1991; vol. 16, pp. 199–221.

Bean, C.R. "European Unemployment: a Survey." *Journal of Economics Literature*. 1994; vol. 32, pp. 573–619.

Bernard, A., and Jones, C.I. "Comparing Apples to Oranges: Product Convergence and Measurement Across Industries and Countries." CI (Stanford). *Discussion Paper*. 1994; 389.

Blanchard, O. "Unemployment: Getting the Questions Right – and Some of the Answers." In Drèze, J.H. and Bean, C.R. eds., *Europe's Unemployment Problem*. Cambridge, MA: MIT Press; 1990.

Bosworth, B., and Perry, G.L. "Productivity and Real Wages: Is the puzzle?" *Brookings Papers on Economic Activity*. 1994; vol. 25, pp. 317–44.

Branson, W., and Rotemberg, J.J. "International Adjustment with Rigidity." *European Economic Review*. 1980; vol. 13, pp. 317–44.

Bruno, M., and Sachs, J.D. *Economics of World Stagflation*. Cambridge, MA: Harvard University Press; 1985.

Card, D. "Do Minimum Wages Reduce Employment? A Case Study of California, 1987–89." *Industrial and Labor Relations Review*. 1992; vol. 46, pp. 38–54.

Card, D., and Krueger, A. "Minimum Wages and Employment: a Case Study of the Fast Food Industry in New Jersey and Pennsylvania." *American Economic Review*. 1994; vol. 84, pp. 772–93.

Card, D., Katz, L.F., and Krueger, A.B. "An Evaluation of Recent Evidence on the Employment Effects of Minimum and Subminimum Wages." *NBER Working Paper*, Cambridge, MA: NBER; 1993, 4528.

Crafts, N. "Productivity Growth Reconsidered." *Economic Policy*. 1992; vol. 15, pp. 387–426.

Dickens, R., Machin S., and Manning, A. "The Effects of Minimum Wages on Employment: Theory and Evidence from the UK." *Discussion Paper*. London School of Economics, Centre for Economic Performance; 1993.

Elemeskov, J., and MacFarlan, M. "Unemployment Persistence." *OECD Economic Studies*. 1993; vol. 21, pp. 57–88.

Franz, W., and Gordon, R.J. "Wage and Price Dynamics in Germany and America: Differences and Common Themes." *European Economic Review*. 1993; vol. 37, pp. 719–54.

Freeman, R.B. "How Labor Fares in Advanced Economies." In Freeman, R.B. ed. *Working Under Different Rules*. New York: Russell Sage Foundation; 1994.

Gordon, R.J. "The Jobless Recovery: Does It Signal a New Era of Productivity-Led Growth?" *Brookings Papers on Economic Activity*. 1993; vol. 24, pp. 271–316.

Gordon, R.J., and Baily, M.N. "Measurement Issues and the Productivity Slowdown in Five Major Industrial Countries." In Bell, G. ed. *Technology and Productivity: The Challenge for Economic Policy*. Paris: OECD; 1991, pp. 187–206.

Grubb, D., and Wells, W. "Employment Regulation and Patterns of Work in EC Countries." *OECD Economic Studies*. Paris: OECD. 1993; vol. 21, pp. 7–58.

Johnson, G.E., and Stafford, F.P. "International Competition and Real Wages." *American Economic Review, Papers and Proceedings*. 1993; vol. 83, pp. 127–30.

Krueger, A.B. "The Effect of the Minimum Wage When It Really Bites: a Reexamination of the Evidence from Puerto Rico." *NBER Working Paper*. Cambridge, MA: NBER. 1994; 4757.

Krugman, P. "Slow Growth in Europe: Conceptual Issues." In Lawrence, R.Z., and Schultze, C.L. *Barriers to European Growth: A Transatlantic View*. Washington, DC: The Brookings Institution; 1987; pp. 48–75.

Layard, P.R.G., Nickell, S.J., and Jackman, R.A. *Unemployment: Macroeconomic Performance and the Labour Market*. Oxford: Oxford University Press; 1991.

Lindbeck, A. "The Welfare State and the Employment Problem." *Seminar Paper*. Institute for International Economic Studies, Stockholm. 1994; 561.

"The Unemployment Problem." *Seminar Paper*. Institute for International Economic Studies, Stockholm. 1994b; 575.

Sachs, J.D. "Wages, Profits, and Macroeconomic Adjustment: a Comparative Study." *Brookings Papers on Economic Activity*. 1979; vol. 10, pp. 269–319.

Saint-Paul, G. "Searching for the Virtues of the European Model." CEPR. *Working Paper*. London: CEPR. 1994; 950.

Simon, J. "The Case for Greatly Increased Immigration." *The Public Interest*. 1991; 102, pp. 89–103.

CHAPTER 6

Forward into the Past: Productivity Retrogression in the Electric Generating Industry

The worldwide slowdown in productivity growth since the early 1970s has continued to puzzle economists. The failure to identify any convincing single cause has led to a shift in research away from aggregate studies toward more detailed research at the industry level.[1] Along with construction and mining, the electric utility industry is one of three U.S. industries that have suffered the sharpest deceleration of productivity growth and thus is a natural candidate for detailed study.

Three special advantages commend the electric utility industry for analysis. First, its output is unusually homogenous, thus minimizing the usual problem of errors in measuring output. Second, as a regulated industry, the production process of electric utility generation is documented in an unusually detailed body of micro data at the establishment level. Third, electric utilities should be a fertile ground to test several of the most prominent single-cause theories of the aggregate productivity slowdown, including those that emphasize the role of energy prices, capital accumulation, environmental regulation, and the "depletion" of technology.

This paper provides new estimates of factor demand equations for labor and fuel use at the establishment level for fossil-fueled steam-electric generating plants, using a data set that has been newly developed for this study. It

[1] Among the single-cause explanations for the aggregate economy are higher energy prices (Rasche-Tatom, 1981), high raw materials prices (Bruno-Sachs, 1985), slower capital accumulation (Norsworthy, Harper, Kunze, 1979), a decline in capital services relative to the measured capital stock (Baily, 1981), and "depletion" of resources and ideas (Nordhaus, 1980; 1982). Others, including Edward Denison (1985), tend to attribute the slowdown to a multitude of causes.

This research was supported by the National Science Foundation. I am grateful to Thomas Cowing for providing the original pre-1972 data set, to Ross Newman and George Kahn for preliminary work on updating the data, and to Tim Schmidt, Gabriel Sensenbrenner, Dan Shiman, Tim Stephens, Janet Willer, and Gabriel Sensenbrenner for further work on the data and regressions. Victor Li carried out the final update of the regression results with admirable care and attention to detail. Martin N. Baily, Ernst R. Berndt, Edward F. Denison, Frank M. Gollop, Zvi Griliches, and Ariel Pakes provided helpful suggestions on earlier drafts of the paper. (*Source.* "Forward into the Past: Productivity Retrogression in the Electric Generating Industry." Previously unpublished. February 1992; NBER Working Paper no. 3988).

Table 6.1. *Output Per Hour Nonfarm Business and Electric Utilities, and Real Price of Electricity, Various Intervals, 1899–1988*

Interval	Output Per Hour Nonfarm Business	Output per Hour Electric Utilities	Real Price of Electricity
	(1)	(2)	(3)
1899–1923	2.1	5.7	−7.4
1923–1948	2.1	6.1	−6.7
1948–1963	2.6	6.8	−1.3
1963–1973	2.2	5.5	−0.8
1973–1988	1.0	1.2	1.6

Sources by Column.
(1) 1899–1948, Kendrick (1961), Table A-XXIII, pp. 338–40, linked in 1948 to *Economic Report of the President*, 1990, Table C-46.
(2) 1899–1953, Kendrick (1961), Table H-VI, pp. 590–91, linked in 1953 to *NIPA* Table 6.2, line 49 (electric, gas, and sanitary services), linked in 1958 to BLS for electric utilities (1958–63 from BLS Bulletin 2296, February 1988, Table 261, p. 142 and 1963–88 from BLS Bulletin 2349, February 1990, Table 279, p. 150).
(3) 1899–1970, Hirsch (1989), Figure 7, p. 9, linked to *NIPA*, Table 7.10, line 50, divided by Table 7.1, line 1.

attempts to link the results to three strands of literature that have developed largely in isolation, (1) the macro-oriented literature on the economy-wide productivity slowdown, (2) the industrial organization literature on public utility and environmental regulation, and (3) the econometric literature on production technology and factor demand in the electric utility industry.

Standard econometric methodology is used except in one respect, the treatment of outlier observations. Unlike most panel data sets in which the identity of individual observations is unknown, here it is possible to contact plant managers of individual outlier establishments and identify important determinants of input demand, thus illuminating the role of missing variables or mismeasured data. The summary of the telephone interviews represents an important contribution of the research and adds insight that cannot be provided by the econometric coefficient estimates alone.

6.1 ELECTRICITY GENERATION IN THE CONTEXT OF THE ECONOMY-WIDE PRODUCTIVITY SLOWDOWN

The electric utility industry is a prime culprit in the economywide post-1973 productivity growth slowdown. As shown in Table 6.1, growth in labor productivity (output per hour) in the electric utility industry proceeded at a rate triple that of the aggregate economy from 1899 to 1948, and at a rate 2.5 times as fast from 1948 to 1973. After 1973, however, the previously rapid rate of advance for electric utilities came screeching to a halt, as productivity growth slowed to the same low rate as experienced by the aggregate economy.

Table 6.2. *Selected Figures on Industry Output, Productivity and Prices, Levels and Growth Rates, Selected Intervals, 1948–88*

	NIPA Utility Sector			BLS Electric Utilities Output/Hour (1977 = 100)	Relative Price of Electricity (1982 = 1.0)
	Real GNP ($ 1982 Billions)	Hours Worked (Billions)	Real GNP/ Hour ($ 1982)		
	(1)	(2)	(3)	(4)	(5)
A. Levels					
1948	16.3	1.03	15.8	–	0.98
1953	26.5	1.11	23.8	–	0.93
1958	36.5	1.16	31.4	34.7	0.85
1963	49.9	1.17	42.7	51.0	0.80
1968	68.1	1.26	54.1	70.1	0.72
1973	92.6	1.41	65.7	88.4	0.74
1978	97.8	1.48	66.1	96.8	0.87
1983	104.3	1.67	62.5	90.9	0.99
1988	134.3	1.75	76.7	105.6	0.94
B. Annual Rates of Growth					
1948–53	9.7	1.5	8.2	–	−1.0
1953–58	6.4	0.9	5.5	–	−1.8
1958–63	6.3	0.2	6.1	7.7	−1.2
1963–68	6.2	1.5	4.7	6.4	−2.1
1968–73	6.1	2.2	3.9	4.6	0.5
1973–78	1.1	1.0	0.1	1.8	3.2
1978–83	1.3	2.4	−1.1	−1.3	2.6
1983–88	5.1	0.9	4.1	3.0	−1.0

Sources by Column.
(1)–(3) and (5) from *NIPA* as follows, (1): 1948–73, Table 6.2, line 49, linked in 1977 to *Survey of Current Business*, January 1991, Table 6, line 49, p. 34; (2): Table 6.11, line 15; (3) = (1)/(2); (5) Table 7.10, line 50.
(4) Uses the same sources as Table 6.1, col. (2).

Table 6.1 also displays the growth rate of the real price of electricity over the same time intervals. Here the rate of improvement decelerated sharply immediately after World War II, and the historical decline in the real price was replaced by an increase after 1973. The fact that the real price fell so much more before 1948 than after, while growth in labor productivity remained fairly steady through 1973, suggests that other factors must have made a major contribution to the falling real price before 1948, for example, a decline in the relative price of fuel and of quality-adjusted capital input. The declining real price of electricity was an important source of productivity growth in the aggregate economy through the early 1970s, for historically much technical progress has been labor saving and electricity using (Jorgenson, 1984).

A closer look at the postwar period is provided in Table 6.2, which documents the behavior since 1948 of output and productivity in the public utility sector

Table 6.3. *Output Per Employee, Annual Percentage Growth Rates, Selected Intervals, 1948–87*

From	To	NIPA Utility Sector	BLS Utility Sector	All Plants in Sample
1948–1950	1957–1959	6.7	–	7.8
1957–1959	1966–1968	5.3	7.0	7.3
1966–1968	1972–1974	3.9	4.8	2.8
1972–1974	1978–1980	−0.4	1.6	−1.7
1978–1980	1985–1987	0.5	0.1	0.4

Sources by Column.
(1) Output, same sources as Table 6.2, col. (1); employees from NIPA Table 6.10B.
(2) Same as Table 6.2, col. (4).
(3) New data set developed for this paper, see Data Appendix.

as defined in the National Income and Products Accounts (NIPA), and in the electric utility portion of the utility sector. Also shown is the relative price of electricity. The top half of the Table displays levels of variables, and the bottom half displays annual rates of growth over five-year intervals.

Real GNP growth in the utility sector was most rapid before 1953, reached a plateau between 1953 and 1973, almost ceased between 1973 and 1983, and then revived after 1983. The slowdown in labor productivity growth in the sector began earlier than that of output, and productivity growth was actually negative on average between 1973 and 1983, followed by a revival during 1983–8. Productivity growth for electric utilities in column (4) displays roughly the same pattern as for the utility sector in column (3). The final column shows that the period of rapid productivity growth coincided with that of a decline in the relative price of electricity, and the poor productivity decade of 1973–83 coincided with the period of most rapid increase in the relative price of electricity.

Scope of the Study

This essay limits its attention to the production of electricity in steam plants using fossil fuels. Electricity makes up about 70 percent of the "electricity, gas, and sanitary services" industry aggregate in the NIPA, fossil-fuel steam accounts for almost three quarters of electricity generation (the rest is mainly hydro and nuclear), and employees involved in generation make up about one third of all employees on the payrolls of electric utilities.

Despite the relatively small fraction of total utility employment covered, the industry segment analyzed in this paper has experienced a slowdown in productivity growth very similar to that of the utility industry aggregate, as shown in Table 6.3. Here growth rates are computed over intervals between three-year averages of levels to smooth year-to-year variation in our sample of plants. Productivity growth in our sample of generating plants decelerates somewhat faster than the BLS index for the electric utility industry through 1978–80 but was almost identical to the BLS index in the last interval through 1985–7.

Limitations

While the electric generating industry is appealing as a subject for study, our regressions cover an extremely small fraction of U.S. employment and bear on only a small fraction of the total U.S. productivity growth puzzle. A second qualification is that the electric utility industry has entered a relatively "mature" phase of the industry growth cycle, and thus it may not be surprising that its productivity growth would decline over time. However, as we shall see the problems of the industry go far beyond those that can be attributed to maturity alone. A third qualification is that our data set, while it has the great advantage that the majority of generating plants can be identified by vintage and observed over a long period of time, lacks particular explanatory variables that have become important during the productivity slowdown period, especially measures of technical characteristics like pressure, temperature, and the presence of scrubbers and cooling stacks. Other data sets, for example, that of Joskow and Rose (1985), are complementary, having the advantage of including many of the technology variables needed to study the effects of environmental regulation, but lacking the advantage in our data set of the ability to observe a given establishment over a long period of time.

6.2   TECHNOLOGY AND ITS IMPLICATIONS FOR RESEARCH

Characteristics of the Technology

Although electric utilities are monopolists in the local markets they serve, the aggregate number of these individual monopolies is substantial, in contrast to the very small number of major producers of generating equipment. Thus utilities can accurately be described as price takers in the market for new equipment, and they also are "quality takers" in the sense that their choice set is constrained by whatever price-quality combinations are offered by equipment manufactures on the market at any given time. Research and development expenditures have taken place largely in the manufacturing sector, not in the utility industry.[2]

---

[2] This verdict is qualified by Hirsch (1989, p. 71), who argues that "to explain progress in electric power technology simply as a result of research and development performed by manufacturers would be one-sided and misleading." The other side of technical advance is achieved by utility management, 67 percent of which in 1964 consisted of trained engineers. Managers in particular companies perceived themselves as competing for the role of technological leadership and constantly pressed equipment manufacturers to achieve technical advances, taking the risk that unproved technology would be successful. However, this role of management is not counted as research and development (R&D) by normal accounting methods, and Hirsch himself reports that utility-funded R&D in 1970 amounted to only 0.23 percent of gross revenues.

The production process involves the transformation of the internal energy in a fuel source into electrical energy. A power generation "unit" operates independently of any other units at a given plant location and consists of a boiler to burn the fuel and to generate and expand the steam, and a turbo-generator, which converts high-pressure steam into electric energy through the rotary motion of a turbine shaft. A condensor converts the steam into water to complete the cycle. The entire unit is called a "boiler-turbo-generator," or BTG unit. A central measure of the efficiency of this transformation process is the "heat rate" (HR) of the cycle, the ratio of input in British thermal units (Btu) to one kilowatt-hour (KWH):

$$HR = \frac{BTU\ input}{KWH\ output}. \tag{1}$$

Thus the higher the heat rate, the more fuel is being consumed in the production of a given amount of electricity, and the less efficient is the generation process. The heat rate moves inversely to a companion ratio called "thermal efficiency."

Technology and the Sources of Economies of Scale

Until the late 1960s technical change in the design of BTG units was aimed primarily at increasing the size of generators and boilers and at improving the thermal efficiency of the generating cycle by increasing the temperature to which the steam is heated, increasing the pressure of the steam entering the turbine, and reducing the heat which is transferred out of the cycle in the condenser. The technical design frontier was limited by the ability of boilers to withstand high temperatures and pressures, and the frontier was pushed out by incremental advances, particularly in metallurgy involving the development of high temperature steel alloys. Most of the shift to higher temperatures and to reheat cycles was completed during the 1948–57 decade, with little further change thereafter, whereas the increase in pressure rating continued until the late 1960s.

The average scale of BTG units also increased, with 58 percent of new units rated below 50 megawatts in 1948, and 60 percent above 500 megawatts in 1987. The increase in scale proceeded steadily through the mid-1970s and then ceased. Increased scale was interdependent with improved thermal efficiency, since many of the efficiency improvements required greater capital expenditures, the expense of which could be partially offset by increased scale.[3] Cowing (1970) has dubbed this interaction between increasing scale and technical improvements "scale augmenting technical change."[4]

---

[3] Engineers use a "six-tenths" rule for approximating the additional cost of a capacity increase, i.e., a 1 percent increase in capacity increases capital cost by 0.6 percent, reflecting the geometrical fact that a 1 percent increase in the volume of a sphere increases its surface area by about 0.6 percent (Moore, 1959).

[4] As Wills illustrates (1978, p. 500), there is little further improvement in thermal efficiency as unit sizes increase beyond 250 megawatts. Indeed, after increasing from 3 percent in 1880 to

The end of the era of increasing size helps to explain the productivity slow-down, and so it is important to determine whether the sources of the previous growth in scale had primarily been technological advance or the increasing size of the market. The technological hypothesis emphasizes the incremental advance of technology toward a technical ceiling reached in the late 1960s, at the beginning of the slowdown period. In contrast the market hypothesis stresses the role of higher energy prices in the 1970s in reducing the growth in demand for electricity, and predicts that further advances in scale should resume in response to the post-1983 decline in the real price of electricity.

One way to distinguish the two hypotheses is to ask why generator units were so small in the early part of the postwar period. Either manufacturers did not have the technical competence to produce larger units at reasonable cost, or markets were too small to support the purchase of larger units. One indirect piece of evidence that supports the technological explanation is that the average number of units installed per newly constructed plant during the 1947–50 period was 2.0, and six plants in our data set were built with three or four units during that interval. If larger pieces of equipment had been available at a lower cost per unit of capacity, they would have been purchased in place of two or more of the smaller units.

Numerous commentaries attribute the gradual increase in scale to a techno-logical frontier that advanced incrementally. For instance, an engineering study in the early postwar period carried out on units in the range of 50–100 KW stated that: "we have every confidence that continued progress in metallurgy and design skill will make units larger than those now in operation economically feasible" (Kirchmayer *et al.*, 1955, p. 609). One of the conference discussants of the same study stated that "size must not run ahead of our proved progress in metallurgy. From recent evidence it seems that size has now outrun progress" (p. 613). Hirsch emphasizes metallurgy, and attributes advances in size, pres-sure, and temperature in the early postwar years to "advances in metallurgical knowledge gained during the war and used in aircraft and artillery ... newly developed 'super alloy' steels that resisted metal fatigue and cracking, for ex-ample, allowed engineers to design larger components for more power output" (1989, pp. 89–90). Thus the engineering literature appears to support the tech-nological hypothesis over the market hypothesis as the primary source of scale economies achieved prior to 1970.

Technology "Hits the Wall"

Until World War II the traditional approach in achieving improvements in scale and efficiency had been the "design-by-experience" approach in which each step to a new technological plateau was followed by a period of debugging before the next advance occurred. In the postwar period, spurred by the rapidly growing

22 percent in 1947, thermal efficiency leveled off at about 33 percent in the late 1950s and showed no change after than (Hirsch, 1989, Figure 1, p. 4).

demand for electricity, equipment manufacturers shifted to a more aggressive philosophy called "design-by-extrapolation" in which the next advance was planned before operating experience had occurred with the previous step.[5] Much of the pressure for this new approach came from the demand for new equipment by utility management who were struggling to keep up with the demand created by a falling real price of electricity and by their own advertising designed to stimulate the use of electricity.

The first technological barrier to be reached was an effective upper limit to thermal efficiency, which had a natural theoretical limit of about 48 percent. Although a few best-practice plants reached 40 percent, the steeply rising marginal cost of improving efficiency through the use of exotic and expensive steels prevented further progress. Further, experience revealed that the 100° increase in temperature from the typical unit of the 1950s to the 1960s increased corrosive activity fiftyfold, led to the discovery that "we suddenly are susceptible to new diseases like stress corrosion cracking."[6] Increased corrosion, in turn, required increased downtime for maintenance, and this in turn contributed to lower utilization rates on new units.

The arrival of the effective plateau in thermal efficiency in the late 1950s increased the emphasis on scaling-up of boilers and generators, but by the end of the 1960s this had also begun to create unanticipated problems. The scale frontier was reached when utilities discovered that downtime was as much as five times greater for units larger than 600 MW than for units in the 100 MW range.[7] Part of this was directly a function of size, since the time required for units to cool down and heat up is directly related to the mass of the unit, and part related to the greater complexity of the larger units. Further, metallurgical problems cropped up in the huge turbine blades on large units, related to the laws of physics that dictated huge centrifugal forces, as much as 33 tons of force on a 7-pound blade.

The last component of the new technological era involved not just hitting a technological wall but rather amounted to a full-fledged retreat. Design-by-extrapolation led to the development in the late 1950s and early 1960s of the "supercritical" boiler (achieving a pressure above 3200 p.s.i.). However, after reaching a 63 percent share in new installations during 1970–4, the share fell to 6 percent in 1981–2 (Joskow-Rose, 1985, Table 1, p. 4). The backing off from supercritical technology resulted mainly from unanticipated maintenance problems, documented in the interviews at the end of this paper.[8]

---

[5] Where no citations are given, specific details in this section are obtained from Hirsch (1989), Chapters 7–8.

[6] Interview with a plant manager, quoted by Hirsch (1989, p. 93).

[7] Joskow-Rose (1985, p. 23) report that average equipment availability over the 1969–80 period ranged from 82.8 percent for units of 100 MW to only 62.6 percent for units of 900 MW.

[8] The interviews contained in an early draft of this paper are cited as an explanation of the abandonment of supercritical units by Hirsch (1989, pp. 97–9) and Joskow-Rose (1985, p. 23). Note that the Joskow-Rose evidence suggests that the availability penalty of supercritical units of given size is less than the penalty of increasing the size of subcritical units from 500 to 900 MW.

The arrival of a technological frontier interacted with the pitfalls of the design-by-extrapolation approach, which downgraded the importance of waiting for experience to accumulate with new larger units.[9] Yet as time went on many problems developed that could have been alleviated with a more cautious approach, for example, stability problems with turbines, twisted and cracked turbine blades, and ash buildup in furnaces. Because of large costs in downtime, added maintenance, and retrofitting of units with flawed designs, the initial cost of equipment appears significantly to understate the "true" cost of equipment delivered in the 1960s. In more recent years manufacturers have learned from their design failures in 1960s-vintage equipment how to avoid design flaws and improve reliability, and failure rates for 1980s-vintage equipment have declined radically.[10]

A timing argument exempts environmental regulation from any appreciable blame in this technological history. Unanticipated problems developed in a major way with equipment manufactured in the early 1960s, yet the response of utilities to environmental regulation is usually dated from the Clean Air Act Amendments of 1970 (Gollop-Roberts, 1983, p. 654). Yet as the 1970s evolved, environmental regulation played a growing role in the slowdown in labor productivity growth and decline in thermal efficiency experienced by utilities, as regulations induced a shift away from soft coal, required major capital expenditures for scrubbers and other devices, and substantially raised the requirement for maintenance employees. Thus productivity growth was impeded after the early 1970s by both the technological plateau and by environmental regulation, introducing a serious identification problem for any study attempting to explain the productivity growth slowdown.

Technological History and Its Implications for Econometric Research

Previous research on the production process for electricity generation (Cowing and Smith, 1978; Wills, 1978) reached a consensus that the usual economic approach to production, based on the notion of homogeneous, divisible, and highly substitutable factor inputs, does not apply for this industry. Instead, the dominant feature of the production process is heterogeneous capital that incorporates the most efficient technology available at the date of its construction but, once built, embodies fixed technical characteristics that impose very tight constraints on the feasible set of input-output combinations. The firm's choices are decomposed between "ex ante" investment decisions and "ex post" operating decisions, the latter involving the choice of variable inputs needed to produce desired output with existing equipment.

---

[9] Hirsch (1989, pp. 122–5) provides specific citations of overoptimistic predictions made in the 1950s and 1960s of continued steady advances in temperature, pressure, and size.

[10] The "forced-outage" rate after the first year of service for Westinghouse equipment dropped from 9 percent for equipment shipped in 1965–9 to 2 percent in 1975–80 to 0.5 percent in 1980–4.

This two-stage view of the production process leads Barzel (1964), Wills (1978), and others to a two-step econometric procedure. The available opportunities that constrain the firm's investment decision are characterized in a hedonic price function that relates the price of equipment to its attributes. Then the operating decision is described in a regression of fuel, employment, or both, on the main attributes of each installed set of equipment. Wills (1978) concludes, in common with other studies dating back to Komiya (1962), that "substitution opportunities at the plant level between equipment, fuel, and labor are poor."

In light of the availability of recent research on the first-step hedonic regression for equipment prices, this paper concentrates on the second step, the regression equations explaining the usage of labor and fuel inputs for the installed stock of equipment.[11] Such a study seems justified in view of the passage of time since the last round of studies by Cowing (1970, 1974), Wills (1978), and Bushe (1981).[12] Another justification is that new questions have been raised by the productivity slowdown and by environmental regulation. Finally, most of the more recent studies have been based on firm rather than the establishment data used here and have been more concerned with measuring economies of scale than interpreting the productivity slowdown.[13]

6.3   ECONOMETRIC SPECIFICATION AND DATA

The Employment Equation

This section specifies a regression equation in which plant employment is explained by output and by various embodied characteristics of installed BTG units. This corresponds to the "ex post" or "operating" decision that, according to the consensus of previous research, is constrained by previous "ex ante" or "investment" decisions. Labor requirements and fuel use are taken to be endogenous choice variables, and equipment characteristics and output are the exogenous explanatory variables. Plant capacity, fuel type, and location are assumed to be predetermined by previous investment decisions, and output (or utilization), is assumed to be set by an exogenously determined demand for electricity at preset prices.

---

[11] See especially Joskow-Rose (1985) and Gordon (1990), which estimate equipment price indexes that decrease rapidly relative to the corresponding NIPA indexes through the late 1960s and rise much faster thereafter.

[12] The earlier studies are surveyed by Cowing and Smith (1978).

[13] Among these studies are Atkinson and Halvorsen (1984), Gollop and Roberts (1981, 1983), Cowing, Small and Stevenson (1981), and Christensen and Greene (1976). The advantages of plant over firm data are discussed by Cowing and Smith (1978), pp. 175–7, with reference to the papers by Nerlove (1963) and Christensen-Greene (1976). A dissenting opinion is offered by Gollop and Roberts (1981, p. 120), who argue that "producers make input decisions on the basis of technical and market conditions facing the complete system, not isolated plants." However, when plant data are available, there is no reason to make this choice *ex ante*, as aggregation issues can be studied explicitly by estimating firm and establishment effects, as in Table 6.12.

Because causation goes from output to inputs, and because there are two input equations, it is inappropriate to take the estimated coefficients from a single input equation, for example, labor, and attempt to invert them to retrieve the underlying production function. We begin with the employment equation, relate it to previous research, and then subsequently adopt a parallel specification for the fuel input equation. The basic employment regression is estimated below for plant data in the following form:

$$\ln L = \alpha_0 + \alpha_1 \ln C + \alpha_2 \ln \left(\frac{Q}{C}\right)_{10} + \alpha_3 \ln \varepsilon_{HR} \\ + \alpha_4 N + \alpha_5 V + \alpha_6 T + \sum_{i=1} \beta_i D_i + \varepsilon_L, \tag{2}$$

where L is employment, C is capacity, Q is output, ε_{HR} is the "heat rate residual" discussed below, N is the number of units, V is vintage, T is the year of each observation, the D_i are ten dummy variables for type of fuel, type of construction, and location, and ε_L is the error term. It is useful to compare (2) with other specifications of the employment equation, for example, those of Wills (1978, p. 508):

$$\frac{L}{C} = \alpha_0 \frac{1}{C} + \left(\alpha_1 + \sum_{i=1}^{2} \beta_i D_i + \sum_{j=1}^{8} \eta_j \bar{T}_j\right) \frac{C}{C} + \alpha_2 \frac{C^2}{C} + \varepsilon_{L/C}, \tag{3}$$

and of Bushe (1981, p. 194):

$$\ln L = \alpha_0 + \alpha_1 \ln C + \alpha_2 \ln \left(\frac{Q}{C}\right) + \alpha_4 N + \beta_1 D + \varepsilon_L. \tag{4}$$

The additional symbol in the Wills equation is $\bar{T}_j$, which stands for a set of eight overlapping dummy variables for year of observation, in contrast to the linear time trend (T) imposed in (2).[14] The Bushe equation omits vintage effects and instead uses design data to divide up the total sample into seven technically homogeneous cells, and the coefficients in equation (4) are separately for each cell. The log-linear functional form of our specification (2) is shared with (4). In contrast, in (3) Wills begins with a linear form but allows for interaction effects and normalizes by capacity. Bushe also implicitly normalizes by capacity, since the average capacity within his seven separate cells differs by several orders of magnitude.

A basic difference between the three specifications is the allowance for both time and vintage effects in (2), only vintage effects in (3) and only "cell" effects in (4). The vintage variable is included in (2) but not in (3), because the latter includes observations only for newly installed plants, whereas the former includes observations for each year of operation. The Bushe approach

---

[14] The two dummy variables in the Wills equation are for presence of coal burning and of more than one unit, and in the Bushe equation the single dummy variable represents the presence of coal burning.

in (4) appears to be inconsistent, in that data for multiple years of operation are included for each plant but no vintage variable is introduced.[15]

The larger number of dummy variables included in (2) reflects the much larger sample size in our study. Our sample consists of 6,674 observations after editing, in contrast to 163 for Wills and cell sample sizes ranging from 25 to 162 for Bushe. Our larger sample size stems both from the inclusion of each plant for every year of operation (starting from the first complete year), and also the addition of eighteen extra years of data beyond that available to Bushe and Wills.

Because our point of departure is the productivity slowdown, the estimates below of (2) allow the vintage (α_5) and time (α_6) coefficients to shift after 1968. We attempt to identify the sources of these shifts by allowing for interaction effects and by isolating observations that are consistent "outliers." Another difference among the specifications is apparent in Wills's omission of an output or utilization variable, in contrast to its inclusion in equations (2) and (4).

The Fuel Input Equation and the "Heat Rate Residual"

The conventional economic theory of production based on homogeneous and highly substitutable inputs might lead to the expectation of a negative coefficient on the heat rate (energy use divided by output) stemming from substitution between energy and labor. In contrast our basic approach holds that there are few *ex post* substitution opportunities involving energy use. Instead, we view the coefficient on the heat rate in our employment regressions as a proxy for unmeasured design characteristics of plants of a given capacity and vintage. Our treatment of the heat rate variable as an indicator of plant efficiency is consistent with the approach of Schmalensee and Joskow (1985, p. 1), who explicitly list heat rate as one of two "indices of quality," the other being the plant's availability factor.

To embody the idea that the heat rate effect represents unmeasured design characteristics, in the present paper the employment equations include not the heat rate itself, but rather the residual from the fuel input equation, ε_{HR}, which is specified:

$$
\begin{aligned}
\ln HR = {} & \alpha_0 + \alpha_1 \ln C + \alpha_2 \ln \left(\frac{Q}{C} \right)_{10} + \alpha_3 \ln \left(\frac{P_F}{P_L} \right) \\
& + \alpha_4 N + \alpha_5 V + \alpha_6 T + \sum_{i=1}^{10} \beta_i D_i + \varepsilon_{HR}.
\end{aligned}
\tag{5}
$$

The specification of the fuel input equation is identical to that of the labor input equation (2), except that the heat rate term in (2) is replaced by the relative

---

[15] Bushe edits his sample to include observations beginning in the second full year of operation and extending until the end of the sample or two years prior to installation of a new unit. We begin in the first full year of operation and apply a different editing criterion described in the Data Appendix.

price of fuel (P_F/P_L). After (5) is estimated, the residual for each observation is included as an explanatory variable in (2).

Data and Estimation Issues

The data file includes all plants listed in the publication *Steam-Electric Power Construction Cost and Annual Production Expenses* for the period 1948–87. In total 401 individual plants are represented, of which 68 were constructed prior to 1948, 113 during 1948–57, 75 during 1958–67, 97 during 1968–77, and 48 during 1978–86. Since each plant is observed in each successive year starting with the first year after its commencement of operations, the sample is quite large, consisting of 7,701 observations prior to editing. Editing pruned the sample down to 6,656 observations, as described in the Data Appendix to this chapter.

Several features of the data need to be considered when interpreting the econometric results below. The greatest problems are posed by the presence of technically heterogeneous units in some multiunit plants, and by varying technical specifications in new plants of a given vintage. Spurious errors caused by the first of these can be minimized either by editing the sample or by including dummy variables. The second cannot be escaped but should cause no bias in coefficients if the distribution of technical features across plants of a given vintage tends to remain constant over successive vintages. A final data problem involves possible measurement errors in the data on plant employees.[16]

Table 6.4 exhibits for selected intervals, separately for new plants and all plants, the annual average number of plants, and their average capacity (C), utilization rate (Q/C), and output per employee (Q/L). The new plants have a smaller capacity than the average for all plants in several of the early intervals. This apparent discrepancy can be explained by a greater number of small-sized units in existing plants (average units per plant decreased steadily from 11 in pre-1948 plants to 1.5 in plants of the 1986 vintage).[17] Productivity in new plants actually *declined* by two thirds between 1966–8 and 1986–7, while productivity on all plants *increased* by 9 percent. The two final columns exhibit the striking finding that the utilization rate for new plants was higher than for all plants prior to 1968, while the reverse was true beginning in 1969–71.

6.4   ESTIMATED FUEL AND LABOR INPUT EQUATIONS

The Fuel Input Equations

The estimated coefficients for the fuel input equation (5) are presented in Table 6.5 where the three columns report results for all plants in the edited

---

[16] Bushe complains that the labor data are "imprecise" and "misleading" and cites instances of firms that allocate all maintenance labor to one plant. We return to this issue in discussing our interviews with managers of outlier plants.

[17] There were no new plants built in 1987, a fact confirmed by Hirsch (1989, p. 165).

Table 6.4. *Selected Characteristics of New Plants and All Plants, Selected Intervals, 1948–1987*

	Average Annual Number of Plants		Output per Employee (millions KWH)		Average Capacity		Average Utilization Rate (percent)	
	New	All	New	All	New	All	New	All
	(1)	(2)	(3)	(4)	(5)	(6)	(7)	(8)
1948–50	11	70	8.20	6.03	85	139	64	62
1951–53	10	105	11.01	8.13	121	168	67	64
1954–56	9	137	20.39	10.63	259	219	59	59
1957–59	8	157	22.53	12.18	221	254	65	54
1960–62	5	174	29.68	14.63	325	324	62	51
1963–65	8	188	29.50	18.95	347	381	61	53
1966–68	6	203	39.15	23.54	651	462	59	57
1969–71	6	216	33.90	26.00	578	561	48	57
1972–74	8	240	30.87	27.78	862	681	44	53
1975–77	11	260	30.40	27.16	749	769	42	47
1978–80	8	270	18.82	25.09	818	834	42	47
1981–83	5	228	20.33	26.06	794	1009	46	47
1984–85	4	197	18.46	25.71	946	1174	46	47
1986–87	2	194	12.77	25.56	921	1195	35	47

Source. New data set developed for this paper, see Data Appendix.

sample, and for the subset of coal-using and noncoal-using plants.[18] The significance of coefficients is indicated by asterisks, and every coefficient in the table is significant at the 1 percent level, with three exceptions.

The negative coefficient on capacity implies that the well-documented economies of scale in equipment cost and labor use extend to fuel use as well. The negative coefficient on utilization could indicate both that plants which experience a lot of down time are also inefficient users of fuel, and that fuel is wasted when plants are shut down for maintenance and then started up again. The relative price term has the expected negative sign and is much larger for coal than noncoal plants. As would be expected, plants which generate a given output with several small units use more fuel than plants with fewer and larger units.[19]

---

[18] The vintage and time trend shifts are defined in exactly the same way. The vintage trend is centered on 1968, that is, equals -20 in 1948, 0 in 1968, and $+19$ in 1987. The vintage trend shift variable equals zero in all years through 1968, and then equals the trend running from $+1$ in 1969 to $+19$ in 1987. The "base" for the fuel-use dummy variable refers to plants which use both oil and gas.

[19] Building fewer and larger units per plant economizes on capital cost and labor as well as fuel. See Hirsch (1989, p. 43), who also notes that prior to the 1930s as many as eight boilers were necessary per turbine generator, but that by the 1930s firms had learned how to economize with "unit-type" construction, that is, one boiler per generator.

Table 6.5. *Equations Explaining the Log of Heat Rate by Plant, 1948–87*

	All Fuels	Coal Using	Noncoal Using
	(1)	(2)	(3)
1. Log Capacity	−0.084**	−0.083**	−0.078**
2. Log Utilization	−0.127**	−0.147**	−0.104**
3. Relative Price	−0.094**	−0.163**	−0.039**
4. Number Units	0.016**	0.011**	0.024**
5. Vintage			
a) All Vintages	−0.002**	−0.003**	−0.002**
b) 1968–87 Shift	0.007**	0.008**	0.002
6. Time			
a) All Years	−0.008**	−0.013**	−0.003**
b) 1968–87	0.017**	0.025**	0.007**
7. Fuel Type			
a) Coal Using	−0.001**	–	–
b) Oil Only	0.029**	–	−0.006
c) Gas Only	−0.027**	–	−0.018**
$\bar{R}^2$	0.649	0.516	0.586
Standard Error	0.124	0.130	0.099
Observations	6857	4232	2623

Notes. Asterisks indicate 5 percent (*) or 1 percent (**) significance levels.
All equations also include five location dummy variables and two construction-type dummy variables, as well as a constant term.

Both the vintage trend and time trend coefficients have a V-shaped pattern, with a negative overall trend more than offset by a positive post-1968 trend. The trends imply for all plants in column (1), for instance, that a 1948-vintage plant of given size used 2 percent more fuel per unit of output than a 1968 plant, and that a 1987-vintage plant used 9.5 percent more fuel. All of the deterioration after 1968 can be attributed to coal plants, since the two vintage terms for noncoal-using plants are of equal and opposite sign, implying flat fuel use after 1968. The time trend coefficients imply the same V-shaped pattern for plants of a given vintage observed in successive years and are consistent, for instance, with the effect of environmental regulations in causing a shift from high-sulfur to low-sulfur coal and oil requiring more BTUs to generate a unit of output.[20] The results indicate that the experience of coal and noncoal plants differs; the $F_{(19,6819)}$ ratio of 29.1 far exceeds the 1 percent critical value of 1.87, indicating that the data for the two fuel types cannot be pooled as in column (1).

An interesting interaction among the coefficients becomes evident when the equations in Table 6.5 are reestimated with the relative price variable omitted. This causes the time trend and trend shift coefficients to drop by roughly half.

[20] Gollop and Roberts (1985) provide data on the cost of pollution control equipment and required reductions in emissions, but not on the fuel-using effect of shifting to low-sulfur fuel.

Table 6.6. *Equations Explaining the Log of Employment by Plant 1948–87*

	All Fuels	Coal Using	Noncoal Using
	(1)	(2)	(3)
1. Log Capacity	0.539**	0.554**	0.453**
2. Log Utilization	0.120**	0.051**	0.032**
3. Heat Rate Residual	0.219**	0.186**	0.508**
4. Number Units	0.061**	0.060**	0.073**
5. Vintage			
a) All Vintages	−0.015**	−0.014**	−0.011**
b) 1968–87 Shift	0.032**	0.031**	−0.012**
6. Time			
a) All Years	−0.027**	−0.029**	−0.024**
b) 1968–87	0.047**	0.053**	0.032**
7. Fuel Type			
a) Coal Using	−0.004**	−	−
b) Oil Only	−0.188**	−	−0.002
c) Gas Only	−0.213**	−	−0.115**
$\bar{R}^2$	0.782	0.792	0.788
Standard Error	0.373	0.357	0.312
Observations	6674	4181	2491

Notes. Asterisks indicate 5 percent (*) or 1 percent (**) significance levels.
All equations also include five location dummy variables and two construction-type dummy variables, as well as a constant term.

Thus, with the relative price omitted, about half of the pre-1968 improvement in fuel use for plants of a given vintage, and about half of the post-1968 deterioration, is offset by the effect of a falling relative price in stimulating fuel use before the late 1960s and in encouraging fuel conservation after the early 1970s.

The Basic Employment Equation

The first column of Table 6.6 reports the estimated coefficients for the basic employment specification (equation 2 above) for the edited sample of 6,674 observations.[21] The elasticity of employment to capacity changes is 0.54, confirming the substantial economies to scale found in previous studies.[22] The elasticity of employment to utilization is 0.12, indicating that labor requirements fluctuate only modestly in response to demand changes, and thus that labor productivity is highly sensitive to changes in utilization. Taken by itself, this coefficient suggests that labor productivity should have declined in the 1970s in response to decreasing average utilization (shown in Table 6.4).

---

[21] There are fewer observations here than in Table 6.5, because there are some observations which are missing data on employment but not the heat rate.

[22] Joskow and Schmalensee (1983, pp. 48–54) provide a relatively recent survey.

The coefficient on the heat rate residual is positive, suggesting that plants having relatively high energy requirements also have relatively high labor requirements. This coefficient can be interpreted as a proxy for unmeasured design differences among plants of a given vintage and capacity.[23] A plant having a relatively large number of small units requires, understandably, more labor than another plant having the same capacity but a relatively small number of larger units.

In lines 5 and 6 we find that the labor productivity slowdown has occurred across both vintage and date of observation. The vintage trend coefficient is −0.015 for all years, whereas the vintage shift variable has a coefficient of +0.032, indicating a net deterioration of productivity growth during 1968–87 at a rate of 1.7 percentage points per year on successive newer vintages. The productivity of older plants deteriorated as well after 1968. The coefficient for the trend on date of observation is −0.027, and that of the 1968–87 shift variable is 0.047, indicating that after 1968 the productivity of existing plants of *all* vintages deteriorated at a rate of 2 percentage points per year. Overall, successive vintages improved in productivity by 30 percent between 1948 and 1967, after which productivity declined by 32 percent between 1967 and 1987. Plants of all vintages observed in 1967 had a productivity performance 54 percent better than plants observed in 1948, but afterward there was a decline in productivity amounting to 38 percent by 1987. These estimates hold constant the influence of capacity and utilization. Hence in the early years these trends understate the true effect of increasing vintage in contributing to productivity growth, since increased capacity over successive vintages raised productivity until 1968, while after 1968 size leveled off but utilization fell, thus causing the time trend coefficients to understate the true deterioration of productivity.

The final set of coefficients refers to dummy variables for fuel use. Coal use (either by itself or together with other fuels) raises employment requirements by 19 percent compared to oil-only and 21 percent compared to gas-only plants.[24]

The other columns in Table 6.6 exhibit the results for the subsample of coal-using and noncoal-using plants. The major differences are that the utilization effect is smaller for both fuel groups when the sample is disaggregated. The heat rate effect is much higher for noncoal plants, while the post-1968 deterioration in productivity measured by the vintage trend shift applies only to coal plants, since noncoal plants show an acceleration in productivity improvement over successive vintages. The V-shaped time trend coefficients apply to both fuel groups, but the slope of the "V" is steeper for coal plants. The $F_{(18,6636)}$ ratio

---

[23] The estimation of the heat rate residual implies that it is independent of the other explanatory variables in the equation, and hence it is not surprising that there is virtually no change in the other coefficients in the employment equation if the heat rate residual is omitted.

[24] This compares closely with the average of 22 percent for the coal use dummy across the seven cells in Bushe's study (1981, p. 192). The linear specification of Wills's employment equation precludes direct comparisons with his coefficients (Wills, 1978).

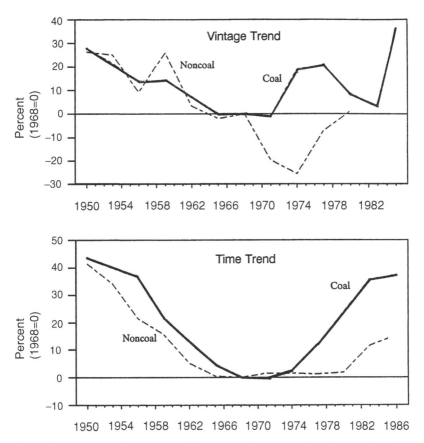

Figure 6.1. Percentage Deviation of Vintage and Time Trend Coefficients from 1968 Level, Employment Regression, Coal and Noncoal Plants

of 71.9, compared to a 1 percent critical value of 1.87, provides strong evidence that the observations for the coal and noncoal plants are not generated from the same relationship.

Variations on the Basic Employment Equations

1.   Year Triplets

The first variant is to replace the simple trend and trend shift terms with separate vintage and time coefficients for successive intervals of three years each ("year triplets"), 1949–51, 1952–54, etc. The results are plotted in Figure 6.1, where the top frame displays the percentage deviation of each vintage coefficient from the 1967–9 coefficient, and the bottom frame shows the same percentage deviation for the time coefficients. The time coefficients in the bottom frame display the same "V-shaped" pattern as the more parsimonious specification in Table 6.6, and repeat our previous finding that the "V" has a steeper slope for coal than for noncoal plants. Also, we can see here that the pattern for the noncoal plants is better described as a "U" than a "V," with a long flat portion between 1965 and 1980.

However, the vintage coefficients in the top frame of Figure 6.1 do not trace out a simple "V-shaped" pattern and indicate that the parsimonious specification of Table 6.6 is oversimplified. The $F(24,4140)$ ratio of 3.29 for coal plants and $F(22,2450)$ ratio of 8.64 for noncoal plants indicates that the employment equation with separate coefficients for the year triplets fits significantly better than the specification in Table 6.6 that imposes two linear trends centered on 1968. However, since the other coefficients in the equations appear to be almost identical whether the Table 6.6 or year-triplet specification is used, we will explore the other variants in this section with the Table 6.6 specification.

2.   *Average Vintage*

The next variant is to move to a more accurate measure of plant vintage. The results in Table 6.6 are based on the vintage listed in the original data source, which is the date when the plant was first constructed. However, this does not take account of the fact that many plants install additional units at a later date. A more accurate vintage measure takes the average vintage of all units in the plant installed as of a given year of observation. The disadvantage of this approach is that it requires throwing away all observations on plants of pre-1948 vintage, since we have no information on the addition of new units before 1948. There are several interesting changes in the coefficients in Table 6.7 as compared with Table 6.6. The utilization coefficient for noncoal plants becomes insignificant, as does the heat rate residual coefficient for coal plants. The "V" of the vintage trends becomes steeper for both fuel types, while the "V" of the time trends becomes flatter for both fuel types.

3.   *Sample Split*

All employment equations thus far force the coefficients other than the vintage and time trends to be identical over the entire 1948–87 sample period. Table 6.8 examines the validity of this constraint by estimating separate equations for 1948–67 and 1968–87, while retaining the measure of average vintage introduced in the preceding section. There are numerous changes in coefficients, indicating a change in structure over the two halves of the postwar period. The capacity coefficients rise in the second half for both fuel types. The utilization coefficient for coal now has the wrong sign in the first half and is insignificant for noncoal in both halves. The heat rate residual coefficient is significant only in the first half for both fuel types, indicating perhaps more heterogeneity in design in the pre-1968 period. However, there is no important change in the vintage or time trend coefficients. Both imply the usual "V-shaped" pattern for both the vintage and time effects. The $F(14,3004)$ ratio of 13.5 for coal and

Table 6.7. *Equations Explaining the Log of Employment by Plant with Vintage Averaging, 1948–87*

	All Fuels	Coal Using	Noncoal Using
	(1)	(2)	(3)
1. Log Capacity	0.580**	0.592**	0.450**
2. Log Utilization	0.088**	0.082**	0.024
3. Heat Rate Residual	0.074	0.004	0.402**
4. Number Units	0.061**	0.067**	0.066**
5. Average Vintage			
a) All Vintages	−0.030**	−0.026**	−0.026**
b) 1968–87 Shift	0.049**	0.047**	−0.014**
6. Time			
a) All Years	−0.014**	−0.019**	−0.011**
b) 1968–87	0.036**	0.045**	0.023**
7. Fuel			
a) Coal Using	−0.343**	–	–
b) Oil Only	−0.065**	–	−0.058**
c) Gas Only	−0.051**	–	−0.112**
$\bar{R}^2$	0.802	0.805	0.790
Standard Error	0.359	0.357	0.313
Observations	5031	3036	1996

Notes. Asterisks indicate 5 percent (*) or 1 percent (**) significance levels.
All equations also include five location dummy variables and two construction-type dummy variables, as well as a constant term.

the $F(14,1960)$ ratio of 5.1 for noncoal indicate that the equations for the two halves of the postwar period cannot be pooled.

4. Interaction Effects

The shift in structure over time suggested in Table 6.8 can be parameterized in a single equation by allowing for interaction effects among fuel type, heat rate, utilization rate, and vintage, that may partially explain some of the behavior of individual coefficients in Tables 6.6 and 6.7. In Table 6.9 heat rates and utilization rates are displayed for new plants built at selected vintage intervals and for three fuel types. For coal-using and oil-only plants, the relationship between vintage and heat rate traces out a backward "J." This reversal still leaves the heat rate in 1983–6 lower (better) than in 1948–52, in contrast to the implication of the vintage trend for coal plants in Table 6.5 (which shows that the reversal more than canceled the 1948–68 improvement). We can reconcile this conflict when we recognize the role of the capacity effect in the regressions, which explains part of the 1948–68 improvement in heat rate by increased scale rather than by the vintage trend.

Exploration of every possible interaction effect for each of the three equations in Table 6.6 is infeasible. Instead, the basic equation for coal-using plants

Table 6.8. *Equations Explaining the Log of Employment by Plant over Split Sample Periods, 1948–67 and 1968–87*

	Coal Using		Noncoal Using	
	1948–67	1968–87	1948–67	1968–87
1. Log Capacity	0.541**	0.665**	0.409**	0.522**
2. Log Utilization	−0.080*	0.150**	0.001	0.022
3. Heat Rate Residual	0.674**	−0.058	0.861**	0.260
4. Units	0.083**	0.053**	0.089**	0.059**
5. Average Vintage				
a. All Vintages	−0.028**	−0.029**	−0.016**	−0.029**
b. 1968–87	–	0.043**	–	−0.018**
6. Time				
a. All Years	−0.013**	0.027**	−0.012**	−0.012**
b. 1968–87	–	–	–	–
7. Fuel				
a. Coal Using	–	–	–	–
b. Oil Only	–	–	0.025	0.057*
c. Gas Only	–	–	−0.147**	−0.116**
$\bar{R}^2$	0.834	0.763	0.837	0.762
Standard Error	0.287	0.373	0.236	0.330
Observations	984	2049	511	1484

Notes. Asterisks indicate 5 percent (*) or 1 percent (**) significance levels.
All equations also include five location dummy variables and two construction-type dummy variables, as well as a constant term.

Table 6.9. *Average Heat and Utilization Rates by Fuel Type, Selected Intervals, New Plants in First Full Year of Operation*

	1948–1952	1953–1957	1958–1962	1963–1967	1968–1972	1973–1977	1978–1982	1983–1986
1. Heat Rate	12.3	10.5	10.0	9.8	10.0	10.4	10.6	10.6
a. Coal Using	12.3	10.4	9.9	9.5	9.9	10.5	10.5	10.6
b. Oil Only	11.6	10.5	10.1	9.2	9.3	10.0	10.9	–
c. Gas Only	12.7	11.6	10.5	10.3	10.2	10.5	10.7	–
2. Utilization Rate	65.1	60.6	64.6	61.7	48.4	42.1	44.5	41.5
a. Coal Using	66.8	56.1	66.9	63.7	47.4	47.3	48.4	41.5
b. Oil Only	65.6	50.7	56.3	68.7	52.4	34.4	18.8	–
c. Gas Only	66.7	61.9	55.3	58.9	46.6	38.0	57.1	–

with average vintages (column 2 in Table 6.7) is presented in Table 6.10 with the addition of various interaction effects. The previous discussion suggests that there may be important interaction effects between vintage and vintage-shift, on the one hand, and capacity, utilization, and heat rate, on the other hand. All six of these possible interaction effects are included in column (2) of

Table 6.10. *Equations Explaining the Log of Employment With Interaction Effects, Coal-Using Plants, 1948–87*

	Basic Equation	Vintage Interaction	Significant Interaction Terms	Add Year Interaction
	(1)	(2)	(3)	(4)
1. Log Capacity	0.592**	0.700**	0.705**	0.623**
2. Log Utilization	0.082**	0.067	0.105**	−0.007
3. Heat Rate Residual	0.004	−0.224	−0.174**	−0.294**
4. Number of Units	0.067**	0.069**	0.069**	0.062**
5. Average Vintage				
a. All	−0.026**	−0.080**	−0.082**	−0.056**
b. 1968–87 Shift	0.047**	0.183**	0.186**	0.193**
c. 1 * 5a (VCAP)	–	0.009**	0.009**	0.004**
d. 1 * 5b (VSCAP)	–	−0.020**	−0.022**	−0.022**
e. 2 * 5a (VUT)	–	−0.001	–	–
f. 2 * 5b (VSUT)	–	0.013	–	–
g. 3 * 5a (VHR)	–	−0.006	–	–
h. 3 * 5b (VSHR)	–	0.122**	0.119**	0.074**
6. Time				
a. All	−0.019**	−0.014**	−0.013	−0.011**
b. 1968–87 Shift	0.045**	0.038**	0.038**	−0.012
c. 1 * 6b (TSCAP)	–	–	–	0.009**
d. 2 * 6b (TSUTIL)	–	–	–	0.013**
e. 3 * 6b (TSHR)	–	–	–	0.039**
$\bar{R}^2$	0.805	0.811	0.811	0.815
Standard Error	0.357	0.351	0.351	0.348
Observations	3036	3036	3036	3036

Notes. Asterisks indicate 5 percent (*) or 1 percent (**) significance levels.
All equations also include five location dummy variables and two construction-type dummy variables, as well as a constant term.

Table 6.10, and three are statistically significant – the log of capacity times the vintage variable and vintage shift variables, and the heat rate residual times the vintage shift variable. Column (3) estimates the same equation with only the five significant interaction variables included from column (2). The first two interaction terms (lines 5c and 5d) indicate that the "V-shaped" pattern of the vintage shift is steeper for small than for large plants.[25] They also imply that the scale coefficient is hump-shaped, rising from 0.54 in 1948 to 0.71 in 1968, and then falling to 0.49 in 1987. The effect of increasing scale on productivity is measured by unity minus this coefficient, and thus is V-shaped. The implication that the productivity benefits of increased scale were

---

[25] The implied vintage and vintage shift coefficients for 200 MW plants are −0.032 and +0.069, and for 2000 MW plants are −0.012 and +0.019.

lowest in 1968 seems consistent with the maintenance problems of large plants built in the late 1960s, as discussed in Section VII. The third interaction effect indicates a more severe adverse vintage shift for plants that are energy inefficient.

We may also inquire which characteristics are correlated with an adverse "time shift," that is, tendency to require more employees with increasing plant age after 1968 as compared to before 1968. The time shift interactions in column (4) indicate that this age deterioration effect was greatest for plants that were relatively large, heavily utilized, and energy-inefficent. The utilization interaction can be described in a second way: The employee requirements imposed by an above-average utilization rate increased after 1968, possibly because environmental regulations raised the employee requirements of maintenance for high-utilization plants. Stated a third and perhaps more appealing way, the employee *savings* made possible by a low utilization rate were greater after 1968, perhaps because plant managers interpreted the low utilization rates as permanent rather than temporary as in the 1950s and reduced their work forces accordingly. It is important to note that the interaction terms in column (4) cause the time shift variable to lose statistical significance.

Implications of the Coefficients for the Productivity Growth Slowdown

The sources of the productivity slowdown in the industry can be decomposed for alternative equations and for alternative sets of years. Lines A and B compare the growth rates of actual and predicted output per employee over the sample of coal-using plants. The predicted value is based on actual output and the equation's prediction of employment based on the estimated coefficients of column (4) in Table 6.10, multiplied by the mean values of each independent variable for the year in question.

The seven lines of Section C of the table decompose predicted productivity growth in each decade among the contributions of the independent variables in the equation. Each contribution is calculated by multiplying the appropriate coefficient times the change in the independent variable over the previous decade. This is done in straightforward fashion for the variables listed in lines C3 through C7, where output is treated as exogenous and every predicted change in employment creates a change in productivity of the opposite sign. The calculation of the effects of changing capacity and utilization require an extra step, since both output and employment are altered. Line 1a shows the direct effect of higher capacity on output, and line 1b subtracts that effect times the estimated coefficient on capacity in the employment equation (0.623). Similarly, line 2a shows the direct effect of changing utilization on output growth, holding constant capacity, while line 2b subtracts the (near-zero) coefficient on utilization in the employment equation. The interaction effects of vintage and time with capacity are grouped together on lines 1c and 1d under capacity,

Table 6.11. *Sources of Productivity Growth, All Coal-Using Plants, by Decade Annual Percentage Rates of Change, Using Equation from Table 10, column (4)*

	1948– 1958	1958– 1968	1969– 1978	1978– 1987
A. Actual	8.83	4.75	−1.88	−0.35
B. Predicted	10.43	4.78	−1.86	−0.43
C. Contribution of				
1. Capacity	3.91	2.71	−2.95	−0.35
a. Effect on Output	10.94	8.94	5.11	6.52
b. Minus Capacity Effect on Employment	−6.82	−5.57	−3.18	−4.06
c. Minus VCAP & VSCAP Effects on Employment	−0.21	−0.66	0.89	4.10
d. Minus TSCAP Effect on Employment	–	–	−5.77	−6.89
2. Utilization	3.35	−0.45	−1.90	1.43
a. Effect on Output	3.33	−0.45	−2.83	0.63
b. Minus Utilization Effect on Employment	0.02	−0.00	−0.02	0.00
c. Minus TSUT Effect on Employment	–	–	0.95	0.80
3. Heat Rate Residual	0.08	0.22	−0.16	0.37
a. Minus HR Effect on Employment	0.08	0.22	−0.02	−0.09
b. Minus VSHR Effect on Employment	–	–	−0.08	0.29
c. Minus TSHR Effect on Employment	–	–	−0.06	0.17
4. Units	−0.53	−0.14	0.05	−0.21
5. Average Vintage	2.90	2.75	0.51	−2.09
a. Basic Effect	2.90	2.75	3.58	3.30
b. 1968–87 Shift	–	–	−3.07	−5.39
6. Time	1.10	1.10	−0.10	−0.10
a. Basic Effect	1.10	1.10	1.10	1.10
b. 1968–87 Shift	–	–	−1.20	−1.20
7. Dummy Variables and Other	−0.38	−1.41	2.69	0.50

and similarly the interaction effect of time with utilization is shown on line 2c, while the heat rate interactions with vintage and time are shown on lines 3b and 3c.

The results in Table 6.11 can be combined in different ways to provide a summary of the causes of the productivity problems of the coal-using steam-electric plants. One useful technique is to divide the causes into three categories, (1) "exogenous" factors including higher fuel prices and macroeconomic business cycles that have caused changes in utilization, (2) "technical design" factors that influence the employment requirements of new equipment, including capacity, heat rate, units, and vintage, and (3) "operating" factors that cause changes in labor requirements on existing equipment represented in our equation by the time effect. As we shall see below, there is substantial interaction between (2) and (3), since extra labor hired on existing equipment may be required to repair problems resulting from design flaws. The following is the breakdown of the factors associated with the productivity slowdown:

	1948–58	1958–68	1968–78	1978–87	Slowdown, 1958–68 to 1968–87
Exogenous	3.35	−0.45	−1.90	1.43	0.13
Technical Design	6.36	5.54	−2.55	−2.26	−7.95
Operating	1.10	1.10	−0.10	−0.10	−1.20
Other + Residual Error	−1.98	−1.44	2.67	0.58	3.12
Equals: Actual Productivity Change	8.83	4.75	−1.88	−0.35	−5.91

The first decade is somewhat unusual, as the "vintage averaging" procedure cuts out all pre-1948 observations and leaves a small and atypical sample of plants in 1948, the first year of observation. Somewhat more instructive is the comparison between the second and the average of the third and fourth periods, that is, between 1958–68 and 1968–87. The total productivity slowdown of 5.91 percentage points at an annual rate is overexplained by the design and operating factors, with virtually no role for the exogenous utilization factor.

6.5   FIRM AND ESTABLISHMENT EFFECTS

This section provides an evaluation of establishment and firm effects. We are interested in determining whether a specification error occurs when the employment equations omit variables with establishment structure, and whether there are firm effects beyond those associated with the regional, fuel, and construction-type dummy variables in the basic specification. The estimation of establishment and firm effects also allows us to deal with the possibility of simultaneity in the employment regressions. While the basic assumption that capacity and output are exogenous in the short run seems convincing, there may be cases where maintenance problems or other factors cause a plant to be taken temporarily out of operation, leading to a simultaneous reduction in employment and output. The exogenous demand would then be satisfied by other plants owned by the firm or by purchases of power from other firms, leading to negative correlation of residuals among plants of a given firm. Another type of "firm effect" would occur if firms operate with different managerial procedures that yield consistently good or poor productivity performance.

The basic specification examined above can be written as the following general linear model:

$$y_{it} = \beta_{0i} + \sum_k^K \beta_k x_{ikt} + \varepsilon_{it}, \quad i = 1, \ldots, N \tag{6}$$

where i indexes individual establishment observations observed at each time period t; there is a vector of K explanatory variables x_{ikt} explaining each observation y_{it}, and the ε_{it} are a set of independent and identically distributed disturbances with zero expectation and a finite variance.[26] The previously estimated employment and fuel use equations (2 and 5) share the feature of (6) that the β_k coefficients are assumed to be identical for all establishments and time periods (except that we have allowed for a vintage shift effect); and that our equations include one or more time trends.

An initial question involves the possible existence of individual establishment effects. Employment in a given establishment might be higher or lower year after year than can be explained by the included x_{ikt} variables, and such an effect could bias any of the estimated coefficients. An establishment effect exists if there is a determinant of establishment employment that has the same value for a given establishment in all time periods but whose value differs between establishments.

The analysis of establishment effects begins by taking the mean over time of the general linear specification in (6). This provides a structural relationship between the mean of the dependent variable over time for each establishment and the means of the right-hand variables over time for each establishment:

$$\bar{y}_i = \beta_{0i} + \sum_{k}^{K} \beta_k \bar{x}_{ik}, \quad \text{where}$$

$$\bar{y}_i = \frac{\sum_t y_{it}}{T}; \quad \bar{x}_{ik} = \frac{\sum_t x_{ikt}}{T} \tag{7}$$

Then the explanation of individual establishment employment (y_{it}) is decomposed into establishment-mean effect and a time-specific effect for each plant. Subtracting (7) from (6), we obtain:

$$y_{it} - \bar{y}_i = \sum_{k}^{K} \beta_k(x_{ikt} - \bar{x}_{ik}) + \varepsilon_{it}. \tag{8}$$

The issue to be explored is the correlation of the individual establishment effects with the mean characteristics of each establishment averaged over time. We investigate the hypothesis that there are establishment effects that are correlated with establishment mean characteristics. The remaining variance of β_{0i} is associated with an independent establishment error term η_i:

$$\beta_{0i} = \beta_0 + \sum_{k}^{K} \phi_k \bar{x}_{ik} + \eta_i. \tag{9}$$

The ϕ_k establishment effect parameters can be estimated directly, and an "establishment effect" is said to occur when the ϕ_k parameters are different from zero.

---

[26] This exposition adapts for time-series purposes the approach developed within the cross-section context by Pakes (1983). I am grateful to Ariel Pakes for his help in developing this exposition.

Substituting (9) into (7), and adding the resulting expression to (8), we obtain a relationship among the underlying observations of the dependent variable (y_{it}):

$$y_{it} = \beta_0 + \sum_k^K \phi_k \bar{x}_{ik} + \sum_k^K \beta_k x_{ikt} + \varepsilon_{it} + \eta_i. \tag{10}$$

The "establishment effect" (ϕ_k) parameters capture the correlation between average plant employment and the average values over time of the other right-hand variables, including capacity, utilization, heat rate, units, vintage, time, and the dummy variables for location, type of fuel, and type of construction. The β_k parameters estimate the remaining response of employment to a unit change in a right-hand variable within a given time period, given the "establishment effect" parameters. Thus the ϕ_k parameters can be thought of as "permanent" effects of changes in the explanatory variables, and the β_k parameters can be treated as "transitory" effects.[27]

By definition, since the vintage observation of a given plant is fixed over time, the vintage trend must be a between-establishment effect, while all the variance of the time trend occurs over time and must then be a within-establishment effect. A plausible outcome for the other coefficients in (10) would be to find that the ϕ_k between-establishment parameters capture all of the influence on employment of capacity, heat rate, and the number of units, while the β_k within-establishment parameters capture the influence from year to year of the utilization and time-trend variables. As is evident from columns (2) and (3) of Table 6.12, however, this sharp dichotomy turns out to be true only for the utilization variable. Capacity and heat rate have both between and within effects, while the coefficients on the number of units are insignificant. The within-establishment effects of capacity and heat rate suggest that additions and retirements of equipment are important causes of changes in employment over time for a given establishment.

Allowing for Firm Effects

The variance in employment can be decomposed into three components, that is, within-establishment-across-time, across-establishments-within-firms, and across firms. One possible type of firm effect might be cross-plant sharing of maintenance or management labor. This is essentially an errors-in-variable problem, in the sense that if employees at one plant are doing maintenance for one or more other plants, the level of capacity relevant for the explanation of employment is incorrectly measured.

---

[27] The specification written in (10) does not represent the only possible method of estimating the ϕ_k establishment parameters. Pakes (1983) suggests a two-step procedure in which one estimates first (6) and then (8), obtaining the ϕ_k estimates as the difference in the β_k estimates from the two stages. But the estimation of (10) directly is both simpler and yields a direct estimate of the standard errors of the ϕ_k parameters.

Table 6.12. *Equations Explaining the Log of Employment Allowing for the Establishment and Firm Effects Unedited Sample for Coal Using Plants, 1948–87*

	Basic Equation	Equation with Establishment Effects		Equation with Establishment and Firm Effects		
		"Within" Effect (β)	"Between" Effect (ϕ)	"Within" Effect (β)	"Betw. Estab." Effect (ϕ)	"Betw. Firm" Effect (Θ)
	(1)	(2)	(3)	(4)	(5)	(6)
1. Log Capacity	0.594**	0.590**	−0.003**	0.601**	0.071*	0.101**
2. Log Utilization	0.068**	0.093**	−0.068	0.077**	−0.105**	0.058
3. Log Heat Rate	0.003**	−0.076**	0.559**	−0.074	0.739**	0.323
4. Number of Units	0.066**	0.034	0.041	0.042*	−0.012	0.129**
5. Vintage						
a) All	−0.026**	–	−0.026**	–	−0.021**	–
b) 1968–87	0.046**	–	0.47**	–	0.044	–
6. Time						
a) All Years	−0.019**	−0.016**	–	−0.016**	–	–
b) 1968–87	0.046**	0.044**	–	0.043**	–	–
$\bar{R}^2$	0.807	0.809		0.827		
Standard Error	0.356	0.354		0.337		
Observations	2990[a]	2990[a]		2990[a]		

Note. Asterisks indicate 5 percent (*) or 1 percent (**) significance levels. All equations also include five location dummy variables and two construction-type dummy variables, as well as a constant term.

[a] Plants with fewer than two observations were excluded.

We can rewrite the basic specification, altering (6) to let j index firms, and i index establishments within firms. Then (6) becomes:

$$y_{ijt} = \beta_{0ij} + \sum_k^K \beta_k x_{ijkt} + \varepsilon_{ijt}. \tag{11}$$

Now we define establishment means over time and firm means over establishments as

$$\bar{y}_{ij} = \sum_t \frac{y_{ijt}}{T}; \ \bar{x}_{ijk} = \sum_t \frac{x_{ijkt}}{T}; \ \bar{y}_j = \sum_t \frac{Y_{ij}}{N_j}; \ \bar{x}_{jk} = \sum_t \frac{\bar{x}_{ijk}}{N_j},$$

where N_j is the number of establishments at firm j. Now the cross-firm relationship and within-firm-over-time relationship can be written as:

$$\bar{y}_i = \beta_{0j} + \sum_k^K \beta_k \bar{x}_{jk} \tag{12}$$

$$\bar{y}_{ij} = \beta_{0ij} + \sum_k^K \beta_k \bar{x}_{ijk}. \tag{13}$$

We now define the establishment effect as in the above analysis,

$$\beta_{0ij} = \beta_{0j} + \sum_k^K \theta_k \bar{x}_{ijk} + \eta_{ij}, \tag{14}$$

and firm effects by analogy:

$$\beta_{0j} = \beta_0 + \sum_k \theta_k \bar{x}_{jk} + \xi_j. \tag{15}$$

Substituting (14) and (15) into (11), we obtain an equation that can provide direct estimates of the establishment and firm effects.

$$y_{ijt} = \beta_0 + \sum_k^K \phi_k \bar{x}_{jk} + \sum_k^K \phi_k \bar{x}_{ijk} + \sum_k^K \beta k x_{ijkt} + \xi_j + \eta_{ij} + \varepsilon_{ijt}. \tag{16}$$

The three right-hand columns in Table 6.12 exhibit the coefficient estimates for the three-way decomposition of within-establishment, between-establishment, and between-firm effects. The β_k coefficients for the within-establishment effects in column (4) are very close to those in column (2). The between-establishment coefficients in column (5) are basically similar to those in column (3), although the capacity coefficient rises from zero to a marginally significant 0.071, and the negative utilization effect becomes significant. This apparently perverse utilization effect means that a plant having a high average utilization rate has a relatively high level of plant productivity, and this correlation may be induced by reverse causation, since high-productivity plants are likely to be the "base load" plants that experience the highest utilization rates.

A broader evaluation of Table 6.12 yields a mixed verdict on the inclusion of the establishment and firm effects. On the one hand, both effects are clearly significant, as is obvious from the high estimated t ratios. Also, a Chow test for the inclusion of the establishment effect in columns (3) and (4) yields a $F(4,2969)$ ratio of 7.8, compared to a 1 percent critical value of 3.32. A test for the inclusion of the firm effect in addition to the establishment effect yields a $F(8,2965)$ ratio of 43.2, compared to a 1 percent critical value of 2.5. On the other hand, the inclusion of the establishment and firm effects does not change any of our previous conclusions regarding the central vintage shift and time shift coefficients. For instance, the vintage shift coefficient in column (1) for the basic equation is 0.046 and is reduced only to 0.044 in the full equation in column (5).

6.6 A SURVEY OF "OUTLIER" PLANTS

Our decomposition of the productivity slowdown at the end of Part V provides a catalogue of factors which, while they help to explain the slowdown, themselves are in need of explanation. To report that productivity growth decelerated because capacity growth decelerated, the heat rate increased, and because there were "vintage shifts" and "time shifts" is not very helpful unless we can begin to understand why these adverse events occurred.

In this section we attempt to learn something about the industry's problems from those most closely involved, the plant managers themselves. The technique is simply to telephone the managers of plants with the largest positive and negative residual errors on average during the last five years of the sample period, in order to learn about their own explanation of the relatively high or low level of employment at their plants. These telephone calls are useful not just in isolating "special factors" that require unusually high levels of employment at some plants, but also in obtaining a set of explanations for the behavior of some of our explanatory variables, particularly capacity, utilization, and heat rate, and the roles of environmental legislation and the "depletion hypothesis" in contributing to that behavior.

Characteristics of Outlier Plants

The telephone interviews were carried out in two steps, once in 1982 for the first draft of this paper, and again in 1990 when the research was updated. In the early interviews outliers were chosen as those with the highest or lowest residuals (actual minus fitted) in the last five years of the sample period, then 1974–8. In the early interviews only positive outliers were telephoned, reflecting our interest in the disappointing productivity performance of the industry. This asymmetry was partly corrected in the second batch of interviews, where more negative than positive outliers were telephoned.[28]

Summary data on the outlier plants are provided in Table 6.13. The early group of plants displays systematic differences, in that the positive outliers

---

[28] The interviews were conducted October 11–18, 1982, and July 9–12, 1990.

Table 6.13. *Summary Information on Outlier Plants*

	Number Telephoned	Average Vintage	Average Capacity	Average Actual Employment	Average Predicted Employment	Ln (Act.) minus Ln (Pred.)
Outliers telephoned in 1982, averages for 1978						
17 positive outliers	12	1963	1179	366	126	1.07
12 negative outliers	0	1946	622	96	178	−0.62
Outliers telephoned in 1990, averages for 1987						
15 positive outliers	4	1968	1473	470	224	0.74
15 negative outliers	8	1966	898	70	169	−0.88

are newer and larger than the negative outliers. In the early group eight of the seventeen positive outliers had vintages of 1968 or newer, while *none* of the negative outliers were post-1968 in vintage (and seven of the twelve were vintage 1950 or earlier). The early group also appears to display a somewhat skewed distribution, in that the average log residual for positive outliers is much larger than for negative outliers. The later group of outliers displays more similarity between the positive and negative averages, with roughly the same average vintage and less skewness.[29] Eight of the positive outliers and nine of the negative outliers are post-1968 in vintage. There is still a tendency, however, for the positive outlier plants to be larger than the negative outlier plants.[30]

The residuals used to choose the early group of outliers come from the original employment equation in Table 6.6, column (1), estimated for the period 1948–78. The later group come from the same equation, estimated for the period 1948–87, and the facts reported in the rest of this paragraph refer to the more recent results. The estimated coefficients in the regression for the complete sample period excluding the thirty outlier plants differ little from those in the equivalent regression for the inclusive group. Obviously, the standard error declines as the outliers are excluded, from 0.373 to 0.348; the unexplained variance is reduced by 22 percent by the exclusion of 8 percent of the plants. The main coefficients of interest, the vintage and time effects and their 1968–78 shifts, change little. The absence of any important change in the 1968–87 year shift effect implies that the role of the outlier plants constructed before 1968 is to raise the residual error in all years, and not to contribute an unexplained increase in employment after 1968.

As indicated in Table 6.13, twenty-four plant managers were contacted, twelve in the early group and twelve in the late group. No individual refused to enter into a discussion. The only limitation on completeness of coverage was the author's own time. There seems to be no other reason in principle why coverage could not be extended to all the outliers or, indeed, to the full sample of plants.[31] In the following analysis of the interviews, plant managers in the

---

[29] There is substantial turnover in the group of positive outliers: of the seventeen plants in the early group identified from data ending in 1978, only five appear in the list of positive outliers based on average residuals during 1983–7. Of the other twelve plants, six disappeared from the data set or changed their identity when small adjacent plants were consolidated; and the average residual for the remaining six in 1983–7 was only 0.12. None of the early group of negative outliers reappeared in the later group.

[30] Why are positive outliers more likely to be large plants? One reason is that large plants are more likely to have supercritical boilers, a technology that (as we see below) led to unanticipated maintenance requirements that raised employment. Rose-Joskow (1990) have studied the diffusion of innovation in the industry and conclude that larger firms were more likely to adopt supercritical units.

[31] In the early interviews an attempt was made to contact all seventeen plants, and plants were excluded only when repeated attempts failed to reach the plant manager. The plants for the later interviews were selected at random, in the sense that one or more phone calls were placed to every plant on the list of thirty. The first twelve plants where the plant manager could be contacted were included; the rest are excluded because of no answer, busy signals, managers who were in meetings or on vacation.

early or later groups, and the sign of the residual error, are distinguished by (pos. 82), (pos. 90), or (neg. 90).

Role of Employees and Extent of Data Errors

An important aspect of the survey is the emphasis by respondents on equipment characteristics and reliability as primary determinants of work-force size and composition. This corroborates the basic distinction in much of the electric utility literature between "ex ante" investment decisions and "ex post" operating decisions, the latter allowing plant managers little freedom to deviate from fixed capital-energy-labor input ratios. Indeed, a striking feature of the data is the tendency for a given plant to experience the same capacity, heat rate, and employment for several years and sometimes decades, with utilization being the only variable experiencing marked year-to-year fluctuations.

The first step in each telephone call was to verify the basic information contained in our data file on plant vintage, units, capacity, and employment. Managers were questioned closely in cases where employment had increased noticeably in the last five years of the sample period without an increase in capacity. In every case but one where a discrepancy was reported, the error could be traced to the government document that provides the source data.

What do plant employees do? Paul Wade at the Bull Run (TN) 1967-vintage TVA plant (pos. 82) decomposed his 1982 work force of 227 people as consisting of 70 involved in maintenance, 55 in operations, 50 in coal handling, 25 in specialized work involving instruments and water quality control, and 15 in administrative capacities (this accounts for 215 of the 227). Twenty-two percent of the work force is cited as being involved in coal handling, very close to the estimated 23 percent employment penalty of coal plants relative to gas plants in column (1) of Table 6.6. Confirmation of this figure also comes from Tim Lovette of the Danskhammer (NY) plant (pos. 90), which shifted from oil and gas to coal in 1986–7 and was forced to raise employment from 101 to 126 as a result.

Omission of Variables

Some, but not all, of the plant managers seemed aware that the level of employment at their plants was "relatively high" or relatively low" and had ready explanations, always involving additional factors that were not identified in the data set. An examination of the following list of factors is somewhat disturbing for the econometrician, in that it suggests that the list of "left-out" variables assembled from a complete set of interviews might exhaust the available degrees of freedom even in this rich data set:

1.   Gas Turbine Unit

Three of the plant managers reported that their employment rolls included people involved in operating and maintaining gas turbine capacity that is not included in the basic data source which covers only steam units. As it happens, all three of these pre-1968 plants added the gas turbine capacity in 1968 or afterward, thus contributing to the significance of the positive 1968–78 time shift coefficient. In every case gas turbine units are used for peaking purposes but nevertheless can add a significant number of employees.

2.   Joint Products

The Warwick (IN) plant was built jointly with an Alcoa aluminum smelter and on average 85 percent of the plant's electric output goes to the smelter rather than to other electric company customers. The particular location and identity of the principal customer would not be important if it were not for the fact that the plant's employment register includes an unspecified number providing specific services to Alcoa, including steam and water treatment services.

3.   Joint Maintenance and Engineering Services

In the later group of interviews all plant managers were questioned about joint maintenance and whether they imported or exported employees. The most common pattern was sharing across plants within the firm with no implications for the regression results if imports of employees for the subject plant's overhaul period are balanced by exports of employees to service other plants. Ron Kilman of the Sooner (OK) plant (pos. 90) stated that he sometimes exported 4–10 employees for minor overhauls and 20–25 for major overhauls, out of a total staff of 220. Melanie Adams-Miller of the Anclote (FL) plant (neg. 90) gets along with only about half the predicted number of employees, partly because her firm has a traveling maintenance crew of 100–120 people who perform overhauls on her plant. Similarly, shift supervisor Wally Ghilani of the Harrison (WV) plant (neg. 90) reports that major maintenance at his plant is performed by "mobile maintenance gangs" employed by a specialist service firm, not by his own utility. Guy Pepipone of the Sammis (OH) plant (pos. 90) was the only manager reporting a major component of employees who performanced services for other plants in the same firm; in his case fully 30 percent of the employees perform engineering and planning services on a per-service fee basis.

4.   Isolated Location

In the later group seven of the fifteen positive outliers, and none of the negative outliers, are located in five mountain-region states (Nevada, Arizona, New Mexico, Wyoming, and Montana), largely because isolated plants are required to be more self-sufficient. The role of this and other omitted variables related to isolation can be illustrated by the example of a consistent top-five outlier, the Navajo (AZ) plant (pos. 82). The 1974-vintage plant is listed as having 615 employees in contrast to the predicted level of 146 in 1978, and by 1987 this had risen to 752 employees versus a predicted level of 310. The plant is in Page, Arizona, near the Arizona-Utah line and east of the Grand Canyon. It faces three separate problems that are directly related to its location. First, its employees run the plant's own railroad to move coal seventy-eight miles from the mine. This factor alone accounts for 100 extra employees. Second, the plant is 300 miles from both Phoenix and Salt Lake City and cannot rely on outside contractors for special maintenance functions. Thus, an undetermined part of its excess staff is explained by the need to include sufficient maintenance employees to handle virtually any conceivable job. A related factor is the dependence of the area on the plant, so that any outage must be repaired more promptly than "plants in the east." Third, the environmental regulations in that area are particularly demanding. Isolation is indirectly related to the high level of employment at the Mohave (NV) plant (pos. 90), due to the use of "slurry" (liquid-form) coal brought in by pipe line. The mechanical process of extracting the water from the coal not only requires extra operating workers, but also "wears the heck out of everything," thus requiring extra maintenance personnel, according to assistant plant manager Don Wilson.

5.   *Old Building*

The data do not distinguish between the vintage of the structure and the vintage of the equipment. Mr. Decker, the Kearney (NJ) plant manager (pos. 82), attributed part of his high employment level to the fact that his steam equipment, of which 52 percent of the current capacity was installed in 1953 and the rest in 1926, was housed in a 1926 building, which required "more maintenance" than a postwar building of similar size.

6.   *New Units After Sample Period*

In the cases of two plants in the early group, a jump in employment in the 1977–8 period was explained by the installation of new units that were actually completed in 1979 or 1980, after the end of the sample period. If also true after the end of the extended 1948–87 sample period, this factor could account for part of the time shift effect.

7.   *Plant Configuration*

Another omitted determinant of employment was identified by Ron Kilman of the Sooner plant. Units of a given-size boiler and generator can be fitted with coal silos of different sizes, and small-sized silos of the type at his plant must be refilled every six to eight hours, as contrasted with other plants of the same size fitted with "twenty-four-hour" silos.

Misgauged Maintenance Burden

A consistent explanation of rising employment relative to capacity was the incorrect anticipation of maintenance requirements. Staffing levels were increased when it was discovered that "the previous force wasn't adequate" and when "deferred maintenance began to build up." This factor would not tend to contribute to our time shift coefficients if it had operated consistently over the postwar period, but it appears to have been concentrated in post-1968 plants. An example of the contribution of maintenance to the time shift coefficient is reported by Guy Pepipone of the Sammis (OH) plant (pos. 90). After installation of seven units over the period 1959–71, employment at his plant had remained at the 450 level through 1978. But then critical maintenance problems began to develop with units 5, 6, and 7 (vintages 1966–71), and employment ballooned to 860 by the early 1980s without any further change in capacity.[32] In this particular case employment overshot and was thereafter steadily reduced by attrition to about 725 in 1990.

Unhappy experiences were reported by Don Wilson of the 1971-vintage Mohave plant. A steam pipe explosion cut output for 1985 almost in half from the average of 1984 and 1986. Unanticipated problems with turbine blades caused substantial shutdowns while the turbine rotors were rebuilt.[33] Related to the role of unanticipated maintenance problems was the shifting division of responsibilities between equipment manufacturers and utilities for troubleshooting and retrofitting. Guy Pepipone reported that "we're not getting as much help from manufacturers as we used to," and he and others attributed this to financial tightness at the manufacturing firms which were faced with a dearth of orders for new equipment after the mid-1970s. Bob Arambel of the Naughton (WY) plant (neg. 90) cited maintenance problems with a coal-pulverizing unit that was "underdesigned" with a firebox that was too small, causing the unit to operate at a too high a velocity and develop "boiler-tube erosion."

Environmental Regulations

The most plausible cause of the adverse time shift effect in our employment regressions is the role of environmental regulations, which fell on electric utilities more heavily than any other industry. Standards for emissions standards dating back to 1970 affected labor productivity at generating plants by forcing plants to shift from high-sulfur to low-sulfur fuel having lower energy content, thus requiring more fuel to be handled per unit of electricity output. Most plants had to install additional capital equipment in the form of electrostatic precipitators or scrubbers, which substantially raised capital cost and also required the addition of maintenance employees. The effects of environmental regulations differ widely in their impact on each plant due to differing emissions standards in different regions (Gollop-Roberts, 1985), different rules applied to plants of different vintages, and variations in the emissions-creating characteristics of the three fuels (coal, gas, and oil).

[32] These were early examples of a new generation of Babcock and Wilcox boilers, and numbers 6 and 7 were supercritical (see below).

[33] The increased size of units created substantial problems with turbine blades, as documented by Hirsch (1989, pp. 105–8).

Among our outlier plants the most common air-pollution-control device is one or more electrostatic precipitators, installed at seven of the twelve plants in the early group and eight of the twelve in the later group (which also contained two plants with scrubbers and two with no emissions control equipment). Although some managers claimed that precipitators were not a major extra source of maintenance employment requirements, thirty-five to forty extra people, or 12 to 13 percent of the work force, were attributed to precipitators at the Gallatin (TN) plant (pos. 82). There first-generation precipitators had proven to be inadequate when emissions requirements were raised from the 95 to the 99 percent level, and new equipment four times as large had to be installed. The need for a quantum jump in the size of precipitators was augmented by the widespread shift to low-sulfur coal. Apparently this type of fuel requires extra precipitator capacity.

At the La Cynge (MO) plant (pos. 82), vintage 1973, two units of roughly the same size experienced quite different employment requirements connected with air pollution equipment. At the first unit, installed in 1973, local high sulfur (5 percent) coal was used, and a "tail-end scrubber" was installed. This required "probably 40–45 people" (25 percent of the average 1974–5 work force) for operations and maintenance.[34] On the second unit, installed in 1977, low-sulfur coal was used, and an electrostatic precipitator instead of a scrubber was included. Extra maintenance requirements of the precipitator are claimed to be only a single person. The trade-off involves a much higher cost of coal for the second unit. At the Sommers (TX) plant (pos. 82) scrubbers installed after 1978 are cited as a "high-cost-maintenance item" that create "sludge that is hard to get rid of." Plant manager Jerry Godwin at the San Juan (NM) plant (pos. 82) reported that scrubbers had been installed on all four of the units installed between 1973 and 1982, as well as a "$93,000,000 zero-discharge water management system," and that fully 17 percent of the level of electric rates charged by his company could be attributed to the expenses of air and water pollution control.

Tony Leavitte of the Gardner (NV) plant (pos. 90) attributed the employment of fifty to sixty people of his 275-person workforce, or 18 to 22 percent, to environmental regulations. These include not only the operation and maintenance of scrubbers, but also water treatment "evaporation ponds." Bob Arambel of the Naughton (WY) plant attributed only 5 percent of employment to environmental regulations, this smaller number reflects the fact that only one of his three units has a scrubber.

A uniquely local form of regulation was cited by Ron Kilman of Sooner. Beginning in 1987 all utility plants in Oklahoma must use 10 percent Oklahoma-mined coal, requiring another feed belt and new automatic controls for blending the Oklahoma coal with the Wyoming coal that was previously used exclusively. Perhaps the extreme case of minimal impact of environmental regulations is

---

[34] The La Cygne plant is the subject of Weaver (1975), which highlights the unanticipated maintenance problems created by scrubbers.

the Anclote (FL) plant (neg. 90), which has no pollution control equipment and manages the burden of obtaining "innumerable permits" and training about regulations with a fixed and relatively small staff.

How do these anecdotes compare with the magnitude of the "time-shift" effect displayed above for the employment equations? To take the equation for coal-using plants with vintage averaging (Table 6.7, col. 2), there was a shift in the time coefficient from -0.019 for 1948–67 to $+0.026$ for 1968–87, for a net deterioration of 0.045 points per year. This would imply that by 1987 fully 85 percent of additional employment could be attributed to the time-shift effect. Since no plant manager cited work force additions connected with pollution control equipment exceeding 25 percent, at a maximum one could attribute only about one third of the time shift effect to environmental legislation, and probably less. This leaves the remainder to be attributed to data errors, unanticipated maintenance, and other undetermined causes. A hint of one of these causes was provided by Jerry Chambers of the Stout (IN) plant (neg. 90), who described an overall shift toward a less productive and more careful response to events: "I've been doing this for twenty-six to twenty-seven years. In those days our main concern was making electricity. If you had a leak, you'd pull off the insulation, patch it, and the repair would be done. Now, you have to call in a contractor to take air samples, you have to be inspected, and it takes two days to do what used to take two hours."

Diminishing Returns to Technical Advance

The interviews revealed substantial evidence of the reversal of vintage-specific technical improvements in the late 1960s and 1970s. The most common feature of the interviews was the uniform report that the technical advance in the 1960s to "supercritical" units (having a pressure of more than 3,200 pounds per square inch) had encountered an unanticipated economic barrier. These units cost too much to build and to maintain, and by 1977–8 subcritical designs were once again the dominant form of new installations (see the discussion in Part III).

Plant managers were outspoken in condemning supercritical units. In comparing his 1973 supercritical unit to his earlier and smaller subcritical units, Jim Smith of the Gaston (AL) plant (pos. 82) commented that the newer unit "blows real crud" that adds substantial maintenance expense. The earlier units are easier to maintain and produce "no filth." Plant manager Cathcart of the Homer City (PA) plant (pos. 82) reported that the supercritical units had been introduced in the early 1960s as the next step in the technical progression that had steadily increased thermal efficiency. But they brought with them "complex valving" with an associated "burden of maintenance." Equipment designers had planned the supercritical units in a "laboratory and had not anticipated the effects of cold and hot weather and of fly ash. The real world is not a laboratory." James Morrison of the Mercer (NJ) plant (pos. 82) commented that most companies had experienced a poor operating record with supercritical units, with a "forced outage rate higher than anticipated." Carl Higgs of the La Cynge (MO) plant (pos. 82) contrasted his "supertroublesome" Westing house Unit #1 with his much more reliable and less labor-intensive General Electric Unit #2. On the same Westinghouse unit the turbine blades had a tendency to keep "falling out."[35] The interviews of negative outliers revealed only one instance of a supercritical boiler, adding further evidence that few if any supercritical boilers achieved a high level of labor productivity.[36]

Advances in metallurgy, which have been credited for allowing larger scale and higher temperatures and pressures, apparently were unable to keep ahead of the needs of plant designers. Wally Ghilani of the Harrison plant cited leaks, overheating, and "fishmouth stress" in his supercritical boilers, as well as the complexity introduced by "so many relays, so much protection" that the problem of false alarms was "phenomenal." Paul Wade of Bull Run also reported gas leaks, which he attributed to "phased pressurized furnaces," "a design that we learned just didn't work." Cathcart of Homer City described considerable extra maintenance connected with "tears in casing" that were related to high furnace pressure.

Most managers agreed that economies of scale had been exhausted. As shown in Table 6.4, the average capacity of new plants reached a plateau at 850 MW by 1972–4 and increased little after that. Carl Higgs of La Cynge felt that the optimal size of a single unit was 600–650 MW, and Paul Wade of Bull run stated that "1,000–1,100 is as large as you can go." Cathcart of Homer City claimed that manufacturers had sold larger units in the 1960s by "extrapolating the features of smaller units and convincing users that they didn't require extra maintenance."

In another comment with important implications for practitioners of the hedonic regression technique, Cathcart contrasted the features of his two 600 MW supercritical units (vintage 1969) with his 650 MW subcritical unit (vintage 1977). In putting out bids for the earlier units, his company had emphasized low cost and had specified only a few basic specifications – temperature, pressure, etc. In contrast, the bidding procedure for the newer unit involved much more detailed specifications, chosen to avoid the maintenance problems encountered in the earlier units. "Wall thickness on tubes was increased from 150 to 200 mils, the maximum velocity of the gas stream was reduced from 85 to 55," and so on. A hedonic regression explaining equipment prices of the type developed in Gordon (1990, Chapter 5) and Joskow-Rose (1985) would treat all three units as essentially identical and would overstate the price increase from 1969 to 1977. Continuing the theme of "learning by doing," James Agnew

---

[35] Interestingly, Westinghouse officials attribute part of their problems to inadequate research and development expenditures in the 1960s. See "The Turbine Troubles that Plague Westinghouse," *Business Week*, April 6, 1984, pp. 54–55.

[36] Another case is the Harrison (WV) plant, which is labeled here erroneously as a negative outlier only because the government data source greatly understated employment in three of the five years 1983–7 (as reported above).

at Cumberland attributed his ability to reduce plant staffing to a gradual process of modifying his 1973-vintage "prototype units" (two enormous units of 1,300 MW each). The furnace had been changed, generating surface had been added to boilers, and precipitator surface had been added.

The later group of interviews did not have quite as gloomy a tone as those conducted earlier. In fact, there are some signs in the interviews (although not yet in our data) that the worst may be over. Several managers cited enthusiastically the role of computerized controls, which can analyze and predict maintenance problems before they occur. Don Wilson at Mohave raved above his training simulator, which could train operators how to handle every eventuality without endangering either of his two large 790 MW units. Tony Leavitte of Gardner cited improved control systems and water-treatment equipment as allowing him to reduce his staff by about 3 percent over the most recent two years. He was also enthusiastic about his CRT-equipped control room which allowed operators to plot the "trend" of numerous variables like temperature and pressure and spot potential problems in advance.

How do plant managers of negative outlier plants explain their low level of employment? Consistent with my earlier research on airlines (1965), managers with poor productivity performance blame outside forces, while managers with a high level of productivity attribute their performance to themselves and their workers. James Stape of the San Tan (AZ) plant (neg. 90) stated flatly that "we're good" and that his employees were a "close-knit" group, the "opposite of Navajo," a plant owned by the same firm that is at the top of our positive outlier list. Rick Smith of the Fort Phantom (TX) plant (neg. 90) cited "the quality of our guys." Tim Lovette attributed the performance of his Danskhammer plant to a "company philosophy to be lean up and down."

Overall, the interviews add up to a convincing case in support of the "depletion hypothesis." Advances in productivity in the first two decades of the postwar era (and before 1948 as well) were made possible by technical improvements that allowed for higher scale, temperatures, and pressure, but this process seems to have come to an end in the late 1960s. The technical barrier represented by supercritical pressure may be likened to the barrier of supersonic speed in the aircraft industry. Coincidentally, the postwar upsurge in aircraft scale and speed also seems to have come to an end around 1970 (Gordon, 1990, Chapter 4). One ray of hope is that, having deteriorated so much from the optimism of 1965 to the gloom of 1982, the conditions for productivity growth do not seem to have deteriorated further during the rest of the 1980s. Plant managers viewed themselves as operating in a difficult environment, but with few exceptions felt that the environment had remained stable over the past five years.

6.7 CONCLUSION

This paper attempts to decompose the sources of the slowdown in labor productivity growth in the steam-electric generating industry among a number of possible causes. Particular emphasis is placed on the separate roles of economies of scale, embodied technical change, and disembodied technical change. The major conclusions can be divided among methodology and substance.

Methodology

1. Data sets that provide information on individual plants observed along the two dimensions of vintage and age are particularly useful in studying the sources of growth. Cross-section data also allow for quantification of scale effects, shifts in the locational mix, and other sources of productivity change that are lumped together as an unexplained "residual" in aggregate studies.

2. In microeconomic research on data sets that identify individual observations, for example, plants or firms, a study of a mysterious phenomenon like the productivity slowdown can benefit from direct personal or telephone contact with plant or firm representatives. Such contact can reveal errors in data or interpretation at previous stages of a particular research study, and can add detail to flesh out an abstract academic conjecture, for example, the "depletion hypothesis."

3. Data sets that identify establishments and firms separately allow for a detailed analysis of "within" establishment and "between" establishment and firm effects. This is an unambiguous advantage of establishment data over the firm data used in many studies, and is only partly offset by measurement errors when separate plants within a firm share employees.

Substantive Results

The steam-electric utility industry experienced a much sharper slowdown in the growth of labor productivity after 1968 than the U.S. economy as a whole. The study identifies four main sources of the growth slowdown, each of which appears to have operated with more severity than in the whole economy.

1. A sharp drop in plant utilization occurred after the late 1960s, resulting both from the two oil shocks that raised the relative price of electricity, and from the slowdown in output and productivity growth in the rest of the economy. Both of these factors caused the growth rate of electricity demand to slacken sharply in the mid-1970s immediately after utilities had been on a binge of purchasing equipment. Our employment regression imply that 92 to 98 percent of any change in utilization flows through to a change in labor productivity in the same direction.

2. The growth of average plant size and unit size decelerated sharply after the late 1960s. Before 1968 rapid increases in the scale of new plants, together with a relatively small elasticity of employment growth to scale growth, allowed for productivity improvements. Earlier increases in scale resulted from incremental improvements in technology, particularly in metallurgy. After 1968, however,

capacity growth appears to have encountered technical constraints. The impact of this source of the productivity slow down is consistent with the "depletion hypothesis" of the overall economy-wide slowdown.

3. There was a disappearance in productivity gains associated with newer plants of a given capacity, that is, the "vintage shift" effect. Plant designers appear to have run into unanticipated technical barriers that caused them to build plants that were too large, too complex, and which required a high and unanticipated level of maintenance expenditures.

4. Beyond the contribution of equipment manufacturing problems to the productivity slowdown, after 1968 the utility industry encountered problems in operating preexisting equipment. Less than one-third of this "time specific" effect can be attributed to environmental legislation. An undetermined part of the rest is due to a previously unanticipated maintenance backlog on plants of earlier generations built when technology arrived at the apparent frontier in the late 1960s and early 1970s.

The regressions in this essay attempt to explain the relation of employment to output by holding constant numerous characteristics of individual plants. If the *only* cause of the slowdown in labor productivity growth in the electric utility industry had been a deceleration in the rate of technical change embodied in new equipment, this would be imply that there had been *no* slowdown in the growth rate of total factor productivity (TFP), since all of the declining growth rate of output per hour would be explained by an equal-size decline in the growth rate of capital's contribution to output. Another implication of this hypothetical finding would be that the source of the productivity problem originates not in the electric utility industry but in the electric equipment industry within the manufacturing sector.

However, a substantial fraction of the overall slowdown in labor productivity in electricity generation can be linked to factors other than embodied technical change, and thus did occur within the utility industry itself. In contrast to labor productivity growth for our sample of plants, which exhibited a deceleration from 7.5 percent per annum in 1948–68 to −0.4 percent per year in 1968–87 (for a total slowdown of 7.9 points), TFP growth using official NIPA deflators for the capital stock slowed from 3.6 to −1.8 percent per year (for a total slowdown of 5.4 points). When the deflator of electric generating equipment is measured by a hedonic index of the type developed by Gordon (1990) and Joskow-Rose (1985), TFP slows from 1.8 to −2.7 points, for a slowdown of 4.5 points.[37] Not coincidentally, the slowdown of 4.5 points is very close to the time shift coefficients in our all-fuel equations in Tables 6.6 and 6.7, ranging from 3.6 to 4.7 points. The fact that TFP slows less than average labor productivity, and that TFP growth in the pre-1968 period was so much slower than the growth of

---

[37] This calculation is not shown in the paper to save space. Output, employment, and nominal equipment cost refer to our sample of plants. The hedonic equipment deflator comes from Gordon (1990), Table 5.9, col. (2), recalculated to 1986 from our revised data.

average labor productivity, underlines the responsibility of capital input growth for much of the industry's outstanding achievements in the first half of the postwar period and for its abysmal performance since then.

This paper represents only a beginning in studying the industry's productivity problems. Much of the large "time-shift" effect remains unexplained. A more complete investigation would incorporate into the data more information on the design characteristics of individual plants, although our interview study suggests that many explanatory factors will inevitably be overlooked. A wider interview survey might reveal a more specific estimate of the impact of air-and-water-pollution-control legislation. Comparisons with foreign countries, using a combination of econometrics and interviews, might reveal the relative roles of design philosophy, equipment reliability, operating procedures, and environmental regulation in explaining why the European and Japanese electric power industries have not exhibited deteriorating performance to the same extent as the American industry.[38] Finally, one might hope that the mixture of econometric and interview techniques utilized here could be fruitfully employed in other industries, and that economists interested in production economics might devote more attention to the possibility of interviewing the business executives whose behavior they are trying to explain.

Data Appendix

Data Source

All data were obtained from the annual publication of the U.S. Energy Information Administration. In 1978 the title of the publication changed from *Steam-Electric Plant Construction Cost and Annual Production Expenses* to *Thermal-Electric Plant and Construction Cost and Annual Expenses*, and then in 1982 to *Historical Plant Cost and Annual Production Expenses for Selected Electric Plants*. In prior years the publication was issued by predecessor agencies, particularly the Federal Power Commission.

The data file contains plants observed from 1948 to 1987, but vintages of these plants extend back to the early years of the century. Data for years through 1971 were obtained from Thomas Cowing, and data for years since 1972 were added by successive research assistants. Most plants added to the original data set had vintage of 1972 or newer, with six exceptions. Some changes in plant identification also occurred as a result of merging of units previously considered as separate plants. The complete data set contains 7,701 observations, with 29 basic variables per observation (including dummies for fuel type, construction type, and regional location), and a number of additional constructed variables.

The 1982 change in the title of the data source also involved a downsizing of the data from a nearly complete census to a sample. Plants excluded in 1982 and

---

[38] The more cautious design philosophy of European manufacturers during the postwar years is discussed by Hirsch (1989), pp. 3, 75.

subsequent years amounted to 25 percent of the plants in the 1981 population, but only 9 percent of the total output of the 1981 population, since the excluded plants were on average only one third as large (measured by either capacity or output) as the average for the 1981 population.

Editing and Adjustments

The total sample of 7,701 was edited down to the 6,674 observations used in the initial regression reported in the first column of Table 6.5. Several criteria were used in editing and apply to the entire data set, not just the new post-1971 observations added for this project.

1.   Cleaning

Observations were excluded when (a) the utilization rate was below 5 percent, (b) when data seemed to be of the wrong order of magnitude, (c) when plant statistics were reported jointly with a nuclear or gas turbine plant, or (d) when data were missing for specific variables needed for a regression. Particular care was taken to make sure that the location, plant construction, and vintage dummies were identical from year to year for each plant, and that there were no implausible jumps in data on capacity and the number of units. In years when plant capacity was missing, this could sometimes be calculated from data on output and the utilization rate.

2.   Adjustments

There were six cases when two or three plants shared a single listed employment figure, and in these cases all variables were aggregated over the plants in question to form a single observation for the hybrid plant. In some recent years data are reported as applying to a percentage "P" of the plant, and quantity data are then divided by "P". Comparisons with adjacent years are made to determine whether "P" applies to all variables, especially employment data. Where some units were indoors and some outdoor, the construction plant dummy was coded "semioutdoor."

3.   Configuration Changes

Plants were included only in the first full year of operation, that is, the year after the vintage year, and were also excluded for years t-1 and t whenever there was a change in year t in either the number of units or a non-negligible change in capacity. This exclusion principle applies both to increases and decreases in units and/or capacity.

4.   Average Vintage

Most of the regression results refer to the "average" vintage of a plant. This is simply the average of the vintage for each unit in the plant. A plant installed in 1955 with five units that adds an additional unit in 1966 would be coded as vintage 1956.8, rounded to 1957.

References

Atkinson, Scott E., and Halvorsen, Robert. "Parametric Efficiency Tests, Economies of Scale, and Input Demand in U.S. Electric Power Generation." *International Economic Review*. October, 1984; vol. 25, pp. 647–62.

Baily, Martin N. "Productivity and the Services of Capital and Labor." *Brookings Papers on Economic Activity*. 1981; no. 1, pp. 1–50.

Barzel, Yoram. "The Production Function and Technical Change in the Steam-Power Industry." *Journal of Political Economy*. April, 1964; vol. 72, pp. 133–50.

Bruno, Michael, and Sachs, Jeffrey. *The Economics of Worldwide Stagflation*. Cambridge, MA: Harvard University Press; 1985.

Bushe, Dennis M. "An Empirical Analysis of Production and Technology Using Heterogeneous Capital: Thermal Electric Power Generation." Unpublished Ph.D. dissertation. New York: New York University; October, 1981.

Christensen, Laurits R., and Greene, William H. "Economies of Scale in U.S. Electric Power Generation." *Journal of Political Economy*. August, 1976; vol. 84, pp. 655–76.

Cowing, Thomas G. "Technical Change in Steam Electric Generation: An Engineering Approach." Unpublished Ph.D. thesis. University of California, Berkeley. 1970.

"Technical Change and Scale Economies in an Engineering Production Function: The Case of Steam Electric Power." *Journal of Industrial Economics*. December, 1974; vol. 23, pp. 135–52.

Small, Jeffrey, and Stevenson, Rodney E. "Comparative Measures of Total Factor Productivity in the Regulated Sector: The Electric Utility Industry." In Cowing and Stevenson. eds. *Productivity Measurement in Regulated Industries*. New York: Academic Press; 1981, pp. 162–77.

and Smith, Kerry V. "The Estimation of a Production Technology: A Survey of Econometric Analyses of Steam-Electric Generation." *Land Economics*. May, 1978; vol. 54, no. 2, pp. 156–86.

and Stevenson, Rodney E., eds. *Productivity Measurement in Regulated Industries*. New York: Academic Press; 1981.

Denison, Edward F. *Trends in American Economic Growth, 1929–82*. Washington: The Brookings Institution; 1985.

Gollop, Frank M., and Roberts, Mark J. "The Sources of Economic Growth in the U.S. Electric Power Industry." In Cowing and Stevenson, eds. *Productivity Measurement in Regulated Industries*. New York: Academic Press; 1981, pp. 107–43.

"Environmental Regulations and Productivity Growth: The Case of Fossil-Fueled Electric Power Generation." *Journal of Political Economy*. November, 1983; vol. 91, pp. 654–74.

"Cost-minimizing Regulation of Sulfur Emissions: Regional Gains in Electric Power." *Review of Economics and Statistics*. February, 1985; vol. 67, pp. 81–90.

Gordon, Robert J. "Airline Costs and Managerial Efficiency." In *Transportation Economics*. New York: Universities-National Bureau Conference Volume. 1965; pp. 61–92.

The Measurement of Durable Goods Prices. Chicago: University of Chicago Press for NBER; 1990.

Hirsh, Richard F. *Technology and Transformation in the American Electric Utility Industry.* Cambridge, U.K.: Cambridge University Press; 1989.

Jorgenson, Dale W. "The Role of Energy in Productivity Growth." *The Energy Journal.* July, 1984; vol. 5, pp. 11–25.

Joskow, Paul L. and Rose, Nancy L. "The Effects of Technological Change, Experience, and Environmental Regulation on the Construction Cost of Coal-burning Generating Units." *Rand Journal of Economics.* Spring 1985; vol. 16, pp. 1–27.

Joskow, Paul L. and Schmalensee, Richard. *Markets for Power: An Analysis of Electric Utility Deregulation.* Cambridge, MA.: The MIT Press; 1983.

Kendrick, John W. *Productivity Trends in the United States.* Princeton, N.J.: Princeton University Press for NBER; 1961.

Komiya, R. "Technical Progress and the Production Function of the United States Steam Power Industry." *Review of Economics and Statistics.* 1962; vol. 44, pp. 156–66.

Moore, F.T. "Economies of Scale: Some Statistical Evidence." *Quarterly Journal of Economics.* May, 1959; vol. 73, pp. 232–45.

Nerlove, Marc. "Returns to Scale in Electricity Supply." In Christ, C. ed., *Measurement in Economics.* Stanford: Stanford University Press; 1963, pp. 167–98.

Nordhaus, William D. "Policy Responses to the Productivity Slowdown." *The Decline in Productivity Growth,* Federal Reserve Bank of Boston. 1980; Conference Series 22, pp. 147–72.

"Economic Policy in the Face of Declining Productivity Growth." *European Economic Review.* May/June 1982; vol. 18, pp. 131–58.

Norsworthy, J.R., Harper, Michael J., and Kunze, Kent. "The Slowdown in Productivity Growth: Analysis of Some Contributing Factors." *Brookings Papers on Economic Activity.* 1979; no. 2, pp. 387–432.

Pakes, Ariel. "On Group Effects and Errors in Variables in Aggregation." *Review of Economics and Statistics.* February, 1983; vol. 65, pp. 168–73.

Rasche, Robert, and Tatom, John. "Energy Price Shocks, Aggregate Supply, and Monetary Policy: The Theory and the International Evidence." In Brunner, Karl and Meltzer, Allan H. eds., *Supply Shocks, Incentives, and National Wealth.* Carnegie-Rochester Conference Series on Public Policy. 1981; vol. 14, pp. 9–93.

Rose, Nancy L. and Joskow, Paul L. "The Diffusion of New Technologies: Evidence from the Electric Utility Industry." *RAND Journal of Economics.* Autumn 1990; vol. 21, no. 3, pp. 354–73.

Schmalensee, Richard, and Joskow, Paul L. "Estimated Parameters as Independent Variables: An Application to the Costs of Electric Generating Units." MIT Sloan School of Management working paper. February, 1985; 1575–84.

Weaver, Paul H. "Behind the Great Scrubber Fracas." *Fortune.* February, 1975; pp. 106–14.

Wills, Hugh R. "Estimation of a Vintage Capital Model for Electricity Generating." *Review of Economic Studies.* October, 1978; vol. 45, no. 141, pp. 495–510.

PART TWO

INTERPRETING PRODUCTIVITY FLUCTUATIONS OVER THE BUSINESS CYCLE

INTRODUCTION

DEBATING THE SOURCES OF BUSINESS CYCLES

In organizing this book it seemed natural to follow the first part on the sources of long-run productivity growth by a second part on cyclical fluctuations in productivity growth. Yet for many readers this would seem like following an elephant with a mouse. Everyone can understand why long-term growth is a compelling topic, but the significance of cyclical fluctuations in productivity growth may be elusive. Why should we care if productivity growth sometimes grows faster or slower than normal for a few quarters or years, when clearly what matters is how fast it grows *on average* over several decades? One answer is that there is a current, hotly debated application, the need for a method of decomposing the cyclical and structural components of the post-1995 productivity growth revival in the United States. To what extent does that revival represent a structural event reflecting an underlying acceleration of technical change, and to what extent was the revival based on unsustainable cyclical factors (e.g., falling unemployment, high-tech stock-market bubble) that allowed U.S. output to grow at faster than its sustainable rate, especially in 1999 and early 2000?[1]

Yet, despite its marginal importance as a macroeconomic phenomenon, the debate about the sources of these cyclical fluctuations in productivity growth has played a surprisingly large role in the development of macroeconomic thought over the two decades after 1980. The traditional "Keynesian" view emerged from the catastrophe of the Great Depression. The economy's failure in the Great Depression was an inadequacy of demand, not an inability to produce, as we soon learned when World War II brought forth unbelievable torrents of production. In a Keynesian depression or recession, supply was ample but demand was insufficient, and so both output and the price level fell. The Keynesian explanation of business cycles began to lose some of its appeal in the early postwar years, as prices kept rising not just during output expansions

---

[1] See Chapter one, Table 1.2, for an estimate of the cyclical component of the post-1995 productivity growth revival.

but also during recessions. The attempt to maintain consistency between ever-positive inflation and the Keynesian emphasis on demand fluctuations led in the late 1950s to the development of the Phillips curve and its associated theory, the topic of Parts Three and Four.

After hanging on by a thread in the 1960s, the Keynesian paradigm appeared to unravel in the1970s. In 1974–5 and again in 1979–82, when output declined in recessions, prices did not just fail to decline, or even to grow at a steady pace, but rather the inflation rate actually increased. For dedicated Keynesians like myself, it was easy to see what had happened. An adverse "supply shock" in the form of a sharp increase in food and oil prices had sapped consumer buying power, leading to a recession as purchases of goods other than food and oil had to decline in order to take up the slack. As a result both unemployment and inflation increased together. The theory and empirical validation of this interpretation is set out below in Chapters Ten, Eleven, and Fourteen.

However, several prominent economists provided a new interpretation of business cycles that differed sharply from the Keynesian approach. This view, instantly dubbed the "Real Business Cycle" (RBC) theory, denied any role to insufficient demand in explaining recessions. Instead, markets cleared, and demand was always equal to supply. Declines of output in recessions were caused by a temporary decline in productivity. Whether positive or negative, the cyclical fluctuations of productivity were slow to evolve (this sluggishness was caused only by positive serial correlation that was an *ad-hoc* addition to the model) and left entirely unexplained. Because the RBC theory assumed that markets clear continuously, that is, that prices are completely flexible, it has been lumped into a category of theories called "New Classical Macroeconomics," together with an earlier market-clearing theory based on mistaken expectations as a source of business cycles. Chapter Seven explains and criticizes the two versions of New Classical Macro, both the expectations version and the RBC version.

The development of the RBC approach brought the cyclical behavior of aggregate productivity out of the shadows. Instead of being a fringe topic of interest mainly to those constructing large-scale econometric models, suddenly everyone became interested in cyclical fluctuations in labor productivity or in MFP, "Solow's residual." For mainstream Keynesians, the topic was *déjà-vu*, long since incorporated in Okun's early-1960s "law" that productivity growth fluctuated relative to its trend by a positive fraction of fluctuations of output relative to its trend, and long since incorporated (or ("buried") within Keynesian structural econometric models.[2]

---

[2] As I learned it in graduate school, a 3 percent positive deviation of output from its trend or "potential" would be accompanied by a 1 percent increase in the employment-population ratio (i.e., one percent decline in the unemployment rate), a 0.5 percent increase in the labor-force participation rate, a 0.5 increase in hours per employee, and a 1 percent increase in output per hour relative to its trend. Okun's Law is known mainly for its 3-to-1 ratio between the rise in detrended output and the decline in the unemployment rate, and it is less well known for the other factors that account for the 2-to-1 excess of detrended output growth relative to unemployment decline.

Part Two of this book is unusual, in that the interpretation of its main subject, cyclical fluctuations in productivity, is set forth initially in Chapter Seven in a playful exercise in academic sociology, not a scholarly analysis of the subject at hand. Yet this sociological introduction seems essential to motivate the other papers in Part Two – why did people care about the sources of productivity fluctuations, and what were the implications of alternative findings? Chapter Seven examines both the 1980s RBC model and also the earlier "mistaken expectations" model developed by Milton Friedman and Robert E. Lucas, Jr. As the chapter explains, its dichotomy between "fresh water" and "salt water" economics, a distinction invented by Stanford's Robert E. Hall, helps to organize a set of issues based on where the protagonists lived in the late 1970s and early 1980s. Fresh water became mixed with salt as protagonists switched universities in the late 1980s and afterward.

The first part of Chapter Seven contains a critical review of both the expectations and RBC versions of the New Classical Macro. The last part of Chapter Seven is an exercise in academic sociology, an attempt to rebut Alan Blinder's dismay that there were hardly, as of 1988 (according to him), any young Keynesians. This section of the paper looks at lists of citations and conference participants and rejects Blinder's assertion. There were plenty of Keynesian-oriented young economists around in the mid-1980s, including several who have since become super stars; the topics treated at macro conferences were mainly about topics for which the fresh/salt water distinction was irrelevant; and the models and concerns of fresh water economists were entirely an American preoccupation that were rejected from the outset by macroeconomists in Europe and elsewhere.

WHY IS PRODUCTIVITY PROCYCLICAL?

There is a loose end here, because productivity growth is undeniably procyclical, at least in the sense (as in Chapter Nine) that productivity grows faster than trend when output grows faster than its trend; the important qualification is that the cyclical relationship involves growth rates, not the *level* of productivity and output. Yet what causes these cyclical fluctuations? Why do not hours and output move in proportion, so that output per hour grows at a steady rate? The RBC approach of the new classical economists offers no answer – the serially correlated "technology shocks" are simply added to the production function without any underlying model to explain them.

Likewise on the Keynesian side, Okun (1962) identified the procyclicality of productivity without explaining it. Simultaneously with Okun's empirical characterization, Walter Oi (1962) added a convincing microeconomic analysis of "labor as a quasi-fixed factor." Because of hiring, firing, and training costs, it was not optimal to allow labor input to move proportionately to every cyclical

The main point is that procyclical fluctuations in productivity growth were a well-established fact two decades before the advent of RBC theory.

fluctuation in output. Some labor would be "hoarded." A standard example developed at that time involved a factory with two assembly lines and one janitor. If one assembly line was shut down in a recession and half the production workers were laid off, there would still be the need for the janitor, since you cannot slice janitors in half.

The phrase "hoarded labor" implies something suspicious or suboptimal. But think of the kinds of job functions that must continue throughout boom and recession. The firm could be bought or could be sued for some past accident or impropriety, requiring an ongoing general counsel's office which needs as much staff in the recession as in the boom. Similarly, there is a pension office which, at least for long-established companies, must pay benefits to retired employees and answer their queries, no matter how depressed business may be today.

In the factory example with half the assembly lines shut down, the janitor will be working only half as hard, and this brings us to the analysis of the causes of procyclical fluctuations in *measured* productivity contained in Chapter Eight. Three ideas are brought together that could be classified as dimensions of mismeasurement of output and inputs; taken together the paper shows that with plausible parameters these three sources of mismeasurement can entirely explain the procyclicality of MFP, or "Solow's residual." The first comes from the janitor example, since we do not measure the fact that the janitor's "work effort" slacks off when one of the assembly lines is shut down. The second is the mismeasurement of output during recessions when fruitful investment activity takes place, perhaps when some of the production workers who are not laid off perform major maintenance activities on the equipment or repaint the factory. The third and doubtless most important is the mismeasurement of capital input by the capital stock rather than the correct measure, that is, the utilized fraction of that stock.[3]

The theory in Chapter Eight is put to test in an empirical study of U.S. quarterly data over the period 1955–92. Using alternative forms of detrending, the results show that hours react with a lag to output rather than vice versa, and that productivity leads output. The business cycle component of productivity can be explained without reliance on technology shocks if capital input depends on utilized capital rather than the capital stock, and if there is any combination of minor measurement errors of output and labor input. A small share of overhead labor and capital is observationally equivalent to mismeasured labor input and provides an alternative explanation of movements at the business cycle frequency.

Going back to the debate between the Keynesians and New Classical economists, the implications of Chapter Eight are significant: The behavior of output and inputs denies the relevance of procyclical technology shocks at the business cycle frequency. The technology shocks that provide the *modus vivendi* of real business-cycle models are absent in U.S. data. Further, the absence of

---

[3] As shown in Chapter Eight, each of the three types of mismeasurement (output, labor, and capital) was examined by previous authors, but the three had not previously been brought together.

procyclicality in properly measured MFP undermines attempts to demonstrate the existence of market power or increasing returns from time-series macro data, as well as the new generation of search models in which "thick markets" boost productivity in booms.[4]

THE FOUR FREQUENCIES OF PRODUCTIVITY

Chapter Nine provides the empirical flesh to cover the theoretical bones of Chapter Eight. It deals entirely with labor productivity (ALP, output per hour), and does not make any attempt – as suggested in Chapter Eight – to correct measures of capital input for changing utilization and thus to arrive at a more accurate measure of fluctuations in MFP. The reason to neglect MFP and focus on ALP (output per hour) is the reality of data timing. Quarterly data on output and hours are released roughly five weeks from the end of the quarter, whereas data on capital input and MFP are only released on an annual basis and usually with a lag of one or two years. There is a need to explain the latest quarterly movements in labor productivity, and this is the task which is tackled in Chapter Nine.

This chapter was written in early 1993 and is based on an earlier paper (Gordon, 1979) that developed the econometric technique and the concepts. It addressed one of the outstanding puzzles of its time, the failure of payroll employment to grow between the trough of the 1990–1 recession in March 1991, and the beginning months of 1993. How could a business-cycle recovery be "jobless," that is, failing to create jobs, unlike any previous such postwar recovery? The corollary of negligible job creation was an explosion of productivity growth during late 1991 and throughout 1992, perhaps the leading edge of a sustained productivity revival from the long and dismal post-1972 productivity growth slowdown discussed in the introduction to Part One.

In the earlier 1979 paper I had developed a way to characterize the cyclical behavior of productivity growth in a simple econometric equation. The growth rate of the deviation of hours growth from its trend was regressed on the deviation of output growth from its (different) trend, and on lagged values of the hours growth deviation to allow for lags in adjustment. That equation had worked well during most of the post-1954 period but had a consistent flaw. At the end of each business expansion (in 1957–8, 1959–60, 1968–70, and later 1978–80 and 1988–90), the equation underpredicted the growth of hours and thus implicitly overpredicted the growth rate of labor productivity.

---

[4] References to this literature are given in Chapter Eight. In a bold stroke of imagination unsupported by facts, Robert E. Hall interpreted the procyclical fluctuations of productivity as providing evidence of increasing returns which in turn was consistent with market power of monopolists. The results of Chapter Eight, showing that the procyclical fluctuations are due almost entirely to measurement errors reduces Hall's claims to irrelevance. Other authors, including Basu (1996) and Burnside-Eichenbaum (1996), have made the same point, especially about capital utilization. For a recent paper on this topic containing a very complete reference list, see Basu-Fernald (2001).

I labeled this error the "end-of-expansion" productivity effect and diagnosed it as resulting from excess optimism by firms at the end of an expansion. At that point in the business cycle new equipment was being purchased, new structures were being built, and new employees were being hired on the assumption that revenue would grow sufficiently rapidly in the future to pay all the costs of the investments. In developing this hypothesis, I was influenced by my own experience as a twenty-year-old intern in the labor relations department of the Pacific Telephone Company in the summer of 1961; where it appeared that hiring plans were made by the "rubber-band" method of statistical extrapolation common in that pre-computer age.[5]

Chapter Nine revives these ideas and the earlier econometric specification to provide an interpretation of the 1991–3 period that was unique at the time.[6] Part of the failure of employment to expand was due to the normal lag of hours behind output, whether in a recession or an expansion. But much of the 1992 bulge in labor productivity was the flip side of the end-of-expansion effect. If firms "over-hire" at the end of an expansion, they must "under-hire" by laying off workers and resisting ambitious hiring plans when the economy begins to recovery. Chapter Nine interprets the 1991–2 surge in productivity growth as a temporary phenomenon, and in retrospect it was quite temporary, followed by near-stagnation of productivity growth in 1992–5. A strength of the 1993 paper reproduced here as Chapter Nine is that a somewhat speculative phenomenon identified in 1979 is shown to have occurred two more times after the publication of the earlier paper, in 1978–82 and 1989–93.

Perhaps the most useful contribution of Chapter Nine is to distinguish four different frequencies over which labor productivity growth varies; the first three are summarized in the conclusion to Chapter Nine and the fourth is added here. The first is the high-frequency movement caused by the relatively short lag of hours behind output; this adjustment in hours is completed within four

---

[5] There are two small autobiographical elements to add to this story. First, my father was also a macroeconomist and demonstrated to me his own version of the "rubber band" version of trend-fitting, with real rubber bands! Second, in relation to the role of the computer in the context of Chapter One, in the summer of 1961 Pacific Telephone was far enough into the computer age to have massive card-sorting machines which sorted the punch-cards that had recorded toll phone calls, and telephone bills for the first time were being prepared by computer. This chronology supports one of the themes of Chapter One, that the greatest impact of the computer on labor productivity was in the 1960s and 1970s when the computer replaced the clerical drudgery previously required to create telephone bills, bank statements, airline reservations, and the like.

[6] One improvement in the 1993 paper compared to the 1979 paper was suggested by James Tobin. Instead of making an "ad-hoc" selection of the dates for the end-of-expansion effect, he suggested that I use the more neutral and less arbitrary device of dating the effect at the period between the end of the "growth cycle" and the end of the "NBER cycle." The growth cycle peaks when output is at its maximum value relative to trend, while the NBER cycle peak occurs in the final month or quarter before output begins its absolute decline (without regard to trend) into the recession. In the late 1980s business cycle, the Tobin criterion dated the end-of-expansion effect as occurring between 1989:Q1 and 1990:Q3, and Chapter Nine discusses the improved results that occur when the effect is dated roughly one year earlier.

quarters after a change in output relative to trend. Second, the adjustment of hours within the first four quarters has a cumulative elasticity to output of roughly 0.75, leaving a positive ALP elasticity of roughly 0.25 to deviations in output from trend that lasts until those deviations disappear. Third, productivity systematically displays an end-of-expansion slump between the peak in the growth cycle and the peak in the NBER cycle; a correction in the two years or so after the NBER peak follows. During this correction period, productivity growth is more rapid than would be predicted on the basis of output growth alone. It is this end-of-expansion phenomenon of overhiring and subsequent correction that is interpreted in Chapter Nine as resulting from systematic overoptimism by business firms. The fourth "frequency" of productivity growth is the very long-run movements over decades and eras, for example, the shift emphasized in Chapter Two above from rapid productivity growth during 1913–72 to slow productivity growth during 1972–95.

References

Basu, Susanto. "Procyclical Productivity: Increasing Returns or Cyclical Utilization?" *Quarterly Journal of Economics*. August, 1996; vol. 111, pp. 719–51.

and Fernald, John. "Why is Productivity Procyclical? Why Do We Care?" In Hulten, Charles R., Dean, Edwin R., and Harper, Michael J., eds. *New Developments in Productivity Analysis*. Chicago: University of Chicago Press for NBER; 2001.

Burnside, Craig, and Eichenbaum, Martin. "Factor-Hoarding and the Propagation of Business-Cycle Shocks." *American Economic Review*. December 1996; vol. 86, pp. 1154–74.

Gordon, Robert J. "The 'End-of-Expansion' Phenomenon in Short-Run Productivity Behavior." *Brookings Papers on Economic Activity*. 1979; vol. 10, no. 2, pp. 447–61.

OI, Walter Y. "Labor as a Quasi-Fixed Factor." *Journal of Political Economy*. December, 1962; vol. 70, pp. 538–55.

Okun, Arthur M. "The Gap between Actual and Potential Output." *Proceedings of the American Statistical Association*. 1962. Reprinted in Edmund S. Phelps, ed. *Problems of the Modern Economy*. New York: Norton, 1965.

CHAPTER 7

Fresh Water, Salt Water, and Other Macroeconomic Elixirs

Viewed from a distance of 10,000 miles, the dominant features of American academic macroeconomics are the worldwide prominence of its leading creative thinkers, and the surprising insularity of its scholastic debates. Nothing seems further from the main macroeconomic concerns of the United States, not to mention of the twenty-three other industrialized nations that constitute the OECD, than the "fresh water, salt water" dichotomy between new-classical and new-Keynesian traditions which has dominated the coffee-break oral tradition of American macroeconomic conferences for the past decade. I suggest here that the "salinity criterion" no longer serves its original purpose of describing the central disputes in American macroeconomics, not only because it is no longer geographically accurate but, much more important, because (1) it leads commentators greatly to exaggerate the influence that new-classical economics *ever* had on the main battlefield of any academic debate – the campaign for the minds of the young, and (2) because it is no longer relevant to the central unsolved puzzles concerning macroeconomic behavior.

7.1 BACKGROUND

More than a decade has now passed since Robert Hall (1976) brilliantly christened the central schism in macroeconomics as a debate between the "fresh water" and "salt water" schools of thought. His nomenclature was based on the geographical location at that time of the three major developers of new-classical macroeconomics (Robert Lucas, Thomas Sargent, and Robert Barro) in four universities placed on or near bodies of fresh water, Carnegie-Mellon, Chicago, Minnesota, and Rochester, and of the major defenders of Keynesian economics

Note. I acknowledge the helpful suggestions of Alan S. Blinder and Robert E. Hall without implicating either of them in the outcome. (*Source.* "Fresh Water, Salt Water, and other Macroeconomic Elixirs." *Economic Record.* March 1989; pp. 177–84).

at universities on either coast.[1] Hall's classification scheme came at or near the high water mark of new-classical economics, which in the late 1970s was creating a near-sensation in macroeconomic conferences and classrooms, with its dramatic "policy-ineffectiveness proposition" claiming that countercyclical monetary policy rules that could be anticipated by the public could have no effect on real output. Since Hall's unpublished paper which introduced the salinity criterion is not well known, it is worth repeating here his evocative characterization (1976, p.1) of the leading figures of the day: "To take a few examples, Sargent corresponds to distilled water, Lucas to Lake Michigan, Feldstein to the Charles River above the dam, Modigliani to the Charles below the dam, and Okun to the Salton Sea."

The Rise

The reasons for the rise and subsequent fall of new-classical macroeconomics are well known and need be summarized here only briefly. Cycles in the acceptance of doctrines often follow the timing of economic events. Just as the undeniable facts of the Great Depression help explain the rapid spread of the original Keynesian doctrine, so the undeniable acceleration of U.S. inflation between 1965 and 1970 quickly undermined the mid-1960s Keynesian orthodoxy. The anti-Keynesian intellectual counterrevolution was particularly swift and powerful because of timing: within two years of Milton Friedman's 1967 Presidential Address to the American Economics Association (1968). United States inflation had accelerated sufficiently to destroy the credibility of the long-run Phillips trade-off and reinstate the classical notion of long-run monetary neutrality. Soon events delivered a second blow to the tattered orthodoxy. Supply shocks, including in the United States not just the first OPEC oil-price hike but also the effects of the imposition and unwinding of price controls, created a positive correlation between inflation and unemployment throughout most of the 1970s that seemed further to sabotage the negative Phillips trade-off idea. In flowery language that amounted to a simultaneous declaration of war and announcement of victory, Lucas and Sargent (1978, pp. 49–50) described "the task which faces contemporary students of the business cycle [as] that of sorting through the wreckage ... of that remarkable intellectual event called the Keynesian Revolution."

Since Friedman had reasoned from theory, while the Keynesians had been destroyed by facts, another implication of the late-1960s debacle was to shift the

---

[1] Four universities get credit for three individuals, since Robert Lucas moved from Carnegie-Mellon to Chicago in 1974, immediately after writing three of the five most influential papers in the development of the new-classical economics, and immediately before the rise of the new-classical school of thought to the peak of its influence in 1976–8 (see footnote 2). My choice of the five most influential papers consists of Lucas (1972, 1973, and 1976), Sargent-Wallace (1975), and Barro (1977). I include Sargent, but not Wallace, among the founders of new-classical macroeconomics, because Sargent wrote a number of other influential pieces by himself, while Wallace did not (see also the discussion to follow on the citation counts).

critical standards of the profession. Supporting facts were no longer enough to validate a paradigm; facts were now expected to be accompanied by a structural model of maximizing behaviour. Lucas's famous econometric "critique" (1976), a formal demonstration that empirically estimated slope parameters were not invariant to policy interventions, both rationalized the demise of the long-run Phillips trade-off and established an "archeological criterion" for future econometric research, which would dig below shallow policy-sensitive relations to uncover "deep parameters" of taste and technology. This meant, in practice, that new-classical macroeconomics consisted of *a priori* theorizing in the analytically convenient setting of "representative agent models," where one could move back and forth between the individual agent and the aggregate economy simply by adding or removing i subscripts, without having to consider such analytically inconvenient issues as coordination failures or the speed of price adjustment.[2]

The original Lucas version of the new-classical macroeconomics combined the undeniable appeal of rational expectations with two more dubious assumptions inherited from Friedman (1968), that is, continuous market clearing and imperfect information, to form the foundation of the famous "Lucas supply function" (more justly, the Friedman-Lucas supply function). Soon Sargent and Wallace (1975) extracted from Lucas's model its implication for monetary policy, the famous "policy-ineffectiveness proposition." The demonstration by Barro (1977) that one could interpret historical U.S. data to be consistent with the proposition and the theory brought new-classical economics to its short-lived period of peak influence.[3]

The Fall

Part of the downfall came early and on theoretical grounds, with the realization that real-world information lags for aggregate variables like the price level and money supply were much too short to rationalize the persistent multiyear deviations from equilibrium that seemed to characterize business cycles in most industrialized countries. The second dubious assumption, continuous market

---

[2] Lucas, Sargent, Barro are undeniably the three most important creators of the new-classical macroeconomics, but we should not overlook a substantial difference in emphasis among them. Lucas in the (1972) and (1973) papers does not mention the policy-ineffectiveness proposition; the explicit statement of the proposition was worked out by Sargent and Wallace (1975). As another difference, of the three Sargent was the most interested in developing theories and methodologies for uncovering deep parameters, and Barro much less so.

[3] The high-water mark can be placed fairly precisely at 8:59 A.M. EDT on Friday, October 13, 1978, at Bald Peak, New Hampshire, just before Robert Barro and Mark Rush began their presentation of an empirical test of the policy-ineffectiveness proposition on quarterly U.S. post-war data that was not only severely criticized by three discussants, but also contained dubious results that seemed questionable even to the authors. Never again after that occasion did any prominent proponent of the central proposition of new-classical macroeconomics even attempt to present empirical evidence in its support, and soon thereafter strong evidence against the proposition was presented by Mishkin (1982) and Gordon (1982).

clearing, was viewed more critically once it was recognized that it was not an inextricable concomitant of rational expectations, especially when Stanley Fischer (1977) and Edmund Phelps and John Taylor (1977) showed that rational expectations could be embedded in a model containing real-world institutional features like multiperiod wage and price contracts to generate nonmarket-clearing behavior. Once Fischer and Phelps-Taylor had shown that rational expectations by itself was a necessary but not a sufficient condition to validate new-classical policy conclusions, the race was on to develop the new-Keynesian theory based on rational expectations and one or another institutional impediment to continuous market clearing. The new-Keynesian theory had the double appeal not only that it seemed better to incorporate whatever adjustment costs led real-world economic agents to constrain their own price-setting behavior by entering into explicit or implicit contractual agreements, but also that it did not require any arbitrary assumptions about information lags.

It is less widely understood that the downfall of new-classical economics was reinforced by its own empirical failure and the simultaneous empirical revival of Keynesian economics. The short-lived attempt to develop an econometric validation of the policy-ineffectiveness proposition by Barro and others was, simply, a research failure. It floundered on their inability to develop a symmetric explanation of output and price behaviour. Barro (1977) showed that output was not related to anticipated monetary changes but could not demonstrate the required corollary – the full and prompt responsiveness of price changes to anticipated nominal disturbances. This failure was not a matter of arcane methodological debates. It was evident in the gross inconsistency of the new-classical bedrock assumption of a perfectly flexible aggregate price level, mandatory in a world of continuous market clearing, with the empirical reality in the postwar U.S. of a time series for the inflation rate that was much more sticky and inertia-prone than the corresponding time series for changes in nominal aggregate demand.

Meanwhile, the effects of supply shocks were absorbed into the empirical Philips curve literature in the late 1970s (see Gordon, 1977, Chapter Fourteen in this book) through the development of a dynamic econometric analogue to the static aggregate demand and supply curves that swept the textbook market at the same time.[4] Since supply and demand shocks entered symmetrically into the determination of the inflation rate, unemployment and inflation could be either positively or negatively correlated in the short run, depending on the dominant source of shocks. The evolution of real world events, which had undermined Keynesian economics in the late 1960s and 1970s, now came to its rescue in the form of a monetary disinflation that had been predicted to be painless by prominent new-classical advocates but quite evidently was not. The precise

---

[4] The distinguishing feature of the Dornbusch-Fischer and Gordon macroeconomics textbooks, first published in 1978, was an explicit dynamic supply and demand model of inflation and unemployment which allowed the events of the 1970s to be explained. Elements of this model were included promptly in prominent elementary textbooks, particularly those by Baumol-Blinder and Dolan.

path of the inflation rate after 1980 depended on a particular combination of monetary disinflation, falling oil prices, and an appreciation of the dollar that no one had predicted in advance. Nevertheless, a crucial implication of the resuscitated 1980-vintage empirical Phillips curves, the value of the "sacrifice ratio" of lost output required to achieve a permanent deceleration of inflation under conditions of variable oil prices and exchange rates, turned out to be surprisingly close to predictions made in advance (Gordon-King, 1982, Chapter Fifteen in this book).

New-classical economics has been undeniably influential, but not in the way that its three prominent creators originally imagined. Its most important contribution to macroeconomics, the assumption of rational expectations, was stolen almost immediately, and applied more fruitfully, by the new Keynesians. As individuals, the three primary creators of new-classical macroeconomics have long since departed for greener research pastures and have left their child, the policy-ineffectiveness proposition, to die neglected and unmourned. Two of the three, Thomas Sargent and Robert Barro, have also physically departed from the nation's fresh-water heartland, the first to a university located a few miles from one of the nation's leading salt farms, and the other to the hotbed of both the old and new versions of Keynesian economics – Cambridge, Massachusetts. Hence my introductory comment that the fresh water, salt water distinction is no longer geographically accurate, at least as a description of the location of the main figures who created new-classical macroeconomics.

Real Business Cycle Theory

Into this vacuum has stepped Edward Prescott, from fresh-water Minnesota, who has picked up the frayed new-classical banner with his "real business-cycle theory." This is based on the core new-classical element of continuous market-clearing but generates a business cycle not from imperfect information, as in the original Lucas-Sargent version, but rather from an autoregressive technology shock process. Believe it or not, the entire explanation for recessions and even the Great Depression in this new-classical macro "Mark II" boils down to technological retrogression, that is, a sustained negative realization of the technology shock. Thus far, Prescott and his small band of followers have understandably shied away from any of the empirical research needed to provide support for their theory, in particular, studies of individual industries to identify the sectoral locus of technological retardation in recessions, and studies of both industry and individual price behavior to isolate the inverse correlation between prices and output that every textbook since Marshall's *Principles* would predict to occur as the counterpart of a technological shock.

Some real-business-cycle proponents defend themselves by claiming that the correlation between prices and output is not foreordained to be negative but rather depends on how the monetary authority responds to real events. I would respond that this "way out" for the real business cycle theorists, to attribute the positive correlation of output and prices that we observe in most historical episodes to procyclical fluctuations of the money supply, just underscores the inadequacy of the empirical research program, which thus far shows no signs of even attempting to estimate models in which output, prices, and money are jointly determined subject to cross-equation restrictions. Even a moment's consideration suggests that such a research program for new-classical macro "Mark II" will fail, as did the attempt to validate the new-classical macro "Mark I."[5] Clearly, price behavior has turned out to be the Achilles heel of new-classical economics, both in its policy-ineffectiveness and in its real-business-cycle incarnations. In fact, to date real business cycle theory has been "price free," which for an economic theory is about as appealing an attribute as "one-armed" would be for a concert pianist.

Fresh-Water Economics: Leaders without Followers

While the basic elements in the rise and fall of new-classical economics are widely understood and have become part of the Conventional Wisdom, even the most perceptive commentators seem to have overstated the influence of fresh-water economics at its peak. The most persistent and articulate chronicler of the revival of Keynesian economics is Alan Blinder, who in the following passage shares the widespread misconception that around 1980 new-classical macroeconomics had swept the younger half of the profession:

> By about 1980, it was hard to find an American academic macroeconomist under the age of 40 who professed to be a Keynesian. That was an astonishing intellectual turnabout in less than a decade – an intellectual revolution for sure ... Thus freed of any need to absorb the knowledge of the past, newly minted Ph.D. economists could concentrate on what they saw as the wave of the future. . . . the young were recruited disproportionately into the new-classical ranks. . . . By 1980 or so, the adage "there are no Keynesians under the age of 40" was part of the folklore of the [American] economics profession (1988, pp. 1, 14).

Was the new-classical "intellectual revolution" really this influential in 1980? First, we need to clarify the use of words. Even those young American economists who believed firmly that markets regularly failed to clear were reluctant in the era 1975–85 to identify themselves as "Keynesians" – that word was always offensive to me, and to other people, because of the intellectual baggage it carried, and indeed only Alan among then-young Americans carried it high. But this was just a name – on any issue of substance there was a large

---

[5] If the procyclical correlation of output and prices is to be explained by a procyclical response of the money supply, a particular set of elasticities is implied. In a recession the aggregate demand curve must shift to the left further than the aggregate supply curve, so that their intersection occurs at a lower price level, implying that supply shocks must regularly induce a response of nominal GNP of greater than unit elasticity to the original real shock, and a response of the money supply that is even greater, given the observation that velocity is procyclical as well. In view of the flexibility of prices intrinsic to the market-clearing framework, an adverse supply shock should show up first in a jump in prices and decline in output, followed by a decline in the money supply and prices.

group which considered sticky prices and failures of market clearing to be an essential part of any satisfactory explanation of business cycles. A big breakthrough came in 1976–8, when Modigliani's Presidential Address (1977) and new macroeconomics textbooks published by Dornbusch-Fischer and myself recast the central policy debate in terms of "monetarists" battling "activists" or "nonmonetarists," rarely if ever mentioning the word "Keynesian."[6]

It is a truism that the influence of an intellectual revolution hinges on its success in the battle to capture the minds of the young. The original Keynesian revolution of 1936 was a near-total success by this criterion. The issue, then, is how influential was new-classical macroeconomics in its heyday of the late 1970s? This turns not on whether young people called themselves "Keynesian," but on what they thought and wrote. I can provide two types of evidence that the inventors of new-classical macroeconomics created much less of a revolution than is generally recognized.

Citation Counts

Nothing is more fun for U.S. economists than to sit in their faculty clubs and chart the fall and rise of doctrines and, even better, individuals. Hence the excitement caused by the recent underground circulation of an unpublished paper by Medoff (1988) that contains by far the most complete count ever carried out on the citations to individual economists over virtually the whole period of existence of the *Social Science Citation Index* (1971–85) which also, luckily, is close to the right period for analyzing the influence of new-classical economics (although the cut-off is too early to evaluate the influence of the "Mark II" version). The Medoff evidence consists of total citation counts, with all self-citations deducted, over 1971–85 for the 150 top-ranked economists (excluding those who had won the Nobel Prize by 1985), a second ranking of the same group by total average citations divided by years since Ph.D., and a third ranking of economists who were forty or under in 1985. One can extract several striking conclusions from these lists, which are all subject to the defect that the source (*SSCI*) counts citations only for the first-listed coauthor and thus it significantly undercounts individuals with names late in the alphabet who have done their most significant work with coauthors. All of the following findings lead me to infer that the three founders of new-classical economics failed to attract a set of influential followers.

1. Looking at the one hundred most-cited economists on the more meaningful second (age-adjusted) ranking, surprisingly few macroeconomists make the list at all, just thirteen out of one hundred. To reach even one fifth of the names, one would have to add five international economists and two public finance specialists who occasionally dabbled in macro.

---

[6] The movement away from the word "Keynesian" started earlier with Okun's classic (1972) analysis of the conditions necessary for what he called "activist" policy prescriptions.

2. The founders of new-classical economics obviously stirred up a ferment with their own work, but that of their followers did not. Barro, Lucas, and Sargent, are respectively ranked 2, 4, and 5, but there is no other name among the remaining ten macroeconomists on the list of the top one hundred who could be labeled as a new-classical proponent.[7]

3. Only six of the fifty most-cited younger economists practice macroeconomics, and none of them could remotely be described as belonging to the new-classical group.[8]

Conference Participants

To provide further documentary evidence on the failure of the new-classical economists to develop influential disciples, much less dominate the profession as Blinder's interpretation would imply, I have collected names of authors from the three major conference volume series through which U.S. macroeconomics is purveyed. On the left, we have the *Brookings Papers on Economic Activity* (BPEA), founded in 1970 by Arthur Okun and George Perry. This group is and always was Keynesian, so much so that Barro, Lucas, Prescott, and Wallace have never been invited to a single meeting of the forty-seven which have been held over the last nineteen years.[9] On the right, we have the Carnegie-Rochester conference series (CRCS), run biennially since 1973 by Karl Brunner and Alan Meltzer, which has cast a wider net than BPEA and has been particularly hospitable to the research of the fresh water macroeconomists. In the middle we have the NBER research group on macroeconomics, admirably run by Robert Hall to include new classicals and new Keynesians alike, which holds about four annual meetings.[10] To decide who was who in U.S. macroeconomics *among young academics who received their Ph.D. degree in the period 1975–85*, I counted from the following documentary material – the tables of contents of all BPEA and CRCS conference volumes published since 1981, and the programs of all NBER economic fluctuations and macroeconomics conference held in the last four years.[11]

---

[7] The closest is B. McCallum, ranked ninety-one. The others in order by the second criterion (and their ranks) are A. Blinder (20), R. Hall (22), R. Solow (26), R. Gordon (32), W. Nordhaus (36), S. Turnovsky (38), S. Fischer (50), R. Fair (66), and B. Friedman (68).

[8] The names and age-adjusted ranks are A. Blinder (3), M. Darby (9), W. Buiter (14), J. Taylor (18), F. Mishkin (25), and L. Summers (35). Excluded from consideration is L. Hansen (7), whom I classify as an econometrician making primarily methodological contributions, just as I have excluded C. Sims (25) from the count of established macroeconomists.

[9] Sargent was invited to participate only in a single year, 1973.

[10] The NBER EF group as such does not have a regular publication outlet for its numerous annual meetings and conferences. Recently a separate annual conference series under NBER auspices, run by Stanley Fischer, has been initiated with its own publication outlet, the *NBER Macroeconomics Annual*.

[11] The count of the NBER meetings includes the Fischer conference plus all meetings of the economic fluctuations group as a whole. Excluded are smaller subgroup meetings, most of which have been held as part of the NBER's Summer Institute.

Perhaps the most surprising result of trying to carry out this exercise is the same as that I reach from the topic count in the next section – far from falling neatly into two lists of "new classicals" and "new Keynesians," most people defy that dichotomy either because they play both sides of the street or, more importantly, the classical/Keynesian distinction is just not relevant for the type of research they do on, say, long-run growth theory or the behavior of asset markets. This leads me to a four-way grouping of young economists who appear at the macro conferences described above: "new-classical," "new-Keynesian," "in-between," and "other-topic." With due apologies to people whom I have omitted for one reason or another,[12] here are the lists:

> *New-Classical:* S. Altug, D. Aschauer, L. Christiano, M. Eichenbaum, R. Flood, L. Hansen, W. Haraf, R. Hodrick, J. Kennan, R. King, J. Long, C. Plosser, K. Singleton, A. Stockman, and R. Townsend.
>
> *New-Keynesian:* L. Ball, R. Barsky, B. Bernanke, O. Blanchard, M. Bils, W. Buiter, D. Carlton, R. Cooper, P. Krugman, G. Mankiw, J. Miron, F. Mishkin, M. Obstfeld, V. Ramey, K. Rogoff, D. Romer, J. Rotemberg, J. Sachs, R. Shiller, J. Stock, L. Summers, M. Watson, and K. West.
>
> *In-Between:* A. Abel, J. Campbell, A. Caplin, P. Evans, R. Farmer, M. Flavin, P. Garber, J. Gray, D. Quah, and M. Shapiro.
>
> *Other-Topic:* D. Bernheim, S. Davis, J. Frankel, R.G. Hubbard, R. Meese, K. Murphy, P. Romer, and Rene Stulz.

My conclusion is simple: new-classical macro did not conquer the new Ph.D.'s during the decade when it was most influential. The "new-classical" list is not only short, but its "tone" is distinctly more technical, particularly in the direction of econometric method, than the "new-Keynesian list." In fact, I conjecture that only about half of the people on the new-classical list would identify their primary field as macroeconomics as opposed to econometrics, international economics, public finance, or microeconomic theory.

7.2 WHICH ARE THE TOPICS OF CENTRAL CONCERN?

Topics of Recent U.S. Research

The attention still given in coffee breaks and written commentaries to the freshwater, salt-water dichotomy seems to imply that the core of U.S. macroeconomics today concerns a debate over the central assumptions of new-classical

---

[12] A helper has checked through this list for date of Ph.D., but not everyone is listed in the AEA Directory that we used as a source. Individuals appearing on the above-listed tables of contents were omitted when I decided that (1) most of their work clearly falls in the micro rather than macro area, or (2) I did not know enough to classify them, or (3) they were based in a foreign university.

macroeconomics, that is, rational expectations, market clearing, and imperfect information, and their implications for the real effects of nominal disturbances. To evaluate this implicit proposition, I went to the place where new-classical macro should have been most dominant, the tables of contents of fifteen volumes of the CRCS published since 1980, containing sixty-seven articles that I could classify. My conclusion is that the central concerns of U.S. macroeconomists in their actual research have not related to new-classical economics, either pro or con, over this period. Here is my count of the topics, with the number of articles in parentheses:

1. Traditional monetary economics (18): institutional aspects of monetary policy, monetary instruments, term structure, money demand, banking deregulation.
2. Real and monetary international economics (10).
3. Evaluations of economic policy in other countries (8), of which five concerned developed countries and three less developed.
4. Public finance, supply-side economics (7).
5. Inflation (7): hyperinflation, costs of inflation, inflation variability, disinflation strategy.
6. Technical issues with no policy content (7): VAR models, overlapping-generation models, pure theory of intermediation, temporal aggregation, optimal prediction.
7. Labor market and productivity (4).

This totals sixty-one of the sixty-seven articles, leaving only six related to the fresh water, salt water dichotomy, and only a few of these pursue the new-classical approach, most notably Prescott (1986).

An Obsolete American Preoccupation?

The fresh water, salt water dichotomy is no longer relevant to the advance of knowledge regarding major unsettled issues in macroeconomics. A poll of U.S. macroeconomists concerning America's greatest unsolved macroeconomic problems would surely emerge with slow productivity growth and the twin deficits (fiscal and foreign trade at the top of the list, and "does money affect output" or "relevance of perfect market clearing" quite far down in rank. New topics have muddied the old distinctions between groups of economists. The now-festering debate over whether the Federal budget deficit is benign or harmful pits such unlikely allies as Robert Eisner, Milton Friedman, Robert Hall, and Paul Craig Roberts into battle with numerous Keynesians centered at the Brookings Institution and Cambridge, Massachusetts.

The continued preoccupation of some American commentators with the small remaining bank of new-classical economists must seem even more bizarre to foreigners. The further one travels from American shores, the smaller appears the relevance of fresh and salt water to central economic problems. A foreigner would note, for instance, that of the 52 items on the reference list of Blinder's recent commentary (1988), 49.5 are by American authors.[13] This could reflect the dominance of Americans in worldwide macroeconomic research, but it also must reflect the fact that foreigners have lost interest. The big events in the world economy – the widely shared slowdown in productivity growth, the rise in unemployment, the debate over classical uemployment in Europe, the policy coordination failures caused by the Reagan deficits, the prominence of the Bundesbank in the European Monetary System, the outstanding export and growth performance of Japan and the Four Tigers, and the ever-worsening Latin American debt overhang – these central concerns are tangential to the aborted new-classical "revolution." Many of the world's major economic problems can be discussed intelligently by a Rip Van Winkle who had a decent graduate education vintage 1970, without a requirement that he read anything published since then, except maybe for the intermediate textbook version of dynamic macroeconomic supply and demand analysis, and a basic textbook presentation on the workings of the flexible exchange rate system, particularly volatility and overshooting.

One response to this accusation of irrelevance is to protest that "policy is not the only thing that macroeconomics is about; macroeconomics is also a science devoted to understanding basic economic phenomena like business cycles." But even by this criterion, when judged by the normal standards for evaluating science, new-classical macro is a scientific failure. We have already seen that the "Mark I" version failed empirically to explain aggregate price behavior, a fatal flaw for a theory with pretensions to science, while the "Mark II" version evasively has nothing to say about price behavior. "Yes, true," the defenders may retort, "but a theory is valuable even if it is wrong, since thinking about why it is wrong may teach us something." By this lower standard we finally arrive at the true contribution of new-classical macro: it has given us all something to argue about.

Redirecting Future Research

Macroeconomics needs to be redirected away from demand and toward supply, but not in the direction suggested by Prescott's attempt to build a model of real business cycles based on wholly exogenous and unexplained technology shocks. Instead, the leading supply-side puzzle concerns the world-wide slowdown in the growth rate of multifactor productivity (MFP), sometimes called "Solow's residual." We need to determine what accounts for the slowdown, and for differences among the major countries. Paul Romer's "Crazy Explanation" and its sequels have shown that research on long-run growth and productivity change can deal with these basic issues and create plenty of controversy along the way. However, the fact that people have been pondering the productivity slowdown for more than a decade without breakthrough helps to explain why so few young people are drawn to this set of research questions: it is hard, and it intrinsically involves messy empirical work that deals with differences among countries and industries.

---

[13] United States' immigrants and recent graduate students are counted as American.

Work also needs to be directed away from the salinity debate toward the long-run implications of the twin deficits. Ultimately we care about the deficits because the accumulation of debt has long-run consequences, and in this sense the deficits fall under the general topic heading of long-run growth and productivity. Both raise awkward questions for economists who would prefer to be tilling in the fields of homogeneous representative agent models. The U.S. fiscal deficit is uniquely persistent for peace time and appears to represent a genuine political innovation, raising questions about the relevance for this episode of recent theorizing on the political determinants of deficits. The trade deficit raises a host of questions about how it will all end in view of the resistance of the deficit to a fall by half in the yen-dollar rate. Why do American firms fail to make well, or make at all, so many of the things that we import from Asia? And how does Japan manage to avoid raising its dollar prices in anything like the proportion by which the dollar has fallen? Indeed, rated by its achievement in achieving low unemployment, low inflation, and rapid productivity growth. Japan scores first by all three criteria in comparison with the United States and any other of the large European nations (albeit Japan ties with West Germany on inflation). How can systematic differences in performance be incorporated in models while retaining rational behavior? Why do not utility-maximizing agents copy whatever elements of policy management or group behavior that underlie the Japanese success?

Extreme cases often provide an essential service in sorting among alternative theories. One such extreme case is the Great Depression, which creates suspicion of any theory like new-classical Mark II, which suggests that factories and workers were idle as the result of a massive supply bottleneck. Rapid economic growth in East Asia is another extreme case that also helps to sort some elements of the productivity story that look more plausible than others. One doubts that high energy prices are a major explanation of the productivity slowdown, given the dependence of these successful countries on imported energy which should have derailed their progress but did not. Rising in plausibility is P. Romer's argument that the return to high rates of capital accumulation is greater than in standard competitive models, and the same may go for accumulation of human and managerial capital (in the pure version of Romer's "crazy" model the elasticity of output with respect to capital input is unity and to labor input is zero). Macroeconomists still have a way to go in building and testing models of growth, debt, and accumulation before we throw in the towel and appeal to the help of other disciplines, particularly comparative sociology and religion, to explain the outstanding economic performance of East Asia.

References

Barro, Robert J. "Unanticipated Money Growth and Unemployment in the United States." *American Economic Review*. March, 1977; vol. 67, pp. 101–15.
Blinder, Alan S. "The Fall and Rise of Keynesian Economics." Invited lecture delivered at 1988 Australian Economics Congress, *Economic Record*; December, 1988.

Fischer, Stanley. "Long-Term Contracts, Rational Expectations, and the Optimal Money Supply Rule." *Journal of Political Economy*. February, 1977; vol. 85, pp. 191–205.

Friedman, Milton. "The Role of Monetary Policy." *American Economic Review*. March, 1968; vol. 58, pp. 12–17.

Gordon, Robert J. "Price Inertia and Policy Ineffectiveness in the United States, 1890–1980." *Journal of Political Economy*. December, 1982; vol. 90, pp. 1087–1117.

"Can the Inflation of the 1970s be Explained?" *Brookings Papers on Economic Activity*. 1977; vol. 8, no. 1, pp. 253–77, Chapter 14 in this book.

and King, Stephen R. "The Output Cost of Disinflation in Traditional and Vector Autoregressive Models." *Brookings Papers on Economic Activity*. 1982; vol. 13, no. 1, 205–42, Chapter 15 in this book.

Hall, Robert E. Notes on the Current State of Empirical Economics. Unpublished paper presented at one-day workshop of the Institute of Mathematical Studies in Social Sciences, Stanford University. 1976.

Lucas, Robert E., Jr. "Expectations and the Neutrality of Money." *Journal of Economic Theory*. April, 1972; vol. 4, pp. 103–24.

"Some International Evidence on Output-Inflation Tradeoffs." *American Economic Review*. June, 1973; vol. 63, 326–34.

"Econometric Policy Evaluation: A Critique." In Brunner, K. and Meltzer, A. eds. *The Phillips Curve and Labor Markets*. Carnegie-Rochester Series on Public Policy. A supplementary series to the *Journal of Monetary Economics*. North-Holland. January 1976; vol. 1, pp. 19–46.

and Sargent, Thomas J. "After Keynesian Macroeconomics." In *After the Phillips Curve: Persistence of High Inflation and High Unemployment*. Federal Reserve Bank of Boston; 1978, pp. 49–72.

Medoff, Marshal. "The Ranking of Economists." Working paper.

Mishkin, Frederic S. "Does Anticipated Monetary Policy Matter? An Econometric Investigation." *Journal of Political Economy*. February, 1982; vol. 90, pp. 22–51.

Modigliani, Franco. "The Monetarist Controversy, or, Should We Forsake Stabilization Policy?" *American Economic Review*. March, 1977; vol. 67, pp. 1–19.

Okun, Arthur M. "Fiscal-Monetary Activism: Some Analytical Issues." *Brookings Papers on Economic Activity*. 1972; vol. 3, no. 1, pp. 123–63.

Phelps, Edmund S., and Taylor, John B. "Stabilizing Powers of Monetary Policy under Rational Expectations." *Journal of Political Economy*. February, 1977; vol. 85, pp. 163–90.

Prescott, Edward C. "Theory Ahead of Business Cycle Measurement." *Carnegie-Rochester Conference Series on Public Policy*. Autumn, 1986; vol. 25, pp. 11–44.

Romer, Paul M. "Crazy Explanations for the Productivity Slowdown." In Fischer, S. ed. *NBER Macroeconomics Annual 1987*. Cambridge, Massachusetts: M.I.T. Press; 1987, pp. 163–201.

Sargent, Thomas J., and Wallace, Neil. "Rational Expectations, the Optimal Monetary Instrument, and the Optimal Money Supply Rule." *Journal of Political Economy*. April, 1975; vol. 85, pp. 241–54.

CHAPTER 8

Are Procyclical Productivity Fluctuations a Figment of Measurement Error?

INTRODUCTION

Multifactor productivity (MFP), or "Solow's residual," exhibits pronounced procyclical fluctuations in official data for the United States, Japan, and most other countries. These procyclical fluctuations have come to play a central role in recent macroeconomic debates. They provide the *modus vivendum* of the real business cycle (RBC) model, as well as the basis for Robert Hall's (1986, 1988) interpretation that the procyclicality of MFP demonstrates the existence of market power and/or increasing returns. They are also cited to support recent search models which demonstrate increasing returns in the form of "thick market externalities."[1]

Scattered through the literature of the past three decades are suggestions that the mismeasurement of output, capital input, or of labor input, might contribute to the observed procyclicality of MFP. However, each of these three mismeasurement sources was examined singly by different authors. This essay is the first to study the potential for all three sources of mismeasurement, interacting together, fully to explain the procyclicality of MFP.

The essay begins with a theoretical analysis that places the potential sources of mismeasurement in an explicit technological context. Part of the observed procyclicality of MFP may indeed be due to mismeasurement, but part may represent the overhead nature of some portion of both labor and capital, due to technological indivisibilities. We set out a model that allows separate roles for several cyclical phenomena that have often been confused in the literature

[1] This phrase is Hall's; the theoretical literature on this type of search model begins with Diamond (1982).

Note. This research has been supported by the National Science Foundation. I am grateful for helpful comments and suggestions to Mark Bils, Alan Blinder, Martin Eichenbaum, Zvi Griliches, Robert Hodrick, Julio Rotemberg, Robert M. Solow, Mark Watson, and to other participants in the Northwestern macro workshop and a NBER Economic Fluctuations Research Meeting. Christy Romer (1986) provided the title. George Williams and Dan Aaronson compiled the data and updated the regression results. (*Source.* "Are Procyclical Productivity Fluctuations a Figment of Measurement Error?" Previously unpublished, November, 1992.)

on procyclical MFP, including labor hoarding, variable work effort, variable capital utilization, overhead labor, and overhead capital.

While measured output, labor input, and capacity utilization can be observed, several concepts in the thoretical analysis are unobservable, for example, the share of overhead labor and capital and the elasticity of unobserved labor effort to observed labor input. The empirical analysis combines data on observables with alternative assumed values of unobservables to provide a menu of plausible parameters that eliminate procyclical technology shocks as an explanation of the procyclicality of observed MFP.

The Rediscovery of Procyclical MFP

More than three decades ago Hultgren (1960) called attention to the procyclicality of labor productivity and the difficulty of reconciling its procyclical behavior with the neoclassical theory of production. His observation spawned substantial research in the 1960s, including suggestions that mismeasurement of labor or capital might help to explain the paradox.

Since the late 1960s macroeconomic debates in the United States have centered on the competing interpretations of the new classical and new Keynesian macroeconomics. The initial new classical model developed in the early 1970s by Robert E. Lucas, Jr., combined market-clearing, imperfect information, and rational expectations. After much testing, it was eventually rejected in the late 1970s for failing to explain why business cycles lasted on average four years while information delays lasted only a few weeks. It was soon replaced by a second new classical approach, the Real Business Cycle (RBC) model, which was also based on continuous market clearing and competitive equilibrium, but now generated the business cycle through serially correlated procyclical technology shocks. For the RBC model to maintain its validity, the observed procyclicality of MFP must be driven by a technological shift parameter, and not by such phenomena as mismeasurement or overhead labor.[2]

A second approach is embodied in the recent work of Robert Hall (1986, 1988). In Hall's interpretation, the procyclicality of MFP demonstrates market power and/or increasing returns. Since microeconomists have long known that market power existed, their interest in Hall's finding is primarily methodological, since his evidence for market power is based on macro time-series data rather than the usual micro approach grounded in the analysis of cross-sections of observations on individual firms.[3]

Both the RBC and market power interpretations of procyclical MFP fluctuations have been resisted by some critics. The RBC model has been subject to

---

[2] Eichenbaum (1991) develops a hybrid model that incorporates labor hoarding into the RBC model and shows that this reduces the ability of technology shocks to account for aggregate productivity fluctuations by 30 to 60 percent, depending on the sample period.

[3] Domowitz, Hubbard, and Peterson (1988) use Hall's technique to explore the sensitivity of his results to an alternative set of time series data at the firm level.

many criticisms, including skepticism of the fast-paced technological regress and revival required for technology shocks to explain the time path of productivity in typical U.S. postwar recessions or the huge collapse of technology required to explain the Great Depression.[4] Objecting to Hall's market-power interpretation, Rotemberg and Summers (1990) have argued that cyclical MFP fluctuations reflect labor hoarding and price stickiness, rather than providing any evidence in support of market power. In turn, Hall's responses to his critics (1990a, 1990b) dismiss all but two (market power, increasing returns) of eight possible "explanations" of procyclical MFP and deny four "nonexplanations" that include labor hoarding.

Previous Research on Procyclical Productivity

In the mid-1960s the cyclical behavior of productivity arose in three contexts: the paradox of short-run increasing returns to labor, Okun's law, and the labor market of the canonical Keynesian macro model.

The paradox of "SRIRL" (short-run increasing returns to labor) was simple and was recognized almost immediately after Solow's (1957) pathbreaking paper by Hultgren (1960), Oi (1962), Solow himself (1964), and others. Take a constant returns Cobb-Douglas production function with an elasticity of measured output (x) to measured labor input (h) of, say, 0.75, and vary labor while holding capital fixed; output should move less than in proportion to labor, so the average product of labor should move countercyclically. But in the data labor's average product (x/h) moves procyclically, exhibiting increasing returns, with a SRIRL parameter ($\beta = \Delta x/\Delta h$) greater than unity rather than the diminishing returns built into the production function.

The second context was Okun's law, which dates back to Okun's famous (1962) paper on potential output. His law is just a stylized fact, that the unemployment rate varies only 1 percentage point for each 3 percentage point change in detrended output; the other two percentage points are accounted for by procyclical variations in the labor force participation rate, hours per employee, and the average product of labor.[5] The stylized fact of Okun's law provided an explicit measurement of the extent of short-run increasing returns to labor. In

---

[4] Bernanke and Parkinson (1990) show that the pattern of procyclical productivity across industries in the interwar period was similar to that in the postwar. They argue that "under the presumption that the Depression was not caused by large negative technological shocks, these findings are inconsistent with the technological shocks hypothesis and provide evidence against real business cycle theory in general." Plosser (1989) provides a sympathetic exposition of the RBC model and numerous references to the original scholarly literature, while Mankiw (1989) provides a wide-ranging critique.

[5] We have known for a long time that, allowing for lags in the adjustment of labor to output, the elasticity of unemployment to output is closer to 0.45 than 0.33, as shown in Gordon (1984), a paper that relates Okun's Law to the set of identities that link cyclical fluctuations in the unemployment rate to cyclical fluctuations in output, productivity, labor force participation, hours, and other variables. We return below to the estimation of β.

Okun's version, the response of the unemployment rate to changes in measured labor hours was one half, the other half taking the form of changes in participation and hours per employee. The elasticity of measured hours to output ($\Delta h/\Delta x$) was 2/3, with the remainder taking the form of changes in labor's average product. Thus the SRIRL parameter ($\beta = \Delta x/\Delta h$) was 1.5.

The third context was the standard Keynesian macro model of the day, which was internally inconsistent by mixing the multiplier, based on the failure of product markets to clear, with continuous market clearing in the labor market. Firms were described as sliding back and forth along a labor demand curve that sloped down because of diminishing returns, requiring the average product of labor to move countercyclically. The fact of SRIRL conflicted with the labor-market assumptions of the Keynesian model and called attention to its internal inconsistency.

So much for the old puzzles. The old solutions were in place and widely accepted by the end of the 1960s. The way out of the internal contradiction of the Keynesian model was developed in two pieces by Don Patinkin (1965, Chapter 13) and Robert Clower (1965), and then put together by Robert Barro and Herschel Grossman (1971). No longer did the Keynesian model mix a nonmarket clearing multiplier in the product market with equilibrium in the labor market; instead the Barro-Grossman framework was based on consistent non-Walrasian framework, with spillovers and rationing in all markets.

The Barro-Grossman model straightened out the theoretical contradiction of the Keynesian model but shed no light on the paradox of short-run increasing returns. One solution proposed by Fair (1969) was that hours actually worked differ from hours paid for, and so short-run increasing returns are exaggerated when labor's average product is measured by hours paid for. Thus Fair's solution was that the paradox was explained by mismeasurement of labor. The second line of work goes back at least to Zvi Griliches (1964) and argues that standard data on the capital stock mismeasure the true input of capital services in the production function, and that the correct measure is the capital stock times the utilization rate of capital.[6] If output fluctuates more than labor input because the input of capital services also fluctuates more than labor input, much of the SRIRL paradox disappears.[7]

---

[6] Griliches (1964) developed several ideas that were then applied to the estimate of MFP growth in Jorgenson and Griliches (1967), including the adjustment of capital input for varying utilization, based on data on the power consumption of electric motors. More recently, Griliches (with Abbott and Hausman, 1988 and also in Eden-Griliches, 1991) has criticized Hall's research on several grounds, one of which is a failure to allow for variable capacity utilization. A research team which early recognized the importance of capital utilization in creating a bias in the estimated SRIRL parameter was Ireland and Smyth (1970), who latter in Ireland, Briscoe, and Smyth (1973) used electricity consumption data to correct the bias. Other references on utilization include Prucha and Nadiri (1991).

[7] In view of this background, Hall's recent work misleads the reader that a new topic has been discovered. He writes (1990b) that "users ... have always been aware that the Solow residual ... fluctuates markedly, but until recently the higher-frequency movements were considered irrelevant noise," thus ignoring all of the 1960s literature on SRIRL, Okun's law, and mismeasurement. In fact, the emphasis on mismeasurement in this paper was anticipated by Evsey

The core of this paper shows how measurement errors in output, labor, and capital, can interact to provide a full explanation for the procyclicality of conventionally measured changes in MFP. It also shows why mismeasurement of labor is observationally equivalent to the existence of an overhead component of labor and perforce of capital. Empirical evidence is provided to pin down the values of the key theoretical parameters. The implications of our analysis are significant: plausible parameters of measurement error and/or overhead labor can extinguish the procyclical technology shocks that provide the *modus vivendum* of RBC models and Hall's market power interpretation, as well as the new generation of search models characterized by productivity-boosting "thick markets" in economic expansions.

8.1   THE ALGEBRA OF MISMEASUREMENT AND OVERHEAD FACTOR INPUTS

The standard approach to production theory in macroeconomics is to write down an equation like:

$$Q_t = Z_t F(N_t, K_t); \quad F_N > 0, F_{NN} < 0, F_K > 0, F_{KK} < 0. \quad (1)$$

Here Q_t is output, N_t and K_t are labor and capital input, and Z_t is a technology shift factor (i.e., Hicks-neutral technical change). Equation (1) is assumed to hold equally in the short and long run.

To adopt the notation used in the rest of this paper, lower-case letters represent logs; Δq, Δz, Δn, and Δk are log first differences of the variables in (1); hereafter we drop the t subscripts. When joined with the assumptions of constant returns and competitive factor pricing, (1) implies that the standard technique for calculating MFP (or Solow's residual, Δm) accurately measures the technological shift term:

$$\Delta m = \Delta q - \alpha \Delta n - (1 - \alpha)\Delta k = \Delta z. \quad (2)$$

where α is labor's income share.

Production in the Short Run

However fruitful may be equation (1) in describing the long-run evolution of output and inputs, its widespread use to describe the short-run production process is contradicted by both macroeconomic and microeconomic evidence. At the macroeconomic level, if the aggregate price level is sticky, then nominal aggregate demand shocks automatically become real aggregate demand shocks.[8] Firms are no longer price takers and quantity setters, as assumed by

---

Domar in a remark delivered to both Hall and myself in our first MIT graduate macroeconomics class: "changes in the utilization of capital and of labor explain cyclical variations in total factor productivity" (class notes, October 26, 1964).

[8] In its assumption of price stickiness, this analysis shares the same starting place as Rotemberg-Summers (1990). But we rely on price stickiness only to support the assumption that firms

(1), but rather are price setters and quantity takers. Having set prices, their remaining decisions are described by input demand equations for labor and capital. If input demand exhibits an elasticity to these exogenous changes in output of less than unity, measured MFP will vary procyclically even in the absence of technology shocks.

In microeconomic analysis we find a consensus going back more than two decades that the usual economic approach to production, based on the notion of homogeneous, divisible, and highly substitutable factor inputs, does not apply in most of the economy, including manufacturing, communication, transportation, and utilities. Instead, the dominant feature of the production process is heterogeneous capital that incorporates the most efficient technology available at the date of its construction but, once built, embodies fixed technical characteristics that impose tight constraints on the feasible set of input-output combinations. In the language of the 1960s, capital is putty-clay. The firm's choices are decomposed between "ex ante" investment decisions and "ex post" operating decisions, the latter involving the choice of variable inputs needed to produce desired output with existing equipment.[9]

Thus microeconomic production theory conflicts with the maintained assumption in the RBC literature and Hall's research that perfect substitution among inputs applies in the shortest run.[10] For instance, Hall claims (1990b) that "as long as capital has no pure user cost, it is reasonable to assume that all capital available is in use," that is, utilization is always 100 percent. Yet this prediction is contradicted by data published by regulatory agencies for airlines, utilities, and other owners of capital equipment; the utilization of specific capital equipment types (for example, Boeing 737-300s) is highly variable over the days of the week, seasons of the year, and phases of the business cycle, simply because labor and capital are not substitutable once the labor requirements of capital equipment are "designed in."

Mismeasurement Parameters

Since our topic is the nature of fluctuations of MFP over the business cycle, we need to separate short-run (cyclical) variation from long-run trends. The subsequent empirical analysis employs several methods of detrending, including one or two log-linear trends, piecewise linear trends that allow a separate trend for

are quantity takers and make input demand decisions. Rotemberg and Summers go further and use the assumption of price stickiness to argue that price (P) is typically above marginal cost ($W \Delta N / \Delta Q$) in recessions. This requires the auxiliary assumption that the wage rate is as sticky as the price level, so that there is no cyclicality in W/P; only on this condition is a statement that P/MC is procyclical equivalent to the statement that labor productivity ($\Delta Q / \Delta N$) is procyclical.

[9] The distinction between the ex ante and ex post production decision is incorporated formally in almost all econometric work on the electric utility industry spanning the last three decades. See especially Wills (1978) and the survey paper by Cowing-Smith (1978).

[10] For instance, Braun and Evans (1991a, 1991b) attempt to apply the neoclassical growth model with fully substitutable inputs at the seasonal frequency.

each business cycle, and the Hodrick-Prescott filter. In this section we interpret all log first differences, for example, Δq, as the first difference in the log ratio of a variable to its trend. Our analysis assumes that the technological shift term, Z_t in (1), changes only at trend frequencies but exhibits no cyclical variation. Our task is to examine the extent of mismeasurement and/or overhead factor inputs required to make the observed procyclical variations of MFP compatible with the maintained assumption of no technological shifts at the cyclical frequency.[11]

Labor and capital input are treated symmetrically. We allow for overhead components of both labor and capital input, and for mismeasurement of each. Measured capital input (Δj) is interpreted as the capacity of the capital stock in place to produce output, for example, available seat miles flown by the airline industry or electric generating capacity in megawatts times the number of hours per year.[12] Actual capital input (Δk) is divided into the measured (Δj) change in capacity and the unmeasured change in capacity utilization (Δu):

$$\Delta k \equiv \Delta j + \Delta u. \tag{3}$$

Similarly, changes in true labor input (Δn) are divided into a measured component (Δh) and a component (Δf) representing unmeasured changes in work effort:

$$\Delta n \equiv \Delta h + \Delta f. \tag{4}$$

Now we need to parameterize the measured and unmeasured components of input fluctuations. For labor, we denote by e^N the "labor mismeasurement" parameter, that is, the fraction of true fluctuations in labor input taking the form of unmeasured changes in labor input:

$$\Delta f = e^N \Delta n; \quad \Delta h = (1 - e^N)\Delta n; \quad 0 \preceq e^N \preceq 1. \tag{5}$$

Similarly, we denote by e^K the "capital mismeasurement" parameter, that is, the fraction of true fluctuations in capital input taking the form of unmeasured changes in capital utilization:

$$\Delta u = e^K \Delta k; \quad \Delta j = (1 - e^K)\Delta k; \quad 0 \preceq e^K \preceq 1. \tag{6}$$

---

[11] Evans (1991) shows that between one quarter and one half of the variance of Solow's residual can be explained by explicit demand variables, including money, interest rates, and government spending. This does not rule out our presumption that the rest of the variance can be explained by demand variables that Evans does not include, such as inventory cycles, fixed investment cycles, and exogenous changes in net exports.

[12] In the airline example, there is a distinction between the capacity of the measured gross capital stock (all aircraft which are on the books and have not been sold or otherwise retired) and the capacity actually flown, that is, available seat miles. The capacity of the gross capital stock shows little if any procyclical movement, while there are procyclical movements in capacity actually flown, since hours flown per plane vary with the cycle (and the seasons). This distinction between the two concepts of measured capital is eliminated to simplify the analysis; maintaining this distinction would add notational clutter without changing any of the results. The distinction between capacity and capital utilization is made by Hilton (1970).

For completeness we add the possibility of mismeasured output fluctuations when some labor effort in recessions is devoted to maintenance, training, and building new facilities, and when these forms of investment are deferred in booms. Such investment-related activities in recessions imply that true output fluctuations (Δq) are smaller in amplitude than measured output fluctuations (Δx):

$$\Delta q = (1 - e^Q)\Delta x, \quad 0 < e^Q < 1. \tag{7}$$

The parameter e^Q represents the ratio of unmeasured investment activities to measured output, and we will investigate the difference made when $e^Q = 0$, or instead e^Q is set at a small fraction like 0.05 or 0.10.

Overhead Labor and Capital

In every industry labor input is divided between a variable portion that changes in response to changes in output and a quasi-fixed portion required to run and maintain the capital stock, often called "overhead labor." For instance, each type of commercial aircraft has a cockpit constructed to require either two or three pilots, independently of how many seats are filled. Pilot requirements are fixed once capacity is determined, while the number of flight attendants, gate agents, baggage handlers, etc., varies with output.[13] Similarly, each railroad locomotive and freight truck has a technical requirement for one or more drivers, while loading personnel vary with the amount of freight actually carried. Assuming that all cyclical movements of labor input can be classified as fully variable or fully fixed, and denoting by v^N the fraction of variable labor, we have:

$$\Delta n = v^N \Delta q + (1 - v^N)\Delta j; \quad 0 \le v^N \le 1. \tag{8}$$

Available data on capacity utilization assume that all of true capital input is variable. However, if there is some overhead labor, there must be some overhead capital as well. Following Rotemberg-Summers (1990), who treat capital input for airlines as seats occupied, the seats occupied by passengers represent variable capital input, while the seats occupied by pilots, schedulers, lawyers, and executives represent fixed capital input. Thus over the cycle true capital input responds partly to output and partly to capacity:

$$\Delta k = v^K \Delta q + (1 - v^K)\Delta j; \quad 0 \le v^K \le 1. \tag{9}$$

Hall (1990b) refers to the variations of true capital relative to true labor input as the "capital-labor complementarity" parameter and assumes that this parameter is unity. However, the above analysis implies that this parameter (σ) is:

$$\sigma = \frac{\Delta k}{\Delta n} = \frac{v^K}{e^K v^N + (1 - e^K)v^K} \tag{10}$$

[13] Williams (1992) has collected labor requirement functions for major categories of airline employment; baggage handlers represent fully variable labor, pilots fully fixed, while flight attendants are an intermediate category with a minimum number required for each aircraft type regardless of passengers, but the number varies above the minimum as a linear function of extra passengers.

In the simple case in which capacity does not vary over the business cycle ($e^K = 1$, implying that $\Delta j = 0$) then (10) reduces to $\sigma = v^K/v^N$, that is, the share of variable capital to the share of variable labor. There is no reason for these two shares to be the same, and hence for σ to equal unity. For instance, low-paid assembly-line workers (variable labor) might work with expensive machines like power cranes and forming presses (variable capital), while high-paid lawyers and executives (overhead labor) might work with relatively cheap capital (desks and notepads). In this example, the share of variable capital is higher than that of variable labor, implying that $\sigma > 1$.

Implications for the Measured Procyclicality of MFP

Now we can take this model in which by assumption there are no cyclical technology shocks ($\Delta z = 0$) and show the conditions required for conventionally measured MFP to be procyclical. The usual methods compute MFP (Δm) by subtracting from measured output (Δx) the change in measured inputs weighted by labor's share:

$$\Delta m = \Delta x - \alpha \Delta h - (1 - \alpha)\Delta j$$
$$= \Delta q \left[\frac{1}{1 - e^Q} - \alpha v^N (1 - e^N) \right.$$
$$\left. - \frac{v^K (1 - e^K)\{1 - \alpha[v^N + (1 - v^N)e^N]\}}{e^K + v^K(1 - e^K)} \right]. \tag{11}$$

If there were no mismeasurement ($e^Q = e^N = e^K = 0$) and if measured labor and capital were entirely variable ($v^K = v^N = 1$), then measured output and both measured inputs would exhibit the same variability as true output ($\Delta x = \Delta h = \Delta j = \Delta q$), and clearly there would be no cyclicality to measured MFP growth ($\Delta m = 0$).

The complexity of the second line of equation (11) arises from interaction effects among capital and labor mismeasurement, and capital and labor fixity. Some intuition is provided in Table 8.1, which calculates the elasticity of measured MFP growth to true output growth ($\Delta m/\Delta q$) for each type of measurement and fixity taken one at a time. There are two columns in the table, the first corresponding to the case of no capital mismeasurement and the second to the case of complete mismeasurement. The second column of complete capital mismeasurement is of particular interest, because conventional measures of the capital stock are computed from perpetual inventories (cumulations of past investment) that by design allow for no cyclical variability of capital input. If there is no capital fixity, then complete capital mismeasurement means that true capital input varies in proportion to true output, and all of this variation takes the form of changes in the utilization of the capital stock ($\Delta k = \Delta u = \Delta q$).

Line 1 of the table shows in the first column that with no mismeasurement or input fixity, the measured MFP elasticity would be zero in a world without technological shocks. But with complete capital mismeasurement the ellasticity would be substantial, equal to capital's share ($1 - \alpha$). Line 2 shows that output

Table 8.1. *Measured Elasticity of MFP to True Cyclical Changes in Output for Specified Parameters of Mismeasurement and of Input Fixity*

Deviation from Perfect Measurement and from Complete Input Variability	Measured MFP Elasticity ($\Delta m / \Delta q$)			
	Case when no Capital Mismeasurement ($e^K = 0$)		Case when Complete Capital Mismeasurement ($e^K = 1$)	
($e^Q = e^N = 0; v^N = v^K = 1$)	Formula	Example	Formula	Example
1. None	0	0.00	$1-\alpha$	0.25
2. Output Mismeasurement ($e^Q \neq 0$; *example* $e^Q = 0.1$)	$\dfrac{e^Q}{1-e^Q}$	0.11	$\dfrac{1-\alpha(1-e^Q)}{1-e^Q}$	0.36
3. Labor Mismeasurement ($e^N \neq 0$; *example* $e^N = 0.1$)	αe^N	0.08	$1-\alpha(1-e^N)$	0.33
4. Labor Partly Fixed ($v^N \neq 1$; *example* $v^N = 0.75$)	0	0.00	$1-\alpha v^N$	0.44
5. Capital Partly Fixed ($v^K \neq 1$; *example* $v^K = 0.75$)	0	0.00	$1-\alpha$	0.25

Notes. 1. All examples assume $\alpha = 0.75$.

2. When all inputs are variable and only capital is mismeasured, the elasticity of MFP is $e^K(1 - \alpha)$.

mismeasurement adds to line 1 an additional component of elasticity equal to the ratio of mismeasured to measured output variation ($e^Q/(1 - e^Q)$). Labor mismeasurement adds a component equal to the mismeasurement fraction times labor's share.

Lines 4 and 5 of the table show that labor and capital fixity do not matter if capital is properly measured. Our concept of fixity (equations 8 and 9 above) involves a dependence of true labor or capital input on the measured capital stock, i.e., capacity. If this is measured correctly, then the true capital stock must vary in proportion to output.[14] Stated another way, if measured capacity varies in proportion to true capital input, the concept of fixity is meaningless. However, with complete capital mismeasurement in the second column of Table 8.1, labor fixity substantially boosts the measured MFP elasticity (by reducing the amplitude of cyclical movements in labor input). Capital fixity does not matter with complete capital mismeasurement, since measured capital is completely fixed by definition ($\Delta j = 0$).

Parameter Tradeoffs

We can narrow the range of plausible parameters if we reverse the question and ask, given what we know about the procyclicality of measured productivity, which combinations of parameters are consistent with the facts? Here we focus not on measured MFP but on the measured cyclicality of average labor

[14] Since perfect measurement means that $\Delta j = \Delta k$, then (9) implies that $\Delta k = \Delta q$.

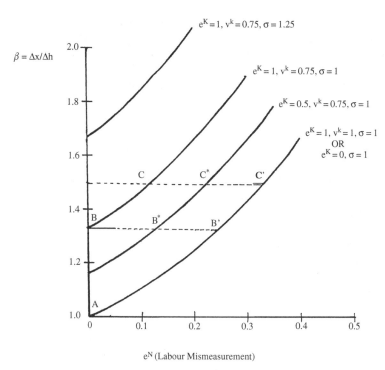

Figure 8.1. Mismeasurement Tradeoffs

productivity ($\beta = \Delta x / \Delta h$, the measured "SRIRL" parameter), simply because the size of β is a widely recognized stylized fact, about 1.5 in Okun's original analysis and between 1.2 and 1.33 in our subsequent empirical examination.

To compute the value of β implied by our model, we can state both Δx and Δh in terms of Δq and then use equations (3) through (10) above to solve for the ratio $\Delta x / \Delta h$, in which the Δq term drops out:

$$\beta = \frac{\sigma [e^K + v^K (1 - e^K)]}{v^K (1 - e^Q)(1 - e^N)}. \tag{12}$$

With no mismeasurement and no input fixity, equation (12) reduces to $\beta = 1$. Figure 8.1 exhibits the interaction among alternative parameter values by plotting β against the labor mismeasurement parameter (e^N) for plausible combinations of the other parameters. We focus on the required amount of labor mismeasurement, simply because the existing literature provides little evidence on the quantitative magnitude of the deviation between measured labor input and true labor input, that is, on the importance of cyclical fluctuations in "labor effort." Each of the schedules assumes that output is perfectly measured; subsequently we return to the question of output mismeasurement.

The lowest curve plots equation (12) on the assumptions of strict capital-labor complementarity ($\sigma = 1$), and either (a) perfect capital measurement (in which case capital fixity is irrelevant) or (b) complete capital mismeasurement and fully variable capital ($v^K = 1$). This case requires large amounts of labor mismeasurement in order to explain Okun's β value of 1.5 (this requires $e^N = 0.33$ at point C') or the more empirically relevant value of 1.33 (this requires $e^N = 0.25$ at point B').

However, with the same capital-labor complementarity parameter and the fraction of variable inputs reduced from 1.0 to 0.75 ($v^K = v^N = 0.75$), Okun's β value can be explained with relatively little labor mismeasurement ($e^N = 0.11$ at point C), and the empirically relevant value of β can be explained with no labor mismeasurement at all (shown at point B). With slightly more variability in capital than in labor, for instance $\sigma = 1.25$, we obtain the highest curve, showing that empirical estimates of β can be explained without any reliance on labor or output mismeasurement. The curve going through points B^* and C^* shows that with 0.75 variable inputs, a reduction in capital mismeasurement from 1.0 to 0.5 raises the amount of labor mismeasurement that is required to explain the facts, as contrasted to points B and C.

The amount of required labor and capital mismeasurement is even less than shown in Figure 8.1 if there is any output mismeasurement, since this shifts each curve upward by $e^Q/(1 - e^Q)$. If we take e^Q to be 0.1, as suggested by Hall (1990) from the work of Fay and Medoff (1985), then this (along with the assumption that $\sigma = 1$) means that the empirical value of $\beta = 1.33$ can be explained with any combination of factor fixity and labor mismeasurement adding up to 0.165, for instance zero labor mismeasurement and 0.165 of labor and capital fixed, or completely variable labor and capital with labor mismeasurement of 0.165.[15] It is in this sense that we subsequently refer to labor fixity and labor mismeasurement as "observationally equivalent" (note that the fixity and mismeasurement parameters appear multiplied together in equation 11).

Hall's Defense Against the Mismeasurement Argument

As we have seen, plausible mismeasurement parameters imply that observed productivity movements can be explained without any reliance on technological shocks, market power, or increasing returns, and what Hall calls "invariance" is upheld. How then does Hall (1990a, 1990b) dismiss the obvious force of the mismeasurement argument? His case depends both on exaggerating the size of β that needs to be explained, and also by treating each type of mismeasurement *ad seriatim* rather than jointly, thus ignoring interaction effects.

---

[15] The Fay-Medoff results for all respondents (1985, Table 2, p. 647) indicate that in the "most recently completed cyclical downturn" shipments fell by 30 percent, while 3 percent of "normal hours" were assigned to "worthwhile other work," implying $e^Q = 3/30 = 0.1$. A possible qualification is that the Fay-Medoff survey applies only to manufacturing. Nevertheless, there are many service industries where employees may have an opportunity to work in investment-type activities during downturns, including deferred maintenance by workers in transportation, communication, and utilities, sales calls by brokers, and store refurbishment in retail trade. Fair (1985) shows that the Fay-Medoff results are consistent with an update of his earlier work (1969).

Hall examines capital mismeasurement on the assumption of no mismeasurement of labor or output. He claims that capital utilization would have to exhibit an elasticity of 5 to true labor input to be the entire explanation of procyclical MFP fluctuations, a number far above his favored elasticity of unity. His method of derivation implies that β has to be 2, which would require an Okun's law response of 4-to-1, rather than Okun's 3-to-1 or the empirical value around 2.5-to-1. And his method involves the nonsensical implicit assumption that capital utilization exhibits cyclical fluctuations 2.5 times as great as those of output itself.[16] In our model the only way capital can vary five times as much as labor input is if all capital is variable while only 20 percent of labor is variable, but this requires a β of 5.

Turning now to Hall's dismissal of errors in measurement of labor, we have to deal both with facts and theories. Hall's discussion is carried out on the assumption that there is no mismeasurement of capital or output, and, as indicated in the last paragraph, that $\beta = 2$. In our analysis of Figure 8.1 these assumptions require that the labor mismeasurement parameter (e^N) must be 0.5 to eliminate cyclical fluctuations in Solow's residual. Yet Hall's dismissal of labor mismeasurement is implicitly based on a much more extreme value of e^N than implied by our analysis or by his other assumptions. He states that unmeasured work effort must have been "10 percent above normal for three successive years" in the mid 1960s to explain all of the procyclical fluctuation in Solow's residual (1990b, p. 24). But this number is too high by a factor of 2.5. Output peaked at 6 percent above normal in the mid-1960s, and measured labor input peaked at 4 percent above normal, half consisting of unemployment 2 percent below normal and half of the usual participation and hours effects. So, with a e^N parameter of 0.5, unmeasured work effort would have been only 4 percent above normal, not 10 percent. And, with the plausible combination of parameters at point C in Figure 8.1, work effort would only have been 0.44 percent above normal.

Hall's discussion of labor mismeasurement cites one additional piece of evidence on work effort. Fay and Medoff (1985) asked their manufacturing plant managers whether the work effort of blue-collar workers increased or decreased in a recession. The answers came out almost in a dead heat, with a slight balance for a countercyclical movement in effort.[17] However, the needed estimate of the labor mismeasurement parameter (e^N) cannot be obtained from

---

[16] Hall's method is to ask what value of $n = \Delta u / \Delta h$ would be necessary to imply

$$\Delta m = 0 = \Delta x - \alpha \Delta h - (1 - \alpha)\Delta u = \Delta h[\beta - \alpha - (1 - \alpha)^n].$$

With a labor's share (α) of 0.75, as we have assumed, Hall's stated value of $n = 5$ requires $\beta = 2$. But it also requires that with $\Delta x / \Delta h = 2$ and $\Delta u / \Delta h = 5$ we must have $\Delta u / \Delta x = 2.5$.

[17] Fay-Medoff (1985, p. 648, footnote 30) report that there was no difference in effort in the subset of their plants that hoarded labor, i.e., maintain more workers in a recession than was technically necessary. For this subset, the tally was 34 respondents reported more effort in the recession, 35 less effort, and 45 no difference. For plants that did not hoard labor, the score was 23 more, 14 less, and 17 no difference. The overall tally indicates 34 percent more, 29 percent less, and 37 percent no difference, which is not a difference significant enough to make a case either way.

survey evidence of "effort," which in a questionnaire may be viewed by worker respondents as synonymous with personal worth and by employer respondents as indicating more about cooperativeness and morale than an actual count of hand motions per hour. Flight attendants on planes are paid the same, but work less hard, when planes are empty. Operators at electricity generating stations are paid the same, but work less hard, when the generating unit cycles down periodically in response to slack demand. Cashiers, baggers, and stockers in supermarkets work less hard when lines are short or empty than when lines are long. In none of these situations do employees feel less worthy nor do employers sense a lack of cooperation (in fact people may seem to be "trying harder"). Consequently, it will require new and better research to reveal from surveys the counterpart of the theoretical concept of work effort.

Dynamics

The previous theoretical analysis assumes that all cyclical fluctuations occur simultaneously. It thus ignores dynamics, and in particular the lagged adjustment of labor input to changes in output. Lagged labor adjustment was a phenomenon known long before the development of sophisticated econometric tools for the analysis of time-series dynamics or even before Hultgren's discovery of the SRIRL puzzle. For instance, Burns and Mitchell recognized that employment lagged output, and the Commerce Department has long classified unemployment as among its set of lagging indicators.

As we shall learn in the empirical section, once a low frequency trend is established, the procyclicality of productivity occurs at two higher frequencies. At the highest frequency labor input lags behind changes in output, with an adjustment speed of about three quarters. After this initial adjustment is completed, there is a remaining procyclical component due to the fact that the full adjustment of labor over the first three quarters occurs with an elasticity to output that is less than unity. This remaining component of procyclical productivity occurs at the business cycle frequency. Henceforth, we will refer to the high-frequency component of procyclical productivity (neglected in the above analysis) as due to "costly adjustment," a separate source of procyclicality from the components that occur at business cycle frequencies due, as shown above, to mismeasurement and to overhead labor.

8.2   ECONOMETRIC ISSUES

The aim of the empirical work in this paper is twofold. First, we estimate the elasticity of measured output to measured hours (β), one of the central parameters in the theoretical analysis summarized in Figure 8.1. Second, we develop an empirical counterpart to the theoretical analysis. Using actual data on output, hours, and utilization, we show which parameters of unobserved output mismeasurement, labor mismeasurement, or labor fixity are required to eliminate the procyclicality of Solow's residual. In contrast to the work of Hall and his followers based solely on annual data, all estimates here are based on quarterly data, both for the nonfarm private economy and for the manufacturing sector, using BLS data on output, hours, capital stock, and labor's share.[18]

Specification

The use of quarterly data allows us to revive familiar dynamic issues that were much discussed in the 1970s (Sims, 1974; Gordon, 1979) but have been neglected by most papers in the recent revival of this topic.[19] In particular, the earlier work concluded from symmetric two-sided tests that hours respond to changes in output, rather than vice versa, and so hours rather than output should be the dependent variable in productivity regressions. This finding has been ignored in the recent work of Hall and his followers. Here we start with Hall's specifications, then examine the effects of reversing dependent and independent variables, and subsequently provide estimates and an evaluation of each approach.

Hall's empirical work estimates two types of equations, with all variables expressed in first differences. One type (1988) regresses output on hours, which, using the above notation, involves the estimating equation:

$$\Delta x_t = \beta \Delta h_t + \tau + u_t^x. \tag{13}$$

Here τ is the productivity trend, which was assumed to be zero in the theoretical analysis above. The second type of equation (1990a, 1990b) regresses the Solow residual on output, as in:

$$\Delta m_t = \lambda \Delta x_t + \tau + u_t^s, \quad \text{where } \Delta m_t \text{ is computed as:}$$
$$\Delta m_t = \Delta x_t - \alpha_t \Delta h_t - (1 - \alpha_t) \Delta j_t. \tag{14}$$

In both (13) and (14) the error term is interpreted as an unobserved productivity shock. The joint dependence of the dependent variable, independent variable, and error term is offered as a justification for the use of instrumental variables. To purge the independent variable of any correlation with the error term, Hall uses three instruments that, he claims, are affected only by demand shocks, and are thus uncorrelated with productivity shocks. These are the change in real military spending, the change in the (nominal) world oil price, and a dummy for the political party of the President.[20]

---

[18] Quarterly data on output and hours come from a BLS diskette corresponding to the standard BLS quarterly releases on labor productivity and compensation. Data on capital and labor's share are available annually from the BLS multifactor productivity project and are interpolated to yield quarterly values.

[19] While quarterly data are an improvement on annual data, Sims (1974) argued that errors introduced by temporal aggregation make monthly data superior to quarterly data.

[20] In Hall's first published paper on this topic (1986) the empirical results were of the first type, with output regressed on hours, but no instruments were used. See Shea (1991) for a criticism that Hall's military spending variable is of little use, because of its low correlation with output at the industry level, as well as an attempt to create new demand instruments for particular industries.

Abbott, Griliches, and Hausman (1988) have argued that one would expect the OLS estimate of the coefficient in (13) to be an upward biased estimate of the true parameter.[21] The argument carries over to (14), since a favorable productivity shock to u_t^s will boost output for any given amount of factor input. However, Abbott, Griliches, and Hausman show that the instrumental variable estimate of (13) yields a higher estimate of β than OLS and consider the possibility that the instruments are positively correlated with the disturbance.[22]

Detrending

The difficulties raised by unobserved productivity shocks are related to the issue of detrending. In the work of Hall and most of his critics only a single constant is included to represent the productivity trend, as in (13) and (14), with no allowance for changes in the productivity trend. If unobserved productivity shocks occur not for a quarter or two, but rather persist for years, then the failure to allow for changing trends will bias upward the coefficient on output in (14), since the missing trend slowdown variable in a period with slow productivity growth like 1973–9 will be positively correlated with the output variable.

This essay uses two different methods to separate trend from cycle. The first method computes (separately for output, hours, and capital) a log-linear piecewise trend that runs through quarters when the actual unemployment rate was equal to the "natural" unemployment rate, roughly 6 percent.[23] During the 1955–92 sample period there are seven different trends subtracted from all variables, so that in first difference form there are implicitly seven constant terms with values fixed by the growth rates of trends through benchmark quarters. The use of piecewise loglinear detrending implicitly involves the same method of separating trend and cycle as the more formal approach of Blanchard and Quah (1989), and this is to assume that the unemployment rate is stationary in the long run, that output is not, and that demand disturbances can be represented

---

[21] Abbott, Griliches, and Hausman argue for (13) that if there is an unobserved demand shock, both output and factor input will increase, leading to an upward biased coefficient. For the case of a productivity shock they show that if the elasticity of demand is greater than unity, the productivity shock will have a positive correlation with changes in the variable factors of production, including h.

[22] Abbott, Griliches, and Hausman based their critique on an early version of Hall (1988) in which the single instrument for Δh in (9) was the change in real GNP. Their argument carries through to the three instruments listed above that are used in the published version of Hall (1988) and in the (1990a) and (1990b) papers as well.

[23] The "natural" unemployment rate is the rate which is consistent with steady inflation and is "backed out" of an equation for price change that includes various lags of price change, the deviation of unemployment from the natural rate, and various measures of supply shocks. The method is developed in Gordon (1982) and Gordon-King (1982). The benchmark quarters are 1949:Q1, 1954:Q1, 1957:Q3, 1963:Q3, 1970:Q2, 1974:Q2, 1979:Q3, 1987:Q3, and 1990:Q4. For all detrended variables, the growth rate of the trend after 1990 is taken to be the 1987–90 rate.

by shocks that occur in common to unemployment and to deviations of output from trend.

A special case of this technique is the allowance for a single break in the productivity trend, as in Rotemberg-Summers (1990). Below we show that estimates of the key parameters (β, λ) are little affected by the choice between a single break or multiple breaks, but that the fit of the equations is improved by multiple breaks.

Alternatively we use the Hodrick and Prescott (1981) filter, which allows the trend to move continuously. The main limitation of the Hodrick and Prescott filter is that the user's choice of the smoothness parameter can yield any arbitrary trend series ranging from a single straight line to a trend that is so variable that it precisely mimics the series being detrended. For instance, one can obtain a Great Depression of arbitrarily small size by setting the Hodrick and Prescott smoothness parameter at a sufficiently low value. In the opposite direction one can obtain detrended values that are almost perfectly correlated with those yielded by the piecewise loglinear trends when a sufficiently high value of the smoothness parameter is used. Thus the use of the Hodrick and Prescott filter involves the imposition of a subjective choice, whereas the piecewise trends have the advantage that they are anchored in the behavior of the unemployment rate.[24] A further advantage of piecewise trends is that there is one trend per business cycle, thus achieving a clean break between the business cycle frequency represented by deviations from trend and the lower frequency changes in the trends from one business cycle to the next.

The top frame of Figure 8.2 compares the two methods of detrending for output and the bottom frame does the same for hours. The differences can be easily explained – the techniques provide a similar interpretation of relatively short-duration business cycles (1955–61, 1971–8, 1987–92) but differ on the long-duration expansion of the 1960s and slump of 1980–6. The piecewise loglinear technique, using "outside information" that unemployment was persistently low during the 1960s and persistently high during 1980–6, transfers this information to conclude that output was persistently away from trend. The Hodrick and Prescott technique allows an acceleration of the trend in the 1960s

---

[24] Hodrick and Prescott (1981, pp. 5–8) provide a justification of a value for their smoothness parameter of 1600, and this has been used in their subsequent work (e.g., Prescott, 1986) and that of most other Hodrick and Prescott users. Yet this justification is based entirely on a subjective statement: "Our prior view is that a five percent cyclical component is moderately large as is a one-eighth of one percent change in the growth rate in a quarter. This led us to select $\sqrt{\lambda} = 5/(1/8) = 40$ or $\lambda = 1600$ as a value for the smoothing parameter." A value of 10 eliminates the business cycle, while a value of 100,000 reproduces the piecewise loglinear detrending procedure and a value of infinity yields a single trend. To interpret their "prior," consider the Great Contraction of 1929–33 (when real GDP fell 34 percent below a 2.5 percent per year loglinear trend extending from 1928 to 1948). We can multiply their example of $5/(1/8)$ by 5, for a cyclical component of 25 percent and a reduction in the growth trend of 5/8 percent per quarter or 2.5 percent per year; thus in their interpretation the growth component had zero growth between 1929 and 1933 despite continued growth in the working-age population and in the productivity that would have been observed at a constant unemployment rate.

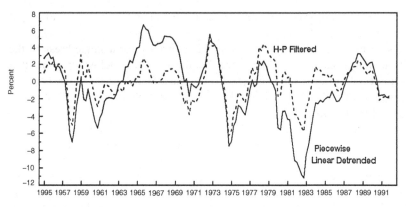

Figure 8.2a. Deviations from Trend of Output, Piecewise Loglinear and Hodrick-Prescott Detrending, Nonfarm Private Economy, 1955:1–1992:1

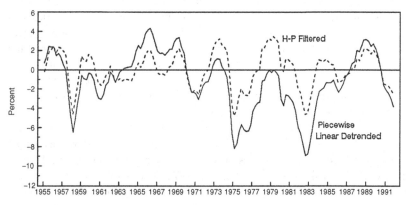

Figure 8.2b. Deviations from Trend of Hours, Piecewise Loglinear and Hodrick-Prescott Detrending, Nonfarm Private Economy, 1955:1–1992:1

and deceleration in the 1980s to absorb much of this cycle.[25] More important for this paper, the Hodrick and Prescott technique transfers different amounts of the output and hours deviations from cycle to trend, thus "flattening out" hours and output deviations so that they look the same. Consequently, as we shall see below, the Hodrick and Prescott filter consistently provides an estimate of $\beta(\Delta x / \Delta h)$ that is closer to unity than the piecewise loglinear technique; hence our preference for the latter approach works against our case that procyclical productivity fluctuations are due to mismeasurement of output and inputs.

---

[25] Using the same smoothness parameter, Kydland and Prescott (1990, Chart 2, p. 9) illustrate the log levels of actual and trend real GNP and show how almost all of the boom of the 1960s is interpreted as an acceleration of the trend rather than a deviation of actual above the trend.

Instruments and Reverse Causation

Both methods of detrending eliminate coefficient bias introduced when only a single trend is imposed on the entire postwar period. But we must still deal with the potential problem of coefficient bias caused by unidentified productivity shocks at business-cycle frequencies. One response is to deny that these are important, on the ground that for a productivity shock to account for more than a trivial amount of the sharp decline in output in a typical recession would require an implausible degree of technological regress or "forgetfulness." While I find this argument convincing, I welcome any remaining bias, because it actually makes the argument of this essay stronger. As we learned from Figure 8.1, any tendency for β to be overestimated makes it harder to accept our basic premise that mismeasurement can explain the procyclicality of MFP. Thus, if we can make the case for mismeasurement with OLS estimates of β, that case becomes even stronger for anyone concerned that β may be upward biased. Finally, if a correctly measured MFP series yields a zero coefficient (λ) on measured output, then the concern about upward bias vanishes. A zero coefficient is not biased away from zero.

In principle one may estimate β either from (13) or from the reciprocal of the coefficient yielded when that regression is run in reverse:

$$\Delta h_t = \gamma \Delta x_t - \tau + u_t^h, \tag{15}$$

where $\gamma = 1/\beta$. While either (13) or (15) may give equivalent answers when responses are instantaneous, they will not yield equal estimates of β in the presence of lags. As Sims (1974) showed in monthly data, the data imply that hours respond to output, rather than vice versa. This is evident from Figure 8.3a, where one can see clearly the lag of hours behind output (in Figures 8.3 and 8.4 the data plotted are four-quarter changes in percentage deviations of log levels from the log-linear piecewise trend). A corollary of lagged hours adjustment is that average labor productivity leads output, as shown in Figure 8.3b. It is well known that the *level* of productivity is related to the first derivative of output, not just the level, and similarly we shall see that the *first difference* of productivity responds to both the first and second derivatives of output.[26] This statistical fact buttresses the case for high-frequency adjustment costs as the basic cause of observed quarterly movements in productivity and weakens the case for any explanation that requires the level of output and productivity to move together, such as increasing returns or "thick market externalities."

Figure 8.4a exhibits the strongly procyclical changes in MFP (Solow's residual, or Δmt). When MFP is calculated with a series on capital input that exhibits

---

[26] Using the Hodrick and Prescott filter with the standard smoothness parameter (1600), Kydland and Prescott (1990) provide cross correlations of output with current and lagged values of many macro variables in quarterly data over the period 1954–89. They (Table 1, p. 10) confirm our finding that establishment hours lag output and that the Hodrick and Prescott technique provides a series for hours at time $t + 1$ that is almost perfectly correlated (0.92) with output at time t. They also show a strong two-quarter lead for productivity ahead of output.

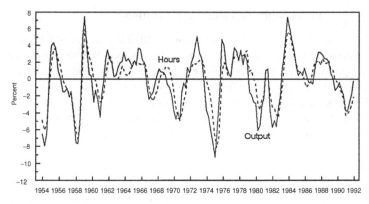

Figure 8.3a. Four-Quarter Change in Deviations from Trend of Output and of Hours, Piecewise Loglinear Detrending, Nonfarm Private Economy, 1955:1–1992:1

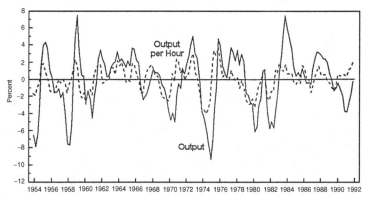

Figure 8.3b. Four-Quarter Change in Deviations from Trend of Output and of Output per Hour, Piecewise Loglinear Detrending, Nonfarm Private Economy, 1955:1–1992:1

little cyclical variation, it is obvious that MFP must be much more procyclical than labor's average product. This can be easily seen in the extreme case in which detrended measured capital changes are zero ($\Delta j = 0$), since then:

$$\Delta m_t = \Delta x_t - \alpha \Delta h_t = \frac{(\beta - \alpha)}{\beta} \Delta x_t, \text{ implying that}$$

$$\lambda = 1 - \frac{\alpha}{\beta}, \tag{16}$$

which must be less than the coefficient of labor's average product on output $[1 - (1/\beta)]$ as long as $\alpha < 1$.

An interesting aspect of the basic data is shown in Figure 8.4b, where actual output changes are contrasted with the changes predicted by Hall's

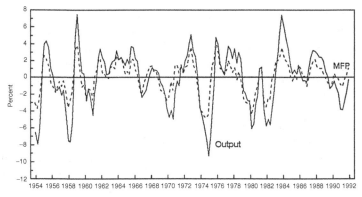

Figure 8.4a. Four-Quarter Change in Deviations from Trend of Output and of MFP, Piecewise Loglinear Detrending, Nonfarm Private Economy, 1955:1–1992:1

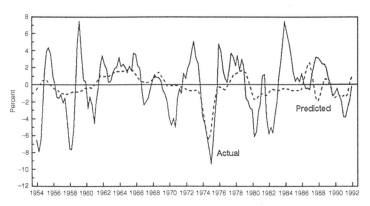

Figure 8.4b. Four-Quarter Change in Deviations from Trend of Output and of Output Predicted by Hall Instruments, Piecewise Loglinear Detrending, Nonfarm Private Economy, 1955:1–1992:1

instruments.[27] The chart helps us to understand why a shift from OLS to instrumental variables estimation always leads to an *increase* in the measured β coefficient, as Abbott, Griliches, and Hausman found and as we discover below.[28] Simply put, the instruments do a very bad job of tracking shifts in output

---

[27] To adopt Hall's instruments for quarterly data, we first correct his mistake of using the nominal rather than the real oil price, and then use the four-quarter change in the real oil price, the four-quarter change in real defense spending, and a dummy for the political party of the President (this equals unity for the quarters 1961:1–1968:4 and 1977:1–1980:4 and is zero otherwise).

[28] A sequel to the Abbott, Griliches, and Hausman paper which confirms their results is Eden and Griliches (1991).

or in hours.[29] The $\overline{R}^2$ in an equation explaining changes in detrended output by a constant and the three instruments is just 0.07, and in an equation explaining changes in detrended hours just 0.05. The oil price change is highly significant with the correct (negative) sign, the political dummy is marginally significant with a large positive coefficient (implying that a Democratic president boosts the growth rate of output by 1.9 percent per annum), while the military variable is wrong-signed and insignificant. The only recession which is decently tracked is 1973–4, an achievement of the oil price instrument. For the other recessions, which are demand phenomena dominated by the yo-yo effect of inventory decumulation on growth, especially 1958–9, 1980–1, and 1982–3, the instruments capture almost none of the variance of output. And in 1986–7 the correlation is negative. Since the instruments "track the interior" of the business cycle, a regression like (14) of MFP change (Figure 8.4a) on the change in output predicted by the instruments (Figure 8.4b) requires a larger coefficient to capture the cyclical effect than would an OLS regression on the actual change in output (the upward bias in the coefficient would be even larger if it were not partially offset by the negative correlation of output and the instruments in 1986–7).[30]

8.3   ESTIMATION

The SRIRL Parameter

We first provide estimates of the SRIRL parameter β alternatively from a regression of hours on output (as in equation 15) and output on hours (as in equation 13). Eight versions of (15) are shown in Table 8.2, both OLS and IV estimates with four alternative methods of detrending. In all regressions the output variable is entered as the current and three lagged values of the quarterly change. The first pair of columns enter actual first differences with a single constant to control for the trend; the second pair allows two trends; the third pair uses data predetrended by the piecewise loglinear technique, and the fourth pair uses data predetrended by the Hodrick and Prescott filter. The standard errors indicate that allowance for one break in trend is important, but that the fit is improved only marginally by allowing for further breaks as in the third pair. The lower S.E.E. of the Hodrick and Prescott filter versions (columns 7 and 8) results from the tendency of that filter to prefit part of the within-cycle variance

---

[29] Another frequently cited series of papers uses Hall's instruments to measure external effects on industry productivity (see for instance Caballero-Lyons 1991). The argument of this section suggests that such estimates of external effects are biassed upward.

[30] Hall defends his use of the oil price variable as a demand shift variable by stating that "changes in factor prices do not shift production functions." For his statement to be true, MFP would have to be measured net of all inputs which have changing prices, that is, Solow's residual would have to be measured net of energy and materials inputs, not just net of labor and capital. Hall's statement is false in the context of all his empirical work, in which measured inputs include only labor and capital, since an increase in oil prices can reduce his measure of Solow's residual by reducing the input of energy per unit of labor and capital.

Table 8.2. *Regressions for First Differences of Hours, Without and with Predetrending, 1955:2–1992:1*

	One Trend		Two Trends		Piecewise Loglinear Detrending		HP Filter, Smoothness Parameter = 1600	
	OLS	IV	OLS	IV	OLS	IV	OLS	IV
	(1)	(2)	(3)	(4)	(5)	(6)	(7)	(8)
Constant Term	−1.07**	−1.02	−1.88**	−2.49**	−0.04	0.15	−0.03	0.14
Slowdown (= 0 1955–73; = 1 1974–92)	–	–	1.34**	1.54*	–	–	–	–
Change in Output	0.85**	0.87**	0.90**	1.13**	–	–	–	–
Change in Output Deviation from Trend	–	–	–	–	0.87**	1.05**	0.90**	1.14**
$\bar{R}^2$	0.74	0.15	0.77	0.18	0.76	0.18	0.76	0.16
S.E.E.	1.86	3.35	1.75	3.29	1.76	3.25	1.69	3.14
D.-W.	1.50	0.91	1.73	0.95	1.65	0.95	1.83	1.02

Notes. ** and * indicate significance of sum of coefficients at 1 percent and 5 percent, respectively.
Coefficients shown are sums of coefficients on lags 0–3 of quarterly log difference in output or output deviation. All quarterly log differences are expressed as annual percentage rates.

Table 8.3. *Regressions for First Differences of Output, with Piecewise Loglinear Predetrending, 1955:2–1992:1*

	Without Leads		With Leads	
	OLS	IV	OLS	IV
	(1)	(2)	(3)	(4)
Constant Term	0.02	0.26	0.03	0.34
Change in Hours Deviation				
Current and Lagged (0 to 3)	0.81**	1.50**	0.34**	−0.05
Leads (−3 to −1)	–	–	0.77**	1.78*
Total	0.81**	1.50**	1.11**	1.73**
$\overline{R}^2$	0.69	0.11	0.72	0.11
S.E.E.	2.67	4.50	2.54	4.54
D.-W.	2.10	1.34	2.22	1.34

Notes. ** and * indicate significance of sum of coefficients at 1 percent and 5 percent, respectively. Coefficients shown are sums of coefficients on lags 0 to +3, −3 to −1, and −3 to +3 of quarterly log difference in the hours deviation. All quarterly log differences are expressed as annual percentage rates. Sample period ends in 1991:Q2 for equations with leads.

of both hours and output, leaving less variance remaining to be explained by the regressions in Table 8.2.

As expected, the instrumental variables versions fit extremely poorly and yield higher coefficients on output than the OLS versions. Finally, the OLS versions yield stable estimates of $\gamma = 1/\beta$, implying β values in the range 1.11–1.18.

In view of the lagged adjustment of hours to output (emphasized by Sims, 1974), we regard Table 8.2 as representing the correct method of estimating β. Nevertheless, it is instructive to see how an investigator could be misled by running regressions of output on hours, as in Hall (1988) and equation (13) above. To show the importance of feedback from output to hours, in Table 8.3 we enter hours in the first two columns with the current and three lagged values only (as in Table 8.2), and in the second pair of columns reestimate the same equation with three leading values added. When leads are excluded, as in column (1) of Table 8.3, the OLS estimate of β is much lower than implied by Table 8.1. Inclusion of leads yields an OLS estimate of β in column (3) of 1.11, very close to estimate of 1.15 implied by column (5) of Table 8.2 that uses the same piecewise loglinear detrending. Once again, the instrumental variables versions fit extremely poorly and yield estimates of β that are far above the OLS estimates. The sum of coefficients on the poorly fitting IV estimate in column (4) of Table 8.3 is 1.73, somewhat below the value of $\beta = 2$ that Hall implicitly assumed when dismissing the importance of measurement errors.

Table 8.4 provides a summary of alternative estimates of β, for both nonfarm business and manufacturing sectors, for both equations (13) and (15), with leads excluded and included, for both the piecewise loglinear and Hodrick and Prescott detrending techniques. Ignoring the third line, which is misspecified

Table 8.4. *Summary of OLS Estimates of the SRIRL Parameter β by Sector, with Hours and Output as Dependent Variables, without and with Leads, 1955:2– 1992:1*

	Nonfarm Private Business Sector	Manufacturing Sector
	(1)	(2)
Piecewise Loglinear Detrending		
Hours Regressed on Output		
Lags 0 to 3	1.15	1.24
Leads 3 to 1, Lags 0 to 3	1.30	1.28
Output Regressed on Hours		
Lags 0 to 3	0.81	1.03
Leads 3 to 1, Lags 0 to 3	1.11	1.10
HP Filter, Smoothness = 1600		
Hours Regressed on Output		
Lags 0 to 3	1.11	1.20
Leads 3 to 1, Lags 0 to 3	1.26	1.18
Output Regressed on Hours		
Lags 0 to 3	0.76	0.99
Leads 3 to 1, Lags 0 to 3	1.08	1.02

Note. Sample period ends in 1991:Q2 for equations with leads.
Source. Tables 8.2 and 8.3, and equivalent regressions for manufacturing.

by excluding feedback from output to hours, the top half of the table based on piecewise loglinear detrending exhibits estimates of β that cover a surprisingly narrow range from 1.10 to 1.30. The range in the bottom half (excluding again the third line) is from 1.02 to 1.26; as expected the Hodrick and Prescott filter dampens within-cycle movements of output more than hours and hence reduces within-cycle fluctuations of productivity. All these estimates are below the value of 1.33 called the "empirically relevant" value in the theoretical analysis of Part II; thus that theoretical analysis overstate the amount of mismeasurement that is consistent with an absence of technology shocks. Hall's dismissal of the mismeasurement approach, implicitly based on β values of 2, seems far off the mark and reflects in large part the poor explanatory power of his instruments and his failure to allow for the lag of hours behind output.

Within-Sample Stability

We now ask whether there is any difference in the cyclical behavior of labor productivity in the two halves of our sample period (1955–73 and 1974–92). We know that the second half was characterized by large oil price shocks, adverse in 1974–5 and 1979–80, and beneficial in 1986. The first half was more clearly dominated by demand shocks. Those who interpret the cyclical behavior of productivity as caused mainly by supply disturbances would expect the cyclical productivity coefficient (β) to be substantially higher in the second half of the

Table 8.5. *Summary of OLS Estimates of the SRIRL Parameter β by Sector, with Hours as Dependent Variable, without and with Leads, Alternative Sample Periods, 1955:2–1992:1*

	Nonfarm Private Business Sector	Manufacturing Sector
	(1)	(2)
Piecewise Loglinear Detrending		
Lags 0 to 3		
1955:2–1992:1	1.15	1.24
1955:2–1973:4	1.14	1.29
1974:1–91992:1	1.15	1.18
Leads 3 to 1, Lags 0 to 3		
1955:2–1991:2	1.30	1.28
1955:2–1973:4	1.25	1.28
1974:1–1992:1	1.33	1.28
HP Filter, Smoothness = 1600		
Lags 0 to 3		
1955:2–1992:1	1.11	1.20
1955:2–1973:4	1.08	1.25
1974:1–1992:1	1.14	1.13
Leads 3 to 1, Lags 0 to 3		
1955:2–1991:2	1.26	1.18
1955:2–1973:4	1.17	1.20
1974:1–1991:2	1.32	1.18

Source. Regressions in Table 8.2 rerun with alternative lags and sample periods as shown.

sample period.[31] The interpretation in this paper, based on an absence of shifts in the production function at cyclical frequencies, together with mismeasurement and fixity of labor and capital, would predict no noticeable changes in the estimated β.

Estimates for the full sample period and each half are shown in Table 8.5. In column (1) for the nonfarm business sector the estimated β rises slightly from the first to the last half but falls in column (2) for manufacturing. However, none of these changes are statistically significant. For instance, a Chow test on the shift from 1.17 to 1.32 in column (1), bottom section, yields a $F(8,129)$ ratio of 0.34, compared to the 5 percent critical level of 2.63.

Once hours are chosen as the dependent variable, should the specification include leads? Here the evidence favors excluding the leads. In exclusion tests leading values of the output change variable are jointly insignificant in all the equations for manufacturing, and in all for nonfarm private business that cover the two subsets of the sample period. Leads are significant only for nonfarm private business when a single equation is run across both halves of the sample

---

[31] For instance, Finn (1991, p. 26) develops a RBC model with the explicit prediction that "energy price shocks enhance the volatility of Solow residual growth."

period, presumably indicating a shift in the lag structure over time without a significant change in the sum of coefficients.

The "End-of-Expansion" Effect

In each business cycle expansion there tends to be an initial rapid phase, a point at which the ratio of actual to trend output reaches its peak, and then a slow "plateau" phase through the point at which the actual level of output reaches its peak (this is the business cycle peak as defined in the standard NBER chronology). In (1979) I identified an "end-of-expansion" (EOE) effect in the systematic tendency for firms to increase hours excessively during the plateau phase, so that observed productivity tends to be relatively low during this phase. Then this "overhiring" is corrected after six quarters, so that productivity growth is relatively high (given the normal lagged response of hours to output) in the following two years. This effect was identified in first-difference equations for hours like those estimated in Table 8.2, column (5), with detrending by the piecewise loglinear method.

To examine the robustness of this effect with thirteen years of additional data, I replicated the exact method of the earlier paper. The EOE effect is measured by the coefficient on a single step-like dummy variable that sums to zero. The variable is defined as $+4/6$ for six quarters beginning in the quarter after the peak in detrended output (i.e., covering the plateau phase), as $-4/8$ for the following eight quarters, and as zeros otherwise.[32] When added to the equation in Table 8.2, column (5), this single variable reduces the unexplained variance by 12 percent, has a t ratio of 4.4, and has a coefficient of 1.4, indicating a tendency for firms to overhire cumulatively 1.4 percent more labor input than needed in the plateau phase, followed by an eight-quarter period in which they shed the unneeded labor. The slow productivity growth observed in 1989–90 and the substantially higher growth observed (together with much publicized "restructuring layoffs") in 1991–2 are consistent with the continued relevance of the EOE effect.

Which Parameter Values Extinguish the Procyclicality of MFP?

Our theoretical analysis of Figure 8.1 concluded that an observed $\beta = 1.33$ could be explained with any combination of factor fixity and labor mismeasurement adding up to 0.165, for instance zero labor mismeasurement and 0.165

---

[32] The variable is defined as 4/6 and 4/8 rather than 1/6 and 1/8, because all our log first difference data have been multiplied by 400 to convert them into percentage growth at annual rates. The peak quarters after which the plateau begins are the same as those chosen in (1979) – 1955:Q4, 1959:Q2, 1968:Q3, 1973:Q1, 1978:Q4, plus the addition of 1989:Q1. Following the earlier paper, the phases in the first cycle following 1955:Q4 are reduced from 6 and 8 to 4 and 6 quarters, respectively.

Table 8.6. *Sums of Coefficients (λ) on Quarterly Change in Output Deviation in Regressions Explaining Quarterly Change in Multifactor Productivity Deviation by Sector, with Piecewise Loglinear Predetrending, without and with Alternative Measurement Adjustments, 1955:2–1992:1*

	(1)	(2)	(3)	(4)	(5)
Utilization Multiplied by	0	$1 - \alpha$	$1 - \alpha$	$1 - \alpha$	$1 - \alpha$
Output Mismeasurement Parameter (e^Q)	0	0	0	0.10	0.05
Labor Mismeasurement Parameter (e^N)	0	0	0.166	0	0.10
Nonfarm Business					
Sum of Coeff. on Output Deviation	0.40	0.12	0.02	0.02	0.01
Significance of Sum	0.0E-35	0.5E-02	0.65	0.66	0.82
Manufacturing					
Sum of Coeff. on Output Deviation	0.43	0.12	0.02	0.03	0.02
Significance of Sum	0.3E-54	0.2E-03	0.50	0.45	0.66

Notes. Explanatory variables include a constant and lags 0–3 of quarterly log difference in output deviation.

of labor and capital fixed, or completely variable labor and capital with labor mismeasurement of 0.165. Since we have found that the estimated value of β is less than 1.33 in almost every cell of Table 8.5, even less mismeasurement or fixity is required to eliminate procyclical fluctuations in MFP (Δm_t).

While neither the amount of capital and labor fixity nor the amount of mismeasurement can be observed, we can combine the observed procyclicality of measured MFP with alternative assumptions to bracket the required amount of mismeasurement and/or fixity. Our technique is to begin by assuming that capital and labor are entirely variable, and that measured MFP cyclicality combines capital mismeasurement with labor and/or output mismeasurement. With no overhead capital, it follows that true capital input is totally variable and moves in proportion with output. Accordingly, we correct measured changes in capital input for changes in utilization, using the Federal Reserve Board index of capacity utilization. Then we experiment to find values of the other unobserved mismeasurement parameters that will reduce the coefficient on output change (λ) to statistical insignificance in an equation like (14) above that explains cyclical changes in MFP.[33]

The results are summarized in Table 8.6, with results for the nonfarm private economy shown above and for manufacturing shown below. When

---

[33] Unfortunately, the capacity utilization index is available only for manufacturing as well as for mining and utilities, but not for the rest of the nonmanufacturing sector. To create a proxy that reflects the smaller amplitude of cyclical volatility outside of manufacturing, we proxy unobserved aggregate utilization with manufacturing utilization times the estimated elasticity (0.46) of aggregate output changes to manufacturing utilization changes (both detrended).

no adjustments are made for mismeasurement, the respective cyclical coefficients (λ) are large and highly significant, 0.40 and 0.43 for the two sectors, respectively. When the capital stock is adjusted for changes in utilization, the estimated value of λ falls by more than two thirds but is still highly significant. Columns (3) through (5) show the effects on the estimated λ of assuming labor mismeasurement ($e^N = 0.166$), or output mismeasurement ($e^Q = 0.1$), or a combination of both together ($e^N = 0.1$ and $e^Q = 0.05$). All three of these assumed parameter values render λ close to zero and statistically insignificant in both the nonfarm private sector and in manufacturing.

How plausible are these parameters? We earlier interpreted the much-cited results of Fay and Medoff (1985) as implying that $e^Q = 0.1$. More recent evidence by Shea (1990) indicates that accident rates are procyclical. He shows that this can be interpreted to imply either that labor effort is procyclical or that output is mismeasured through the omission of investment-type activities in recessions on which the risk of accidents is lower. Shea shows that the introduction of accident rates can explain 26 percent of the procyclicality of Solow's residual in manufacturing (1990, p. 23). Since the procyclicality coefficient for manufacturing in Table 8.6, column (1) is 0.43, explaining 26 percent of this would yield a contribution of 0.11, almost identical to the contributions of the parameter combinations in Table 8.6, cols. (3) through (5).

As shown in the theoretical analysis, labor fixity is observationally equivalent to labor measurement error. Both taken separately cause measured labor input to fluctuate less than output and thus contribute to the observed procyclicality of labor productivity and of MFP. An alternative interpretation of column (3) in Table 8.6 is that the procyclicality of MFP can be extinguished with no measurement error in output and labor input, but with some fraction of labor input fixed and the remaining fraction variable. With strict capital-labor complementarity ($v^K = v^N$ and $\sigma = 1$), the same fraction of capital input would be fixed as well under this interpretation. The required overhead (i.e., fixity) fraction to eliminate MFP procyclicality is 0.375 with no output measurement error and 0.22 with an output measurement error of $e^Q = 0.05$.[34] An even smaller fraction of overhead labor is required if we allow drop the assumption of strict capital-labor complementarity and allow the share of overhead capital to be smaller than the share of overhead labor.

These results, like all those reported in Table 8.6, are based on piecewise linear detrending. Even smaller amounts of mismeasurement are required with Hodrick-Prescott detrending. This relationship occurs, as we noted in commenting on Tables 8.4 and 8.5, because Hodrick and Prescott detrending tends to adjust intracycle movements in output and hours by different amounts, thus

---

[34] Given the estimates presented in Table 8.6, a general formula for the parameter values needed to extinguish procyclicality is:

$$0 = 0.12 - 0.6(e^N - (1 - v^N)) - e^Q + 0.28(1 - v^K).$$

With strict capital-labor complementarity, this is solved for $v^K = V^N$.

Table 8.7. *Coefficients on Quarterly Change in Output Deviation, in Equation Explaining Quarterly Change in MFP, Adjusted as in Table 8.6, column (5), 1955:2–1992:1*

	Nonfarm Private Business Sector	Manufacturing Sector
	(1)	(2)
Coefficient and [t ratio] on Lag		
0	0.348 [10.61]	0.203 [8.02]
1	−0.203 [−5.80]	−0.093 [−3.28]
2	−0.052 [−1.48]	−0.051 [−1.80]
3	−0.082 [−2.54]	−0.043 [−1.73]
Sum	0.010 [0.23]	0.015 [0.44]

Source. Quarterly change in multifactor productivity (Δm_t) is adjusted by the parameter values shown in Table 8.6, column 5.

generating smaller intracycle procyclicality in labor productivity and MFP that require an explanation.

High-Frequency Movements in MFP

Above we noted (in discussing Figures 8.3b and 8.4a) that the level of productivity is related to the change in output, and the change in productivity is related to the second derivative of output. This phenomenon comes out clearly in our econometric results. Even though the equations in columns (3) through (5) of Table 8.6 yield an insignificant *sum* of current and lagged coefficients on output, the individual coefficients are highly significant. As an example, the individual coefficients for the particular parameter choices of Table 8.6, column (5), are recorded separately in Table 8.7. We interpret this result as showing that a demand shock is accompanied by faster response of output than of hours, leading to a transitory positive response in MFP that is completely reversed by the end of the third quarter, eliminating the cyclical correlation in less than one third of the average duration of a business cycle phase.[35] This "acceleration" effect is consistent with the hypothesis of costs of adjustment in labor input, but not with a procyclical "level" effect that lasts for the full extent of the business cycle, as required by Hall's market power explanation, by the real business cycle theory, and by theories of "thick market" externalities.

8.4 CONCLUSION

This essay distinguishes among three different frequency distributions of changes in labor productivity and multifactor productivity (MFP). At low

---

[35] There were seven complete peak-to-peak business cycles between 1953:2 and 1990:3, for an average duration of 21 quarters per cycle, or an average of 10.5 quarters in each cycle of above-average and below-average output growth.

frequencies (longer intervals than the business cycle) productivity grows at variable rates, not a single steady trend, and the most important aspect of this variability has been the post-1973 productivity growth slowdown that has now lasted through more than three business cycles. The secular or low frequency component of MFP movements is identified in this paper alternatively through piecewise loglinear detrending, with one loglinear segment per business cycle, or alternatively by the Hodrick and Prescott filter that allows the trend component to vary within individual business cycles. At the other extreme is the high-frequency component of movements in productivity that we capture by allowing the first difference of hours to take three quarters to adjust to changes in output. In between is the true medium-frequency component associated with the business cycle; it lasts longer than three quarters and has a duration equal to the typical length of a business cycle phase. This paper identifies the high-frequency component with costs of adjustment that lead to a lagged reaction of hours to output that is extremely stable throughout the postwar period. The business cycle component is explained by the mismeasurement of capital input by the stock of capital rather than the utilized portion of that stock, together with modest amounts of mismeasurement of output and/or labor.

With allowance for changes in capital utilization, it takes only a 5 percent mismeasured component of output taking the form of investment or maintenance of physical and human capital in recessions, together with only a 10 percent unmeasured variation in labor effort as a percentage of cyclical variations in true labor effort, to extinguish the procyclicality of MFP at the cyclical frequency. These mismeasurement effects are consistent with the evidence of Fay and Medoff (1985) on countercyclical variations in unmeasured investment activities and of Shea on the procyclicality of accident rates.

Alternatively, there may be no mismeasurement at all of output or labor input, while both capital and labor can be divided into a component varying with output and incorporating 5/8 of input, while a remaining 3/8 component consists of overhead labor and capital that vary with capacity rather than output. Adding a small 5 percent component of mismeasured output, the required breakdown of labor and capital shifts to 4/5 variable input and 1/5 overhead input.

The implications of our analysis are significant: the behavior of output and inputs over the business cycle denies the relevance of procyclical technology shocks at business-cycle frequencies. The technology shocks that provide the *modi vivendi* of RBC models are absent in U.S. data. Further, if productivity does not exhibit procyclical fluctuations, there is no empirical support for the new generation of search models in which "thick markets" boost productivity in booms. And, if we conclude that there are no cyclical movements in MFP after allowing for modest components of mismeasurement and/or overhead inputs, Hall's attempt to link aggregate MFP cycles to market power becomes a theory unsupported by fact.

If there is no evidence in aggregate time series data in support of market power or increasing returns, what are we to make of the ample evidence in the micro IO literature that firms do set prices and are monopolistic competitors in product markets? There is an old literature dating back to the 1920s concluding that a company like General Motors sets price to earn a normal profit at a normal level of capacity utilization, that is, its price is rigid in the sense stressed by Rotemberg and Summers.

However, the fact that price fluctuates less than marginal cost over the business cycle has no necessary implications for the short-run response of labor input to changes in the demand for output.

Instead, the major implication of price rigidity is to make output, as well as correctly measured inputs, more variable than they would be otherwise, since price rigidity causes a given fluctuation in nominal income to be accompanied by a greater change in output than if prices were flexible. This paper shows that, once price rigidity translates nominal demand shocks into real demand shocks, procyclical variations in productivity can be entirely explained by the mismeasurement of capital input as a stock rather than as a utilized stock, together with surprisingly small components of mismeasurement of output, and/or mismeasurement of labor effort, and/or overhead components of labor and capital.

References

Abbott, T. A. III, Griliches, Z., and Hausman, J. A. "Short-Run Movements in Productivity: Market Power versus Capacity Utilization." Working paper without place or date. 1988.

Barro, Robert J., and Grossman, Herschel I. "A General Disequilibrium Model of Income and Employment." *American Economic Review*. 1971; vol. 61, no. 1, pp. 82–93.

Bernanke, Ben S., and Parkinson, Martin L. "Procyclical Labor Productivity and Competing Theories of the Business Cycle: Some Evidence from Interwar U.S. Manufacturing Industries." NBER working paper 3503. October, 1990.

Blanchard, Olivier J., and Quah, Danny. "The Dynamic Effects of Aggregate Demand and Supply Disturbances." *American Economic Review*. September 1989; vol. 79, pp. 655–73.

Braun, R. Anton, and Evans, Charles L. "Seasonal Solow Residuals and Christmas: A Case for Labor Hoarding and Increasing Returns." Federal Reserve Bank of Chicago. Working paper 91–20. October, 1991a.

"Seasonality and Equilibrium Business Cycle Theories." Federal Reserve Bank of Chicago. Working paper 91–23. December, 1991b.

Caballero, Ricardo J., and Lyons, Richard K. "External Effects in U.S. Procyclical Productivity." Columbia University. Unnumbered working paper.

Clower, Robert W. "The Keynesian Counterrevolution: A Theoretical Appraisal." In Hahn, F., and Brechling, F. *The Theory of Interest Rates*. London: Macmillan; 1965.

Cowing, Thomas G., and Smith, Kerry V. "The Estimation of a Production Technology: A Survey of Econometric Analyses of Steam-Electric Generation." *Land Economics*. May, 1978; vol. 52, no. 2, pp. 156–86.

Diamond, Peter. "Aggregate Demand Management in Search Equilibrium." *Journal of Political Economy*. October, 1982; vol. 90, pp. 881–94.

Domowitz, Ian; Hubbard, R. Glenn; and Petersen, Bruce C. "Market Structure and Cyclical Fluctuations in U.S. Manufacturing." *Review of Economics and Statistics*. February, 1988. vol. 70, pp. 55–66.

Eden, Benjamin, and Griliches, Zvi. "Productivity, Market Power and Capacity Utilization when Spot Markets are Complete." NBER working paper 3697. May, 1991.

Eichenbaum, Martin. "Real Business-Cycle Theory: Wisdom or Whimsy?" *Journal of Economic Dynamics and Control*. 1991; vol. 15, pp. 607–26.

Evans, Charles L. "Productivity Shocks and Real Business Cycles." Federal Reserve Bank of Chicago. Working paper 91–22. December, 1991.

Fair Ray C. *The Short-run Demand for Workers and Hours*. Amsterdam: North-Holland; 1969.

"Excess Labor and the Business Cycle." *The American Economic Review*. March, 1985, vol. 75, pp. 239–45.

Fay, Jon, and Medoff, James. "Labor and Output over the Business Cycle." *American Economic Review*. September, 1985; vol. 75, pp. 638–55.

Finn, Mary G. "Energy Price Shocks, Capacity Utilization, and Business Cycle Fluctuations." Federal Reserve Bank of Minneapolis, Institute for Empirical Macroeconomics. Discussion Paper 50. September, 1991.

Gordon, Robert J. "The 'End-of-Expansion' Phenomenon in Short-Run Productivity Behavior. *Brookings Papers on Economic Activity*. 1979; vol. 10, no. 2, pp. 447–61.

"Inflation, Flexible Exchange Rates, and the Natural Rate of Unemployment." In Baily, M.N., ed. *Workers, Jobs, and Inflation*. Washington: Brookings, 1982, pp. 88–152.

"Unemployment and Potential Output in the 1980s." *Brookings Papers on Economic Activity*, 1984; vol. 15, no. 2, pp. 537–64.

Gordon, Robert J., and King, Stephen R. "The Output Cost of Disinflation in Traditional and Vector Autoregressive Models." *Brookings Papers on Economic Activity*. 1982; vol. 13, no. 1, pp. 205–42, Chapter 15 in this book.

Griliches, Zvi. "Notes on the Measurement of Price and Quality Changes." In *Models of Income Determination*. Conference on Research in Income and Wealth. Princeton, N.J.: Princeton University Press for NBER; 1964, no. 28, pp. 381–404.

Hall, Robert E. "Market Structure and Macroeconomic Fluctuation." *Brookings Papers on Economic Activity*. 1986; vol. 17, no. 2, pp. 285–322.

"The Relation between Price and Marginal Cost in U.S. Industry." *Journal of Political Economy*. October, 1988; vol. 96, pp. 921–47.

"Invariance Properties of Solow's Productivity Residual." In Diamond, Peter A., ed. *Growth/Producitivity/Unemployment: Essays to Celebrate Bob Solow's Birthday*. Cambridge MA: MIT Press; 1990a, pp. 71–112.

"Econometric Research on Shifts of Production Functions at Medium and High Frequencies." Paper presented to Barcelona World Congress of the Econometric Society. August, 1990b.

Hilton, K. "Capital and Capacity Utilization in the United Kingdom." *Oxford Bulletin of Economics and Statistics*. August, 1970; pp. 187–217.

Hodrick, Robert, and Prescott, Edward C. "Postwar U.S. Business Cycles: An Empirical Investigation." Carnegie-Mellon discussion paper. May, 1981; no. 451.

Hultgren, Thor. "Changes in Labor Cost during Cycles in Production and Business." NBER Occasional Paper. 1960; no. 74.

Ireland, N. J., and Smyth, D. J. "The Specification of Short-run Employment Model." *Review of Economic Studies*. April, 1970; pp. 281–5.

Ireland, N. J., Briscoe, G., and Smyth, D. J. "Specification Bias and Short-run Returns to Labour: Some Evidence for the United Kingdom." *The Review of Economics and Statistics*. February, 1973; vol. 55, pp. 23–7.

Jorgenson, Dale W., and Griliches, Zvi. "The Explanation of Productivity Change." *Review of Economic Studies*. July, 1967; vol. 34, pp. 249–83.

Kydland, Finn E., and Prescott, Edward C. "Business Cycles: Real Facts and a Monetary Myth." *Federal Reserve Bank of Minneapolis Quarterly Review*. Spring, 1990; pp. 3–18.

Mankiw, N. Gregory. "Real Business Cycles: A New Keynesian Perspective." *Journal of Economic Perspective*. Summer, 1989; vol. 3, pp. 79–90.

Oi, Walter Y. "Labor as a Quasi-Fixed Factor." *Journal of Political Economy*. December, 1962; vol. 70, pp. 538–55.

Okun, Arthur M. "The Gap between Actual and Potential Output." *Proceedings of the American Statistical Association*, 1962. Reprinted in Phelps, Edmund S. ed. *Problems of the Modern Economy*. New York: Norton, 1965.

Patinkin, Don. *Money, Interest, and Prices*. Second edition. New York: Harper and Row; 1965.

Plosser, Charles I. "Understanding Real Business Cycles." *Journal of Economic Perspectives*. Summer, 1989; vol. 3, pp. 51–77.

Prescott, Edward C. "Theory Ahead of Business Cycle Measurement." *Carnegie-Rochester Conference Series on Public Policy*. Autumn, 1986; vol. 25, pp. 11–44.

Prucha, Ingmar R., and Nadiri, M. Ishaq. "Endogenous Capital Utilization and Productivity Measurement in Dynamic Factor Demand Models: Theory and an Application to the U. S. Electrical Machinery Industry." NBER working paper. 3680. April, 1991.

Romer, Christina D. "Is the Stabilization of the Postwar Economy a Figment of the Data?" *American Economic Review*. June, 1986; vol. 76, pp. 314–34.

Rotemberg, Julio, and Summers, Lawrence H. "Inflexible Prices and Procyclical Productivity." *Quarterly Journal of Economics*. November, 1990; vol. 105, pp. 851–74.

Shea, John. "Accident Rates, Labor Effort, and the Business Cycle." University of Wisconsin. SSRI working paper 9028. November, 1990.

"Do Supply Curves Slope Up?" University of Wisconsin SSRI. working paper number 9116. Revised version. November, 1991.

Sims, Christopher A. "Output and Labor Input in Manufacturing." *Brookings Papers on Economic Activity*. 1974; vol. 5, no. 3, pp. 695–728.

Solow, Robert M. "Technical Change and the Aggregate Production Function." *Review of Economics and Statistics*. August, 1957; vol. 39, pp. 312–20.

"The Short-run Relation between Employment and Output." Draft of Presidential Address to the Econometric Society. 1964.

Williams, George. "Explanations of Procyclical Productivity in the Airline Industry." Northwestern University Ph.D. Dissertation. August, 1992.

Wills, Hugh R. "Estimation of a Vintage Capital Model for Electricity Generating." *Review of Economic Studies*. October, 1978; vol. 45, no. 141, pp. 495–510.

CHAPTER 9

The Jobless Recovery: Does It Signal a New Era of Productivity-Led Growth?

By far the most widely noted and puzzling aspect of the current economic recovery is its failure to create jobs. While payroll employment in seven previous recessions increased a full 7 percent in the first twenty-three months following the National Bureau of Economic Research (NBER) business cycle trough, such employment increased by only 0.8 percent – just over one tenth as much – from March 1991 to March 1993.[1] Part of the explanation of negligible job growth lies in the recovery's relatively slow pace of output growth, which has been little more than one third the usual postwar pace.[2]

The remaining part of the job puzzle stems from the ebullient performance of productivity – that is, output per hour in the nonfarm business sector – which registered a growth rate of 3.2 percent in the four quarters ending in 1992:4, the most rapid rate recorded in any similar period for more than sixteen years.[3] The *share* of output growth accounted for by productivity growth in the current recovery is 112 percent, far exceeding the 47 percent average of the previous postwar recoveries at the same stage.[4] For any given pace of output growth,

---

[1] The seven previous troughs are those from 1949 to 1982, with the exception of July, 1980. See Ritter (1993).

[2] The annual growth rate of nonfarm business output (Bureau of Labor Statistics measure) was 2.42 percent at an annual rate in the first seven quarters of the 1991–3 recovery, only 39 percent of the 6.25 percent annual rate achieved in the first seven quarters of seven previous postwar recoveries (including all but the abortive 1980–1 recovery).

[3] The 3.2 percent four-quarter rate achieved in 1992:4 was most recently exceeded by a rate of 4.8 percent in 1976:1. The highest rate achieved in the previous business cycle was 4.8 percent in 1973:1.

[4] In the first seven quarters of the recent recovery, the annual growth rates of nonfarm business output and output per hour were 2.42 and 2.71 percent, respectively. The unweighted averages of seven previous postwar recoveries were 6.25 and 2.94 percent, respectively.

Note. This research has been supported by the National Science Foundation. Dan Aaronson provided able research assistance, and Sandy Choi typed the tables with admirable speed and accuracy. Martin N. Baily, Michael Harper, Jack E. Triplett, and participants in a NBER Productivity Research Meeting and at an American Economics Association session on productivity provided helpful comments on earlier drafts. (*Source.* "The Jobless Recovery: Does It Signal a New Era of Productivity-Led Growth?" *Brookings Papers on Economic Activity.* 1993; vol. 24, no. 1), pp. 271–316.

more rapid productivity growth by definition implies less rapid growth in labor input. This suggests that the recent revival in productivity growth may be the key to understanding the puzzling absence of job creation in the recovery.

Productivity-led growth is nothing but good news. In the two decades ending in mid-1992, the nonfarm business sector registered an average annual productivity growth rate of less than 1 percent: 0.85 percent, to be exact.[5] Imagine the benefits to the economy if the recent good news on productivity were to imply, as some have suggested, a doubling in productivity growth to a rate of 1.7 percent over the next decade.[6] For any given path of labor input, nonfarm private business output in the year 2003 would be almost 9 percent larger – some $450 billion more – allowing that much more private and/or public spending. Productivity-led growth does not imply a jobless recovery in anything but the shortest run. Instead, any beneficial shock to productivity growth sets the stage for lower inflation that enables policymakers to stimulate output growth sufficiently to create the same number of jobs that would have occurred in the absence of the shock. If the jobless character of the 1991–3 recovery indeed has been caused by a benign productivity shock, then its jobless character implies that there has been too little stimulus to output growth, not that a productivity surge must necessarily rob the nation of jobs.

Alternative Interpretations: A New Era versus the Usual Cyclical Rebound?

This paper takes a skeptical view of the widely held belief that a new era of faster productivity growth is at hand. Weighed against the innumerable tales of corporate restructuring and downsizing is a much more pessimistic story told by the official data on productivity growth over the last few years.

The Case for a New Era

The universal theme of recent commentaries is that this recovery is unique in the continuing onslaught of permanent job terminations, mainly by large corporations, and the apparent refusal of employers (large and small) to hire new employees. The *Economist* prompted the title of this essay when it argued, "America is enjoying its first productivity-led recovery for many decades."[7] Secretary of Labor Robert Reich has expressed concern about "job gridlock."[8]

---

[5] This is the annual growth rate between 1972:2 and 1992:2. When the most recent two quarters are included, the growth rate rises to 0.92. The quarter chosen for this comparison, 1972:2, is judged to be a "cyclically neutral" quarter, as discussed in Table 9.3. As I discuss, weighting problems bias downward the measured rate of productivity growth before 1987.

[6] Stephen S. Roach of Morgan Stanley predicts that nonfarm business productivity will grow at the rate of 1.7 to 1.8 percent per year during the 1990s. See Sylvia Nasar, "U.S. Output per Worker Is Growing: Recent Data Show Productivity Is Up," *New York Times*, November 27, 1992, p. D9.

[7] "America the Super-fit," *Economist*, February 13, 1993, p. 67.

[8] See "Biggest Rise Since '72 for Productivity," *Chicago Tribune*, March 10, 1993, p. 3.

Lawrence Mishel and Jared Bernstein have highlighted the fact that roughly three-quarters of the rise in unemployment in the early 1990s has been due to permanent job loss, so that the absolute magnitude of permanent job loss has been as great in this relatively mild recession as in the much deeper 1981–2 recession.[9] While a productivity surge during the recovery is normal, Stephen S. Roach has argued that "there is reason to believe that what's happening this time is different ... a job shakeout that is an inevitable byproduct of market globalization."[10] The *Wall Street Journal* has heralded an "age of angst" and announced that a "workplace revolution boosts productivity at [the] cost of job security."[11]

A particular aspect of the recent recovery has been the disproportionate share in corporate layoffs of white-collar workers and of workers in the service sector, in contrast to the decimation of manufacturing employment and of the Rust Belt that characterized employment adjustments a decade ago. As Roach has argued, "Corporate America can no longer afford to subsidize the bloat of unproductive workers. ... These efficiency breakthroughs have taken a steep toll on an entirely new class of victims – white-collar workers. White-collar unemployment now exceeds blue-collar joblessness by 200,000 workers, the first such gap on record."[12]

The Opposing View: A Normal Cyclical Rebound

Journalistic accounts focus on corporate downsizing of particular firms having unusual problems, such as IBM and Sears, and leave out the much less dramatic humdrum everyday business of gains in sales and employment by their competitors. As American Enterprise Institute economist Marvin Kosters has noted, "Sears announces job cutbacks. Ever see any references to Wal-Mart hiring anyone? I never heard of Microsoft ever hiring a worker, but they must have."[13]

Moving from anecdotal evidence to the hard facts, journalistic accounts have highlighted only the heady numbers of recent productivity performance over the past four quarters without lingering on the dismal performance of the four years before that. In contrast to the long-run growth rate since 1972 of slightly less than 1 percent per year, the annual growth rate of nonfarm private productivity recorded for the four years ending in 1991:4 was virtually zero: 0.11 percent per year, to be precise. The big boom of 3.2 percent for the following four quarters

[9] See Mishel and Bernstein (1992, p. 5).

[10] Stephen S. Roach as paraphrased by *Forbes*. See "What's Ahead for Business," *Forbes*, March 1, 1993, p. 37.

[11] G. Pascal Zachary and Bob Ortega, "Age of Angst: Workplace Revolution Boosts Productivity at Cost of Job Security," *Wall Street Journal*, March 10, 1993, p. A1.

[12] Stephen S. Roach, "The New Majority: White-Collar Jobless," *New York Times*, March 14, 1993, p. E17.

[13] Quoted in Jerry Flint, "Keep a Resume on the Floppy, But Don't Panic," *Forbes*, April 26, 1993, p. 69.

only brought the rate for the past five years up to 0.74 percent, still below the 1972–87 average.

It is always tempting to proclaim a new era on the basis of a few months or quarters of macroeconomic data. Yet the productivity record viewed over any period longer than the last four quarters displays faint support for a new era. Because the actual rate of productivity growth achieved through the end of 1992 over the past five years is below, not above, the lamentable pace of 1972–87, those claiming that the trend rate has increased must be assuming that the actual *level* of productivity in 1992:4 was well below the new rapidly growing trend. Any assessment of the new era approach requires a model of the cyclical deviation of productivity from trend at each stage of the business cycle. What is a plausible estimate of the deviation of actual productivity below its trend at this stage of the business cycle? The econometric analysis of this paper provides an answer to this and other related questions.

Separating Trend and Cycle

At least since the early 1960s, when Thor Hultgren[14] and Arthur M. Okun[15] published their analyses, macroeconomists have known that productivity exhibits procyclical fluctuations. Any evaluation of the long-term productivity performance of the economy requires that the underlying trend be unscrambled from quarter-to-quarter cyclical movements. This task cannot be achieved simply by measuring productivity growth between successive NBER-demarcated cyclical peaks or between successive troughs, for at least three reasons. First, productivity is a leading indicator and reaches its peak at a different point in the cycle from the official NBER peak. Second, cycles are of different durations and amplitudes, and so the relationship of the productivity peak to the NBER peak is variable, rather than fixed. Third, the last stage of the business cycle expansion is marked by a regular phenomenon that I have previously called the end-of-expansion effect, the unusually slow productivity growth that seems to occur in the last year or two before the NBER peak.[16]

The importance of separating trend from cycle is motivated by many considerations in addition to the natural interest in whether the economy's long-term productivity performance has gotten better or worse. First, any evaluation of past economic policies, such as the effect of supply-side tax cuts or R&D tax credits, requires a measure of their effect on cyclically adjusted productivity growth. Second, assessments of the performance of political eras, such as the Eisenhower era or the Reagan-Bush era, must refer to productivity purged of purely cyclical effects. Finally, estimates of future growth in potential output (that is, trend productivity plus trend hours) are needed to project the federal budget,

---

[14] Hultgren (1960).
[15] Okun (1962).
[16] Gordon (1979).

the likely path of unemployment, and even the inflationary consequences of alternative monetary policies.

This paper's basic purpose is to develop a method for determining what information about the underlying trend is provided by the latest data on actual productivity movements. The second part begins with data issues, which play a surprisingly important role in assessing the validity of the interpretation of a new era. The third part then assesses two alternative detrending techniques and describes the data on actual and trend movements in average labor productivity (ALP) and multifactor productivity (MFP). The fourth part sets out the specification of a time-series regression equation that identifies the cyclical parameters and also presents the estimated equations. The fifth part then provides alternative measures of the underlying trend for 1987–92 that result in the best fit to the cyclical adjustment model. The section also computes forecasts of productivity growth over the 1993–4 period. The sixth and final part presents conclusions.

All the empirical analysis is carried out for three sectors – nonfarm business, manufacturing, and the nonfarm nonmanufacturing business sector (NFNM). While historical growth rates are displayed for both average labor productivity and multifactor productivity, the econometric analysis concentrates entirely on average labor productivity.

9.1 DATA AND DETRENDING

There are three official sources of data on productivity for the U.S. economy. Annual data on gross product originating (that is, value added) and hours worked are part of the National Income and Product Accounts (NIPA).[17] Unfortunately, the NIPA data for output by industry are not currently available after 1989. The Bureau of Labor Statistics (BLS) provides data on gross output, employment, and (in some cases) hours worked for a long list of industries in both the manufacturing and nonmanufacturing sectors; these are available through 1990 (or, in some cases, 1991). But the BLS provides no aggregates corresponding to its industry-by-industry measures. Both the NIPA and BLS industry measures share a defect; they are available only annually and thus are not suitable for a study of high-frequency time-series dynamics.

Thus by default this study uses the third data source based on *Productivity and Costs,* the BLS quarterly series on output and hours worked in the private nonfarm economy and in manufacturing. The BLS also publishes annual series for these two sectors on capital input and capital's income share – required ingredients in computing its annual measures of MFP. Here I interpolate the capital input and income share data from the annual to the quarterly

---

[17] Hours worked are provided for major industrial sectors at roughly the one-digit level (NIPA Table 6.11), while output (NIPA Table 6.2) and persons engaged (NIPA Table 6.10b) are provided for a much longer list of two-digit industries. Table numbers refer to those using 1982 as the base year.

frequency (using overlapping four-quarter moving averages) in order to compute a quarterly series on MFP for each sector.

While the BLS does not publish series for the NFNM sector, these can be calculated as a residual. I calculate NFNM by multiplying the BLS index numbers for the aggregate series and for manufacturing by the Bureau of Economic Analysis (BEA) absolute levels of output, hours, and capital input in 1982. The NFNM totals are then obtained by subtraction and are converted back to index numbers.

The underlying source for the BLS output measure in the private nonfarm sector is the NIPA quarterly series on GDP, minus general government, farm output, output of nonprofit institutions, output of paid employees of private households, the rental value of owner-occupied dwellings, and the statistical discrepancy. The hours data are obtained from the monthly payroll employment survey, combined with hours per employee from the BLS hours at work survey. Adjustments are made to exclude from labor input the same sectors that are subtracted from GDP in obtaining the output series. The annual capital input and capital share are recomputed by the BLS from BEA data.

To obtain quarterly data on manufacturing output, the BLS takes quarterly movements in the Federal Reserve Index of Industrial Production (IIP) and adjusts these to the annual manufacturing output levels in the NIPA. Because the NIPA do not yet include annual series on manufacturing output for the period after 1989, the BLS extrapolates the NIPA output series with the IIP.

Data Issues

By far the most important data issue for the results of this paper is the so-called base-year weighting bias. This bias understates the growth rate of productivity before 1987. This substantially raises the hurdle to be leaped by those who would proclaim a new era of productivity growth, because the economy's productivity performance during the slowdown from 1972 to 1987 was substantially better than is indicated by the currently published official data.

The Base-Year Weighting Bias

The BLS output data used in this paper for the aggregate economy (that is, the nonfarm business sector) reflect the rebasing of output deflators from 1982 to 1987 prices. While the BEA has not yet published manufacturing output data for the 1987 base year, it has prepared for the BLS productivity program an unpublished series of revised 1987-weighted manufacturing output data covering 1977–89.[18] Thus the BLS output data used in this paper provide a consistent

---

[18] I am grateful to Michael Harper for providing me with a BLS press release dated March 26, 1992, that describes the special BEA series on manufacturing output used by the BLS productivity program.

treatment of the aggregate economy and of manufacturing, which allows non-farm nonmanufacturing output to be extracted as a residual.

However, as is well known, output measures based on the fixed weights of a single year lead to a systematic bias: for products such as computers with a rapidly declining relative price, the share of output in higher aggregates (such as manufacturing, producers' durable equipment, and GDP) will be exaggerated in each year after the base year and understated in each year before the base year. The base-year bias correspondingly causes the annual growth rate of output and of productivity to be understated in each year prior to the base year and overstated in each year after the base year.

Table 9.1 summarizes what is known about the base-year bias in the BEA output series for the aggregate economy for the 1959–90 period and for manufacturing during the 1977–87 period. Bias is measured here by the difference between the data based on 1987 weights and on data calculated using BEA's benchmark-year series. The latter is based on a geometric mean of indexes from succeeding BEA benchmark years, which are five years apart.[19] I have supplemented published BEA estimates of the base-year bias by providing an estimate of the manufacturing bias for 1972–7, derived the implied base-year bias for nonfarm nonmanufacturing for 1972–87, and then applied these bias figures to the published growth rates of the BLS series on output per hour. For the aggregate economy, productivity growth is understated by about 0.3 percent per year during 1959–87 and is overstated by 0.1 percent per year during 1987–90. Manufacturing productivity growth is overstated during 1972–87 by a much larger 1.0 percent per year, while there appears to be little if any bias in nonmanufacturing productivity growth.

While no estimate is available of the base-year bias for manufacturing after 1987, one would assume that it might be relatively large for 1987–92, the first five years after the base year. The best guess that might pin down the approximate size of the bias comes from the BEA's estimate that with 1982 weights, the growth in manufacturing output for 1982–7 is overstated by 0.8 percent per year.[20] However, a mitigating factor is that the BEA has not calculated manufacturing output after 1989, and instead the BLS extrapolates the 1989–92 values using the IIP, which is not subject to the same type of base-year bias.

IIP Use of Employment Data

Monthly changes in the IIP are partly based on employment data. To the extent that productivity is procyclical, output measures based on the IIP will understate the degree of cyclicality. Assuming that quarterly fluctuations in GDP are accurate, the use of IIP to create the manufacturing output series leads to an understatement of the procyclicality in manufacturing productivity and the

---

[19] See Young (1992) for more detailed information about fixed-weight and benchmark-years indexes.

[20] Young (1992, Exhibit 1, p. 34).

Table 9.1. *Effect of Alternative Weighting Systems on Aggregate and Sectoral Productivity, 1959–90*
Percent per year

Sector	Period	Output			Output Per Hour	
		Fixed 1987 Weights Index	Benchmark-Years Index	Difference (Bias)	Fixed 1987 Weights Index	Implied Benchmark-Years Index[a]
Aggregate economy	1959–72	3.7	4.1	0.4	2.4	2.8
	1972–77	2.6	2.9	0.3	1.3	1.6
	1977–87	2.6	2.9	0.3	0.7	1.0
	1987–90	2.5	2.4	−0.1	0.0	−0.1
Manufacturing	1972–77	2.8	3.8[c]	1.0[c]	2.5	3.5
	1977–87	1.6	2.6	1.0	1.8	2.8
Nonmanufacturing[b]	1972–77	2.9	2.8[c]	−0.1[c]	0.8	0.7
	1977–87	3.1	3.2	0.1	0.2	0.3

[a] The implied benchmark-years index for productivity is the sum of the fixed 1987 weights index for output per hour plus the bias in output between the fixed weight and benchmark years indexes.

[b] Nonmanufacturing output is aggregate real GDP minus manufacturing real GDP.

[c] Manufacturing output data for 1972–7 have not been published with 1987 fixed weights and are available only with 1982 fixed weights. The problem is to estimate the base-year bias for 1972–7 with 1982 fixed weights. This is the same number of years prior to the base year as 1977–82 with 1987 fixed weights, for which Young (1992, exhibit 1, p. 34) provides an estimated base-year bias of 1.4 percentage points per year. To be conservative, and because computers are less important in earlier years, these 1.4 percentage points are reduced to the 1.0 percentage point bias shown in the third output column labeled "Difference" for manufacturing during 1972–7.

Source. Author's calculations using the following sources. Aggregate economy refers to real GDP, from Young (1992, Table A, p. 36). Manufacturing for 1972–7 is estimated as described in note b below. Manufacturing for 1977–87 is also from Young (1992, Exhibit 1, p. 34). The 1982 values of manufacturing real GDP are obtained from *Survey of Current Business* (January 1991, Table 6, p. 34); values for other years are obtained by multiplying the BLS output series (expressed as an index with 1982 = 1.0) by the 1982 values. Output per hour for manufacturing was obtained from Bureau of Labor Statistics, *Productivity and Costs*, various issues, as described in the text. Hours data for manufacturing are from *Survey of Current Business*, Table 6.11, various issues, using 1982 as the base year.

opposite bias for NFNM productivity, because the latter is calculated as a residual. More generally, the calculation of NFNM data as a residual will lead to measurement errors that go in the opposite direction from errors in the manufacturing data. However, because the NFNM sector is three times larger than the manufacturing sector in absolute size, any such measurement errors in *percentage change data* for NFNM will be one third the size of the corresponding errors in manufacturing.

Payroll Employment versus Household Employment

As indicated in the introduction, payroll employment stagnated during the 1991–3 recovery, with growth between March 1991 and March 1993 of only 0.8 percent. This contrasts with growth of 1.5 percent – almost twice as fast – in civilian employment from the household survey. This contrast appears to be a normal feature of business cycles.[21] A more convincing hint that the payroll employment numbers grow too slowly is provided by the discrepancy between the national total published by the BLS and the sum of estimates issued by individual states. By one estimate, this discrepancy could lead to a subsequent upward revision to payroll employment of as much as 0.7 percent.[22]

Detrending

The basic question addressed by this paper is whether the underlying trend of average labor productivity has accelerated in recent years. Much recent empirical work in macroeconomics uses the Hodrick-Prescott filter, which allows the trend to move continuously.[23] The trend that emerges from the Hodrick and Prescott filter calculation depends on the user's choice of a smoothness parameter. At one extreme, the choice of a parameter of zero yields a trend that exactly tracks every value of the series being detrended. At the other extreme, a parameter of infinity yields a single straight loglinear trend. Between zero and infinity, a relatively low value for the smoothness parameter creates a trend series that bends frequently in response to changes in the actual series and hence implies relatively small deviations from trend; a high parameter value creates a relatively smooth trend and relatively larger deviations from trend. The parameter endorsed by Hodrick and Prescott is a relatively low value (1,600) that

---

[21] To assess the normal cyclical fluctuations in the ratio of civilian household to nonfarm payroll employment, this ratio was regressed in annual data for 1972–92 on a constant, a trend, one lagged value of the dependent variable, and the current and one lagged value of the unemployment gap (the actual unemployment rate minus my estimate of the natural unemployment rate). The residual for 1992 is close to zero and less than half of the standard error of the equation.

[22] See Gene Koretz "New Numbers Are Brightening the Employment Outlook," *Business Week*, May 3, p. 22. Koretz reported that the growth from September 1991 to January 1993 of the national payroll employment estimate was 0.5 percent and the sum of the individual states estimate was 1.1 percent.

[23] Hodrick and Prescott (1981).

Table 9.2. *Trend Growth Rates of Labor Productivity Using Hodrick and Prescott Filter*

Sector	Smoothness Parameter	1972:2–1987:3	1987:3–1990:3	1990:3–1992:4
Nonfarm business	None (actual values)	0.99	−0.23	1.95
	400	0.96	0.21	1.01
	1,600	0.95	0.45	0.66
	6,400	0.93	0.62	0.59
	25,600	0.93	0.68	0.62
	102,400	0.97	0.66	0.60
Manufacturing	None (actual values)	2.13	2.49	2.31
	400	2.07	2.37	2.34
	1,600	2.07	2.53	2.31
	6,400	2.04	2.66	2.47
	25,600	2.05	2.60	2.49
	102,400	2.11	2.36	2.28
Nonfarm nonmanufacturing business	None (actual values)	0.48	−1.10	1.86
	400	0.23	−0.35	0.60
	1,600	0.20	−0.10	0.20
	6,400	0.16	0.06	0.11
	25,600	0.17	0.09	0.10
	102,400	0.24	0.04	0.04

Source. Based on author's calculations using five alternative values of a smoothness parameter for the Hodrick and Prescott filter as described in the text. Actual data are taken from Bureau of Labor Statistics, *Productivity and Costs*, various issues.

implies implausibly large accelerations and decelerations of the trend within each business cycle.[24]

Table 9.2 compares actual growth rates of average labor productivity for three periods – 1972–87, 1987–90, and 1990–2 – with computed Hodrick and Prescott trends for ALP, using five alternative values of the smoothness parameter. This

[24] Hodrick and Prescott (1981, pp. 5–8) provide a justification of a value for their smoothness parameter of 1,600, and this has been used in their subsequent work (such as Prescott, 1986) and the work of most other Hodrick and Prescott users. Yet this justification is based entirely on a subjective statement: "Our prior view is that a five percent cyclical component is moderately large as is a one-eighth of one percent change in the growth rate in a quarter. This led us to select $\sqrt{\lambda} = 5/(1/8) = 40$ or $\lambda = 1,600$ as a value for the smoothing parameter." To interpret their prior, consider the Great Depression of 1929–33 (when real GDP fell 34 percent below a 2.5 percent per year loglinear trend extending from 1928 to 1948). One can multiply their example of 5/(1/8) by 5, for a cyclical component of 25 percent and a reduction in the growth trend of 5/8 percent per quarter or 2.5 percent per year. Thus in their interpretation, the computed trend had zero growth between 1929 and 1933 despite continued growth in the working-age population and in the productivity that would have been observed at a constant unemployment rate.

Index, 1982 = 100

Figure 9.1. Labor Productivity and Hodrick and Prescott Trend for Nonfarm Business[a]

[a] The Hodrick and Prescott smoothness parameter is set to 25,600.

Source. Author's calculations based on Bureau of Labor Statistics. *Productivity and Costs*, various issues.

comparison is displayed from the top to the bottom of Table 9.2 for the three sectors (nonfarm business, manufacturing, and NFNM). As would be expected, the coherence of the H-P trend with the growth rates of the actual values is greatest for the lowest numerical value of the smoothness parameter. As the smoothness parameter increases, the computed trend is equalized across the three subperiods. Despite these patterns, the choice of the smoothness parameter does not appear to make much difference; for the nonfarm business sector in the top section of the table, any parameter of 1,600 or more yields a trend for 1990–2 of only 0.6 percent at most – well below the 0.99 percent actual rate recorded from 1972–87. In the NFNM sector, the Hodrick and Prescott trends of around 0.1 percent per year are also well below the actual 1972–87 rate of 0.48 percent. Only in manufacturing is there a post-1987 acceleration, and here the actual value grows so smoothly that all the alternative Hodrick and Prescott trends grow at a rate roughly similar to that of the actual value.

Figure 9.1 displays one of the computed Hodrick and Prescott trends for the nonfarm business sector (this series assumes a smoothness parameter of 25,600) and compares it with the actual values over the 1972–92 period. Note that the actual value in late 1992 rises well above the Hodrick and Prescott trend, in contrast to the 1983–4 recovery when the actual value did not significantly exceed the trend. This contrast suggests that the computed Hodrick and Prescott trends for the recent period may grow too slowly. But Figure 9.1 also illustrates a basic dilemma in assessing the recent episode. Because actual productivity growth was so slow over the 1987–91 period, almost any trend line must interpret much or all of the 1992 acceleration as simply a catchup, rather than representing the beginning of a new faster trend. The 1992 acceleration has not yet lasted long enough to provide reliable evidence that the trend has accelerated relative to the 1972–87 growth rate of about 1 percent per year (as measured by the

Index, 1972:2 = 100

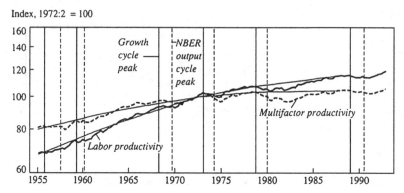

Figure 9.2. Productivity in Nonfarm Business[a]

[a] Vertical bars designate end-of-expansion intervals. The solid line represents the growth cycle peak when output reaches its highest level relative to trend or potential output. The dashed line represents the NBER-dated output cycle peak, except for the line for 1974:2, when the NBER peak was dated as occurring in 1973:4.

Source. Author's calculations based on Bureau of Labor Statistics, *Productivity and Costs*, various issues. See the text for more details on source information and for an explanation of the author's methodology.

official 1987-fixed-weight data, or 1.3 percent with the alternative benchmark-weighted data).

The alternative detrending technique used in the rest of this essay is to draw piecewise loglinear trends through selected benchmark quarters. This technique has the advantage that it can use outside information on variables other than the one being detrended – for example, such variables as unemployment and the capacity utilization rate – to select benchmark quarters having similar cyclical characteristics.[25] A further advantage of piecewise trends is that there is one trend per business cycle, thus achieving a clean break between the business cycle frequency represented by deviations from trend and the lower frequency changes in the trend from one business cycle to the next.

The business cycle in productivity differs from that in output. Figure 9.2 shows two measures of productivity and the dating of the expansion effects. Note that by this dating, productivity leads the output cycle, which is marked by the dashed vertical lines that identify NBER peaks. Productivity tends to reach its peak relative to trend when output is growing most rapidly. Further, productivity

[25] In contrast, the univariate Hodrick and Prescott technique ignores outside information. For instance, using the same smoothness parameter as that recommended by Hodrick and Prescott (1,600), Finn E. Kydland and Edward C. Prescott (1990, Chart 2, p. 9) illustrate the log levels of actual and trend real GNP and show that almost the entire boom of the 1960s is interpreted as an acceleration of the trend, rather than a deviation of actual above the trend. This ignores outside information, such as the fact the that the unemployment rate in the mid-1960s was unusually low and that the capacity utilization rate was unusually high.

Table 9.3. *Selected Variables in Benchmark Quarters*

Business Cycle (Peak to Peak)	Quarter Selected[a]	Unemployment Rate	Capacity Utilization Rate	Gordon Output Ratio[b]
1948–53	1950:2	5.6	77.9	100.2
1953–57	1954:4	5.3	79.7	100.1
1957–60	excluded	...	...	...
1960–69	1963:3	5.5	83.6	100.0
1969–73	1972:2	5.7	82.0	101.1
1973–80	1978:3	6.0	85.1	101.0
1980–81	excluded	...	...	...
1981–90	1987:3	6.0	80.2	100.0

[a] Criteria for selection are as follows: the unemployment rate, U_t, is as close as possible to the natural rate of unemployment as calculated in Gordon (1993, appendix Table A-2); the unemployment rate is falling; and the end-of-expansion effect dummy is nonoperative ($D_k = 0$ in equation 1 of the text).
[b] The output ratio is the ratio of actual to natural output.
Source. Unemployment rate is from Bureau of Labor Statistics, *Employment and Earnings*, various issues. Capacity utilization rate is from *Federal Reserve Bulletin*, various issues. Gordon output ratio is from Gordon (1993, appendix Table A-2).

tends to perform poorly at the end of expansions. These observations suggest that benchmark quarters should be chosen by three criteria: to maintain roughly the same *level* of utilization of resources across cycles; to choose points at which the *growth* characteristics of output are roughly similar; and to exclude end-of-expansion periods. Six benchmark quarters that meet these criteria are displayed in Table 9.3. Note that I exclude the short business cycles containing the incomplete recoveries of 1958–59 and 1980–1.

For the remaining six cycles, I choose quarters in which the unemployment rate was roughly equal to the natural rate identified in my previous research on inflation.[26] Two such quarters occur in each cycle: one when unemployment is falling and another when unemployment is rising. I chose the former quarter. Hence my benchmark quarters tend to be periods when output is rising relatively fast and thus productivity is relatively high. As a result, actual productivity is below trend on average over the postwar period. Table 9.3 also presents two other cyclical indicators, the Federal Reserve capacity utilization rate and the ratio of actual to natural output as calculated from my past research. Because unemployment is currently well above the natural rate of about 6 percent, there is no benchmark quarter to establish the trend for the period since 1987. Determination of the post-1987 trend is the task of the final part of this paper.

[26] For example, see Gordon (1982).

Index, 1972:2 = 100

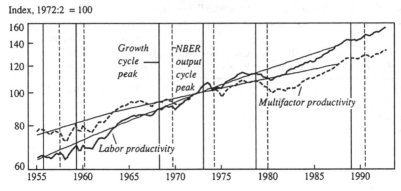

Figure 9.3. Productivity in Manufacturing[a]

[a] Vertical bars designate end-of-expansion intervals. The solid line represents the growth cycle peak when output reaches its highest level relative to trend or potential output. The dashed line represents the NBER-dated output cycle peak, except for the line for 1974:2, when the NBER peak was dated as occurring in 1973:4.

Source. Author's calculations based on Bureau of Labor Statistics, *Productivity and Costs*, various issues. See the text for more details on source information and for an explanation of the author's methodology.

9.2   THE HISTORICAL BEHAVIOR OF PRODUCTIVITY

Now equipped with a consistent set of benchmark quarters, one can examine plots of actual data and trends in the official data (ignoring for now the effects of the 1987 base-year weighting bias). The actual and trend values of ALP and MFP are shown for the three sectors in figures 9.2, 9.3, and 9.4. The post-1987 trends are omitted, and for ALP, will be determined in the final part below. (This essay does not discuss the post-1987 trend of MFP.) The solid vertical lines in the figures mark off the end-of-expansion periods highlighted in the regression analysis below.

Several facts about the nonfarm business sector stand out in Figure 9.2. The ALP trend decelerates after 1972 and decelerates further after 1978, indicating that the secular productivity slowdown worsened in the 1980s. The end-of-expansion periods marked by the solid vertical lines illustrate a phenomenon that appears to recur in each business cycle, with zero or negative ALP growth in 1959–60, 1968–9, 1973–4, 1978–80, and 1989–90. MFP growth subtracts from output a weighted average of labor input and capital input growth. Because capital grew rapidly in the late 1960s, the slowdown in MFP growth began earlier than the slowdown in ALP growth.

Figure 9.3 for manufacturing contrasts sharply with Figure 9.2; no slowdown appears to have occurred in the trend growth of ALP. The amplitude of cyclical fluctuations is greater, particularly during the period of weak growth in 1955–61, the 1973 bulge, and the 1977–80 decline. However, the cyclical fluctuations surrounding the latest recessions have been more moderate than in the total

Index, 1972:2 = 100

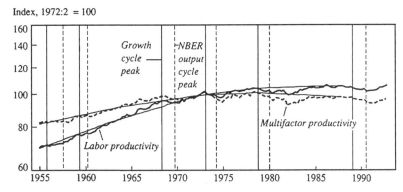

Figure 9.4. Productivity in Nonfarm Nonmanufacturing Business[a]

[a] Vertical bars designate end-of-expansion intervals. The solid line represents the growth cycle peak when output reaches its highest level relative to trend or potential output. The dashed line represents the NBER-dated output cycle peak, except for the line for 1974:2, when the NBER peak was dated as occurring in 1973:4.

Source. Author's calculations based on Bureau of Labor Statistics, *Productivity and Costs*, various issues. See the text for more details on source information and for an explanation of the author's methodology.

economy. The straight trend for ALP in manufacturing contrasts with the evidence for MFP, where a slowdown in growth seems to have occurred between 1967 and the early 1980s, followed by a robust recovery. The rapid growth of ALP in manufacturing in the late 1980s and early 1990s is qualified by the base-year data bias, which affects manufacturing to a greater extent than the aggregate economy.

Because NFNM constitutes three quarters of output in the private nonfarm sector, it is not surprising that Figure 9.4 looks much like Figure 9.2, but with a sharper slowdown in trend ALP growth. Cycles in both ALP and MFP mimic those in Figure 9.2.

Table 9.4 displays the annual average growth rates between benchmark quarters of output, hours, capital input, ALP, and MFP for all three sectors. Also shown in the right-hand column are growth rates from the most recent benchmark quarter, 1987:3, to the most recent quarter with available data, 1992:4. Among the important facts about the private nonfarm sector are the two-stage slowdown in ALP after 1972 and again after 1978, and the three-stage slowdown of MFP (with almost zero growth during 1978–87). After 1987, the growth rates of output, inputs, and ALP all decelerated, while MFP recovered a bit.[27] Presumably, a good part of the deceleration in output and inputs was caused by the 1990–1 recession and slow pace of the 1991–3 recovery, but it remains to be seen how large the cyclical component in ALP is.

[27] Capital input through 1991 is from the BLS, *Productivity and Costs*, various issues. Capital input for 1992 is based on a regression of capital input growth on the share of NIPA net investment in GDP from 1959 to 1991.

Table 9.4. *United States Input and Output Growth Rates, 1954–92*
Percent per year

Sector		1950:2–1954:4	1954:4–1963:3	1963:3–1972:2	1972:2–1978:3	1978:3–1987:3	1987:3–1992:4
Nonfarm business	Output	3.64	3.28	3.82	3.31	2.44	1.31
	Hours	1.39	0.88	1.69	2.05	1.64	0.57
	Capital	3.85	3.31	4.83	4.14	3.86	1.89
	Labor productivity	2.25	2.40	2.13	1.26	0.79	0.75
	Multifactor productivity	1.28	1.50	1.09	0.62	0.12	0.37
Manufacturing	Output	4.17	3.23	3.68	3.12	1.38	1.59
	Hours	1.59	0.62	1.15	0.99	−0.75	−0.86
	Capital	4.92	2.76	4.92	3.96	2.46	1.27
	Labor productivity	2.58	2.61	2.53	2.13	2.13	2.45
	Multifactor productivity	1.37	1.88	1.37	1.30	1.29	1.87
Nonfarm nonmanufacturing business	Output	3.45	3.30	3.88	3.38	2.79	1.23
	Hours	1.28	1.02	1.97	2.54	2.56	1.02
	Capital	3.56	3.45	4.81	4.18	4.21	2.04
	Labor productivity	2.17	2.27	1.91	0.83	0.23	0.21
	Multifactor productivity	1.27	1.38	0.95	0.33	−0.27	−0.08

Source. Author's calculations based on Bureau of Labor Statistics, *Productivity and Costs*, various issues, and NIPA. See Table 9.1 for methodology.

In manufacturing, the most striking facts are slow output growth since 1978, negative labor input growth since 1978, the acceleration in ALP growth after 1987 when compared to 1972–87, and the faster rate of MFP growth after 1987 than that achieved over the entire 1963–87 period. Corresponding to the relatively robust performance of manufacturing, particularly since 1987, is the pathetic performance of the NFNM sector. Here ALP growth has been essentially zero since 1978, while MFP growth has been negative since 1978, and the same three-stage deceleration in MFP growth occurred after 1963, 1972, and 1978. All comments are qualified by the previous remarks on base-year data bias.

9.3 ECONOMETRIC SPECIFICATION AND ESTIMATION

The rest of the paper is limited to an analysis of ALP; the same technique can be applied to MFP. To the extent that MFP is a more fundamental measure of underlying technical progress, my examination of ALP must be treated as an approximation. However, two problems arise with MFP that give ALP priority. First, several additional measurement errors enter into the calculation of MFP: errors in capital input and in capital's income share as a proxy for the true elasticity of output to capital. In addition, the maintained assumption of constant returns to scale may involve an error. Also, to develop predictions of future growth in potential output needed for forecasts of the federal budget, unemployment, and so on, an estimate of future MFP growth must be supplemented with predictions of growth in both labor and capital input. In contrast, in order to predict future growth in potential output, a forecast of future ALP growth needs to be joined only by a forecast of trend hours growth, which is less subject to error and does not require forecasts of investment behavior.

Dynamic Specification and the End-of-Expansion Effect

Following the 1974 work of Christopher Sims and my own 1979 work,[28] I estimate equations in which the dependent variable is the first difference of the log of hours relative to its trend ($\Delta h - \Delta h^*$). This is regressed on a series of lagged dependent variable terms and on the first difference of deviations of the log of output from its trend ($\Delta q - \Delta q^*$). The output deviation variable in principle can enter with leads, the current value, and lags. The lags can be interpreted as reflecting adjustment costs: that is, delays in hiring and firing. The use of leads was introduced by Sims in the context of his analysis of Granger causality between hours and output.[29] A structural interpretation of leading output variables is that the choice of labor input is based in part on a forecast of future changes in output.

[28] See Sims (1974) and Gordon (1979).
[29] Sims (1974).

Two additional variables are added to the traditional regression that relates first differences of hours deviations to first differences of output deviations. The first is an error-correction term. Recently, the concept of error correction has been linked to that of cointegration, which can be defined informally as the notion that a linear combination of two series – for example, the hours deviation and the output deviation – is stationary.[30] When two such variables are cointegrated, a regression consisting entirely of differenced data will be misspecified, while a regression consisting entirely of level data will omit important constraints. The solutions is to estimate a regression of the first difference of one variable on the first difference of the other, plus an error correction variable consisting of the lagged log ratio of one variable to the other.[31]

In my 1979 work, I identified a tendency for labor input to grow more rapidly than can be explained by output changes in the late stages of the business expansion.[32] I dubbed this tendency toward overhiring the end-of-expansion effect and argued that it was balanced by a tendency to underhire in the first two years or so after the end of the expansion. In this paper, I adopt a more systematic approach to defining and interpreting the EOE effect. According to the NBER definition, the expansion ends when real output (actually a collection of coincident indicators) reaches its absolute peak. This can be distinguished from the earlier peak of the growth cycle when output reaches its highest level relative to trend or potential output. The EOE period is defined here as the interval between the peak of the growth cycle and the peak of the NBER cycle; by definition, it is a period when output displays positive but subnormal growth. The overhiring that consistently occurs during the EOE period can be interpreted as resulting from individual firms incorrectly expecting that their output will keep rising at or above trend, while output for the aggregate economy turns out to grow more slowly than its trend rate.

The EOE effect is introduced into the regression equation through a set of six dummy variables. These are not 0, 1 dummies; rather, they are in the form $1/M$, $-1/N$, where M is the length in quarters of the period of the initial interval of excessive labor input growth and N is the length of the subsequent correction. By forcing the sum of coefficients on each variable to equal zero, any overhiring in the initial phase is subsequently corrected. The length of the first period, M, is the number of quarters between the peak in the growth cycle and the peak of the NBER cycle.[33] The timing and duration, N,

---

[30] For the formal definition of stationarity and cointegration, see Engle and Granger (1987, pp. 252–53).

[31] A complete taxonomy of the possible forms of dynamic specification in a bivariate model is presented in Hendry, Pagan, and Sargan (1984, pp. 1040–49).

[32] Gordon (1979).

[33] The peak of the growth cycle is defined by the ratio of real GDP to natural real GDP; the latter measure is taken from Gordon (1993, appendix Table A-2). In the 1960s, peaks occurred in 1966:1 and 1968:2. I chose the latter. I chose the termination date of the fourth EOE episode to be 1974:2, rather than the NBER peak of 1973:4, because output remained at a plateau in the first half of 1974, rather than declining as it normally does in a recession.

of the subsequent correction period is determined by examining residuals in equations that omit the dummies entirely.[34] The amplitude of the end-of-expansion effect is allowed to differ across business cycles by allowing the dummy variable for each episode to have its own separate coefficient. (I subsequently test whether these coefficients are significantly different from each other.)

Combining these explanatory variables, the basic equation to be estimated is

$$(\Delta h - \Delta h^*)_t = \mu + \sum_{i=k}^{L} \alpha_i (\Delta h - \Delta h^*)_{t-i} + \sum_{j=M}^{N} \beta_j (\Delta q - \Delta q^*)_{t-j}$$

$$+ \phi[(q - h) - (q^* - h^*)]_{t-1} + \sum_{k=1}^{6} \gamma_k D_k + \epsilon_t, \quad (1)$$

Where $D_k = 0$ in all quarters except the end-of-expansion and subsequent correction period, which are as follows:

k	M	$D_k = 1/M$ during	N	$D_k = -1/N$ during
1	8	1955:4–1957:3	3	1957:4–1958:2
2	5	1959:2–1960:2	9	1960:4–1962:4
3	7	1968:2–1969:4	6	1970:2–1971:3
4	6	1973:1–1974:2	7	1974:4–1976:2
5	6	1978:4–1980:1	8	1981:1–1982:4
6	7	1989:1–1990:3	8	1991:4–1993:3

Here μ is the constant term; the α_i are the coefficients on the lagged dependent variable; the β_j are the leading, current, and lagged coefficients on the change in the output deviation from trend; ϕ is the coefficient on the error-correction term; and the γ_k are the coefficients on the end-of-expansion dummies. The γ_k coefficients indicate the cumulative amount of excess labor hired in a particular end-of-expansion episode, measured as a percent, and typical estimates below are in the range of 2.5 percent cumulative overhiring at the end of the expansion balanced by a cumulative −2.5 percent adjustment in hours during the subsequent recession and early stages of the recovery.[35]

(The level of real GDP in 1974:2 was only 0.3 percent below the annual average for the year 1973.)

[34] The timing of the 1991–3 correction period is somewhat arbitrary. To avoid interpreting the 1992 productivity spurt entirely as the result of the EOE effect, the correction period is extended to 1993:3. But to prevent too sharp a jump in the growth of predicted hours from 1993 to 1994, the correction effect is allowed to taper off through 1993. (The correction part of the sixth dummy variable is defined as 1/6.5 for 1991:4–1992:4; 0.75/6.5 for 1993:1; 0.5/6.5 for 1993:2; and 0.25/6.5 for 1993:3).

[35] The dummy variable is defined as −1/M and −1/N when I use annual data, and 4/M and −4/N with quarterly data.

Table 9.5. *Estimated Equations for Change in Nonfarm Business Hours Relative to Trend, 1954:4–1992:4[a]*

Independent Variable	1954:4–1992:4	1954:4–1992:4	1954:4–1992:4	1954:4–1972:4	1973:1–1992:4
Constant	0.31	0.13	...	...	...
	(1.82)	(0.82)			
Lagged dependent	0.18	−0.29	−0.32	−0.40	−0.25
$(\Delta h - \Delta h^*)$	(1.62)	(−2.47)	(−2.75)	(−2.21)	(−1.63)
Output deviation	0.67	0.91	0.95	0.95	0.93
$(\Delta q - \Delta q^*)$	(6.49)	(9.34)	(10.9)	(6.55)	(8.23)
Error-correction term	0.26	0.08	...	...	...
	(2.65)	(0.94)			
End-of-expansion dummies					
γ_1 (1955–58)	...	2.25	2.30	2.62	...
		(3.37)	(3.47)	(3.54)	
γ_2 (1959–62)	...	1.95	1.97	2.01	...
		(2.65)	(2.69)	(2.63)	
γ_3 (1968–71)	...	2.71	2.80	2.98	...
		(3.89)	(4.08)	(4.04)	
γ_4 (1973–76)	...	3.24	3.35	...	3.13
		(4.37)	(4.58)		(3.86)
γ_5 (1978–82)	...	2.65	2.84	...	2.60
		(3.42)	(3.81)		(3.22)
γ_6 (1988–92)	...	3.01	3.15	...	2.95
		(3.86)	(4.11)		(3.54)
Summary Statistic					
$\bar{R}^2$	0.77	0.83	0.83	0.81	0.83
SER	1.72	1.50	1.50	1.51	1.54
SSR	422	309	311	141	164
Addendum					
All γ constrained to be					
equal	...	2.57	2.68	2.54	2.89
γ coefficient		(6.98)	(7.55)	(5.18)	(5.25)
SER	...	1.49	1.48	1.49	1.52

[a] The regressions estimate variations of equation 1 in the text: $(\Delta h - \Delta h^*)_t = \mu + \sum_{i=k}^{L} \alpha_i (\Delta h - \Delta h^*)_{t-i} + \sum_{j=m}^{N} \beta_j (\Delta q - \Delta q^*)_{t-j} + \phi[(q - h) - (q^* - h^*)]_{t-1} + \sum_{k=l}^{6} \gamma_k D_k + \epsilon_t$. The dependent variable is the change in the log of hours relative to trend. The numbers in parentheses are t-statistics.

Source. Author's regressions using data described in Table 9.1.

Estimation: Nonfarm Private Business

Now that the trends for hours and output have been determined, along with the configuration of the end-of-expansion dummies, estimation of Equation 1 is straightforward. Results for the nonfarm private business sector are displayed in Table 9.5. Changes in structure are tested by estimating over the entire sample

period, 1954:4 to 1992:4, as well as for two subperiods broken roughly in half at
1972:4. The first three regressions display results for three variants that include
the error-correction term and end-of-expansion dummies both separately and
together. Prior testing not reported in the table determined that the current
value and three lagged values of the output deviation variable are significant,
but further lags are not; leading values (that Sims and I found to be significant)[36]
lose their significance in the presence of *either* the error-correction term or end-
of-expansion dummies. Thus in everything that follows, the line labeled output
deviations refers to the sum of coefficients on lags 0-3, and leading values are
omitted.

The most important conclusions from the first three regressions are that
the end-of-expansion dummies are highly significant, as is the error-correction
parameter, ϕ, by itself; however, in combination with the end-of-expansion
dummies, the error-correction parameter becomes insignificant. The constant
term, μ, is always insignificant and is omitted in the last three columns. Hence
my preferred specification is that shown in the third regression of Table 9.5.
Noting that the end-of-expansion coefficients on the six separate episodes are
of roughly the same size, I reran the equations to constrain the six separate
γ_i coefficients to be the same and determined that they are not significantly
different from one another.[37] The constrained value of γ is about 2.7, as shown
in the bottom section of Table 9.5, implying cumulative overhiring of 2.7 percent
during the EOE period, followed by a subsequent correction of 2.7 percent.

The last two regressions show that the coefficients for the two subperiods
are very close to those for the entire 1954–92 period. A Chow test fails to reject
the hypothesis of structural stability; the F test (8, 131) is 0.49, compared to
the 5 percent critical value of 2.01. Finally, the sums of the α and β coefficients
imply that the elasticity of hours deviations to output deviations is $\beta/(1 - \alpha) =$
0.72, and hence the response of ALP to output deviations from trend has an
elasticity of 0.28. A dynamic simulation of the estimated equation indicates
that initially hours adjust by less than this response, and that four quarters are
required for the response of hours deviations to output deviations to arrive at
the value of 0.72.

Summarizing the Specification: The Four Frequencies
of Productivity

The specification of hours adjustment in Equation 1 implies that there are four
different time frequencies relevant for productivity analysis. At the highest frequency, the deviation from trend of labor input adjusts with a lag distribution
spreading over four calendar quarters to deviations from trend of output, and

---

[36] Sims (1974) and Gordon (1992).

[37] The F(5, 139) ratio for the difference in fit between the equations in the third column of table 5,
using six different EOE coefficients and a single EOE coefficient, is 0.24, as compared to the
5 percent critical value of 2.27.

as a result, productivity movements *lead* those in output by a few months. This high-frequency movement occurs with the same lead-lag pattern whether the business cycle lasts two years or ten. The second frequency is cyclical and reflects the fact that hours respond to a sustained movement of output away from trend with an elasticity below unity, about 0.72. Thus ALP responds to a sustained movement of output away from trend with an elasticity of about 0.28. The third frequency is also cyclical. This is the end-of-expansion effect: the slump in productivity that appears to occur repeatedly between the peak of the growth cycle and the peak of the NBER cycle. Finally, the fourth frequency is the trend itself that emerges when the parameters governing the other three frequencies are identified; the loglinear trends-through-benchmarks technique allows the trend to vary from one business cycle to the next.

Estimation: The Two Subsectors

Table 9.6 and 9.7 display estimated parameters in the same format as Table 9.5 for the manufacturing and NFNM sectors. As would be expected, because NFNM makes up three-quarters of the nonfarm business aggregate, the results in Table 9.7 are quite similar to those in Table 9.5. The elasticity of hours to output, β, is lower, possibly reflecting measurement error, the goodness of fit is worse, and the end-of-expansion dummies tend to have lower t-ratios than in Table 9.5.[38]

Table 9.6 reflects the higher volatility of manufacturing hours and output; both the $\bar{R}^2$ and the standard error of estimate are higher than in Table 9.5. In all columns of Table 9.6, the response of hours deviations to output deviations is smaller over the first four quarters than for the nonfarm business sector in Table 9.5; this implies that, on average, productivity displays a larger response to cyclical output deviations in the manufacturing sector than in the total economy.

An interesting result is that in the 1988–92 cycle, the end-of-expansion effect in manufacturing is unusually low and in NFNM is unusually high. In contrast, the end-of-expansion effect in manufacturing was unusually high for 1978–82, the "Rust Belt" episode. These estimated coefficients support the thrust of popular commentary. The early 1980s witnessed an unusually savage downsizing of manufacturing employment, whereas the early 1990s have witnessed a corporate downsizing movement in the NFNM sector. The difference between the journalistic version of these episodes and my econometric version, however, is that in each case there was end-of-expansion overhiring that preceded the downsizing. Journalists, by contrast, focus on the firings and layoffs, while omitting mention of the overhiring that came earlier.

---

[38] The EOE dummies are identical in the two subsectors as in the aggregate; no searching was done to locate the best-fitting timing of the correction period.

Table 9.6. *Estimated Equations for Change in Manufacturing Hours Relative to Trend, 1954:4–1992:4*[a]

Independent Variable	1954:4– 1992:4	1954:4– 1992:4	1954:4– 1992:4	1954:4– 1972:4	1973:1– 1992:4
Constant	0.38	0.20	...	...	...
	(1.63)	(0.86)			
Lagged dependent	0.37	0.12	0.09	0.03	0.05
$(\Delta h - \Delta h^*)$	(3.77)	(1.14)	(0.85)	(0.22)	(0.59)
Output deviation	0.48	0.62	0.66	0.74	0.66
$\Delta q - \Delta q^*)$	(5.47)	(6.84)	(7.89)	(5.87)	(5.77)
Error-correction term	0.20	0.10	...	...	...
	(2.39)	(1.33)			
End-of-expansion dummies					
γ_1 (1955–58)	...	1.98	2.11	2.00	...
		(1.98)	(2.12)	(2.01)	
γ_2(1959–62)	...	1.35	1.44	1.13	...
		(1.22)	(1.30)	(1.05)	
γ_3(1968–71)	...	2.70	2.79	2.71	...
		(2.60)	(2.70)	(2.64)	
γ_4 (1973–76)	...	2.45	2.60	...	3.33
		(2.21)	(2.36)		(2.72)
γ_5 (1978–82)	...	3.74	4.24	...	4.46
		(3.13)	(3.72)		(3.65)
γ_6 (1988–92)	...	1.35	1.50	...	1.82
		(1.22)	(1.36)		(1.60)
Summary Statistic					
$\bar{R}^2$	0.86	0.88	0.88	0.89	0.87
SER	2.40	2.29	2.28	2.16	2.31
SSR	824	716	725	290	368
Addendum					
All γ constrained to be					
equal	...	2.16	2.37	1.96	3.10
γ coefficient		(4.18)	(4.72)	(3.00)	(3.94)
SER	...	2.27	2.28	2.15	2.32

[a] The regressions estimate variations of equation 1 in the text: $(\Delta h - \Delta h^*)_t = \mu + \sum_{i=k}^{L} \alpha_i (\Delta h - \Delta h^*)_{t-i} + \sum_{j=m}^{N} \beta_j (\Delta q - \Delta q^*)_{t-j} + \phi[(q - h) - (q^* - h^*)]_{t-1} + \sum_{k=l}^{6} \gamma_k D_k + \epsilon_t$. The dependent variable is the change in the log of hours relative to trend. The numbers in parentheses are t-statistics.

Source. Author's regressions using data described in Table 9.1.

9.4 THE UNDERLYING TREND IN LABOR'S AVERAGE PRODUCT, 1987–92

The specification of the econometric equation estimated in the previous section requires that the first difference of hours and of output be expressed as deviations from trend. For the period through 1987, loglinear trends are extended between the benchmark quarters listed in Table 9.3. However, there is no benchmark

Table 9.7. *Estimated Equations for Change in Nonfarm Nonmanufacturing Business Hours Relative to Trend, 1954:4–1992:4*[a]

Independent Variable	1954:4–1992:4	1954:4–1992:4	1954:4–1992:4	1954:4–1972:4	1973:1–1992:4
Constant	0.23	0.13	...	...	...
	(1.27)	(0.75)			
Lagged dependent	0.08	−0.36	−0.40	−0.60	−0.30
($\Delta h - \Delta h^*$)	(0.70)	(−2.51)	(−2.86)	(−2.60)	(−1.66)
Output deviation	0.59	0.71	0.77	0.65	0.81
($\Delta q - \Delta q^*$)	(5.68)	(6.98)	(8.49)	(3.99)	(7.10)
Error-correction term	0.27	0.15	...	...	...
	(2.67)	(1.51)			
End-of-expansion dummies					
γ_1 (1955–58)	...	1.98	2.06	2.86	...
		(2.37)	(2.46)	(2.84)	
γ_2 (1959–62)	...	2.19	2.21	2.52	...
		(2.37)	(2.39)	(2.50)	
γ_3 (1968–71)	...	2.13	2.37	2.72	...
		(2.46)	(2.79)	(2.91)	
γ_4 (1973–76)	...	2.75	2.97	...	2.65
		(2.96)	(3.24)		(2.82)
γ_5 (1978–82)	...	2.05	2.28	...	1.86
		(2.13)	(2.39)		(1.92)
γ_6 (1988–92)	...	3.79	4.03	...	3.56
		(3.69)	(3.96)		(3.36)
Summary Statistic					
$\bar{R}^2$	0.47	0.54	0.54	0.40	0.63
SER	2.03	1.89	1.89	1.98	1.84
SSR	592	490	498	242	234
Addendum					
All γ constrained to be equal	...	2.34	2.52	2.69	2.60
γ coefficient		(5.09)	(5.60)	(4.20)	(3.85)
SER	...	1.88	1.88	1.95	1.84

[a] The regressions estimate variations of equation 1 in the text: $(\Delta h - \Delta h^*)_t = \mu + \sum_{i=k}^{L} \alpha_i (\Delta h - \Delta h^*)_{t-i} + \sum_{j=m}^{N} \beta_j (\Delta q - \Delta q^*)_{t-j} + \phi[(q - h) - (q^* - h^*)]_{t-1} + \sum_{k=l}^{6} \gamma_k D_k + \epsilon_t$. The dependent variable is the change in the log of hours relative to trend. The numbers in parentheses are t-statistics.

Source. Author's regressions using data described in Table 9.1.

quarter after 1987, because at the end of the sample period in late 1992, the unemployment rate remained well above its natural rate of about 6 percent.[39]

---

[39] Recall that the criteria for a benchmark quarter are that the unemployment rate is close to the natural rate, currently about 6 percent; that the unemployment rate is falling (thus ruling out the

All the estimates discussed in the previous section assume arbitrarily that the productivity trend recorded in 1972–87 continues during 1987–92.[40] In this section, I search for the optimal 1987–92 productivity trend that yields the best-fitting equations estimated for the period 1973–92.

Cumulative 1987–92 Errors in Alternative Equations

To illustrate the sensitivity of the results to the form of the specification, Figure 9.5 displays cumulative forecasting errors over the 1987:4–1992:4 period for the nonfarm business sector. There are three frames in the diagram, corresponding to three different versions of the equation, each estimated over the 1973–92 interval. In each frame, cumulative errors are shown for three different assumptions about the 1987–92 productivity trend.

The top frame uses the version of the equation that excludes the end-of-expansion terms but includes the error-correction term. (This version corresponds to the first regression of Table 9.5, reestimated for the shorter 1973–92 period.) No matter whether the assumed 1987–92 productivity trend is 0.75, 1.00, or 1.25 percent per year, this version of the equation makes large positive forecasting errors, implying that the growth of actual labor input during 1987–91 is substantially larger than the equation predicts. Furthermore, the cumulative error is eliminated by slow hours growth of 1992 only when the 1987–92 productivity trend is set at a relatively low 0.75 percent per year.

The middle frame uses the version of the equation that excludes the error-correction term and includes the end-of-expansion dummy variables. (This frame corresponds to the last regression estimated in Table 9.5.) The cumulative errors plotted in the middle frame are much smaller than those in the top frame because much of the excess growth of hours in the 1989 90 period is explained by the end-of-expansion dummy (which has its "on" phase during 1989:1–1990:3). The cumulative error at the end of the period in 1992:4 is closest to zero with a relatively slow assumed productivity trend of 1 percent per year.

However, in the middle frame the cumulative errors display a consistent hump-shaped pattern that is independent of the assumed trend. This occurs because the equation cannot explain why hours growth was so rapid (or productivity growth was so slow) during 1988, before the onset of the EOE

period in late 1990 when the unemployment rate was 6 percent but unemployment was rising); and that the end-of-expansion effect is nonoperative.

[40] More precisely, a trend for hours is established for each of the three sectors, and then the output trend is equal to the hours trend plus the assumed productivity trend. To fix the hours trend in all the regressions estimated in Table 9.4–9.7, I assumed that a 6 percent unemployment rate (in contrast to the 7.3 percent unemployment rate recorded in 1992:4) would require a level of hours 1.6 percent higher than actually occurred in 1992:4. Of this 1.6 percent difference, 1.2 percent is required to reduce the unemployment rate to 6 percent, and the remaining 0.4 percent is assumed to be reflected in some combination of higher hours per employee and a higher labor force participation rate. The implied annual trend growth rate of hours during 1987:3–1992:4 is 0.87 percent for nonfarm business, −0.56 for manufacturing, and 1.32 percent for NFNM.

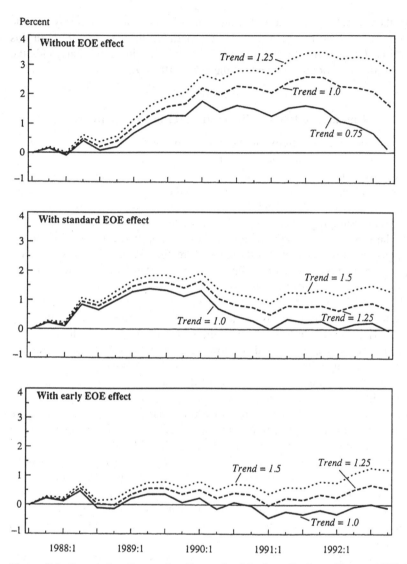

Figure 9.5. Cumulative Forecasting Errors for Nonfarm Business Hours, 1987:4–1992:4[a]

[a] Each panel depicts the forecasting errors using three different assumptions about the 1987–92 productivity trend. The panels differ in terms of equation specification as follows. The first panel uses the specification of the first regression estimated in Table 9.5 with an error-correction term and no EOE dummies, but estimates it for the shorter period of 1973:1–1992:4. The second panel uses the specification of the last regression estimated in Table 9.5, which includes EOE dummies but excludes an error-correction term. The third panel's specification is similar to second panel's, except that the EOE term has its "on" phase one year earlier, from 1988:1–1989:3.

Source. Author's calculations.

Table 9.8. *Best-Fitting Productivity Growth Trends*[a]
Percent per year

| Sector | Equation Type | Actual Growth Rate 1972:2–1987:3 | | Optimal Trend, 1987:3– 1992:4 | Mean Residual, 1992:1– 1992:4 |
		Official	Benchmark Reweighted		
Nonfarm	No EOE effect	0.98	1.28	0.73	−1.16
business	With EOE effect	0.98	1.28	1.10	−0.27
Manufacturing	No EOE effect	2.13	3.13	2.51	0.46
	With EOE effect	2.13	3.13	2.65	−0.45
Nonfarm	No EOE effect	0.48	0.46	0.03	1.04
nonmanufacturing business	With EOE effect	0.48	0.46	0.66	−0.32
Nonfarm business	No EOE effect	0.98	1.28	0.78	0.86
aggregated from subsectors	With EOE effect	0.98	1.28	1.26	−0.36

[a] All equations are estimated from 1973:1–1992:4. The best-fitting trends are those that minimize the root squared error of the particular equation over 1987:4–1992:4.

Source. Author's calculations based on Bureau of Labor Statistics, *Productivity and Costs.*

interval. To determine how this early initiation of overhiring interacts with the underlying trend, I define an alternative EOE variable which has its "on" phase one year earlier (1988:1–1989:3) than the standard variable, but retains the same definition of the correction ("off") phase. The cumulative errors with this alternative early EOE variable are plotted in the bottom frame of Figure 9.5 and are much closer to zero. There is little impact on the trend; the trend that brings the cumulative error closest to zero in 1992:4 is 1.00 percent per year, just as in the middle frame with the standard EOE definition.

Searching for the Optimal Trend

Figure 9.5 displays various assumed trends. The analysis can be extended by conducting a grid search for the best-fitting trend for each sector and for each version of the specification. Table 9.8 displays the actual 1972–87 growth rates of productivity with and without correction for the base-year data bias, the optimal 1987–92 trends resulting from the grid search, and the residual for each equation during the final four quarters of the sample period ending in 1992:4. A negative residual means that hours growth is overpredicted in 1992: that is, productivity grew faster than the equation can explain.

The first section of the table displays results for the nonfarm business sector – the same sector displayed in Figure 9.5; the results are consistent with that graph. The optimal 1987–92 trend is only 0.73 percent when the EOE effect is excluded, but a more robust 1.10 percent when the EOE effect is included. The 1992 residual with the EOE effect is only −0.27 percent.

The second and third sections of Table 9.8 display optimal trends for the manufacturing and NFNM sectors. For each sector, the inclusion of the EOE effect raises the optimal 1987–92 trend. The inclusion of the EOE effect reduces the residuals for 1992, making them negative in both sectors. The EOE effect makes little difference to the *absolute* size of the manufacturing residual for 1992 but substantially reduces the *absolute* size of the 1992 residual in the NFNM sector. The fourth section of the table displays the weighted average of the two subsectors; the implied optimal productivity trend for the nonfarm business sector is 1.26 percent per year, more rapid than the direct estimate of 1.10 percent in the first section. In view of the numerous sources of measurement error in the subsector data, the direct estimates in the first section are probably more reliable than the estimates in the fourth section based on subsector data.

Interpreting Cyclical Fluctuations in Productivity

The distinguishing feature of productivity change in the aggregate economy over the past five years is a long period of zero growth during 1987–91, followed by a sharp upsurge in 1992. Can this record be interpreted as normal cyclical behavior? The performance of the basic equation (with the standard EOE effect and optimal 1987–92 trend of 1.10 percent) is plotted in Figure 9.6. The actual and predicted values of labor productivity and the deviation of productivity from its assumed trend are displayed.

The equation does an acceptable job of tracking cyclical fluctuations in productivity, and in fact performs better in 1987–92 than in previous cyclical episodes. The appearance of serial correlation in the plot reflects the fact that the equation is estimated in first differences (where no serial correlation exists), but plotted in levels. The errors in Figure 9.6 – the actual values minus the predicted values – are computed by cumulating the first-difference equation residuals beginning in the first quarter of the sample period (1973:1). These errors are thus equivalent to the cumulative errors plotted in Figure 9.5. The equations tend to predict too large a decline in productivity and subsequent recovery in the 1973–7 period and too small a decline in productivity in the 1982 recession. As noted above, the equation with the standard timing of the 1989–90 EOE effect also misses the overhiring that occurred in 1988, and hence its prediction of the late 1980s decline in productivity occurs about a year too late. However, the prediction of the 1991–2 recovery of productivity is right on track. The predicted deviation of productivity from trend in 1992:4 is −2.5 percent, implying that there is substantial room for productivity growth to proceed at a rate above the assumed 1.1 percent trend during 1993–5 without implying a need to reassess the trend.[41]

---

[41] Productivity growth during the three years 1993–5 at a rate of 1.93 percent per year would bring the deviation from trend back to zero in 1995:4.

Index, 1972:2 = 100

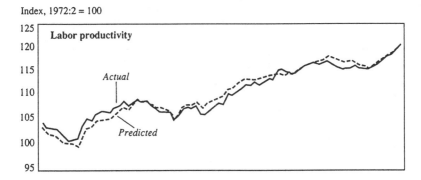

Percent

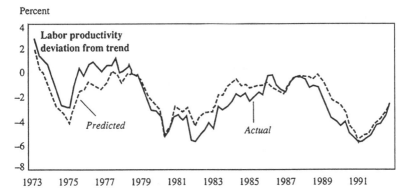

Figure 9.6. Actual and Predicted Productivity for Nonfarm Business, 1973–92[a]

[a] The 1987–92 assumed productivity trend is 1.1, and the equation estimated includes standard-timing EOE effects.

Source. Author's calculations.

Forecasts for 1993–4

For any assumed growth rate of output in 1993–4, each of the equations can be used to divide output between a predicted path of hours growth and a residual path of productivity growth. For output growth, I assume a steady annual growth rate during the eight quarters of 1993–4 of 3.2 percent per year, the current consensus of the blue chip group of economic forecasters. The productivity trend is the optimal rate listed in the first section of Table 9.8.

As shown in Table 9.9, all equations forecast substantial growth in hours, in contrast to the zero growth that characterized 1992. The two alternative equations – based on standard and early EOE effects – predict productivity growth in the range of 1.5–1.7 percent for 1993 and 1.3–1.4 percent for 1994. These relatively slow rates of productivity growth would leave the deviation from trend (as plotted in the bottom of Figure 9.6) still from −1.7 to −1.9 percent in 1994:4. The failure of productivity to recover to its trend is the counterpart

Table 9.9. *Alternative Growth Rate Forecasts for Nonfarm Business, Four Quarters Ending 1993:4 and 1994:4*[a]

Percent per year

	Hours		Output Per Hour	
Forecast Specification	1993:4	1994:4	1993:4	1994:4
No EOE effect and productivity trend of 0.73	2.48	2.53	0.72	0.67
Standard EOE effect and productivity trend of 1.10	1.68	1.89	1.52	1.32
Early EOE effect and productivity trend of 1.10	1.53	1.84	1.67	1.36

[a] The assumed output growth rate is 3.2 percent per year.

Source. Authors calculations.

of the assumed 3.2 percent growth rate of output, a much slower rate than at the same stage of previous business-cycle expansions.

9.5 CONCLUSION

The performance of average labor productivity and multifactor productivity in the U.S. economy was dismal from 1972 to 1991. Does the relatively rapid growth in ALP and MFP experienced in 1991–2 warrant optimism that relief has arrived from the two-decade-long productivity growth slowdown? The answer depends on whether the recent experience represents an acceleration in the underlying long-term trend or just a normal cyclical upturn that is similar to behavior in previous business cycles. To provide the answer, this paper proposes a method for separating trend from cycle.

I show that cyclical productivity does not simply parallel the cycle in output that determines the dates of NBER peaks and troughs. Instead, productivity displays complex cyclical behavior that can be decomposed into three different time frequencies. First is the high-frequency movement caused by the relatively short lag of hours behind output; this adjustment in hours is completed within four quarters after a change in output relative to trend. Second, the adjustment of hours within the first four quarters has a cumulative elasticity to output of 0.72, leaving a positive elasticity of ALP to deviations in output from trend that lasts until these deviations disappear – that is, for the duration of the business cycle. Third, productivity systematically displays an end-of-expansion slump between the peak in the growth cycle (the peak for detrended output) and the NBER peak (defined for the absolute level of output); a correction in the two years or so after the NBER peak follows; during this correction period, productivity growth is more rapid than would be predicted on the basis of output growth alone. I interpret this phenomenon as the result of overoptimism by business firms that is subsequently corrected.

This essay provides strong support for the end-of-expansion effect. This phenomenon, originally proposed in 1979 and based largely on cyclical behavior through the mid-1970s, has now recurred in two more cyclical episodes, 1978–82 and 1989–93. Equations that include the end-of-expansion effect provide a much improved fit of the data and are quite robust, passing a test for structural stability over the full 1954–92 period. The 1988–91 decline in productivity relative to trend and the subsequent 1991–2 recovery are tracked quite accurately. As a byproduct, inclusion of the end-of-expansion effect provides a more optimistic interpretation of the trend in productivity growth over the past five years than an equation that omits this effect.

For two alternative definitions of the end-of-expansion effect, the best-fitting 1987–92 productivity trend for the private nonfarm economy is 1.1 percent per year. When the best-fitting trends are determined separately for the manufacturing and nonfarm nonmanufacturing sectors and then aggregated, the result is 1.26 percent per year. Both of these rates are below the actual 1972–87 growth rate of 1.28 percent per year obtained by correcting the bias in the official data that arises from its fixed 1987 weighting scheme. The best-fitting 1987–92 trends at the sectoral level imply that there has been a substantial 0.5 percent per year *deceleration* in the growth rate of manufacturing productivity as compared to the 1972–87 growth rate corrected for the base-year data bias, offset by a modest 0.2 percent acceleration for the nonfarm nonmanufacturing sector.

How does the econometric investigation assess the widespread journalistic view that a new era of productivity-led growth is at hand? The only way to emerge with an optimistic conclusion is to focus entirely on 1991–2 and ignore the productivity stagnation of 1987–91. Those who would argue that there was a one-shot jump of productivity in 1992, as opposed to a normal cyclical correction of the type that has occurred repeatedly in past cycles, are forced to conclude that the trend from 1972 to 1991 is even more dismal than previously believed.

However, the detailed analysis does provide a few glimmers of support for some aspects of the popular view. First, the end-of-expansion effect estimated for the 1989–92 episode is among the largest on record, with an estimate of 3.2 percent cumulative overhiring (followed by a cumulative 3.2 percent decline during 1991–3 in labor input relative to the level implied by output growth). Second, the end-of-expansion effect in the recent episode has been much smaller than usual in manufacturing and much larger than usual in NFNM. Both these conclusions support the journalistic view that the current wave of corporate downsizing and restructuring is unusual, both in its size and in its concentration in the service sector and in white-collar occupations.

What the popular view misses quite consistently, however, is that the wave of downsizing does not emerge out of thin air but is the direct result of extensive overhiring in the NFNM sector during the late 1980s. If the economic difficulties of the early 1990s come to be labeled generally as an economic hangover, then the jobless recovery of 1991–2 can be viewed as a hangover reaction to a binge of overhiring in the late 1980s – just as sluggish spending by consumers and business firms has come to be viewed widely as a hangover reaction to excess indebtedness incurred in the mid- to late 1980s. Perhaps the business press could be urged to replace the common expression "corporate restructuring" with the more appropriate phrase, "correcting our past mistakes."

References

David, Paul A. "The Dynamo and the Computer: An Historical Perspective on the Modern Productivity Paradox." *American Economic Review, Papers and Proceedings.* 1990; vol. 80, no. 2, pp. 355–61.

Engle, Robert F., and Granger, C. W. J. "Co-Integration and Error Correction: Representation, Estimation, and Testing." *Econometrica.* 1987; vol. 55, no. 2, pp. 251–76.

Gordon, Robert J. "The 'End-of-Expansion' Phenomenon in Short-Run Productivity Behavior." *BPEA.* 1979; vol. 2, pp. 447–61.

"Inflation, Flexible Exchange Rates, and the Natural Rate of Unemployment." In: Baily, Martin N., ed. *Workers, Jobs, and Inflation.* Washington: Brookings; 1982.

"Are Procyclical Productivity Fluctuations a Figment of Measurement Error?" Working paper. Evanston, Ill.: Northwestern University. August, 1992, Chapter 8 in this book.

Macroeconomics. Sixth edition. New York: Harper Collins; 1993.

Hendry, David F., Pagan, Adrian R., and Sargan, J. Denis. "Dynamic Specification." In: Griliches, Zvi, and Intriligator, Michael D. *Handbook of Econometrics,* Amsterdam: North-Holland; 1984.

Hodrick, Robert J., and Prescott, Edward C. "Postwar U. S. Business Cycles: An Empirical Investigation." Discussion Paper 451. Minneapolis, Minn.: University of Minnesota. May, 1981.

Hultgren, Thor. "Changes in Labor Cost during Cycles in Production and Business." Occasional Paper 74. New York: National Bureau of Economic Research. 1960.

Kydland, Finn E., and Prescott, Edward C. "Business Cycles: Real Facts and a Monetary Myth." *Federal Reserve Bank of Minneapolis Quarterly Review.* 1990; vol. 14, no. 2, pp. 3–18.

Mishel, Lawrence, and Bernstein, Jared. "Job Destruction: Worse Than We Thought." *Challenge.* 1992; vol. 35, no. 5, pp. 4–8.

Okun, Arthur M. "The Gap between Actual and Potential Output." *Proceedings of the American Statistical Association.* 1962. Reprinted in, Phelps, Edmund S. ed. *Problems of the Modern Economy.* New York: Norton; 1966.

Prescott, Edward C. "Theory Ahead of Business Cycle Measurement." In: Brunner, Karl, and Meltzer, Allan H., eds. *Real Business Cycles, Real Exchange Rates and Actual Policies. Carnegie-Rochester Conference Series on Public Policy.* 1986, vol. 25.

Ritter, Joseph A. "The Delayed Recovery of Employment." *National Economic Trends, Federal Reserve Bank of St. Louis.* February, 1993, p. 1.

Sims, Christopher A. "Output and Labor Input in Manufacturing." *BPEA.* 1974; vol. 3, pp. 695–728.

Young, Allan H. "Alternative Measures of Change in Real Output and Prices." *Survey of Current Business.* 1992; vol. 72, no. 4, pp. 32–38. 72(4):32–48.

PART THREE

THE THEORY OF THE INFLATION-UNEMPLOYMENT TRADEOFF

INTRODUCING SUPPLY SHOCKS INTO MACROECONOMICS

The Keynesian interpretation of business cycles as reflecting swings in aggregate demand, relative to a relatively stable capacity to supply goods and services, received a body blow in the early 1970s. If demand is moving back and forth along a stable supply curve, then output and price movements should be positively correlated. If supply is moving back and forth along a stable demand curve, then output and price movements should be negatively correlated. The deep recession in 1974–5 was accompanied by an explosion of inflation and thus seemed to deny the Keynesian emphasis on demand fluctuations. In the words of Robert E. Lucas, Jr., and Thomas J. Sargent, quoted in Chapter Seven, "the task which faces contemporary students of the business cycle [is] that of sorting through the wreckage . . . of that remarkable intellectual event called the Keynesian Revolution. . . ."

Yet those of us faced at the time with the need to find an interpretation of the 1974–5 episode could not toss out demand as a primary mover of the business cycle. How else, after all, could we interpret the Great Depression, with its bank failures, apple-sellers, and legions drifting from town to town looking for jobs, as anything other than a massive insufficiency of aggregate demand? What event could have restricted aggregate supply to such an extent – bombing raids reduced the productive capacity of the United Kingdom, Japan, and Germany during 1940–5, but not that of the United States in 1929–33? There was only one conclusion to be reached from an attempt to explain 1929–33 in the same consistent model as 1974–5. Once recognized, it was blindingly obvious, especially to those who regularly taught a course in elementary principles of economics. Just as the output and price of corn or wheat could be positively or negatively correlated depending on the importance of microeconomic demand or supply shocks, so the aggregate level of output and price of goods and services could be positively or negatively correlated, depending on the relative importance of aggregate demand or supply shocks.

The catalyst for this line of thinking began in the early 1970s when a series of events (poor harvests in the U.S. and the U.S.S.R and weather-related problems elsewhere) caused the price of farm products to jump by 50 percent during 1972–3. Soon afterward the upward pressure on raw materials prices was amplified by the 1973–4 OPEC oil embargo and subsequent near-quadrupling of crude oil prices. Keynesian economics had been based on the assumption of fixed or sticky prices and wages outside the raw materials sectors, and thus it seemed clear that the sharp upward jolt in farm and oil prices could not be offset by a sharp downward movement in the prices of other goods and services. The initial insight that an adverse supply shock created a "macroeconomic externality" came from Arthur M. Okun, who argued that the demand for farm and oil products was price-inelastic, and to pay the higher prices in a world of rigid wages, households would be forced to cut back, perhaps drastically, on their real purchases of other products besides farm and oil-related products.

EMERGENCE OF THE THEORY
OF SUPPLY SHOCKS

Okun discussed his ideas informally at conferences but did not write them up as a formal article.[1] The first version of my paper, reproduced here as Chapter Ten, was presented at the Brookings Panel in early December 1974, just as the U.S. economy was exhibiting a dramatic "free fall" into the worst postwar recession to that time. Okun, one of the editors of the Brookings Panel, did not feel that my paper was ready for publication at that time; what appears here as Chapter Ten is a revised version presented in April 1975 and published soon thereafter. The example in the paper focuses on a supply reduction in the farm sector, for example, caused by a drought or crop failure, and this was motivated by the agricultural supply problems of 1972–3 that had caused farm prices to rise by 50 percent in a short period. Its analysis is equally applicable to a restriction in the supply of oil such as that initiated by OPEC in 1973.

Chapter Ten analyzes the response of a simple two-sector "farm" and "nonfarm" economy to a decline in output in the farm sector, where the price adjusts instantly to clear markets. No problems arise if wages and prices are fully flexible and markets clear in the nonfarm sector. These wages and prices drop instantly to clear markets, and the optimal policy response is a reduction in nominal income to hold the aggregate price index constant (that is, a constant average of rising farm prices and declining nonfarm prices).

In contrast, when the nonfarm wage and price levels are rigid and nominal income is held fixed, the supply reduction in the external sector has a multiplier effect, since the rising share of income required to purchase the farm products leaves a smaller nominal (and real) amount remaining to purchase nonfarm products. The size of this multiplier effect varies inversely with the price elasticity of demand for farm products (see Chapter Ten, equation 9). The social

---

[1] Okun's informal discussion is cited in Chapter Eleven, footnote 2.

cost of the reduction in aggregate output exceeds the value of the lost farm output by the value of the nonfarm output that is squeezed out.

Now the optimal policy response becomes more complicated, depending on the exact nature of the price- and wage-setting process in the nonfarm sector. If nonfarm wages are totally rigid, then policy makers can "accommodate" the shock, boosting nominal income without fear of raising nonfarm prices or wages. If, however, there is a channel by which farm prices feed through to wages (for example, by formal or informal indexation), then an accommodative policy that raises nominal income will permanently raise the rate of inflation. The paper concludes by highlighting the dangers of wage indexation in combination with supply shocks, and indeed numerous economies, for example, Brazil and Israel, found themselves in damaging inflationary spirals in the mid-1970s as a result of the potent inflationary mixture of supply shocks, wage indexation, and accommodative policy.

While my paper (Chapter Ten this book) was the first theoretical analysis of the macroeconomic externality from supply shocks to appear in print, independently Edmund S. Phelps (1978) had worked out a complementary analysis that appeared three years later, due to the delays inherent in the refereed journal submission process. Our analyses differed in two dimensions that made each paper more complex than necessary. Phelps's paper incorporated a neoclassical production function that allowed basic results to be stated as a function of the change in the income share of the "shocked" (raw material) sector, whereas my similar conclusions stated as a function of the price elasticity of demand for the raw material emerged in a more complex form. However, Phelps introduced two needless complexities. First, his production process included capital input, which can be safely neglected for this problem. Second, his policy variable was the money supply rather than nominal GDP, introducing variations in the income velocity of money as an additional source of complexity.

Chapter Eleven, written in 1984, merges the best features of the Chapter Ten model with Phelps's framework and yields a stunningly simple result that appears as equation (9). The condition to avoid a macroeconomic externality from a supply shock is that the growth rate of nominal income minus the growth rate in the nominal wage rate equals the change in the income share of the raw material. Thus, if the price elasticity of demand for the raw material is less than unity, so a supply reduction raises its income share, a "wedge" must open up between the growth rates of nominal GDP and the nominal wage rate. If the wage rate is fixed, then the growth rate of nominal GDP must increase sufficiently to "pay for" the higher expenditures on the raw material. If conversely the growth rate of nominal GDP is fixed, then the growth rate of the nominal wage rate must fall by an equivalent amount.

The appeal of this result is that it is both simpler and more general than anything in Chapter Ten or in the Phelps (1978) paper. There is no need to assume that nominal GDP or the nominal wage rate are fixed. The condition applies to either a market-clearing or nonclearing economy. The relevance of hinging the analysis on the changing income share of the raw material is evident in the tripling of energy's income share between 1972 and 1981. Chapter Eleven also probes further into the interplay between supply shocks and wage indexation. With lagged wage indexation (today's wage change depending on last year's inflation) accommodative policy that raises nominal GDP growth will permanently increase the rate of inflation following any supply shock that permanently boosts the raw material income share. The size of the macroeconomic externality depends on the slope of the Phillips curve, that is, how much the recession in the noncommodity sector pulls down the inflation rate to counterbalance the inflation impact of the supply shock. The optimal policy response in any given nation may differ, depending on the nature of its Phillips curve and its wage indexation regime, and these response parameters may in turn change in response to the shock and its aftermath.

Taken together, Chapters Ten and Eleven helped to unify the teaching of macroeconomic theory with that of microeconomics, since basic results in both subjects could now be summarized with supply and demand curves. Business cycles could be caused by any combination of demand and supply shocks, and inflation could be either positively or negatively correlated with output changes. Finally, supply shocks raised questions about the optimality of decentralized and uncoordinated wage and price setting. Whatever the virtues of decentralization for microeconomic efficiency, some coordination and centralization might be needed to obtain an improved macroeconomic response to supply shocks.

THE DYNAMIC MODEL OF AGGREGATE SUPPLY AND DEMAND

The idea that supply shocks and demand shocks were parallel and complementary causes of business cycles was not explicit in Chapter Ten's analysis, but soon this idea fundamentally changed the teaching of macroeconomics at every level, from the principles course for freshmen to the level of advanced graduate topics classes. The integration of demand and supply shocks in a formal dynamic algebraic model may be unique in the annals of economic thought, as it was achieved first in textbooks prior to the publication of scholarly articles on the theory or econometric validation of the theory. The textbooks by Rudi Dornbusch and Stan Fischer (1978) and by myself (Gordon, 1978) appeared almost simultaneously, and both used alternative versions of a simple diagram that can be traced back to a classroom handout that Dornbusch had used at the Chicago Business School in early 1975. The diagram, which had the inflation rate on the vertical axis and either the unemployment rate or the output gap on the horizontal axis combined three elements – the expectational Phillips curve developed by Milton Friedman and Phelps in the late 1960s, an identity that decomposed nominal GDP growth into inflation and output growth, and Okun's insight that supply shocks can have macroeconomic externalities.[2]

---

[2] The only difference in the two expositions is that I took "excess" nominal GDP growth (in excess of growth in potential real GDP) as exogenous, wheas Dornbusch took excess monetary growth

The earliest known version of this model to appear in an academic journal is reproduced here as Chapter Twelve. This paper was presented at the AEA meetings in October 1976, and published early in 1977. Its model looks remarkably like the algebraic model that appears in the latest (2003) edition of my macro textbook. Inflation is driven by the excess growth in nominal GDP relative to growth in potential output. An Okun's law relation relates changes in the unemployment rate to changes in the output gap. This dynamic demand equation connecting the inflation rate with changes in nominal GDP growth and changes in the unemployment rate is then joined with a dynamic supply relationship in equation (13), an expectational Phillips curve with a shift term to represent supply shocks, "whether cost-push pressure by unions, oil sheiks, or bauxite barons."[3]

The paper in Chapter Twelve lays out the model but does not put it through its paces to show the dynamic adjustment of the economy to a demand or supply shock, temporary or sustained. As a sign of the times in the 1970s, the paper feels obliged to provide a critique of the Lucas expectational-error version of New Classical Macroeconomics. Interestingly, that critique does not appear in the subsequent Chapter Thirteen, perhaps because it was written well after the demise of the Lucas model (see Chapter Seven, footnote 5). Chapter Twelve contains a brief conclusion asserting that the new framework does not free policymakers in an inflationary environment from a tradeoff, in the sense that a permanent reduction in the inflation rate requires creation of a recession "which might last for years" and create a permanent loss of wealth. It dismisses price controls on the usual allocative grounds and because controlling wages is politically infeasible, and discusses the interplay between the costs of ongoing inflation, supply shocks, and the benefits of widespread indexation.

THE "TRIANGLE" MODEL OF INFLATION

Chapter Thirteen, written in 1989, is the last paper in Part Three and provides a summary view of developments in the study of the inflation-unemployment tradeoff that had occurred since the 1960s. Since some of these developments are discussed earlier in this introduction, here the summary is limited to other aspects of Chapter Thirteen. The basic features of the inflation model developed in 1976 are in Chapter Thirteen more clearly described by the phrase "triangle model," with its three essential elements of supply shocks, demand shocks (represented by the level and change of the unemployment gap), and inertia (represented by the influence of lagged inflation on current inflation).[4] All three

as exogenous. My version eliminated the unnecessary (and inaccurate) step of assuming that velocity growth is constant.

[3] I later showed (see Chapters Seventeen and Eighteen) that changes in labor's share achieved by labor market events like, say, the French General Strike of 1968, operated exactly like oil price shocks in shifting the Phillips curve.

[4] The phrase "triangle model" originated in Gordon (1983).

sides of the triangle are equally important – the influence of supply shocks is needed to explain the twin peaks of inflation and unemployment in 1974–5 and 1979–81, the influence of demand shocks is needed to explain why inflation accelerated in the late 1960s and late 1980s, and decelerated from 1981 to 1985, and the role of inertia explains why, as a result of expectation formation and long-term contracts, inflation incorporates Keynesian rigidities and tends to adjust slowly when buffeted by shocks.

Also emphasized is the need for a dichotomy in macroeconomics between the causes of demand shocks, which the triangle model does not address, and their consequences, which it does address. Nominal GDP is taken to be exogenous ("which admittedly sweeps two thirds of macroeconomics under the rug"), and it is admitted that this practice ignores channels of feedback between inflation and nominal GDP growth, as would occur with an accommodative monetary policy. Because inertia, the third side of the triangle, sets a limit on the speed with which inflation can adjust to any supply or demand shock, the triangle model is resolutely Keynesian. Agents are implicitly price setters and quantity (demand) takers. Agents are pushed off "notional" supply and demand curves by constraints that spill over from rationed markets, that is, firms which cannot sell all they want may ration the number of jobs they offer to a number smaller than the supply of labor at the going real wage.

Chapter Thirteen emphasizes three important differences between the triangle model and pre-1974 empirical work on the Phillips curve. First, it takes a neutral view of the role of the lagged inflation variable by calling it "inertia" rather than "expectations." Much ink had been spilled on the distinction between adaptive and rational expectations, yet numerous economists later showed that price and wage inertia of the type embedded in the triangle model is compatible with rational expectations. The speed of price adjustment and the speed of expectation formation are two different issues. Price adjustment can be delayed by wage and price contracts, and by the time it takes for firms to react when notified by their suppliers of cost increases.

The second omission is to leave the unemployment rate out of the model and focus directly on the relationship between inflation and the output gap. Chapter Thirteen argues that the unemployment rate is a bad cyclical indicator, and that detrended output or the rate of capacity utilization are superior. This theme is picked up in Chapter Seventeen below, which shows the starkly different behavior of the unemployment rate and rate of capacity utilization in the late 1990s. The third and perhaps most notable omission from the triangle model is wages. By condensing the supply side of the model into a single equation in which inflation is related to lagged inflation, demand shocks, and supply shocks, the slippage between prices and wages embodied in pre-1974 econometric models is avoided. Put another way, the standard price markup equation that translated Phillips curve wage equations into inflation equations embodies an assumption that labor's share is constant in the long run, and this did not turn out to be true either in the late 1960s or the 1990s.

Chapter Thirteen concludes with some thoughts about the Phillips curve which may be more acceptable today than they were in 1989 or would have been in 1979. "Why has the Phillips curve become the black sheep of macroeconomics? Economists under the age of forty seem afraid to touch it." When Chapter Thirteen was written the Phillips curve had died out as an empirical topic, and the paper speculates that this occurred because it is not supported by a model of rational maximizing behavior by individual agents. Yet the Phillips curve is a description of an economy-wide relationship that is aggregated over millions of agents, none of whom has a reason to believe that he or she is behaving exactly like all the others.

Fortunately, my pessimism in Chapter Thirteen about the lack of widespread interest in the Phillips curve was not borne out in the 1990s. Several of the best and brightest young econometricians, particularly James Stock and Mark Watson, in a series of papers studied the inflation-output-unemployment relationship intensively during the 1990s and helped to develop new statistical tools for understanding it. As we shall see in Part Four below, when reviewing my econometric work on inflation behavior, a fruitful complementarity between my work and that of Stock and Watson emerged. They improved the statistical tools but took as their point of departure my triangle model from the early 1980s. Emerging from both their empirical work and mine was the long-lasting utility of the triangle framework. The puzzle of high inflation combined with high unemployment in the 1970s was replaced by the puzzle of low inflation combined with low unemployment in the late 1990s. An era of adverse supply shocks had been replaced by an era of beneficial supply shocks. The triangle model emerged basically intact from this challenge posed by new data.

CONCLUSION

To conclude this introduction to Part Three, we can briefly summarize the main implications of the triangle model as set forth in Chapter Thirteen. (1) Milton Friedman had written in 1963 that "inflation is always and everywhere a monetary phenomenon," but the triangle model replaces this with "always and everywhere an excess nominal GDP phenomenon." (2) There is no special connection between the growth in the money supply and inflation; any effect of money on inflation is shared by a similar effect of velocity on inflation. Stated another way, an increase in monetary growth must boost nominal GDP growth if inflation is to be impacted, and increases in monetary growth like those of 1985–6 that are accompanied by a slump in velocity growth do not cause the inflation rate to increase. (3) Fluctuations in excess nominal GDP growth lead to counterclockwise loops on a diagram plotting inflation against the output gap, due to the role of inertia in spreading out the impact of any demand or supply shock. A sharp increase in nominal GDP growth, as occurred in the mid-1960s, leads first to a rising output gap and then to a shrinking output gap, labeled then and since as "stagflation."(4) Supply shocks tend to cause negative comovements of inflation and output or positive comovements of inflation and unemployment. The triangle model interprets the "twin peaks" of inflation and unemployment in 1974–5 and 1980–2 as part of the same phenomenon as the "valley" of low inflation and unemployment in 1998–9. The mechanism was the same but operated in the opposite direction.

References

Dornbusch, Rudger, and Fischer, Stanley. *Macroeconomics*. New York: McGraw-Hill; 1978.

Gordon, Robert J. "Alternative Responses of Policy to External Supply Shocks." *Brookings Papers on Economic Activity*. 1975; vol. 6, no. 1, pp. 183–206.

Macroeconomics. Boston: Little-Brown; 1978.

"'Credibility' vs. 'Mainstream': Two Views of the Inflation Process." In Nordhaus, W.D. ed. *Inflation: Prospects and Remedies, Alternatives for the 1980's*. Center for National Policy. October, 1983; no. 10, pp. 25–34.

"Supply Shocks and Monetary Policy Revisited." *American Economic Review Papers and Proceedings*. May, 1984; vol. 74, pp. 38–43.

Macroeconomics, Ninth edition. Boston: Addison-Wesley-Longman; 2003.

Phelps, Edmund S. "Commodity-Supply Shock and Full-Employment Monetary Policy." *Journal of Money, Credit, and Banking*. May, 1978; vol. 10, pp. 206–21.

CHAPTER 10

Alternative Responses of Policy to External Supply Shocks

During 1973 and 1974 reductions in supplies of food (through natural causes) and of oil (through unnatural causes) simultaneously lowered the real income of U.S. nonfarm workers and raised the rate of inflation. An inflation-cum-recession induced by lower supplies of raw materials may call for a policy response different from the traditional tonic of demand restriction called for by a "garden-variety" inflation generated by excess demand.

In light of the novelty of the 1974 situation, the sharp divergence of policy recommendations among economists is not surprising. Some analyzed the episode within the context of standard macroeconomic demand analysis, treating the 1973–4 acceleration of inflation as a delayed consequence of the acceleration in monetary growth during 1972, and the 1974–5 recession as a delayed consequence of the sharp deceleration in monetary growth that began in June 1974. The policy advice of this group, consisting largely of economists generally identified as "monetarists," was to maintain a constant or even slightly reduced rate of growth of the money supply.[1] Arthur Okun put forth the contrasting view that an attempt by policymakers to maintain fixed growth in nominal

---

[1] See Allan Meltzer, "A Plan for Subduing Inflation" (a dialogue between Allan H. Meltzer and two editorial staff members of *Fortune*), *Fortune*, vol. 90 (September 1974), pp. 112ff. In the same month, when the money supply (M_1) had risen 5.8 percent over the preceding twelve months, Milton Friedman wrote that "until a few months ago at best, these high interest rates have been accompanied by extremely high rates of monetary growth.... Recent rates of monetary growth are not too low. If anything they are still too high to bring inflation to an end in a reasonable period of time." See Milton Friedman, "Is Money Too Tight?" *Newsweek*, vol. 84 (September 23, 1974), p. 82. Friedman's stand on monetary policy was taken despite his recognition that special factors had contributed to the 1974 inflation. He attributed roughly half of it to increases in oil and food prices, to the lifting of price controls, and to precautionary increases against renewed price controls. See Milton Friedman, "Inflation Prospects," *Newsweek*, vol. 84 (November 4, 1974), p. 84.

Note. This paper was supported by National Science Foundation Grant GS-39701. It was inspired, as was a previous paper in another area, as an attempt to reconcile the views of Milton Friedman and Arthur Okun. I am grateful to Michael Parkin and participants in the Brookings panel for helpful suggestions. (*Source.* "Alternative Responses of Policy to External Supply Shocks." *Brookings Papers on Economic Activity* 1975; vol. 6, no. 1, pp. 183–206.)

income ignored the "macroeconomic externalities" of commodity shortages: total real output falls by more than the decline in farm output, through an extra induced loss of nonfarm output.[2] An implication of Okun's argument is that, while stabilization policy cannot recreate the lost farm output, it can minimize or eliminate the induced loss of nonfarm output by promoting a higher growth rate of nominal income.

The inflation in 1973 and 1974 can be regarded as a combination of an underlying "hard-core" inflation, inherited from the 1960s and perhaps aggravated by the rapid pace of economic expansion between 1971 and 1973, with a set of four temporary "bubbles": (1) the 1972–4 shortfall of farm supplies to U.S. consumers, caused in the first two years by buoyant foreign demand and in the third by domestic supply shortages; (2) the restriction of oil production enforced by the cartel of the Organization of Petroleum Exporting Countries (OPEC); (3) the end of price and wage controls in 1974; and (4) the devaluations of the dollar in 1971 and 1973. Although these events may have permanently raised the price *level*, such a one-shot rise generates only a temporary increase in the rate of inflation.[3]

This paper deals with the issues raised by an inflation initiated not by excess demand but by commodity shortages. Although its formal analysis treats an external shock that takes the form of a decline in farm output, its basic conclusions apply with only minor changes to the cases of oil and devaluation. What policies are available to minimize the indirect effects on output? What are the conditions under which expansive policy actions taken to counteract a temporary decline in farm output will cause a permanent increase in the rate of inflation? What are the relative advantages and disadvantages of income-tax reductions, food subsidies, and expansive monetary policy as policy responses? Finally, how would universal escalation (or "indexation") of wage contracts affect the results of the analysis?

10.1   THE POLAR CASES

To establish the range of possibilities, the following two sections compare the responses of two hypothetical economies, one with perfect flexibility of prices and wages and the other with absolute rigidity in the nonfarm sector. These cases serve to illuminate the more complicated and relevant analysis of a realistic economy in which nonfarm prices and wages are neither perfectly flexible nor absolutely fixed.

---

[2] Arthur Okun, "Incomes Inflation and the Policy Alternatives," in "The Economists Conference on Inflation," September 5, 1974, Washington, D.C. A formal analysis of the externality argument is presented below.

[3] The list could perhaps be expanded by two smaller bubbles – the increases in prices in fear of reimposition of controls, and the overshooting of commodity prices beyond the levels justified by shortages due to speculative inventory hoarding.

Perfect Price Flexibility

The economy encounters no problems in adjusting to an external shock – say, a crop failure – if both farm and nonfarm prices and wages are perfectly flexible. In this case the market for nonfarm goods and labor always clears, and no involuntary unemployment can arise. A brief examination of this case serves as a point of comparison with the diametrically opposite case of fixed prices.

The treatment of all cases incorporates several common assumptions. The economy is closed, with all output of both sectors produced and consumed in the domestic economy. Farm output is exogenous, produced by a factor that is not mobile between the two sectors and consumed entirely in the nonfarm sector. The exogenous supply of farm output, Q_F, is equated to the demand:

$$Q_F = AQ_N{}^{a_0} \left(\frac{P_F}{P_N} \right)^{-a_1},$$

(1)

where A is a constant, a_0 is the nonfarm income elasticity of demand for farm products, a_1 is the absolute value of the price elasticity (which throughout the paper is assumed to be less than unity), and P_F and P_N are, respectively, price indexes for farm and nonfarm output. A rearrangement of (1) relates the market-clearing relative price, P_F/P_N, to the exogenous supply of farm output and the level of nonfarm output, Q_N:

$$\frac{P_F}{P_N} = \left[\frac{AQ_N{}^{a_0}}{Q_F} \right]^{1/a_1}.$$

(2)

For any given supply of farm products, an increase in nonfarm output raises the demand for farm products, and hence the relative price, by an amount that depends positively on the income elasticity, a_0, and negatively on the price elasticity, a_1. The relative price depends, in part, on the level of nonfarm output, except in the special case of a zero income elasticity.

Nonfarm output is assumed to be produced with labor and some other fixed factor, like capital. Knowledge and technology is assumed fixed, so that labor input determines nonfarm output. Given the population, if the supply of labor does not respond to changes in the real wage, both labor input and nonfarm output are fixed. In this case, a crop failure changes the relative price of farm products but not the level of nonfarm output. Since the wage rate that nonfarm firms can afford to pay to a given number of workers is limited by nonfarm prices, any increase in the relative price of farm products reduces the real wage of workers, when the latter is defined in terms of a consumer price index including both farm and nonfarm products.

If, however, a lower real wage causes workers to reduce their labor input, either by withdrawing from the labor force or by working fewer hours per week, a crop failure must reduce nonfarm output.[4] This response in the nonfarm labor

---

[4] A third case, not discussed here, is a negatively sloped labor supply curve. Most cross-section evidence for the United States appears to support a vertical curve for adult male workers, a

market thus provides a second relationship between nonfarm output and the relative price of farm products, in addition to equation (2) above, allowing the simultaneous determination of both variables.[5] Hence, output and relative prices in each sector are beyond the control of policymakers. If the choices of individuals between leisure and labor are socially accepted, any reduction in employment caused by the voluntary withdrawal of labor input in response to a lower real wage is of no concern for stabilization policy, since that reduction is purely voluntary.

What, if anything, can stabilization policy accomplish when nonfarm prices are perfectly flexible? Aggregate-demand policy controls the level of nominal income (that is, gross national product in current dollars), which is sufficient to set the nominal nonfarm price level since the values of all real variables have been determined. If policymakers follow a rule that calls for constant nominal income, then a crop failure must cause nominal nonfarm prices to fall, but the overall average price level must rise.[6] If, on the other hand, policymakers achieve constant overall prices by reducing nominal income, they would prevent a redistribution of income from creditors and pensioners to debtors. Even if the expected rate of inflation and the level of the interest rate are unaffected, the higher the price level, the smaller the fraction of income a debtor will require to service his debts.

Whether or not the labor supply shrinks in the flexible-price case, the welfare of nonfarm workers is reduced.[7] Not only does a crop failure reduce total real output, but also, as long as the demand for farm products is price inelastic, it transfers income from workers to farmers, who enjoy a windfall. While the problem is not one of stabilization, society might wish to reduce or eliminate the transfer by a redistributive tax policy that, for example, levies a windfall-profits tax on farmers to finance a subsidy on nonfarm products purchased by nonfarm workers. However, the case for redistributive tax-subsidy schemes is not obvious, nor is there an obvious line between temporary events justifying redistribution and those that do not.

---

positively sloped response of women and teenagers to an increase in their own real wage, and a negative response of wives to an increase in their husbands' real wage. See the evidence cited in Robert J. Gordon, "The Welfare Cost of Higher Unemployment," *BPEA* (1:1973), Table 2, p. 159.

[5] The exact form of the second relationship is:

$$Q_N = D \left(\frac{kP_F}{P_N} + 1 - k \right)^{-e(b-1)/(b+e)},$$

where D is a constant, k is the share of farm products in consumer expenditures, and b and e are, respectively, the elasticities of the nonfarm labor demand and supply curves.

[6] The nonfarm price level falls if the price elasticity of demand for farm products is (approximately) less than unity; the overall price level must rise, because real output has fallen and nominal income is assumed constant.

[7] Although workers who reduce labor input obtain leisure worth the real wage at the margin, they lose part of their producers' surplus earned on inframarginal units of work. In parallel fashion, farmers gain a producers' surplus from the increase in the relative price of their output.

Complete Wage and Price Rigidity

In the case of perfect price flexibility, nonfarm output is either fixed or determined by workers' decisions about labor supply, leaving the nonfarm price level to be determined by stabilization policy. If, on the other hand, the nonfarm wage rate is rigid and nonfarm prices are "marked up" over the wage rate by a constant fraction, then nonfarm prices are fixed and nonfarm real output is determined by stabilization policy.

Nominal income, Y, is the sum of total nominal spending in each sector:

$$Y = P_F Q_F + P_N Q_N; \tag{3}$$

equation (2) can be substituted into (3) to obtain

$$Y/P_N = \left[A Q_N{}^{a_0} Q_F{}^{-(1-a_1)} \right]^{(1/a_1)} + Q_N. \tag{4}$$

When nominal income is held fixed by a policy rule, the wage rate and nonfarm prices are rigid, and the demand for farm products is income and price inelastic ($a_0 < 1$ and $a_1 < 1$), then nonfarm output varies in the same direction as farm output, *even if the supply of nonfarm labor is completely unresponsive to changes in the real wage*. Since the value of farm output rises and nominal income is fixed, the value of nonfarm output must fall. With nonfarm prices rigid, nonfarm output must drop, causing involuntary unemployment. The crop failure thus carries with it a real "multiplier" effect. Just as stabilization policy can alter nominal nonfarm spending and the price level of the nonfarm sector in the flexible-price case, so it can alter that sector's nominal spending, real output, and employment in the rigid-wage case.

In this extreme case, the multiplier can be derived when the market-clearing condition for farm output, (2) above, is written in the form of percentage changes:

$$p_F - p_N = \frac{-q_F + a_0 q_N}{a_1}, \tag{5}$$

where lower-case ps and qs denote percentage changes between the initial situation and the new situation after the crops have failed:

$$P_F = (P_{F_1} - P_{F_0})/P_{F_0}.$$

If policymakers hold nominal income constant, the change of nominal income – that is, a weighted average of spending in the two sectors as defined in (3) above – must be zero:

$$y = 0 = k(p_F + q_F) + (1 - k)(p_N + q_N), \tag{6}$$

where k is the share of farm spending in total spending. Substituting (5) into (6) yields, after some rearrangement, the percentage change in nonfarm output relative to the exogenous change in farm output:

$$\frac{q_N}{q_F} = \frac{k(1 - a_1)}{k a_0 + (1 - k) a_1}. \tag{7}$$

To take a simple example, assume that the initial share of expenditure in the farm sector, k, is 10 percent, and that the income and price elasticities are, respectively, zero and 20 percent ($a_0 = 0$ and $a_1 = 0.2$). In this case the elasticity of nonfarm output to a change in farm output is 4/9. With initial levels of expenditure of $100 billion and $900 billion in the two sectors, a 10 percent loss in farm output ($10 billion) causes a 4.44 percent decline in nonfarm output ($40 billion). Thus the social cost, C, of the $10 billion crop failure is

$$C = -[kq_F + (1-k)q_N]Y = \frac{-kq_F Y}{a_1} \tag{8}$$

$$= \frac{\$10 \text{ billion}}{0.2} = \$50 \text{ billion}.$$

Since the nonfarm price level is rigid, policymakers can fully offset the multiplier effect of the crop failure on nonfarm output with no deleterious side effects. Nominal income must simply increase sufficiently to leave nonfarm output unchanged by the crop failure. This "fully accommodating" policy response can be calculated from (6) when q_N (as well as p_N) is equal to zero:

$$y = k(p_F + q_F) = -q_F \frac{k(1-a_1)}{a_1}. \tag{9}$$

With the parameters of the previous example, nominal income should be raised by 4 percent – $40 billion – to counteract the $40 billion loss of nonfarm output that would have occurred had nominal income been allowed to remain fixed.

The consumer price index, an average of the fixed nonfarm price and the higher farm price, must rise, and policymakers cannot avoid accepting this higher overall price level, just as they cannot re-create the lost crops.[8] But stabilization policy *can* eliminate the wasteful "multiplier" loss in nonfarm output and associated involuntary nonfarm unemployment by providing enough extra nominal income to make room for both the original level of nonfarm spending (fixed price and initial real output) and the higher level of spending on farm products.[9]

---

[8] A positive value for the income elasticity of demand for farm products reduces the multiplier, since lower nonfarm output moderates the increase in the relative price needed to clear the farm output market, and this in turn releases more of the fixed level of nominal income for the support of nonfarm output. When $a_0 = 0.2$, the elasticity of nonfarm output is reduced from 4.44 to 4.0 percent, the social cost from $50 billion to $46 billion, and the necessary nominal income offset from $40 billion to $36 billion.

[9] Nonfarm output might have fallen as in the flexible-price case if the supply of labor were voluntarily reduced in response to the lower real wage.

10.2 PARTIAL PRICE ADJUSTMENT

No Cost-of-Living Effect on Wages

At this point the policymaker is torn between the conflicting advice of the flexible-price model, which recommends a *reduction* in nominal income to stabilize the price level, and that of the rigid-price model, which recommends an *increase* in nominal income to avoid involuntary unemployment. The simplest intermediate model allows the rate of change of nonfarm prices (p_N, where small letters now denote percentage changes per unit of time) to adjust by a fraction, λ, of the difference between the market-clearing value of the flexible price, $\hat{P}_N$, and the current price, P_N:

$$p_N = \lambda(\hat{P}_N - P_N). \tag{10}$$

When nominal income is held constant, $\hat{P}_N$ during the period of the crop failure lies below the initial nonfarm prices level (P_{N_0}) and the rate of change of nonfarm prices is negative until they are brought into line with $\hat{P}_N$. Since P_{N_0} lies above the market-clearing value, $\hat{P}_N$, the initial consequence of the crop failure is a decline in nonfarm output and the creation of involuntary unemployment, as in the rigid-price analysis of the previous section. Through time, however, downward adjustment of the nonfarm price level makes more of nominal income available for nonfarm output, and the severity of the recession is gradually mitigated. Finally, P_N ends its decline when it reaches its market-clearing level, $\hat{P}_N$, at which point involuntary unemployment is eliminated. The process is reversed when the crops return to normal; at the low nonfarm price level, $\hat{P}_N$, the constant level of nominal income allows nonfarm output to rise above its initial value, and an output and employment "boom" continues until P_N has returned to P_{N_0}.

The temporary recession, as well as the subsequent temporary boom in output, can be eliminated, as described in the previous section, by a policy of accommodating nominal income. If nominal income is raised by the amount calculated in equation (9), the market-clearing value of $\hat{P}_N$ during the period of the crop failure is by definition equal to the initial price level, P_{N_0}, and no downward adjustment in nonfarm prices takes place. Now a policy of accommodating nominal income imposes on society the cost of a higher price level than one that aims at constant nominal income, and a more substantial (albeit temporary) redistribution from creditors and pensioners to debtors. The choice between the policies has no long-run consequences for the level of prices or output, or for the rate of inflation.[10]

---

[10] Such consequences might ensue to the extent that the recession-inducing policy cuts real investment and thus endows future generations with a lower capital stock.

Some Cost-of-Living Effects on Wages

The previous section assumes that higher farm prices have no direct effect on nonfarm wages and prices, and thus ignores the possibility that a policy of accommodating nominal income may permanently increase the rate of inflation. As a point of departure for developing a more realistic mechanism for adjusting nonfarm prices, which allows for the possibility of an equilibrium nonzero inflation rate, (10) may be reformulated as

$$p_N = p_N^* + jZ, \tag{11}$$

where p_N^* is the rate of change of the expected nonfarm price level, Z is the excess demand for labor, and j is an adjustment coefficient. Assume that the expected level of nonfarm prices remains constant ($p_N^* = 0$) after a crop failure. Then, so long as the price level is above its market-clearing value – $P_N > \hat{P}_N$ in (10) – the resulting involuntary nonfarm unemployment means that $Z < 0$ in (11).

Equation (11) is simply an "expectational Phillips curve," the properties of which have received extensive analysis and empirical testing in recent years. A slightly more complicated but substantially more realistic version can be developed if (ignoring productivity change) it is assumed that the rate of growth of the wage rate, w, is equal to that of the expected price level plus a fraction, j, of the excess demand for labor, Z:

$$w = p^* + jZ. \tag{12}$$

The expected price level relevant for wage decisions is a weighted average of the expected nonfarm price, P_N^*, which defines the value of labor's marginal product, and the expected consumer price index, P_C^*, adjusted for the payroll-tax factor, T^*, used by workers to calculate their real after-tax wage rate. Thus (12) becomes[11]

$$w = g(p_C^* + t^*) + (1 - g)p_N^* + jZ. \tag{13}$$

When the coefficient g is greater than zero, the wage rate depends not only on the nonfarm product price, but also on farm prices and the payroll tax rate. In the extreme case, when g has a value of unity, all of the increase in consumer prices relative to nonfarm product prices resulting from a crop failure is passed through to the wage rate, and real wages do not fall. When the wage equation is interpreted as the adjustment path in a neoclassical model of the labor market, the parameter g is the ratio of the elasticity of the labor supply curve to the sum of that elasticity and the elasticity of the demand curve, and is zero when the

---

[11] Equation (13) has been estimated in Robert J. Gordon, "Inflation in Recession and Recovery," *BPEA* (1:1971), Table 1, equation (11). The equation has also been used in empirical work for the United Kingdom by Michael Parkin and his collaborators and has been derived explicitly in Michael Parkin, Michael T. Sumner, and R. Ward, "The Effects of Excess Demand, Generalized Expectations, and Wage-Price Controls on Wage Inflation in the U.K." In Karl Brunner (ed.), a conference volume on controls (Amsterdam: North-Holland, 1975), forthcoming.

supply of labor does not respond to changes in the real wage.[12] But in alternative labor market settings the value of g might be nonzero even if labor were supplied inelastically. In unionized industries, for instance, the strike weapon might be used to pass through some or all of an increase in farm prices in higher wages. Quite apart from unions, competitive firms might offer risk-averse employees a wage contract indexed to the consumer price index, trading this real-wage insurance for a reduction in the average real wage.[13] The following analysis will discuss the consequences of different values of g as though they result from an expectational mechanism in wage bargaining, but the interpretation could readily be adapted to cover other cases.

An equation for the price of output in the nonfarm sector is now required. In line with considerable evidence, the nonfarm price level is set as a "markup fraction" multiplied by "standard" unit labor cost – that is, the wage rate divided by productivity at some "standard" level of capacity utilization – with the size of the markup fraction dependent on the demand for commodities.[14] Assuming a constant level of standard productivity (equal to 1.0), the price equation becomes

$$P_N = W X^c, \tag{14}$$

where X is an index of excess commodity demand and c is the percentage response of the inflation rate to the rate of growth of output.

When the wage and price equations are combined with the definition of consumer prices,

$$P_C = P_F^k P_N^{(1-k)}, \tag{15}$$

a relationship between changes in nonfarm and farm prices is obtained:

$$p_N = (1 - gk)p_N^* + g(kp_F^* + t^*) + jZ + cx. \tag{16}$$

As in equation (11), the basic force that allows involuntary unemployment to persist is the partial downward adjustment of prices in the face of excess labor (and commodity) supply. What difference is made by a value of g greater than zero? The analysis is identical to that of (11), of course, if the expected farm price is unaffected by a temporary increase in the actual level. On the other hand, a crop failure may lead individuals to revise upward the level of farm

---

[12] A more complex version with several varieties of taxes, cyclical variations in productivity growth, and other complications, is analyzed in Robert J. Gordon, "Interrelations between Domestic and International Theories of Inflation." In R. Z. Aliber (ed.), *The Political Economy of Monetary Reform* (1977).

[13] The idea of "wage insurance" as an explanation of rigid wages was developed simultaneously and independently by C. Azariadis, "Implicit Contracts and Underemployment Equilibria," *Journal of Political Economy*, December 1975, vol. 83, no. 6, pp. 1183–1202; Martin N. Baily, "Wages and Employment under Uncertain Demand," *Review of Economic Studies*, January 1974, vol. 41, pp. 37–50; and Donald F. Gordon, "A Neo-Classical Theory of Keynesian Unemployment," in Karl Brunner and Allan Meltzer (eds.), *The Phillips Curve and Public Policy*, Carnegie-Rochester Conference Series, vol. 1, Amsterdam: North-Holland, 1975.

[14] See the evidence presented in Gordon, "Inflation in Recession and Recovery," p. 129.

prices that they expect during their wage contracts (in 1972–4, U.S. domestic food consumers had "three lean years"). In this case a "wage push" is exerted by farm prices, which raises the nonfarm price level above the adjustment path described by (10) and (11), in turn "using up" more of the fixed level of nominal income, raising the multiplier, and aggravating the recession.

If g is positive and if expected farm prices respond to the higher actual level, the results depend on how expectations adjust to price changes in the nonfarm sector. One possibility is that expectations adapt to past changes in nonfarm prices. The expected *level* of nonfarm prices for the next period would then be set equal to the current level extrapolated by an expected rate of nonfarm inflation estimated from its past rate. Just after a crop failure, such adaptive nonfarm expectations would worsen inflation, since nonfarm price expectations would be raised in response to the higher current price level caused by the feed through of farm prices to wages.[15] And, if nominal income is held constant, the higher level of nonfarm prices worsens the initial stages of the recession. But soon the adjustment of nonfarm price expectations would begin to operate in the opposite direction, reducing inflation and the magnitude of the recession, since it would amplify the downward adjustment of nonfarm wages and prices in response to excess labor supply.

In short, adaptive nonfarm price expectations amplify the fluctuations in nonfarm output and prices in response to a crop failure as long as nominal income is held constant. If, on the other hand, policymakers pursue a fully accommodating policy for nominal income, which prevents the emergence of excess labor supply, adaptive expectations raise expected nonfarm prices – the "base" around which the adjustment of prices takes place – and endow the economy with a permanently higher price *level*. So long as the crop failure is temporary, the rate of inflation is not permanently affected, since the decline in farm prices at the end of the failure feeds through to expectations and ends the upward adjustment of expected nonfarm prices. But an accommodating policy for nominal income *would* permanently raise the rate of inflation in the case of a permanent supply reduction, brought about, for example, by an eternal oil cartel.

The Potential for Tax Policy

In any realistic case, a policy accommodating nominal income (such as an increase in the money supply sufficient to eliminate the nonfarm multiplier effect of a crop failure) has the disadvantage of raising the price level relative to

---

[15] Corresponding to (7) above is a multiplier formula that takes into account the feedthrough of farm prices to wages (but not the effect on prices of excess labor or commodity supply):

$$\frac{q_N}{q_F} = \left\{ \frac{k[(1-a_1)(1-gk)+g]}{a_0gk + [ka_0 + (1-k)a_1](1-gk)]} \right\}.$$

Compared to the case $a_1 = 0.2$, $a_0 = 0.2$, and $g = 0$, which yields an elasticity of 0.4, the 0.2 value for g (assumed in the simulation below) increases the elasticity to 0.492.

an alternative policy aimed at constant nominal income. Changes in tax rates and subsidies, on the other hand, not only operate on income but also can directly alter the price level. A reduction in the payroll tax rate, for instance, narrows the "wedge" between market prices and after-tax factor cost, and hence allows firms to charge a lower price while paying workers the same after-tax wage rate. Along with a reduction in tax rates, policymakers must take steps (cutting government expenditures or the money stock, for example) to maintain, as I shall assume, an unchanged path of nominal income.[16]

A reduction in taxes will lower consumer prices most if applied to those taxes whose burden is borne by consumers rather than factors of production. At one extreme, changes in state sales taxes are probably shifted forward to consumer prices by nearly 100 percent, while at the other extreme, changes in the corporation income tax affect mainly capital income and do not appear to be substantially shifted forward.[17] The personal income tax is an intermediate case and appears to be shifted forward to consumers by roughly 20 percent.[18] In the absence of a universal federal sales tax, the policy option that would yield the greatest reduction in prices for a given loss of revenue would be a federal government bribe to induce reductions in state and local sales taxes. If this mechanism were rejected as administratively clumsy or politically infeasible, the federal government could subsidize *nonfarm* output to offset the impact of the higher farm prices on the consumer price index.[19] A constant nominal income would thereby be sufficient for both the higher farm-price level needed to clear that market *and* the original level of nonfarm output, since the after-subsidy nonfarm price would be pushed down to the market-clearing level, $\hat{P}_N$. The size of the required subsidy relative to GNP is given by equation (9) – for instance, $40 billion in the simple example spelled out above.

Possibly, such a subsidy could be financed by a windfall-profits tax on farmers if society felt this temporary event justified income redistribution. Another alternative would be bond finance, which would redistribute income from future generations to present ones. Still another solution would be the establishment of a "price stabilization fund" that would pay nonfarm subsidies in years of low farm production, financed by a nonfarm sales tax in years of bumper crops and low farm prices.[20] Symmetric supply fluctuations would allow this

---

[16] In principle, if no offsetting action is taken, the price level may be either raised or lowered. See Alan S. Blinder, "Can Income Tax Increases Be Inflationary? An Expository Note," *National Tax Journal*, vol. 26 (June 1973), pp. 295–301.

[17] Robert J. Gordon, "The Incidence of the Corporation Income Tax in U.S. Manufacturing, 1925–62," *American Economic Review*, vol. 57 (September 1967), pp. 731–58.

[18] See Gordon, "Inflation in Recession and Recovery," Table 1, where the tax coefficient refers to the personal income tax plus the social security tax paid by employees.

[19] A subsidy for farm products would raise demand above the reduced supply and hence would be infeasible without a commodity inventory or buffer stock. A subsidy for nonfarm products would not require higher nonfarm output than initially, but would simply offset the multiplier effect and allow the original full employment level of nonfarm output to be maintained.

[20] Inventories of farm products are ruled out by the assumption that the supply shock is sufficiently severe to exhaust them.

remedy, but asymmetric events like those engendered by the OPEC oil cartel would not.

The Inflationary Consequences of an Accommodating Policy

A nonfarm subsidy appears to be almost ideal in principle, eliminating involuntary nonfarm unemployment and averting most (but not all) of the increase in consumer prices.[21] But its rapid implementation may pose administrative or political issues, and its financing raises difficult problems. An alternative is an accommodating policy for nominal income, which could eliminate involuntary nonfarm unemployment at the cost of a higher price level.

A rough numerical estimate of these inflationary consequences is presented in Figure 10.1. A simple model has been simulated to illustrate the consequences of a hypothetical 10 percent decline in farm output lasting twelve quarters. The model consists of the farm market-clearing equation (2) combined with the nonfarm price adjustment equation (16). The simulated response of the rate of wage increase to excess labor supply is relatively slight, as U.S. evidence suggests, but excess commodity demand is assumed to have a substantial impact on nonfarm prices relative to wages. Other parameters are identical to those used in the multiplier examples in the previous section (details are spelled out in the appendix).

The "basic" simulation, A, illustrated by the solid line in Figure 10.1, shows that a crop failure accompanied by a policy of constant nominal income creates a recession, the severity of which gradually eases as nonfarm prices adjust downward in response to excess supply. The "optimistic accommodation" simulation, B, assumes that policymakers raise nominal income to maintain the original level of nonfarm output and that the expected level of farm prices is adjusted upward to the higher actual farm price, but that individuals maintain their expectations about nonfarm prices. The "pessimistic accommodation" simulation, C, assumes that the expected level of nonfarm prices is adjusted adaptively to *all* changes in actual nonfarm prices, whether associated with temporary or permanent events. Simulation B illustrates that an accommodating policy buys full employment at the cost of a *temporary* increase in the price level and in the rate of inflation; but it permits more deflation after the crops return to normal, leaving the consumer price index the same ten years after the initial shock. In simulation C, the inflation *rate* increases by more than it does in the optimistic case but nevertheless temporarily; the consumer price index is permanently increased by almost 4 percent as the result of the gradual upward adjustment of the expected rate of nonfarm inflation during the period of the crop failure.

The Consequences of Wage Indexing

The computer simulation program can also be used to evaluate the consequences of an external shock for an economy in which wages are indexed. Wage indexing can be represented by a new wage equation to replace (13):

[21] See footnote 6, this chapter.

Base = 1.00

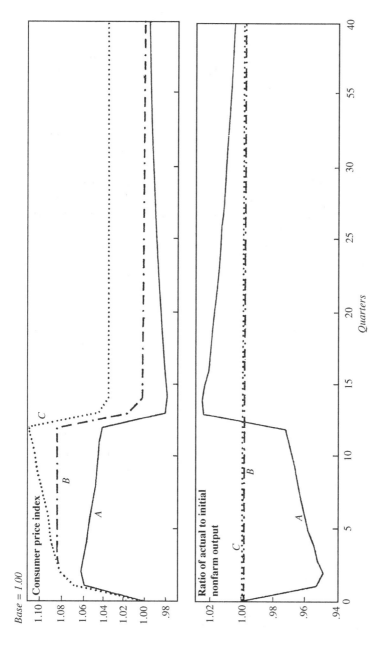

Figure 10.1. Effects on Prices and Output Ratios over a Ten-Year Period of a 10 Percent, Twelve-Quarter Drop in Farm Output[a]

[a] The curves represent the results of simulations as follows: *A* assumes fixed nominal income and fixed nonfarm price expectations; *B* assumes accommodating nominal income and fixed nonfarm price expectations; *C* assumes accommodating nominal income and adaptive nonfarm price expectations.

Source. Author's simulation.

$$w = p_C + jZ. \tag{17}$$

The rate of change of the real wage rate ($w - p_C$) now depends only on excess labor demand. By increasing the stability of the real wage, wage indexing makes wages and prices more responsive and real output less responsive to "nominal" shocks – that is, variations in monetary growth. At the same time, however, the built-in rigidity of the real wage impedes the economy's adjustment to "real" shocks, which require a change in the real wage.[22] In (17) the reduction in the real wage needed to clear the market for farm output calls for a deeper recession with indexing than without.

Figure 10.2 contrasts the path of the consumer price index and nonfarm output in the basic nonindexed simulation *A* from Figure 10.1 with two indexing simulations. The behavior of the wage rate under indexing is represented by (17), adjusted to make the current rate of wage change equal to the rate of change of the CPI in the *previous* period, adjusted for that period's excess labor demand. Curve *D* in Figure 10.2 traces the effects of wage indexing when policymakers hold nominal income constant. The increase in farm prices during the crop failure feeds through much more completely to wages and nonfarm prices when wages are indexed, using up more of the fixed nominal income and requiring a much more substantial decline in real output (reaching a maximum of nearly 15 percent) than in the basic simulation. Eventually, the deep recession brings down the price level, freeing more of nominal income to support real output. When the crop failure ends, a very large excess demand for labor develops. In short, wage indexing makes both prices and unemployment substantially less stable when nominal income is held constant in the presence of an external supply shock.

As before, policymakers can raise nominal income to accommodate both higher farm prices and the original level of nonfarm output. But this policy has very serious inflationary consequences under wage indexing, since it prevents the emergence of the excess labor supply required in the lagged version of (17) to lower the real wage. As illustrated by curve *E* in Figure 10.2, the result is a geometric increase in the consumer price index (a steady 6.0 percent *quarterly* rate of inflation) until farm output returns to its initial level in the thirteenth quarter, by which time the consumer price index has doubled. Only a bumper crop or a policy-induced recession can reverse the process and bring the consumer price index back down.

10.3 SUMMARY AND CONCLUSIONS

This essay analyzes the response of a simple two-sector economy to a decline in output in an external sector where the price is assumed to clear markets. Its

---

[22] The sentence summarizes the major conclusion of Joanna Gray in "Wage Indexation: A Macroeconomic Approach" (1976).

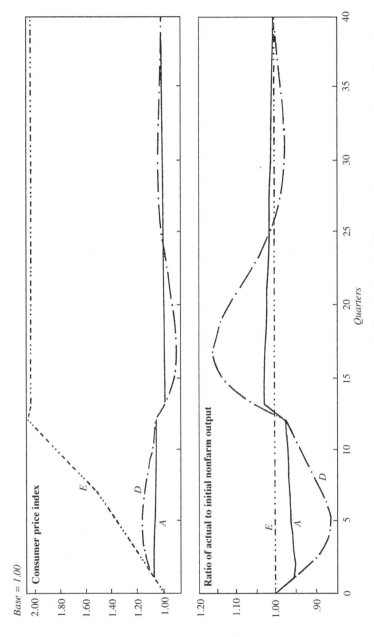

Base = 1.00

Consumer price index

Ratio of actual to initial nonfarm output

Quarters

Figure 10.2. Effects on Prices and Output Ratios over a Ten-Year Period of a 10 Percent, Twelve-Quarter Drop in Farm Output with Wage Indexing[a]

[a] The curves represent the results of simulations as follows: *A* assumes fixed nominal income and no indexing; *D* assumes fixed nominal income and lagged wage indexing; *E* assumes accommodating nominal income and lagged wage indexing.

Source. Equation (17), with adjustments as described in the text.

major conclusions are, first, that no problems arise if wages and prices in the internal sector instantly fall to clear the market. Any reduction in employment is purely voluntary. The optimal policy is a *reduction* in nominal income to hold the aggregate price index constant and avoid a temporary increase in its level.

Second, when nonfarm wage and price levels are absolutely rigid, and when nominal income is held fixed, the supply reduction in the external sector has a multiplier effect, causing a recession and involuntary unemployment in the internal sector. The "social cost" of the supply reduction then exceeds the value of lost external output by the value of the nonfarm output that is squeezed out. The optimal policy is an *increase* in nominal income designed to accommodate both the higher external price level and the original level of internal output; a temporary increase in the aggregate price level cannot be avoided since the internal price level is fixed.

Third, when wages and prices are partially responsive to excess labor and commodity demand but wages do not respond directly to higher external prices, the initial effect of the external supply reduction is the same as in the rigid-price case. If nominal income is held constant, a recession will continue until the nonfarm price has fallen to its market-clearing level. As in the rigid-price case, the recession can be avoided by an accommodating policy for nominal income, which temporarily (but not permanently) raises the price level compared with the case when nominal income is held constant.

Fourth, when wages and prices are partially responsive to excess labor and commodity demand, and in addition external prices feed through directly to wages, the inflation and recession caused by the external supply shock are both aggravated. A policy aimed at an accommodating nominal income raises the price level temporarily but not permanently higher than would one of nonaccommodation *if* expectations of the nonfarm price level do *not* extrapolate the inflation that occurs during the period of the supply reduction. On the other hand, adaptive nonfarm expectations would cause the price level (but not the rate of inflation) to remain permanently higher when an accommodating policy is pursued. Moreover, in the event of a permanent reduction in supply (such as one enforced by an unbreakable oil cartel), a policy of accommodating nominal income would raise permanently the rate of inflation of the consumer price index.

For the case of the temporary crop failure, a superior policy in principle would be a subsidy to nonfarm products that would avert both the recession entailed by nonaccommodation, and the higher price level required by accommodation. The major obstacles to a subsidy are the administrative and political difficulties of its prompt implementation, and the costs of financing it.

Finally, the analysis of this paper raises serious questions about the merits of the full indexation of wage contracts, which would shorten the lag in the adjustment of wages to changes in external prices and would thus inhibit the decline in the real wage required by an external supply shock. If policymakers attempt to stabilize nominal income in a wage-indexed economy, any external shock will destabilize both prices and output more than it would in an unindexed economy. Any attempt to accommodate the higher prices by raising nominal income under indexing will impose on the economy a substantially higher inflation rate for the duration of the external supply reduction. These disadvantages of wage indexation seem to me persuasive, but do not weaken my previously stated support for fully indexed government bonds, tax exemptions, and tax brackets.

Appendix
Model Used for Simulations

In this description of the model, superscripts refer to sectors, and subscripts to time periods. (The basic parameter assumptions and their justifications are listed at the end of this appendix.) Farm output, Q_t^F, depends on its base-period level, adjusted by a percentage crop failure, v:

$$Q_t^F = (1 - v)Q_0^F. \tag{A-1}$$

From (2) in the text,

$$P_t^F = P_{t-1}^N \left[A\left(Q_t^N\right)^{a_0} / Q_t^F \right]^{1/a_1}. \tag{A-2}$$

From (13),

$$w_t = p_t^{N*} + jZ_{t-1} + g\left(kp_t^F + t\right), \tag{A-3}$$

where the expected farm prices and the tax rate are set at their actual values, and the symbols are as defined in the text equations. With the rate of growth of output as a proxy for the rate of growth of excess commodity demand, from (14):

$$p_t^N = w_t + cq_{t-1}^N. \tag{A-4}$$

The consumer price index is

$$P_t^C = kP_t^F + (1 - k)P_t^N. \tag{A-5}$$

(I have omitted equations that convert levels to rates of growth, and vice versa.) When expectations are adaptive, the expected level of nonfarm prices is extrapolated from the actual level of the previous period by an expected inflation rate that is a distributed lag of past inflation rates, with weights from my "Inflation in Recession and Recovery," Table A-1, truncated to the first ten values and constrained to add to unity:

$$P_{t+1}^{N*} = P_t^N \left(1 + \sum_{i=1}^{10} u_i p_{t-i}^N \right), \tag{A-6}$$

where the u_i, are the weights. The expected farm price level, P_t^{F*}, is always equal to its actual value, P_t^F.

In the simulations that hold nominal income, Y_t, constant, the level of non-farm output is a residual, and labor demand fluctuates by a fraction, n, of the change in output, while labor supply is assumed constant:

$$Q_t^N = \left(Y_0 - P_t^F Q_t^F\right)/P_t^N; \tag{A-7}$$

therefore, the excess demand for labor, Z_t, is

$$Z_t = Z_{t-1}\left(1 + nq_t^N\right). \tag{A-8}$$

In the simulations that vary nominal income to hold real nonfarm output constant, (A-7) and (A-8) are replaced by

$$Y_t = P_t^F Q_t^F + P_t^N Q_0^N, \tag{A-9}$$

and

$$Z_t = 0. \tag{A-10}$$

In the simulations of wage indexing, (A-3) is replaced by

$$w_t = p_{t-1}^C + jZ_{t-1}. \tag{A-11}$$

The basic parameter assumptions and their justifications are as follows:

a_1, the price elasticity of demand for farm products, is 0.2, a value suggested to the author by Dale E. Hathaway. Hathaway also suggested 0.2 as a value for the income elasticity, a_0.

v, the percentage reduction in farm output, is 0.10, an arbitrary choice.

j, the percentage change in wage growth for a change of 1 percentage point in the excess demand for labor, is set equal to 0.13, to correspond to the more pessimistic assumption in Tobin's recent *BPEA* paper.[23] (Note, however, that Tobin allows for no reaction in the price equation.)

g, the response of wage change to changes in farm prices, is 0.2, roughly consistent with my evidence in "Inflation in Recession and Recovery," Figure 10.1.

c, the percentage response of the inflation rate to the rate of growth of output, holding wage growth constant, is 0.15. This implies that a 10 percent reduction of output relative to trend reduces the price-wage ratio by 1.5 percent. This is somewhat larger than the 1 percent estimate implied by the coefficient on the

---

[23] James Tobin, "Monetary Policy in 1974 and Beyond," *BPEA* (1:1974), pp. 229–30.

ratio of unfilled orders to capacity in "Inflation in Recession and Recovery," because of my finding in after research that the transactions prices of producers' durable goods are flexible relative to the list prices used in that earlier paper.

k, the share of the farm sector in initial spending, is 0.10, an arbitrary choice.

n, the share of a change in output taking the form of a change in labor input, is set at 0.5, allowing half of the output fluctuation to be reflected in productivity.

CHAPTER 11

Supply Shocks and Monetary
Policy Revisited

A macroeconomic supply "disturbance" or "shock" is any event which creates an autonomous shift in the aggregate supply curve relating the economywide price level to the level of output or utilization. The autonomous nature of such shifts distinguishes them from other movements in the supply curve that represent the consequences of a current or prior changes in aggregate demand. The distinction between supply and demand shocks is valid only with reference to their *origin*, whereas the *consequences* of supply shocks for output and inflation depend fundamentally on the aggregate demand policies that are pursued in their wake.

This paper was written almost a decade after the first attempts in 1974 to develop a theory of policy response to supply shocks.[1] It provides a simple algebraic framework that facilitates a summary of the central issues posed by supply shocks for macroeconomic policy. Primary emphasis is placed on the case for and against monetary accommodation, on the nature and extent of wage indexation, and on the distinction between permanent and transitory shocks. A tight space constraint precludes more than passing mention of cost-oriented fiscal policy, oil tariffs, buffer stocks, and other policies that mainly influence the magnitude of the shocks themselves rather than their consequences for macroeconomic performance. Given the difficult trade-offs faced by monetary policy-makers considering the merits of accommodation, these supply-side alternatives may actually represent the best available policy options. The first line of defense against a real disturbance is a real policy.

---

[1] Edmund S. Phelps (1978, p. 206) lists the 1974 conferences at which he and I independently developed what Edward Gramlich later called the "Gordon-Phelps model." I discovered after writing this paper that Stanley Fischer (1983) developed an analysis that is compatible with my Section I but is both more complex and more general.

Note. This research has been supported by the National Science Foundation. I am grateful to Robert Flood for helpful discussion, and to Glenn Hubbard and Allan Meltzer for comments on a first draft. (*Source.* "Supply Shocks and Monetary Policy Revisited." *American Economic Review Papers and Proceedings*. May 1984; vol. 74, no. 2, pp. 38–43.)

11.1   A SIMPLIFIED HYBRID MODEL

The original case for the monetary accommodation of an adverse supply shock, as developed by my 1975a paper and by Edmund Phelps, rests on a "macroeconomic externality," that is, a spillover from the unavoidable loss of output in the shocked sector of the economy to a loss of output in the unshocked sector that may be avoidable by monetary accommodation. The case for accommodation is strongest in a model with rigid or sluggishly adjusting nominal wages in the unshocked sector, is weaker in the presence of partial wage indexation, and is nonexistent in the presence of complete wage indexation or instantaneous market clearing achieved by perfectly flexible wages. Here I set out a hybrid model, sharing Phelps's one-sector production technology with my exogenous nominal *GNP* assumption, that allows the analysis of macroeconomic externalities and monetary accommodation to be presented in a more transparent fashion than in the two original papers.

Consider an economy that produces output (Q) using only labor (N) and a raw material (σ):

$$Q = F(N, \sigma), \quad F_N > 0, F_\sigma > 0. \tag{1}$$

The supply of labor in the economy is fixed at N^*, and so "natural" (or "full employment" or "potential") output is

$$Q^* = F(N^*, \sigma). \tag{2}$$

Note that no capital is used in production. Capital appears in Phelps' model, but its only role there is to introduce a set of complex and ambiguous impacts of supply shocks on the real rate of interest and on velocity. Here these second-order effects are neglected through the assumption that nominal *GNP* (Y) is exogenous. The economy's demand price (P^d) is then simply nominal GNP divided by actual real *GNP*:

$$P^d = Y Q^{-1} = Y [F(N, \sigma)]^{-1}. \tag{3}$$

Assuming that the product market always clears and labor is paid its marginal product, the economy's supply price (P^s) is equal to the nominal wage rate divided by the marginal product of labor:

$$P^s = W [F_N(N, \sigma)]^{-1}. \tag{4}$$

The conditions for a macroeconomic externality can now be examined by subjecting this economy to a single comparative static experiment, a change in the raw material input σ, caused by some unexplained event. A macroeconomic externality is defined as occurring when, starting in equilibrium with $Q = Q^*$, the percentage change in Q needed to keep $P^d = P^s$ is not equal to the change in Q^*. Here I shall use the "dot" notation for percentage changes ($\dot{Q} = dQ/Q$), and so the difference between the rate of actual and natural output change is, from (3):

$$\dot{Q} - \dot{Q}^* = \dot{Y} - \dot{P}^d - \dot{Q}^*. \tag{5}$$

The condition necessary for this to be zero can be worked out by setting $\dot{P}^d = \dot{P}^s$, and by noting that if the change in actual *GNP* is equal to that in natural real *GNP*, then both output change terms can be evaluated by assuming that labor input remains at N^*, that is, that $\dot{N} = 0$. We have from (2) and (4):

$$\dot{Q} - \dot{Q}^* = \dot{Y} - \dot{P}^s - \dot{Q}^*$$
$$= \dot{Y} - \dot{W} + (F_{N\sigma}/F_N)d\sigma - (F_\sigma/F)d\sigma. \qquad (6)$$

Thus the condition for real *GNP* to remain at equilibrium can be written

$$\dot{Y} - \dot{W} = -(F_{N\sigma}/F_N - F_\sigma/F)d\sigma. \qquad (7)$$

That is, that the *difference* between the percentage change in nominal *GNP* and that in the nominal wage rate remain equal to the right-hand side of (7).

And what is this unfamiliar-looking term? We can write the income share of the raw material (α) as unity minus the share of labor: $\alpha = 1 - F_N N/F$, so that $\dot{\alpha} = -(\dot{F}_N + \dot{N} - \dot{F})$. Because at Q* there is no change in labor input ($\dot{N} = 0$), the change in the raw material share is just

$$\dot{\alpha} = -(\dot{F}_N - \dot{F})$$
$$= -(F_{N\sigma}/F_N - F_\sigma/F)d\sigma. \qquad (8)$$

Thus substituting (8) into (7), we have the condition:

$$\dot{Y} - \dot{W} = \dot{\alpha}. \qquad (9)$$

While it is completely consistent with the analysis in the original Gordon and Phelps papers, the appeal of (9) is that it is both simpler and more general. There is no need to assume that nominal *GNP* or the nominal wage rate is fixed. Condition (9) applies to either a market-clearing or nonclearing economy. In a market-clearing economy the perfectly flexible wage can adjust downward by any amount needed to open up the required "wedge" between dY/Y and dW/W when the raw material share increases, and there is no necessity for monetary accommodation. However, a rigid or sticky nominal wage rate and an increase in the raw material share together imply that full employment can be maintained only if policymakers generate a sufficient increase in nominal *GNP*. And the relevance of an increasing share is clear, given the actual tripling of energy's value share between 1972 and 1981.[2]

11.2 ACCOMMODATION AND INDEXATION

The theory of monetary policy responses to supply shocks is clear-cut in unrealistic extreme cases and ambiguous in more realistic intermediate cases. Here I ignore effects of supply shocks on the velocity of money, allowing us to link

---

[2] The share index is calculated by multiplying total real energy consumption by the composite energy deflator (both from the *Statistical Abstract of the United States*, 1982–83, pp. 572–73), dividing by nominal *GNP*, and setting 1972 as the base of the index.

central bank control of the money supply with control over the growth rate of nominal *GNP* ($\dot{Y}_t$). Effects of indexation are examined in a mechanical adjustment equation which allows changes in wage rates to depend only on current and past price changes, on past wage changes, and on the output ratio (Q_t/Q_t^*):

$$\dot{W}_t = \beta \dot{P}_t + \gamma \dot{P}_{t-1} + (1 - \beta - \gamma) \dot{W}_{t-1} + \phi(\dot{Q}_t/Q_t^*). \tag{10}$$

This equation is not intended to represent the outcome of maximizing behavior, but rather to allow examination of a taxonomy of consequences of an accommodating monetary policy that maintains full employment, that is, $Q_t = Q_t^*$. In each of the following cases, I normalize on an assumed situation in the period prior to the shock in which $\dot{W}_0 = \dot{Y}_0 = \dot{Q}_0^* = 0$, and assume that the supply shock has a permanent impact on the level of the raw material share only in period one ($\alpha_0 < \alpha_1 = \alpha_2 = \ldots = \alpha_n$). Thus the only nonzero value of $\dot{\alpha}_t$ is $\dot{\alpha}_1 > 0$. Note also that for full employment to be maintained, $\dot{P}_t = \dot{Y}_t - \dot{Q}_t^*$. Substituting (10) into (9) gives

$$\dot{Y}_t = [\dot{\alpha}_t - \beta \dot{Q}_t^* + \gamma(\dot{Y}_{t-1} - \dot{Q}_{t-1}^*)$$
$$+(1 - \gamma - \beta)\dot{W}_{t-1} + \phi(Q_t/Q_t^*)]/1 - \beta. \tag{11}$$

When wage changes depend only on their own past values and on the output ratio ($\beta = \gamma = 0$), full monetary accommodation is clearly optimal. During period one $\dot{W}_1 = 0$, so that an accommodative policy would set $\dot{Y}_1$ to equal $\dot{\alpha}_1$. The opposite extreme occurs with complete indexation of wage changes to current changes in the price level, $\beta = 1$ while $\gamma = 0$. Now the right-hand side of (11) becomes infinite, implying that there is no change in nominal *GNP* that will maintain full employment. Full indexation in the presence of supply shocks is clearly suboptimal, as pointed out by Joanna Gray (1976) and by Stanley Fischer (1977).

Another possible case is that wage changes are indexed fully to lagged price change ($\beta = 0$ while $\gamma = 1$). In this case (11) reduces to the following, when we note that from (2) that $\dot{Q}_t^* = \dot{F}_t$:

$$\dot{Y}_t = \dot{Y}_{t-1} + \dot{\alpha}_t - \dot{F}_{t-1}.$$

In the example of a one-period supply shock, in the first period, $\dot{W}_1 = 0$, and this requires the same accommodative policy as if $\gamma = 0$, that is, $\dot{Y}_1 = \dot{\alpha}_1$. In the second period, however, lagged indexation prevents nominal wage and *GNP* growth from returning to zero. Instead, from (8),

$$\dot{Y}_2 = \dot{W}_2 = \dot{Y}_1 - \dot{F}_1 = \dot{\alpha}_1 - \dot{F}_1 = -\dot{F}_{N_1}.$$

In all future periods,

$$\dot{Y}_t = \dot{W}_t = \dot{P}_{t-1} = -\dot{F}_{N_1}.$$

That is, maintenance of full employment requires a permanent acceleration of inflation and in the growth of nominal wages and *GNP* following any supply shock that permanently shifts the raw material share. In this plausible case of lagged indexation, supply shocks pose a trade-off between a permanent acceleration of inflation and a temporary loss of output. The severity and duration of the output loss depend on the Phillips curve parameter ϕ or, more generally, on the economy's "sacrifice ratio" (my article with Stephen King, 1982). For the U.S. case I showed (1982, p. 134) that an accommodative policy that cumulatively raised the money supply by 9 percent in 1975–80 compared to an alternative hypothetical constant-growth money path would have resulted in 1.9 percentage points more inflation in 1980 with the benefit of 3.2 fewer point-years of unemployment during 1975–80 (an output gain of 8 percent of a year's *GNP*).

In the realistic case of a permanent shock and partial and/or lagged wage indexation, the optimal degree of accommodation depends on a finely balanced comparison of the welfare costs of inflation and unemployment. The optimal outcome is different in a society like the United States in 1973–5, where inflation had high costs due to nonneutral tax rules and binding financial rate ceilings, than in a society like Israel or Brazil, in which real interest rates and tax rates were much more neutral with respect to inflation. In a sense there is a cumulative interaction, as I suggested earlier (1975b), between monetary accommodation, behavior regarding contract lengths and the Phillips curve parameter (ϕ above), and institutional rules regarding tax rates and financial regulations. Inflation begets a neutralized institutional environment, which begets accommodation and more inflation.

11.3 THE PERSISTENCE OF SHOCKS AND THE FORMATION OF EXPECTATIONS

In the above example an adverse supply shock causes a permanent reduction in the economy's productive capacity. Another possibility is that the shock is temporary, as in the case of an agricultural drought or freeze. In this case the trade-off with partial or lagged indexation is between a temporary output loss and a temporary rather than permanent acceleration of inflation. Even a temporary upsurge in the inflation rate is not without welfare costs, since it causes a permanent increase in the price level at every date in the future and a corresponding loss in the wealth of holders of high-powered money (effects on interest-bearing assets and liabilities cancel out).

Thus far nothing has been said about inflation expectations. If the indexation parameters β and γ are set by legislation, then wage changes would evolve mechanically in the aftermath of a supply shock, as described above. If β and γ are relatively low at the time of the shock, for example, if wage changes are determined mainly by their own past values, then the decline in the real wage rate associated with the shock may create political pressure to have indexation legislation changed. Indeed the percentage "pass through" of price changes in the Italian *scala mobile* indexation agreement was raised in 1975 after the first oil shock. However, in most countries indexation parameters are not set in legislative stone, but are subject to frequent negotiation between workers and firms. Multiperiod wage agreements achieved in delicate negotiations would not tend to be altered in response to a temporary shock that is expected to leave output and the real wage unaffected after a transition period of a few months or a year.

But a shock expected to have a permanent effect on output and the real wage poses a serious dilemma for the parties in wage negotiations, and may well lead to a change in any or all of the parameters of (11). As depicted in the model of John Taylor (1980), newly negotiated contracts depend not just on the current state of demand, as in (11), but also on the expected *future* state of demand. Taylor's agents are "forward looking," not "backward looking" as in mechanical formulae like (11). Workers with forwardlooking expectations can calculate the future consequences of maintaining high β and γ indexation parameters in the face of a permanent supply shock – permanently higher inflation of the policy authorities accommodate, and a period of low aggregate demand (Q/Q^*) if they do not accommodate. Faced with this unpleasant trade-off, rational workers would suspend indexation and allow the real wage to fall by the required amount. Hence the rational expectations response to a permanent shock merges together with the market-clearing outcome described above.

The painless transition implied by quickly adjusting forward-looking expectations to a permanent shock has not been observed in fact. As Jeffrey Sachs (1979) has emphasized, unemployment increased in virtually all OECD countries after the 1973–4 oil shock, reflecting a combination of nonaccommodative aggregate demand policies, and an excess of real-wage growth over productivity growth. One possible explanation for this outcome is that economic agents initially thought the oil shock would be temporary and were slow to learn that it was permanent. Karl Brunner, Alex Cukierman, and Allan Meltzer (1980) show that, even within the context of a market-clearing model, a permanent reduction in productivity can cause stagflation, because agents only gradually learn the permanent values of real variables and only gradually adjust their anticipations. Consistent with their analysis is my 1983b finding that real wage growth in most large European countries was much more moderate after the 1979–80 oil shock than after the initial 1973–4 shock. Having seen the effects of the first shock persist, agents were more prepared to believe that the second would persist as well.

11.4 IMPACT ON DOCTRINAL DEBATES

Supply shocks have helped to unify the teaching of macroeconomic theory with that of microeconomics, since basic results in both subjects can be summarized with supply and demand curves. Undergraduates are now taught that unemployment and inflation may be either negatively or positively correlated. Following an autonomous shift in demand, the extent and duration of any change in unemployment depends on the length of wage contracts and the adjustment of expectations, while following an autonomous shift in supply, the extent and duration of any change in unemployment depends on the interaction of wage indexation and monetary accommodation. The recognition that inflation depends on shifts in both demand and supply, not just on past changes in the money supply, has facilitated econometric explanations of the inflation process that appear able to explain why in the 1970s U.S. inflation was so variable and why in 1981–3 it decelerated so rapidly.[3]

The positive correlation of inflation and unemployment in the 1970's brought forth many responses. In a famous polemic (1978), Robert Lucas and Thomas Sargent used this positive correlation to challenge the application of "Keynesian" models to macroeconomic policymaking. Their stated intent was "to establish that the difficulties are *fatal*: that modern macroeconomic models are of *no* value in guiding policy and that this condition will not be remedied by modifications along any line which is currently being pursued" (p. 50). Especially with respect to the issue at hand, this dismissal is inappropriate. Observations in the inflationunemployment quadrant can represent the interaction of demand and supply curves. The Lucas-Sargent challenge failed to notice the concurrent development of new "Phillips curve" formulations which combined the effects of supply and demand shifts with that of sluggish price adjustment, the basic element in Keynesian economics. As put forth in my article with King, the U.S. Phillips curve appears to be one of the most stable empirical macroeconomic relationships of the postwar era, one that shows no sign as of yet of being subject to Lucas' econometric critique.[4] In basing their attack on Keynesian economics on the alleged collapse of the Phillips curve, Lucas and Sargent seem in retrospect like teenage pranksters who scare everyone by crying "wolf" and then flee the scene when it is discovered that there is no wolf.

Finally, supply shocks have raised the perennial question of the optimality of decentralized and uncoordinated wage and price setting. Decentralization ("the invisible hand") is usually supported by economists as required for *microeconomic* efficiency, yet coordination and centralization may be needed to obtain an improved *macroeconomic* response to supply shocks. In the past decade economists have debated the merits of alternative responses that would have required coordinated action, including a onetime real wage reduction to match the decline in productivity caused by the 1973–4 and 1979–80 oil shocks, changing indexation formulae to exclude oil prices and indirect taxes from the price measure used for escalation, and oil import taxes balanced by reductions in other indirect taxes to put downward pressure on the world oil price and to discourage consumption.

[3] Models that combine demand and supply elements include those of Otto Eckstein (1980), my 1982 article, and my article with King. Readable descriptions of the role of supply shocks in the inflation of the 1970s are provided by Alan Blinder (1979, 1982). An evaluation of the 1981–3 disinflation is provided by the three papers in the volume edited by William Nordhaus (1983).

[4] The stability of the inflation equation to changes in sample period is examined by myself and King (p. 218) and related to the Lucas critique (pp. 224–9). Structural shifts in the twentieth century prior to 1954 are discussed in my 1983a article and by Meltzer (1977).

References

Blinder, Alan S. "The Anatomy of Double-Digit Inflation in the 1970s." In Hall, R. E. ed. *Inflation: Causes and Consequences.* Chicago: University of Chicago Press, NBER; 1982, pp. 261–82.

Economic Policy and the Great Stagflation. New York: Academic Press; 1979.

Brunner, Karl; Cukierman, Alex; and Meltzer, Allan H. "Stagflation, Persistent Unemployment and the Permanence of Economic Shocks." *Journal of Monetary Economics.* October, 1980; vol. 6, pp. 467–92.

Eckstein, Otto. *Core Inflation.* Englewood Cliffs: Prentice-Hall; 1980.

"Supply Shocks, Wage Stickiness, and Accommodation." Working Paper No. 1119. National Bureau of Economic Research; May, 1983.

Fischer, Stanley. "Wage Indexation and Macroeconomic Stability." In Brunner, K. and Meltzer, A. eds. *Stabilization of the Domestic and International Economy.* Vol. 5, Carnegie-Rochester Conferences on Public Policy. *Journal of Monetary Economics.* Supplement. 1977; pp. 107–47.

Gordon, Robert J. "Alternative Responses of Policy to External Supply Shocks." *Brookings Papers on Economic Activity.* 1975a; vol. 6, pp. 183–206, Chapter 10 in this book.

"The Demand for and Supply of Inflation." *Journal of Law and Economics.* December 1975b; vol. 18, pp. 807–36.

"Inflation, Flexible Exchange Rates, and the Natural Rate of Unemployment." In Baily, Martin N. ed. *Workers, Jobs, and Inflation.* Washington: The Brookings Institution; 1982, pp. 89–158.

"A Century of Evidence of Wage and Price Stickiness in the United States, the United Kingdom and Japan." In Tobin, J. ed. *Macroeconomics, Prices, and Quantities.* Washington: The Brookings Institution; 1983a, pp. 85–121.

"The Wage and Price Adjustment Process in Eight Large Industrialized Countries." Working Paper. October, 1983b.

and King, Stephen R. "The Output Cost of Disinflation in Traditional and Vector Autoregressive Models." *Brookings Papers on Economic Activity.* 1982; vol. 13, pp. 205–42, Chapter 15 in this book.

Gray, Joanna. "Wage Indexation: A Macroeconomic Approach." *Journal of Monetary Economics,* April 1976; vol. 2, pp. 221–35.

Lucas, Robert E. Jr., and Sargent, Thomas J. "After Keynesian Macroeconomics." *After the Phillips Curve.* Federal Reserve Bank of Boston Conference Series. 1978; no. 19, pp. 49–72.

Meltzer, Allan H. "Anticipated Inflation and Unanticipated Price Change." *Journal of Money, Credit and Banking.* Part 2; February, 1977; vol. 9, pp. 182–205.

Nordhaus, William D. *Inflation Prospects and Remedies, Alternatives for the 1980s.* Washington, Center for National Policy, 1983; no. 10.

Phelps, Edmund S. "Commodity-Supply Shock and Full-Employment Monetary Policy." *Journal of Money, Credit, and Banking.* May, 1978; vol. 10, pp. 206–21.

Sachs, Jeffrey D. "Wages, Profits, and Macroeconomic Adjustment: A Comparative Study." *Brookings Papers on Economic Activity.* 1979; vol. 2, pp. 269–319.

Taylor, John B. "Aggregate Dynamics and Staggered Contracts." *Journal of Political Economy.* February, 1980; vol. 88, pp. 1–23.

U.S. Bureau of the Census. *Statistical Abstract of the United States.* Washington, D.C. 1982–83.

CHAPTER 12

The Theory of Domestic Inflation

Authors and readers of the thousands of articles and books published on inflation during the past decade may regard as audacious any attempt to survey the theory of domestic inflation in 3,000 words. But far from requiring an apology, this format forces concentration on central issues and justifies skipping second-order questions. More leisurely expositions and extensive bibliographies are provided in recent surveys by David Laidler and Michael Parkin and by Robert J. Gordon (1976). The ground rules for this paper are a limitation to theory rather than empirical tests, to closed rather than open economies, and to causes of inflation rather than costs, consequences, or cures.

12.1 INFLATION AND MONEY IN THE LONG RUN

A simple set of definitions helps to separate noncontroversial from controversial issues. We begin with a national income identity, expressed in growth-rate form:

$$y \equiv p + q, \tag{1}$$

where lower-case letters represent rates of growth, and y, p, and q stand for, respectively, the rates of growth of nominal income, the aggregate price deflator, and real output. Subtracting the long-term trend growth rate of capacity (q^*) from both sides of (1), we obtain:

$$y - q^* \equiv p + q - q^*, \tag{2}$$
$$\text{or} \quad \hat{y} \equiv p + \hat{q},$$

where $\hat{y} = y - q^*$, and $\hat{q} = q - q^*$. Arthur Okun (1962) was the first to establish the statistical relation now widely known as "Okun's Law" between the current unemployment rate (U), last period's unemployment rate (U_{-1}), and the output growth deviation ($\hat{q}$):

$$U = U_{-1} - \hat{q}/a, \tag{3}$$

Source. "The Theory of Domestic Inflation." *American Economic Review Papers and Proceedings.* February 1977, vol. 65, no. 1, pp. 128–34.

where a is a constant, roughly equal to 3.0 in the United States. When (3) is solved for $\hat{q}$, the result is substituted into (2), and then (2) is solved for the rate of inflation (p), we have:

$$p = \hat{y} + a\,(U - U_{-1}). \tag{4}$$

The sources of change in y can be decomposed if we once again invoke an identity:

$$\hat{y} \equiv \hat{m} + v, \tag{5}$$

where $\hat{m}$ is the growth rate of money adjusted for capacity growth ($\hat{m} = m - q^*$), and v is the growth rate of velocity. Combining (4) and (5), we obtain:

$$p = \hat{m} + v + a(U - U_{-1}). \tag{6}$$

Once the economy has settled down at any given unemployment rate ($U = U_{-1}$), the rate of inflation depends only on the adjusted growth rate of money ($\hat{m}$) and the growth rate of velocity (v). Shifts in fiscal policy can cause one-time-only changes in velocity, as even Milton Friedman (1966b) recognized long ago, but cannot cause permanent changes in the growth rate of velocity. Innovations in transactions technology, as well as an income elasticity of the demand for money differing from unity, could make v positive or negative, but these factors appear to exhibit only modest changes insufficient to account for marked accelerations or decelerations in inflation.

Changes in the adjusted growth rate of money are thus isolated as a necessary concomitant of long-run changes in the inflation rate. It is in this carefully qualified sense that Friedman (1966a, p. 18) correctly labeled inflation as "always and everywhere a monetary phenomenon." But despite the attempts of some less subtle monetarists to treat this quotation as settling all questions, in fact it represents only a starting point. Accelerations in monetary growth are not usually autonomous whims of central bankers. In most classic wartime or postwar money-fueled inflations and hyperinflations, the role of the monetary authority has been passively to finance deficits resulting from the unwillingness or inability of politicians to finance expenditures through conventional taxation. In the same way, a "cost push" by unions or firms must be ratified continuously by the monetary authority if inflation is to continue.

A more general view, explicitly set out in Melvin Reder's classic analysis, attributes inflation to the passivity of the monetary authority in the face of a "tripartite" set of pressures emanating from all groups in society – labor, management, and government. R.J. Gordon (1975c) extends this theme by distinguishing the "demand for inflation," i.e., monetary accomodation, caused by government's refusal to tax and by pressure groups which attempt to increase their income share, from the "supply of inflation," the degree of response to these pressures, a result of the political balancing of the votes likely to be lost from higher inflation, as against the vote cost of the higher unemployment consequent upon a policy of nonaccomodation.

12.2 THE "MISSING EQUATION"

For anything other than long-run analysis, equation (6) is incomplete. Even if $\hat{m}$ and v are known, there are two remaining unknowns (p and U) but only one equation. A decade ago it was usual to close the model by adding a Phillips curve:

$$p = bp^e + f(U), 0 < b < 1, f' < 0. \tag{7}$$

Together (6) and (7) determine a menu of p, U combinations for different $\hat{m}$. It was common in the United States for economic advisers to Democratic Presidents to recommend a combination with higher p and lower U than the target of Republican advisers.

Friedman (1966a, p. 60) was the first explicitly to reject (7) and to state that "there is no long-run, stable trade-off between inflation and unemployment." On the grounds that workers supply labor by evaluating the expected real value of a wage offer, and that the expected and actual price levels cannot diverge in equilibrium, Friedman (1968) and Edmund Phelps argued that in equilibrium with $p = p^e$ only a single "natural rate of unemployment" (U^N) is possible:

$$p = p^e + g(U - U^N), \quad g' < 0, g(0) = 0. \tag{8}$$

The "natural rate hypothesis" (NRH) as embodied in (8) completely changed the framework of stabilization policy. No longer could an administration choose its own favorite point on the p, U trade-off curve. A rate of unemployment below U^N could not be achieved by aggregate demand policy through manipulations of $\hat{m}$, because inflation would continuously accelerate as long as p^e responds to past changes in p:

$$p^e = h(P_{-1}, P_{-2}, \ldots). \tag{9}$$

A permanent reduction in actual unemployment could be achieved without accelerating inflation only by operating directly on U^N, through manpower programs and other subsidies to reduce worker-job mismatch, and through reductions in the minimum wage and in other barriers to the flexibility of relative wages. It was not widely understood that the NRH did not establish a link between inflation and money where none existed before. Instead, p and $\hat{m}$ are linked together in (6), whether or not the "missing equation" is provided by the old-fashioned trade-off curve (7) or the NRH (8).

12.3 SHORT-RUN PRICE INFLEXIBILITY AND THE ROLE OF CONTRACTS

An important criticism of the NRH has been its apparent lack of validation in recession and depression episodes.

Combining (8) and (9), a deceleration of inflation requires that actual U exceed U^N, since p^e cannot fall until p itself first experiences a decline. A period during which U remains above U^N for a substantial period should be characterized by an accelerating decline in p. But during the Great Depression the unemployment rate remained above 8.5 percent for twelve straight years in the United States without the slightest sign of such an acceleration. If the function $g()$ in (8) were completely flat for high values of U, the NRH would remain valid only as long as U were kept below the flat range. Even if $g()$ retains its negative slope in the range of U relevant for current policy, a relatively gentle slope nevertheless would make extremely costly any attempt to "beat the inflation out of the system" by the deliberate creation of a recession.

Until recently the apparent downward inflexibility of prices during periods of high unemployment constituted an empirical phenomenon in search of a theory. Okun (1975) distinguishes between "auction" markets (wheat, peso futures) with instantaneous market clearing and "customer" markets in which economic incentives induce long-term contractual arrangements, infrequent price changes, and quantity rationing. Costly search makes customers willing to pay a premium to do business with customary suppliers. Firms, in turn, have an incentive to maintain stable prices to encourage customers to return, using yesterday's experience as a guide. "A kind of intertemporal comparison shopping" discourages firms from raising price in response to short-run increases in demand or decreases in productivity in order to avoid giving customers an incentive to begin exploring. Prices are not completely sticky, however. Widespread knowledge shared by customers and firms that costs have increased permanently allows price increases without providing an incentive for search, as was evident in the rapid response of final goods prices to the energy cost explosion of 1974.

While R. J. Gordon's (1975b) results support at least some role for changes in demand, nevertheless Okun's basic message is validated by the overwhelming share of the total variance of aggregate price inflation which is explained by changes in "standard" unit labor cost (defined for trend rather than actual productivity). Thus the search for an adequate theory of the downward inflexibility or inertia of inflation in the face of deep recessions and depressions turns to the labor market. Substantial attention has been attracted by the theory of implicit labor contracts independently developed by Costas Azariadis, Martin Baily, and Donald Gordon. Firms and workers engage in long-term contractual arrangements, which may be implicit and unwritten, and which specify wage rates in advance. Entrepreneurs are self-selected individuals who are relatively indifferent toward risk and are willing to provide insurance services for their risk-averse employees in the form of a fixed wage rate.

At present the wage contract models are incomplete and subject to criticism. R. J. Gordon (1976, p. 209) pointed out that the Azariadis-Baily-D. Gordon theory could not explain fixed-wage contracts without relying on government transfer payments paid to workers during unemployment, thus providing them with a higher total income over the cycle than they would receive if the wage varied to clear the labor market continuously. But government transfers would induce firms to respond to a recession in demand by laying off workers rather than cutting their wages even without any contractual arrangements, making the contract idea itself irrelevant. Robert Barro also makes the important point that the adoption of fixed-wage contracts imposes dead-weight losses on participants by creating a divergence between the marginal product of labor and the marginal value of time. It is to the advantage of both firms and workers to maintain employment at its market-clearing level to maximize the total available product pie.

Ongoing theoretical work attempts to "rescue" the fixed-wage contract from these and other criticisms. Herschel Grossman has analyzed the attempt by firms to minimize the "default risk" of workers jumping from the fixed-wage labor contract into the auction part of the labor market when demand is high. Fruitful ideas introduced by various authors include the preference by firms for the relative certainty of the cost reduction achieved by layoffs compared to the uncertainty of the worker's response to a wage cut, and perhaps most important, the role of employer profits made on the specific human capital of experienced employees, leading firms to maintain the wage rate of experienced employees, while achieving lower costs in a recession by laying off the least profitable inexperienced employees. The consensus appears to be shifting toward worker heterogeneity in the form of differential risk of default, and differential endowments of specific human capital, as the most important elements motivating sticky wages, layoffs, and implicit contracts, and away from the completely homogeneous risk-averse workers featured in the earlier Azariadis-Baily-D. Gordon approach.

Whatever the precise details of the theory which explains wage and price inflexibility, the implications of such stickiness have been worked out in great detail by Barro and Grossman. Starting from an initial level of output (Q_0) and prices (P_0), let a decline in aggregate demand cut the "market clearing" price level (P^*) at which Q_0 would be purchased. If the price level remains at P_0, firms want to produce as much as before but face a constraint on the amount which can be sold. Even if P drops below P_0, there will still be a sales constraint as long as P remains above P^*. In the labor market the sales constraint forces firms to hire fewer workers than they would prefer at today's too-high sticky wages and prices. The requirement for the sales constraint to be lifted, and for firms, to resume operating on their voluntary output supply and labor demand schedules, are (a) an increase in aggregate demand which raises P^* back up to P, or (b) the passage of enough time to allow P to sink down to equal P^*.

12.4   THE CHALLENGE OF RATIONAL EXPECTATIONS

The Application of Rational Expectations to Economic Policy (*AREEP*) constitutes a radical contribution to the theory of the *short-run* determinants of unemployment and inflation. The *AREEP* model begins with (6) above, often assuming $v = 0$ to simplify the exposition, and thus has no bearing on our previous analysis of the *long-run* connection between p and $\hat{m}$. Equation (6) is combined with the "Lucas supply function" (see Robert Lucas), which limits the source of output and unemployment changes to purely voluntary responses of firms and workers to deviations between actual and expected inflation:[1]

$$U = U^N + g^{-1}(p - p^e). \tag{10}$$

The supply function (10) is simply an inverted version of (8), describes the same long-run equilibrium conditions, and is implicit in expositions of the *NRH* by Friedman (1968) and others. While the idea of rational expectations has been fruitfully applied to the behavior of financial, primary commodity, and other "auction" markets, we argue here that *AREEP* goes badly astray by using (10) as a description of the conditions necessary for short-run output changes in the portion of the economy dominated by "customer" or "contract" markets and sluggish price adjustment.

Expectations are rational when the expectational error $(p - p^e)$ is unrelated to all information (I_{-1}) available when expectations were formed, including the autoregressive structure of all variables. The information set I_{-1} includes (6), which (when $v = 0$ and U is constant) implies:

$$p = \hat{m}, \text{ and } P^e = \hat{m}^e. \tag{11}$$

Substituting (11) into (10), we have:

$$U = U^N + g^{-1}(\hat{m} - \hat{m}^e) \tag{12}$$

Thus the monetary authority cannot influence unemployment, even in the short run, unless it acts in an unpredictable way. If it simply responds to an event by a formula known to the public in the previous period as part of the information set I_{-1}, the public will shift its expectation $\hat{m}^e$ by the exact amount of the change in $\hat{m}$, the difference $(\hat{m} - \hat{m}^e)$ will be zero, and unemployment will not change.

The preceding argument has received widespread attention since its formalization by Thomas Sargent and Neil Wallace. It requires for its validity that the price level (P) respond instantaneously to any change in the market-clearing price (P^*), as occurs in (11). When P is sticky and fails to drop instantly to P^*, the firm faces a sales constraint and cannot operate along its voluntary Lucas supply curve (10). Price inflexibility rules out the supply curve and with it the expositions of *AREEP*, all of which to date are built on it. The U.S. evidence in favor of sluggish price adjustment is strong. Two of the many studies include my (Gordon, 1975b) reduced-form regression between p and past values of $\hat{m}$ in the postwar United States, which has a mean lag of four years.[2] And Robert Hall has shown that only 2 percent of the quarterly variation in United States

---

[1] It is customary to include stochastic error terms in the structural equations (6) and (10), but no essential conclusions are changed by omitting these terms in this exposition.

[2] Some *AREEP* theorists have pointed out another interpretation of my equation, that it represents a relation between p and m^e, with the lag distribution on m representing the adaptive formation of the expectation m^e. It is true that the long lag might represent expectation formation, not sluggish price adjustment. But then why should expectations on money take many years longer to form than expectations on inflation itself, which in interest rate regressions appears to be described by a mean lag of one year or less?

unemployment during 1954–74 remains unexplained in a simple two-quarter autoregression, in contrast to (10) above, in which U can differ from U^N only by the serially uncorrelated random error $(p - p^e)$.

Bennett McCallum has tried to argue that "recognition of price level stickiness does not, in and of itself, negate the Lucas-Sargent Proposition." His argument and its defects are most transparent for the extreme case of completely rigid prices in which $p = 0$ and a rational expectation $p^e = 0$ as well. The expectation error $(p - p^e)$ in (10) is zero, and thus unemployment is unaffected by any aggregate demand policy. But consider a policy which cuts nominal expenditure by half from E_0 to $.5E_0$. According to the McCallum argument, if prices are rigid the price level (P), unemployment, and output (Q) remain at their original level. If originally $E_0 = P_0Q_0$, now $E_1 = .5P_0Q_0$. Production is double the level of sales, and so an involuntary accumulation of inventories occurs and continues as long as E remains low and P remains rigid. Retention of the Lucas supply function in the face of price rigidity thus leads to the counter-factual conclusion that businessmen never cut production in response to involuntary inventory accumulation.

There is nothing wrong with the assumption of rational expectations itself, nor with its fruitful application to financial markets. But in light of widespread evidence that, except in a few scattered auction markets, prices adjust sluggishly to the market-clearing level in response to demand and supply shocks, it is hard to avoid the conclusion that for short-run analysis the Lucas supply function and with it *AREEP* should be relegated to the same scrap heap of discarded ideas where lie the earlier classical models of perfect market clearing laid to rest by Keynes forty years ago.

12.5   COST PUSH, CONTROLS, AND SUPPLY SHOCKS

Much attention in the popular press has been devoted to the positive correlation of inflation and unemployment during some years of the 1970s, and the alleged failure of economists to explain it. The straw man being attacked has only one arm, equation (8) of our two-equation inflation model, and lacks its other arm, equation (4). Further, inflation is necessarily negatively correlated with unemployment in (8) only when p^e is fixed. Inflation can increase while unemployment is rising, as in 1970 and early 1971, if expectations are formed adaptively and p^e is still rising in response to past realizations of p.

In contrast to equation (8), the dynamic supply schedule which plots a negative relation between p and U for given p^e and U^N, equation (4) is a dynamic demand schedule which plots a *positive* relation between p and U for given $\hat{y}$ and U_{-1}. Any event which shifts the supply curve up a fixed demand curve raises p and U simultaneously. We introduce the shift factor (Z) explicitly into (8):

$$p = p^e + g(U - U^N) + Z. \tag{13}$$

Z might be a cost-push pressure by unions, oil sheiks, or bauxite barons. As long as the authorities hold $\hat{y}$ constant, inflation and unemployment will increase simultaneously. The imposition of price controls may introduce a negative value of Z, which with $\hat{y}$ constant will cause inflation and unemployment to decrease simultaneously, as in the preelection boom of 1971–2. The termination of controls raised inflation and unemployment simultaneously in 1974. R. J. Gordon (1975a) has shown in this context that crop failures or other supply shocks in general have multiplier effects which spread the loss of output into the nonfarm sector.

12.6 INERTIA AND POLICY OPTIONS

The same downward inertia of price adjustment which vitiates the conclusions of *AREEP* poses obstacles for policymakers. An economy inheriting a substantial fully anticipated inflation and operating at the natural unemployment rate has two problems – how to achieve price stability and how to reduce U^N to allow the creation of jobs for disadvantaged groups suffering from high unemployment rates. The direct remedy for inflation is the creation of a recession, which reduces p below p^e and allows the adaptive expectation of p^e to drift downward. The permanent benefits of lower inflation must be weighed not only against the transitory output costs of a recession which might last for years, but against the permanent wealth loss caused by the recession-induced drop in saving.

Another remedy is the direct control of wages and prices. Price controls by themselves misallocate resources without permanently reducing inflation, because prices tend to be tied so closely to wage costs. Wage controls by themselves have proven to be politically infeasible; the present British experiment is possible only because it is structured to achieve a massive redistribution of income away from the rich. Recent proposals to "sell" wage controls include clever tax schemes designed to offset the inevitable short-term losses of real income of workers who agree to allow their wages to be controlled.

Finally, the ongoing inflation can be accepted rather than resisted by allowing for the full indexing of financial assets, labor and product contracts, and all nominal dollar amounts (tax brackets, maxima, minima) written into private and government regulations. Preliminary research by Joanna Gray and others indicates that full indexing increases macroeconomic stability if the economy only suffers from demand shocks, but in the presence of supply shocks aggravates both inflation and recession. Thus from a social standpoint full indexing is not optimal, but as yet economists have failed to explain why private institutions have provided such an incomplete menu of indexed assets, liabilities, and contracts.

References

Azariadis, Costas. "Implicit Contracts and Underemployment Equilibria." *J. Polit. Econ.* December, 1975; vol. 83, pp. 1183–1202.

Baily, Martin N. "Wages and Employment Under Uncertain Demand." *Rev. Econ. Stud.* January, 1974; vol. 41, pp. 37–50.

Barro, Robert J. "On Long-Term Contracting and the Phillips Curve." University of Rochester. Unpublished. December 1975.

Barro, Robert J. and Grossman, H. *Money, Employment, and Inflation.* Cambridge; 1976.

Milton Friedman. "What Price Guideposts?" In Shultz, G. P. and Aliber, R. Z., eds. *Guidelines: Informal Controls and the Market Place.* Chicago; 1966a, pp. 17–39 and 55–61.

"Interest Rates and the Demand for Money," *J. Law Econ.*, Oct., 1966b, 9.

"The Role of Monetary Policy." *Amer. Econ. Rev.* March, 1968; vol. pp. 1–17.

Gordon, Donald F. "A Neo-classical Theory of Keynesian Unemployment." *Econ. Inquiry.* December, 1974; vol. 12, pp. 431–59.

Gordon, Robert J. "Alternative Responses of Policy to External Supply Shocks." *Brookings Papers.* 1975a; vol. 6, pp. 183–206, Chapter 10 in this book.

"The Effect of Aggregate Demand on Prices." *Brookings Papers.* 1975b; vol. 6, pp. 613–62.

"The Demand for and Supply of Inflation." *J. Law Econ.* December, 1975c; vol. 18, pp. 807–36.

"Recent Developments in the Theory of Inflation and Unemployment." *J. Mon. Econ.*, April, 1976; vol. 2, pp. 185–219.

Grossman, Herschel. "Risk Shifting and Reliability in Labor Markets." *Scand. J. Econ.* Forthcoming. 1977.

Gray, Joanna. "Wage Indexation: A Macroeconomic Approach." *J. Mon. Econ.*, April, 1976; vol. 2, pp. 221–36.

Hall, Robert E. "The Rigidity of Wages and the Persistence of Unemployment." *Brookings Papers.* 1975; vol. 6, pp. 301–35.

Laidler, David, and Parkin, J. Michael. "Inflation: A Survey." *Econ. J.* December, 1975; vol. 85, pp. 741–809.

Lucas, Robert E. Jr. "Expectations and the Neutrality of Money." *J. Econ. Theory*, April, 1972; vol. 4, pp. 103–24.

McCallum, Bennet. "Price Level Stickiness and the Feasibility of Monetary Stabilization Policy with Rational Expectations." *J. Polit. Econ.* Forthcoming.

Okun, Arthur. "Potential GNP: Its Measurement and Significance." *Proc. Amer. Statist. Assn.* 1962; pp. 98–116.

"Inflation: Its Mechanics and Welfare Costs." *Brookings Papers.* 1975; vol. 6, pp. 351–90.

Phelps, Edmund S. "Phillips Curves, Expectations of Inflation, and Optimal Unemployment Over Time." *Economica.* August, 1967; vol. 34, pp. 254–81.

Reder, Melvin W. "The Theoretical Problems of a National Wage-Price Policy." *Can. J. Econ.* February, 1948; pp. 46–61.

Sargent, Thomas J. and Wallace, Neil. " 'Rational' Expectations, the Optimal Monetary Instrument, and the Optimal Money Supply Rule." *J. Polit. Econ.* April, 1975; vol. 83, pp. 241–57.

CHAPTER 13

The Phillips Curve Now and Then

Almost thirty years ago Paul Samuelson and Bob Solow coined the term "Phillips curve" at the 1959 AEA meetings, reacting promptly to the publication of Phillips's (1958) article. For many years afterward Solow thought and wrote about the Phillips curve and many of the unsettled research puzzles that economists had struggled to resolve under that general heading. As Olivier Blanchard and Peter Diamond remind us, the Samuelson and Solow AEA paper (1960) was farseeing, anticipating many of the major issues that arose later when the Phillips curve started shifting. So it is fitting to take a look at the current state of the Phillips curve in economic research and its evolution since the seminal Phillips and Samuelson and Solow papers.

13.1 THE PHILLIPS CURVE NOW

To determine the difference between present views and those of the 1960s, and to highlight remaining puzzles, I take as my point of departure the current mainstream view of the U.S. inflation process.[1] To find this mainstream view, you can look it up in any of the three best-selling intermediate macroeconomics textbooks. Here we find what I call the "triangle" model of inflation – inflation depends on three basic sets of factors: demand, supply, and inertia.

Formally, this model consists of two equations, the modern Phillips curve and a second equation, which, at least in my version, is a pure identity splitting the rate of nominal GNP growth in excess of potential output growth (this is "excess nominal GNP growth") between inflation and changes in the output gap (i.e., in the log ratio of actual to potential output). In fact, some French authors have dubbed this model of the Phillips curve plus an identity as the "split" model. The

---

[1] Here the adjective "U.S." must be emphasized, as the nature of the inflation process in Europe is currently the subject of controversy that does not apply to the United States.

Source. "The Phillips Curve Now and Then." In Diamond, P. ed. *Growth, Productivity, Unemployment: Essays in Honor of Bob Solow's 65th Birthday.* Cambridge, MA: MIT Press; 1990, pp. 207–17.

first equation, the modern Phillips curve, is where the triangle appears. Inflation is explained by three sets of variables, demand, supply, and inertia. Demand enters through the level and change of the output gap, or, equivalently, the level and change of the unemployment gap. Supply enters through one or more exogenous shift variables to convey the effect of supply disturbances like oil shocks, import prices, and price controls. Inertia enters through a set of lagged inflation variables. In the textbook version the lagged inflation coefficients are *assumed* to sum to unity, and in the econometric version they *actually do* sum to unity. When the two equations are solved simultaneously, they determine inflation and the output gap, for any given history of inflation, any set of supply shocks, and any rate of excess nominal GNP growth.

Taking excess nominal GNP growth as exogenous admittedly sweeps two thirds of macroeconomics under the rug, but this is the kind of assumption that Solow might endorse, because it makes the model simple enough to focus attention on the basic determinants of inflation and to allow side issues to be ignored. This assumption imposes a kind of dichotomy on macroeconomic discourse. Under this dichotomy one group of economists is assigned the task of understanding how excess nominal GNP growth is determined by monetary and fiscal policy, by the dynamics of investment and inventory behavior, by the demand for alternative types of assets, and other factors. Then another group of economists is assigned the task of understanding how excess nominal GNP growth is split between inflation and changes in the output gap. Among the members of this second group are practitioners of the "New Keynesian Economics," the current attempt to build the microeconomic foundations of price stickiness; in this context price stickiness can be interpreted simply as the failure of price changes to mimic excess nominal GNP growth.

The dichotomy admittedly ignores channels by which inflation feeds back into the determination of nominal GNP, which may cause econometric bias in versions in which nominal GNP appears directly as an explanatory variable. This raises the question as to whether the triangle equation should be estimated with nominal GNP appearing directly as an explanatory variable, as I have done in some papers focussing on century-long annual data, or in an alternative version with real GNP or unemployment as an explanatory variable and with nominal GNP omitted (using the identity). As a general proposition, in the presence of contemporaneous feedback from inflation to nominal GNP and of supply shocks that are imperfectly measured, estimates of the triangle-type inflation equation will yield a coefficient on nominal GNP, which is biased away from zero, and on real GNP or unemployment which is biased toward zero. The bias in the latter case, which applies to most published estimates for quarterly data, is likely to be small when a full set of supply-shock variables is included.

It should be emphasized that the triangle approach does not require impos-ing the dichotomy. In fact, it is possible to build large and complex econo-metric models that simultaneously express relationships among a large number of common variables, and that allow for two-way feedback between nomi-nal GNP growth and inflation. The purpose of the dichotomy, and the simple

two-equation inflation model that it makes possible, is both to facilitate exposition and to allow us to understand historical events in a simpler and clearer
way than is possible with the large models.

Once this dichotomy is accepted, the mainstream triangle model has at least
five clear implications.

1. In the long run, inflation is "always and everywhere an excess nominal
GNP phenomenon." To control inflation, policy needs a nominal anchor. Correspondingly, there has been growing support for a policy of nominal GNP
growth as the core target of monetary policy by economists as diverse as
Robert Hall, Bennett McCallum, John Taylor, James Tobin, and myself. Because of inertia, the model instructs the Fed to start targeting nominal GNP
growth when the economy has a zero output gap, which I estimate to have
occurred in the third quarter of 1987, and to choose a number for nominal
GNP growth equal to potential output growth plus inherited inertial ("core")
inflation. The choice of any other number will lead to output fluctuations as
the economy overshoots in its struggle to establish a new core rate of inflation. Adopted in late 1987, this approach would have chosen a growth rate
of 6.5 percent for nominal GNP (2.5 percent for potential output growth and
4.0 percent for the inherited "core" inflation rate at that time). Achieving that
target would have required somewhat tighter monetary policy in 1988 and
1989 than has occurred, given the fact that actual nominal GNP growth between 1987:Q3 and 1989:Q2 has turned out to be 7.5 percent at an annual
rate.

2. There is no special connection between growth in the money supply and
inflation; any effect of money on inflation is shared by a similar effect of velocity
on inflation. Stated another way, a change in the money supply must induce a
change in nominal GNP if it is to affect inflation, whereas if that change in
the money supply is offset by a movement of velocity in the opposite direction
(as in 1985–6 for M1), there will be no response of inflation.

3. In the short run, fluctuations in excess nominal GNP growth lead to counterclockwise loops on a diagram plotting inflation against the output gap. The
loops come from inertia. An acceleration of excess nominal GNP growth causes
a loop on the diagram from six o'clock to three o'clock to twelve o'clock, with a
low-inflation boom followed by stagflation. This happened in 1964–71 and a
milder version is in progress today. A deceleration of excess nominal GNP
growth causes a loop from twelve o'clock to nine o'clock to six o'clock, with
a recession followed by an expansion in which inflation may decelerate. This
happened between 1981 and 1986.

4. Supply shocks cause other patterns. An adverse oil shock can cause the
economy to shoot off to the northwest, as in 1974–5. Price controls or a beneficial
oil shock can push the economy to the southeast, as in 1971–2 or 1986–7. The
point on the compass depends not just on the nature of the supply shocks, but
also on the policy response. The northwest movement following an adverse
supply shock assumes that policymakers hold excess nominal GNP growth

fixed. A restrictive policy response would tilt the economy's movement toward the west and an accommodative response would lead the economy's movement to be more northward than westward.

5. The triangle model is resolutely Keynesian. Prices are prevented from mimicking changes in nominal GNP growth both by inertia – the presence of lagged inflation – and by the finite Phillips curve adjustment coefficient (that is, the coefficient on the output gap variable). With excess nominal GNP growth treated as exogenous, the output gap is determined as a residual. One can use the second equation (that is, the identity) to write an equation for the output gap that is the dual to the Phillips curve, showing that changes in output depend positively on excess nominal GNP growth and negatively on lagged inflation. The negative effect of inflation inertia on output is the identifying restriction that allows this model of ouput to be distinguished from the Lucas supply equation approach.

What theoretical story is consistent with the mainstream triangle model? Agents implicitly are price-setters and demand-takers. Although the Patinkin, Clower, Barro, and Grossman disequilibrium framework has no model of price setting, it is the right model of quantity determination given whatever sources of inertia and finite Phillips slopes prevent prices from clearing markets. Agents are pushed off notional supply and demand curves by constraints that spill over from rationed markets. Today's macroeconomists who write survey papers tend routinely to brush off the disequilibrium framework because it has no theory of price determination, while forgetting that it has the right theory of output determination. When these economists say things like "long-lasting effects of money require flat supply curves for goods and labor" (Blanchard 1987), they forget that output and employment are not choice variables and that their movements cannot be interpreted as responses of economic agents along supply curves.

13.2 ORIGINS AND PERFORMANCE OF THE MAINSTREAM TEXTBOOK MODEL

In the history of economic models, the triangle model may be unique in that its textbook version came first, and the econometrics and theory came after that. The textbooks were published in 1978; the basic equations were set out in 1976;[2] and the diagrammatic version originated in a classroom handout that Rudi Dornbusch developed at the Chicago Business School in early 1975. Both my version and that of Dornbusch combined the Friedman-Phelps Phillips curve and a nominal GNP-type identity with Okun's insight that supply shocks have macroeconomic externalities.[3]

---

[2] Gordon (1977, Chapter Twelve in this volume). This paper was presented at the AEA meetings in October 1976.

[3] The only difference is that I took excess nominal GNP growth as exogenous and Dornbusch took excess monetary growth. My version eliminates the unnecessary (and inaccurate for the 1980s) step of assuming that velocity growth is constant.

In contrast to empirical work on Phillips curves in the 1960s and early 1970s, when every year there was a paper explaining why last year's paper had underpredicted the inflation rate, the triangle framework has remained stable for almost fifteen years. The textbook version survives totally intact. The econometric version, developed and refined in the late 1970s, has been validated in the 1980s. The cumulative output gain or loss caused by a permanent acceleration or deceleration of nominal GNP depends on two sets of parameters in the Phillips curve equation, the demand coefficient (that is, the Phillips curve slope) and the inertia coefficients on one or more lags of inflation. A widely used summary statistic that combines the effects of the demand and inertia coefficients is the "sacrifice ratio" (i.e., the ratio of the cumulative output gain or loss to the permanent increase or decrease in the inflation rate). The predictive power of the mainstream model was demonstrated in 1981–7, when the actual sacrifice ratio (roughly six) turned out to be almost exactly what had been predicted in advance on the basis of parameters estimated through the end of 1980.[4]

More recently there has been another empirical validation. We only learn the value of potential or natural output, and of the constant-inflation rate of unemployment, by inverting the empirical Phillips curve. This told us in 1985 and 1986 that inflation was not decelerating fast enough to be consistent with a constant-inflation unemployment rate below 6 percent. And, lo and behold, when unemployment did go below 6 percent in late 1987, price inflation started to accelerate, and in 1988 wages joined in. These validations of the mainstream model warrant rejecting Arthur Okun's (1980, p. 166) skeptical view, expressed a decade ago, that "since 1970 the Phillips curve has become an unidentified flying object."

This history of the triangle model reveals a wonderful irony. A central point of departure for Lucas's new classical revolution was the failure of the 1960s Phillips curve. We all remember the flowery language of Lucas and Sargent (1978, p. 49–50), "that these predictions were wildly incorrect, and that the doctrine on which they were based is fundamentally flawed, are now simple matters of fact . . . the task that faces contemporary students of the business cycle [is] that of sorting through the wreckage . . . of that remarkable intellectual event called the Keynesian Revolution." The irony is that the triangle model was in print in its present form before Lucas and Sargent spoke these lines. It has survived and thrived, while the wreckage consists of the empirical attempts by Robert Barro and others to validate the new classical policy ineffectiveness

---

[4] Using the series for the output ratio given in my textbook (Gordon, 1990, Appendix A), the cumulative deviation of actual from potential output during the period 1980–7 was 26.2 percent. Although many different measures could be chosen for the "permanent" reduction of inflation during this period, I prefer to take the average annual rate of change of the fixed-weight consumption deflator in 1979–80 (8.25 percent) minus the average for 1985–6 (4.15 percent), for a reduction of 4.1 percent and a sacrifice ratio of 6.4 percent. This is remarkably close to the sacrifice ratio of 6.2 estimated by Gordon and King (1982) on the basis of data for 1954–80 (this is the undiscounted sacrifice ratio from Table 5, line 3, where the reasons for preferring line 3 are given on p. 237).

proposition, which ran aground on the bedrock of inflation inertia. In fact, the Lucas imperfect information version of new-classical macroeconomics has even been abandoned in print by one of its most prominent developers.[5]

13.3 THE TRIANGLE MODEL FROM AN EARLIER PERSPECTIVE: OMITTING EXPECTATIONS, UNEMPLOYMENT, AND WAGES

Viewed from the perspective of the triangle model, much of the pre-1974 empirical work on the Phillips curve seems quaint and anachronistic. We cannot blame our own youthful transgressions for neglecting supply shocks because there had been no prior oil shocks of any importance; and in fact there was ample attention to Kennedy-Johnson guideposts and Nixon price controls as variables that could shift the Phillips curve down in just the same way as oil shocks later shifted it up.

But there are other major differences between the earlier writing and the triangle model. The original Phillips article was, after all, about the relationship between wage changes and unemployment. Later, expected inflation was added and we had the expectational Phillips curve. But the triangle model as summarized here has no expectations, no wages, and no unemployment. These are issues of substantive significance.

The omission of expectations is deliberate. Much time was wasted and ink spilled in the late 1960s and early 1970s trying to interpret the lagged effect of prices on wages as reflecting adaptive lags in the formation of expectations. But if we have learned anything from the new Keynesian economics of Fischer, Taylor, Blanchard, and their younger followers, it is that price and wage inertia is compatible with rational expectations. The speed of price adjustment and the speed of expectation formation are two totally different issues. Price adjustment can be delayed by wage and price contracts, and by the time needed for cost increases to percolate through the input-output table, and yet everyone can form expectations promptly and rationally based on full information about the aggregate price level.

The omission of unemployment at one level is trivial; it allows us to write the model as two equations. To include unemployment requires the addition of a third "Okun's law" equation to link the output and unemployment gaps. But at a more profound level the omission of unemployment is desirable, for the unemployment rate is a bad cyclical indicator. This is one of the main points made by Blanchard and Diamond. The raw unemployment rate mixes up what they call aggregate activity and reallocation shocks, and one needs a careful econometric study like theirs to achieve the needed decomposition

---

[5] Recently Barro (1989, abstract page) has written, "The new classical macroeconomics began at about that time [the 1970s], and focused initially on the apparent real effects of monetary disturbances. Despite initial successes, this analysis ultimately was unsatisfactory as an explanation for an important role of money in business fluctuations."

of unemployment into its cyclical and structural components. George Perry (1970) taught us that you cannot take the raw unemployment rate off the shelf and stick it into a Phillips curve – you need a demographic adjustment. But the events of the last decade have taught us that the demographic adjustment is not enough either. The natural unemployment rate has not fallen in response to the demographic reversal of the 1980s. By leaving unemployment out of the triangle model, we avoid having to deal with all that. The output gap will do just fine, and if you want a variable that can be taken off the shelf from the government statisticians without any fine tuning, the Fed's capacity utilization rate captures the impact of the business cycle on the inflation process without the need for any adjustment or decomposition at all.[6]

More important than the omission of unemployment is the omission of wages in the triangle model. We now realize that the earlier fixation on wages was a mistake. Back in the bad old days, all the Phillips curve action was assumed to take place in the wage equation, which was assumed to represent a structural relationship in the labor market. Prices were determined by a markup equation, which was generally assumed to tell us something about the product market and to be a sideshow to the main arena, the labor market. The mistake was to assume that the markup fraction, while allowed to vary over the business cycle, was stable on average across cycles. If the markup of prices over unit labor cost was stable across cycle averages, then so by definition was labor's income share. But this turned out to be incorrect. When we cumulate the wage, price, and productivity data that we have all used in Phillips curve estimation, we see that labor's income share exhibits a strong upward secular movement between the mid-1960s and late 1970s and a strong downward movement since then.[7] The Federal Reserve's goal is to control inflation, not wage growth, so these changes in labor's income share across business cycles imply that wage equations are useless in explaining inflation if they are combined with price markup equations that assume a constant markup across business cycles. As I wrote in 1988 in an overstatement intended to dramatize this issue, "The markup hypothesis is dead."

It appears in retrospect that those large increases in wages in 1969–1971, which forced us to write new articles on the Phillips curve every year, reflected in substantial part the secular upswing in labor's share. And it appears that those small increases in wages in the last five years, when wages by some measures have actually increased less than inflation despite positive growth in productivity, are part of the secular reversal of the previous upswing in labor's share. This is important, because every economist who reached the misguided conclusion that the natural rate of unemployment fell below 6 percent in the mid-1980s did so on the basis of a wage equation; such a conclusion cannot be reached from evidence on price behavior and hence is of little interest to the Federal Reserve.

---

[6] See the estimated equations in my comment on Shapiro, 1989.
[7] The data are plotted in Gordon, 1988.

I credit Christopher Sims with the major role in purging wages from the triangle model. His contribution came not just from his invention of the Vector Autoregressive (VAR) format for estimation, which puts a premium on pruning the list of variables, but also from his consistent position as a critic at the Brookings Panel, where he steadfastly refused to accept any structural interpretations of wage and price equations and insisted that a price equation is a wage equation stood on its head, and vice versa.[8] To their credit, Samuelson and Solow in their original paper presented their famous stylized Phillips curve in the price-unemployment quadrant. The earliest credit for ignoring wages is claimed by Irving Fisher (1926), whose neglected article discovered the Phillips curve in the form of a relationship between the unemployment rate and price changes, not wage changes.

13.4 THE PLACE OF THE PHILLIPS CURVE IN MACROECONOMICS

Despite its success with postwar U.S. data, the triangle model does not settle everything. There are still big puzzles to be explained through history and across countries, especially the hysteresis-like disappearance of the Phillips curve in the interwar United States and United Kingdom and in most of Europe over the last decade.[9] Nevertheless, the postwar U.S. success is there, and the econometric version of the triangle model is absolutely central to any current U.S. discussion of inflation, unemployment, or monetary policy. This then leads me to ask, as my last issue, why has the Phillips curve become the black sheep of macroeconomics? Economists under the age of forty seem afraid to touch it, and as a result miss the chance to tackle the big remaining puzzles. Why?

The answer, I believe, is that the young are irresistibly drawn to models of maximizing behavior. This is nothing new. In our childhood term papers, some of which became part of the MPS model, we MIT graduate students followed Jorgenson and others by starting from a marginal condition for an individual agent and then jumping to aggregate data to which we attached a structural interpretation. Today this fixation on the representative agent leads not just Minnesota graduates but even a few from MIT to develop equilibrium business cycle models that are in fundamental conflict with the nonmarket-clearing implications of price inertia.

I think we should just face the fact that we will probably never have an adequate theory of the Phillips curve slope at the level of the representative agent. As Bob Solow (1976) said in his "gun-and-camera" paper, "it did not occur to me then that the Phillips curve ... needed any subtle theoretical justification. It seemed reasonable in a commonsense way...." The common sense Phillips

---

[8] See Sims's comments on my paper in *Brookings Papers on Economic Activity,* 1977, no. 1, and on Blanchard's paper in 1987, no. 1.

[9] Samuelson and Solow (1960, p. 188) spotted the disappearance of the Phillips relation during the Great Depression and dismissed the 1933–41 observations as *sui generis.*

curve slope comes from aggregation over millions of decisionmakers, looking forward and backward in the input-output table at both costs and demand, trying to anticipate aggregate events without letting prices get out of line with slowly adjusting costs.

Representative agent theorists, if they want to expose themselves briefly to the real world, might benefit from a recent case study in the *Wall Street Journal* (Wessel, 1989). One of the examples in the article goes as follows: a paper box company plans to raise prices on January 1, but in fact it does not because it learns competitors will not follow. One month later, on February 1, it tries again; this time the increase sticks, but at 7.3 percent rather than the 9.7 percent originally planned for January 1. Try to model that, and then try to aggregate it.

We would all be better off if we recognized with Solow that it is common sense that demand matters, and that the Phillips curve should have a slope, but that the exact value of that slope depends on aggregation over millions of decisions each of which is based on a set of complex criteria. Any apparent stability of that slope tells us more about the law of large numbers than about microeconomic behavior. With luck the law of large numbers may help us to escape the bite of the Lucas critique and use the triangle model for policy. We will always need to be vigilant, however, because our luck could run out, as it did in the Great Depression, and as it has in Europe more recently.

References

Barro, Robert J. "New Classicals and Keynesians, or the Good Guys and the Bad Guys." *University of Rochester Working Paper.* May, 1989; no. 187.

Blanchard, Olivier Jean. "Why Does Money Affect Output? A Survey." *NBER Working Paper* 2285. June, 1987. Forthcoming in Friedman, B., and Hahn F. eds. *Handbook of Monetary Economics.* North-Holland.

Fisher, Irving "A Statistical Relation between Unemployment and Price Changes," in *International Labor Review.* June, 1926; vol. 13, pp. 785–92. Reprint, *Journal of Political Economy.* March/April, 1973; vol. 81, pp. 496–502.

Gordon, Robert J. "The Theory of Domestic Inflation." In *American Economic Review Papers and Proceedings.* February, 1977; vol. 67, pp. 128–134, Chapter 12 in this book.

"The Role of Wages in the Inflation Process." In *American Economic Review Papers and Proceedings.* May, 1988; vol. 78, pp. 276–283.

Macroeconomics. 5th ed. Glenview, IL: Scott, Foresman; 1990.

Gordon, Robert J., and King, Stephen R. "The Output Cost of Disinflatior in Traditional and Vector Autoregressive Models." *Brookings Papers on Economic Activity.* 1982; vol. 13, no. 1, pp. 205–242, Chapter 15 in this book.

Lucas, Robert E., Jr., and Sargent, Thomas J. "After Keynesian Macroeconomics," In *After the Phillips Curve: Persistence of High Inflation and High Unemployment.* Boston: Federal Reserve Bank of Boston; 1978, pp. 49–72.

Okun, Arthur M. "Postwar Macroeconomic Performance." In Feldstein, Martin S., ed. *The American Economy in Transition.* Chicago: University of Chicago Press for NBER; 1980, pp. 162–9.

Perry, George L. "Changing Labor Markets and Inflation." *Brookings Papers on Economic Activity.* 1970; vol. 1, no. 3, pp. 411–48. 1, 3, 411–448.

Phillips, A. W. "The Relation between Unemployment and the Rate of Change of Money Wage Rates in the United Kingdom, 1861–1957." *Economica.* November, 1958; vol. 25, pp. 283–299.

Samuelson, Paul A., and Solow, Robert M. "Analytical Aspects of Anti-Inflation Policy." *American Economic Review Papers and Proceedings.* May, 1960; vol. 50, pp. 177–94.

Shapiro, Matthew D. "Assessing the Federal Reserve's Measures of Capacity and Utilization." *Brookings Paper on Economic Activity.* 1989; vol. 20, no. 1, pp. 181–225.

Solow, Robert M. "Down the Phillips Curve with Gun and Camera." In Belsley, David A.; Kane, Edward J.; Samuelson, Paul A.; and Solow, Robert M. eds. *Inflation, Trade and Taxes: Essays in Honor of Alice Bourneuf,* Columbus: Ohio State University Press; 1976.

Wessel, David. "Seeking Better Prices, Firms Haggle a Lot, Affect Inflation Rate." *Wall Street Journal.* April 14, 1989.

PART FOUR

EMPIRICAL STUDIES OF INFLATION DYNAMICS IN THE UNITED STATES

EMPIRICAL IMPLEMENTATION OF THE TRIANGLE MODEL

Time-series econometrics lives a life of its own. When I started running Phillips curve regressions, the sample period was 1954–69, a mere 64 quarters of data, and many fewer degrees of freedom once current and lagged explanatory variables are included. My latest work, still in progress, covers the sample period 1954–2002, fully three times as many quarters of data. Why should any empirical paper be included in this volume other than the latest, since the latest overlaps the time coverage of the earliest and provides far more scope to explore stability and changes in parameters?

Part Four includes as Chapter Seventeen the latest (1998) published empirical paper on the dynamics of inflation behavior. However, more is involved in understanding empirical work than archiving the old framework in order to pursue the new framework. The first two papers included in Part Four (Chapter Fourteen, published in early 1977, and Chapter Fifteen, published in 1982) taken together helped to reorient the econometrics of the Phillips curve toward the specification and format that has become standard since the early 1980s. This specification has been fruitfully used to study the sources of low inflation in the 1990s not just by myself, but also by Douglas Staiger, James Stock, Mark Watson (1997, 2001), and others.

The framework introduced in Chapters Fifteen and Sixteen contrasts sharply with the standard approach of inflation studies dating back to the earliest econometric models of the late 1950s and early 1960s. These always took wage formation and price formation to be two different topics. Following Phillips' original work (1958), the dynamic element was restricted to the wage equation, in which the *rate of change* of wage rates was dependent on the level of the unemployment rate. To explain the change in prices, that is, the inflation rate, a second equation had to be introduced, often called in those days the "markup equation," in which the price *level* was determined as a multiple or "markup" over some definition of labor cost (the wage rate adjusted for productivity) and other variables representing demand shifts, usually quite different than the demand variable in the wage equations. There was nothing in these models tying together the demand variable in the wage equation (usually, the unemployment rate, with or without a demographic adjustment) and the price equation (usually, a variable describing only manufacturing rather than the whole economy, for example, the ratio of unfilled orders to shipments).

With two separate equations, each prone to error, the estimated inflation rate could drift substantially from the actual rate. In fact, the first sentence of Chapter Fourteen cites the marked increase in forecasting errors in inflation equations in "the past six years" (for example, 1971–6). The paper in Chapter Fourteen makes only an incremental change from previous practice. It still is divided into two sections, corresponding to the "structural" price equation and the "structural" wage equation. Nevertheless it moves toward the improved 1980s specification in several dimensions. First, it includes several versions that replace the unemployment rate with the output gap (both level and change) in the wage equation and replace idiosyncratic demand variables (e.g., unfilled orders) with the output gap in the price equation. By eliminating a different set of demand variables in the wage and price equations, Chapter Fourteen represents a step on the way to a single reduced-form inflation equation that eliminated the distinction between separate price and wage equations. Second, the results show that wage behavior depends more on product prices than consumer prices, indicating that the demand for labor is a more important determinant of wages than autonomous reactions by workers based on consumer price behavior. Third, the paper shows that wage changes incorporated virtually none of the increases in food or oil prices from 1973–4, supporting an accommodative policy in the context of the theoretical analysis of supply shocks in Chapters Eleven and Twelve. However, the slope of the Phillips curve, now defined for the output gap rather than the unemployment rate, was sufficiently steep that the paper accurately predicted that inflation was about to accelerate from its 5 percent rate in 1976 to "6 or 7 percent." Today's data show that this conclusion was quite accurate, with inflation rates in the GDP deflator of 6.4 percent for 1977 and 7.1 percent for 1978.

Chapter Fourteen was still "traditional" in that it had separate price and wage equations with no attempt to merge them. Everyone remembers his favorite critic, and my favorite comment from the published discussion of Chapter Fourteen was that "Christopher Sims expressed some amusement that the best wage equation had no labor market variables in it. This result conformed with his belief that wage and price equations cannot be distinguished as applying to different categories of behavior. It was preferable to consider them as interesting statistical reduced-form summaries of the dynamic relationship among the variables."[1]

---

[1] Sims's comment appears in the general discussion of Chapter Fifteen as it appeared in the *Brookings Papers on Economic Activity*, 1977, no. 1, p. 279.

USING VAR METHODOLOGY TO REFINE
THE INFLATION EQUATION

Sims's comment contributed one step in helping me break free from the two-equation approach in which wage and price behavior were described by separate equations with different variables representing demand and supply shocks. The second and perhaps more important step was also associated with Sims and his co-authors who introduced the vector-auto-regressive (VAR) methodology into macroeconomics in the late 1970s and early 1980s. The essence of the VAR approach was to create a symmetric model containing just a few variables, all of which were treated as endogenous, and all of which were explained by themselves and the other variables. By choosing the order of the equations, the investigator could choose the direction of causation between the error terms in one equation (e.g., oil prices) and the next (e.g., GDP prices).

Chapter Fifteen represents a much sharper break with the previous Phillips curve literature than does Chapter Fourteen.[2] It uses VAR methodology selectively both to edit down the long list of variables that traditionally had been involved in explaining wage and price behavior, and also to treat several of the important "supply-shock" variables as endogenous rather than exogenous. Because the VAR methodology introduces a number of lags on all variables alike, data limitations on available degrees of freedom force the investigator to pare the list of endogenous variables to a small number, seven in this case. In condensing the list of variables, the first to be dropped is the wage rate, leaving only a reduced-form inflation equation as the core of the "triangle" model, and second to be dropped was the distinction between unemployment and the output gap (not to mention unfilled orders) as alternative demand variables. Okun's law had already taught us that there was a strong and systematic negative correlation between the unemployment rate and the output gap, and so little was lost by eliminating the unemployment rate from the model.

The incorporation of the VAR methodology provided a payoff by indicating that two supply-shock variables, the relative price of imports and of food and energy, could be usefully treated as endogenous rather than exogenous. However at a broader level the paper concluded that the VAR technique had a "low benefit-cost ratio." By insisting that all variables be treated as endogenous, it omitted key variables, especially the wage-price-control dummy variables, that were clearly exogenous. This and other omissions caused a bias in other coefficients and in particular yielded "coefficients that are severely biased and imply a Phillips curve with a perverse slope."[3]

---

[2] Chapter Sixteen is one of only two chapters in this book that are coauthored. Stephen R. King is a full collaborator and in particular wrote the initial methodological section that explains the VAR methodology. Several prominent economists at the time told me that his exposition is a masterful presentation, the most comprehensible that had appeared to that time.

[3] Intuitively, the Phillips curve is a positive relationship between inflation and the output gap. If other "supply shock" variables are relevant, they can explain a negative correlation between inflation and the output gap without biasing the Phillips curve slope itself. However, omitting

The other main novelty of Chapter Fifteen is its detailed attention to the "sacrifice ratio," the ratio of the cumulative percentage loss in output required to reduce inflation by 1 percent, according to a dynamic simulation. Published in 1982 at the beginning of the disinflation of 1981–6, the paper accurately predicted that the sacrifice ratio of roughly 3 (Chapter Fifteen, Table 15.5, line 1) was substantially lower than the value of 10 than had been previously estimated by Okun.[4] The much lower ratio resulted from three channels of "international feedback" incorporated into the model – tight money, by boosting (1) the exchange rate of the dollar, reduced both (2) the relative price of imports and (3) the relative price of food and energy. Artificially suppressing these three channels resulted in a sacrifice ratio of 9.9, close to Okun's value.

Chapter Sixteen, along with Chapter Five discussed earlier, are the only papers included in this book, among the many that I have written, to make explicit econometric comparisons across countries.[5] The aim of Chapter Sixteen is to develop an econometric model of the inflation process that is appropriate for examining the very different evolution of the inflation-unemployment tradeoff in Germany and the United States through the early 1990s. This paper goes back to treating price and wage inflation in two separate equations but does so within the context of Sims's critique cited above. Following his suggestion that it was incredible for different variables to appear in the price and wage equations, both equations included the same list of variables, and feedback from wages to prices, or vice versa, was introduced by solving the wage and price equations for a definitional relationship involving labor's share.[6] The resulting inflation equation was the same as that in the triangle model, but changes in labor's share became a new source of supply shocks, having potentially the same effects as an increase in the relative price of food or energy.

Another change in Chapter Sixteen is to incorporate an error-correction term, so that inflation responds both to the change in labor's share and as well to any

those variables can cause the slope of the Phillips curve to be biased toward zero or even to have the wrong sign.

[4] A retrospective comparison of the output loss during the 1980–6 period with the permanent decline of inflation yields a sacrifice ratio of 3.3. The cumulative output gap in those seven years was 19 percent (Gordon, 2000, Table A-1) and the reduction of inflation in the chain-weighted GDP deflator was from 9.2 percent in 1980 to 3.4 percent in 1988, for a reduction of 5.8 percent (*Economic Report of the President*, January 2001, Table B-3). The Okun evidence is cited in Chapter Fifteen, footnote 1, in a 1978 paper that is usually cited as originating the term "sacrifice ratio."

[5] Chapter Seventeen is also, along with Chapter Sixteen, the only coauthored papers in the volume. The first-listed coauthor in the published journal version is Wolfgang Franz.

[6] See Chapter Seventeen, equations (7) through (9). The change in labor's share is equal by definition to the change in unit labor cost minus the inflation rate, and so one can specify a relationship in which inflation depends on a weighted average (weights summing to zero) of lagged inflation and lagged unit labor cost, and solve to replace lagged inflation and lagged unit labor cost by lagged inflation (now with a sum of coefficients of unity) and the change in labor's share.

excess of the level of labor's share above its equilibrium level. Thus far, two new variables have been added to the triangle model, in addition to lagged inflation, a demand gap variable, and a set of supply shock variables, namely the change in labor's share as well as its deviation from its equilibrium value. Finally, to address the "hysteresis" hypothesis regarding high European unemployment, as to whether the natural rate of unemployment (or NAIRU) in Europe evolved in response to changes in the actual value of the unemployment rate, the model replaces the traditional output gap with the unemployment rate as the demand variable.[7] As shown in equations (16) through (19), a parameter indicating the presence of hysteresis can be defined by including both the level and change of the unemployment rate in the inflation equation.

The empirical research in Chapter Sixteen reaches two striking conclusions. The first is that during 1973–1990 German wage behavior was remarkably similar to that in the United States, with almost identical estimates of the Phillips curve slope, of the hysteresis effect, and of the NAIRU emerging from the respective wage equations. In particular, both countries were characterized by partial but not full hysteresis in the wage equations, and the NAIRU indicated by the wage equations was about 6 percent in both countries in 1990, a result consistent with the empirical findings for the United States in Chapter Seventeen.

But the second conclusion indicates an important difference between the two countries. In Germany (not the United States), we found no feedback from wages to prices. Thus the relatively optimistic estimates of the German NAIRU emerging from the wage equation are irrelevant to the determination of inflation. Instead the inflation rate was found to have a stable relationship to the capacity utilization rate. Because the capacity utilization rate was relatively high in 1989–90, inflation accelerated.

Chapter Sixteen puts a new interpretation on the divergence between U.S. and German unemployment behavior in the 1980s. American inflation fell after 1982–3, because a sharp demand contraction sent unemployment far above the NAIRU, and the economy slid down a relatively steep short-run Phillips curve. There is no evidence of unique weakness of labor unions in the 1980s. Labor's income share hardly fell at all in the United States in the 1980s, and in fact declined much more in Germany. The American problem of slow real-wage growth was a productivity problem, not a wage negotiation phenomenon.

The paper concludes that the puzzle of high unemployment in Germany in the 1980s can be "repackaged" as why the unemployment rate consistent with the mean rate of capacity utilization("MURU") increased so much, especially during 1980–6. In Germany there was a growing mismatch between the size of the labor force and the availability of industrial capacity. Germany failed to invest sufficiently to provide the industrial capacity required by its labor force.

---

[7] "NAIRU" stands for the Non-Accelerating Inflation Rate of Unemployment.

WHY WAS U.S. INFLATION SO LOW IN THE LATE 1990s?

The last paper in the book in Chapter Seventeen attempts to explain why inflation and unemployment were both so low in the late 1990s. The basic answer is that the late 1990s were the mirror image of the 1970s. Exactly the same econometric approach can be used to explain the "twin peaks" of inflation and unemployment in 1974–5 as the "valley" of inflation and unemployment that reached its trough in early 1998. The basic model used in Chapter Seventeen to study the late 1990s (actually, fitting equations to the period 1962–98) is the same as that developed in Chapter Fifteen, with two exceptions. First, alternative versions are estimated that allow for mutual feedback among inflation and changes in unit labor costs, using the same specification as in Chapter Sixteen.[8] Perhaps more important, as in Chapter Sixteen, the demand variable is switched back from the output gap to the unemployment gap, and the natural rate of unemployment or NAIRU is allowed to vary over time.

The story of the time-varying NAIRU is simply told. The Chapter Fifteen specification of the domestic U.S. inflation process had been developed in 1980–2 and had been left unchanged from then until the mid-1990s. Until 1994–5, this inflation equation could be subjected to dynamic simulations (that fed back the endogenously estimated lagged inflation variable) for as long as seven years after the end of the sample period without developing any substantial "drift" away from the actual values. In light of the instability of many other macroeconomic relationships, including equations for the demand for money or investment, the success of the triangle inflation model seemed remarkable.[9] Yet toward the end of 1994, after the actual unemployment rate fell below the previously assumed NAIRU of 6 percent, the simulated inflation rate began to drift up relative to the actual inflation rate.[10]

The time had come to abandon the previously innocuous practice of assuming that the NAIRU was a constant and to estimate changes in its value. My work during 1996–7 was complementary with that of Staiger, Stock, and Watson (1997) – they developed the method for allowing the NAIRU to vary over time and applied it to my reduced-form "triangle" equation for the inflation process, and I borrowed their technique to develop further my own inflation specification, including the process of wage-price feedback discussed above in the context of Chapter Sixteen. The results were published in the same journal issue in 1997

---

[8] Chapter Seventeen includes the change in labor's share, using the same derivation as in Chapter Sixteen, but does not take the extra step of included the error-correction mechanism.

[9] I once enjoyed hearing Robert E. Hall refer to this approach to modeling inflation dynamics as "one of the great successes of postwar time-series econometrics."

[10] During the long post-1982 period of stable simulations of the equation, alternative versions were run with the output gap or unemployment gap (that is, actual unemployment rate minus the NAIRU) as alternative demand variables. The NAIRU was simply assumed to remain at a constant level of 6.0 percent continuously after 1978, and the natural level of output was assumed to grow at a fixed logarithmic growth rate between benchmark quarters when the unemployment rate was roughly 6 percent, e.g., 1978:Q2, 1987:Q3, and 1994:Q3.

(see references below) and found similar results, that the NAIRU had declined from roughly 6.5 percent in the mid-1980s to 5.5 percent in the mid-1990s. More recent work, still unpublished, suggested that the NAIRU settled down to the range of 5.0 to 5.2 percent in 1999–2000.

Chapter Seventeen takes the two 1997 papers as a point of departure and develops further three aspects of the analysis. First, in parallel to the adverse supply shocks of the 1970s, a longer list of beneficial supply shocks is developed and quantified for the late 1990s. Two of these are the "old" supply shocks, the relative prices of imports and of food and energy. Two are "new," namely an acceleration in the rate of decline of computer prices and a temporary hiatus during 1996–8 in ongoing medical care inflation. The last is not properly termed a supply shock but operates in the same way, namely changes in measurement techniques that reduced the measured rate of inflation relative to the true rate of inflation in several stages between 1991 and 1998. When these five elements were quantified in Chapter Seventeen, they can account for most but not all of the low rate of inflation in early 1998. But this quantification requires that the NAIRU be allowed to decline and leaves open a question of why it did. Part of the explanation was the "new" supply shocks and the measurement changes that were not included explicitly in the equation.[11] Other changes in labor markets that helped to reduce the NAIRU were examined in a subsequent paper by Lawrence Katz and Alan Krueger (1999).

The second primary contribution of Chapter Seventeen is to explore for the United States further some of the feedback channels between prices and labor costs that were initially developed in Chapter Sixteen. The results indicate that feedback makes a contribution, with one exception, to each of the equations estimated. The results suggest that the deceleration of inflation in 1994–8 helped to keep wages from accelerating more than they actually did, and that the acceleration of wages helped to keep prices from decelerating more than they actually did.

The third contribution is to contrast the unemployment rate and capacity utilization rate as alternative demand variables. Here Chapter Seventeen is complementary to Chapter Sixteen but reaches the opposite conclusion for the United States in the 1990s as for Germany in the 1980s. In the earlier decade Germany experienced a marked increase in the unemployment rate that was consistent with a constant rate of capacity utilization. In the 1990s the United States experienced a sharp decline in the unemployment rate that was consistent with a steady rate of capacity utilization. Since the utilization measure applies only

---

[11] The NAIRU is estimated on the assumption of zero values for the supply shock variables that are included in the quation, namely changes in the relative price of imports and of food and energy. Any tendency of the relative price of imports or of food-energy to decline, as in 1997–8, reduces the inflation rate consistent with a given unemployment rate or, alternatively, allows the unemployment rate to decline without causing an acceleration of inflation. The additional elements – computer prices, medical care prices, and measurement changes – were not included in the estimated equations of Chapter Seventeen and so implicitly reduce the NAIRU when they shift in a beneficial direction.

to manufacturing, mining, and utilities, and not to the vast service sector, this contrast may point to developments in the labor market in the service sector, which have generated an increased demand for labor without creating additional pressure on industrial capacity.

It is tempting to speculate that the resolution of the unemployment-utilization discrepancy lies in the much-discussed ability of the American economy (in contrast to the rich nations in Europe) to provide abundant jobs in the service sector for hamburger flippers, grocery baggers, parking lot attendants, valet parkers, and bus-people without placing pressure on capacity in the manufacturing sector. These were central theories of Chapter Five. It also raises a central question that remains unanswered in Chapter Seventeen: Was the big puzzle of the 1990s the fact that inflation was so low, or that unemployment was so low, that is, that the unemployment rate declined so much relative to what would have been predicted from the behavior of the rate of capacity utilization?

References

Gordon, Robert J. "The Time-Varying NAIRU and its Implications for Economic Policy." *Journal of Economic Perspectives*. February, 1997; vol. 11, pp. 11–32.

Katz, Lawrence F., and Krueger, Alan B. "The High-Pressure U. S. Labor Market of the 1990s." *Brookings Papers on Economic Activity*. 1999; vol. 30, no. 1, pp. 1–65.

Phillips, A. W. "The Relation Between Unemployment and the Rate of Change of Money Wage Rates in the United Kingdom, 1861–1957." *Economica*. November, 1958; vol. 25, pp. 283–99.

Staiger, Douglas, Stock, James H., and Watson, Mark W. "The NAIRU, Unemployment, and Monetary Policy." *Journal of Economic Perspectives*. Winter, 1997; vol. 11, pp. 33–49.

"Prices, Wages, and the U. S. NAIRU in the 1990s." in Alan B. Krueger and Robert M. Solow, eds., *The Roaring Nineties: Can Full Employment Be Sustained?* New York: The Russell Sage Foundation and the Century Foundation Press, pp. 3–60.

CHAPTER 14

Can the Inflation of the 1970s be Explained?

By many standards inflation has been a "surprise" during the past six years. Errors in forecasting inflation have increased markedly compared with earlier periods. For instance, during the interval 1971:3 to 1975:4 the root mean-square error of the Livingston panel of economists in forecasting the consumer price index six months ahead was 3.5 percentage points at an annual rate, compared with an error of 1.6 percentage points over the previous seventeen years.[1] Not only did the panel forecasters fail to predict the increased variance of the inflation rate in the 1970s, but also they fell far short in predicting the cumulative total price change between 1971 and 1976 – 24 percent compared with the actual change of 34 percent.[2] Most of the error occurred during the four quarters of 1974, with an actual increase of 11.6 percent, almost twice the 6 percent increase forecast six months in advance.[3]

---

[1] The Livingston forecasts were obtained from John A. Carlson, "A Study of Price Forecasts," *Annals of Economic and Social Measurement*, vol. 6 (Winter 1977), Table 1, pp. 33–4. I calculated the errors by comparing the six-month-ahead forecasts with the change in the consumer price index in the two relevant quarters. For instance, Carlson's calculation of the predicted quarterly rate of change between December 1973 and June 1974 is compared with the average quarterly rate of change of the CPI in the first and second quarters of 1974. The "previous seventeen years" runs from 1954:1 to 1971:2.

[2] The actual figure refers to the sum of the quarterly rates of change of the CPI in the interval 1971:3 through 1976:2. The forecast figure is the sum of the six-month predicted changes calculated by Carlson from the Livingston panel data for the ten surveys between June 1971 and December 1975.

[3] The errors for the forecasts from five large-scale models compiled by McNees were similar. The four-quarter-ahead forecast made in 1973:4 for the change in the GNP deflator to 1974:4 was 6.04 percent; the actual was 11.04 percent. See the revised reprint of Stephen K. McNees, "An Evaluation of Economic Forecasts: Extension and Update," *New England Economic Review* (September/October 1976), pp. 30–44.

This research has been supported by the National Science Foundation. I am grateful to my research assistant, Joseph Peek, for his superb efficiency in compiling and creating the complex data base on which the paper depends. Helpful suggestions were received from participants in seminars at Northwestern, the University of California at Berkeley, and the Federal Reserve Banks of San Francisco and Philadelphia. (*Source.* "Can the Inflation of the 1970s be Explained?" *Brookings Papers on Economic Activity*, 1977; vol. 8, no. 1, pp. 253–77).

In searching for an explanation for this inflation, this paper can be likened to an investigative report following a railroad or airline crash. The news of the disaster – in this case, the failure to forecast inflation accurately – was reported long ago and by now is well known. But what can we say beyond the fact that the disaster occurred? Just as transportation investigations attempt to determine which specific parts of the machine failed, and to recommend improvements, so here the relationship of the inflation rate to other important economic variables is studied to determine as precisely as possible what was different about the experience of the 1970s, and what lessons can be learned from past mistakes. Which theories and structural relationships relevant for predicting inflation remain intact, and which require surgery or euthanasia? What are the implications for policy?

Most econometric models base their inflation forecasts on structural price and wage equations, either a single pair for the aggregate economy, or a larger set of disaggregated equations. In my own past work on inflation, I have specified and estimated aggregate price and wage equations, and have studied the sensitivity of the results to alternative specifications, estimation methods, and sample periods. This paper investigates the performance of my price-wage model in tracking the inflation of the 1970s, and studies the implications of its successes and failures for the future conduct of economic policy.

The paper is divided into three sections, one on the price equation, one on the wage equation, and one on dynamic simulations in which the two equations interact.

1.   Structural Price Equation

An equation that explains price change with wage change as a predetermined variable is a component of almost all large-scale econometric models of the U.S. economy. In a previous paper I argued that the total increase in prices relative to wages between mid-1971 and late 1975 was almost exactly what would have been predicted by a structural price equation fitted to the 1954–71 period, and that the timing of postsample errors was consistent with the hypothesis that prices had been held down by controls in 1971–2 and then rebounded when controls were terminated in 1974.[4] This paper extends this test through the end of 1976, notes the effects of recent data revisions on the original price equation, and explores alternative explanations of its overprediction of price change in 1975 and 1976.

2.   Structural Wage Equation

Can a wage equation specified in 1971 and estimated for pre-1971 data explain the behavior of wage change since 1971? What was the impact of 1973–4 "supply shocks" on wage change, and how should policy respond to future supply

---

[4] Robert J. Gordon, "The Impact of Aggregate Demand on Prices," *BPEA, 3:1975*, pp. 613–62.

shocks?[5] Has high unemployment during 1975 and 1976 held down wage increases by more or less than would have been expected on the basis of pre-1971 relationships? Finally, can the pre-1971 data or the 1971–6 experience distinguish among the various proxies for labor-market tightness used by different econometric investigators?[6]

3.   *Dynamic Simulations*

How potent are high unemployment and a slack economy in slowing the inflation rate? What would have been the consequences for inflation of an alternative expansionary policy in 1974? Is the Carter administration's planned economic recovery consistent with its goal of decelerating inflation? A dynamic simulation in which the price and wage equations interact can provide answers to these questions.

14.1 BEHAVIOR OF THE MAIN VARIABLES, 1969–76

Table 14.1 displays the behavior over the 1969–76 period of several important measures of changes in prices, wages, money, and nominal demand. The figures are annual rates of change. The first column covers the ten quarters prior to the imposition of the controls program in 1971, the second column covers the two quarters influenced by the 1971 freeze, and the next five columns show for the five years 1972–6 the sum of the quarterly rates of change for the four quarters of each year.

The official price indexes displayed in the first four lines uniformly record little price change in late 1971 and 1972, double-digit inflation in 1974, and a return in 1976 to rates similar to or below those of 1969–71. The fifth line displays the "nonfood, net of energy" deflator that I developed earlier, as recomputed from the revised national income accounts and extended to the end of 1976.[7] This index misses double-digit inflation in 1974 by only a hair.

Two wage indexes are displayed next. The first is compensation per manhour, with an adjustment for overtime and shifts in the interindustry employment mix; this is used as an independent variable in the structural price equation. The second is the official index of adjusted hourly earnings compiled by the Bureau of Labor Statistics, further adjusted here to include fringe benefits; this is the dependent variable in the wage equation. The most notable difference between wage and price behavior over this period has been the lower variability of wage change – less slowdown during late 1971 and 1972, less acceleration in 1974, and less deceleration between 1974 and 1976. As in the case of prices, wage

---

[5] See Robert J. Gordon, "Alternative Responses of Policy to External Supply Shocks," *BPEA*, *1:1975*, pp. 183–204, Chapter 10 in this book.

[6] Robert J. Gordon, "Inflation in Recession and Recovery," *BPEA, 1:1971*, pp. 105–58.

[7] Gordon, "Impact of Aggregate Demand," pp. 622–9, 656–60.

Table 14.1. *Annual Rates of Change in Major Economic Measures Before, During, and After Wage and Price Controls, 1968:4–1976:4* Percent[a]

Measure	Before Controls 1968:4–1971:2	Freeze 1971:2–1971:4	Full Controls 1971:4–1972:4	Relaxed Controls 1972:4–1973:4	After Controls			Total Change, 1971:2–1976:4
					1973:4–1974:4	1974:4–1975:4	1975:4–1976:4	
Price index								
Gross national product	5.24	3.43	4.10	7.30	11.04	6.95	4.55	35.66
Consumption	4.36	3.52	3.43	7.31	11.45	5.86	4.64	34.45
Consumer prices	5.22	3.13	3.38	8.18	11.55	7.13	4.92	36.72
Nonfarm business	4.76	2.88	2.93	5.91	12.14	6.48	4.88	33.78
Nonfood business net of energy	5.06	2.75	3.07	5.33	9.97	6.27	5.12	31.14
Wage index[b]								
Compensation per manhour adjusted	6.71	5.55	5.77	7.78	10.68	9.12	7.19	43.31
Hourly earnings adjusted	7.18	5.51	7.16	7.58	9.56	8.03	7.01	42.09
Final demand and money supply								
Nominal final sales	6.65	7.80	10.69	9.40	8.29	10.24	9.16	51.68
M_1 (currency plus demand deposits)	5.14	4.63	8.15	6.11	4.97	4.30	5.55	31.39
M_2 (M_1 plus time deposits)	6.95	7.78	10.75	8.56	7.47	8.07	10.41	49.15

[a] Calculated as sums of quarterly rates of change, converted to annual rates in first two columns.

[b] Adjusted for overtime and shifts in the interindustry employment mix; for hourly earnings, also adjusted for fringe benefits.

Sources. With the exceptions noted, the data are from U.S. Bureau of Economic Analysis, *The National Income and Product Accounts of the United States, 1929–74: Statistical Tables* (GPO, 1977), and *Survey of Current Business*. The consumer price index and money supply are official data from the U.S. Bureau of Labor Statistics and the Federal Reserve Board, respectively.

The deflator for nonfood business product net of energy and the adjusted measures for compensation per manhour are constructed using the methodology explained in Robert J. Gordon, "The Impact of Aggregate Demand on Prices," *BPEA, 3:1975*, pp. 613–62. Adjusted hourly earnings is constructed as explained in Robert J. Gordon, "Inflation in Recession and Recovery," *BPEA, 1:1971*, pp. 153–54. The sources for the last three measures are extensions of those given in the previous papers cited here and incorporate the 1976 Department of Commerce revisions of the national income accounts.

change in 1976 returned to roughly the same rate as in 1969–71 – a bit higher for compensation, and a bit lower for average hourly earnings.

The final section of Table 14.1 displays the growth of final demand and two measures of the money supply. In none of these was growth nearly as variable as price change. The difference between the minimum and maximum annual rates of change in the 1972–6 period was 2.4 percentage points for demand, 3.8 for M_1, 3.3 for M_2, but 6.9 for the GNP deflator and 8.2 for the CPI. Simple reduced-form regressions in which price change is regressed on a distributed lag of past changes in money or final sales confirm that virtually none of the variance of inflation in the 1970s can be attributed to the behavior of money or final sales. When estimated for 1954–71, and extrapolated to 1976, such reduced-form regressions can explain at most one sixth of the acceleration of inflation from the 5 percent range in 1969–71 to double digits in 1974, and the subsequent deceleration back to 5 percent in 1976.

14.2   STRUCTURAL PRICE EQUATIONS

In an earlier paper I estimated structural price equations that exhibited relatively strong effects of aggregate demand on the price "markup," that is, on the relationship of the aggregate price level to the aggregate wage level. These equations appeared able to explain the cumulative 1971–5 inflation using coefficients estimated through 1971:2. Although the postsample prediction errors were large, their timing was consistent with the interpretation that the controls had temporarily held down the price level. In Table 14.2, the first column lists the coefficients of a version of the "core" equation as published in 1975.[8]

The specification of the various price equations presented in Table 14.2 corresponds to that derived in my 1975 paper. The price level net of excise and sales taxes is marked up over total cost by a margin that depends on the level of excess demand for commodities. Total cost in turn consists of unit labor cost, materials prices, and the user cost of capital. After each variable is transformed into a percentage rate of change, and when technical change is assumed to be labor-augmenting, an equation is derived in which the rate of change of prices depends on each of the variables listed in Table 14.2: (1) the rate of change of an excise-tax term; (2) the rate of change of the relative price of materials; (3) the deviation of the growth rate of actual productivity from its trend; (4) the rate of change of wages minus the trend growth rate of productivity – "trend unit labor cost"; (5) the rate of change of the relative price of capital goods; and (6) a proxy for the excess demand for commodities, either the rate of change of the ratio of unfilled orders to capacity (UFO/C), or the rate of change of the gap between actual and potential output.

While in the earlier paper equations including the two alternative proxies were essentially identical, the same cannot be said of the equations reestimated

---

[8] See Gordon, "Impact of aggregate Demand," pp. 634–5, for the equations, and p. 639 for an illustration of the prediction errors of one equation.

Table 14.2. *Structural Price Equations and Extrapolation Errors, Alternative Variants*[a]

	Sample Period and Type of Equation						
	1954:2–1971:2					1954:2–1976:4	
	Original Equation						
Independent Variable (Quarterly Rate of Change) and Regression Statistic	As Published in 1975 (1)	With Revised Data (2)	UFO/C Replaced with Gap (3)	Demand Variables Excluded (4)	Constrained Coefficient on Trend Unit Labor Cost[b] (5)	Unconstrained with Gap (6)	Constrained Coefficient on Trend Unit Labor Cost[b] (7)
Independent Variable							
1. Indirect tax rate	0.402	0.048	0.271	0.148	0.427	0.239	0.212
	(2.09)	(0.22)	(1.31)	(0.68)	(2.18)	(1.21)	(1.11)
2. Materials prices	0.025	0.014	0.019	0.043	0.026	0.035	0.031
	(1.46)	(0.69)	(1.13)	(2.52)	(1.74)	(2.91)	(2.98)
3. Deviation of productivity from trend	−0.024	−0.049	−0.118	−0.047	−0.093	−0.145	−0.152
	(−0.77)	(−1.12)	(−2.11)	(−1.03)	(−1.70)	(−2.91)	(−3.18)
4. Trend unit labor cost	1.090^c	1.076^c	1.074^c	1.021^c	1.000^c	0.963^c	1.000^c
	(19.2)	(19.9)	(20.96)	(20.0)	...	(20.59)	...
Mean lag	[4.8]	[5.3]	[4.8]	[4.3]	[4.8]	[3.2]	[3.2]
5. Relative price of capital goods	0.401^c	0.290^c	0.385^c	0.235^c	0.499^c	0.134^c	0.088^c
	(3.37)	(2.07)	(2.75)	(1.66)	(4.34)	(1.05)	(0.84)

6. Ratio of unfilled orders to capacity	0.065^c (2.74)	0.052^c (2.08)	...	...	...	...
7. Output gap	...	...	-0.324^c (-3.27)	-0.256^c (-3.05)	-0.195^c (-2.15)	-0.218^c (-2.72)
8. Dummy = 1.0, 1971:3–1972:4	...	...	...	...	-0.330 (-2.73)	-0.350 (-3.10)
9. Dummy = 1.0, 1974:2–1975:1	...	...	...	...	0.510 (2.28)	0.460 (2.21)
Regression Statistic						
10. Standard error	0.207	0.244	0.235	0.254	0.234	0.261	0.259
11. Postsample root mean-square error (1971–76)	...	0.599	0.676	0.507	0.667	...	...
12. Cumulative error	...	-4.61	-3.65	-4.68	0.77	...	...

a The dependent variable is the deflator for nonfood business product net of energy. The numbers in parentheses are *t* ratios.

b The constraint is applied in columns 5 and 7 by taking the distributed-lag coefficients estimated in columns 3 and 6, respectively, dividing each coefficient by the sum of the coefficients, and subtracting the result from the dependent variable.

c The figure is the sum of a set of distributed-lag coefficients, and the number in parentheses below is the *t* ratio indicating the statistical significance of the sum of the coefficients.

Sources. Column 1, Gordon, "Impact of Aggregate Demand on Prices," Table 3, equation 3.5: for the other columns, the equations were reestimated using revised and extended data from the sources in ibid., appendix B. The methods used to construct the variables are identical to those used in ibid.

All distributed lags in this paper are estimated by the polynominal distributed-lag technique, with the lag coefficients constrained to lie along a third-degree polynomial, and with the far end constrained to be zero. The lag length is allowed to extend over twelve quarters on line 4 and eight quarters elsewhere.

with new data from the 1976 revision of the national income accounts. The data revisions reduce the statistical significance of most variables when either demand proxy is used, but the version using *UFO/C* is affected most adversely (compare columns 2 and 3). The output-gap equation is superior on almost every count, with a lower standard error of estimate and higher t ratios on every independent variable.

In contrast to the initial core equation, which tracked the cumulative post-sample price change very closely, both of the new equations in columns 2 and 3 overpredict inflation during 1971–6 very substantially. The problem is not that inflation has been mysteriously low over the five-year extrapolation interval, but rather that the sum of coefficients on labor cost (line 4) is so far above 1 that a significant overprediction builds up. The same cumulative postsample overprediction is exhibited in column 4, where both demand variables are excluded. An interesting feature of the no-demand version is the higher coefficient on materials prices, which in the postsample extrapolation captures more of the 1974 upsurge in prices and allows the equation to achieve a lower postsample root mean-square error. But the higher coefficient on materials prices adds to the overprediction of the equation in column 4, offsetting the lower coefficient on labor cost.

The postsample performance of the best equation – that in column 3 – is markedly improved when the sum of coefficients on labor cost is constrained to equal precisely 1. The constrained equation in column 5 fits the sample period about as well as the unconstrained version. While the root mean-square extrapolation error is only slightly improved in the constrained version, the cumulative overprediction disappears.

The actual change in the deflator for nonfood product net of energy and the predicted value from the constrained equation of column 5 are displayed in Figure 14.1. A comparison of the curve marked "actual" (solid line) and that labeled "fitted values (1954:2–1971:2 sample period)" (dotted line) reveals that the equation underpredicts inflation at the end of its sample period in early 1971, but then overpredicts in late 1971 and throughout 1972 by a cumulative 2.44 percentage points. If interpreted as a measure of the effect of the controls program, that figure lies at the low end of the range estimated in my previous papers.

Next, the cumulative underprediction error in the two years ending in 1975:1 is 6.13 percentage points, more than double the 1971–2 overprediction. That finding is not consistent with my previous interpretation that all of the 1973–5 underprediction can be attributed to the effect of the unwinding of controls. A more plausible interpretation is that the equation goes astray by exaggerating the lag between wage and price changes in an abnormal period in which firms recognized that controls had ended and reacted to postcontrol wage increases by passing them forward to customers much faster than they normally would have done.

A final puzzle is why the inflation rate in 1976 was consistently below the prediction of the equations – in Figure 14.1 the cumulative overprediction is

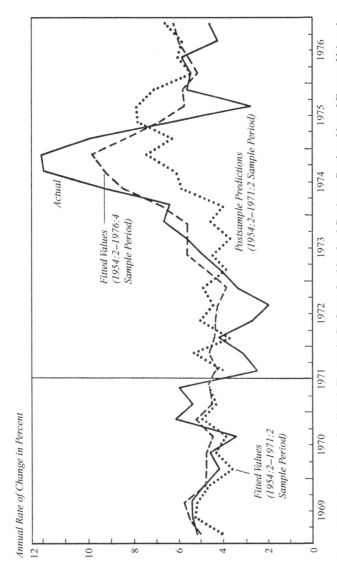

Figure 14.1. Actual and Predicted Change in Deflator for Nonfood Business Product Net of Energy Using the Specifications of the Structural Price Equations, 1969–76

Sources. Actual, see Table 14.2 sources; predicted and fitted, Table 14.2, columns 5 and 7.

0.92 percent. One way to isolate any recent change is to examine the predictions of a similar structural price equation reestimated through the end of 1976.

Column 6 in Table 14.2 reports the coefficients of the extended equation. The effect of price controls is captured by two dummy variables, one covering the six-quarter interval beginning in 1971:3, and the second covering the four-quarter interval beginning in 1974:2. The coefficients of the dummy variables are highly significant and cumulate to a value of −1.98 percent of the controls period and +2.04 for the postcontrols rebound (there is no constraint imposed to force these cumulative totals to equal each other).

Column 7 amends column 6 by constraining the sum of the coefficients on trend unit labor cost to equal 1. To highlight the differing time paths of the two sets of predictions, based on columns 5 and 7, respectively, fitted values for the extended equation are displayed in Figure 14.1 with the impact of the dummy variables excluded. The major differences occur in the 1973–5 period, when the extended equation does a much better job of capturing the timing of the acceleration and subsequent deceleration of inflation. This performance is achieved by three shifts in coefficients when the equation is extended. First, the coefficients on labor cost shift sufficiently to reduce the mean lag by 1.6 quarters.[9] This allows more of the postcontrols, 1974 bulge in wage change to influence price change in 1974, rather than in 1975. Second, the coefficient on materials prices is higher, which raises predicted inflation in 1973–4 while reducing it in 1975. Third, the coefficient on current productivity change is higher, allowing the negative values of productivity change in late 1973 and throughout 1974 to boost predicted price change.

What is the proper interpretation of the shifts in coefficients when the sample period is extended? Any coefficient in a time-series regression is sensitive to conditions inside the sample period. Thus it is not surprising that an equation estimated for the relatively placid 1954–71 period misses some aspects of the timing of pricing decisions by firms during 1971–6, a period that included price and wage controls, a tremendous surge in materials prices, and an unprecedented slump in productivity.

14.3 STRUCTURAL WAGE EQUATIONS

Structural wage and price equations suitable for estimating the surprising aspects of the 1971–6 inflation are contained in a paper that I wrote in early 1971.[10]

---

[9] The mean lag of 4.8 quarters in the 1954–71 equation seems unreasonably long. When that sample period is split in half, the mean lag falls to 2.9 quarters for 1954–62 but rises to 8.1 quarters for 1963–71. A close examination of the data leads me to suspect that erratic movements of the series on compensation per manhour (CMH) in the latter period forced the computer to "stretch out" the lags. The alternative wage index, average hourly earnings (AHE), moved more smoothly and actually is more successful as the wage variable for the equation in column 5. It cuts the standard error from 0.234 to 0.213, and the mean lag from 4.8 to 4.0 quarters. I now believe that, despite its narrower scope, AHE is the preferable wage variable for price (as well as wage) equations, returning to a judgment reflected in my 1971 paper.

[10] "Inflation in Recession and Recovery."

While the specification of the structural *price* equations reported in Table 14.2 and Figure 14.1 was altered somewhat in 1975 and thus incorporates knowledge of events to that point, no such reevaluation of the 1971 *wage* equations has yet been carried out.[11] Thus this section on wage behavior in the last five years can identify genuine "surprises" relative to 1971 expectations.

The first column of Table 14.3 presents the relevant statistics of the "final" 1971 wage equation.[12] The dependent variable is the *two-quarter* rate of change in a private hourly earnings index, the *AHE* variable mentioned above, which is adjusted by the Bureau of Labor Statistics to exclude the effects of changes in overtime and of interindustry employment shifts, and which incorporates as well an adjustment to include the effects of changes in fringe benefits (including employer contributions for social security).

Coefficients for two of the independent variables in the equations are not listed in Table 14.3, the constant term and the constrained effect of changes in the social security tax rate. The first three listed independent variables are proxies for labor market tightness – unemployment dispersion among demographic subgroups, the "disguised unemployment rate" (the difference between the actual labor force and its trend), and the "unemployment rate of hours" (the difference between private hours per week and its trend). The official unemployment rate does not appear in the equation; the three labor market variables are all correlated with it and incorporate its influence. Although only current values of the three variables are included in the wage equation, each of the three reacts to changes in output with a differing lag pattern, allowing output changes and thus changes in labor market conditions to influence wages with a distributed lag.

Two price variables are listed (lines 6 and 7). The first is a distributed lag of past changes in the personal consumption deflator, with lag weights obtained from a separate regression of the nominal interest rate on past inflation. The second is the difference between changes in the "product price" (nonfarm deflator) and the consumption deflator. The final variable (line 9) is the rate of change in the employee-tax variable, the sum of the effective tax rate on personal income and the employee's effective social security tax rate.[13]

Data revisions between 1971 and 1976 alter the coefficients and their statistical significance, as is evident in comparing column 1, which is based on

---

[11] Detailed comparisons of the performance of the 1971 wage equations with alternative versions proposed by other authors are contained in Robert J. Gordon, "Wage-Price Controls and the Shifting Phillips Curve," *BPEA, 2:1972*, pp. 385–421.

[12] This information is copied from "Inflation in Recession and Recovery," Table 1, equation 11.

[13] The 1971 specification, with the social security tax appearing both as a constraint on the left-hand side of the equation and as part of the employee-tax variable on the right-hand side, allows measurement error to bias downward the coefficient on the employee-tax variable. In columns 2 through 7 this bias is eliminated by defining the employee-tax variable as the two-quarter change in $1/(1 - \tau_p)$, where τ_p is the effective personal income tax rate. This and the replacement of the nonfarm deflator by the deflator for nonfood business product net of energy are the only changes in specification in moving from column 1 to column 2. Each equation includes a constant term and a social security tax constraint, not shown in Table 14.3.

Table 14.3. *Structural Wage Equations and Extrapolation Errors, Alternative Variants*[a]

	Sample Period and Type of Equation							
	1954:1–1970:4		1954:1–1971:2				1954:1–1976:4	
	Original Equation				Output Gap			
Independent Variable and Regression Statistic	As Published in 1971 (1)	With Revised Data (2)	Original Specification (3)	Constrained Sum of Coefficients on Price (4)	Unconstrained Prices (5)	Constrained Prices (6)	Original Specification (7)	Output-Gap Version (8)
Independent Variable								
1. Unemployment dispersion	0.018 (2.3)	0.019 (0.86)	−0.009 (−0.39)	−0.016 (−0.86)	...	...	0.005 (0.25)	...
2. Disguised unemployment rate	−0.278 (−4.3)	−0.111 (−1.57)	−0.170 (−2.63)	−0.153 (−2.52)	...	...	−0.187 (−2.85)	...
3. Unemployment rate of hours	−0.086 (−1.0)	−0.133 (−2.34)	−0.162 (−2.79)	−0.043 (−0.78)	...	...	−0.144 (−2.78)	...
4. Output gap					−0.011 (−1.04)	−0.008 (−1.31)		−0.023 (−2.89)
5. Change in output gap					−0.069 (−2.71)	−0.063 (−2.70)		−0.055 (−2.14)
6. Change in consumption deflator	0.600[b] (4.0)	1.006[b] (8.67)	1.085[b] (11.55)	...	...		...	...
7. Change in product price minus consumption deflator	0.596[c] (2.8)	1.343[c] (5.41)	0.974[c] (6.69)	−0.220[c] (−1.55)	−0.067[c] (−0.38)	−0.035[c] (−0.27)	−0.110[c] (−0.87)	−0.103[c] (−0.80)

	(1)	(2)	(3)	(4)	(5)	(6)	(7)	(8)
8. Change in product price	...	...	...	1.000[d]	1.136[c] (15.81)	1.000[d]	0.939[c] (16.95)	1.008[c] (22.06)
9. Change in employee tax rate	0.169 (3.3)	0.080 (1.24)	0.061 (0.96)	0.064 (1.08)	0.061 (1.03)	0.032 (0.54)	0.035 (0.72)	0.035 (0.74)
10. Dummy = 1.0, 1971:3–1972:4	...	...	...	...	...	...	0.331 (2.37)	0.312 (2.25)
11. Dummy = 1.0, 1974:2–1975:1	...	...	...	...	...	...	0.018 (0.06)	−0.012 (−0.04)
Regression Statistic								
12. Standard error	0.261	0.278	0.275	0.271	0.263	0.267	0.299	0.303
13. Root mean-square error (1971–76)[e]	...	...	0.754 / 1.059	0.664 / 0.913	0.644 / 0.962	0.539 / 0.807	...	...
14. Cumulative error (actual minus predicted)[e]	...	...	−2.91 / −13.05	−1.30 / −7.03	−4.23 / −11.17	0.11 / −6.70	...	...

[a] The dependent variable is the two-quarter rate of change in the private hourly earnings index. The numbers in parentheses are *t* ratios.

[b] Lag coefficients estimated from an equation relating the nominal interest rate to past price change reported in "Inflation in Recession and Recovery," appendix A (cited in sources). This set of lag coefficients remains unchanged in columns 1 through 3.

[c] The sum of a series of distributed-lag coefficients estimated by the polynomial-distributed-lag method, with details of estimation the same as in Table 14.2. The lag length is eight quarters in line 7 and twelve quarters in line 8.

[d] The sum of a series of twelve lag coefficients is constrained to equal 1.

[e] The upper figure in each column is derived from an equation using the deflator for private nonfood business product net of energy. The coefficients reported in lines 1–11 for equations in columns 2–8 are all from equations using that deflator. The lower figure is derived from an equation using the deflator for private nonfarm business as the product price.

Sources. Column 1, Gordon, "Inflation in Recession and Recovery," Table 1, equation 11; for the other columns the equations were reestimated using revised and extended data from the sources in ibid., pp. 155–8. See Table 1 above for sources for revised national income accounts data. The gap variable is the same as Table 14.2 above, line 7. The data used for the product-price variable are those for the deflator for private nonfood business product net of energy – that is, the dependent variable in Table 14.2.

the original data, and column 2, which is based on the most recently revised data. Ironically, the "natural rate hypothesis," in the form of a coefficient of unity on price inflation, is vindicated by the revisions in the official data. The unemployment-dispersion variable becomes insignificant while the coefficient on inflation increases in lines 6 and 7; as I showed in 1972, the dispersion variable and high coefficients on inflation are substitute explanations of wage change in the 1954–70 sample period.[14]

When the sample period is extended by two quarters, in column 3, co-efficients shift further but the results are reasonably satisfactory. Although the unemployment-dispersion variable has faded away, the coefficient of the disguised-unemployment variable remains significant and that of unemploy-ment of hours is considerably increased and enhanced in statistical significance as compared with column 1. The coefficients on the price variables strongly indicate that wage change fully incorporates changes in price inflation and that it is influenced by changes in product prices, not consumer prices.

As in the case of the structural price equations, the postsample extrapolation errors of the wage equation are vastly larger than the in-sample standard error (lines 12 and 13 of column 3). Two separate extrapolations are performed; the lower figures in lines 13 and 14 result from using the nonfarm business deflator as the "product price" while the upper figures result from using the deflator of nonfood business product net of energy.[15] The cumulative overprediction given in line 14 is much higher when the nonfarm deflator is used. This is the first indication of a conclusion that emerges very strongly in this section: *none* of the 1973–4 inflation in food and energy prices "got into" wages, and all pre-1971 wage equations that allow any influence of food and energy prices drastically overpredict the cumulative 1971–6 wage increase.

Just as the postsample extrapolations of the structural price equation were superior when the sum of labor-cost coefficients was constrained to be 1, the extrapolations of the wage equation improve when the sum of the price coef-ficients is constrained to be 1. The constraint is introduced by changing the arrangement of the price variables. Since the result in column 3 indicates that only the product price "matters" – since the 1.085 coefficient on the consump-tion deflator in line 6 is virtually canceled by the 0.974 coefficient on "minus" the consumption deflator in line 7 – the product price is entered directly in line 8 with the sum of coefficients constrained to equal 1. Now the size of the coefficient on line 7 measures (with reverse sign) the separate influence of the consumption deflator; a coefficient of 0 would indicate that only product prices matter, and a coefficient of −1 that only consumption prices matter.

The constrained equation in column 4 fits the sample period slightly better than the unconstrained version does, and achieves a marked improvement in the postsample root mean-square error. The cumulative postsample overprediction

---

[14] See my "Wage-Price Controls," Figure 1, p. 402.
[15] The coefficients in columns 2 through 8 are based on the deflator for nonfood business product net of energy.

is cut to slightly more than 1 percentage point when the deflator for nonfood business product net of energy is used as the product price. Nevertheless, the postsample performance is by no means perfect, as is clear in Figure 14.2 from a comparison of the solid, "actual," line with the dotted line representing the postsample predictions of column 4. The equation underpredicts in 1972 and 1973. Although the similar underprediction in the four quarters prior to controls in 1970–1 complicates the verdict, the performance suggests that the controls program did not reduce wage change at all; beyond that, wage change during the controls program did not even reflect the deceleration of prices. The other major error in the extrapolation is a substantial overprediction of wage change during 1975 and 1976. A possible interpretation of the pattern of these errors is presented below.

The strong evidence that product prices and not consumer prices matter suggests that the major determinant of wage behavior is the demand for labor by firms, not the needs of workers or union aggressiveness. That, in turn, raises the question of whether wage changes depend basically on demand conditions in the product market rather than exclusively in the labor market.

Considerable experimentation with lag structures suggests that the effect of the commodity market on wages can be represented by a pair of proxies for excess demand: (1) the gap between actual and potential output, and (2) the first difference in the gap (the same variable used in the price equation).[16] When the pair of output-gap variables replaces the three labor market variables of the original specification, the standard errors of estimate improve slightly (compare columns 3 and 5). The same holds true for a comparison of the respective versions with constrained price coefficients in columns 4 and 6. The postsample performance of the constrained output-gap version in column 6 is markedly better than that reported in column 4 by the criteria of both the root mean-square error and the cumulative error. When the product price is represented by the deflator for nonfood business product net of energy, the output equation in column 6 can track cumulative wage change between 1971 and 1976 to within 0.1 percent.

The output-gap equation in column 6 is remarkable in attributing virtually all of the impact of the demand for commodities on wages to the *change* in the output gap. The coefficient on the level of the output gap is so small, and so weak statistically, that it plays only a trivial role, implying that an economy with output gaps of 6 percent and −6 percent would have almost exactly the same rates of wage inflation, given the rate of price inflation. This implication of the output-gap version in column 6 conflicts with the vast body of previous

---

[16] The output gap is equal to potential output minus actual output, with the difference divided by potential output. The level of potential output is a trend that equals actual output when unemployment equals the natural rate of unemployment. Details of the methodology for estimating the natural unemployment rate are contained in Robert J. Gordon, "Structural Unemployment and the Productivity of Women," in Karl Brunner and Allan H. Meltzer, eds., *Stabilization of the Domestic and International Economy*, Carnegie-Rochester Conference Series on Public Policy, vol. 5 (Amsterdam: North-Holland, 1977), pp. 181–229.

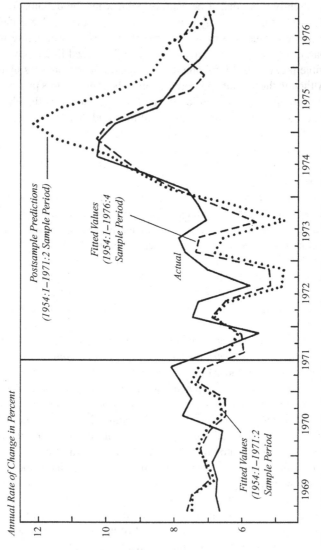

Figure 14.2. Actual and Predicted Change in Adjusted Hourly Earnings Index Using the Specifications of the Structural Wage Equations, 1969–76

Sources. Actual, see Table 14.3 sources; predicted and fitted, Table 14.3, columns 4 and 7.

research, including the original specification in columns 1 and 4, in which the dominant labor market variable is disguised unemployment, which tends to be correlated more with the *level* of total unemployment than with its rate of change.

Finally, in constructing Table 14.3, I extended the sample period of the wage equations to the end of 1976. Results for the unconstrained versions are shown in columns 7 and 8. Dummy variables for the controls are included in the equation for the same time intervals as in Table 14.2, and imply not only that controls in 1971–2 did not hold down wages, but that wages increased *more* than would have been expected in light of the moderating impact of the controls on price inflation. The improvement in fit in the extended version with the original specification is evident in the contrast between the dotted and dashed lines in Figure 14.2. At the cost of only a slight deterioration in the tracking of wage change in 1969–71, the extended equation is able to cut drastically the overprediction of wage change in 1975.

Other than the inclusion of dummy variables, the main difference in the extended equation in column 8 is a marked increase in the absolute value of the coefficient on the level of the output gap. The recession appears to have been more effective during 1975–6 in holding down wage change than would have been predicted from the sample period ending in 1971:2. The output-gap equations estimated for the 1954–71 period tend to exhibit a relatively flat short-run Phillips curve, because of the influence of the rapid wage change during the recession of 1970–71. Equations estimated to the full 1954–76 period display a higher coefficient on the level of the output gap, reflecting the reduced rates of wage change in 1975–6. The same contrast is evident in a comparison of the coefficient on the unemployment of hours in columns 4 and 7, the two equations that are plotted in Figure 14.2. Is it the 1970–1 period that should be considered the outlier, or 1975–6? Some previous research suggests an unusual spread in 1970–1 between union and nonunion wage change which may be associated with the timing of union negotiations over the 1967–71 period. Based on this evidence, I tend to favor the interpretation that the 1970–1 period was unusual, and hence to prefer the coefficients in the extended equations in columns 7 and 8.

Some authors have developed models of wage-setting behavior in which wage change depends not on price change, as in Table 14.3, but only on the past behavior of wages. While it is plausible to argue that both firms and workers base wage changes on wage changes recently granted to comparable employees in other firms or industries, both theory and the data decisively support a role for price change.[17] When a distributed lag on past changes in wage rates is substituted for price change in the 1954–71 period, using the specification of column 5 in Table 14.3, the sum of squared residuals *triples*. For the longer 1954–76 period, the sum of squared residuals rises by 59 percent. Further, the

---

[17] See particularly Robert E. Hall, "The Process of Inflation in the Labor Market," *BPEA, 2:1974*, pp. 343–93, and my criticisms of that paper, pp. 394–99.

pattern of residuals indicates that the "wage-wage" version cannot explain any of the acceleration of wage change between 1973 and 1974.

14.4 POLICY SIMULATIONS

A dynamic simulation of the wage and price equations, which allows for the effects of wages on prices and prices on wages, provides an assessment of the inflationary implications of alternative paths of economic recovery and of the required duration of a "stable prices at any cost" policy that *prevents* recovery and maintains today's output gap.

Policy simulations with a two-equation wage-price model have both disadvantages and advantages as compared to simulations using the large-scale forecasting models. The main disadvantage is that the specification must be restricted to rely (largely if not entirely) on a single exogenous variable – for example, the output gap – which "drives" the simulation. Offsetting advantages are that the simulation results may be more easily studied, interpreted, and understood, and that the equations that underlie the simulations are similarly "open for inspection."

The policy simulations derive alternative paths of inflation in the nonfood sector net of energy implied by alternative exogenous paths of the output gap. Since relative energy prices are likely to rise over the next few years, the corresponding paths for the GNP deflator would all lie above that presented in Figure 14.3.

Because the previous analysis leads to the conclusion that the extended-period price equation contains a more plausible lag pattern on trend unit labor cost, and that the steeper Phillips curve in the extended-period wage equation is likely to be more accurate, the simulations presented here are based on the price equation in Table 14.2, column 7, and the wage equation in Table 14.3, column 8. The wage equation that uses the output gap rather than the unemployment variables of the original specification is employed to avoid the problem of creating equations that link those unemployment variables to the output gap.

Tax rates were all assumed to remain unchanged at their values in 1976:4, and the change in the relative prices of capital and consumption goods was set equal to zero in all simulations. Simple equations were developed to relate changes in materials prices and the change in the productivity deviation to the change in the output gap. Further adjustments were made to ensure that the inflation rate would neither accelerate nor decelerate when the output gap was zero. To obtain this result in dynamic simulations, it is not enough to constrain the sum of coefficients on wages in the price equation, and on prices in the wage equation, to be equal to 1. Three other important restrictions must be imposed: First, the trend rate of productivity growth in the price equation must be set equal to the constant term in the wage equation. This switch, from 1.96 to 2.13 percent annually, is small enough to be acceptable and within the range of the standard error in the equation originally used to estimate the productivity trend. Second, the growth rate of the wage variable in the price equation must equal

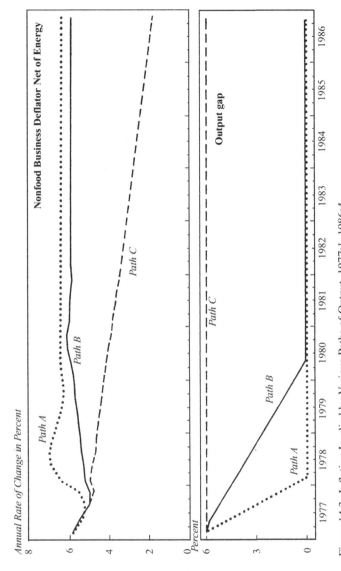

Figure 14.3. Inflation Implied by Various Paths of Output, 1977:1–1986:4
Source. Based on Table 14.2, column 7, and Table 14.3, column 8.

385

that of the wage variable in the wage equation. Third, there must be no change in relative materials prices.

Figure 14.3 corresponds to these assumptions and displays three combinations of inflation and unemployment. Path A is an implausibly rapid recovery that reduces the output gap from its 6.2 percent rate at the end of 1976 to zero by 1978:1. At first inflation is predicted to slow down moderately, benefitting from the lagged influence of low rates of change in wages and prices in 1976, but then an acceleration begins. The "rate of change" effects of a rapidly falling output gap push inflation close to 7 percent in late 1978, followed by an adjustment to the long-run "steady state" rate of 6.4 percent.

A slower recovery, path B, reaches a zero gap in 1980, rather than in early 1978. Slower growth has both transitory and permanent benefits. Inflation is lower by as much as 1.3 percentage points at an annual rate in late 1978, and the long-run "steady state" rate of inflation is 0.4 point slower.[18]

Since path B corresponds most closely to the recovery path apparently desired by the Carter administration, this "optimistic" simulation conflicts with the administration's avowed aim of reducing unemployment while simultaneously achieving a deceleration of inflation to 4 percent. Even on the optimistic assumption of zero change in relative energy and food prices, the administration's policy goals are inconsistent.

The third alternative in Figure 14.3, path C, shows the rate of deceleration of inflation that would obtain if the output gap were held permanently at 6.2 percent. The inflation rate would fall rapidly during 1977, reflecting the delayed impact of the lower-than-predicted actual rates of wage and price change during 1976. Subsequently, a further modest slowdown of inflation would occur, beginning with a 0.24 percentage point drop in the inflation rate in 1978, widening to a deceleration of 0.36 percentage point per year in 1986. This turtle-like deceleration of inflation reflects the extremely weak effect of a high output gap on wage behavior, and the absence of any effect of a maintained gap on price behavior.

In my own judgment, the assumptions underlying the simulations reflected in the figure lean toward the optimistic side. First, as noted they ignore the prospect of rising relative prices of energy over the years ahead. Second, they assume no upward trend in relative materials prices, in contrast with the actually observed trend of 2.0 percent a year for 1963–76 (adjusted to a constant output gap). Third, they assume that compensation per man hour and average hourly earnings will grow at equal rates, when in fact the former has outpaced the latter by 0.3 percentage point a year on average since mid-1971. If that trend were assumed to continue, it would put added upward pressure on the price equation for any path of average hourly earnings predicted by the wage equation. Alternative,

---

[18] As an example of a more optimistic conclusion, a "control solution" published by Data Resources, Inc., predicted that the economy could reach 5.5 percent unemployment in 1980, a path roughly equivalent to my path B, with only a 5.4 percent change in the GNP deflator in 1980. See Otto Eckstein and others, *Economic Issues and Parameters of the Next 4 Years* (Data Resources, Inc., 1977), table 6, p. 30, solution "CONTROL1229."

more pessimistic, assumptions could easily add 1 to 2 points to the inflation rate by 1980 and as much as 3 to 4 points by 1986.

14.5 CONCLUSION

All approaches fail to explain the increased variance of inflation during 1971– 6 as compared to the pre-1971 period. But overall, the *cumulative* amount of inflation since 1971 can be explained – even overexplained – by established econometric procedures. Both the structural price and the structural wage equations can track the cumulative change in the prices of nonfood business product net of energy and in wages to within a percentage point, once they incorporate the sensible constraint that sums of coefficients of prices on wages and wages on prices equal unity.

The analysis of this paper leads to the following interesting conclusions.

First, the short-run Phillips curve relating wage change to unemployment or the output gap may well be steeper than implied by equations estimated for sample periods ending in 1971. While this result helps to explain why wage changes were so moderate in 1976, it implies that a rapid economic recovery may bring about a greater acceleration in inflation than some commentators appear to anticipate.

Second, the speed of recovery matters, in both the price and the wage equations. It is the rate of change of the output gap that influences the rate of change of prices relative to wages, and there is also a partial impact from the speed of the change in output in the output-gap version of the wage equations.

Third, the ability of product prices and the output gap alone to explain wage behavior suggests that the demand for labor by firms is the main determinant of wages, and that autonomous actions or reactions by workers have little impact.

Fourth, I conclude that price controls worked temporarily, with a decline in the price level followed by a rebound, but that wage controls had if anything a perverse effect. Why the effectiveness of the controls program should have been limited to prices is a puzzle that others may be better able to answer. The implications for wage guidelines or jawboning are not reassuring.

Fifth, none of the increases in food or oil prices in 1973–4 appears to have been incorporated into wages. In the context of my previous study of supply shocks, this implies that policymakers could have stimulated nominal income growth to accommodate some of the effect of food and oil prices without setting off an endless inflationary spiral. But the strong demand effects exhibited in the equations of this paper suggest that such a policy of accommodation would have substantially lessened the deceleration of inflation between 1974 and 1976.[19]

[19] A hypothetical accommodative policy that maintained the output gap at zero in 1974–76 would have caused substantial extra inflation, reaching a peak in mid-1975 of 3.8 percentage points over that which actually occurred, and then tapering off to an excess of 2.0 percentage points in late 1976. This conclusion is based on a dynamic simulation of the same equations as are used in Figure 14.3.

Sixth, perhaps most important, the outlook for inflation is rather grim. Despite the continuing output gap, the statistical evidence presented above indicates that any further deceleration in inflation is highly unlikely. On the contrary, it points to the probability of some acceleration as the economy continues its recovery. While the extent of that acceleration will depend on the speed of the recovery, inflation rates of 6 or 7 percent seem likely for the next several years, compared with the 5 percent rate during 1976. Any serious effort to eliminate inflation through demand restraint would be exceedingly costly; a strategy of maintaining the late 1976 output gap might bring the inflation rate down to 2 percent by the mid-eighties, but only through a loss of output that would substantially exceed $1 trillion.

Finally, as a corollary to this unpleasant verdict, the recovery itself is likely to require a maintained growth of monetary aggregates above rates that now seem acceptable to the Federal Reserve, in order to finance an annual growth of nominal gross national product of 12 or 13 percent during the rest of the decade. How the makers of monetary policy will react to this dilemma remains to be seen.

CHAPTER 15

The Output Cost of Disinflation in Traditional and Vector Autoregressive Models

With Stephen R. King

The speed of adjustment of the aggregate price level to demand and supply shocks has long been a leading topic of controversy in macroeconomics. Among the many issues requiring for their resolution solid empirical evidence on the dynamics of price adjustment is the prediction of the output loss that would accompany a strategy of monetary disinflation. In 1978 Arthur M. Okun surveyed a variety of econometric evidence and reached the pessimistic conclusion that the inflation process in the postwar United States is so inertia prone that the cumulative sacrifice of 10 percent of a year's GNP would be required to achieve a permanent 1 percentage point reduction in the inflation rate.[1]

This paper compares the dynamic response patterns of prices and output that emerge from two quite different approaches to time-series econometrics, the traditional structural framework imbedded in most econometric models, and the more recent nonstructural or atheoretical vector autoregressive (VAR) technique. Both approaches reach conclusions by imposing restrictions of different types; by assessing the validity of these restrictions, we are able to compare the merits of each methodology. Of equal importance are new estimates of the speed of price adjustment in the postwar United States, which we summarize in a single number called the sacrifice ratio that measures the output loss required to eliminate permanently one point of inflation. By introducing several channels of monetary influence on the inflation process that are often overlooked, we conclude that the sacrifice ratio is roughly half that suggested by Okun's survey.

Although they are often regarded as radically different, both the traditional and VAR approaches to time-series econometrics essentially carry out the same task of allocating zero restrictions in the face of scarce degrees of freedom. With

[1] Arthur M. Okun, "Efficient Disinflationary policies," *American Economic Review*, vol. 68 (May 1978, *Papers and Proceedings, 1977.*), pp. 348–52.

This research was supported by the National Science Foundation. We appreciate the comments on an early draft of this paper by Jorge Braga de Macedo, Robert B. Litterman, Bennett T. McCallum, and especially Stanley Fischer. We are also indebted to Thomas Doan and members of the Brookings panel for helpful suggestions. (*Source. "The Output Cost of Disinflation in Traditional and Vector Autoregressive Models." Brookings Papers on Economic Activity.* 1982; vol. 13, no. 1, pp. 205–42.)

only 140 quarterly observations available in the postwar U.S. national accounts data for 1947–81, an econometric model containing sixteen endogenous and exogenous variables would have only four degrees of freedom remaining if each variable were entered with eight lagged values on the right-hand side of each equation.[2] The traditional approach uses theory to exclude all but a few variables from each equation – for instance, the investment tax credit matters for investment but not for wages – while price control dummies and energy prices matter for prices but not for consumption, and so on. This method of imposing zero restrictions allows econometric models to become very large and, if necessary, to contain more variables than there are sample observations available.

In contrast, the typical small-scale VAR model treats all variables symmetrically by including each on the right-hand side of every equation and by allowing each explanatory variable to enter with the same number of lagged values. This symmetry forces investigators to limit the total number of variables in the model to an arbitrary subset believed to be important for the economy as a whole (interest rate, money, price level, output) and to exclude variables that the traditional approach typically includes in individual equations (investment tax credit, control dummies, energy prices).[3]

Christopher Sims has argued convincingly that many of the zero restrictions embodied in traditional models are "incredible," particularly because any lagged variable may influence the formation of expectations. Our paper makes the reverse criticism that the zero restrictions embodied in VAR models are equally dubious because the pursuit of symmetry has usually led investigators to exclude explanatory variables that other research demonstrates to be highly significant statistically in some equations, and to have a strong theoretical presumption of relevance. Our preferred hybrid strategy for model specification uses the VAR approach to evaluate conventional restrictions and exogeneity assumptions, but then includes a second step that "edits" insignificant variables and lag lengths, as well as nominal variables from equations explaining relative price variables, to obtain a model of tractable size that yields plausible relations in long-run simulations.

Our use of alternative models to calculate sacrifice ratios for hypothetical *future* policy regimes is subject to the Lucas critique that parameters estimated from sample-period values may not be invariant to arbitrary shifts in policy.

---

[2] With eight lagged values, the first observation of each equation would be 1949:1, leaving 132 observations in the sample period.

[3] The current popularity of VAR models attests to the influence of two papers by Christopher Sims, "Macroeconomics and Reality," *Econometrica*, vol. 48 (January 1980), pp. 1–48, and "Comparison of Interwar and Postwar Business Cycles: Monetarism Reconsidered," *American Economic Review*, vol. 70 (May 1980 *Papers and Proceedings, 1979*), pp. 250–7. Some of the methodology was developed in Robert B. Litterman. "Techniques of Forecasting Using Vector Autoregressions." Working Paper 115 (Federal Reserve Bank of Minneapolis, 1979). Recent applications of the technique include Stanley Fischer, "Relative Shocks, Relative Price Variability, and Inflation." *BPEA, 2:1981*, pp. 381–431, and Benjamin Friedman. "The Roles of Money and Credit in Macroeconomic Analysis." Working Paper 831 (National Bureau of Economic Research, 1981).

Most papers using the VAR technique have avoided this critique by constructing multivariate exogeneity and causality tests for small innovations to money or other variables assumed to occur within the historical sample period. We defend our excursion into the future against the Lucas critique by pointing to the stability of parameters in our basic inflation equation over a historical sample period during which the response of monetary policy to output and inflation underwent significant changes.

15.1 THE VAR METHODOLOGY

Estimation

The VAR methodology begins with the concept of a covariance-stationary time series, one that has a mean and an autocovariance at all lags that are constant through time.[4] By Wold's theorem any such time-series process, say x_t, can be decomposed into two components. The first, η_t, is linearly deterministic, that is, exactly predictable given a linear combination of its own past values; the second is a moving average, possibly of infinite length, of white noise errors, ϵ_t:[5]

$$x_t = \eta_t + A(L)\epsilon_t, \quad E(\epsilon_t) = 0$$

$$E(\epsilon_t \epsilon_{t-h}) = \begin{cases} \Omega & k = 0 \\ 0 & k \neq 0, \end{cases} \tag{1}$$

where $A(L)$ is a polynomial in the lag operator.

When the polynomial $A(L)$ is invertible,[6] an autoregressive representation of equation 1 exists and can be written as

$$A(L)^{-1}x_t = A(L)^{-1}\eta_t + \epsilon_t. \tag{2}$$

By moving the lagged x's to the right-hand side of the equation and combining them with the η's, which, by definition, are linear functions of lagged x's, we obtain the system of equations,

$$x_t = B(L)x_t + \epsilon_t = \sum_{j=1}^{N} B_j L^j x_t + \epsilon_t. \tag{3}$$

---

[4] Covariance stationarity is not an innocuous assumption, but it can often be approximated for macroeconomic time series by defining variables as first differences.

[5] White noise errors, like covariance stationary series, have constant autocovariances, but in addition have all covariances identically zero. That is, there are no systematic components that would enable a white noise process to be predicted from its own past.

[6] Invertibility of $A(L)$ rules out cases in which x_t, depends to a greater extent on past innovations than on current ones. For example, if equation I were univariate. $\eta_t = 0$, and $A(L) = 1 - aL$, that equation would be $x_t = \epsilon_t, -a\epsilon_{t-1}$. Successive substitutions to eliminate the lagged error terms would yield

$$x_t + ax_{t-1} + a^2 x_{t-2} + \cdots + a^m x_{t-m} = \epsilon_t - a^{m+1}\epsilon_{t-m-1}.$$

If a is greater than 1, the last term does not vanish as m increases, so no autoregressive representation exists. In this case, the requirement of invertibility for the polynomial $A(L) = 1 - aL$ is that a is less than 1 in absolute value.

In general, N, the lag length of the autoregressive representation in 3, will be infinite, but in practice it is generally truncated to some number that is both small enough to be computationally feasible and large enough to ensure that the equation residuals are approximately white noise. In this case, 3 is the basic form of a vector autoregression in which each regressor x_{it}, an element of the vector x_t, is a linear function of its own lagged values, the lagged values of all other regressors in the system, and a white noise error term. If there are M time-series variables in the model, then the coefficient matrix B_j is of dimension M by NM. As a consequence, every variable in the model is treated as being endogenous, and each has two components – its best linear predictor given information available one period previously, and its linearly unpredictable "innovation."

An example of the general form of 3 can be seen in a hypothetical VAR model containing only two variables, growth of the money supply, m_t, and p_t, the GNP deflator:[7]

$$m_t = b_{mm} m_{t-1} + b_{mp} p_{t-1} + \epsilon_{mt} \tag{4a}$$

$$p_t = b_{pm} m_{t-1} + b_{pp} p_{t-1} + \epsilon_{pt}. \tag{4b}$$

Here each variable is explained by one lag ($N = 1$) of each of the two ($M = 2$) variables in the model and an error or "innovation" term (ϵ_t) that represents that part of the dependent variable not predictable from knowledge of lagged values of the regressors. Since we have two equations and one lagged value, the coefficient matrix B is of dimension 2×2.

Equation 3 and the example (4a and 4b) take the form of the multivariate regression model, and the presence of identical sets of regressors for each of the M equations ensures that the coefficients may be estimated consistently by single-equation least squares.[8] If it is further assumed that the innovations, ϵ_t, are not only white noise but are also normally distributed, then the estimates of the B_j coefficients are asymptotically efficient.

The testing of restrictions in a VAR is quite different from standard econometric methodology because it involves considering the impact of a given restriction on the model as a whole, rather than on each individual equation.[9] For

---

[7] Throughout this paper lowercase variables denote rates of growth; uppercase denote levels.

[8] Peter Schmidt, *Econometrics* (Marcel Dekker, 1976), pp. 78–80.

[9] Tests of restrictions on the model can be carried out by comparing the determinants of the restricted and unrestricted covariance matrices of the equation errors. The test statistic a can be computed as

$$a = (T - k)(\log |\Omega^R| - \log |\Omega^U|),$$

where T is the number of observations, k is the number of estimated parameters in each equation, and $|\Omega^R|$ and $|\Omega^U|$ denote, respectively, the determinants of the contemporaneous covariance matrix of the residuals of the restricted and unrestricted models. This statistic a is distributed as x^2 with r degrees of freedom, where r is the number of restrictions imposed. If the Ω matrices are diagonal (implying that residuals are mutually uncorrelated across equations) the relevant determinants are simply the product of the residual sums of squares from each equation and the statistic a clearly interpretable as the deterioration in fit caused by imposing the restrictions. If

instance, the test of truncation restrictions has generally been to test the joint significance of longer lags (such as eight versus four quarters) on all variables in all equations. Yet this procedure may reject longer lags that are unimportant in all equations except one, the one in which the lags may have a significant explanatory role. This is an example of how substantive economic issues become intertwined with restrictions that are said to be introduced simply to reduce complexity.

Simulations

All simulations calculated in VAR studies must grapple with the treatment of contemporaneous correlation among innovations. In conventional model building this issue is often suppressed by arbitrary restrictions that constrain the contemporaneous correlation between two variables to be unidirectional. This occurs, for instance, in models in which the money supply is treated as exogenous, and current money changes are included in an equation for price changes. In the VAR framework both prices and money are assumed to be endogenous, and because contemporary right-hand variables are omitted at the estimation stage, any contemporaneous correlation shows up as a correlation between the current innovations in the price and money equations.

Simulations of the effect of an exogenous shock require that some assumption be made about the causal ordering of the relation. Investigators can avoid an arbitrary choice about causal ordering only if they have a single-equation model, or if they are fortunate enough to find that the innovations in each equation, for instance, ϵ_{mt} and ϵ_{pt} in the example 4a, 4b are contemporaneously uncorrelated. In this lucky case, the estimated equations 4a and 4b can be inverted to compute the moving-average response of p_t to current and past innovations,

$$p_t = \epsilon_{pt} + b_{pp}\,\epsilon_{p,t-1} + (b_{pp}^2 + b_{pm}b_{mp})\epsilon_{p,t-2} + \dots$$
$$+\, b_{pm}\,\epsilon_{m,t-1} + (b_{pm}b_{mm} + b_{pp}b_{pm})\epsilon_{m,t-2} + \dots, \qquad (5)$$

and a symmetric response for m_t. In 5 a monetary innovation in period t has no effect on prices until period $t + 1$, and vice versa for the effect of a price innovation on money. More generally, the estimated system of equations given by 3 can be inverted to compute x_t as a moving average of past errors:

$$x_t = (I - B(L))^{-1}\epsilon_t. \qquad (6)$$

If, however, the innovation processes are contemporaneously correlated, investigators must decide how to treat this correlation. In our two-equation

there were only one equation the statistic would reduce to approximately

$$\frac{(SSR^R - SSR^U)}{SSR^U/(T - k)},$$

where SSR denotes the sum of squared residuals. This statistic is easily seen to be r multiplied by the conventional F-statistic for testing restrictions in a single regression-equation.

example, there are two obvious alternatives. First, the error in the money equation can be decomposed into a portion explained by the price innovation and a remaining independent portion, u_{mt}:

$$\epsilon_{mt} = c_{mp}\epsilon_{pt} + u_{mt}; \quad \epsilon_{pt} = u_{pt}, \tag{7}$$

where c_{mp} is the estimated coefficient in a regression of ϵ_{mt} on ϵ_{pt}. The second alternative is to assume that the price error can be decomposed in the opposite direction:[10]

$$\epsilon_{pt} = c_{pm}\epsilon_{mt} + u_{pt}; \quad \epsilon_{mt} = u_{mt}. \tag{8}$$

Now consider introducing a shock, s_m, into the money equation equal to one sample-period standard deviation of the error, ϵ_m, and comparing this event with another hypothetical situation in which no such shock occurs. The calculated effect of this on prices in the initial period would be $\Delta p_t = 0$ under the alternative of 7 and in the second period would be $b_{pm}s_m$. In contrast, if the alternative of 8 were used, the initial-period response of prices would be $c_{pm}s_m$, and the second period response would be $(b_{pm} + b_{pp}c_{pm})s_m$. Thus it is likely that the simulation of a monetary disinflation using 8 would yield a larger and faster dynamic response of prices than an alternative simulation using 7.

At first glance it might seem preferable to avoid the choice between 7 and 8 by ignoring the contemporaneous correlation, that is, by setting both c_{mp} and c_{pm} equal to zero even though they are known to be nonzero.[11] This third choice would be tantamount to the selection of 7 for the simulation of a monetary shock, since the price responses in the first two periods would be, respectively, zero and $b_{pm}s_m$. And the use of the same criterion for the simulation of the effects of a price innovation would lead investigators into an inconsistency, since in this case they would have switched in midstream from 7 to 8. In short, the third choice is even more arbitrary than the first two. It is both inconsistent and involves throwing out known information.[12]

---

[10] Note that these two alternatives, and the third choice discussed below, do not exhaust the plausible assumptions about causality between contemporaneous errors. It would also be possible to assume that each error helps to explain the others. Then, however, regression techniques could not be used, and the size of each error's effects on the others would have to be known a priori.

[11] In this example, c_{mp} and c_{pm} are the regression coefficients from equations 7 and 8: hence,

$$c_{mp} = \sum_{t=1}^{I} \epsilon_{mt}\epsilon_{pt} / \sum \epsilon_{pt}^2 = \omega_{mp}/\omega_{pp},$$

where ω_{ij} is the i, jth element of Ω.
In general, the C matrix can be calculated recursively from the identity $(I - C)\epsilon_t = u_t$, and hence the identity

$$(I - C)^{-1}uu'(I - C)^{-1} = \Omega$$

[12] In general, any linear combination of c_{pm} and c_{mp} would be acceptable, since equations 7 and 8 are both unidentified, but in looking at the extremes we are able to examine the full effect of the ordering assumption on the properties of the system.

The assumption about causal ordering of contemporaneous errors in a VAR system amounts to a decision about admitting current variables into the estimating equation. To see this, return to the general VAR model in 3 and decompose each error term, ϵ_{it}, into a part explained by the other innovations, ϵ_{jt}, and a remaining component that is orthogonal to them, u_t.

Following the analysis given above for the two-variable case, we assume that if ϵ_{jt} affects ϵ_{it}, there is no reverse causality. We order the variables so that a given error affects only errors that are lower in the list; that is, ϵ_{jt} affects ϵ_{it} only if $j < i$. This ordering is called a triangularization of the system. In matrix notation we can write a set of M regression equations analogous to 7 and 8:

$$\epsilon_t = C\epsilon_t + u_t, \tag{9}$$

where C is a lower triangular $M \times M$ matrix with zeros on the diagonal, and whose i, jth element is the regression coefficient of ϵ_i on ϵ_j for $j < i$. Since the ϵ_t vector is orthogonal to all of the regressors in equation 3, the B and C coefficients could also be obtained by fitting the set of regressions,

$$x_t = \sum_{j=1}^{N} B_j L^j x_t + C\epsilon_t + u_t, \tag{10}$$

where each equation except the first includes in the list of regressors the residuals from each previous regression. It is easy to show that identical residuals, u_t, to those in 10 will be obtained from an alternative set of regressions that directly include, in all equations except the first, the current values of the dependent variables from each previous equation,

$$x_t = \sum_{j=1}^{N} D_j L^j x_t + G x_t + u_t, \tag{11}$$

where D_j is the $M \times M$ matrix of coefficients on variables lagged j periods, and G is the lower triangular matrix of coefficients on included current variables.[13] In terms of the simple model of equations 4a and 4b, if the money equation were ordered first the two equations would be estimated as

$$m_t = d_{mm} m_{t-1} + d_{mp} p_{t-1} + u_{mt} \tag{12a}$$

$$p_t = d_{pm} m_{t-1} + d_{pp} p_{t-1} + g_{pm} m_t + u_{pt}. \tag{12b}$$

---

[13] This can be seen by substituting each equation of 10 into every equation with a lower order. The D and G matrices are related to B and C matrices by the following identities:

$$G(i, m) = C(i, m) - \sum_{k=1}^{i-1} C(k, m)$$

$$B_j(i, m) = B_j(i, m) - \sum_{k=1}^{i-1} C(k, m) D_j(k, m),$$

where $x(i, m)$ represents the (i, m)th element of x.

Table 15.1. *A Three-Equation VAR Model*

Dependent	Number of Coefficients on Explanatory Variables					
	Lagged			Current		
Variable	M	Q	P	M	Q	P
M	N	N	N	...	...	...
Q	N	N	N	1	...	...
P	N	N	N	1	1	...

Here the money equation contains only lagged values, but the inflation equation also includes the contemporaneous value of money.

The outcome of all this is that when contemporaneous errors have been causally ordered, a VAR model of the form of equation 3 is equivalent to the system of equation 10 or 11, or the simple example of equation 12. And these systems look a lot more like a "conventional" econometric model than 3 because they include both current and lagged values of right-hand variables. The main differences between conventional models and triangularized VAR models are that the latter include all lagged regressors in each equation, impose equal lag lengths, and allow current right-hand variables to enter only in a recursive fashion.

The question remains of how to order the equations. The recursive form (11) suggests that, recalling that G is lower triangular, those variables that respond most to current events, such as changes in exchange rates and interest rates, should be placed at the bottom of the equation list so that their values reflect contemporaneous realizations of variables of a higher order. Conversely, those variables thought by the investigator to be least sensitive to current innovations would be placed at the top; this is consistent with the ordering used by Sims.[14] The ordering chosen clearly depends on the investigator's previous beliefs for, while it seems reasonable to order interest and exchange rates at the bottom of the list, the relative positions of money, output, and prices are controversial.

The implicit appearance of contemporaneous variables in 11 allows us to use a simple tabular device to describe any of the models examined below by indicating which variables contribute coefficients to the D and G matrices. For instance, Sims's simple three-equation model for the levels of money, M, output, Q, and prices, P, can be displayed as in Table 15.1.[15]

The table states that the three equations explaining M, Q, and P, respectively, each contain N lagged values of M, Q, and P, while in addition the Q equation contains the current value of M, and the P equation contains the current values

---

[14] Sims, "Macroeconomics and Reality."
[15] Sims. "Interwar and Postwar."

of M and Q. The M equation contains no current values. If the right-hand (G) matrix were to contain elements above the diagonal, the model would not be recursive and would have to be solved simultaneously.

15.2 GRADUAL ADJUSTMENT OF PRICES TO DEMAND AND SUPPLY SHOCKS

Whereas the VAR model of the previous section is minimally restricted and atheoretical, this section introduces a more traditional model with many restrictions – both in the construction of variables and in the introduction of particular variables and lag lengths into individual equations – which reflect a mixture of previous beliefs and empirical experimentation. The VAR model is symmetric in variables, whereas the central focus here is on the specification of an equation explaining the rate of change of the aggregate price level. Each additional equation is provided solely to make endogenous a variable that appears on the right-hand side of the inflation equation, rather than for its intrinsic interest. These auxiliary equations are deliberately constructed to avoid the introduction of any additional endogenous variables into the model beyond those appearing in the inflation equation.

Specification of the Inflation Equation

The aggregate supply sector of traditional econometric models has typically included two separate equations describing wage and price behavior, with the former including a variable such as the unemployment rate measuring labor market tightness, and the latter involving a variable such as the rate of capacity utilization measuring product market tightness. Yet in the presence of gradual adjustment of wages and prices that is generally assumed in such econometric research, the relevant theoretical framework is a model without market clearing characterized by spillovers between the product and labor market that imply a high correlation between the unemployment of labor and the utilization of capacity.[16] Indeed, as Okun's law would lead one to expect, the level and change in the ratio of actual to "natural" real GNP (hereafter the output ratio, $\hat{Q}_t$) can explain changes in both wages and prices as well as variables traditionally identified with particular markets, such as the unemployment rate and ratio of unfilled orders to capacity.[17]

---

[16] The spillover model is analyzed in John Muellbauer and Richard Portes, "Macroeconomic Models with Quantity Rationing," *Economic Journal*, vol. 88 (December 1978), pp. 788–821. The sources of gradual wage and price adjustment are examined in Arthur M. Okun, *Prices and Quantities: A Macroeconomic Analysis* (Brookings Institution, 1981), and Robert J. Gordon, "Output Fluctuations and Gradual Price Adjustment," *Journal of Economic Literature*, vol. 19 (June 1981), pp. 493–530.

[17] Robert J. Gordon, "Can the Inflation of the 1970s Be Explained?" *BPEA. 1:1977*, pp. 253–77. The shift from the more structural interpretation of wage and price equations present in Gordon's earlier papers to the present interest in the VAR approach can be traced to those 1977 results and

The inflation equation developed here is designed to suppress wage changes as both a dependent and independent variable.[18] Wage and price markup equations are specified with restrictions on lags that allow the wage variable to drop out of the model, leaving inflation specified as a function of its own past values, a demand pressure variable, x_t, and a vector of various supply shift variables, z_t, that may influence the determination of wages, prices, or both:

$$p_t = \gamma_0 + \gamma_1(L)p_{t-1} + \gamma_2(L)x_t + \gamma_3(L)z_t + \epsilon_t. \tag{13}$$

Here each L in parenthesis indicates that the set of coefficients is allowed to be a polynomial in the lag operator. Each component of the z vector is defined to equal zero when a particular supply shift is absent, allowing a zero value for the sum of the x_t, term and the constant term to be interpreted as a "no-shock natural rate" situation compatible with steady inflation ($p_t = p_{t-1}$).

In the research paper that developed the particular form of the inflation equation used here, the proxy for x_t was George Perry's demographically weighted unemployment rate, U_t^W.[19] The natural weighted unemployment rate can be calculated from 13 as

$$U^{W*} = -\gamma_0 \Big/ \sum_{j=1}^{N} \gamma_{2j},$$

where the γ_{2j} are the individual coefficients in the $\gamma_2(L)$ distribution.[20] In this paper we simplify the presentation by omitting the unemployment rate and substituting the highly correlated log output ratio, $\hat{Q}_t$. Because the natural unemployment rate and the natural real GNP levels are defined by the same criterion, the log output ratio is zero in equilibrium, allowing the constant term to be excluded from 13.[21]

Table 15.2 presents estimates of 13 for the sample period 1954:2 through 1980:4 and for the first and last halves of the period separately. The estimation

particularly to Christopher Sims's published remarks on that paper (in that same *BPEA* volume, p. 279): "Christopher Sims expressed some amusement that the best wage equation had no labor market variables in it. This result conformed with his belief that wage and price equations cannot be distinguished as applying to different categories of behavior. It was preferable to consider them as interesting, statistical reduced-form summaries of the dynamic relationships among the variables."

[18] Robert J. Gordon, "Inflation, Flexible Exchange Rates, and the Natural Rate of Unemployment," in Martin Neil Baily, ed., *Workers, Jobs, and Inflation* (Brookings Institution, 1982), pp. 88–155. That paper tests and rejects the inclusion of lagged wages in the wage equation.

[19] George L. Perry, "Changing Labor Markets and Inflation," *BPEA, 3:1970*, pp. 411–41.

[20] Gordon in "Inflation, Flexible Exchange Rates" tests and rejects the hypothesis that the natural weighted unemployment rate shifted upward in the 1970s.

[21] Natural real GNP, Q_t, is set equal to actual real GNP, Q_t, in years when the actual weighted unemployment rate was equal to the estimated natural weighted unemployment rate. It is interpolated for intervening years, and is assumed to grow after 1979:1 at an annual rate of 2.75 percent. Our resulting Q_t series is $1,520 billion in 1980 and thus is even more pessimistic than the recent $1,546 billion estimate in John A. Tatom, "Potential Output and the Recent Productivity Decline," *Review of the Federal Reserve Bank of St. Louis*, vol. 64 (January 1982), p. 16.

Table 15.2. *Basic Equation Explaining Quarterly Change in the Fixed-Weight GNP Deflator, Alternative Sample Periods, 1954:2 through 1980:4[a]*

Independent Variable or Summary Statistic[b]	1954:2–1980:4	1954:2–1966:4	1967:1–1980:4
Independent variable			
Lagged dependent variable, p_{t-1}			
1954:2–1966:4	0.88**	0.89*	...
Mean lag	(14.6)	(13.7)	
1967:1–1980:4	1.01*	...	1.04*
Mean lag	(8.9)		(7.6)
Output ratio, $\hat{Q}_t$	0.35*	0.42*	0.32*
Nixon control dummies, z_{1t}			
Controls "on"	−1.49*	...	−0.96***
Controls "off"	2.47*	...	1.77***
Deviation in productivity growth, z_{2t}	−0.19*	−0.08	−0.31*
Relative price of food and energy, z_{3t}	0.60*	0.56	0.37
Relative price of imports, z_{4t}	0.06**	−0.10	0.08***
Effective exchange rate for 1975–80, z_{5t}	−0.10*	...	−0.07***
Effective minimum wage rate, z_{6t}	0.03*	0.04*	0.04
Effective social security tax rate, z_{7t}	0.33***	0.05	−0.11
Summary statistic			
$\bar{R}^2$	0.956	0.859	0.940
Standard error of estimate	0.740	0.623	0.868
Sum of squared residuals	39.4	8.9	18.8

[a] The output ratio. $\hat{Q}$, is the log of the ratio of real GNP to natural real GNP. The latter is set equal to real GNP in years when the actual weighted unemployment rate was equal to the estimated natural weighted unemployment rate, is interpolated for intervening years, and is assumed to grow after 1979:1 at an annual rate of 2.75 percent.

The z_{1t} Nixon control dummies are defined to sum to 4, since the dependent variable is the quarterly change multiplied by 4. Specifically, the Nixon "on" variable is defined as 0.8 for the five quarters 1971:3–1972:3, while the Nixon "off" variable is defined as 0.4 for 1974:2 and 1975:1, and 1.6 for 1974:3 and 1974:4.

The remaining variables are defined as follows: z_{2t}–the difference between the rate of growth of nonfarm business productivity and a trend that is allowed to decelerate from 2.56 percent a year during 1956–64, to 2.11 percent for 1964–72, to 1.22 percent for 1972–78, and to 0.5 percent for 1978–81: z_{3t}–the rate of growth of the fixed weight personal consumption expenditure deflator minus the growth in the same fixed weight consumption deflator stripped of food and energy: z_{4t}–the difference between the rates of growth of the fixed weight import deflator and the fixed weight GNP deflator: z_{5t}–the change in the index combining the exchange rates between U.S. dollars and seventeen other major currencies with weights derived from the International Monetary Fund's Multilateral Exchange Rate Model: z_{6t}–the difference between the rate of growth of the statutory minimum wage and average hourly earnings in the nonfarm economy: and z_{7t}–the percentage change in $(1/(1 - t))$. where t is the ratio of total federal and state and local social security contributions to total wage and salary income. All variables, except for the output ratio and the Nixon control variables, are expressed as rates of change. Quarterly changes are at annual rates.

[b] The lagged dependent variable, p_{t-1}. is the sum of coefficients of a twenty-four quarter lag distribution constrained to lie along a fourth-degree polynomial with a zero end-point constraint (with mean lags in parentheses): $\hat{Q}_t$ and z_{3t} are the sums of coefficients of an unconstrained lag distribution including the current and four lagged values: z_{2t} is the sum of coefficients of an unconstrained lag distribution including the current and one lagged value: z_{4t}, z_{6t}, and z_{7t} are the sums of coefficients of an unconstrained lag distribution including four lagged values: and z_{5t} is the coefficient on one lagged value.

Source. All data are from the national income and product accounts except the effective exchange rate and wage and hourly earnings data, which are from International Monetary Fund. *International Financial Statistics* and U.S. Bureau of Labor Statistics, respectively.

* Significant at the 1 percent level.
** Significant at the 5 percent level.
*** Significant at the 10 percent level.

for the full sample period allows one parameter change in the middle of the period, a shift in the coefficients on the lagged dependent variable; this sum of coefficients increases modestly in the last half, and the mean lag of the distribution shortens substantially from 14.6 to 8.9 quarters. The shift is highly significant, with $F(4,72) = 4.20$ exceeding the 1 percent critical value of 3.59, and may be due to the increased proportion of workers covered by cost-of-living agreements in the last half of the sample period.

The output ratio entry shows a highly significant sum of coefficients. The remainder of the table lists the sums of coefficients on the various supply-shift variables, z. The results for the full sample period in the first column can be summarized as follows. The Nixon-era price controls are estimated to have held down the price level by 1.5 percentage points, and their removal to have raised the price level by 2.5 points. It appears that this estimated effect from removing controls combines the effect of ending controls with the cumulative impact of the 1971–74 depreciation of the dollar, the main effect of which was delayed by the controls until 1974.[22] The coefficient on the deviation of actual productivity growth from its trend implies that firms base 20 percent of their price-setting decisions on actual productivity changes, and the remaining 80 percent on trend productivity growth.[23] Changes in the relative prices of food and energy are defined as the difference between the growth rates of the deflator for personal consumption expenditures, respectively including and excluding expenditures on food and energy. If the dependent variable were the change in the total consumption deflator, and if the other explanatory variables influenced only the consumption deflator net of food and energy with no impact on the difference between the two deflators, the coefficient on this variable in Table 15.2 would be 1. The actual coefficient of 0.6 results from some combination of, first, the effect of our choice of the fixed-weight GNP deflator as dependent variable, particularly the exclusion from this variable of oil and other imports; and second, the possible negative correlation between other explanatory variables in Table 15.2, such as the output ratio, and the difference between the deflators with and without food and energy.

Two other variables, changes in the relative price of imports and in the effective exchange rate of the dollar, reflect the sensitivity of U.S. inflation to international events.[24] Last, the equation includes two domestic supply-shift

---

[22] This interpretation is explained in Gordon's "Inflation, Flexible Exchange Rates" as due to the fact that the exchange rate is allowed to have an impact only beginning in 1975:2. Thus the controls "off" coefficient combines the effect of ending controls with the cumulative impact of the 1971–4 depreciation of the dollar.

[23] The productivity growth trend is allowed to decelerate from 2.56 percent a year during 1954–64 to 2.11 percent for 1964–72, to 1.22 percent for 1972–78, and to 0.5 percent for 1978–81. The estimated coefficient on the productivity growth deviation of -0.19 is remarkably close to the figure of -0.24 estimated more than a decade ago in Robert J. Gordon. "Inflation in Recession and Recovery." *BPEA. 1:1971*, p. 129.

[24] The former is defined as the difference between the quarterly rates of change of the fixed-weight import deflator and fixed-weight GNP deflator. The latter is defined as the change in

variables, changes in the effective minimum wage rate and in the effective social security tax rate. The coefficient on the latter indicates that about one third of an increase in the combined payroll tax (employee plus employer share) is shifted forward to prices, and the burden of the remainder falls on profits and wages.

Structure of the Model

The small econometric model designed to calculate the output and price effects of a monetary deceleration adds to 13 the minimum number of equations needed to explain its endogenous explanatory variables. Unlike the VAR approach, in which all variables are usually treated as endogenous, here some of the relevant variables are assumed to be exogenous:

Endogenous	*Exogenous*
Food-energy effect, z_{3t}	Adjusted money-supply growth, $\hat{m}_t$
Change in relative price of imports, z_{4t}	Price control dummies, z_{1t}
	Change in effective minimum wage, z_{6t}
Adjusted nominal GNP growth, $\hat{y}_t$	
Output ratio, $\hat{Q}_t$	Change in effective social security payroll tax, z_{7t}
Deviation in productivity growth, z_{2t}	
Inflation rate, p_t	
Change in U.S. effective exchange rate, z_{5t}	

The endogenous variables are arranged in an order that treats the food-energy effect and relative price of imports as "most exogenous" and allows the inflation rate and effective exchange rate to be influenced by current innovations in each of the variables listed above them. The variables included in each equation are shown in Table 15.3, which has a format similar to that of Table 15.1.

The first two variables listed, the food-energy effect and the relative price of imports, are often treated as exogenous. Here each of the two is allowed to depend on its own lagged values, the lagged values of the other, and the lagged effective exchange rate. Money, nominal GNP, and inflation are excluded from the equations for these two variables because in simulations of future policies we do not want the rate of relative price change to be influenced permanently by changes in the growth rates of nominal money and GNP.[25]

The sums of coefficients for these equations and those for the nominal GNP and labor productivity equations are set out in Table 15.4. It can be seen that the

---

the effective exchange rate using the IMF Multilateral Exchange Rate Model weights: see International Monetary Fund. *International Financial Statistics*, line am.x.

[25] Although the effective exchange rate is also a nominal variable, the equation describing its determination is neutral in the long run with respect to changes in the growth rate of nominal money. Our justification for this specification is given below.

Table 15.3. The Basic Restricted Model[a]

	Lagged Coefficients										Current Coefficients									
	Endogenous							Exogenous			Endogenous							Exogenous		
Dependent Variable	z_3	z_4	$\hat{y}$	$\hat{Q}$	z_2	p	z_5	$\hat{m}$	z_6	z_7	z_3	z_4	$\hat{y}$	$\hat{Q}$	z_2	p	z_5	$\hat{m}$	z_1	z_8
Relative price of food and energy, z_3	4	4	…	…	…	…	4	…	…	…	…	…	…	…	…	…	…	…	…	…
Relative price of imports, z_4	4	4	…	…	…	…	4	…	…	…	…	…	…	…	…	…	…	…	…	…
Adjusted nominal GNP growth, $\hat{y}$	…	…	4	…	…	…	…	4	…	…	1	…	…	…	…	…	…	1	…	…
Output ratio, $\hat{Q}$	…	…	…	1	…	…	…	…	…	…	…	…	1	…	…	1	…	…	…	…
Productivity growth deviation, z_2	2	…	…	4	…	…	…	…	…	…	1	…	…	1	…	…	…	…	…	…
Fixed-weight GNP deflator, p	4	4	…	4	1	24	1	4	4	4	1	1	…	1	…	…	…	…	…	…
Effective exchange rate, z_5	…	…	4^b	…	…	…	4	8^b	…	…	1	…	1^b	…	…	…	…	1^b	1	1

[a] See definition of variables in Table 15.2, note a. The growth rates of M1 and nominal GNP, less the growth rate of natural real GNP, are denoted by $\hat{m}$ and $\hat{y}$, respectively. The dummy variables in the exchange rate equation are indicated by z_8 and defined as $D72 = 1.0$ in 1972:1 and zero otherwise and as $D73 = 1.0$ in 1973:1 and 1973:2 and zero otherwise.

[b] For this equation $\hat{m}$ is actually $\hat{m}$, the deviation of actual money growth from its three-year moving average, and $\hat{y}$ is the deviation of velocity growth from its long-run trend. See the discussion of equation 15 in the text.

relative price of food and energy, z_3, depends most significantly on the foreign exchange rate, z_5. By contrast the relative price of imports, z_4, depends little on the exchange rate directly, but is very strongly influenced by its own lagged value and by the food-energy variable. The high coefficient on current and lagged food and energy prices appears to be due to the unusual and correlated movements of oil prices, import prices, and the exchange rate in the 1970s. In view of the possible spuriousness of this coefficient for long-run simulations, we later examine the sensitivity of the results of our model's simulation to the exclusion of the food-energy and import price equations.

Because the model is designed to trace the output and price effects of alternative deterministic monetary growth paths, money growth is treated as an exogenous variable. The growth rates of money and the nominal GNP are adjusted by netting out the growth of natural real GNP ($\hat{m}_t = m_t - q_t^*; \hat{y}_t = y_t - q_t^*$). This allows us to move back and forth between these nominal growth rates and the output ratio, using the basic identity,

$$\hat{Q}_t \equiv \hat{Q}_{t-1} + \hat{y}_t - p_t. \tag{14}$$

To avoid introducing any additional variables relevant to the determination of aggregate demand, the adjusted growth rate of nominal GNP is determined in a bivariate Granger-type VAR equation in which the only explanatory variables are lagged values of adjusted nominal GNP and current and lagged adjusted money growth. Then the inflation equation 13 and the identity 14 are solved simultaneously to split current nominal GNP growth between inflation and changes in the output ratio.

This leaves three endogenous variables in Table 15.3 to be determined. Deviations in productivity growth from trend (row 5) depend on lags in firing and hiring, which make the productivity variable a function of current and past changes in the output ratio.[26] The productivity variable is also allowed to be influenced by the food-energy effect. The coefficient sums in Table 15.4 show the food-energy effect on productivity, but mask the influence of output movements that primarily influence productivity in proportion to the rate of change of the output ratio rather than to its level. The actual coefficients imply that a 1 percent increase in the output ratio would be associated with a transitory 2.4 percent increase in productivity, which is then reversed in the following five quarters.

The inflation equation (row 6) is the same as that displayed in the first column of Table 15.2. The specification of changes in the foreign exchange rate is quite unconventional, as it is motivated by a desire to keep interest rates and foreign money and income variables out of the model. Clearly, the exchange rate should appreciate in response to a deceleration in domestic money growth, but a constraint is needed in future simulations to keep the exchange rate from appreciating forever.

---

[26] This specification and the timing of the slowdown in the trend are consistent with the empirical description of cyclical productivity effects in Robert J. Gordon, "The 'End-of-Expansion' Phenomenon in Short-Run Productivity Behavior," *BPEA, 2:1979*, pp. 447–61.

Table 15.4. *Auxiliary Equations for the Basic Model, 1954:2 through 1980:4[a]*

Sums of Coefficients on Current and Lagged Variables and Summary Statistic	Dependent Variable			
	Relative Price of Food and Energy, z_3	Relative Price of Imports, z_4	Adjusted Nominal GNP Growth, $\hat{y}$	Productivity Growth Deviation, z_2
Sums of Coefficients				
z_3	0.10	3.36*	...	−0.43
z_4	0.05	0.35*	...	...
$\hat{y}$	...	...	−0.14	...
$\hat{Q}$	...	...	...	−0.10*
z_5	−0.17*	−0.02	...	...
$\hat{m}$	...	...	1.27*	...
Summary Statistic				
$\bar{R}^2$	0.53	0.61	0.52	0.62
Standard Error of Estimate	0.95	5.1	3.1	2.0

* Significant at the 1 percent level.
[a] See the definitions of variables in Table 15.2, note a. and Table 15.3 note a.
Source. Same as Table 15.2.

The equation summarized in row 7 of Table 15.3 introduces $\tilde{m}_t$, the deviation of actual money growth from its three-year moving average, where the latter may be considered a proxy for foreign money growth and represents the idea that a monetary deceleration in the United States will be followed in due course by a deceleration in foreign money growth. The deviation of velocity growth from its long-run trend ($y_t - m_t - 3.2$) is also included, along with the food-energy variable and two dummy variables for the sharp correction in the overvaluation of the dollar that occurred after the Smithsonian Agreement and in early 1973. The estimated equation for the 1972:1–1980:4 sample period is

$$z_{5t} = \sum_{i=1}^{9} \beta_i \tilde{m}_{t-i+1} + \sum_{i=1}^{5} \delta_i (y_{t-i+1} - m_{t-i+1} - 3.2)$$
$$+ 2.07^{**}z_{3t} - 16.6^* D72 - 33.6^* D73 \tag{15}$$
$$R^2 = 0.75, \text{ standard error} = 7.5, \Sigma\beta_i = -4.3^{**}, \Sigma\delta_i = 1.4^{**}.$$

where $\tilde{m}_t = m_t - (1/12)\sum_{i=1}^{12} m_{t-i}$, $D72 = 1.0$ in the first quarter of 1972 (0 otherwise), and $D73 = 1.0$ in the first and second quarters of 1973 (0 otherwise), and the asterisks have the same meaning as in Table 15.2. The resulting equation for exchange rate has the property that the exchange rate appreciates while money growth decelerates, but reaches a new steady-state level when money growth arrives at its final constant growth rate in the simulations reported below.

Overall, the model is similar in structure to those that have been used to simulate the effects of monetary policy in our previous work. The main innovation here is the treatment of the food-energy and import variables as endogenous.[27] Compared to an unconstrained VAR model including the same variables, the main justification for the many zero restrictions in the model shown in Table 15.3 is a conscious attempt to separate real from nominal effects, so that the numerous variables representing relative price changes approach zero in the long run in simulations of alternative nominal money-growth paths.

15.3 CONCEPTUAL ISSUES IN SIMULATING FUTURE POLICIES

The Lucas Critique

Some economists, following the lead of Robert Lucas, object to econometric simulations of hypothetical future policy actions based on parameters estimated from a historical sample period when a different policy regime may have been in effect. In the specific case we examine, the dynamic response of output and price adjustment to a hypothetical future monetary deceleration depends mainly on the parameters in an inflation equation estimated for the 1954–80 sample period. Critics might argue that the inflation equation 13 is misspecified; in place of the $\gamma_1(L)$ lag distribution on past inflation should be substituted the expected rate of inflation, say Ep_t. Because no sustained monetary deceleration was ever actually carried out within the sample period, they would claim we have no evidence to rule out a much more prompt response of Ep_t to the announcement of a monetary deceleration in 1981 – the Volcker policy – than would be indicated by the historical lag distribution on past inflation rates.

Our willingness to take seriously simulations of hypothetical future monetary policies rests on the parallel nature of the hypothetical 1981–86 monetary deceleration and the actual 1965–70 monetary acceleration. Our argument in the following paragraphs can be divided into three components. There was a monetary "regime shift" in the mid-1960s that was more significant statistically than that implied by the Volcker monetary slowdown. Economic agents would have taken several years to recognize a regime shift in the mid-1960s and, presumably, a shift in the opposite direction in 1981. And, perhaps most important, the structure of our basic inflation equation exhibits structural stability when estimated across two subperiods (1954–66 and 1967–80) that bracket the mid-1960s monetary regime shift, thus yielding no presumption that a structural shift in that equation would occur in the early 1980s, even after the several years that would elapse before such a shift could be recognized.

---

[27] A similar model is displayed in Gordon. "Inflation in Recession and Recovery," appendix B. A similar treatment of the foreign exchange rate was introduced in "Inflation, Flexible Exchange Rates," equation A.5.

In the literature on the Lucas critique a monetary regime is in effect over a given time interval if the evolution of monetary growth can be described by a feedback rule having stable parameters. It is taken for granted in existing studies of monetary regime shifts, such as that of Thomas Sargent and Salih Neftci, that a change in regime can be identified econometrically by applying a Chow test to an equation in which the growth rate of the money supply is the dependent variable, and both the lagged dependent variable and other key macroeconomic aggregates to which the monetary authority might react are on the right-hand side of the equation.[28] Indeed, when equations explaining quarterly M1 growth for the three alternative sample periods 1954–80, 1954–66, and 1967–80 are estimated with four lags of M1 growth, inflation, and the output ratio as explanatory variables, a Chow test confirms that a structural shift at the beginning of 1967 is significant; the $F(13, 81)$ ratio is 2.26, compared to a 5 percent critical value of 1.87.

Is such a shift in structure implied by the deterministic money growth paths used to generate the post-1980 simulations in the next section? When the 1981–92 series of assumed money growth paths are treated as a dependent variable, and the generated values of inflation and the output ratio are treated as explanatory variables (along with the lagged dependent variable), a Chow test comparing the stability of 1981–92 coefficients with 1967–92 coefficients reveals no shift in structure in either the control or Volcker solutions. For the control solution path the $F(13, 91)$ ratio is 0.38, compared to a 5 percent critical value of 1.86, and for the Volcker solution the analogous F-ratio is 1.73.

The Lucas critique implies that a recognized shift from the stable parameters in one monetary regime to another set of stable parameters for a second monetary regime should lead to an instantaneous shift in the behavior of private agents. Yet a crucial flaw in this argument is the assumption of instant recognition that a regime change has occurred: how does one recognize such a change?

Consider the monetary regime shift at the beginning of 1967, described in the previous section, that can be recognized by the econometrician performing tests on data available in 1982. Could such a shift have been recognized and thus have been a source for a behavioral parameter change in 1967? Using currently available data, we can compare M1 equations estimated for the full period from 1954 to the end of the year L and two equations extending from 1954 to $L - 5$ and from $L - 5$ to L. We find that, while the Chow test reveals a structural shift significant at the 10 percent level as early as $L = 1968$, a structural shift is identified using the more conventional 5 percent significance level only when several more years have passed and $L = 1972$. With such flimsy evidence available in the interim between 1968 and 1972, our hypothetical "yeoman agent-econometrician" would have had no

---

[28] Salih Neftci and Thomas J. Sargent. "A Little Bit of Evidence on the Natural Rate Hypothesis from the U.S.," *Journal of Monetary Economics*, vol. 4 (April 1978), pp. 315–19.

firm reason for changing price-and-wage-setting practices and institutions in the interim.[29]

These yeoman-agent–econometricians would not only have trouble distinguishing a regime change if one were to occur in 1981, but would also have no precedent for shifting their wage-setting and price-setting behavior in response to such a shift. Table 15.2 presents inflation equations for the 1954–66 and 1967–80 subperiods corresponding to the apparent monetary regime change that occurred at the beginning of 1967.[30]

What seems remarkable to us is, despite a few minor exceptions, the overall stability of the sums of coefficients in the inflation equation across the two subintervals. The only significant coefficient shift, that in the distribution on the lagged dependent variable, is already included in the full-period equation. A Chow test confirms that there is no significant change in structure when the other coefficients are allowed to shift in 1967:1; the $F(24,48)$ ratio is 0.85, compared to a 10 percent critical value of 1.53.

Thus, even if the post-1980 monetary deceleration were sufficiently dramatic to be interpreted by agents, perhaps with a lag of two to five years, as a regime change, we are left with no solid reason to think there would be a marked change in the structure of the inflation equation, and thus in the estimated "sacrifice ratio." The only change in the inflation process after 1967 was a shortening of the lag distribution. If a policy shift caused history to "rewind" to the longer lag distribution in effect before 1967, our simulations would be too optimistic, not too pessimistic as the critics suggest.[31]

---

[29] The phrase "yeoman-agent–econometrician" combines three essential elements of the new classical equilibrium macroeconomics associated with the names of Lucas, Sargent, and Barro. First, their microeconomic behavioral models are most appropriate for price-taking "yeoman farmers," as pointed out by Alan S. Blinder and Stanley Fischer in "Inventories, Rational Expectations and the Business Cycle," *Journal of Monetary Economics*, vol. 8 (November 1981), pp. 277–304. Second, the individuals making decisions in the Lucas, Sargent, Barro literature are almost always described as agents. Third, the reliance of such yeoman agents on Chow tests to identify shifts in regimes implies that they have all received a rudimentary education in econometrics.

[30] We identify such a policy shift by a significant change in parameters, not by an explicit announcement of a policy shift by the Board of Governors. The 1967 shift involved a significant reduction of the previously negative coefficient on the inflation rate in the M1 equations; this suggests that the Federal Reserve's behavior shifted through its failure significantly to decelerate monetary growth in response to the upsurge of inflation that occurred in the 1966–8 interval. It is unlikely that a new policy involving the "failure to fight inflation" would have been announced explicitly by the Board.

[31] Cross-country historical evidence from the last century suggests that inflation inertia is a unique phenomenon of the postwar United States and that the timing of parameter shifts is consistent with the view that the institution of staggered three-year wage contracts is the main culprit. There is no reason to believe that a drastic shift would occur in the structure of the inflation equation until a regime shift far more drastic than that in 1967 were to cause multiyear contracts to be abandoned. See Robert J. Gordon. "Why U.S. Wage and Employment Behavior Differs from that in Britain and Japan." *Economic Journal*, vol. 92 (March 1982). pp. 13–44.

Some skeptics may resist the preceding analysis, which follows Neftci-Sargent by basing its assessment of regime shifts entirely on the behavior of the money supply. Instead one could examine the behavior of interest rates and might conclude that the willingness of the Federal Reserve to tolerate high interest rates since its announced November 1979 policy shift, despite relatively high unemployment, is unprecedented.[32] The widespread wage concessions and contract renegotiations of 1981–2 seem consistent with widespread perception of a new toughness in the Federal Reserve's stance. Yet the implication that our simulations may be too pessimistic is not supported by the data for 1981:1 through 1982:1. Our basic model of Table 15.3, row 1, when simulated using the actual monetary growth rates between 1981:1 and 1982:1, underpredicts both the inflation rate (an average predicted rate of 7.7 percent versus the actual 8 percent) and the unemployment rate (predicted 7.4 percent versus the actual 7.8 percent).[33]

Finally, we can concede that the structure of the inflation process might change in some unpredictable way after sufficient time, say five years, has passed for a monetary regime shift to be identified; indeed, the twelve-year interval between 1981 and 1992 *is* a long time to look into the future. But a structural change after five years would not alter our conclusion that stopping inflation is costly simply because most of the output cost occurs early in the simulation interval (91 percent of the cost occurs in the first five years along path 1 in Figure 15.1, and 56 percent along path II).

The Sacrifice Ratio

Arthur Okun computed the output loss from reducing inflation implied by a number of Phillips curve models and came up with estimates of the output cost of reducing inflation by 1 percentage point of between 6 and 18 percent of a year's GNP, with a mean of 10 percent.[34] Those estimates were based on a ratio between the loss of output, in percent of GNP, and the reduction in inflation, in percentage points, occurring in the first year of a disinflation experiment. This

---

[32] As evidence that the shift in Federal Reserve interest rate policy in November 1979 was not perceived to be permanent, we can cite Fair's published belief that the policy shift was temporary and had ended in mid-1980. See Ray C. Fair, "Estimated Effects of the October 1979 Change in Monetary Policy on the 1980 Economy," *American Economic Review*, vol. 71 (May 1981 *Papers and Proceedings*, 1980), pp. 160–5.

[33] The error in predicting unemployment was quite large in 1982:1, when the basic model predicted an unemployment rate of 7.6 percent along the Volcker path in Figure 15.1 as contrasted with the 8.8 percent rate that actually occurred in that quarter. Most of this error is caused by our simplistic equation that translates money growth into nominal GNP growth, not by the inflation equation itself that predicts inflation given unemployment. The forecast error of 1.2 percentage point of unemployment can be decomposed as follows: actual quarterly path of M1 growth in 1981 in contrast to the constant 5 percent rate assumed in figure 1, 0.2 extra point of unemployment: slowdown in velocity growth not predicted by nominal GNP equation, 0.6 point: underprediction of unemployment rate, with corresponding overprediction of output ratio, 0.3 point: and error in unemployment equation for a given output ratio, 0.1 point.

[34] Okun. "Efficient Disinflationary Policies."

Percent

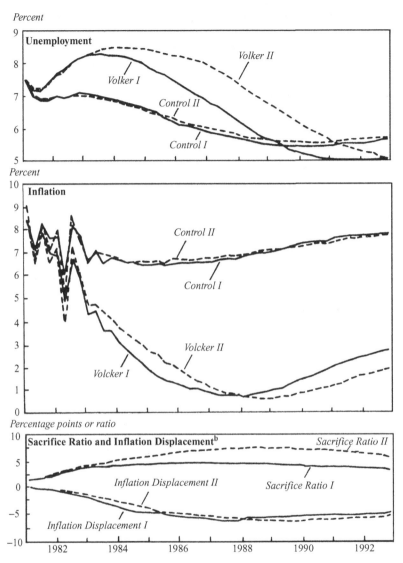

Figure 15.1. Effects of Different Monetary Policies on Unemployment, Inflation and the Sacrifice Ratio, Alternative Models, 1981–1992[a]

[a] Path 1 is the one presented as the basic model in Table 15.5, row 1. Path II holds constant the relative prices of imports and food and energy, as presented in Table 15.5, row 3.

The control solution sets the growth rate of M1 at 6.6 percent a year. The Volcker solution sets 5 percent for 1981. 4 percent for 1982, and then decelerates by 0.5 point a year to a rate of 2 percent for 1986 through 1992.

[b] The sacrifice ratio is undiscounted. The inflation displacement is the difference in the inflation path between the control and Volcker solutions.

method of calculation does not, however, take into account the possibility of changes in the ratio as the disinflation experiment proceeds.

Here we investigate a disinflationary monetary strategy and calculate the ratio of the present discounted value of the cumulative output loss to the average discounted reduction in inflation. While these might, in principle, be computed for an infinite time horizon, we economize on computation cost by calculating the ratio of terms discounted forty-eight quarters into the future as

$$S_{10} = \frac{\sum_{t=1}^{48} \left(\hat{Q}_t^1 - \hat{Q}_t^0 \right)/4(1 + r)^t}{\left(\sum_{t=1}^{48} (p_t^1 - p_t^0)/(1 + r)^t \right) \bigg/ \sum_{t=1}^{48} (1 + r)^{-t}} \tag{16}$$

where the superscript 1 refers to a control simulation and 0 refers to a simulation perturbed by a deterministic money-growth deceleration. In 16 the cumulative output loss is divided by four to convert it to an annual basis, and the denominator is divided by $\sum_{t=1}^{48}(1 + r)^{-t}$ in order to average the inflation rate, so that, for example, if $P_t^1 - p_t^0$ were constant at a rate π, the denominator would just equal π.

Obviously the choice of discount rates is crucial once we use a procedure that takes account of developments over several years. The analogous procedure to Okun's would be to ignore the relative timing of costs and benefits and simply to divide the cumulative output loss after twelve years by the permanent reduction in inflation. We report results on this basis ($r = 0$) and also with a positive annual discount rate ($r = 3$), which provides a better starting point for welfare analysis.

An important issue raised by this set of calculations involves the limitation of the horizon to twelve years. As we show here, our disinflationary monetary strategy overshoots the equilibrium output ratio and inflation rate by varying amounts in the different simulations, and in most cases the economy has not settled down by the end of 1992. This causes an overstatement in our sacrifice ratio by excluding the discounted benefit of lower inflation after 1992, as well as any possible increase in the growth rate of "natural" output, which is assumed below to be exogenous. It also, however, understates the sacrifice ratio by failing to include the post-1992 recession that arises from overshooting, the cost to society of the instability in both output and inflation that is caused by the disinflationary strategy, and any diminution in the capital stock due to low investment during the 1981–5 slump. We assume that the net effect of these distortions is small enough so that our results are not significantly biased. As further justification for a truncated horizon, we feel that it is unwise to give too much weight to the parts of the simulation that are remote in time from the starting date and therefore subject to large forecasting errors.[35]

---

[35] For a more detailed discussion of the welfare costs of disinflation, see Okun, *Prices and Quantities*. Chapters 7 and 8. In particular, we follow Okun in treating a positive log output ratio as creating a benefit for society, due to the role of the tax "wedge" that makes labor's marginal product exceed its opportunity cost at a zero log output ratio. For a detailed analysis, see

It is instructive to consider the implications of a discounted sacrifice ratio of, say, 6. Such a ratio would imply that in order to achieve a long-run reduction in the inflation rate of 5 percentage points, the economy would have to sacrifice output with a present value of 30 percent of a year's natural GNP, roughly $1,000 billion at current prices, or about $4,000 per capita.

However large, the output loss from disinflation does not by itself contain implications for economic policy. An assessment must be made of the welfare cost of lost output and the welfare benefit of lower inflation. Consideration of the value of the leisure time gained by the unemployed reduces the loss of $1,000 billion in domestic output to about $860 billion.[36] Lowering inflation would yield benefits to society reflecting the nonneutral impact of financial regulation and the tax system. For example, Stanley Fischer estimates the annual gain from a 5 percentage point reduction of inflation as 0.30 percent of GNP. This reflects reduced distortion in holdings of noninterest-bearing money and interest-bearing assets subject to interest rate ceilings.[37] The gain from lower inflation can be boosted to as much as 1 percent of GNP by considering the effects of inflation on saving, although all of this added effect hinges on the assumption that tax reform is infeasible. Were the total annual gain from reducing inflation by 5 points to amount to as much as 1 percent of GNP ($30 billion), the present value of the gain from reducing inflation would be $1,000 billion, exceeding the present value of the output loss of $860 billion. But we do not believe that tax distortions should be treated as unalterable and permanent.

The Control and Volcker Solutions

To carry out a simulation whose results are directly relevant to the contemporary policy debate, we compare a control solution with an approximation of the current official policy of the Federal Reserve Board. The control solution sets the annual growth rate of M1 permanently at its 1980 average of 6.6 percent a year. The alternative disinflationary Volcker solution sets 1981 growth at the actual average of 5 percent, sets 1982 growth at the midpoint of the official target range, 4 percent, and then allows M1 growth to decelerate by 0.5 percentage point a year to a final rate of 2 percent for 1986 through 1992.[38]

An alternative to this comparison of solutions would be the "innovation accounting" approach generally used in the evaluation of VAR models. A

Robert J. Gordon. "The Welfare Cost of Higher Unemployment," *BPEA, 1:1973*, pp. 133–95. A comprehensive analysis of the costs of inflation is contained in Stanley Fischer, "Towards an Understanding of the Costs of Inflation: II," in Karl Brunner and Allan H. Meltzer, eds., *The Costs and Consequences of Inflation*. Carnegie-Rochester Conference Series on Public Policy, vol. 15 (Amsterdam: North-Holland, 1981), pp. 5–41.

[36] Gordon, "The Welfare Cost of Higher Unemployment," p. 164.

[37] Fischer, "Towards an Understanding," pp. 17–19.

[38] The 1980 and 1981 actual figures are fourth quarter to fourth quarter, as reported in Board of Governors of the Federal Reserve System, "Monetary Policy Objectives for 1982," February 10, 1982, pp. 6–7. The 1981 "shift adjustment" of M1B is ignored.

downward innovation in M1 growth could be introduced in the first quarter of the simulation, equal in size to one sample-period standard deviation, and the subsequent adjustment of the output ratio and inflation rate could be calculated. Because the shock occurs for only one period, the resulting sacrifice ratio would differ from that in the control and Volcker simulations because there would be more time for the overshooting cycles to dampen. These differences are difficult to explain in a compact way, however, and we choose to limit the size and complexity of the paper by presenting simulation results only for the control and Volcker alternatives.

15.4 SACRIFICE RATIOS IN ALTERNATIVE MODELS

Table 15.5, which summarizes the simulation results and implied sacrifice ratios, is divided into two sections. Rows 1 through 4 use alternative versions of the basic model from Table 15.3. The remainder of the table shows how the results are altered when we convert our basic model, step by step, into a simple VAR model. Each line of the table displays goodness-of-fit statistics for the inflation equation in the first two columns, the undiscounted cumulative twelve-year output loss in the third column, and the average reduction of the inflation rate in the fourth column. The last two columns show the sacrifice ratio from equation 16 with the undiscounted ratio ($r = 0$) and the sacrifice ratio discounted at an annual rate of 3 percent ($r = 3$).

The first row of the table shows that the basic model of Table 15.3 generates a cumulative output loss of 13.4 percent of a year's GNP to reduce inflation by an average of 4.4 percentage points a year for sacrifice ratios of 3.0 (undiscounted) and 4.3 (discounted). Discounting raises the ratio, of course, because the output loss comes relatively early in the 1981–92 period, and the benefit of lower inflation comes later. The permanent reduction in the inflation rate in equilibrium is 4.9 percent, and it is accompanied by a 4.6 percentage point reduction in M1 growth and a 0.3 point reduction in velocity growth.

The economy's dynamic adjustment is illustrated in Figure 15.1, where the solid lines indicate the simulations being discussed here. Because the unemployment rate is a more familiar statistic than the output ratio, we display in the top panel the implied unemployment rate profile for 1981–92 under the control and Volcker simulations.[39] Whereas the control unemployment rate remains in

---

[39] The unemployment rate is calculated from the following Okun's Law equation estimated in Gordon's "Inflation. Flexible Exchange Rates":

$$U_t^W = 3.96 - 0.243\hat{Q}_t - 0.142\hat{Q}_{t-1} - 0.040\hat{Q}_{t-2}$$
$$(46.2) \quad (-12.0) \quad (-6.39) \quad (-1.78)$$

$\bar{R}^2 = 0.976$, Durbin-Watson $= 1.55$, Standard error $= 0.178$.

where numbers in parentheses are t-ratios.

To convert from the weighted to the official unemployment rate, the constant is changed from 3.96 to 6.00 percentage points.

Table 15.5. *Alternative Models: Sample Period Goodness-of-Fit Statistics for the Inflation Equation and Implied Sacrifice Ratios, 1981–2*

	Inflation Equation in Sample Period		Control versus Volcker Money Path[b]			
Model Description[a]	Sum of Squared Residuals	Standard Error of Estimate	Cumulative Output Loss (Percent)	Average Inflation Reduction (Percentage Points)	Sacrifice Ratio	Discounted Sacrifice Ratio[b]
Basic model						
1. Same model as Table 15.3	39.4	0.74	13.4	4.4	3.0	4.3
2. z_4 exogenous	39.4	0.74	21.0	4.4	4.8	5.8
3. z_3, z_4 exogenous	39.4	0.74	27.5	4.5	6.2	7.2
4. z_3, z_4, z_5 exogenous	39.4	0.74	37.9	4.5	8.4	9.9
Symmetric VAR models[c]						
5. Variables same as in Table 15.3	46.1	0.90	−0.5	4.3	−0.1	1.7
6. Variables same as preceding row, excluding $\hat{m}$ from inflation equation	47.3	0.90	−0.5	4.3	−0.1	1.8
7. Variables same as in Table 15.3, four lags on all variables	71.8	0.98	−0.3	4.1	−0.1	1.2
8. Same as preceding row, with reverse ordering	82.5	1.04	−7.2	4.3	−1.7	0.0
9. Only $\hat{m}$, $\hat{Q}$, p, z_4 included	94.1	1.03	−3.8	4.6	−0.8	1.0
10. Only m, q, p, $z_4 + p$ included	95.6	1.04	24.5	4.5	5.5	6.1
11. Only M, Q, P, PZ_4 included	103.4	1.08	144.7	3.5	41.7	34.2

[a] Variables are defined as in Table 15.2, note a, and table 3, note a. In models 10 and 11, q indicates the rate of growth in actual real GNP, and capital letters indicate the levels of the variables.

[b] For a definition of the sacrifice ratio, see the text. The discounting was done at an annual rate of 3 percent.

[c] In VAR models each variable appears in each equation with four lags except where noted.

[d] Twenty-four quarter lagged dependent variable and lags zero through four on $\hat{m}$ in the inflation equation.

Source. Simulations by the authors.

the range of 5.5 to 7.4 percent, the Volcker unemployment rate peaks at 8.3 percent in 1983 and then drops rapidly to a trough of 5 in 1991, substantially overshooting its natural rate of 6 percent and implying additional instability for the post-1992 period. In the second panel the relatively stable control inflation rate is contrasted with the plummeting Volcker inflation rate, which hits a trough of 0.7 percent in 1987. The last panel shows the undiscounted sacrifice ratio and the displacement of the inflation rate between the control and Volcker projections.[40] If the variance rather than the mean of the inflation rate is what matters for its welfare cost, a defect of the Volcker policy is the extra instability that it creates for inflation over this period.

International Effects

Why is the sacrifice ratio on row 1 of Table 15.5, both with and without discounting, so much lower than the ratio of 10 reported in Okun's survey? Our more optimistic set of results reflects three channels of "international feedback" included in the basic model. The Volcker simulation reduces the inflation rate not only through the traditional channel of lower output, but also by causing a reduction in the relative price of imports and in the relative price of food and energy, as well as an appreciation in the effective exchange rate. The impact of these channels of monetary influence is demonstrated in Table 15.5. In row 2 the relative import price change variable, z_4, is set at zero during the 1981–92 simulation, in contrast to its endogenous response allowed in row 1. The consequence of imposing exogeneity on the z_4 variable is an increase in the discounted sacrifice ratio from 4.3 to 5.8. In parallel fashion, row 3 treats both the relative import price and food-energy, variables z_4 and z_3, as exogenous, raising the discounted sacrifice ratio to 7.2. Finally, in row 4 all three international feedback variables are made exogenous in the simulation, resulting in a discounted sacrifice ratio of 9.9 that is close to Okun's summary estimate of 10.

Since the endogeneity of the international variables accounts for the more optimistic results in row 1 as compared to row 4, we may ask whether the behavior of the international variables in the two simulations, as summarized in the following, is plausible:

	Cumulative Changes, 1981–92 (Percent)		
	Control	Volcker	Difference
Food-energy effect	−3.8	−6.0	2.2
Relative price of imports	−7.7	−32.3	24.6
Effective exchange rate	4.6	20.8	16.2

---

[40] The plotted undiscounted sacrifice ratio is based on a separate calculation for each period. Thus the plotted value for 1992:4 corresponds to that listed in the fifth column of Table 15.5.

Although the food-energy change seems minor, the exchange rate difference of 16.2 is substantial. It is quite close, however, to the 13.7 percent cumulative appreciation of the same exchange rate measure that actually occurred between 1980:4 and 1981:4. Since the cumulative displacement of the domestic price level between the two simulations is 53.2 percent, the exchange rate results would be consistent with the long-run achievement of purchasing power parity if the Volcker policy caused a cumulative displacement of the foreign price level by 37 percent (53.2 minus 16.2), that is, by about two thirds of the U.S. displacement. In this case, by 1992 the real U.S. exchange rate would have returned to its 1980 value.[41]

The 24.6 point displacement of the relative import price may be questioned. Added to the 53.2 percentage point cumulative displacement of the domestic price level, the implied displacement of the nominal price of imports would be 77.8 percent in dollars or 61.6 percent in foreign currency (77.8 minus 16.2). Achievement of purchasing power parity, as suggested in the last paragraph, would require a displacement of the foreign price level by 37 percent. Thus in foreign currency those foreign goods purchased by the United States would fall in price by 24.6 percent relative to all other foreign goods. Although some raw materials purchased by the United States may have low price elasticities of demand and may exhibit a relative price decline in response to a U.S. recession, the 24.6 percent relative price shift appears implausibly large for U.S. imports taken as a whole. As suggested above in our discussion of Table 15.4, we believe that the large coefficients in the import price equation on the food-energy variable reflect a particular concurrence of events in 1974 that is unlikely to be repeated, and believe that the simulation of the basic model in the first row of Table 15.5 may be too optimistic.

Exogenous International Prices

The projections given by the dashed lines in Figure 15.1, path II, correspond to the intermediate model of row 3 in Table 15.5, which treats the two relative price variables, z_3 and z_4, as exogenous, but allows the exchange rate–which exhibits plausible behavior–to remain endogenous. Now there is a greater difference between the unemployment rates in the control and Volcker solutions, with the latter yielding a peak unemployment rate of 8.5 percent in 1984:2. The undiscounted cumulative output loss in the dashed-line projections is double that in path I, and the unemployment rate remains above 7 percent until 1988 instead of 1986. At the end of the simulation the Volcker unemployment rate has reached 5.1 percent and is still falling very rapidly, implying substantial instability after 1992.

---

[41] See the related discussion in Willem H. Buiter and Marcus Miller, "Real Exchange Rate Over-shooting and the Output Cost of Bringing Down Inflation," in *European Economic Review*, vol. 18 (May–June 1982), pp. 85–130.

Symmetric VAR Models

In contrast to the model described in Table 15.3, which exhibits many empty cells indicating that a particular set of coefficients has been set to zero in a particular equation, the VAR model reported in row 5 of Table 15.5 includes four lagged values in all equations, except that for inflation, which includes twenty-four lagged values of the dependent variable.[42] Current values are included in the recursive manner of Table 15.1, except that inflation and the output ratio are simultaneously determined. Another difference is the appearance of M1 growth in all equations including that explaining the inflation rate. This VAR system produces a total lack of significance of money changes in the inflation equation: none of the coefficients on current or lagged money is individually significant, even at the 10 percent level, and the F-ratio on the inclusion of the current and lagged values is only 0.28. Corresponding to this lack of significance is the identical set of simulation results on rows 5 and 6 of Table 15.5, which respectively include and exclude money from the inflation equation.

More interesting are the much lower sacrifice ratios, both with and without discounting, for the VAR models on rows 5 and 6 as compared to the most closely corresponding restricted model in row 1. The VAR results appear implausible because they imply continuous drifting of real endogenous variables through 1992, even though the growth rate of M1 under both simulations is constant after 1985. For instance, in 1992 under the control simulation the relative price of imports is steadily rising at an annual rate of 4 percent a year with a constant exchange rate, whereas under the Volcker simulation the relative price of imports is rising at the same 4 percent rate but the exchange rate is depreciating steadily at 4 percent a year. By 1992 the *level* of the exchange rate has actually depreciated in the Volcker simulation compared to the control simulation, implying that in the long run restrictive monetary policy *raises* foreign inflation. Further, the cumulative 1981–92 displacement of the relative price of imports is 53.1 percent, which is more than twice as much as in the basic model of the first row in the Table and is thus even more implausible than the result that we questioned above.

By making small changes in the VAR model, it is possible to obtain even lower sacrifice ratios. Row 7 shortens the distribution on the lagged dependent variable in the inflation equation from twenty-four to four quarters, thus quickening the overall responsiveness of the model. Then in row 8 the ordering is reversed from that in Table 15.3, with the exchange rate first, the inflation rate next, and so on. This version actually yields a zero discounted sacrifice ratio.

---

[42] There are a few remaining asymmetric features of the VAR model in row 5 of Table 15.5 that are necessitated by the limited degrees of freedom. The 1972 and 1973 dummy variables appear only in the exchange rate equation; the Nixon dummy variables appear only in the inflation equation; and, because of its limited 1972–80 sample period, there are only two lags on each variable in the foreign exchange equation.

Finally, rows 9 through 11 make a gradual transition to the more conventional VAR models estimated by Sims and others. Row 9 takes the row 7 model and excludes all supply variables except for the relative price of imports (the latter variable is retained because it is used in the six-variable model in Sims's original VAR paper "Macroeconomics and Reality"). This smaller model in row 9 retains the basic properties of row 7, with little change in the discounted sacrifice ratio. But the model of row 9 would never be chosen by a VAR afficionado, since our previous research has been used to introduce the natural output "adjustments" to the $\hat{m}$ and $\hat{Q}$ variables, as well as to state the import price variable in relative rather than nominal form. The last two rows, row 10 in first differences and row 11 in levels, eliminate these adjustments. The model in row 11 seems to us a good example of the folly of the atheoretical VAR approach when it is unencumbered by common sense. The discounted sacrifice ratio is an enormous 34.2, and the implied unemployment rate in the model grows steadily to almost 15 percent by 1992. Why? The specification in levels rather than growth rates mixes up trend and cycle phenomena. It yields a *negative* coefficient on output and a negligible positive coefficient on money in the price equation, which as a result is little more than an autoregression in which the inflation rate responds very sluggishly to restrictive monetary policy.[43]

Overall, we find little to dissuade us from our preference for the basic model. It is based on an inflation equation that is stable over the 1954–80 sample period and in which coefficients have correct signs and are of reasonable size. The auxiliary equations added for the policy simulations yield plausible paths for the endogenous variables, except for the excessive response of the relative price of imports. The version shown in row 2, which restricts the growth rate of the relative import price variable to be zero during the simulation period, omits this implausible import-price pattern and thus seems to us to be the most reliable indication of the consequences of the control and Volcker policies. The VAR models of rows 5 and 6 lack plausibility, since they yield continuous long-run drift in real variables many years after the growth rate of M1 in our simulations has arrived at its steady-state value. Finally, we find the VAR models of rows 7 through 11 inferior due to the omission of significant variables.

15.5 CONCLUSIONS

The Chapter has attempted to provide new measures of the output cost of disinflationary monetary policy using traditional and vector autoregressive techniques and to use this substantive issue as an occasion to provide an assessment of alternative econometric methodologies. Our conclusions are divided between those of methodological interest and those that relate to the estimated sacrifice ratios and their policy implications.

---

[43] The model shown in the last row of Table 15.5 with variables stated as log levels is the same as that in Sims. "Interwar and Postwar," with his interest rate replaced by our import deflator.

Methodology

Although to date VAR models have mainly been used for multivariate exogeneity and causality analysis, they also serve in testing the specification of traditional econometric models. Thanks to the discipline imposed by the VAR technique, we have discovered that the relative price of imports, and of food and energy, both usually treated as exogenous, can be partially explained by lagged values of other variables. As a result, the estimated response of inflation to restrictive monetary policy is amplified.

The traditional and VAR approaches can be viewed as selecting different methods of allocating zero restrictions in the face of scarce degrees of freedom. Like any trade-off in economics, the best way to allocate these restrictions should depend on an assessment of benefits and costs. We find that the VAR technique, although a useful tool for checking traditional specifications, has a low benefit-cost ratio. The pursuit of symmetry leads an investigator to omit "special variables" that matter for particular equations such as the effect of the Nixon controls in the inflation equation or the investment tax credit in investment equations. By clinging to published data and eschewing our natural output adjustments, VAR models also tend to mix secular and cyclical effects and to yield biased coefficients for key relations. As an example, the endogenous treatment of food-energy and import prices suggested by the VAR technique yields an implausibly large response of the latter variable in our simulations.

A VAR enthusiast might be willing to admit that a pure VAR model is of limited usefulness for studying our particular substantive question over a long postsample time horizon and to retreat into a defense of VAR models for multivariate exogeneity and causality testing. But, as the example on row 11 of Table 15.5 illustrates, a VAR model not unlike those published in the literature can yield coefficients that are severely biased and imply a Phillips curve with a perverse slope. This is quite likely to influence the results of exogeneity and causality testing.

The Output Cost of Disinflation

The discounted sacrifice ratio that emerges from our basic model is 4.3 with the relative import price variable included and 5.8 with that variable excluded. The latter estimate, which we prefer, suggests that to achieve by restrictive monetary policy a long-run reduction in the inflation rate of 5 percentage points the nation must choose to give up output having a present value of 29 percent of a year's natural GNP, almost $1,000 billion at current prices.

Disinflationary monetary policy in the United States is likely to create similar conditions abroad. Without estimating separate equations for the rest of the world, we cannot conjecture about the size of the additional output lost elsewhere. To the extent that nominal wages and prices are less sticky in other countries, the adjustment process may be less painful there than in the United States. But there is no doubt that the $1,000 billion figure understates the worldwide output loss imposed by the current official monetary policy of the U.S. government.

The output loss from disinflation, however large, does not by itself contain implications for economic policy. The discounted welfare gain from a permanent reduction of the inflation rate by 5 percentage points is unlikely to approach $1,000 billion unless nonneutral tax distortions and financial regulations are assumed to be permanent. We find such a presumption implausible. Further, we believe that the public aversion to inflation largely reflects a confusion between the effects of inflation itself and the real income loss caused by the oil price shocks and productivity slowdown of the 1970s. Economists have a responsibility to educate the public about the true costs of inflation in a neutral tax and regulatory environment and about the output cost of reducing inflation.

Our paper also has implications for the literature on inflation and Phillips curves. By including the exchange rate and import prices in the U.S. inflation equation, we tie the study of inflation in the United States more closely to the literature on international monetary economics than has traditionally been the case. Just as foreign economists have long recognized, the mix of monetary and fiscal policy, through its effect on the exchange rate, matters for the short-run inflation adjustment process.

Finally, we find the stability of our basic inflation equation before and after 1967 to be encouraging and offer this evidence in rebuttal to those economists who specialize in "sorting through the wreckage" of earlier Phillips curves and prematurely announcing the demise of Keynesian economics.[44]

---

[44] See especially Robert E. Lucas, Jr., and Thomas J. Sargent, "After Keynesian Macroeconomics," in Federal Reserve Bank of Boston, *After the Phillips Curve: Persistence of High Inflation and High Unemployment*, Conference Series 19 (FRBB, 1978), pp. 49–72.

CHAPTER 16

German and American Wage and Price Dynamics: Differences and Common Themes
With Wolfgang Franz

Persistent Unemployment and Europessimism

Economic pessimism in Europe has been substantially based on the contrasting evolution of unemployment during the 1980s between Europe and the United States. While the U.S. unemployment rate fell from over 10 percent in early 1983 to nearly 5 percent in 1988–1990, the rate for the EC remained above 10 percent for six straight years (1983–8) and fell only modestly thereafter.[1] The causes of high European unemployment have been posed as a choice between restrictive demand policies and structural impediments at the microeconomic level. Published economic research, so far mainly based on data through the mid 1980s, has as yet reached no consensus on the relative persuasiveness of these two explanations. The economic recovery of several European countries in the late 1980s has generated new data that might break through this stalemate.

Given the new weight of the German economy within Europe, its role as the anchor of the EMS, and the recent controversy created by the antiinflationary policies pursued by the Bundesbank, it seems natural to choose Germany for a detailed comparative study with the United States. Following 1960, for almost fifteen years extremely low unemployment rates of about 1 percent were at the core of the German economic "miracle" and provoked transatlantic envy when contrasted with the average 5 percent American unemployment rate over the

[1] By "commonly used definitions," the EC unemployment rate peaked at 11 percent in 1985, and fell below double digits to 9 in 1989, 8.4 in 1990, and 8.8 in 1991. See *OECD Economic Outlook*, June 1992, Table R19.

Note. Franz's research is supported by the Deutsche Forschungsgemeinschaft and by the European Community, and Gordon's by the National Science Foundation. This research is part of the CEPR research program in International Macroeconomics and the NBER research program in Economic Fluctuations. Any opinions expressed are those of the authors and not those of the Centre for Economic Policy Research nor of the National Bureau of Economic Research. The authors are grateful to Dan Aaronson and Werner Smolny for excellent research assistance, to Sandy Choi for typing the tables, and to David Coe, Michael Funke, and seminar participants at the International Seminar on Macroeconomics and at the Bank of Canada for numerous helpful suggestions. (*Source.* "German and American Wage and Price Dynamics: Differences and Common Themes." *European Economic Review.* May 1993, vol. 37, pp. 719–54.)

same period. But after 1973 German unemployment rose steadily and exceeded American unemployment during each year between 1984 and 1990. Further, the long-term (one year and longer) component of German unemployment rose markedly relative to the United States in the 1970s and 1980s.

Phillips Curves, the NAIRU and New Theories of the Labor Market

Why did German authorities not combat unemployment with a more expansionary monetary and fiscal policy? A common method to evaluate the scope for demand expansion is to compare the actual unemployment rate with the "nonaccelerating inflation rate of unemployment," the infamous NAIRU. Since the technology for calculating the NAIRU requires an estimated relation between inflation and the unemployment rate, the policy implications of the NAIRU are inextricably linked to dynamic Phillips curve equations for price and wage changes.

As usual, new economic events (in this case high European unemployment) have generated new economic ideas. In Europe, the apparent increase in the NAIRU spawned the hysteresis interpretation: the NAIRU is not a number fixed by a given set of microeconomic distortions, but rather tags along in the wake of the actual unemployment rate, as in the famous American song "Me and my Shadow." Hysteresis is a mechanical hypothesis, positing in the limit that inflation depends on the *rate of change* of unemployment and not (as in the standard Phillips curve) on the *level* of unemployment. But hysteresis needs an underlying economic explanation, for which the leading proposed candidate is the insider–outsider theory, which stresses the disenfranchisement of the long-term unemployed from the wage-setting process.

The Plan

We employ a common theoretical framework and a set of comparable data to investigate similarities and differences in wage and price dynamics in Germany and the United States. The point of departure is a set of nonstructural reduced forms that identify broad differences in behavior without restrictions tied to particular theories. Particular attention is paid to the related nonstructural concepts of cointegration and error correction. The second step is to examine structural tests that have been proposed by developers of specific theories and to determine whether key parameters suggested by these theories can be identified.

The essay begins with an examination of the facts and the puzzles that they suggest for further analysis. Section 2 begins the theoretical treatment with a nonstructural analysis of the interplay between wage and price dynamics, cointegration and error correction, changes in labor's share, the NAIRU, supply-shift variables, and hysteresis. Then in section 3 the theoretical analysis turns to structural models, starting with a traditional Phillips curve model that allows changes in relative prices and tax rates to influence wage behavior, and then proceeding

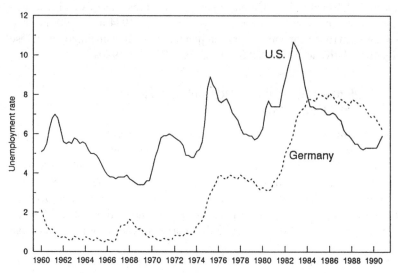

Figure 16.1. Official Unemployment Rates: Germany and the United States, 1960–90.

to the identification of structural hypotheses like the insider–outsider model
and real-wage bargaining model. Section 4 contains the empirical estimates of
parameters in the wage and price equations and performs dynamic simulations
that identify the NAIRU in both countries. Section 5 draws the results together
and concludes.

16.1   SOME FACTS AND PUZZLES

The Time Path of the Unemployment Rate

Figure 16.1 and the first two columns of Table 16.1 display the evolution of the
unemployment rate in the United States and Germany. While the unemployment
rate in the United States declined from about 5 percent in the early 1960s to
3.5 percent in 1968–9, Germany experienced virtually no unemployment until
1973. During 1962 to 1972 the average unemployment rate was below 1 percent
in every year but the recession period of 1967–8, when the rate increased only
to 1.8 percent. The German labor market was characterized by excess demand
which was partly accommodated through the employment of "guest-workers,"
i.e. foreign workers, which increased from 1.3 percent to 10 percent of total
employment between 1960 and 1973.

The spurt in the German unemployment rate began in 1974. While unemployment in the United States evolved more cyclically, with peaks in 1975 and
1982–3, Germany experienced a rise in unemployment in two steps, roughly
in the same years, but with little decline between 1975–80 and 1983–8. During
1983–90 the German unemployment rate was above that in the United States,

Table 16.1. *Summary Measures of Unemployment, Employment and Hours*[a]

Average Over Interval	Official Unemployment Rate		Share of Long-Term Unemployed		Employed Persons (Millions)		Annual Hours per Worker	
	FRG (1)	U.S. (2)	FRG (3)	U.S. (4)	FRG (5)	U.S. (6)	FRG (7)	U.S. (8)
1961–1964	0.6	5.8	n.a.	n.a.	20.2	62.5	2,081	1,799
1965–1969	1.0	3.8	9.1	2.1[b]	20.2	70.5	2,003	1,816
1970–1973	0.8	5.4	7.1	3.5	20.8	77.9	1,909	1,796
1974–1979	3.5	6.8	15.3	5.5	20.1	88.0	1,803	1,759
1980–1984	6.0	8.3	23.2	8.9	20.3	97.6	1,734	1,722
1985–1990	7.3	6.1	35.8	7.5	20.8	110.1	1,675	1,709

[a] Notes by column number in parentheses. Numbered sources in brackets identified at end of notes.
Germany. (1) Registered unemployed persons as a percentage of civilian labor force (including self-employed) [1]. (3) Percentage of unemployed more than one year. Figures prior to 1966 are not available [1]. (5) Including self-employed persons; private non-farm sector [2]. (7) Per year; aggregate economy; including self-employed persons [2].
United States. (2) Unemployed persons as a percentage of civilian labor force [7]. (4) Percentage of unemployed more than one year. Figures prior to 1967 are not available [7]. (6) Including self-employed persons; private non-farm sector [4]. (8) Per year; aggregate economy; including self-employed persons [5].
[b] Refers to 1967–1969 only.
Sources. [1] Official News of the Federal Labor Office, Germany. [2] German Institute of Economic Research, quarterly national accounts. [3] IFO-Institute, Munich. [4] *Economic Report of the President*, February 1992. [5] *Survey of Current Business.* [6] *Economic Indicators.* [7] Bureau of Labor Statistics. [8] *Federal Reserve Bulletin.*

which would not have been so remarkable except for the stark contrast in the opposite direction during the 1960s and 1970s.

Table 16.1 shows also the high and growing share of long-term unemployment in Germany, compared to its small share in the United States. There has been a sharp contrast between negligible growth in German employment and huge American growth (76 percent between the first and last period). As well, annual hours per employee in Germany have fallen from 16 percent above the U.S. level to 2 percent below.

NAIRU: Alternative Estimates and Concepts

The two countries differ not only with respect to the development of actual unemployment but also with respect to the time pattern of the natural rate. According to Gordon (1990), the U.S. natural rate was roughly stable at about 6 percent throughout the period 1975–90, having gradually risen from 5.2 to 6 percent during the two decades before 1975. Estimates of the NAIRU for Germany are much more controversial. While most auhors estimate a NAIRU of some 2 percent at the beginning of the 1970s (Coe, 1985, Franz, 1987), the range of NAIRU estimates in the second half of the 1980s is between 5.5 percent (Franz and Hofmann, 1990) and nine percent (Funke, 1991). Common to all studies is, however, the much more substantial increase of the NAIRU in Germany than in the United States.

As we shall see, one explanation for the divergence of German NAIRU estimates is the failure to distinguish alternative NAIRU concepts, particularly the distinction between a NAIRU calculated alternatively holding constant or ignoring the effects of supply shocks, and alternatively incorporating or ignoring the effects of hysteresis. The failure to distinguish alternative NAIRU concepts helps to explain the range in NAIRU estimates for Germany and for the eighties mentioned above: tentative estimates for 1986 wind up with a contemporaneous and steady-state NAIRU of 8.8 and 5.7 percent, respectively (Franz, 1987). Given the evolution of additional data since this and other studies, it may be possible now to provide a narrower band of estimates of the German NAIRU.

Alternative Theories

Table 16.2 displays data on wage and price changes and productivity growth. Wage and price changes in the United States decelerated markedly in the second half of the 1980s despite higher capacity utilization than in the first half, which may be explained by lagged wage and price adjustment to earlier low utilization, as well as by lower oil prices. The figures for Germany in the eighties show relatively low and stable wage and price inflation with relatively high capacity utilization. Given the persistently high unemployment rate, the time pattern of those variables cannot be explained by the standard Phillips curve model unless it is claimed that the actual unemployment rate coincided with the NAIRU.

If hysteresis is present in fact, this calls for a theoretical explanation.[2] The insider-outsider model of wage determination shows how employed insiders are able to convert a favorable demand or supply shock into wage increases for themselves rather than into new jobs for the unemployed. The target real-wage bargaining model goes in the same direction. In addition to total unemployment in the Phillips curve approach, nominal wage increases are influenced by the deviation of real wages or of labor's income share from target levels. If the target level of labor's share responds hysteresis-like to its actual level, then any pressure on wages stemming from deviations of the actual share from the target share gradually disappears.

Interpreting Changes in Labor's Share

Standard neoclassical theory emphasizes that the equilibrium level of labor's share is determined largely by the elasticity of output to changes in labor input, leading one to expect that the actual labor share would fluctuate around its equilibrium level. In contrast, the hypothesis that Europe suffered from classical

---

[2] A wide variety of theoretical and empirical papers on hysteresis is found in Cross (1988) and Franz (1990).

Table 16.2. *Summary Measures of Wages, Prices, Productivity, and Labor's Share (Annual Percentage Growth Rates)*[a]

Average Over Interval	Nominal Wage Growth		Growth Rate of GDP Deflator		Growth Rate of Real Product Wage		Actual Productivity Growth		Change in Labor's Share	
	FRG (1)	U.S. (2)	FRG (3)	U.S. (4)	FRG (5)	U.S. (6)	FRG (7)	U.S. (8)	FRG (9)	U.S. (10)
1961–1964	9.4	3.3	3.6	1.0	5.8	2.3	4.9	3.4	1.0	−1.0
1965–1969	7.3	5.3	2.7	2.9	4.6	2.4	5.2	1.8	−0.6	0.6
1970–1973	12.4	7.0	6.3	3.8	6.1	3.2	4.6	2.3	1.4	0.9
1974–1979	7.9	8.2	4.5	6.6	3.4	1.6	3.7	0.6	−0.4	1.0
1980–1984	5.0	7.3	3.9	6.3	1.1	1.0	1.6	0.9	−0.5	0.1
1985–1990	4.3	4.1	2.5	3.7	1.8	0.4	2.4	0.6	−0.6	−0.2

[a] Notes by column number in parentheses. Numbered sources in brackets identified at end of notes.
Germany. (1) Hourly nominal wage costs including employer's contributions to social security; private nonfarm sector [2]. (5) = (1)–(3). Private nonfarm sector [2]. (7) Real value added per hour worked, 1985 = 100, private nonfarm sector [2]. (9) = (5)–(7).
United States. (2) Employment cost index linked to average hourly earnings index times compensation of employees divided by wages and salaries. Includes employer costs for employee benefits; private nonfarm sector [5] and [7]. (4) Private nonfarm sector [5]. (6) = (2)–(4). (8) Output per hour, private nonfarm business sector [7]. (10) = (6)–(8).

Sources. [1] Official News of the Federal Labor Office, Germany. [2] German Institute of Economic Research, quarterly national accounts. [3] IFO-Institute, Munich. [4] *Economic Report of the President*, February 1992. [5] *Survey of Current Business*. [6] *Economic Indicators*. [7] Bureau of Labor Statistics. [8] *Federal Reserve Bulletin*.

unemployment in the 1980s was based on a disequilibrium interpretation that the real wage was boosted artificially above labor productivity, resulting in an increase in labor's income share (see Schultze, 1987). The first two columns in Table 16.3 display gross labor compensation as a share of national income and indicate the reverse of the pattern that one might expect.[3] The German labor share has fluctuated around its mean of 67.8 percent but shows no trend, that is, it is roughly equal to its mean in both 1961–4 and 1985–90. In contrast the U.S. labor share exhibits a one-time jump in the early 1970s, with little movement in other periods. Given the widespread characterization of the German labor movement as strong and the American as weak, it is clearly surprising to find that the German labor share declined much more in the late 1980s than did the American.

In contrast to the data in columns (1) and (2), copied directly from the National Income Accounts (NIA), column (3) and (4) show an alternative labor's share concept implied by the set of wage, price, and productivity data entered into our estimated wage and price equations. One can cumulate changes in the real product wage minus average labor productivity and convert them into an "Adjusted Labor Share Index," with the *level* of the adjusted share set to equal the NIA share in 1987. Since different data are used to construct the adjusted share, for example, for the nonfarm private sector rather than the total economy, data differences can create a difference between the NIA and adjusted share measures.

Fortunately, a comparison of the share concepts shows a reasonably consistent picture. The adjusted German share peaks in the late 1970s rather than the early 1980s for the NIA concept, and the adjusted share in the late 1980s is distinctly lower than in any earlier period. For the United States the adjusted share rises steadily from the late 1960s to the early 1980s, in contrast to the one-shot jump for the NIA share in the early 1970s.

In addition to the disequilibrium real wage hypothesis, there are several other reasons why the equilibrium level of labor's share may not be determined solely by competitive factor pricing given a particular production function. The wedge between the before-tax product wage and the after-tax consumption wage may play a role. Table 16.3 decomposes the total wedge into that portion due to changes in the ratio of consumer prices to product prices (the "price wedge") and the remaining portion due to changes in taxes (the "tax wedge"). The German price wedge, expressed on a 1987 base, shows a sharp downward jump in the early 1970s as a result of the appreciation of the DM during the transition from the Bretton Woods regime to the flexible exchange rate regime. In addition the upward bulge in the German price wedge in the late 1970s and

---

[3] A qualification to the labor share data in Table 16.3 is that no attempt is made to allocate self-employment ("proprietors") income among labor and capital. One attempt to do so (Gordon, 1987) concludes that such adjustments create a secular downward adjustment in the German labor share relative to the U.S. labor share, thus accentuating the contrast already evident in Table 16.3.

Table 16.3. *Summary Measures of Labor's Share, Wedge Variables, and the Output Ratio*[a]

Average Over Interval	Labor's Share		Adjusted Labor's Share		Price Wedge (1987 = 100)		Tax Wedge		Capacity Utilization (Dev. from Mean)	
	FRG (1)	U.S. (2)	FRG (3)	U.S. (4)	FRG (5)	U.S. (6)	FRG (7)	U.S. (8)	FRG (9)	U.S. (10)
1961–1964	67.6	69.0	69.9	67.2	110.3	92.9	139.4	123.1	2.7	0.0
1965–1969	63.2	70.0	69.5	66.3	109.1	92.6	142.9	125.9	0.7	6.7
1970–1973	66.9	73.3	71.3	70.0	101.9	94.2	155.0	128.8	3.7	-0.3
1974–1979	69.8	73.5	71.7	72.6	102.7	97.0	167.2	131.7	-3.5	-0.8
1980–1984	71.5	74.6	71.0	75.3	104.7	98.9	173.4	134.3	0.3	-3.6
1985–1990	67.9	73.2	67.1	73.6	101.1	99.8	179.7	135.5	2.0	-0.9

[a] Notes by column number in parentheses. Numbered sources in brackets identified at end of notes.

Germany. (1) Unadjusted labor's share as displayed in the national accounts, i.e. total wage bill divided by national income; aggregate economy [2]. (3) Cumulated index of Table 16.2, col. (9), set equal to Table 16.3, col. (1) in 1987. (5) Ratio of consumer price index to value added deflator of private nonfarm sector, 1987 = 100 [2]. (7) Gross wage costs per hour divided by net take home pay per hour [2]. (9) Capacity utilization rate for industry, based on business survey data; deviation from 1960–1990 mean [3].

United States. (2) and (4), same as Germany. (6) Ratio of fixed weight consumption deflator to the fixed weight GDP deflator, 1987 = 100 [5]. (8) Gross compensation of employees divided by net take home pay. Net take home pay is defined as one minus personal tax and nontax payments divided by personal income times compensation of employees minus contributions for social insurance [4]. (10) Federal Reserve Board capacity utilization rate for industry [8].

Sources. [1] Official News of the Federal Labor Office, Germany. [2] German Institute of Economic Research, quarterly national accounts. [3] IFO-Institute, Munich. [4] *Economic Report of the President*, February 1992. [5] *Survey of Current Business*. [6] *Economic Indicators*. [7] Bureau of Labor Statistics. [8] *Federal Reserve Bulletin*.

early 1980s reflects higher oil prices. The behavior of the U.S. price wedge reflects both the decline in the dollar and fluctuations in oil prices; the increase in the late 1980s indicates that the sharp post-1985 decline in the dollar more than offset the benefit of lower oil prices. The tax wedge shows a monotonic upward trend for both countries, but at about triple the rate in Germany as in the United States.

16.2 WAGE–PRICE DYNAMICS AND LABOR'S SHARE: A NONSTRUCTURAL APPROACH

Our theoretical treatment integrates the traditional literature on the Phillips curve and hysteresis with the more recent attention to cointegration and error correction. We distinguish between separate wage and price equations, thus allowing us to incorporate dynamic feedback between wages and prices, and the possibility that the NAIRU emerging from the wage equation is not the same as the NAIRU which matters for monetary policy, that is, that which emerges from the price equation.

Price and Wage Equations

A general specification relates current and lagged price changes (p) to current and lagged wage changes (w), an index of excess demand (X, normalized so that $X = 0$ indicates the absence of excess demand), a vector of other relevant variables (z), and a serially uncorrelated error term (e):

$$a(L)p_t = b(L)w_t + g(L)X_t + d(L)z_t + e_t. \tag{1}$$

In our notation upper-case letters designate logarithms of levels and lower-case letters designate first differences of logarithms. The vector z_t includes "supply shift" variables that can alter the rate of inflation at a given level of excess demand, for example, changes in the "price wedge" or "tax wedge." All components of z_t are expressed as first differences and normalized so that a zero value indicates an absence of upward or downward pressure on the inflation rate. Except for its distinction between growth rates and log levels, required to define the "natural rate" of the excess demand variable X_t, (1) is a general form that can encompass nonstructural VAR models or, with restrictions, can be made to resemble traditional "structural" price and wage equations.[4]

---

[4] Note that the entry of the level of X_t does not require that a "level demand effect" be present; if the estimated coefficients display an alternation of a positive contemporaneous coefficient and negative lagged coefficient (with all coefficients summing to zero), this would indicate the presence of a "rate of change demand effect" and would be compatible with what we define below as "full hysteresis." Symmetrically, as we shall see below, the inclusion of an error-correction term allows an expression specified in first differences to recover a relationship between the levels (rather than first differences) of two variables.

The coefficients $a(L)$, $b(L)$, $g(L)$, and $d(L)$ are polynomials in the lag operator L, and $a(L)$ can be normalized so that its first element equals unity.[5] With this normalization, the term $a(L)p_t$ can be rewritten as

$$a(L)p_t = p_t + a'(L)p_{t-1}. \tag{2a}$$

Similarly,

$$b(L)w_t = b_0 w_t + b'(L)w_{t-1}. \tag{2b}$$

Substituting (2a) and (2b) into (1), we have a more transparent version of the price change equation:

$$p_t = -a'(L)p_{t-1} + b_0 w_t + b'(L)w_{t-1} \\ + g(L)X_t + d(L)z_t + e_t. \tag{3}$$

Here we see that the price equation includes not just lagged values of price and wage change, but also the current value of wage change.

What about the wage equation? The price equation (3) has the startling implication *that there is no such thing as a separate wage equation*. Equation (3) is a price and wage equation at the same time, which can be seen when (3) is renormalized as

$$w_t = -\left(\frac{1}{b_0}\right)[b'(L)w_{t-1} - p_t - a'(L)p_{t-1} \\ + g(L)X_t + d(L)z_t + e_t]. \tag{4}$$

Thus, without further restrictions, the "price equation" (3) and the "wage equation" (4) are alternative "rotations" of the same equation.[6]

Two main approaches are available to identify separate price and wage equations. First, different sets of X_t and z_t variables could be assumed to enter the price and wage equations. However, this is implausible a priori, since any variable relevant as a determinant of price change may also be relevant for participants in the wage-setting process, and vice-versa for prices.

A second approach is to restrict the contemporaneous coefficient on w_t in the price equation or on p_t in the wage equation, since it is likely that there is a contemporaneous correlation between w_t and the error term e_t in (3), or similarly for p_t in (4).[7] Some past papers have set the contemporaneous

---

[5] The analysis in this section is adapted for this paper from Gordon (1990). Up to this point, the notation and normalization follow Blanchard (1987), except for the distinction here between demand and supply variables and the interpretation of the demand variable as a level rather than a first difference.

[6] This insight and the term "rotation" come from Sims's comment on Blanchard (1987).

[7] Some papers in this literature cite Kuh (1967), who proposed a "productivity theory of wage levels," that is, that the change in the wage rate was explained by a distributed lag of changes in productivity, and hence that the level of the wage was related to the level of productivity. However, a modern rereading of Kuh reveals that his econometric investigation is plagued by simultaneity, with the current value of both the consumer price index and the current output deflator entered as explanatory variables for the current wage rate (pp. 347, 350).

coefficient to a particular value or to zero in one of the two equations; in this paper the price and wage equations are placed on an equal footing by excluding the contemporaneous wage and price terms from both equations:

$$p_t = a^{\mathrm{p}}(L)_{t-1} + b^{\mathrm{p}}(L)(w - \theta)_{t-1}$$
$$+ g^{\mathrm{p}}(L)X_t + d^{\mathrm{p}}(L)z_t + e_t^{\mathrm{p}}, \tag{5}$$

$$(w - \theta)_t = b^{\mathrm{w}}(L)(w - \theta)_{t-1} + a^{\mathrm{w}}(L)p_{t-1}$$
$$+ g^{\mathrm{w}}(L)X_t + d^{\mathrm{w}}(L)z_t + e_t^{\mathrm{w}}. \tag{6}$$

The first bit of structure is imposed here by replacing the wage change variable in (3) and (4) by the wage change minus the change in labor's average product $(w - \theta)$, that is, the change in nominal unit labor cost. Two very different rates of wage change would be consistent with the same inflation rate if they were offset by a difference in productivity growth by the same amount.

Interpreting Changes in Labor's Share

Implicit in (5) and (6) is a relationship between inflation and changes in labor's share, since the change in labor's share (s_t) is defined as

$$s_t = w_t - \theta_t - p_t. \tag{7}$$

The effects of changes in labor's share in the inflation equation become transparent if (5) is rewritten in the following form, adding and subtracting $b^{\mathrm{p}}(L)p_{t-1}$ and using the definition (7):

$$p_t = [a^{\mathrm{p}}(L) + b^{\mathrm{p}}(L)]p_{t-1} + b^{\mathrm{p}}(L)s_{t-1} + g^{\mathrm{p}}(L)X_t$$
$$+ d^{\mathrm{p}}(L)z_t + e_t^{\mathrm{p}}. \tag{8}$$

Similarly, for labor cost, we have

$$(w - \theta)_t = [a^{\mathrm{w}}(L) + b^{\mathrm{w}}(L)](w - \theta)_{t-1} - a^{\mathrm{w}}(L)s_{t-1}$$
$$+ g^{\mathrm{w}}(L)X_t + d^{\mathrm{w}}(L)z_t + e_t^{\mathrm{w}}. \tag{9}$$

The effect of a change in labor's share on inflation depends on the sum of coefficients $(\sum b_i^{\mathrm{p}})$ in (8). If that sum is a positive fraction between zero and unity, then an increase in labor's income share becomes a source of "cost push" that is on an equal footing with any other type of adverse supply shock. If that sum is zero, then wage changes are irrelevant for inflation, meaning that the counterpart of an increase in labor's share is a profit squeeze rather than upward pressure on the inflation rate. This would imply a dichotomy between the time-series processes determining inflation rate and wage changes; wage behavior would be irrelevant in determining the inflation rate and the natural rate of unemployment, and the wage equation would be of interest only for its description of changes in the distribution of income.

Cointegration and Error Correction

The previous exposition of dynamic adjustment expresses the price and labor cost variables only in first differences, allowing only for a single "level" variable, excess demand (X) to represent a disequilibrium that may lead to wage and price adjustment. However, there is a long literature going back to Phillips (1957) and Sargan (1964) that allows for "error correction," in this context the deviation of the real wage from some normal or equilibrium level is allowed to enter as a separate measure of disequilibrium in an equation relating wage changes to price changes or vice versa. For instance, an increase in the real wage caused by "wage push" (as happened in some European countries in the late 1960s), or a decrease in the real wage caused by an oil shock (as happened in the United States in the mid 1970s) may have created pressure for adjustment in both wages and prices independently of the evolution of the excess demand variable, for example, the unemployment rate.[8]

More recently, the concept of error correction has been linked to that of cointegration, which can be defined informally as the notion that a linear combination of two series, say the price level and unit labor cost, is stationary.[9] When two such variables are cointegrated, a regression consisting entirely of differenced data will be misspecified and a regression consisting entirely of level data will omit important constraints. The solution is to estimate a regression of the first difference of one variable on the first difference of the other, plus an error correction variable consisting of the lagged log ratio of one variable to the other.[10] Omitting the lag operators to simplify, an error correction version of (8) and (9) is

$$p_t = (a^p + b^p)p_{t-1} + b^p s_{t-1} + c^p (S - S^*)_{t-1}$$
$$+ g^p X_t + d^p z_t + e_t^p, \tag{10}$$

where $S_t = W_t - \theta_t - P_t$ is the log level of labor's share and S_t^* is the equilibrium log level of labor's share. Thus the error-correction term generates an increase in the rate of price change whenever labor's share exceeds its equilibrium level, and similarly a decrease in the rate of change of labor cost:

$$(w - \theta)_t = (a^w + b^w)(w - \theta)_{t-1} - a^w s_{t-1} - c^w (S - S^*)_{t-1}$$
$$+ g^w X_t + d^w z_t + e_t^w. \tag{11}$$

When the relation between cointegration and error correction is recognized, then a two-step procedure is indicated. First, the price and labor cost variables

---

[8] The basic theoretical reference on error-correction is Hendry et al. (1984) and the references contained therein. The relationship between error-correction and cointegration is explored in Engle and Granger (1987).

[9] For the formal definition of stationarity and cointegration, see Engle and Granger (1987, pp. 252–3).

[10] A complete taxonomy of the possible forms of dynamic specification in a bivariate model is presented in Hendry et al. (1984, pp. 1040–9). A simple exposition in the context of the demand for money is contained in Gordon (1984, pp. 419–23).

must be tested empirically for cointegration. If they are indeed cointegrated, then the specification must follow the error-correction format of (10) and (11) rather than the simple first-difference format of (8) and (9).[11]

The NAIRU and "Hysteresis"

A simplified version of eq. (10) illustrates alternative definitions of the NAIRU. We restrict the coefficient on lagged inflation to unity; include only a single lagged labor's share term (s_{t-1}) and a single supply shock term (z_t); and proxy the excess demand term by a constant and the current unemployment rate (U_t):

$$p_t - p_{t-1} = g_0 - g_1 U_t + d_1 s_{t-1} + d_2 (S - S^*)_{t-1} + d_3 z_t + e_t. \tag{12}$$

Using (12), we can define the "shock" NAIRU (U_t^s) as that which is consistent with steady inflation ($p_t = p_{t-1}$) and includes the higher level of unemployment needed to offset any upward push on inflation coming from the labor's share, error-correction, and supply shock terms in (10), but omits the error term, which is assumed to be serially uncorrelated with mean zero:

$$U_t^s = \frac{g_0 + d_1 s_{t-1} + d_2 (S - S^*)_{t-1} + d_3 z_t}{g_1}. \tag{13}$$

The "no shock" NAIRU (U_t^{NS}) is the concept that "controls" for the influence of changes in labor's share, the error-correction term, and supply shocks:

$$U_t^{NS} = \frac{g_0}{g_1}. \tag{14}$$

Policy discussions are not always clear regarding the concept of the NAIRU that is relevant for policymaking. To keep inflation from responding at all to an increase in labor's share or an adverse supply shock, policymakers must apply an "extinguishing" policy contraction that raises the unemployment rate from the "no shock" NAIRU in (14) to the "shock" NAIRU in (13).[12]

Hysteresis as applied in this context represents the hypothesis that the no-shock NAIRU responds fully or partially to the lagged actual unemployment rate:

$$U_t^{NS} = U_t^* + \phi(U_{t-1} - U_t^*). \tag{15}$$

U_t^{NS} is the "quasi-equilibrium" or "contemporaneous" NAIRU which is conditional on the history of unemployment, and U_t^* is the "steady state" NAIRU, i.e. the NAIRU sustainable in the long-run equilibrium. When (14) and (15) are substituted into the simplified Phillips curve (12), we have

---

[11] We are grateful to our discussant Michael Funke and to Mark Watson for stressing the imperative of the error-correction specification in this context.

[12] Gramlich (1979) introduced the distinction between accommodative, neutral, and extinguishing responses to supply shocks. An extinguishing response attempts to set the actual unemployment rate equal to the "shock" NAIRU.

$$p_t - p_{t-1} = g_1[U_t^* + \phi(U_{t-1} - U_t^*) - U_t] + d_1 s_{t-1}$$
$$+ d_2(S - S^*)_{t-1} + d_3 z_t + e_t. \tag{16}$$

Rearranging, we see that the change in the inflation rate now depends on the steady-state NAIRU, the lagged *level* of the unemployment rate, and the current *change* in the unemployment rate:

$$p_t - p_{t-1} = -g_1[(1 - \phi)(U_t - U_t^*) + \phi \Delta U_t] + d_1 s_{t-1}$$
$$+ d_2(S - S^*)_{t-1} + d_3 z_t + e_t. \tag{17}$$

Three cases are of interest.

1. *Full hysteresis.* If $\phi = 1$, then the "level effect" vanishes and the change of inflation depends only on the change in unemployment and the additional terms in (17).

2. *No hysteresis.* If $\phi = 0$, then the change term drops out, and (17) becomes identical to (12), with $U^* = g_0/g_1$. This is the case of the pure "level" or "Phillips curve" mechanism.

3. *Intermediate case: persistence.* If $0 < \phi < 1$ we have the intermediate "persistence" case, in which both the level and rate of change effects matter, and in which the contemporaneous NAIRU can drift away from the steady state NAIRU.

To estimate the parameters of interest and determine which case is consistent with the data, we can run the following regression:

$$p_t - p_{t-1} = h_0 - h_1 U_t - h_2 \Delta U_t + d_1 s_{t-1}$$
$$+ d_2(S - S^*)_{t-1} + d_3 z_t + e_t. \tag{18}$$

The parameters to be identified are the hysteresis coefficient (ϕ), the coefficient of response of the inflation rate to unemployment (g_1), and the "steady state" NAIRU (U_t^*). These can be computed from the estimated coefficients in (18) as

$$\phi = \frac{h_2}{h_1 + h_2}, \quad g_1 = h_1 + h_2, \quad U^* = \frac{h_0}{h_1}. \tag{19}$$

The interpretation of these is straightforward; note that U^* cannot be defined when there is no level effect ($h_1 = 0$), since in this case the NAIRU freely floats in response to the past behavior of actual unemployment. If there is a level effect and U^* can be identified, the determinants of U^* are assumed to be "microeconomic structure" and are not explained.

16.3 STRUCTURAL INTERPRETATIONS OF WAGE BEHAVIOR

Thus far we have presented nonstructural price and wage equations which contain only lagged prices and wages, an error-correction term, a demand term (e.g., the level and/or change of the unemployment rate), and an unspecified "supply shift" term. We turn now to a structural wage equation that allows us (1) to specify the form of the supply shift variable; (2) to contrast the previous nonstructural equations with the traditional "expectational Phillips curve" approach; and (3) to specify forms of the insider–outsider and real-wage bargaining models that are suitable for testing.

How the Price and Tax Wedge Enter the Phillips Curve

The Phillips curve hypothesis is based on the idea that wages adjust to eliminate any excess demand or supply in the labor market.[13] The demand for labor is determined by setting the expected real before-tax wage equal to the marginal product of labor and solving for the quantity of labor as a function of the expected real before-tax wage. With a Cobb–Douglas production function (written in logs as $Y = \theta + \gamma N$, where θ is the productivity shift factor and N is labor input), the demand for labor is

$$N^d = \alpha(\gamma + \theta + P^e + T^i - W - T^f). \tag{20}$$

Here α is $1/(1 - \gamma)$, the elasticity of labor demand with respect to the (inverse of the) real wage, P^e is the expected product price, T^i is the indirect or value-added tax factor, and T^f is the employer-paid payroll tax factor.[14] Labor supply is

$$N^s = \beta(W + T^p - R - C^e), \tag{21}$$

where T^p is the personal tax factor (including both personal income taxes and the employee portion of the payroll tax), R is the "aspiration real wage" that governs labor supply, and C^e is the expected consumption price deflator.

Using X as before to represent excess demand, we can define the log level (X) and rate of change (x) of excess demand as

$$X = N^d - N^s, \quad x = n^d - n^s. \tag{22}$$

The Phillips curve hypothesis is that the excess demand for labor is eliminated at a rate which is proportional to its own level, i.e.:

$$x = -gX. \tag{23}$$

When we take the time derivative of the difference between the labor demand and supply functions in (20) and (21), we obtain an expression for the change in excess demand, which in turn can be substituted into the adjustment equation (23). When solved for $w - \theta$, this directly yields the "expectational

---

[13] The particular formulation set out here dates back to Gordon (1977) and earlier authors, including Lipsey and Parkin.

[14] $T^i = 1 - \tau^i$ and $T^f = 1 + \tau^f$, where τ represents the appropriate tax rate.

Phillips curve" wage equation:

$$w - \theta = p^e + \frac{1}{\alpha + \beta}[\beta(r - \theta + c^e - p^e - t^p)$$
$$+ \alpha(t^i - t^f) + gX]. \quad (24)$$

In equilibrium, labor demand equals labor supply and tax rates remain unchanged, hence $t^p = t^i = t^f = X = 0$. If the reservation wage rate increases at the same rate as the productivity shift term $(r = \theta)$ and $c^e = p^e$, then $w - \theta = p^e$, that is, the growth rate of nominal unit labor cost equals the inflation rate of output prices. Under these conditions, in equilibrium labor's income share is constant. A general expression for the equilibrium level of labor's share, S^*, can be obtained by setting (20) equal to (21) and solving:

$$S^* = \frac{1}{\alpha + \beta}[\alpha\gamma + \beta(R - \Theta + C - P - T^p) + \alpha(T^i - T^f)]. \quad (25)$$

From (25) it is clear that the equilibrium labor share becomes a constant $[\alpha\gamma/(\alpha + \beta)]$ if $R = \theta$, the product price and consumption price indexes are identical, and if there are no taxes. For small values of the real wage elasticity of labor supply, β, labor's share equals γ, the exponent on labor in the production function.

Estimated Form of the Wage Equation

Section 3 developed a nonstructural wage equation (11) which made the rate of change of unit labor cost depend on its own lagged values, lagged changes of labor's share, an error-correction term (the deviation of labor's share from its equilibrium value), current and lagged values of an unspecified excess demand variable (X), and current and lagged changes in an unspecified supply shift variable (z). Our discussion of hysteresis suggested that the excess demand variable could be proxied by a constant, the level of unemployment, and the change in unemployment, as in equation (18). Our structural Phillips curve model suggests that the rate of change of the price wedge and tax wedge, appropriately defined, are the appropriate supply shift variables, as in (24). Taken together, the wage equation becomes

$$(w - \theta)_t = [a^w(L) + b^w(L)](w - \theta)_{t-1} - a^w(L)s_{t-1}$$
$$- c^w(S - S^*)_{t-1} + h_0^w - h_1^w U_t - h_2^w \Delta U_t$$
$$+ d_1^w(L)\pi_t + d_2^w(L)\omega_t + e_t^w. \quad (26)$$

Here π_t and ω_t are, respectively, the rates of change of the price wedge and tax wedge.

Alternative Hypotheses

Insider–Outsider

Long-term unemployed persons may not exert a strong influence on wage determination, if any at all. This view rests on the hypothesis that long-term unemployed persons are imperfect candidates for filling vacancies. Their human capital and work attitudes may have deteriorated during their extended spell of unemployment, or they may suffer from discrimination, based on false beliefs about the deterioration of their skills. To allow for this approach, we define the "true" unemployment variable (U') that enters eq. (26) as

$$U'_t = U^s_t + \psi U^L_t. \tag{27}$$

This formulation introduces a parameter (ψ) to indicate the extent to which the long-term unemployed are perfect substitutes for the short-term unemployed, which requires ($\psi = 1$). When the "true" unemployment concept defined in (27) is substituted into (26), the weight on long-term unemployment may be calculated. This provides a test of the insider–outsider model.

Real-wage Bargaining Model

As formulated by Coe and Krueger (1990), who in turn attribute the idea to Sargan (1964), the real-wage bargaining model involves introducing an error-correction term into the wage equation, which we have already carried out above. To understand this interpretation, we can refer to a simple version of equation (11) above:

$$(w - \theta)_t = p^e_t - g_1(U - U^*)_t - g_3(S - S^*)_{t-1}, \tag{28}$$

where as above $S = W - P - \theta$, the log level of labor's share. When $g_3 = 0$, this is a stripped-down expectational Phillips curve relating the growth rate of unit labor cost to the level of the gap between actual and natural unemployment. In contrast, when $g_3 > 0$ the equation is converted from a growth-rate relationship to a level relationship among the same variables. This is evident in the long-run version of (28) in levels that assumes $p = p^e$:

$$S = S^* - \left(\frac{g_1}{g_3}\right)(U - U^*). \tag{29}$$

The target real wage model implies that the target level of labor's share (the right-hand side of (29)) is equal to the equilibrium level (S^*) adjusted for the effect of the unemployment gap, which "can be thought of as a proxy for the bargaining power of labor" (Coe and Krueger, 1990, p. 6). In contrast to the Phillips curve model of (28) with $g_3 = 0$, which can be in long-run equilibrium only with unemployment at the natural rate, the economy in (29) can be in a long-run "quasiequilibrium" as long as the real wage relative to trend productivity has been pulled down below S^* by a level of unemployment held above the natural rate.

In this approach, since the *level* of real wages is related to the *level* of unemployment, the *growth* of real wages is related to *changes* in unemployment. This might appear to make the real wage bargaining model observationally equivalent to the full hysteresis approach developed above. However, full hysteresis requires that the "level" effect of unemployment be absent, that is, that $g_1 = 0$ in (28) and (29). Thus if $g_1 > 0$ it is possible that the real-wage bargaining model could be validated even if there is no hysteresis, full or partial. Just as hysteresis is a hypothesis that provides a structural interpretation for the entry of a term in the change of the unemployment rate, so the real-wage bargaining hypothesis provides a structural interpretation of the error-correction term that should enter any equation relating two cointegrated series.

Estimated Form of the Price Equation

The price equation is estimated in the same format as the wage equation (26), with the rate of change of an aggregate price index (p) replacing the rate of change of unit labor cost ($w - \theta$). While in principle the same variables that matter for the wage equation could matter for the price equation, in practice there are differences. Because price changes are determined in the product market rather than the labor market, we replace the unemployment rate with two alternative demand variables, (1) the log output ratio (i.e., detrended output), and (2) the capacity utilization rate. Also, a different set of supply shift variables may enter the price equation, particularly changes in the relative prices of oil and/or imported materials. Since expectations of price setters are influenced by the variables that enter the wage equation and vice versa, in principle all supply shift variables relevant for either equation should enter into both. In practice there are insufficient degrees of freedom for everything to be included, particularly when lagged effects are present, and so we experiment to find the best set of supply shift variables for each equation in each country, starting from a set that includes the change in the tax and price wedges, as in (26), and changes in the relative prices of imports, imported materials, energy, and in the real exchange rate (the initial list of candidates differs slightly between Germany and the United States, reflecting data availability).

16.4   ESTIMATED WAGE AND PRICE EQUATIONS

Data and Lag Lengths

The basic format for wage change is equation (26) and for price change (26) with the price and labor cost variables interchanged as in (10) and (11). Equations are estimated on quarterly data with sample periods ending in 1990:4 and beginning at the earliest possible date consistent with the 1960:1 starting date of the

German data, allowing for lag lengths. The data sources for the wage, price, productivity, price wedge, and tax wedge variables are listed in the notes to Tables 16.2 and 16.3. All quarterly change variables are defined in percent at annual rates, that is, as the first difference of the log times 400. All U.S. variables are seasonally adjusted by official agencies; most of our German data contain strong seasonal patterns that we correct prior to running the regressions.[15]

Change in Labor Cost $(w - \theta)$

The wage is gross of payroll taxes. Following Gordon (1971) and subsequent papers, the productivity variable relevant for wage and price setting is a weighted average of a spline trend and the deviation of actual productivity from that trend, or in our notation for rates of change, $\theta' = \theta^* + \eta(\theta - \theta^*)$. By defining the wage change variable in the form of $w - \theta^*$ and entering $(\theta - \theta^*)$ as a separate variable, the parameter η can be estimated freely (rather than imposed, as in many studies).[16]

Change in Price (p)

The product price is represented by the GDP deflator, implicit for Germany and fixed-weight for the United States. The price wedge is the ratio of the consumption deflator to the same product price term (again, implicit for Germany and fixed-weight for the United States).

Excess Demand Variable

The unemployment rate is the demand variable entering into the wage equations. Outsider ineffectiveness is assessed by splitting the total unemployment rate into the long-term (U^L) and residual (U^S) components and estimating the weight (ψ) attributable to long-term unemployment as in (27) above. For the price equations two alternative demand variables are used, the log output ratio and the rate of capacity utilization. The log output ratio for Germany is the deviation from a spline trend running through 1960, 1972, 1979, and 1990, and for the United States uses particular quarters in the years 1957, 1963, 1972, 1979, 1987, and 1990 (Gordon, 1990). For both countries the capacity utilization rate is entered as the deviation from the 1960–90 mean of that series (as displayed in Table 16.3).

---

[15] Seasonal adjustment is carried out in the RATS regression program using the option of "trend exponential smoothing."

[16] The benchmark dates for the spline productivity trend are for Germany 1960:1, 1970:1, 1979:1, and 1990:4. For the United States they are the same as in Gordon (1990), 1954:2, 1964:3, 1972:1, 1978:4, 1986:4, and the additional date 1990:4.

Tax Wedge

The tax wedge is the ratio of gross-of-tax employer labor cost to net-of-tax employee take-home pay. Specific definitions for the two countries are provided in the notes to Table 16.3.

Lag Lengths

In recent work Gordon (1990) found that very long lag lengths of up to 24 quarters were required in estimating equations like (26) for the United States. Most previous work on Germany has used much shorter lag lengths, and in one extreme case lag lengths are restricted to a single quarter.[17] The algebra in (8) and (9) that replaces lagged prices and labor cost by the change in labor's share requires identical lag lengths on the lagged dependent variable and on the lagged change in labor's share. Lag lengths for these two variables in the estimated equations are chosen by starting with long lags and then truncating the length of the distribution, based on formal exclusion tests. This procedure chooses lag lengths for the lagged dependent variables and the change in labor's share of four quarters for Germany and twelve quarters for the United States. Lag lengths are chosen for other variables by estimating initially with a four-quarter length and then truncating insignificant terms.[18]

Cointegration and Error-Correction

Before estimating wage and price equations, we tested for the cointegration of the price and unit labor cost variables. Cointegration was not rejected for either country by any of the first three tests listed by Engle and Granger (1987, pp. 264–8; these include the Dickey–Fuller and augmented Dickey–Fuller tests), and accordingly all equations include an error-correction term. Our formulation in (26) calls for this to be entered as the difference between the log level of labor's share and its equilibrium value; in order to avoid an iterative procedure (determining the value of the equilibrium share from estimated parameters), we simply define the required difference as the deviation of labor's share from its sample mean.

Dummy Variables

Much of the previous literature on German wages allows for a "wage push" dummy for one or more quarters in 1970. In our case the dummy variable is defined for the period 1970:Q1–1971:Q1. Some previous literature also allows

[17] This is the basic equation (2) that Coe and Krueger (1990) use to show the significance of the target-real-wage bargaining term, i.e., that $h_3 < 0$.

[18] The excess demand variables (unemployment, the output ratio, or capacity utilization) are initially entered with lags 0–3. The coefficients always change sign, indicating the presence of both level and change effects; the significance of these coefficients then determines which lag applies when the level and change are entered separately as in (26).

for a "strike dummy" in 1984:1, and we define a dummy variable equal to +1 in 1984:1 and −1 in 1984:2. We also allow the estimated NAIRU to change in selected equations for both countries by including separate dummy variables for 1973–90 and 1981–90 and then reestimating to exclude insignificant dummies. As in previous papers for the United States, the effect of the Nixon-era price controls is assessed with dummy variables.[19]

Within-Sample Stability

The use of dummy shift variables for 1973–90 and 1981–90 implicitly allows the constant term in the equation to shift while forcing all other coefficients to remain constant. To tests for shifts in all coefficients, we run Chow tests on the stability of the specification in the 1962–72 and 1973–90 subperiods. The break in 1973:1 is chosen so that the two subperiods can be interpreted as applying to the fixed and flexible exchange rate regimes. As we shall report below, the German wage and U.S. price equations fail the test for stability, and accordingly we base our conclusions on the versions estimated for the 1973–90 subperiod. The U.S. wage and German price equations pass the test for stability, indicating that the parameters estimated for the full 1962–90 period remain stable.

Estimated Wage Equations

The estimated wage equations for Germany are summarized in Table 16.4; here we discuss the main features of the coefficients and defer to Table 16.8 a discussion of the estimated NAIRUs and adjustment parameters. Significant values for coefficients or sums of coefficients are indicated by (*) or (**), as indicated in the notes to the Table. Lag lengths are listed on the left of the Table; when more than one lag is included on a particular line, the listed numbers and significance levels refer to the sum of coefficients. For the full sample period 1962–90 column (2) differs from column (1) only by excluding insignificant variables or lags.[20] Because a Chow test rejects stability over a break of the 1962–90 sample period in 1973, we focus primarily on the results for 1973–90 shown in columns (3)–(5).[21] The unusual nature of the 1962–72 period is evident in Figure 16.2, which plots the labor cost, price, and income share variables for Germany. Highly volatile wage behavior in the 1967–8 recession and in the 1970–71 "wage explosion" period was not repeated after 1972. Figure 16.3 shows the same variables on the same scale for the United States and displays much more persistent and less volatile wage behavior.

---

[19] As in Gordon (1990, notes to Table 16.3) and previous papers by Gordon cited there, the Nixon controls "on" dummy variable is entered as 0.8 for the five quarters 1971:1–1972:3. The "off" variable is equal to 0.4 in 1974:2 and 1975:1 and to 1.6 in 1974:3 and 1974:4.

[20] The tax wedge is included for 1962–90 because it is highly significant for 1973–90 in columns (3)–(5).

[21] The $F(17, 77)$ ratio for a structural break in the equation in column (1) is 3.20, as compared with the 1 percent significance level of 2.13.

Table 16.4. *Estimated Equations for Quarterly Change in Trend Unit Labor Cost* $(w - \theta^*)$, *Germany*[a]

Variable	Lags	1962:2–1990:4		1973:1–1990:4		
		(1)	(2)	(3)	(4)	(5)
1. Δ Labor cost	1–4	1.32**	1.28**	0.83**	0.82**	0.80**
2. Δ Labor share	1–4	−0.87**	−0.82**	−0.66*	−0.57*	−0.76*
3. Δ Unemployment	0–3	−0.25	−0.31**	−0.66**	–	–
4. Δ Unemployment	3	–	–	–	−0.64**	–
5. ST unemployment	3	–	–	–	–	−0.93**
6. LT unemployment	3	–	–	–	–	−0.10
7. Δ Unemployment	0	–	–	–	−0.84**	−0.81**
8. Error-correction term	1	−0.17**	−0.17**	−0.23**	−0.22**	−0.18*
9. Δ Prod. deviation	0–1	0.07	–	–	–	–
10. Δ Price wedge	1–4	0.29*	–	–	–	–
11. Δ Price wedge	2	–	0.25**	0.14	0.14*	0.17*
12. Δ Tax wedge	1–4	0.07	0.09	0.35**	0.30**	0.32**
13. Constant	–	−2.18	−2.05**	4.57**	4.54**	4.65**
14. Shift 1973–1990	–	3.10	3.36**	–	–	–
15. Shift 1981–1990	–	−0.12	–	–	–	–
16. Shift 1970:1–1971:1	–	4.37**	4.42**	–	–	–
17. Shift 1984:1(+1), 1984:2(−1)	–	2.57**	2.60**	2.46**	2.68**	2.62**
$\bar{R}^2$		0.85	0.85	0.86	0.86	0.86
S.E.E.		1.23	1.22	0.82	0.83	0.83
S.S.R.		131.8	140.8	36.1	37.6	37.1

[a] * Indicates that coefficient or sum of coefficients is significant at 5 percent level;
** at 1 percent level.

441

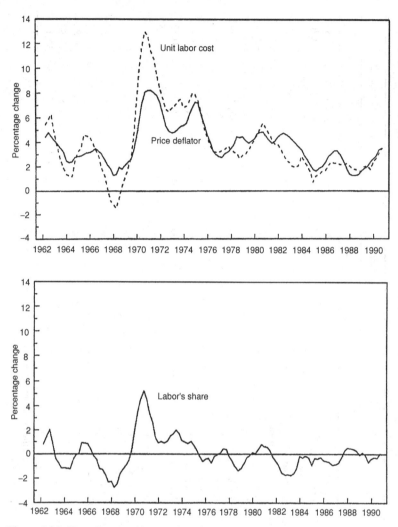

Figure 16.2. Four-Quarter Changes in Price Deflator, unit Labor Cost and Adjusted Labor's Share: Germany, 1962:1–1990:4

The 1973–90 German wage equation in column (3) corresponds exactly to the 1962–90 equation in column (2), except for the exclusion of inapplicable dummy shift variables. Column (4) shifts from four lagged values of the unemployment to single terms in the level and change of unemployment. Finally, column (5) splits the level of unemployment between short-term and long-term unemployment. The significance of the change in labor's share on line 2 indicates feedback from prices to wages; in column (5) labor cost depends only on lagged prices, not at all on lagged wages. Both the level and change in unemployment are highly significant, indicating partial hysteresis, while the

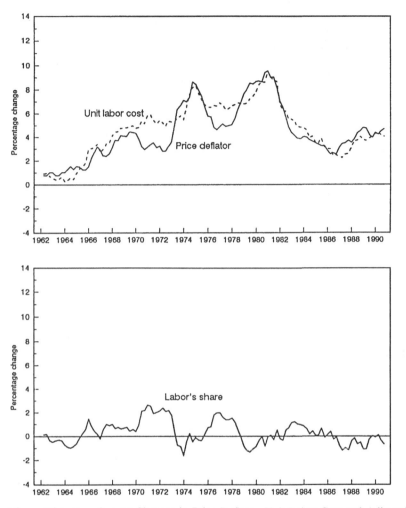

Figure 16.3. Four-Quarter Changes in Price Deflator, Unit Labor Cost and Adjusted Labor's Share: United States, 1962:1–1990:4

insignificance of long-term unemployment supports the insider–outsider hypothesis (the estimated ψ parameter is 0.1, as compared to the value of $\psi = 1.0$ required for full outsider effectiveness). The error-correction term is significant with the correct sign in all equations, supporting Coe–Krueger and their interpretation of the real-wage bargaining hypothesis. The price and tax wedge terms enter with the correct signs, and the latter is highly significant in the 1973–90 period. The dummy shift term for 1981–1990 is insignificant and is omitted.

Table 16.5 presents several alternative wage equations for the United States. Unlike Germany, the list of supply shock terms includes two additional variables relevant in principle for price behavior, that is, changes in the relative price of food and energy, and in the relative price of imports. Starting from the basic

Table 16.5. *Estimated Equations for Quarterly Change in Trend Unit Labor Cost*
(w − θ), United States*[a]

| Variable | Lags | 1962:2–1990:4 | | | 1973:1–1990:4 |
		(1)	(2)	(3)	(4)
1. Δ Labor cost	1–12	1.33**	1.32**	1.32**	1.49**
2. Δ Labor share	1–12	−0.90**	−0.79**	−0.77*	−0.93*
3. Unemployment	0–3	−1.05	−0.96**	–	–
4. Unemployment	0	–	–	−0.95**	−1.17**
5. Δ Unemployment	0	–	–	−0.81**	−0.71
6. Error-correction term	1	−0.01	−0.01	−0.01	−0.02
7. Δ Prof. deviation	0	0.07*	0.07*	0.07*	0.10
8. Δ Price wedge	1–4	0.23	–	–	–
9. Δ Price wedge	4	–	0.21*	0.19	0.28*
10. Δ Tax wedge	1–4	0.10	–	–	–
11. Δ Food–energy relative price	1–4	0.31	–	–	–
12. Δ Food–energy relative price	3	–	0.30**	0.30**	0.16
13. Δ Imported relative price	1–4	0.10*	–	–	–
14. Δ Imported relative price	2	–	0.06**	0.06**	0.06**
15. Constant	–	5.24**	4.69**	4.63**	5.20**
16. Shift 1973–1990	–	−0.09	–	–	–
17. Nixon 'on'	–	0.14	0.47	0.48	–
18. Nixon 'off'	–	1.15	1.23**	1.23**	1.27*
$\bar{R}^2$		0.88	0.89	0.89	0.87
S.E.E.		0.84	0.81	0.80	0.80
S.S.R.		45.9	51.4	52.1	25.1

[a]* Indicates that coefficient or sum of coefficients is significant at 5 percent level;
** at 1 percent level.

equation in column (1), column (2) drops insignificant variables and lag lengths, column (3) shifts to a single level and change of the unemployment rate, and column (4) shows for comparison the results for 1973–1990 (although stability in the 1962–90 period is supported).[22] Comparing column (3) with the German results in Table 16.4, column (4), there is similar feedback from prices to wages (although a higher U.S. sum of coefficients on lagged wages), and strikingly similar effects of the level and change of unemployment. The persistence of the

[22] Because of the long lag lengths in the U.S. equation, there are insufficient degrees of freedom to run equations for the 1962–72 subperiod. Since data are available for the entire postwar period, we test structural breaks here and in Table 16.7 by running the same equations over the 1954–90, 1954–72, and 1973–90 subperiods. The $F(46, 52)$ ratio for the equation in Table 16.5, column (1) is 0.89, compared to a 5 percent significance level of 1.62.

U.S. wage process evident in Figure 16.3 is captured by the long 12-quarter lag distribution, while the two humps in 1974–5 and 1980–2 are captured by the significant food-energy and import relative price terms. The main differences in the U.S. equations compared to Germany are the significance of the productivity deviation, the insignificance of the tax wedge, and the significance of the supply shift relative price terms. As we shall see in Table 16.8, the implied NAIRU and Phillips curve slopes are surprisingly similar in the two countries.

Estimated Price Equations

The German price equations are displayed in Table 16.6. Two basic equations are presented, in column (1) with detrended output as the demand variable and in column (2) with the capacity utilization rate. The latter provides a slightly better fit and has the advantage of structural stability across the 1962–90 period.[23] The most important result in all the German price equations is the insignificance of the lagged labor share variable, implying an absence of feedback from wages to prices. Taken at face value this preliminary result means that the NAIRU refers to the capacity utilization rate and can be computed directly from the price equation without reference to the wage equation.

Other results evident in Table 16.6 are the role of partial hysteresis, the insignificance of the error-correction term when demand is measured by capacity utilization, and the significant and correctly signed productivity deviation and imported materials relative price terms.[24] An adverse shift in the capacity utilization NAIRU for 1973–90 is implied by the pattern of shift dummies on lines 11 and 12.

The American price results in Table 16.7 present several variants for the 1973–90 subperiod, since structural stability over the 1962–90 period is rejected.[25] The results indicate substantial feedback from wages to prices in both the change term on line 2 and the error-correction term on line 9. The demand effects of capacity utilization, and the support for partial hysteresis, parallel the German price results, as does the significant and correctly signed productivity deviation variable. The change in the relative price of food and energy and the change in the real effective exchange rate enter as significant and correctly signed supply shift terms. The constant and 1973–90 shift terms are insignificant in columns (5) and (6), and the equations are reestimated with these terms omitted.

---

[23] The absence of a structural break in 1973 is barely rejected for the utilization version; the $F(27, 57)$ ratio is 1.32 compared with the 5 percent critical value of 1.65. With the log output ratio the $F(27, 57)$ ratio is 2.27.

[24] A coefficient of -0.10 on the deviation of productivity from trend means that 10 percent of a cyclical increase in productivity takes the form of lower prices and the remaining 90 percent takes the form of higher profits.

[25] As in Table 16.5, the Chow test is conducted for a break in 1973 over the period 1954–90. The $F(25, 84)$ ratio for the output ratio version in Table 16.7, column (1), is 1.88 and for the utilization version in column (2) is 2.65, both higher than the 5 percent critical value of 1.65.

Table 16.6. *Estimated Equations for Quarterly Change in Product Price Deflator (p), Germany*[a]

		1962:2–1990:4		1973:1–1990:4		
Variable	Lags	(1)	(2)	(3)	(4)	(5)
1. Δ Product price	1–4	0.92**	0.98**	0.98**	0.99**	0.87**
2. Δ Labor share	1–4	0.04	0.01	0.01	-0.10	-0.12
3. Output ratio	0–3	0.05	–	–	–	–
4. Capacity utilization	0–3	–	-0.09*	–	–	–
5. Capacity utilization	1	–	–	0.08**	0.09**	0.14**
6. Δ Capacity utilization	1	–	–	0.13**	0.16**	0.08*
7. Error-correction term	1	-0.24**	-0.12	-0.12	0.01	0.16
8. Δ Product deviation	0	-0.08	-0.11*	-0.10*	-0.10*	-0.07
9. Δ Imported materials relative price	1–4	0.02**	0.02**	0.02**	0.02**	0.01
10. Constant	–	-0.27	-0.34	-0.34	0.15	0.38
11. Shift 1973–1990	–	1.30**	0.87*	0.86*	–	–
12. Shift 1981–1990	–	-0.58	-0.41	-0.41	–	–
13. Shift 1970	–	1.42*	1.35*	1.34*	1.58**	–
$\bar{R}^2$		0.82	0.82	0.83	0.82	0.82
S.E.E.		0.80	0.79	0.78	0.79	0.68
S.S.R.		59.9	58.0	58.0	60.5	25.7

[a] Indicates that coefficient or sum of coefficients is significant at 5 percent level; ** at 1 percent level.

Table 16.7. Estimated Equations for Quarterly Change in Product Price Deflator (p), United States[a]

		1962:2–1990:4			1973:1–1990:4		
Variable	Lags	(1)	(2)	(3)	(4)	(5)	(6)
1. Δ Product price	1–12	0.78**	0.77**	0.88**	0.97**	0.78**	0.85**
2. Δ Labor share	1–12	0.72**	0.69**	0.61**	0.51**	0.51**	0.39*
3. Output ratio	0–3	0.08	–	0.15	–	–	–
4. Output ratio	3	–	–	–	0.17*	–	–
5. Δ Output ratio	0	–	–	–	0.15**	–	–
6. Capacity utilization	0–3	–	0.15**	–	–	0.11	0.15**
7. Capacity utilization	3	–	–	–	–	–	0.13**
8. Δ Capacity utilization	0	–	–	–	–	–	0.22**
9. Error-correction term	1	–0.07	–0.02	0.46**	0.39**	0.27**	–
10. Δ Productivity deviation	0–1	–0.19**	–0.16**	–0.20*	–0.17*	–0.17*	–0.12*
11. Δ Tax wedge	0–1	0.17*	0.13	0.15	–	0.12	–
12. Δ Price wedge	1–4	0.53*	0.59**	–0.10	–	0.01	–
13. Δ Food-energy relative price	0–3	0.61**	0.52**	1.28**	0.86**	0.88**	0.50*
14. Δ Import relative price	0–3	–0.07	–0.05	0.03	0.02	0.02	0.03
15. Δ Real exchange rate	2–5	–0.03*	–0.03*	–0.05**	–0.03**	–0.03*	–0.02*
16. Constant	–	–0.04	2.19	–1.19	–1.31*	–	–
17. Shift 1973–1990	–	1.09	0.99	–	–	–	–
18. Nixon 'on'	–	–0.94	–0.42	–	–	–	–
19. Nixon 'off'	–	0.27	0.18	1.23	1.12*	0.62	0.93*
$\bar{R}^2$		0.89	0.91	0.94	0.94	0.95	0.94
S.E.E.		0.79	0.72	0.54	0.53	0.49	0.53
S.S.R.		38.9	32.1	6.1	8.3	5.4	8.4

[a] * Indicates that coefficient or sum of coefficients is significant at 5 percent level;
** at 1 percent level.

447

Table 16.8. *Parameter Values Implied by Tables 16.4–7*

Dependent Variable:	Trend Unit Labor Cost $(w - \theta)$		Price Deflator (p)	
Activity Variable:	Unemployment Rate		Utilization Rate	
Equation	Germany; Table 4, Column (4)	U.S.; Table 5, Column (3)	Germany; Table 6, Column (5)	U.S.; Table 7, Column (6)
Phillips curve slope (g_1)	1.48	1.76	0.22	0.28
Hysteresis coefficient (ϕ)	0.57	0.46	0.36	0.46
'Natural rate' of unemployment or utilization (1973–1990)[a]	6.20	6.22	84.7	81.7
Actual rate of unemployment or utilization, 1990:4	6.22[b]	5.90	90.4[b]	80.8

[a] Natural rates are computed from versions of each equation that constrain the sum of coefficients on the lagged dependent variable to be unity.

[b] Seasonally adjusted by the authors.

Estimated Parameters: Adjustment, Hysteresis, and NAIRU

The estimated coefficients in Tables 16.4–7 can be unscrambled to reveal the main parameters of interest, using the relationships displayed in equation (19). These determine the coefficient of response (g_1) of wages or prices to a deviation of actual unemployment from the contemporaneous no-shock natural rate of unemployment (U_t^{NS}), the hysteresis coefficient (ϕ), and the steady-state no-shock NAIRU (U_t^*). Analogous parameters are presented for the price equations, where capacity utilization is the preferred demand variable.

The first section of Table 16.8 shows that the estimated response coefficient (g_1) is quite similar for the two countries in both the wage and price equations. The absolute size of the response coefficient is lower for the price equation, simply because the demand variable in these equations (the capacity utilization rate) is more volatile than the unemployment variable entered into the wage equations. The estimated hysteresis coefficients in the next section of Table 16.8 indicate surprisingly similar behavior in both Germany and the United States, and in both the wage and prce equations.

NAIRU estimates require reestimation of each equation with the sum of coefficients on the lagged dependent variable restricted to sum to unity, as assumed in the algebra of equations (12) through (19) above, and the results are shown in the third section of Table 16.8. Perhaps the most surprising result of this paper is that the NAIRU implied by the German and American wage equations is identical over the entire 1973–90 period at about 6.2 percent. The

Table 16.9. *Mean Errors (ME) and Root Mean-Squared Errors (RMSE) from Dynamic within-Sample Simulations, 1981:1–1990:4*[a]

	Rate of Change of Price Deflator		Rate of Change of Trend Unit Labor Cost	
	ME	RMSE	ME	RMSE
Only lagged dependent variable endogenous				
Germany	0.46	0.75	0.06	0.80
United States	0.22	0.42	0.06	1.18
Both price and labor cost endogenous				
Germany	0.38	0.69	0.34	0.89
United States	0.16	0.62	0.20	1.20

[a] The simulations are based on the same equations listed in Table 16.8. The coefficients on the lagged dependent variable are freely estimated rather than restricted to sum to unity.

natural rate of capacity utilization for the United States is simply the mean value of 81.7 percent, since the constant term is insignificant and excluded from the relevant equation. The natural rate of capacity utilization for Germany is close to its mean value of 84.4 percent in the restricted equation estimated for the 1973–90 sample period.

While the estimated NAIRU from the German wage equation provides the optimistic interpretation that German unemployment had not fallen below the NAIRU by the end of the sample period in 1990:4, this optimism is tempered by the pessimistic conclusion of the price equation. Utilization was more than five points above the natural rate, according to the price equation, and this is what counts in view of the absence of feedback from wages to prices.

Dynamic Simulations

To test the stability of these wage and price equations, we subjected them to dynamic simulations for the ten years beginning in 1981:1. The upper part of Table 16.9 displays simulations that feed back the equation's own prediction of the lagged dependent variable (prices or labor cost), while holding the change and level of lagged labor's share exogenous. The lower part is a more demanding test, calculating both wages and prices together. In such simulations it is possible for the computed inflation rate to drift substantially away from the actual 1981–90 values. The most important statistic is the mean error of the simulation; a large positive or negative value of this statistic indicates that the simulated values drift substantially away from the actual values. Shown also are the root-mean-squared errors.

The results are encouraging, particularly the extremely low mean errors for the wage equations in both countries. There is moderate drift in the Germany

Table 16.10. *Forecast of Inflation Rate for Selected Quarters for Different Paths of Unemployment and Utilization, 1991:1–2000:4[a]*

	1990:4	1992:4	1994:4	2000:4
Both wage and price endogenous, price equation reestimated with unemployment replacing utilization				
Germany				
Path B	3.5	4.5	4.2	3.9
Path A	3.5	4.0	3.6	3.5
Difference, Path B – Path A	0.0	0.5	0.6	0.4
United States				
Path B	4.7	4.8	5.9	12.9
Path A	4.7	3.9	3.8	4.2
Difference, Path B – Path A	0.0	0.9	2.1	8.7
Price equation alone with utilization variable				
Germany				
Path B	3.5	4.8	5.8	7.1
Path A	3.5	3.3	3.4	3.4
Difference	0.0	1.5	2.4	3.7

[a] The simulations are based on the same equations listed in Table 16.8, and the coefficients on the lagged dependent variable are freely estimated rather than restricted to sum to unity. In the upper part of the Table the price equations are reestimated with the unemployment rate replacing the utilization rate; Path A has 6 percent unemployment throughout, Path B reduces unemployment to 5 percent by 1991:4. In the bottom part Path B maintains 89 percent utilization throughout, Path A arrives at 85 percent utilization by 1991:4.

price equation, with an average underprediction of actual 1981–90 inflation by almost half a percentage point at an annual rate. The U.S. equations stay on track remarkably well in the dynamic simulations in the bottom part of the table.

Implied NAIRU from Dynamic Simulations

What are the implications of these equations for the NAIRU? We would like to use the estimated coefficients in the wage and price equations to simulate the effects of different paths of the unemployment rate over the period 1991–2000, both to check the values of the NAIRU and to measure how rapidly inflation accelerates when unemployment is reduced below the NAIRU. However, since the wage equations use unemployment and the price equations use the capacity utilization rate, a full dynamic simulation of the inflation rate implied by alternative unemployment rates would have to add a separate "Okun's law" equation linking capacity utilization to unemployment.

To avoid adding complexity to the model, as an expedient we reestimate the price equation for each country (using the particular variant listed in Table 16.8 and 9), replacing the capacity utilization rate by the unemployment rate. The top part of Table 16.10 shows the inflation rate for selected periods for two alternative paths of the unemployment rate, a path "A" which holds the rate constant at 6 percent and another path "B" that reduces it to 5 percent by the end of 1991 and holds it there through the year 2000. The contrast between the German and U.S. results is remarkable. While inflation is stable in both countries at a 6 percent unemployment rate, the path B demand expansion causes a slow but steady acceleration in the U.S. that is absent in Germany. This contrast might cause us to leap to the conclusion that German policymakers can expand the economy as much as they want without adverse inflationary consequences.

However, an alternative procedure tempers this optimism. Since our estimates found no feedback from wages to prices in Germany, we can simulate the price equation by itself, using utilization as the demand variable and ignoring the wage equation and the unemployment rate. Now the expansionary path B holds the utilization rate at 89 percent (a bit below the 90.4 percent rate achieved in 1990:4), while the "natural rate" path A reduces the rate to 85 percent by the end of 1991 and holds it there through the year 2000. The four-point difference between paths A and B (compared to one-point difference in the top part of the Table) reflects the fact that utilization is about four times as volatile as unemployment over the typical business cycle in Germany.

The results are shown in the bottom section of Table 16.10; the predicted inflation along path A is roughly the same as in the top part of the Table, but inflation accelerates significantly along path B. The acceleration (measured by the difference between inflation along paths B and A) starts faster than the U.S. result in the upper part of the Table, but cumulates less by the year 2000. The difference reflects the persistence of the U.S. inflation process, with its long lags and mutual feedback between wages and prices.

Why do the two procedures for Germany yield such different results? The reason is that the top part of the Table replaces the utilization rate, the demand variable that "belongs" in the price equation, with the unemployment rate. The fit deteriorates, and most notably the "level effect" of unemployment almost disappears, leaving an equation that displays nearly full hysteresis and hence for which the NAIRU cannot be defined. In contrast, there is a significant "level effect" in the version that uses utilization (e.g., Table 16.6, column [5]), and this equation should be viewed as more reliable. The utilization version is more reliable both because it fits better, and also because the relationship between utilization and unemployment in Germany is dominated by a strong trend (implying misspecification of an inflation equation that uses unemployment as a demand variable but omits the role of this trend).

As shown in Figure 16.4, the German "Mean-Utilization Rate of Unemployment" (MURU), the unemployment rate consistent with the 1962–90 average mean utilization of 84.4 percent, rose from 2 percent in 1973 to 3.4 percent in 1980 to 8 percent in 1986, before falling to 7.3 percent in 1990:4.[26] Since the

---

[26] The German MURU is calculated by running a set of regressions of the unemployment rate on lags 0–3 of the deviation of utilization from its 1962–90 mean and two piecewise trends. The MURU is equal to the fitted coefficients of the trends, plus the residual in the equation. Equations

Figure 16.4. Mean-Utilization Rate of Unemployment: Germany and the United States, 1962–90

inflation equation is stable with respect to the utilization rate, this series for the MURU represents our final estimate of the German NAIRU. It implies that in the 1989–90 period, when unemployment fell to 6.2 percent and utilization rose above 90 percent, the Germany economy became significantly overheated. The German MURU is contrasted in Figure 16.4 with the MURU for the United States, which is stationary and displays long swings in the range of 5 to 7 percent, with troughs in 1969–72 and 1987, and a peak in 1978–81.

16.5 CONCLUSIONS

The essay provides a new interpretation of wage and price dynamics. Its non-structural analysis integrates a number of concepts that have been treated separately in much of the literature, including Phillips curve "level effects," hysteresis "change effects," the error-correction mechanism, and the role of changes in labor's share in acting as a supply shock in the inflation process. Its structural analysis is complementary, deriving a role for changes in the tax and price wedge terms as supply shift variables, and showing how the insider–outsider

are estimated over four overlapping sample periods; by running separate equations we allow the cyclical response of unemployment to utilization to vary over time, and by overlapping the equations we can blend the predicted MURU from one equation smoothly into the prediction from the next equation. The equations are estimated for 1962–73, 1972–80, 1979–85, and 1984–90. The two piecewise trends in the four equations are broken respectively in 1968:4, 1975:4, 1982:4, and 1985:4. The same procedure is used for the U.S. MURU, with four equations estimated for 1955–64, 1963–71, 1970–79, and 1978–90, with breaks in 1959:2, 1974:2 and 1984:2 (no break is found necessary in the second equation for 1963–71).

and real-wage bargaining models may be interpreted in the more general context of the nonstructural approach.

An important analytical conclusion that builds on prior literature is the distinction among the shock, no-shock, and contemporaneous concepts of the NAIRU. The no-shock NAIRU relevant for monetary policy can be overstated in the presence of adverse supply shocks, unless variables are included in wage and price equations to control for such shocks. More novel is the stress on feedback between the wage and price equations, achieved by an algebraic transformation that introduces changes in labor's share as the primary feedback variable, with an additional role for the log level of labor's share as the error correction term. Since the primary target of monetary policy is inflation itself, not changes in labor cost, the wage equation is irrelevant to the estimation of the NAIRU if there is no feedback from wages to prices.

In this light the essay reaches two striking conclusions. The first is that during 1973–90 German wage behavior was remarkably similar to that in the United States, with almost identical estimates of the Phillips curve slope, of the hysteresis effect, and of the NAIRU emerging from the respective wage equations. In particular, both countries are characterized by partial but not full hysteresis in the wage equation, and the NAIRU indicated by the wage equation is about 6 percent in both countries in 1990.

But the second conclusion indicates an important difference between the two countries. In Germany (not the United States) we found no feedback from wages to prices. Thus our relatively optimistic estimates of the German NAIRU emerging from the wage equation are irrelevant to the determination of inflation and to an evaluation of the monetary policy of the Bundesbank. Instead, we find that inflation has a stable relationship to the capacity utilization rate, and that the "natural rate of capacity utilization" of about 85 percent is well below the actual rate of 90 percent reached in 1990. The economy was overheated and inflation accelerated, justifying the subsequent monetary tightening by the Bundesbank. The implied NAIRU consistent with steady inflation in Germany was 7.3 percent in 1990; this is the unemployment rate consistent with mean utilization (MURU) in that year. This estimate lies in the middle of the estimated NAIRU range of 5.5 to 9 percent appearing in the recent German literature.

Because there is mutual feedback between wages and prices in the United States, both the wage and price equations matter for inflation dynamics and monetary policy. Fortunately, both the wage and price equations tell a consistent and familiar story. The U.S. NAIRU is estimated from the wage equation to be roughly 6 percent, the same finding as in previous research. The equilibrium rate of U.S. capacity utilization in the price equation is about 82 percent, almost precisely the rate that is consistent with a 6 percent unemployment rate. Because of long lags in wage and price formation, policymakers face considerable danger in allowing the unemployment rate to fall much below 6 percent. A decade of 5 percent unemployment is estimated to cause a slow but powerful acceleration of inflation which eventually reaches double digits. The counterpart of this result is that the two years of unemployment above 6 percent in 1991–2 have achieved a permanent deceleration of U.S. inflation that will not be reversed even when the unemployment rate recovers to 6 percent, as long as it does not go below that rate.

Unlike the traditional assumption that the United States has a uniquely flat Phillips curve, we find that its wage and price adjustment to a change in utilization or unemployment is as great as in Germany and shows more of a tendency to cumulate. This puts a new interpretation on the divergence between U.S. and German unemployment behavior in the 1980s. American inflation fell after 1982–3, because a sharp demand contraction sent unemployment far above the NAIRU, and the economy slid down a relatively steep short-run Phillips curve, bringing inflation down fast in 1981–3. During the 1987–9 boom American unemployment barely fell below the 6 percent NAIRU, and hence the post-1986 acceleration of inflation was modest. A surprise for the United States is that there is no evidence of unique weakness of labor or labor unions in the 1980s. Labor's income share hardly fell at all in the United States in the 1980s, and in fact declined much more in Germany. The American problem of slow wage growth is a productivity problem, not a wage negotiation phenomenon.

Finally, the essay does not solve the mystery of why the German NAIRU rose from the 1960s to the 1980s, but it provides a new twist. Since inflation maintains a stable relationship with the rate of capacity utilization, the German puzzle can be repackaged as the mystery of why the mean-utilization unemployment rate (MURU) increased so much, particularly in the interval 1980–6 (since 1986 the MURU has declined slightly from about 8 to 7.3 percent). Here the contrast with the United States is startling. The relationship between U.S. unemployment and capacity utilization was absolutely the same in 1990 as two decades earlier, while in Germany there evolved a remarkable mismatch between the size of the labor force and the availability of industrial capacity.[27] In view of America's longstanding concern over its low rate of investment, it seems ironic that Germany emerges as a country that did not invest enough to provide the capacity required by its labor force.

The inadequacy of investment in Germany required tight monetary policy which, through the role of the Deutsche mark as the anchor of the European Monetary System, spilled over to the rest of Europe. To answer the question posed at the beginning of this paper, as to whether high European unemployment was due to restrictive demand or structural impediments, we conclude that both explanations are crucial. Structural factors interacting with restrictive demand policies depressed investment and slowed the growth of industrial capacity, leaving Europe in the 1980s without enough capital fully to employ its labor force. In the end, the core explanation of high European unemployment in the decade in the 1980s is a capital–labor mismatch.

---

[27] The U.S. capacity utilization rate was 84.3 percent in 1972 and 83.0 percent in 1990. The respective unemployment rates in these two years were 5.5 and 5.4 percent.

References

Blanchard, Olivier J. "Aggregate and Individual Price Adjustment." *Brookings Papers on Economic Activity.* 1987; vol. 18, no. 1, pp. 57–109.

Branson, William H., and Rotemberg J. "International Adjustment with Wage Rigidity." *European Economic Review.* 1980; vol. 13, pp. 309–332.

Coe, David T. "Nominal Wages, the NAIRU, and Wage Flexibility." *OECD Economic Studies.* 1985; vol. 5, pp. 87–126.

Coe, David T., and Krueger, Thomas. "Why is Unemployment So High at Full Capacity?" *The Persistence of Unemployment, the Natural Rate, and Potential Output in the Federal Republic of Germany.* Working paper 90/101. Washington, DC, IMF Research Department: October, 1990.

Cross, Rod, ed. *Unemployment, Hysteresis, and the Natural Rate Hypothesis.* Oxford and New York: Basil Blackwell; 1988.

Engle, Robert F., and Granger, C.W.J. "Co-integration and Error Correction: Representation, Estimation, and Testing." *Econometrica.* March, 1987; vol. 55, no. 2, pp. 251–76.

Franz, Wolfgang. "Hysteresis, Persistence, and the NAIRU: An Empirical Analysis for the Federal Republic of Germany." In: Layard R. and Calmfors, L. eds. *The Fight Against Unemployment.* Cambridge, MA: MIT; 1987, pp. 91–122.

Franz, Wolfgang. "Hysteresis Effects in Economic Models." *Empirical Economics* Special issue. 1990; vol. 15, no. 2, pp. 107–29.

Franz, Wolfgang, and Hofmann, Thomas, "Eine Schätzung der inflationstabilen Arbeitslo-senquote mit Hilfe von Preiserwartungen des IFO-Konjunkturtest." *IFO-Studien.* 1990; vol. 36, pp. 211–227.

Funke, Michael, "Das Hysteresis-Phänomen, Zeitschrift für Wirtschafts- und" *Sozialwissenschaften.* 1991; vol. 111, pp. 527–551.

Gordon, Robert J. "Inflation in Recession and Recovery." *Brookings Papers on Economic Activity.* 1971; vol. 2, no. 1, pp. 105–166.

"Interrelations Between Domestic and International Theories of Inflation." In: Aliber, Robert Z. ed. *The Political Economy of Monetary Reform.* New York: Macmillan; 1977, pp. 126–154.

"The Short-Run Demand for Money: A Reconsideration." *Journal of Money, Credit, and Banking.* November, 1984; vol. 16, no. 4, part 1, pp. 403–434.

"Productivity, Wages, and Prices Inside and Outside of Manufacturing in the U.S., Japan, and Europe." *European Economic Review,* April 1987; vol. 31, no. 3, pp. 685–733.

"U.S. Inflation, Labor's Share, and the Natural Rate of Unemployment. In: H. König, ed. *Economics of Wage Determination.* New York: Springer-Verlag; 1990, pp. 1–34.

Gramlich, Edward M. "Marco Policy Responses to Price Shocks." *Brookings Papers on Economic Activity.* 1979; vol. 10, no. 1, pp. 125–178.

Hendry, David F.; Pagan, Adrian R.; and Sargan, Denis J. "Dynamic Specification." In: Griliches, Zvi and Intriligator, Michael D. eds. *Handbook of Econometrics.* Amsterdam: Elsevier Science Publishers; 1984, pp. 1022–1100.

Kuh, Edwin. "A Productivity Theory of Wages Levels – an Alternative to the Phillips Curve." *Review of Economic Studies.* October, 1967; vol. 34, no. 4, pp. 333–60.

Phillips, A.W. "Stabilization Policy and the Time Forms of Lagged Responses." *Economic Journal.* 1967; vol. 67, pp. 265–277.

Sachs, Jeffrey D. "Wages, Profits, and Macroeconomic Adjustment: A Comparative Study." *Brookings Papers on Economic Activity*. 1979; vol. 10, no. 2, pp. 269–319.

Sargan, Denis J. "Wages and Prices in the United Kingdom: A Study in Econometric Methodology." In: Hart, P.E., et al., eds. *Econometric Analysis for National Economic Planning*. Colston Papers. London: Bullerworths; 1964, vol. 16, pp. 25–54.

Schultze, Charles L. "Real Wages Real Wage Aspirations, and Unemployment in Europe. In: Lawrence Robert Z. and Schultze, Charles L. eds. *Barriers to European growth: A Transatlantic View*. Washington, DC: Brookings; 1987, pp. 230–91.

CHAPTER 17

Foundations of the Goldilocks Economy: Supply Shocks and the Time-Varying NAIRU[1]

The American Economy of the mid-1990s has been a source of envy for the world and of puzzlement for macroeconomists. The civilian unemployment rate has remained below 5 percent for one year and below 6 percent for almost four years. Despite near universal forecasts in 1994 of accelerating inflation that would accompany a dip of the unemployment rate below 6 percent, inflation actually decelerated significantly between 1994 and 1998. This benign outcome for inflation stands in contrast to the significant acceleration that occurred when unemployment last dipped below 6 percent, in the late 1980s.[1]

The failure of inflation to accelerate allowed the Federal Reserve to avoid raising short-term interest rates after early 1997, and even to lower them in late 1998. Freed from the restraint of restrictive monetary policy that had choked earlier expansions, and with its fires stoked by the lowest medium-term and long-term nominal interest rates in three decades, the economy charged ahead and achieved a state of high growth – noninflationary bliss that some have dubbed the "Goldilocks economy" (neither too hot nor too cold, but just right). Low interest rates and low inflation combined to propel the American stock market to valuation levels without precedent, along the way creating $10 trillion of wealth in barely four years, and most of this wealth was still intact after the market correction in the summer and fall of 1998. Overcome

---

[1] The four-quarter rate of change of the chain-weighted GDP deflator decelerated from 2.5 percent in 1994:3 to 1.0 percent in 1998:2, in contrast to its acceleration from 3.1 percent in 1987:3 to 4.2 percent in 1990:2 (see Table 17.1).

Note. This research is supported by the National Science Foundation. I am grateful to William Nordhaus and to participants of the Brookings Panel meeting for helpful comments. Christian Ehemann and Steven Landefeld were invaluable, both in providing data and helping me to understand them. Aarti Dhupelia, Tominori Ishikawa, and Stuart Gurrea provided excellent research assistance. Above all, I am greatly indebted to James Stock for his role in developing the methodology adopted in this paper, and for his instant and insightful responses to my endless queries about how to merge his new techniques with my traditional specification of the Phillips curve. (*Source.* "Foundations of the Goldilocks Economy: Supply Shocks and the Time-varying NAIRU" *Brookings Papers on Economic Activity.* 1998; vol. 29, no. 2, pp. 297–333).

with enthusiasm, one distinguished economist gushed, "This expansion will run forever."[2]

While some observers have attributed the miracle economy to the Fed's brilliant monetary policy, it is clear that the true heroine of the drama is the deceleration of inflation, and the basic challenge for economists is to explain that deceleration.[3] Proposed explanations can be divided among three groups.[4] The first view announces a revolution and the arrival of a "new economy": the rapid growth of production of high-technology products, many of which enjoy continuing declines in prices, has rendered obsolete previous capacity constraints associated with the Phillips curve, while globalization has provided low-technology products in infinite quantity at ever-lower prices.[5] The second, which also denounces the Phillips curve view, argues on econometric grounds that the NAIRU (or "nonaccelerting inflation" rate of unemployment), natural rate hypothesis, and short-run Phillips curve have never existed, even prior to 1990.[6]

The third view defends the natural rate version of the Phillips curve and explains recent events as consistent with a decline in the NAIRU. Using techniques developed by Douglas Staiger, James Stock, and Mark Watson, I have elsewhere provided estimates that the NAIRU in the United States declined by a full percentage point between the mid-1980s and mid-1990s. In this interpretation, inflation accelerated in 1987–9 but not in 1995–8, because the actual unemployment rate was significantly below the NAIRU in the previous episode but not in the recent period.[7]

The first round of papers on the time-varying NAIRU (hereafter TV-NAIRU) in 1997 identified the phenomenon of the declining NAIRU in the 1990s but did not explain it. This paper takes the next step. The list of candidate explanations

---

[2] Rudiger Dornbusch, "Growth Forever," *Wall Street Journal*, July 30, 1998, editorial page.

[3] Compare the two-year period ending in 1998:2 with the last two years of the previous expansion, ending in 1990:2. The annual rate of nominal GDP growth was considerably slower in the recent period than in the earlier period (5.0 percent compared with 7.0 percent), but inflation was so much lower (1.5 percent compared with 4.3 percent) that the annual rate of real GDP growth was higher (3.5 percent compared with 2.7 percent). Correspondingly, the unemployment rate fell by more over the most recent two-year period, from 5.4 to 4.4 percent, than the slight decline from 5.5 to 5.3 percent observed in the earlier two-year period.

[4] While the present account places primary emphasis on inflation behavior, there is also an independent view of monetary policy that predicts steady expansion based on the long-term bond market acting as an automatic stabilizer, thus making discretionary action by the Fed unnecessary; see Gene Koretz, "A Golden Age of Steady Growth?," *Business Week*, March 10, 1997, p. 22.

[5] The new economy advocates are led by Edward Yardeni, chief economist of Deutsche Morgan Grenfell. A skeptical view is provided in "Too Triumphalist by Half," *Economist*, April 25, 1998, p. 29.

[6] A leading proponent of this view is my colleague at Northwestern University, Robert Eisner. For instance, see his article "The Economy is Booming. So Why Are Economists Glum?," *Wall Street Journal*, July 29, 1998, editorial page. See also Levy (1997).

[7] Staiger, Stock, and Watson (1997); Gordon (1997). The time series for the time-varying NAIRU created by Staiger, Stock, and Watson is very similar to mine when the same definition of inflation is used. See also Stock (1998); Stock and Watson (1998b).

is long and can be roughly grouped into three sets: a first, general group of explanations not directly related to wage or price behavior; a second group related to wage behavior; and a third related to price behavior.

General candidates include vague references to the new economy or "a mysterious X factor that Alan Greenspan believes is boosting the economy."[8] These hypotheses run aground on the failure of measured productivity growth to accelerate significantly in the 1990s.[9] Another general candidate is the set of international crises – in Asia, Russia, Latin America, and elsewhere – which have created a flight to quality and the American "safe haven" in world capital markets, resulting in the appreciation of the dollar and the reduction of both interest rates and import prices in the United States.

Hypotheses involving wage behavior point to weak labor unions, a secular decline in the real minimum wage, "heightened job insecurity," and falling benefit costs due primarily to the revolution in medical care through the development of health maintenance organizations (HMOs).

Hypotheses involving price behavior are the main focus of this paper, which suggests that the low inflation of the mid-1990s resulted from the confluence of no fewer than five beneficial supply shocks, each working to reduce the inflation rate consistent with any given unemployment rate. Two of these beneficial shocks are the familiar pair – changes in real food and energy prices and in real import prices – that working in reverse played such a large role in creating the twin peaks of unemployment and inflation in 1974–5 and 1979–81, and have now helped to create an inflation-unemployment valley. The other three are of more recent origin: a sharp incease in the rate of deflation of real computer prices, a sharp reduction in the rate of inflation in real medical care prices, and a reduction in measured inflation relative to true inflation achieved by improvements in the measurement of official price indexes.

Three of these beneficial supply shocks are complementary with others cited above. The flight of capital to a safe haven explains much of the decline in real import prices. The role of computer prices provides a quantifiable measure of the role of at least part of the new economy. And the HMO-driven decline in real medical care inflation is the flip side of the decline in the rate of change of fringe benefits that has held down the growth rate of employee compensation.

---

[8] Andy Serwer, "The 'X Factor'? It's My Pal Bedford," *Fortune*, August 17, 1998, p. 233.

[9] Since the task is to explain the *officially measured* deceleration of inflation, it is the officially measured rate of productivity growth that matters; any suspected measurement error would reduce the inflation rate and raise the rate of productivity growth by exactly the same amount for any specified sector of the economy – for example, the nonfarm private business sector – and thus would not contribute an explanation for the measured decleration of inflation. Supporting the view that the officially measured rate of productivity growth has not accelerated, the private nonfarm business productivity trend used below to create the productivity deviation variable and also to compute trend unit labor cost registers an annualized rate of increase over 1987–98 of only 1.06 percent per year. Over the shorter six-year period ending in 1998:2, the annualized growth rate is 1.11 percent per year. As interpreted by my detrending procedure, the level of productivity was above trend by 0.5 percent in 1992:2 and by 0.9 percent in 1998:2.

Thus far, I have characterized the major surprise in the Goldilocks economy as the low rate of inflation given the low rate of unemployment, and indeed, this has been the focus of the media as well. But combined with that surprise there have been several central macroeconomic relationships that are not surprises, and the task of explaining the contrast between the surprises and "nonsurprises" creates a complex and subtle interpretation of the Goldilocks economy. While inflation has been low given the behavior of unemployment, inflation has not been surprisingly low given the behavior of an alternative measure of the economy's tightness: the rate of capacity utilization.

A parallel phenomenon is that the behavior of wages has not been surprising given unemployment. Unemployment has been low and, as would be predicted by the standard Phillips curve, wage rates have accelerated substantially between 1994 and 1998. Thus creating a two-by-two matrix consisting of two inflation measures, price changes and wage changes, and two measures of economic tightness, the capacity utilization rate and the unemployment rate, gives two surprises – low inflation despite low unemployment and accelerating wages despite relatively low utilization – and two nonsurprises – accelerating wages responding to low unemployment and low inflation responding to relatively low capacity utilization. Stated another way, the real questions about the Goldilocks economy are why inflation has been so low relative to changes in wages and why the unemployment rate has declined when utilization has not increased.[10]

The aspect of these puzzles involving the relation between price and wage changes reveals a limitation of previous work by myself and others on the TV-NAIRU. This research has focused entirely on equations in which inflation is explained by lagged inflation, the unemployment gap, and various supply shocks, paying no attention at all to wages. This paper is the first in the literature to devote parallel attention to wages and prices, and also to consider mutual feedback between wages and prices. Can the inflation rate be explained entirely by lagged inflation and other variables, or does feedback from wage behavior play a role? Can wage changes be explained entirely by lagged wage changes and other variables, or does feedback from price behavior play a role?

I begin with a brief review of my traditional inflation model and extend it to provide a simple method of estimating feedback between wage and price changes. In the following section I look briefly at the data that document the deceleration of inflation and at the quite different behavior of wage indexes that include or exclude benefits, and contrast wage and price behavior in 1994–8 with that in 1987–90. I then develop quantitative measures of the extent to which the behavior of price inflation in 1993–8 represents a surprise.

The next section quantifies the roles of the traditional import price and food-energy price supply shocks in the 1990s. In the following section, I assess the roles of computers, medical care, and measurement changes in price changes by stripping these effects from the official GDP and personal consumption expenditure (PCE) deflators. I then estimate new TV-NAIRUs to demonstrate the

---

[10] I owe this characterization to James Stock's comments on the meeting draft of the paper.

roles of these three more recent supply shocks. In the next section, I review tests of feedback among wage and price equations and provide alternative estimates of the TV-NAIRU taking these estimates into account. Finally, I summarize what is known about the likely behavior of both the older and the more recent supply shocks over the next few years, and the implications for the evolution of inflation and of the TV-NAIRU.

17.1 MODELING INFLATION, THE TV-NAIRU, AND MUTUAL WAGE-PRICE FEEDBACK

The Phillips curve has become a generic term for any relationship between the *rate of change* of a nominal price or wage and the *level* of a real indicator of the intensity of demand in the economy, such as the unemployment rate. In the 1970s the simple Phillips relation was amended by incorporating supply shocks and a zero long-run trade-off. What emerged was an interpretation of the Phillips curve that I have called the triangle model of inflation, in reference to the three basic determinants of the inflation rate: inertia, demand, and supply.[11]

For example, a general specification of this framework would be

$$p_t = a(L)p_{t-1} + b(L)D_t + c(L)z_t + e_t, \tag{1}$$

where lower-case letters designate first differences of logarithms, upper-case letters designate logarithms of levels, and L is a polynomial in the lag operator. The dependent variable p_t is the inflation rate. Inertia is conveyed by the lagged rate of inflation p_{t-1}. D_t is an index of excess demand, normalized so that $D_t = 0$ indicates the absence of excess demand; z_t is a vector of supply shock variables, normalized so that $z_t = 0$ indicates an absence of supply shocks; and e_t is a serially uncorrelated error term.[12]

Usually, equation 1 will include several lags of past inflation rates, reflecting the influence of several past years of inflation behavior on current price setting, through some combination of expectation formation and overlapping wage and price contracts. If the sum of the coefficients on these lagged inflation values equals unity, there is a "natural rate" of the demand variable (D_t^N) consistent with a constant rate of inflation.[13] Subsequently, I provide alternative versions of equation 1 that explain wage changes, with and without two-way feedback

---

[11] Gordon (1977, 1982) and Gordon and King (1982) develop a model of the inflation process driven by these three factors. The term "triangle model" was first used in Gordon (1983). The origins of the triangle model and additional perspective are provided in Gordon (1997). Stock (1998, p. 3) cites Gordon (1982) as the source of the framework that Stock, Staiger, and Watson have used in estimating the TV-NAIRU, See Chapters Fourteen and Fifteen in this book.

[12] The theory of real output, inflation, and policy responses to supply shocks was developed independently by Gordon (1975) and Phelps (1978), and is integrated and summarized in Gordon (1984), See Chapters Ten and Eleven in this book.

[13] While the estimated sum of the coefficients on lagged inflation is usually roughly equal to unity, that sum must be constrained to be exactly unity for a meaningful "natural rate" of the demand variable to be calculated.

between prices and wages. The basic equations estimated in this paper use current and lagged values of the unemployment gap as a proxy for the excess demand parameter D_t, where the unemployment gap is defined as the difference between the actual rate of unemployment and the natural rate, and the natural rate is allowed to vary over time. Use of the unemployment rate as a predictor of inflation can be justified, for example, by the work of Robert King and Watson, who find that unemployment causes inflation in the Granger-causation sense, by preceding it in time.[14] Alternatively, the capacity utilization rate is used as a proxy for the excess demand parameter D_t, and the natural rate of the capacity utilization rate is also allowed to vary through time.

The structure of the triangle model, with its distinction between demand and supply shocks, suggests a particular conception of the NAIRU. The standard concept is the unemployment rate that is consistent with steady inflation in the absence of supply shocks. To put it another way, if the inflation rate suddenly exhibits a spike that is entirely explained by the z_t supply shock variables in equation 1, the standard conception of the NAIRU measures the unemployment rate that would be compatible with steady inflation in the absence of those supply shocks. Without this qualification, the NAIRU would jump around as supply shocks came and went, which is not what most economists are trying to convey when they speak of the natural rate of unemployment.

Allowing the NAIRU to Vary over Time

The estimation of the time-varying NAIRU (U^N) combines inflation equation 1, with the unemployment gap serving as the proxy for excess demand, and a second equation that explicitly allows the NAIRU to vary with time:

$$p_t = a(L)p_{t-1} + b(L)\left(U_t - U_t^N\right) + c(L)z_t + \epsilon_t, \tag{2}$$

$$U_t^N = U_{t-1}^N + \eta_t, E\eta_t = 0, var(\eta_t) = \tau^2. \tag{3}$$

When τ in equation 3 is equal to zero the natural rate is constant, and when it is positive the model allows the NAIRU to vary by a limited amount each quarter. If there was no limit on the ability of the NAIRU to vary each time period, the time-varying NAIRU would jump up and down and soak up all the residual variation in the inflation equation.

---

[14] See King and Watson (1994). Inflation depends on both the level of and change in the demand variable. I first noted the importance of the rate of change effect in Gordon (1977, pp. 270–1). The rate of change effect is automatically allowed to enter as long as the gap variable is entered with more than one lag; in other words, if the gap variable is entered as, say, the current value and one lagged value, this formulation contains precisely the same information as entering the current level and change from the previous period. The change variable is incorporated in the present paper, as in previous papers, by including the current and four lagged values of the unemployment rate; the zig-zag in the current and lagged coefficients reflects the change effect, whereas the significant sum of coefficients reflects the level effect.

The Interaction of Wage and Price Behavior

Recent discussions of the time-varying NAIRU have focused on equations explaining price inflation, because this concept of inflation is the most directly relevant to monetary policy. However, ever since Keynes's *General Theory*, the rate of change of wages has been believed to play a central role in aggregate supply behavior. One direct indicator of the role of wages in the inflation process is provided by labor's share in national income. The change in labor's share (s_t) is by definition equal to the growth rate of the real wage $(w_t - p_t)$ minus the growth rate of labor's average product (θ_t):

$$s_t = w_t - \theta_t - p_t. \tag{4}$$

It can be shown that changes in labor's share become a source of "cost push" that is on an equal footing with any other type of supply shock; an increase in labor's share pushes upward on the rate of inflation at any given level of the unemployment gap.[15]

The well-known stability of labor's share in the United States since the early 1970s suggests that wage behavior has not played much of an independent role in the inflation process. Nevertheless, it is informative to create estimates of the NAIRU corresponding to the same dynamic estimation framework developed above. A straightforward analogy to the basic inflation equation 2 is an equation explaining changes in wage rates (w_t) relative to trend productivity (θ_t^*) by its own lagged values and the same set of demand and supply variables that enter into the price equation. The difference between the growth rates of wage rates and trend productivity is often called the growth rate of trend unit labor cost $(w - \theta^*)$. Thus

$$(w - \theta^*)_t = g(L)(w - \theta^*)_{t-1} + h(L)\left(U_t - U_t^N\right)$$
$$+c(L)z_t + \epsilon_t. \tag{5}$$

As originally suggested by Christopher Sims, the identification of a wage equation that is separate from the price equation is problematic.[16] One approach might be to include in the wage equation different sets of demand and supply terms as explanatory variables from those included in the price equation. But this is implausible a priori, since any variable relevant as a determinant of price change may also be relevant for participants in the wage-setting process, and vice-versa for prices. Another approach might be to restrict the contemporaneous coefficient of wages on current prices or prices on current wages, but this is arbitrary as well. In this paper, I estimate the time-varying NAIRU based on equation 5, which is a direct analogy to equation 2 and includes the same explanatory variables, on the grounds that the variables relevant for wage behavior are similarly relevant for price behavior.

---

[15] See Franz and Gordon (1993), Chapter Sixteen in this book.
[16] Sims (1987).

However, equation 5 is restrictive in that it does not allow for feedback from prices to wages. In the present context, it is of particular interest whether wage changes were restrained by the beneficial supply shocks that reduced the rate of price inflation, and whether price changes were restrained by factors that limited wage changes, for example, worker insecurity. An alternative wage equation, leaving open the relative importance of wage-wage and price-wage feedback, can be written as follows:

$$(w - \theta^*)_t = g(L)(w - \theta^*)_{t-1} + h(L)p_{t-1}$$
$$+ b(L)\big(U_t - U_t^N\big) + c(L)z_t + e_t. \tag{6}$$

Equation 6 is the same as equation 5 but with the addition of the lagged price inflation terms. A simple method of estimating the relative importance of lagged wage and price inflation is to transform equation 6 by adding and subtracting $h(L)$ times the lagged trend unit labor cost terms:

$$(w - \theta^*)_t = [g(L) + h(L)](w - \theta^*)_{t-1} - h(L)(w - \theta^* - p)_{t-1}$$
$$+ b(L)\big(U_t - U_t^N\big) + c(L)z_t + e_t. \tag{7}$$

The sum of $g(L)$ and $h(L)$ coefficients can be constrained to equal unity, which imposes the natural rate hypothesis. The freely estimated sum of coefficients (Σh) indicates the weight on lagged prices in the determination of trend unit labor cost, while $1 - \Sigma h$ indicates the weight to be applied to wage-wage feedback. Henceforth I call the $w - \theta^* - p$ term the change in trend labor share; note that this differs from the change in labor's share in equation 4 only through the replacement of actual productivity change (θ) by trend productivity change (θ^*). By analogy, feedback from wages to prices can be estimated by the "dual" to equation 7:

$$p_t = [g(L) + h(L)]p_{t-1} + h(L)(w - \theta^* - p)_{t-1}$$
$$+ b(L)\big(U_t - U_t^N\big) + c(L)z_t + e_t, \tag{8}$$

where the change in trend labor share appears with a positive sign, in contrast to its negative sign in equation 7.

To summarize, there are four sets of equations to estimate. While they all contain the unemployment gap and the same set of supply shock terms, they differ in the dependent variable, lagged dependent variable, and lagged trend labor cost term, as follows:

Dependent Variable	Lagged Dependent Variable	Trend Labor Share?
Price change	Price change	No
Trend unit labor cost change	Trend unit labor cost change	No
Price change	Price change	Yes
Trend unit labor cost change	Trend unit labor cost change	Yes

Table 17.1. *Basic Data, Selected Quarters*[a]
Percent

Variable	1987:3	1990:2	1994:3	1998:2
Excess demand[b]				
Civilian unemployment rate	6.0	5.3	6.0	4.4
Capacity utilization rate	81.7	82.8	83.2	82.1
Prices[c]				
GDP deflator	3.1	4.2	2.5	1.0
PCE deflator	4.0	4.4	2.7	0.8
CPI-U-X1	4.2	4.5	2.8	1.6
Wages and productivity[c]				
ECI-total compensation[d]	3.2	5.0	3.2	3.4
ECI-wages and salaries[d]	3.3	4.3	3.1	3.9
Compensation per hour	3.3	5.5	1.5	4.2
Average hourly earnings	2.7	3.8	2.5	4.2
Output per hour	−0.3	1.0	0.4	1.9

[a] See text for basis for selection of quarters.
[b] Levels.
[c] Four-quarter rates of change.
[d] Employment Cost Index.
Source. Data are from the worldwide web pages of the Bureau of Economic Analysis and the Bureau of Labor Statistics.

17.2   BASIC DATA AND THE EXTENT OF THE INFLATION SURPRISE

The postwar inflation experience in the United States is well known. There are three basic price indexes for final goods: the chain-weighted GDP deflator, the chain-weighted deflator for personal consumption expenditures, and the version of the Consumer Price Index (CPI) that incorporates the current treatment of shelter costs back to 1967, the so-called CPI-U-X1. When four-quarter moving average rates of change are plotted, the differences among these indexes are minor. Each has twin peaks in 1974–5 and 1980–1 and substantial accelerations of inflation in periods of relatively low unemployment, especially 1956–7, 1965–72, and 1987–90. Common valleys are evident as well, most notably in 1960–5; 1972–3, presumably influenced by the Nixon price controls; 1986, when oil prices collapsed; and 1997–98.

Although I do not present such a plot, for reasons of space, the recent behavior of these price indexes and several wage indexes over the two most recent business cycles is summarized in Table 17.1. The table also shows the behavior of the two main tightness measures examined in this paper: the unemployment rate and the rate of capacity utilization. The unemployment rate is reported for four calendar quarters: 1987:3 and 1994:3 are chosen for being quarters when the unemployment rate first reached 6 percent along a cyclical path toward lower values, 1990:2 is the cyclical peak quarter of the previous business expansion, and 1998:2 is the most recent quarter. Between 1994 and 1998 the unemployment rate declined by more than twice as much as between 1987 and 1990. In contrast, the rate of capacity utilization reveals a reduction in cyclical tightness in the more recent period but an increase in tightness in the earlier period.

For the selected price deflators, Table 17.1 displays the four-quarter changes ending in the same four quarters designated above. All three deflators exhibit a deceleration during 1994–8 that contrasts with an acceleration between 1987 and 1990, although the earlier accelerations for the PCE deflator and the CPI are quite modest. The Table also presents four-quarter changes in four wage indexes and a productivity index. The contrast between wage and price behavior is quite marked. All four wage indexes accelerated in 1994–8. Further, the 1994–8 accelerations in compensation per hour and average hourly earnings were actually greater than for the same indexes in 1987–90. Productivity accelerated in both business cycles over the periods shown.

Quantifying the Price Surprise

Table 17.1 suggests that the puzzle of low inflation in the mid-1990s applies to price behavior but not necessarily to wage behavior. Price inflation decelerated sharply as unemployment fell during 1994–8, whereas wage inflation accelerated in all four wage indexes shown – by much more in compensation per hour and average hourly earnings than in either Employment Cost Index (ECI) measure used. How much of a surprise was the inflation deceleration of the mid-1990s?

One straightforward way to quantify the inflation surprise is to compute the forecasting error in my standard inflation equation 2 when the NAIRU is maintained at a constant value throughout the 1980s and 1990s. The exercise can be carried out with the arbitrary NAIRU series that I used in research in the 1980s and early 1990s and published in successive editions of my macroeconomics textbook until 1993, henceforth the "textbook NAIRU." This series rose gradually from the 1950s through the late 1970s, to reflect demographic changes, and after 1978 was fixed at 6 percent. As recently as 1994, I assessed the accuracy of this series by running postsample dynamic simulations of equation 2 and noted the absence of substantial drift of predicted from actual values.[17]

Throughout this paper, equations are estimated using a uniform sample period, set of supply variables, and set of lag lengths, chosen to conform with my inflation research since 1982.[18] The wage data refer to the Employment Cost

---

[17] Gordon (1994). I found no evidence that the actual inflation rate was drifting down relative to the predicted inflation rate that assumed a fixed NAIRU of 6 However, it soon became evident that the fixed NAIRU approach should be abandoned, and my first paper on the TV-NAIRU was presented less than a year later (Gordon, 1995).

[18] That is, since Gordon (1982). The one change is that the present paper uses a shorter sample period, beginning in 1962:1. Thus it is no longer necessary to link the Bureau of Economic

Table 17.2. *Actual and Simulated Values of Price and Wage Changes, Using Alteranative Indexes and Constant NAIRU[a]*
Units as indicated

	1998:2 Results[b]			Dynamic Simulation Errors	
Index	Actual	Simulated	Error	Root Mean-Squared Error	Mean Error
GDP deflator	1.01	2.31	−1.30	0.82	−0.46
PCE deflator	0.85	2.86	−2.01	1.24	−1.01
CPI-U-X1	1.61	3.19	−1.58	0.89	−0.59
Trend unit labor cost					
ECI–total compensation	2.35	3.13	−0.78	0.99	−0.52
ECI–wages and salaries	2.87	1.98	0.89	0.77	0.47

[a] Specification of equations given by equations 2 and 5 in text: sample period is 1962:1–1992:4. Dynamic simulation is from 1993:1 to 1998:2. See Appendix A for details of variables and lag lengths.
[b] Four-quarter percent changes.
Source. Author's calculations.

Index, with ("ECI-TC") and without ("ECI-WS") employee fringe benefits. For details, see Chapter appendix A.

The results of the inflation surprise computations are presented in Table 17.2, which shows the actual and fitted values of equation 2 estimated with each of the three price indexes shown in Table 17.1, and the actual and fitted values of equation 5 for both versions of the ECI. In the case of each dependent variable, the textbook NAIRU is used to compute the unemployment gap, and the sample period ends in 1992:4. Fitted values starting in 1993:1 are computed in a dynamic simulation that feeds back the estimated, rather than actual, values of the lagged dependent variable.

The largest simulation errors in Table 17.2 are for the rate of change of the PCE deflator (below, I present the complementary result that the estimated TV-NAIRU for the PCE deflator declines more than for the other price indexes between the late 1980s and 1998). Errors for the two-trend unit labor cost variables are much smaller, and indeed, the error is positive for the ECI-WS, indicating that the acceleration in the ECI for wages and salaries after 1992:4 has been greater than would have been predicted by equation 5 on the basis of a fixed NAIRU of 6 percent. Correspondingly, I show below that the TV-NAIRU estimated for this wage index lies above 6 percent during the 1990s.

A question raised by Table 17.2 is why the inflation rates predicted for 1998:2 using the price deflators were roughly the same as the actual rates for 1994:3 shown in Table 17.1. Why was there no predicted acceleration of inflation,

Analysis's chain-weighted deflators – available only since 1959 – to the implicit deflators available for the earlier period.

Percent

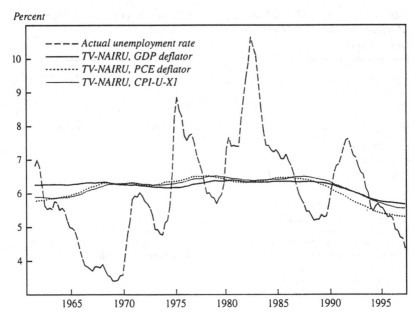

Figure 17.1. Actual Unemployment Rate and TV-NAIRUs for Price Indexes, 1961–98
Source. Worldwide web page of the Bureau of Labor Statistics and author's calculations.

since the natural rate hypothesis forecasts that the actual unemployment rate, continually below the fixed textbook NAIRU of 6 percent after 1994:3, should have caused inflation to accelerate? The simple answer is that an acceleration in the predicted values was prevented by the combined effect of the relative import price and relative food-energy variables, which held down the inflation rate by a large amount. While the impact of these variables can be documented with the textbook NAIRU used to construct the results in Table 17.2, I prefer to quantify their impact using newly estimated time-varying NAIRUs (see Table 17.4).

17.3 NEW TV-NAIRU ESTIMATES FOR INFLATION, STRIPPED INFLATION, AND LABOR COST

The prediction errors for the price indexes displayed in Table 17.2 suggest that the natural rate hypothesis remains valid in the 1990s only if the estimated TV-NAIRU (incorporating equations 2 and 3) declines substantially from its values in the late 1980s. This is indeed the case. Figure 17.1 plots the actual unemployment rate against new TV-NAIRUs for the three basic inflation indexes. The TV-NAIRUs are quite stable, remaining within a narrow band between 5.3 and 6.5 percent throughout the past four decades. Since 1989, the TV-NAIRU for the PCE deflator has been somewhat lower than those for the GDP deflator and the CPI-U-X1, dropping below 5.5 percent in 1995:1 and stabilizing at

5.31 percent in the last four quarters. The TV-NAIRU for the GDP deflator has fallen from a value of 6.36 percent as recently as 1988:3 to reach a final value of 5.68 percent in 1998:2.

The Smoothness Issue

The smoothness issue becomes evident when equations 2 and 3 are examined. One faces the inescapable choice of either setting the NAIRU as a constant and allowing all the residual variation to remain in the error term of equation 2, or allowing some or all of the residual variation to create movements in the TV-NAIRU. In their latest research, Stock and Watson allow the standard deviation term (τ_η) to be estimated.[19] Identifying this parameter does not restrict the relationship between the variances of the error terms in equations 2 or 3; the model is identified by the assumption that the TV-NAIRU is a random walk (or, more generally, integrated of order one). They prove that if the variance of the change in the TV-NAIRU is small relative to the variance of the error in equation 2, their estimator is asymptotically median unbiased.

In the present essay, I adopt this new methodology.[20] My baseline estimates of the TV-NAIRU are based on Stock and Watson's median-unbiased estimator, τ_η; for the GDP deflator, the estimate is 0.090. However, this point estimate changes with the specification and it also has considerable sampling uncertainty. Moreover, it is useful to contrast the TV-NAIRUs obtained by this new method with those obtained using the judgmental method set forth in my previous paper, whereby τ_η is chosen so that the TV-NAIRU is allowed to vary, subject to the constraint that it is not to exhibit short-term reversals.[21] As a sensitivity analysis, therefore, I also consider alternative values for this standard deviation.

Figure 17.2 illustrates the effects of estimating equation 2 for the GDP deflator using four different values for the imposed standard deviation: 0.045, 0.090, 0.136, and 0.271. The solid line plots the TV-NAIRU series that results from imposing a standard deviation of 0.090, as henceforth in this paper.[22] With higher standard deviations, the resulting series exhibit short-term reversals that are slight for a value of 0.136 and increasingly noticeable for a value of 0.271.[23] Imposing a lower standard deviation of 0.045 results in a slightly smoother series.

Clearly, the extent to which the TV-NAIRU declines between the late 1980s and 1998 depends on the choice of smoothness parameter. As the smoothness

---

[19] Stock and Watson (1998b).

[20] The details of this approach as applied to estimation of the TV-NAIRU are laid out in Stock (1998).

[21] See Gordon (1997).

[22] The corresponding coefficients are reported in Table 17.3.

[23] The computer programs that implement the methodology of Stock and Watson (1998b) do not directly constrain the value of the τ parameter, but rather a related parameter, λ. The research in this paper is based on integer values of λ that translate into noninteger decimals for τ.

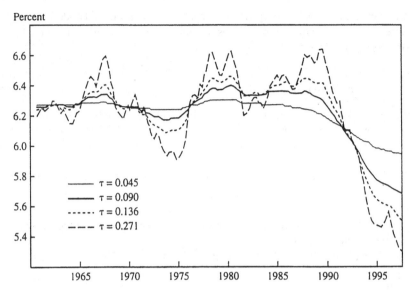

Figure 17.2. TV-NAIRUs for the GDP Deflator, Alternative Standard Deviations, 1961–98

Source. Author's calculations.

parameter is increased across the four alternative values shown in Figure 17.2, the series declines by 0.38, 0.67, 0.84, and 1.15 percentage points, respectively, between 1988:1 and 1998:2. The criterion that the resulting TV-NAIRU series be free of short-term reversals might lead some to stop at a higher standard deviation, such as 0.136 instead of 0.090; and any choice of a higher standard deviation will boost the amount by which the estimated TV-NAIRU declines in the 1990s and reduce the errors reported below in explaining the observed inflation rates of 1998. In the conclusion to this paper, however, I provide a complete decomposition of the inflation surprise of the 1990s, consisting of two error terms, the part of the decline in the TV-NAIRU that the model cannot explain, and the remaining residual error. The higher the assumed standard deviation of the TV-NAIRU, the larger will be the part of the decline that the model cannot explain and the smaller will be the remaining residual error.

Estimated Coefficients

Table 17.3 displays the estimated coefficients for equations 2 and 5 for the GDP and PCE deflators and the two labor cost variables. The coefficients on the deflator equations are similar to my previous research, with those on the sum of lagged dependent variables very close to unity, those on the sum of unemployment gap variables around −0.6, those on the productivity deviation around −0.1, those on the relative import price of 0.1, those on the food-energy effect of about 0.7 for the consumption deflator but an insignificant 0.2 for the

Table 17.3. *Estimated Equations for Quarterly Change in Price and Wage Variable, 1962:1–1998:2*[a]

| | | | Dependent Variable | | |
| | | | | Trend Unit Labor Cost[b] | |
Independent Variable	Lag	GDP Deflator	PCE Deflator	ECI–Total Compensation	ECI–Wages and Salaries
Lagged dependent variable[c]	1–24	1.00**	1.01**	1.00**	1.00**
Unemployment gap	0–4	−0.57**	−0.63**	−0.48**	−0.43**
Change in relative import price	1–4	0.12**	0.11**	0.07**	0.06**
Change in relative food-energy price	0–4	0.15	0.70**	0.30	0.15
Change in productivity deviation	0–1	−0.14**	−0.06	0.05	0.01
Nixon controls on	0	−1.75**	−1.76**	−1.01*	−1.34**
Nixon controls off	0	1.00**	0.55	0.14	0.13
Summary statistic					
$\bar{R}^2$		0.92	0.91	0.86	0.89
Standard error of estimate		0.68	0.76	0.86	0.70
Sum of squared residuals		56.1	71.1	88.0	58.1
Addendum: Dynamic simulation errors[d]					
1993:1–1998:2					
Mean error		−0.25	−0.46	−0.15	0.27
Root mean-squared error		0.60	0.70	0.79	0.64
1998:1–1998:2					
Mean error		−0.99	−1.07	−0.72	0.00
Root mean-squared error		0.99	1.16	1.06	0.36

[a] Specification of equations given by equations 2 and 5 in text. Statistical significance at the 5 percent level is denoted by*; at the 1 percent level, by**.

[b] Regression equations for the trend unit labor cost variables also include three seasonal dummy variables.

[c] Lagged dependent variable is entered as the four-quarter moving average of the dependent variable for lags 1, 5, 9, 13, 17, and 21.

[d] Dynamic simulations are based on regressions for the sample period 1962:1–1992:4, in which the coefficients on the lagged dependent variable are constrained to sum to unity.

Source. Author's calculations.

Percent

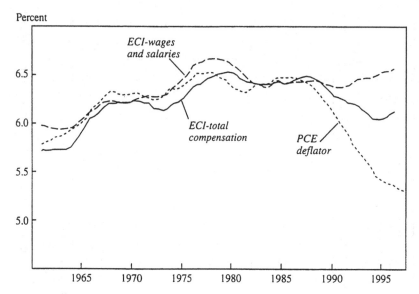

Figure 17.3. TV-NAIRUs for Wage Indexes and the PCE Deflator, 1961–98
Source. Author's calculations.

GDP deflator.[24] The bottom panel of the table displays results of postsample dynamic simulations that truncate the sample period at 1992:4. Both price equations overpredict the rate of inflation in the first half of 1998 by roughly 1 percentage point.

The coefficients for the labor cost equations (using the specification in equation 5) are similar to those in the inflation equations, as are the goodness-of-fit statistics.[25] The slope of the Phillips curve is somewhat flatter, and neither the food-energy nor productivity variables are significant. However, both the import price effect and the "Nixon controls on" variable are significant. It is notable that the mean error of the equation for the ECI-WS is exactly zero in early 1998, highlighting the sharp contrast between the wages and salaries version of the ECI and the other variables already evident in the forecasting errors of Table 17.2.

Figure 17.3 presents the TV-NAIRU estimates for the two trend unit labor cost series in comparison with the basic TV-NAIRU estimate for the PCE deflator. As can be seen, the trend unit labor cost TV-NAIRUs display very

---

[24] See Gordon (1982, Table 17.2, pp. 103–04; 1997, Table 17.1, p. 25). In the present paper, lags thirteen to twenty-four are highly significant in the price equations reported in Table 17.3 and contribute 30 percent and 27 percent of the total sum of lagged coefficients on the GDP and PCE deflator equations, respectively. While the sum of coefficients on the food-energy effect in the GDP deflator equation is insignificant, an exclusion test indicates that this set of lagged variables makes a contribution to the fit of the equation at a better than 1 percent significance level.

[25] The ECI series for total compensation and for wages and salaries extend back only to 1980. For this exercise they are extrapolated back to 1948 with a mix-adjusted average hourly earnings series that I developed in earlier research, which is adjusted for fringe benefits when extrapolating the total compensation ECI. See appendix A for further details.

similar behavior to the series for the PCE deflator until the 1990s, when they diverge markedly. In contrast to the plummeting TV-NAIRU for the PCE deflator, that for ECI-WS creeps up somewhat to 6.55 percent throughout 1996–8, while that for the ECI-TC declines only slightly and reverses itself, to end at 6.13 percent in 1998:2. The fact that the TV-NAIRU for ECI-WS is roughly the same in 1998 as in 1988 indicates that most of the corresponding 0.3 percentage point decline for the ECI-TC can be attributed to the sharp decline in the rate of increase of benefit compensation over the 1990s.

Contribution of Supply Shock Variables

As indicated in Table 17.3, the specification of the basic inflation equation 2 includes four sets of supply shock variables (food and energy prices, import prices, productivity deviation, and Nixon price controls) in addition to lagged inflation and the unemployment gap. In this section I am particularly interested in quantifying the degree to which the significant post-1992 decline in real import prices, reinforced by a decline in real food and energy prices, explains the absence of an accelerating inflation rate in the mid-1990s despite the relatively low unemployment rate.[26] One way to assess the impact of food energy and import prices in holding down inflation is to estimate the basic equation for each price index through 1992:4 and compute a dynamic simulation through 1998:2 using the previously estimated TV-NAIRU but artificially setting the food-energy and import price variables equal to zero. The results of this exercise for both the GDP and PCE deflators are summarized in Table 17.4. The third column displays for 1998:2 the simulation errors with actual values of the import and food-energy effects and, by contrast, the errors when either or both effects are set to zero. The results indicate that the food-energy and import price effects in the four quarters ending 1998:2 were holding down inflation in the GDP deflator by 1.42 percentage points and in the PCE deflator by 1.39 percentage points, and that most of this difference was made by the import price effect. These effects combine the static impact of the coefficients as shown in Table 17.3, which contribute about 0.93 percentage point to the PCE deflator, and the dynamic feedback from the lagged inflation variable, which contributes the remainder.[27]

17.4   EXPLAINING THE DECLINE IN THE NAIRU

I have shown that the combined impact of import prices and food-energy prices helps substantially in the explanation of why inflation did not accelerate in 1996–8. This does not, however, explain the decline in the TV-NAIRU for the

---

[26] The four-quarter rate of change of the relative import price variable was −6.34 percent in 1997:2 and −6.00 percent in 1998:2; the corresponding figures for the food-energy effect were −0.19 percent and −0.39 percent, respectively.

[27] Taking the PCE deflator coefficients in Table 17.3 and the values of the variables reported in the previous footnote, the static import price effect is 0.11 times −6.0, and the food-energy effect is 0.70 times −0.39.

Table 17.4. *Actual and Simulated Values of Price Changes, Using Alternative Indexes and Time-Varying NAIRU*[a]
Units as Indicated

Index	1998:2 Results[b]			Dynamic Simulation Error	
	Actual	Simulated	Error	Root Mean-Squared Error	Mean Error
GDP deflator					
Actual values	1.01	1.78	−0.77	0.60	−0.25
Omitting food-energy effect	1.01	1.91	−0.90	0.65	−0.32
Omitting import price effect	1.01	3.08	−2.07	1.16	−0.85
Omitting both effects	1.01	3.20	−2.19	1.22	−0.91
PCE deflator					
Actual values	0.85	1.90	−1.05	0.70	−0.46
Omitting food-energy effect	0.85	2.29	−1.44	0.96	−0.66
Omitting import price effect	0.85	2.90	−2.05	1.18	−0.95
Omitting both effects	0.85	3.29	−2.44	1.43	−1.14

[a] Specification of equations given by equation 2 in text: sample period is 1962:1–1992:4. Dynamic simulation is from 1993:1 to 1998:2. See Appendix A for details of variables and lag lengths.
[b] Four-quarter percent changes.
Source. Author's calculations.

deflators, since the influence of the supply shock variables is controlled in the process of estimating the TV-NAIRU. Stated another way, the combined impact of import prices and food-energy prices does not help to explain why actual inflation decelerated rather than staying roughly stable. I now consider to what extent the decline in the TV-NAIRU depicted in Figure 17.1 can be attributed to the role of computer prices, medical care prices, and improvements in the measurement of prices.

Table 17.5 provides, for selected quarters, basic data from the Bureau of Economic Analysis (BEA) on the shares of computers and medical care in both GDP and personal consumption expenditure, as well as four-quarter changes in the deflators for GDP, PCE, total computers, consumption computers, and medical care goods and services. In view of the much-hyped new economy, it is surprising to learn that the nominal share of computers (including producers' durable equipment, consumption, government, and net exports) did not grow at all between 1988 and 1998. The share of computers in real GDP grew enormously, from 0.6 to 6.1 percent, but this simply reflects the sharp decline in computer prices rather than an increase in the importance of computer spending. It is the nominal shares that are used in the computation of chain-weighted deflators and that determine the impact of computer prices on overall inflation. The share of medical care is much larger than that of computers in both GDP and PCE, and it grew by a much larger absolute amount between 1988 and 1993, after which it remained on a high plateau.

Table 17.5. *Data on Computers and Medical Care, Selected Quarters*
Percent

Item	1988:1	1993:1	1998:2	Change 1988–98[a]
Nominal expenditure shares				
Total computers in GDP	1.2	0.9	1.2	0.0
Consumption of computers in PCE	0.2	0.3	0.4	0.2
Medical care goods and services in GDP	9.6	12.1	11.9	2.3
Medical care goods and services in PCE	14.4	17.6	17.4	3.0
Four-quarter rates of change of deflators				
GDP deflator	3.0	2.7	1.0	−2.0
PCE deflator	3.7	2.9	0.9	−2.8
Total computers	−9.6	−19.8	−33.5	−23.9
Consumption of computers	−7.7	−29.1	−34.3	−26.6
Medical care goods and services	6.0	6.0	2.1	−3.9

[a] In lower panel, column gives change in the four-quarter rates of change.
Source. Unpublished data provided directly by the Bureau of Economic Analysis.

The growing impact of computers on overall inflation performance reflects not the increase in their nominal share but rather a sharp acceleration in their rate of price decline: from an average annual rate of −13 percent during 1988–93 to −28 percent during 1993–8, reaching a peak of −37 percent in mid-1997. With a share of 1.2 percent in GDP and a rate of price decline of −34 percent in the year ending 1998:2, computers deducted −0.41 percentage point from the rate of change of the GDP deflator, helping to explain why inflation has recently been so low (the actual impact is more severe than −0.4, due to the dynamic contribution of the lagged dependent variable). It is important to note that if both the computer share in spending and the rate of price decline stabilize at present levels, computers will make no further contribution to the deceleration of inflation.

The lower panel of Table 17.5 contrasts the inflation rates of the GDP and PCE deflators with the implicit deflator of medical care. It shows that medical care inflation substantially boosted overall inflation in both 1988 and 1993, with a wedge that declined to zero in 1996–7 but reemerged in 1998 when overall inflation decelerated further but medical care inflation did not.

In addition to computers and medical care, a third factor holding down the measured rate of inflation has been changes in measurement methodology during the 1990s. Measurement improvements in the CPI are estimated to have reduced measured inflation relative to actual inflation by an amount that grew gradually from −0.1 percentage point in 1992 to −0.46 percentage point in early 1998. Moreover, the BEA's 1998 benchmark revision has, in translating price changes for individual CPI components into the measures used in the PCE deflator, introduced several changes in CPI methodology that were applied retroactively as far back as 1995:1. The net impact of these measurement

Table 17.6. *Effects of Computers, Medical Care, and Price Measurement on Inflation and the TV-NAIRU, Selected Quarters*
Percent

Item	1988:1	1993:1	1998:2	Change 1988–98[a]
GDP deflator, impact of stripping				
Computers	−0.15	0.22	−0.40	−0.25
Medical care goods and services	0.30	0.44	0.16	−0.14
Changes in price measurement	0.00	−0.07	−0.36	−0.36
All three components	0.14	0.13	−0.60	−0.74
PCE deflator, impact of stripping				
Computers	−0.03	−0.09	−0.16	−0.13
Medical care goods and services	0.37	0.65	0.23	−0.14
Changes in price measurement methods	0.00	−0.10	−0.52	−0.52
All three components	0.35	0.44	−0.45	−0.80
TV-NAIRU for GDP deflator				
Official	6.36	6.05	5.68	−0.67
Deflator stripped of				
Computers	6.34	6.09	5.76	−0.58
Medical care	6.24	6.05	5.69	−0.55
Measurement adjustments	6.36	6.16	5.86	−0.50
All three components	6.27	6.22	6.03	−0.24
TV-NAIRU for PCE deflator				
Official	6.42	5.77	5.31	−1.11
Deflator stripped of				
Computers	6.44	5.81	5.37	−1.07
Medical care	6.28	5.78	5.40	−0.88
Measurement adjustments	6.46	5.96	5.59	−0.87
All three components	6.29	5.96	5.67	−0.62

[a] Third column minus first column.

Source. Author's calculations based on unpublished data provided directly by the Bureau of Economic Analysis.

changes was to reduce the measured inflation rate in early 1998 by 0.73 point compared with the rate that would have been estimated under the methodology used before 1992.[28]

Table 17.6 computes the contributions of computers, medical care, and the CPI measurement adjustment to GDP and PCE inflation, as well as to the TV-NAIRU, in the four-quarter periods ending 1988:1, 1993:1, and 1998:2. The fourth column measures the change between 1988:1, and 1998:2. Of particular importance are the data showing the impact of the three factors taken together: from 0.14 percentage point in 1988:4 to −0.60 percentage point in 1998:2 for the GDP deflator (a change of −0.74 percentage point), and from 0.35 to −0.45 percentage point for the PCE deflator (a change of −0.80 percentage

[28] See Chapter 17 Appendix A for details and sources for the CPI measurement adjustment.

point). To summarize, it was determined above that the static impact of the import price and food-energy terms was to hold down the rate of change of the PCE deflator by −0.93 percentage point in the four quarters ending 1998:2, and these three "new" supply shocks contribute another −0.80 percentage point in reducing inflation between 1993 and 1998. Thus the total static impact of the five supply shocks is −1.73 percentage points.

To determine how much difference the three new factors make to the TV-NAIRU, one can strip computers, medical care, and the CPI measurement adjustment, as well as all three effects together, from the deflators, and then compute new TV-NAIRUs for each stripped deflator. By comparing each stripped TV-NAIRU to the nonstripped series plotted in Figure 17.1, one can assess the total impact of the three new factors on the TV-NAIRU. Table 17.6 compares each stripped TV-NAIRU with the nonstripped TV-NAIRU and in the fourth column calculates the change between 1988:1 and 1988:2. For the GDP deflator, the stripping process explains −0.43 percentage point of the total decline in the TV-NAIRU of −0.67 percentage point. For the PCE deflator, the stripping process explains −0.49 percentage point of the total TV-NAIRU decline of −1.11 percentage points. Thus the stripping exercise explains 64 percent of the decline in the TV-NAIRU for the GDP deflator and 44 percent for the PCE deflator.

17.5 CONTRASTS BETWEEN WAGES AND PRICES AND BETWEEN UNEMPLOYMENT AND CAPACITY UTILIZATION

The basic data in Table 17.1 and the TV-NAIRUs shown in Figures 17.1 to 3 call attention to a sharp contrast between the behavior of wages and that of prices in the mid-1990s. Far from exhibiting weak behavior as a result of structural factors in labor markets, such as labor insecurity or weak unions, wage changes have if anything accelerated more than would have been expected from the precedent set in the economic expansion of the late 1980s. The TV-NAIRU for the wage and salary component of the ECI drifts up slightly from 1990 to 1998, contrary to the decline in the series for the price deflators; and although the TV-NAIRU for the total compensation ECI measure does decline slightly, this can be entirely attributed to a slowdown in benefit growth, which is largely the counterpart of the moderation in medical care inflation.

The contrasting behavior of prices and wages raises the intriguing issue of how they have interacted. Was there feedback from prices to wages, so that the influence of the five beneficial supply shocks identified above held down wages? Was there feedback from wages to prices such that without the influence of accelerating wages, inflation would have decelerated even more than actually occurred? I test for the presence of feedback effects by estimating equations 7 and 8, which introduce the change in trend labor share (that is, the difference between the changes in trend unit labor cost and in the appropriate inflation rate) into the wage and price equations, respectively. Positive feedback from wages to prices, as in equation 8, should yield a positive sum of coefficients on the change in trend labor's share, whereas positive feedback from prices to wages, as in equation 7, should yield a negative sum of coefficients.

The results of estimating equations 7 and 8 are presented in Table 17.7 which shows the impact of adding eight lages of changes in the trend labor share variable to each of the equations displayed in the first three columns of Table 17.3. The Table reports changes in the regressions' summary statistics, the standard error of estimate and the sum of squared residuals, that result from adding the set of trend labor share lags; it also reports the sums of coefficients, the significance level of the sum, and the significance level of an exclusion test on the set of eight lagged variables. The results indicate that in the wage equations (the last two rows) the sum of coefficients on the feedback terms is highly significant and has the correct sign, whereas in the price equations (the second and fourth rows) the sum of coefficients is not significant. These results suggest that the deceleration of inflation in 1994–8 helped to keep wages from accelerating more than they actually did, but there is no parallel claim that the acceleration of wages helped to keep prices from decelerating more than they actually did.

I have also estimated a full set of TV-NAIRUs (not shown) for each equation summarized in Table 17.7. With wage feedback, in 1998:2 the price equations exhibit TV-NAIRUs that are roughly 0.15 percentage point lower than those displayed in Figure 17.1, indicating that allowing for the acceleration of wages, the puzzle of low inflation would have been even deeper than suggested by the basic equation 2 that ignores wage-to-price feedback. With price feedback from the consumption deflator, the TV-NAIRU for the ECI-TC wage variable is almost identical to the basic result for equation 5 shown in Figure 17.3. With price feedback from the GDP deflator, in 1998:2 the TV-NAIRU is 6.31 percent compared with 6.08 percent with that feedback effect indicating that allowing for the feedback from decelerating prices boosts the extent to which wages exhibit an acceleration.

The Capacity Utilization Rate as an Alternative Demand Variable

The basic data presented in Table 17.1 also display a contrast between the behavior of the unemployment rate and that of the capacity utilization rate (for manufacturing, mining, and utilities) over the past two business expansions. From 1987 to 1990 the capacity utilization rate increased, while from 1994 to 1998 it decreased. It is possible to estimate a NAIRCU (or "nonaccelerating inflation" rate of capacity utilization); the analogy to the sharp decline in the TV-NAIRU in the 1990s for the price deflators would be a sharp increase in the corresponding TV-NAIRCU. However, as illustrated in Figure 17.4, only a mild increase is observed. Since the variance of the capacity utilization rate is about three times that of the unemployment rate, the decline of about 1 percentage point in the TV-NAIRU for the unemployment rate observed for the PCE deflator

Table 17.7. Testing Price-Wage Interaction for Addition of the Trend Labor Share Variable, Alternative Dependent Variables[a]

Dependent Variable	Sum of Coefficients, Lags 1–8	Significance Level		Standard Error of Estimate	Sum of Squared Residuals
		Sum of Coefficients	Exclusion Test		
GDP deflator					
No labor share term	...	...	...	0.68	56.1
With labor share term	0.16	0.43	0.00	0.63	45.0
PCE deflator					
No labor share term	...	...	...	0.76	71.1
With labor share term	0.21	0.22	0.36	0.77	67.5
Trend unit labor cost[b]					
No labor share term	...	...	...	0.86	88.0
Labor share for GDP deflator	−0.44	0.02	0.03	0.82	75.0
Labor share for PCE deflator	−0.45	0.01	0.04	0.83	76.3

[a] Specification of equation given by equation 2, 5, 7, and 8 in the text; sample period is 1962–1998:2. See Chapter 17 Appendix A for details of variables and lag lengths.

[b] Based on the Employment Cost Index for total compensation.

Source. Author's calculations.

Percent

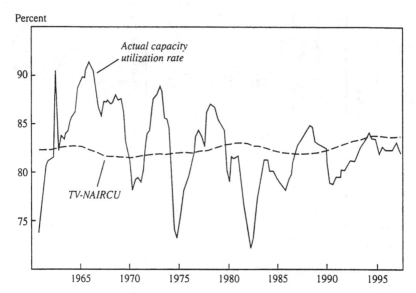

Figure 17.4. Actual Capacity Utilization Rate and TV-NAIRCU for the PCE Deflator, 1961–98

Source. Worldwide web page of the Bureau of Economic Analysis and author's calculations.

in Figure 17.1 and Table 17.6 should have been accompanied by an increase in the TV-NAIRCU of about 3 percentage points. In fact, the TV-NAIRCU increased by about 1 percentage point between 1990 and 1998. Figure 17.4 shows that actual capacity utilization was below the TV-NAIRCU in 1998, consistent with decelerating inflation, whereas in Figure 17.1 the actual unemployment rate was below the TV-NAIRU, implying accelerating inflation.[29]

17.6   CONCLUSION

This paper attempts to explain the outstanding macroeconomic performance of the U.S. economy in the 1990s. The explanation of the so-called Goldilocks economy turns largely, if not entirely, on the explanation of the deceleration of inflation that has accompanied a marked decline in the unemployment rate over 1994–98. The conventional natural rate hypothesis, by contrast, would have predicted that such a decline in the actual unemployment rate would have

[29] Using the methodology of this paper, I have examined an additional measure of demand tightness: the demographically adjusted unemployment rate recently developed by Robert Shimer (forthcoming). My results confirm Shimer's view that changes in the TV-NAIRU can be almost entirely attributed to changes in the age composition of the unemployed – but only through 1990. Contrary to his claim that the same is true of the 1990s, I find that the TV-NAIRU based on Shimer's data on the demographically adjusted unemployment rate actually declines slightly more than the standard TV-NAIRU series for the PCE deflator between 1992 and 1998.

Table 17.8. *Decomposition of the Inflation Surprise in the GDP Deflator, 1998:2*[a]
Percent per Year

Component of Inflation	Change
1. Predicted inflation, constant NAIRU, constant real prices of food, energy, and imports (rows 3 – 2c)	3.73
2. Contribution of traditional supply shocks	
a. Food and energy prices	−0.13
b. Import prices	−1.30
c. Total	−1.42
3. Predicted inflation with actual behavior of supply shocks and constant NAIRU	2.31
4. Contribution of new supply shocks	
a. Computers	−0.06
b. Medical care	−0.02
c. Measurement methodology	−0.10
d. Interaction effect	−0.08
e. Total, working through decline in TV-NAIRU	−0.26
5. Predicted inflation with actual behavior of supply shocks and explained portion of decline in TV-NAIRU (rows 3 + 4e)	2.05
6. Contribution of unexplained decline in TV-NAIRU	−0.27
7. Predicted inflation with actual behavior of supply shocks and estimated TV-NAIRU	1.78
8. Error term in simulation of inflation (rows 9 – 7)	−0.77
9. Actual inflation, four quarter change to 1998:2	1.01

[a] Percent changes are four-quarter moving averages.

Source. Author's calculations. By row, 2 is from Table 17.4, "error for effect" minus "error for actual value": 3 is from the first row of Table 17.2; 4 and 6 are from Table 17.6, change 1993:1–1998:2 in TV-NAIRUs for the GDP deflator, prorated among explained and unexplained components: and 7 and 9 are from the first row of Table 17.4.

been accompanied by an acceleration of inflation if the NAIRU had remained constant.

Decomposition of Proposed Explanations

How great would that predicted acceleration have been, and how can the alternate observed deceleration be explained? A complete decomposition of the contribution of this paper is provided in Table 17.8. I take as a point of departure the textbook NAIRU of an arbitrary and fixed 6 percent that I used in research prior to 1995, which predicts that the inflation rate for the GDP deflator would have accelerated from 2.5 percent in 1994:3 to 3.73 percent in 1998:2 if there had been no change in the real prices of food, energy, and imports (all Figures in this section refer to four-quarter rates of change ending in the designated quarter).

The last row of Table 17.8 reminds one that the inflation rate in 1998:2 was not 3.73 percent but 1.01 percent. This leaves a glaring error of 2.72 percentage points to be explained. Slightly more than half of the required explanation is provided by the contribution of the traditional supply shocks, since the actual declines in the real prices of food, energy, and imports explained a decline in the inflation rate of 1.42 percent. Thus the predicted inflation rate net of the traditional supply shocks that actually occurred was just 2.31 points. Using the estimated TV-NAIRU rather than the fixed NAIRU of 6 percent assumed initially further reduces the predicted inflation rate from 2.31 percent to 1.78 percent; of this additional reduction, about half is explained by the role of computers, medical care, and measurement changes. This leaves an unexplained error of −0.77 percentage point in explaining the actual inflation rate of 1.01 percent.

Thus it appears that what this paper leaves unexplained are the unexplained contribution of the decline in the TV-NAIRU and the pure unexplained residual. These add up to 1.04 percentage points, or 38 percent of the original 2.72 point "surprise" on comparing the prediction of the top row of the Table with the actual result on the bottom row. Clearly, the decomposition of the unexplained 1.04 percentage points depends on the smoothness parameter (τ_η) imposed on the estimation of the model consisting of equations 2 and 3. The larger is the assumed standard deviation, the more of the unexplained component of inflation will be attributed to the unexplained component of the decline in the TV–NAIRU and the less to the pure residual.

However, this decomposition of what remains unexplained is sensitive to the use of the TV-NAIRU methodology. Another approach would be to take the predicted value of inflation net of traditional supply shocks (from Table 17.8) and add to actual inflation the full change between 1993 and 1998 contributed by computers, medical care, and measurement methodology, which is 0.80 percentage point in Table 17.6. This would make actual inflation 1.81 percent rather than 1.01 percent, and would reduce the unexplained component from 1.04 percentage points to 0.50 percentage point (2.31 from Table 17.8 minus the alternative actual of 1.81). This approach would suggest that only 18 percent (0.50/2.72) of the initial inflation surprise remains unexplained.

In other words, the contribution of the three new supply shocks – computers, medical care, and measurement methodology – depends on whether it is fed through the TV-NAIRU and thus is subject to the associated smoothness assumptions, or it is added to the actual inflation rate to create an alternative stripped inflation rate. The new supply shocks make a much bigger difference when this second approach is followed, and this approach is also more symmetrical to the direct treatment of the traditional supply shocks.

This paper goes beyond the attempt to explain the inflation surprise of the 1990s to extend previous work on the TV-NAIRU, which so far has been limited to a model in which price inflation evolves independent of wage changes. Estimates of a model of wage-wage feedback parallel to the standard model of price-price feedback reveals a stark contrast: the estimated TV-NAIRU for total compensation barely declines in the 1990s, and all of the small decline can be attributed to the sharp decline in the rate of change of employee benefits, largely reflecting the transition to HMO-type payment systems for medical care.

I then extend the standard autoregressive price and wage inflation models to allow for wage-to-price and price-to-wage feedback. The sum of the lagged feedback terms is significant only from prices to wages, not from wages to prices. Allowing for such feedback effects alters the estimated TV-NAIRUs only slightly. The results suggest that wages would have accelerated even more during the current economic expansion without the moderating effect of price feedback. Ignoring the insignificant sums of coefficients on the feedback terms in the price equations, prices would have decelerated slightly more without the inflationary impact of wage feedback. Thus when allowance is made for wage-price feedback, the contrast between price and wage behavior deepens.

The Future

To the extent that this paper attributes most of the inflation surprise of the 1990s to five supply shocks, the two traditional shocks (food-energy and import prices) and the three new shocks (computers, medical care, and measurement method-ology), it opens debate regarding the likely evolution of these shocks. The continued arrival of new shocks would be required to continue the deceleration of inflation, given a constant unemployment rate. For instance, at a given share of nominal expenditure for computers, the rate of deflation of computer prices would have to continue to accelerate as it did between 1993 and 1998. Steady deflation of computer prices at 40 percent a year, along with a fixed share of computers, would maintain current inflation without any pressure for renewed deceleration or a reversal toward acceleration.

Viewed in this perspective, between 1993 and 1998 the economy benefited from a powerful and interactive push toward decelerating inflation, resulting from appreciation in the dollar, a decline in real oil prices, an accelerated rate of decline of computer prices, a reduced *relative* rate of inflation in medical care, and a series of measurement improvements in the official price indexes. It is not an unreasonable conjecture that each of these beneficial shocks was temporary, which would imply that inflation in the future will be much more dependent on the gap between the actual unemployment rate and the NAIRU than has heretofore been the case.

The movement of the dollar cannot be forecast; the exchange rate might stabilize and could either depreciate or appreciate. Oil prices may have fallen as far as they can and could exhibit a partial recovery in the next few years. Computer prices may continue to decline at 40 percent per year, but not at 60 percent per year. The medical-care revolution may have reached its limit in cost reductions, and henceforth medical care inflation may once again outpace general inflation – a development that already seems in prospect for 1999.[30]

---

[30] See Milt Freudenheim, "Employees Facing Steep Increases in Health Costs," *New York Times*, November 27, 1998, p. A1.

And the improvements in price measurement may be complete; note, especially, that the national accounts have since 1995 incorporated improvements in CPI methodology that will be implemented only in 1999. Thus the net balance of the supply shocks may be shifting from sharp downward pressure on the inflation rate to neutral or even slight upward pressure.

Alternative Explanations

While this paper explains most of the inflation surprise of the 1990s, it leaves some of it unexplained, and so leaves room for other explanations. The advocates of the new economy view could argue that high-technology innovation has held down inflation. But they must be careful in explaining how the benefits of high-technology products could have held down measured inflation without boosting measured productivity. A complaint that official price indexes miss some of the impact of such innovation (however justified) cannot be part of the explanation of a mysterious deceleration in measured inflation.

Achieving a full explanation of the decline in the TV-NAIRU for measured price inflation may depend on developing better empirical counterparts of the new economy argument. For instance, high technology involves more than the direct production of computers, as included in the national accounts. The pervasive role of electronic components in many other products, ranging from automobiles to supermarket check-out scanners, may have contributed to lower inflation but is not captured by an analysis that limits the computer effect to the narrow 1.2 percent of GDP included in the official definition.

This paper points toward two main areas for future research. The first is to explain the contrast between decelerating prices and accelerating wages. The easy answer that unmeasured productivity growth has accelerated is unconvincing, because the price deceleration has occurred in measured inflation, and this paper has taken fully into account improvements in measurement methods in the CPI and in the deflators. More plausible answers are likely to focus on developments in product markets that do not apply to labor markets, going beyond the aspects of the computer and medical care industries that are explicitly treated here.

A second, parallel contrast deepens the puzzle. Unemployment has fallen much more than the rate of capacity utilization has risen, once one allows for the much higher cyclical volatility of utilization. Since the utilization measure applies only to manufacturing, mining, and utilities, and not to the vast service sector, this contrast may point to developments in the labor market in the service sector that have generated an increased demand for labor without creating additional pressure on industrial capacity. It is tempting to speculate that the resolution of the unemployment-utilization discrepancy lies in the much discussed ability of the American economy (in contrast to the rich European nations) to provide abundant jobs in the service sector–flipping hamburgers, bagging groceries, valet parking, waiting tables–without placing pressure on capacity in the manufacturing sector.

Appendix A
Data Appendix

The following are the common elements of the estimated equations for price and wage change. The sample period is 1962:1 to 1998:2, or 146 quarters. All right-hand-side variables are allowed to enter with lags.[31] Supply shock variables include the change in the relative price of imports and the change in the relative price of food and energy.[32] Dummy variables are included for when the Nixon price controls of 1971–5 went "on" and "off." These dummy variables, and all the other variables, are defined exactly as in all my papers starting with Gordon (1982). An additional explanatory variable is the difference between productivity growth and its trend, reflecting the fact that while the larger part of any cyclical increase or decrease in productivity is reflected in a movement in profits in the same direction, a small fraction remains to influence the inflation rate in the opposite direction.[33]

Five indexes of price and wage change are studied. These are the official chain-weighted GDP deflator, the chain-weighted PCE deflator, CPI-U-X1, trend unit labor cost for the Employment Cost Index–Total Compensation (ECI-TC), and trend unit labor cost for the Employment Cost Index–Wages and Salaries (ECI-WS). ECI-WS differs from ECI-TC by excluding employee benefits. Neither ECI variable is available prior to 1980:1. The ECI series are extrapolated backward using two series developed in previous research. For the ECI-WS, I use an index of average hourly earnings in the nonfarm private economy, adjusted for changes in interindustry employment mix and in

---

[31] Lag lengths are chosen to be identical to those in Gordon (1990). The only smoothing condition imposed on the lag distributions involves the lagged dependent variable, where twenty-four lagged terms enter. Rather than estimating that number of unconstrained coefficients, the lagged dependent variable is entered as a series of fourquarter moving averages of rates of change; for example, the first variable is a fourquarter average of lags $t - 1$ to $t - 4$, the next $t - 5$ through $t - 8$, and so forth. The coefficients on the individual moving averages are unconstrained. Exclusion tests indicate that the moving averages are unconstrained. Exclusion tests indicate that the moving averages representing lags thirteen through twenty-four enter with a significance level of better than 1 percent for each of the three price indexes shown in Figure 17.1 and are thus highly significant. The coefficients on lags thirteen through twenty-four represent 30 percent of the total lagged effect in the equation for the GDP deflator, 24 percent of the total effect for the PCE deflator, and 35 percent of the total effect for CPI-U-X1.

[32] The food-energy effect is defined as the difference of the rate of change of the chain-weighted consumption deflator minus the rate of change of the chain-weighted consumption deflator net of food and energy. Also, the change in the real effective exchange rate, included in previous papers, is found to be insignificant in all versions estimated for this paper, presumably because its effect is swamped by that of the relative import price. I therefore exclude it in the results presented here.

[33] The productivity deviation is defined as the growth rate of the log ratio of actual nonfarm private business output per hour to a log-linear piecewise trend running through 1950:2, 1954:4, 1963:3, 1972:2, 1978:3, 1987:3, and 1996:4. The 1987–96 growth rate of this trend is 1.06 percent per year.

the importance of overtime pay.[34] For the ECI-TC, I use the same index multiplied by the ratio of employee compensation to wages and salaries (both from the National Income and Product Accounts) to adjust it for the effective fraction of employer-paid and employee-paid fringe benefits. Because changes in fringe benefits have almost always occurred in the first quarter of the year, each equation for trend unit labor cost includes seasonal dummy variables.

The seasonal dummies must have mean zero in order not to change the mean of the TV-NAIRU. Hence, taking the first quarter of each year as an example, I use dummies equal to 0.75, -0.25, -0.25, -0.25 rather than the usual 1, 0, 0, 0. As a result, the compensation version of the wage equations has a higher error variance than the wage-salary version. These appear only in the wage equations (for trend unit labor cost), not in the price equations.

Alternative measures of the TV-NAIRU are estimated for both the GDP and the PCE deflators stripped of three different elements. The first element is computer expenditures for total GDP (including PCE, PDE, government, and net exports) and for PCE. The second is total medical care expenditures, which is entirely a component of PCE and consists of both services and goods expenditures. The third is the CPI measurement adjustment.

Time-series expenditures on nominal and real expenditures on GDP and PCE computer expenditures and on PCE total medical care expenditures through 1998:2 were provided by Christian Ehemann of the Bureau of Economic Analysis.

The time series on the price measurement adjustment is taken from the *Economic Report of the President*, February 1998 (Table 2–4, p. 80) with three qualifications. First, I do not include the 1998 component for "updated market basket," since the PCE and GDP deflators are not affected by the updating of "upper-level" weights in the CPI. Second, I add an additional measurement adjustment beginning in 1992:1, based on graph 1 of U.S. Bureau of Labor Statistics (1997), which compares the "test" (that is, constant measurement methods) CPI with the official Laspeyres CPI. This graph appears to show an average difference between the two indexes of about -0.15 percent per year during 1992–4; I reduce this to -0.10, to be conservative. Third, I adjust for the fact that the BEA "backcast" the 1999 implementation of "lower level geometric weights" and several other minor changes to 1995:1. In order to reflect this shift in the measurement methods of the PCE deflator, I take the stated revisions to the PCE deflator in Seskin (1998, Table 4, p. 24) and add the absolute value of these revisions to the CPI measurement series. To summarize, the price measurement adjustment used in this paper is as follows: for 1992:1–1994:4, -0.1 percent; for 1995:1–1995:4, -0.53 percent; for 1996:1–1996:4, -0.73 percent; for 1997:1–1997:4, -0.49 percent; and for 1998:1–1998:4, -0.73 percent. The measurement methodology series for the GDP deflator is

---

[34] See Gordon (1971, pp. 115–8) for a full explanation of the construction of this series and a contrast with the conventional data on compensation per hour.

equal to that for the PCE deflator times 0.7, roughly the share of personal consumption expenditures in GDP.

References

Franz, Wolfgang, and Gordon, Robert J. "German and American Wage and Price Dynamics: Differences and Common Themes." *European Economic Review.* 1993; vol. 37, no. 4, pp. 719–62.

Gordon, Robert J. "Inflation in Recession and Recovery." *BPEA.* 1971; vol. 1, pp. 105–58.

"Alternative Responses of Policy to External Supply Shocks." *BPEA.* 1975; vol. 1, pp. 183–206.

"Can the Inflation of the 1970s Be Explained?" *BPEA.* 1977; vol. 1, pp. 253–77.

"Inflation, Flexible Exchange Rates, and the Natural Rate of Unemployment." In: Baily, Martin N., ed. *Workers, Jobs, and Inflation.* Brookings; 1982.

" 'Credibility' vs. 'Mainstream': Two Views of the Inflation Process." In: Nordhaus William D., ed. *Inflation: Prospects and Remedies, Alternatives for the 1980s.* Washington: Center for National Policy; 1983

"Supply Shocks and Monetary Policy Revisited." *American Economic Review, Papers and Proceedings.* 1984; vol. 74, no. 2, pp. 38–43.

"U.S. Inflation, Labor's Share, and the Natural Rate of Unemployment." In: König, Heinz, ed. *Economics of Wage Determination.* Berlin: Springer-Verlag, 1990.

"Inflation and Unemployment: Where is the NAIRU?" Paper prepared for the Meeting of Academic Consultants to the Board of Governors of the Federal Reserve System. Washington, DC. December 1, 1994.

"Estimating the NAIRU as a Time-Varying Parameter." Paper prepared for the Panel of Economic Advisors to the Congressional Budget Office. November 16, 1995.

"The Time-Varying NAIRU and Its Implications for Economic Policy." *Journal of Economic Perspectives.* 1997; vol. 11, no. 1, pp. 11–32.

Gordon, Robert J., and King, Stephen R. "The Output Cost of Disinflation in Traditional and Vector Autoregressive Models." *BPEA.* 1982; vol. 1, pp. 205–42.

King, Robert G., and Watson, Mark W. "The Post-War U.S. Phillips Curve: A Revisionist Econometric History." *Carnegie-Rochester Conference Series on Public Policy.* 1994; vol. 41, pp. 157–219.

Levy, Mickey D. "Slaying the NAIRU Myth." *Jobs and Capital.* Summer, 1997; vol. 6, pp. 15–19.

Phelps, Edmund S. "Commodity-Supply Shock and Full-Employment Monetary Policy." *Journal of Money, Credit, and Banking.* 1978; vol. 10, no. 2, pp. 206–21.

Seskin, Eugene P. "Annual Revision of the National Income and Product Accounts." *Survey of Current Business.* August, 1998; vol. 78, pp. 7–35.

Shimer, Robert. "Why Is the U.S. Unemployment Rate So Much Lower?" In: Bernanke, Ben S., and Rotemberg, Julio J. *NBER Macroeconomics Annual 1998.* Cambridge. MIT Press; forthcoming.

Sims, Christopher A. "Comment." *BPEA.* 1987; vol. 1, pp. 117–20.

Staiger, Douglas; Stock, James H., and Watson, Mark W. "The NAIRU, Unemployment, and Monetary Policy." *Journal of Economic Perspectives.* 1997; vol. 11, no. 1, pp. 33–49.

Stock, James H. "Monetary Policy in a Changing Economy: Indicators, Rules, and the Shift towards Intangible Output." Paper prepared for Bank of Japan Conference on Monetary Policy in a World of Knowledge-Based Growth, Quality Change, and Uncertain Measurement. Tokyo. June 18–19, 1998.

Stock, James H., and Watson, Mark W. "Forecasting Inflation." Unpublished paper. Harvard University, Kennedy School of Government and the Woodrow Wilson School. 1998a

"Median Unbiased Estimation of Coefficient Variance in a Time-Varying Parameter Model." *Journal of the American Statistical Association.* March, 1998b; vol. 93, pp. 349–58.

U.S. Bureau of Labor Statistics. "The Experimental CPI Using Geometric Means (CPI-U-XG)." Unpublished paper. Department of Labor. April, 1997.

Subject Index

Author Index